CULTURE, PEOPLE, NATURE

Sixth Edition

CULTURE, PEOPLE, NATURE

An Introduction to General Anthropology

MARVIN HARRIS
University of Florida

HarperCollins*College*Publishers

Acquisitions Editor: Alan McClare
Developmental Editor: Marisa L'Heureux
Project Editor: Claire M. Caterer
Design Supervisor: Heather A. Ziegler
Text Design Adaptation: Heather A. Ziegler
Cover Design: Heather A. Ziegler
Cover Photo: Don Klumpp, The Image Bank
Photo Researcher: Mira Schachne
Production Manager/Assistant: Willie Lane/Sunaina Sehwani
Compositor: Publication Services, Inc.
Printer and Binder: R. R. Donnelley & Sons Company
Cover Printer: The Lehigh Press, Inc.
Insert Printer: Southeastern Color Graphics

For permission to use copyrighted material, grateful acknowledgment is made to the copyright holders on pp. 517–522, which are hereby made part of this copyright page.

Culture, People, Nature: An Introduction to General Anthropology, *Sixth Edition*
Copyright ©1993 by HarperCollins College Publishers

93 94 95 9 8 7 6 5 4 3 2

BRIEF CONTENTS

DETAILED CONTENTS

BOXES AND TABLES

TABLES

TO THE INSTRUCTOR

The sixth edition of *Culture, People, Nature* offers the student a comprehensive introduction to anthropology that emphasizes the integration of the different fields. Because it has been written from the standpoint of a consistent theoretical framework it allows instructors and students to see links and connections between apparently disparate topics and issues. Such linkages are needed now more than ever to show that the different fields do indeed complement and support each other and that the four-field approach to anthropology is both useful and viable.

This sixth edition of *Culture, People, Nature* follows its predecessors in attempting to update and freshen the data it presents and the style in which it is written. Extensive new information is presented in numerous new sections, a host of new boxes, and a new chapter 21 on gender roles and human sexuality. New figures complement the new information in the text.

Some of the new sections discuss hominid and chimpanzee sexuality, Neandertal speech and religion, single and multiple origin theories, population increases, gender, age, and hierarchy, the non-complaint Japanese, advocacy anthropology, and the new racism. Some of the new boxes include "DNA Hybridization," "The Wages of Racism," "Kanzi speaks English," "The Economy of Parental Love," "A World of Limited Good, Whose Fault?," "Meat and Politics in Russia," and "Modern Times: Working for a Large Oil Company."

Many people have contributed to the preparation of this edition. A very able group of reviewers made many valuable suggestions. However, problems of space and context made it impossible to implement all their suggestions. Diversity of points of view and differences of opinion also sometimes resulted in one reviewer contradicting another. My inability to respond to all suggestions is not a measure of my appreciation of their work and I especially want to thank

Donald N. Brown, Oklahoma State University
Frank McGlynn, University of Pittsburgh
Susan Meswick, St. John's University
Sue N. Moore, Georgia Southern University
Michael Olien, University of Georgia
Jon A. Schlenker, University of Maine at Augusta
William Torrey, West Virginia University
Arthur Tuden, University of Pittsburgh

Bryan Byrnes and Tim Schwartz, both graduate students in the department of anthropology at the University of Florida, rendered valuable assistance in the preparation of the new, considerably updated bibliography of references cited. I am greatly indebted to all of my colleagues at the University of Florida for providing a congenial intellectual and social environment. I wish especially to thank Alan McClare for his continuing interest and support as the Acquisitions Editor and Claire Caterer, the Project Editor, who worked diligently to keep the book on schedule.

Marvin Harris

TO THE STUDENT

I hope that you will find this textbook both informative and provocative. In keeping with the many different kinds of research that anthropologists carry out, it covers a broad range of subjects spanning millions of years and the entire inhabited globe. Its aim, like that of anthropology, is to provide a scientifically valid account of the evolution of human nature and of human cultures from the remote past to the present. It seeks to answer the most fundamental questions about human existence: where our species came from; what human social life was like in the past; what it is like today; and what it may be like in the future.

As the twentieth century draws to a close, we confront a world in which an understanding of sexual, racial, ethnic, linguistic, and cultural differences is indispensable not only for the welfare of nations but for the survival of our endangered species. To meet global challenges we must learn to think in global terms. And this means that we must acquire an up-to-date scientific knowledge of the processes that have shaped and continue to shape human nature and human cultures. We cannot hope to control these processes if we do not understand them first. In this sense, anthropology is a practical science even when it deals with subjects that are remote in time and space. Its facts and theories are indispensable to everyone who aspires to be a well-informed and responsible partner in the human enterprise.

To serve this aspiration, I have drawn links wherever possible between the subject considered—be it fossil ancestors or the beginnings of agriculture—and the practical problems and dilemmas of modern life, especially those having to do with inequality, poverty, racism, sexism, alienation, and war. Part VII, "Anthropology and Modern Life," should leave no doubt that anthropology is not merely about bones, pots, and exotic customs, but about you and me, our friends and relatives, and our own everyday way of life.

Marvin Harris

CULTURE, PEOPLE, NATURE

Chapter 1

Introduction

Anthropology is the study of humankind—of ancient and modern people and their ways of living. Different branches of anthropology focus on different aspects of the human experience. Some branches focus on how our species evolved from earlier species. Others focus on how we came to possess the facility for language, how languages evolved and diversified, and how modern languages serve the needs of human communication. Still others focus on the learned traditions of human thought and behavior, how ancient cultures evolved and diversified, and how and why modern cultures change or stay the same.

As the world becomes smaller, people from different continents who speak different languages and who possess different values and religions find themselves living together in the same "global village." To all the members of this new human community, anthropology extends a unique invitation to explore the roots of our common humanity as well as the sources of our distinct ways of living.

Most large departments of anthropology in the United States offer courses in five major fields of knowledge about humankind: cultural anthropology (sometimes called *social anthropology*), archaeology, anthropological linguistics, physical anthropology, and applied anthropology (Fried 1972; American Anthropological Association 1991).*

Cultural anthropology deals with the description and analysis of cultures—the socially learned traditions of past and present ages. It has a subdiscipline, ethnography, that describes and interprets present-day cultures. Comparison of these interpretations and descriptions can lead to the formation of hypotheses and theories about the causes of past and present cultural similarities and differences (Fig. 1.1a).

Archaeology and cultural anthropology possess similar goals but differ in the methods they use and the cultures they study. Archaeology examines the material remains that cultures of the past leave behind on or below the surface of the earth. Without the findings of archaeology we would not be able to understand the human past, especially where people have not left any books or other written records (Fig. 1.1b).

Anthropological linguistics is the study of the great variety of languages spoken by human beings. Anthropological linguists attempt to trace the history of all known families of languages. They are concerned with the way language influences and is influenced by other aspects of human life, and with the relationship between the evolution of language and the evolution of our species, *Homo sapiens*. They are also concerned with the relationship between the evolution of languages and the evolution of different cultures (Fig. 1.1c).

Physical anthropology (also called *biological anthropology*) connects the other anthropological fields to the study of animal origins and the biologically determined nature of *Homo sapiens*. Physical anthropologists seek to reconstruct the course of human evolution by studying the fossil remains of ancient humanlike species. Physical anthropologists also seek to describe the distribution of hereditary variations among contemporary populations and to sort out and measure the relative contributions to human life made by heredity, environment, and culture (Fig. 1.1d).

Applied anthropology utilizes the findings of cultural, archaeological, linguistic, and biological studies to solve practical problems affecting the health, education, security, and prosperity of human beings in many different cultural settings.

The combination of all five fields of anthropology is known as *general anthropology*. This book is an introduction to the major findings in all five fields. Hence, it is an introduction to general anthropology.

WHY ANTHROPOLOGY?

Many disciplines other than anthropology are concerned with the study of human beings. Biologists, geneticists, and physiologists study our physical nature. In medicine alone, hundreds of specialists investigate the human body, and psychiatrists and psychologists, rank upon rank, seek the essence of the human mind and soul. Many other disciplines examine our cultural, intellectual, and aesthetic behavior. These

---

*See the first page of the bibliography for an explanation of the system of citations used in this book.

FIGURE *1.1*

ANTHROPOLOGISTS AT WORK
(A) Ethnographer Margaret Mead among the Manus Islanders. **(B)** Jerald T. Milanich, archaeologist, Florida Museum of Natural History, with prehistoric **(A. D.** 200–900) Native American bird vessel. **(C)** Linguist Francesca Merlin with the speakers of a previously unknown language near Mt. Hagen, New Guinea. **(D)** Physical anthropologist Donald Johanson fossil hunting at Olduvai Gorge.

(A)

(C)

(B)

(D)

disciplines include sociology, human geography, social psychology, history, political science, economics, linguistics, theology, philosophy, musicology, art, literature, and architecture. There are also many "area specialists" who study the languages and life-styles of particular peoples, nations, or regions: "Latin Americanists," "Indianists," "Sinologists," and so on. What, then, is distinctive about anthropology?

The distinction of anthropology is that it is global and comparative. Other disciplines are concerned with only a particular segment of human experience or a particular time or phase of our cultural or biological development. But anthropologists never base their findings on the study of a single population, race, tribe, class, nation, time, or place. Anthropologists insist first and foremost that conclusions based on the study of one particular human group or civilization be checked against the evidence of other groups or civilizations. In this way anthropologists hope to control the biases of their own sex, class, race, nation, religion, ethnic group, or culture. In anthropological perspective, all peoples and cultures are equally worthy of study. Thus, anthropology is incompatible with the view of people who would like to have themselves and no one else represent humanity, stand at the pinnacle of progress, or be chosen by God or history to fashion the world in their own image.

Anthropologists believe that a sound knowledge of humankind can be achieved only by studying distant as well as near lands and ancient as well as modern times. By adopting this broad view of the totality of human experience, perhaps we humans can tear off the blinders put on us by our local life-styles and see ourselves as we really are.

Because of its biological, archaeological, linguistic, cultural, comparative, and global perspective, anthropology can answer many fundamental questions. It can contribute to understanding the significance of our species' animal heritage and hence to the definition of what is distinctively human about human nature. It is strategically equipped to study the biological and cultural significance of race in the evolution of cultures and in the conduct of contemporary life. And it also holds the key to understanding the origins of social inequality in the form of racism, sexism, exploitation, poverty, and international underdevelopment.

© Chronicle Features, 1982

"Anthropologists! Anthropologists!"

WHY STUDY ANTHROPOLOGY?

Most anthropologists make their living by teaching in universities, colleges, and junior colleges, and by carrying out university-based research. But a substantial and increasing proportion of anthropologists find employment in nonacademic settings. Museums, for example—especially museums of natural history, archaeology, and art and folklore—have long relied on the expertise of anthropologists. In recent years, anthropologists have been welcome in a greater variety of public and private positions: in government agencies concerned with welfare, drug abuse, mental health, environmental impact, housing, education, foreign aid, and agricultural development; in the private sector as personnel and ethnic relations consultants and as management consultants for multinational firms; and as staff members of hospitals and foundations (see Box 1.1).

In recognition of the growing importance of these nonacademic roles as a source of employment for anthropologists, many university departments of anthropology have started or expanded programs in applied anthropology. These programs supplement traditional anthropological studies with training in

statistics, computer languages, and other skills suitable for solving practical problems in human relationships under a variety of natural and cultural conditions.

Despite the expanding opportunities in applied fields, the study of anthropology remains valuable not so much for the opportunities it presents for employment but for its contribution to the basic understanding of human variations and relationships. Just as the majority of students of mathematics do not become mathematicians, so too the majority of students of anthropology do not become anthropologists. For human relations fields, such as law, medicine, nursing, education, government, psychology, economics, and business administration, anthropology has a role to play that is as basic as mathematics. Only by becoming sensitive to and learning to cope with the cultural dimensions of human existence can one hope to be optimally effective in any of these fields. Multicultural studies began with and are most highly developed within anthropology.

In the words of Frederica De Laguna, "Anthropology is the only discipline that offers a conceptual schema for the whole context of human experience.... It is like the carrying frame onto which may be fitted all the several subjects of a liberal education, and by organizing the load, making it more wieldy and capable of being carried" (1968:475).

BOX *1.1*

AN ANTHROPOLOGICAL SCORECARD

Anthropologists frequently identify themselves with one or more specialized branches of the five major fields. The following is only a partial listing.

CULTURAL ANTHROPOLOGY

Ethnography   Describe contemporary cultures.
Medical anthropology   Study biological and cultural factors in health, disease, and the treatment of the sick.*
Urban anthropology   Study city life, gangs, drug abuse.*
Development anthropology   Study the causes of underdevelopment and development among the less developed nations.*

ARCHAEOLOGY

Historic archaeology   Study cultures of the recent past by means of a combination of written records and archaeological excavations.
Industrial archaeology   Historic archaeology that focuses on industrial factories and facilities.
Contract archaeology   Conduct archaeological surveys for environmental impact statements and protection of historic and prehistoric sites.*

PHYSICAL (BIOLOGICAL) ANTHROPOLOGY

Primatology   Study social life and biology of monkeys, great apes, and other primates.
Human paleontology   Search for and study fossil remains of early human species.
Forensic anthropology   Identify victims of murders and accidents. Establish paternity through genetic analysis.*
Population genetics   Study hereditary differences in human populations.

LINGUISTICS

Historical linguistics   Reconstruct the origins of specific languages and of families of languages.
Descriptive linguistics   Study the grammar and syntax of languages.
Sociolinguistics   Study the actual use of language in the communication behavior of daily life.

*APPLIED ANTHROPOLOGY
Starred items have strong applied focus.

SUMMARY

Anthropology is the study of humankind. Its five major branches are cultural or social anthropology, anthropological linguistics, physical (or biological) anthropology, archaeology, and applied anthropology. Its distinctive approach lies in its global, comparative, and multidimensional perspective. The combined approach of all five fields is known as *general anthropology.*

PART I

PHYSICAL ANTHROPOLOGY

*T*he first part of this book consists of five chapters that ground anthropology in the study of the evolution of humankind's biological characteristics. We shall survey the aspects of human biology that define our place in the animal kingdom, review the genetic and fossil evidence for the time and place of the evolution of our own and earlier species, and investigate the origin and significance of contemporary racial differences.

Organic Evolution

This chapter contains a rapid survey of the basic principles of biological heredity and biological evolution. I know that students without a background in biology will find this to be a difficult chapter. But the topics covered provide indispensable background for understanding how our remote ancestors acquired and passed on the distinctive biological features of our species—a subject we will get into in Chapters 3 and 4. Certainly we all need to understand what is meant by evolution and how it works. Because there is a great deal of misinformation about the scientific status of evolution and natural selection, this chapter includes a discussion of the arguments and theories of anti-evolutionists who claim that creationism offers a better theory of the origins of living and extinct species.

CHROMOSOMES AND DNA

The nucleus of every cell in the human body contains a set of structures known as *chromosomes*. Except when cells are in the process of reproducing themselves, chromosomes come in *homologous pairs* (that is, pairs that have the same length, shape, and sequence of hereditary material). The single member of a homologous pair is known as a *chromatid*. Chromosomes consist of a long strand of *DNA* (deoxyribonucleic acid) wound and folded around beadlike structures called *nucleosomes*. Under an electron microscope, chromosomes normally looks like beaded

filaments. When a cell begins to reproduce itself, however, its chromosomes condense, become tightly folded, and take on a rodlike appearance (Fig. 2.1).

The DNA portion of chromosomes (Fig. 2.2) has two strands that wind about each other to form a spiral "ladder" (or double helix). The side pieces of the DNA ladder consist of sugar (deoxyribose) and phosphate molecules, while each "rung" consists of two kinds of chemical bases bonded at the center by hydrogen. The rungs of the DNA ladder consist of four different kinds of chemical bases: adenine, thymine, cytosine, and guanine, or A, T, C, and G for short. In forming the rungs of the ladder, A can bond only with

FIGURE *2.1*

STRUCTURE OF CHROMOSOMES
At left is highly condensed rodlike form, which under higher magnification is shown to consist of DNA wrapped around nucleosomes. Higher magnification also shows the relationship of the threadlike and beaded filament forms to DNA and the nucleosomes.

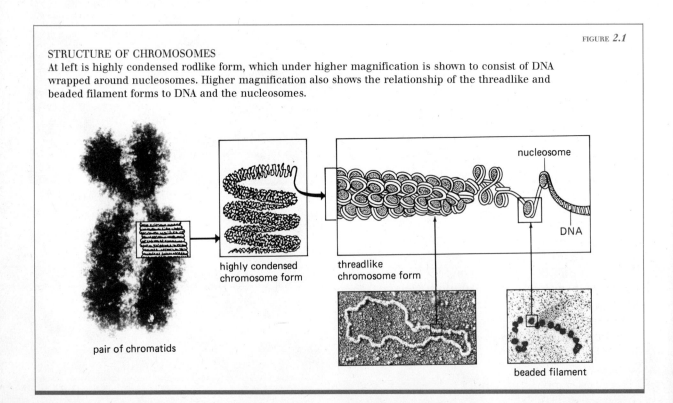

pair of chromatids

highly condensed
chromosome form

threadlike
chromosome form

nucleosome

DNA

beaded filament

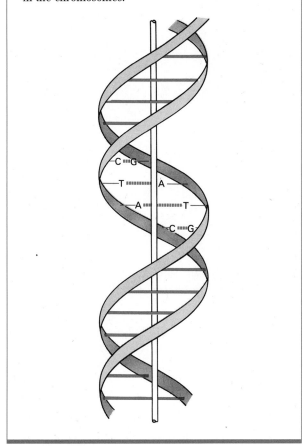

FIGURE *2.2*

DOUBLE HELIX MODEL OF DNA
C = cytosine; T = thymine; G = guanine;
A = adenine. It is the sequence of these chemicals
that determines the message carried by the DNA
in the chromosomes.

different kinds of amino acids. Thus, DNA's codons provide the instructions for assembling amino acids into proteins. Proteins in turn—and there are thousands of different kinds—are the essential constituents of all life processes.

THE INHERITANCE OF GENES

Genes are the fundamental units of heredity. A gene is any sequence of codons providing instructions for the synthesis of a protein that influences an organism's biochemical processes.

To understand how species evolve, one must understand how the chromosomes and their genes are passed along from parent to offspring. As stated above, within ordinary body cells, chromosomes always consist of a pair of homologous chromatids. In sexually reproducing organisms, one chromatid is the contribution of the male parent, and the other chromatid, the contribution of the female parent. Thus, human beings have 46 chromatids, of which 23 are inherited from the father and 23 from the mother (Fig. 2.3). Our hereditary nature is determined when a sperm bearing 23 chromatids unites with an ovum containing 23 chromatids. Soon after this union, the 23 pairs of homologous chromatids from the sperm and ovum jointly communicate their hereditary instructions to the first cells of the new individual, which is called a *zygote*. The zygote proceeds to divide and differentiate until a whole embryo is constructed and a new human being is ready to be born.

Since both parents have 23 chromosomes (46 chromatids), some process must exist to prevent the doubling of chromosomes in each generation. This process takes place during the production of the sex cells in the testes and ovaries. It involves two sequential divisions. As a preliminary to the first division, each of the immature sex cell's 46 chromatids makes a copy of itself, raising their number to 92. The homologous double-stranded chromosomes next line up at the cell's equator and the two members of a pair are pulled to opposite poles of the cell. The cell then divides in half, resulting in two daughter cells that each have 23 pairs of chromosomes (46 chromatids). These daughter cells now undergo a second division in which the members of a chromatid pair are pulled to opposite poles of the cell (23 to a pole, one member of each pair), and the cell then divides in two. This process is called *meiosis* (or reduction division) and occurs only during the formation of the sex cells. Subsequently, when the mature male sex cell (the sperm) fertilizes the mature female sex cell (the

T, and C can bond only with G, so the two sides of the ladder have a different but complementary sequence of bases.

The sequences of bases up and down the ladder constitute coded messages that, upon being copied, transferred out of the nucleus, and "translated," guide the synthesis of chains of amino acids within the cell. It takes sequences of three bases—triplets—to code for an amino acid. For example, the code for the amino acid called methionine is TAC; that for lysine is TTT, TTC; that for argenine, GCA, GCG, GCT, GCC, TCT, TCC. Each triplet of coded instruction is called a *codon*.

There are 20 amino acids. Their importance lies in their being the building blocks of proteins; that is, proteins are merely long chains of

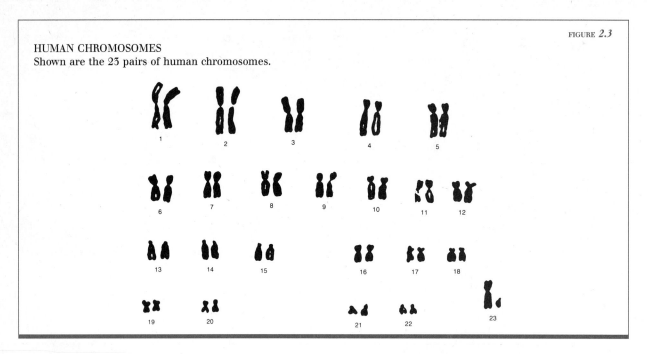

FIGURE *2.3*

HUMAN CHROMOSOMES
Shown are the 23 pairs of human chromosomes.

ovum), the number of chromatids will be restored to 46 (23 + 23 = 46).

During meiosis when the number of chomatids in the daughter sex cells is reduced from 46 to 23, it is entirely a matter of chance whether the member of a pair that has been contributed by the individual's father or the individual's mother is drawn to the cell's north or south pole. Each new sex cell thus contains a new assortment of hereditary material created by the shuffling of the homologous chromatids—some coming from the mother and the rest from the father in a proportion governed by chance (Fig. 2.4).

The fact that the father-derived and mother-derived chromatids are shuffled by chance during meiosis of the sex cells (reduction from 46 to 23 chromosomes) means that although one-half of our chromatids come from our father and one-half from our mother, there is no guarantee that one-quarter of our chromatids come from each of our grandparents, and it is unlikely that precisely one-eighth of our chromatids come from each of our great-grandparents. On the fifth ascending generation, where we theoretically could have as many as 64 grandparents, it is possible that some of these "ancestors" may not have contributed any genes at all to our heredity. This should have a sobering effect on people who delight in tracing their "roots" more than four generations back to royalty, first settlers, or other dignitaries.

The situation would be even more bleak for people interested in identifying their remote family an-cestors were it not for the fact that homologous chromatids exchange segments with each other. This phenomenon, known as *crossing over* (Fig. 2.5), takes place just before the first division of the sex cells. Because of crossing over, the chromatids contributed by any particular ancestor do not remain intact from one generation to another. Thus, several different ancestors may contribute genes to each of the 46 chromatids possessed by one of their descendants, making it likely that each of as many as 64 ancestors could have contributed some genes to their great-great-great-great-grandchild. That their contribution would be exactly $\frac{1}{64\text{th}}$, however, is highly unlikely.

Genotype

When the genes at the same *locus* (place) on a pair of homologous chromatids contain precisely the same sequence of base pairs (see p. 11), the individual is said to be *homozygous* for the trait controlled by those genes. Often, however, the two genes will differ slightly and the individual is said to be *heterozygous*. The variant genes found at a given locus are called *alleles*. During meiosis, as we have just seen, the mother-derived alleles and the father-derived alleles on each chromatid pair are segregated from each other and end up in different sex cells. This is a basic genetic principle known as the law of *segregation*. A second basic principle of genetics is known as the law of *independent assortment*. This states that the alleles located on nonhomologous chromatids are

FIGURE *2.4*

MEIOSIS

Schematic representation of steps responsible for the reduction and assortment of parental chromosomes in an individual's sex cells.

1.

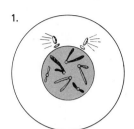

Chromosomes become visible as long, well-separated filaments; they do not appear double-stranded, although other evidence indicates that replication has already occurred.

2.

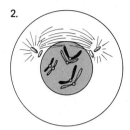

Homologous chromosomes pair and become shorter and thicker.

3.

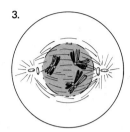

Chromosomes become clearly double-stranded. Nuclear membrane begins to disappear.

4.

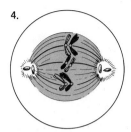

Each pair moves to the center of the cell. Chance determines which member of each pair lines up on right or left.

5.

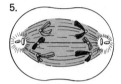

Double-stranded chromosomes move apart to opposite poles.

6.

New nuclei form. Chromosomes are double-stranded.

7.

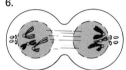

Cell divides. Each cell has a different set of chromosomes.

8.

Cells begin to divide again.

9.

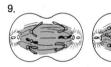

Each daughter cell receives same chromosomes as parent cell.

10.

Reduction division is complete. Sex cells are ready to combine with sex cells of another individual to restore full number of chromosomes.

assorted independently of each other in the formation of the sex cells.

These principles make it possible to predict the probable proportions in which two or more alleles will occur in the children of groups of fathers and mothers whose genetic types are known. For example, suppose that a particular population (interbreeding group) has two alleles: A and a on homologous chromatids. Because of the law of segregation, three kinds of individuals may occur: AA, Aa, and aa. Each of these combinations is called a *genotype*. The proportion in which genotypes will occur can be calculated from a simple device known as a Punnett square. If ovum and sperm have an equal chance of possessing either allele, the zygote has a one-half chance of being heterozygous Aa or aA, a one-quarter chance of being homozygous AA, and a one-quarter chance of being homozygous aa. The following Punnett square shows that the three genotypes can be expected to occur in the ratio 1AA : 2Aa : 1aa.

OVA

	A	**a**
A	**AA**	**Aa**
a	**aA**	**aa**

SPERM

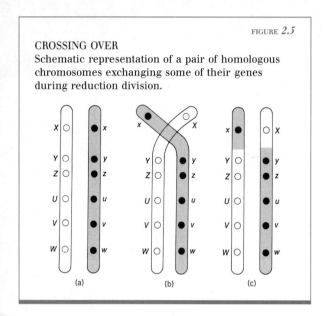

FIGURE *2.5*

CROSSING OVER
Schematic representation of a pair of homologous chromosomes exchanging some of their genes during reduction division.

(a)   (b)   (c)

Note that because of the law of independent assortment, these ratios do not depend on the sorting of alleles on the other pairs of homologous chromatids.

Phenotype Versus Genotype

As the zygote matures, and as the organism is born, grows, and dies, its genetic traits interact with the environment of its particular life experiences. The interaction of genes with environment produces the organism's *phenotype*—its appearance. Organisms having similar genotypes may have dissimilar phenotypes, and vice versa. For example, people who are disposed by heredity to accumulate fat may keep themselves thin by strict dieting, while others predisposed by heredity toward thinness may make themselves fat by overeating. The important lesson here is that no organism is a product of its purely hereditary nature, nor is any organism purely the product of its environmental life experience. Rather, all individuals are products of the interaction of their genes and their environment.

DOMINANT AND RECESSIVE GENES

Individuals who are heterozygous for a trait cannot always be identified as such by their appearance. Some alleles seem to have no effect on the appearance of a trait if they are in a heterozygous condition. Such alleles are said to be recessive. The alleles paired with recessives are said to be dominant.

In the previous example, suppose that A is dominant and a is recessive. The ratio of the genotypes will not change, but individuals AA, Aa, and aA will all have the same phenotype (under similar environmental conditions).

This discovery was first made by Gregor Mendel, the founder of scientific genetics. Crossing red-flowered peas with white-flowered peas, Mendel obtained a generation of peas all of which had red flowers:

	w	w
R	Rw	Rw
R	Rw	Rw

The reason for this is that all the white-flowered peas were homozygous for the recessive gene w, and all the red-flowered peas were homozygous for the dominant gene R. None of the phenotypes shows the presence of the recessive gene. Then, by crossing the red-flowered heterozygotic peas with each other, Mendel showed that the recessive gene was still present in the genotype:

	R	w
R	RR	Rw
w	wR	ww

Approximately one out of every four pea plants—those homozygous for the recessive w—now bore white flowers. Note that the genes for red and white did not blend together but remained separate and distinct.

Although this Punnett square indicates three genotypes, which occur in the ratio 1 : 2 : 1, there are only two phenotypes, which occur in the ratio 3 : 1. Many human traits—such as eye color and color blindness, as well as hemophilia, sickle-cell anemia, and other hereditary diseases—are governed by systems of dominant and recessive genes in which heterozygous individuals are phenotypically indistinguishable from those who are homozygous for a dominant allele. This often makes the heterozygotes carriers of harmful traits. In some instances, however, the heterozygotes have an advantage over the homozygote dominants even though the homozygote recessives may be the victims of fatal diseases. The resistance against malaria enjoyed by persons heterozygous for sickle-cell anemia is a classic instance of heterozygous superiority (see p. 89). It should be emphasized that not all recessive genes are harmful.

Contrary to popular notions about heredity, dominant alleles do not tend to become more frequent in a population as time goes by. In the absence of the forces that promote evolution, dominant and recessive alleles maintain the same frequency of occurrence within a given population.

THE FORCES OF BIOLOGICAL EVOLUTION

Evolution in its broadest sense denotes the change of old forms or structures into new forms or structures. This kind of change takes place among many different "levels" of phenomena, including human ways of living. We shall turn our attention to cultural evolution in Chapter 9. For the moment, however, we shall be concerned with biological evolution. Biological evolution—the change of one kind of organism into another—takes place when the frequency of new or old genes in a population is altered. Any process that changes the frequency of genes in a population is an evolutionary force. Biologists generally identify four major evolutionary forces.

1. Drift The proportions of genes in each generation may differ purely as a result of chance. The frequencies of alleles predicted by the laws of independent assortment and segregation presume the existence of large populations. If a population is very small, there may not be enough matings for these laws to operate. Suppose, for example, that in an isolated population only one individual out of a total population of 100 is carrying an allele for curly hair. By chance, it might happen that the individual dies childless or that his or her children do not inherit the curly hair allele. As a result, there could no longer be any people with curly hair in that population. Another form of drift known as the *founder effect* may occur when a small part of one population migrates and takes with it to its new homeland a pool of genes that is not representative of the original group. One of the migrants, for example, might be carrying a recessive gene for a rare eye disease. Upon arriving in a previously uninhabited island, this individual might have many children, thereby raising the frequency of the allele to a high level. This is the story of what actually happened during the settlement of the South Atlantic island of Tristan da Cunha. The island was settled in 1817 by a single Scottish family, one of whose members carried the gene for the eye disease retinitis pigmentosa. The descendants of the original settlers intermarried with shipwrecked sailors, and their offspring carried the allele with a much higher fre-

quency than found among their ancestors in Scotland (Birdsell 1981:64–65; Nelson and Jurmain 1988:124).

2. Gene flow Since populations that make up a species are never completely isolated from one another, there is usually some interbreeding between them. When interbreeding takes place on a large scale, many alleles may occur in new proportions in the new gene pool. For example, as a result of gene flow, the population of modern Brazil has gene frequencies that were not characteristic of the Africans, Europeans, and native Americans who contributed to the formation of the population of Brazil.

As the example of Tristan de Cunha indicates, migrations need not lead to gene flow. Drift and gene flow therefore are not the same process. In drift, random changes in gene frequencies result from genetic "bottlenecks" that constrict the variety of genes transmitted through a small number of individuals, while in gene flow, large populations interbreed and give rise to new genotypes.

3. Mutations Mutations are alterations or "errors" in the DNA code, or changes in the structure or number of chromosomes, that result in new alleles or new chromosomes. Many physical and chemical factors may play a role in the failure of a gene or of a whole chromosome to duplicate itself. Radiation, for example, is a well-known cause of mutations in many species. Under natural conditions, human mutations may occur anywhere from once every 20,000 duplications to once every 10 million duplications. High rates of mutation will tend to alter the makeup of the gene pool. Regardless of their rate of occurrence, however, mutations may constitute the raw material for extensive evolutionary change if they are advantageous.

4. Natural selection The most powerful force for evolutionary change arises from the variable fitness of genes and alleles. *Fitness* refers purely to the number of surviving progeny—the reproductive success—associated with the alleles at a particular locus. The more progeny that survive, the higher the fitness. Alleles associated with higher fitness will increase in frequency, at the expense of alleles having lower fitness. The process by which high-fitness genes replace low-fitness genes is called natural selection. Natural selection denotes any change in gene frequency brought about by differential fitness. Natural selection may act on mutations or on the existing repertory of genes. When acting on mutations, natural selection can rapidly increase the frequency of a new allele even if the mutation recurs only once in a million duplications. If environmental conditions change to favor alleles already present in the gene pool, natural selection can rapidly raise their frequency also. An example of the power of natural selection to raise the frequency of a rare gene is the evolution of penicillin-resistant strains of bacteria. The alleles conferring resistance are present in normal populations of bacteria but in only a small percentage of individuals. As a result of the differential reproductive success of such individuals, however, the resistant genotype soon becomes the most common genotype.

As a result of natural selection, organisms may be said to become *adapted* to the needs and opportunities present in their environments. An adaptive trait is one that confers relatively high levels of fitness. It is important to remember that there is no absolute fixed level of fitness that guarantees the perpetuation of a species. The essence of organic evolution is its opportunism. A vast range of natural experiments is always being carried out, leading inevitably to the modification and replacement of hitherto highly adapted species (Mayr 1982). As a result of changes in the physical and organic environments, traits that were once adaptive may become maladaptive. The evolutionary record shows that as conditions change, better-adapted species replace those that are less well adapted or maladapted. In most instances these new species cannot be regarded as either more or less complex, "advanced," or "efficient" than their predecessors. They are simply better adapted under the circumstances.

NATURAL SELECTION AND THE "STRUGGLE FOR SURVIVAL"

The information contained in the genes is not sufficient to produce a new organism. For that, the genes need space, energy, and chemical substances. These vital ingredients must be obtained from the environment according to directions contained in the genes. Unless a parent organism dies immediately after producing a single copy of itself, reproduction tends to increase the size of a population. As a population increases, a point is reached sooner or later at which the space, energy, and chemical substances needed for constructing new organisms become more difficult to obtain. If each organism produces several copies of itself, population expansion can occur very rapidly. In a short time there are not sufficient space, energy, or chemical nutrients to permit all the members of the population to reproduce at the same rate. Some genotypes, enjoying greater fitness, will come to constitute an increasing proportion of the population—they will be selected by natural selection.

Fitness is associated with many different kinds of factors. It may be related to the organism's ability to resist disease, to gain or hold space more securely, or to obtain energy in larger or more dependable amounts, as well as to the increased efficiency and dependability of some aspect of the reproductive process itself.

It was Charles Darwin and Alfred Wallace (Box 2.1) who formulated the basic principles of how organic evolution could result from natural selection. Under the influence of the prevailing philosophy of economic competition, however, both Darwin and Wallace accepted Thomas Malthus's concept of a "struggle for survival" as the main source of selection for reproductive success. Thus, in the nineteenth century, natural selection was pictured incorrectly as the direct struggle between individuals for scarce resources and sexual partners, and even more erroneously as the preying upon and destruction of one another by organisms of the same species. Although within-species killing and competition sometimes do play a role in organic evolution, the factors promoting differential reproductive success are in the main not related to an organism's ability to destroy other members of its own population or to prevent them from obtaining nutrients, space, and mates.

Today, biologists recognize that natural selection favors cooperation within species as often as it favors competition. In social species the perpetuation of an individual's genes often depends as much on the reproductive success of its close relatives as on its own survival and reproduction. Many social insects even have "altruistic" sterile "castes" that assure their own genetic success by rearing the progeny of their fertile siblings (see p. 478).

SPECIATION: FAST OR SLOW?

Darwin pictured evolution taking place as a result of the slow accumulation of slight adaptive changes. Eventually, enough differences would accumulate in a population so that it gradually became unable to interbreed with or have fertile offspring with other populations. As a result of this increasing degree of reproductive isolation, a new species would emerge. This view of speciation is called *phyletic gradualism.* It has recently been criticized for its failure to account for certain aspects of the fossil record namely, the long periods during which many species do not seem to change at all and the suddenness with which new species often appear.

An alternative view of speciation is called *punctuated equilibrium.* According to this view, species are not always accumulating new adaptive changes; they

A GREAT MOMENT IN SCIENCE

On the Tendency of Species to form Varieties; and on the Perpetuation of Varieties and Species by Natural Means of Selection. By Charles Darwin, Esq., F.R.S., F.L.S., & F.G.S., and Alfred Wallace, Esq. Communicated by Sir Charles Lyell, F.R.S., F.L.S., and J. D. Hooker, Esq., M.D., V.P.R.S., F.L.S. &c.*

[Read July 1st, 1858.]

London, June 30th, 1858.

MY DEAR SIR,—The accompanying papers, which we have the honour of communicating to the Linnean Society, and which all relate to the same subject, viz. the Laws which affect the Production of Varieties, Races, and Species, contain the results of the investigations of two indefatigable naturalists, Mr. Charles Darwin and Mr. Alfred Wallace.

These gentlemen having, independently and unknown to one another, conceived the same very ingenious theory to account for the appearance and perpetuation of varieties and of specific forms on our planet, may both fairly claim the merit of being original thinkers in this important line of inquiry; but neither of them having published his views, though Mr. Darwin has for many years past been repeatedly urged by us to do so, and both authors having now unreservedly placed their papers in our hands, we think it would best promote the interests of science that a selection from them should be laid before the Linnean Society.

*Darwin's friends, Lyell and Hooker, interceded to protect Darwin from being upstaged by Wallace. This is one of the most remarkable cases of simultaneous independent invention (see p. 111).

SOURCE: *Journal of the Proceedings of the Linnean Society—Zoology* 3(1859):45–46.

are already very well adapted and hence are in "equilibrium" with their habitats. Only after millions of years, and sometimes tens of millions of years, will this equilibrium be "punctuated" by a species-forming "event." Such an event might be triggered by a change in environment or an opportunity to utilize a new habitat, and might at one extreme take only a few hundred years to complete (Eldredge and Gould 1972; Eldredge and Tattersall 1982:59). Although punctuated equilibrium has been represented by the popular media as a fundamental challenge to Darwin's view of evolution, it is in reality no such thing (Gould 1987). Most biologists find no difficulty in accepting the possibility of both gradual and sudden speciation events, with most new species originating over intermediate time spans (hundreds of thousands of years). The most important point about speciation is not the rate at which it occurs but that it occurs as a result of the four major natural forces of evolution—drift, gene flow, mutation, and natural selection—and not as a result of divine intervention, as scientists once believed.

SCIENTIFIC CREATIONISM

Scientific creationism denies the validity of anthropological theories of biological and cultural evolution. The aim of scientific creationists is to compel the public schools either to stop teaching evolutionism or to give equal time to their views. They seek to achieve this aim by labeling evolutionism as "theory, not fact."

This argument contains a grain of truth. All scientific "facts," "theories," and "laws" are held provisionally and are subject to being overturned by new evidence, so it cannot be denied that evolutionism is "theory, not fact." But the theories that scientists teach are those that have withstood rigorous testing and are supported by the greatest amount of evidence. Creationist theory is not acceptable as science because it has not withstood rigorous testing and is contradicted by an enormous amount of evidence. No student should be prevented from reading about scientifically discredited theories, but no teacher should be compelled to teach every theory that has ever been proposed and discredited. (There are still people who believe that the earth is flat. Should their views be given equal time in an astronomy class?)

Scientific creationism claims that the entire universe—including all the galaxies, stars, planets, minerals, plants, and animals—was created in six 24-hour days. These six days of creation allegedly took place no more than 10,000 years ago. Modern human types and every kind of animal now extinct such as dinosaurs were once alive at the same time. All species at one time ate only plants and were capable of living forever. Even wolves and tigers had to be vegetarians in those earliest times, for no animals could die. But then, 8,000 years ago, the entire earth was flooded to a height of over 17,000 feet in 40 days. At the end of a year, all this water flowed into ocean basins that had not previously existed. All present-day land-animal species were saved from this flood by being taken on board a wooden barge that alone survived the catastrophic winds and waves that swept over the entire globe (Godfrey 1981; Morris 1974a, 1974b).

According to the Institute for Creationist Research, most of the earth's water was contained in a vapor "canopy" in the upper atmosphere and in underground reservoirs. The flood was initiated by the volcanic eruption of the underground waters, which caused turbulence in the atmosphere and "broke the water canopy." Almost every land animal died. The creatures killed by the flood were then washed into lower elevations, buried by sediments, and fossilized. The first to be buried and fossilized were creatures that lived on the bottom of the sea—shells and other invertebrates; fish were buried next; then amphibians and reptiles (because they lived at "higher elevations"); finally mammals and birds ("because of their greater mobility"). The last to die were human beings—in fact, they were seldom buried by sediments but lay on top of the ground, where their bodies decayed rather than fossilized—and that accounts for there being few fossilized human bones mixed in with those of extinct animals. Moreover, everywhere smaller and lighter creatures succumbed first and were buried deepest, while stronger and larger creatures were buried in the higher sediments. Thus, the flood produced the general order of fossils in the geological strata, from simple to complex and from small to large, with humans on top. It is this layering that the scientific establishment has mistaken for evidence of evolution, the creationists assert.

This scenario lacks scientific credibility. There is no physical evidence for a water canopy, no geophysical explanation why the supposed underground reservoirs should have suddenly erupted simultaneously all over the earth, and no known geophysical processes that could account for the sudden formation of ocean basins into which the flood waters conveniently drained at the end of one year. Moreover, geological strata contain numerous formations that could not conceivably have been produced by raging floodwaters, such as desert sandstones complete with salt deposits indicative not of floods and rapid draining but of slow evaporation from ancient lakes, for example, and fossilized forest covered by layers of volcanic ash left intact by the supposed floodwaters.

The attempt to explain why the deepest strata contain the simplest forms of life, and why fossil vertebrates appear above invertebrates, amphibians above fish, reptiles above amphibians, and mammals above reptiles, is logically inconsistent. Why should land mammals have survived the 40 days of rains and floods better than sharks, whose fossil remains are first found far below those of mammals? The same question applies to fossil reptiles, including aquatic dinosaurs and giant crocodiles and turtles. How could the land mammals, struggling up the face of the tallest mountains (against torrents of hot brine spewing down on them) survive while the sharks, dinosaurs, and crocodiles drowned, sank to the bottom, and were buried? Evolutionary theory of course has no difficulty in explaining the relative positions of invertebrates, fish, reptiles, mammals, and humans in the earth's geological strata—that is the sequence in which they evolved (see p. 41).

Creationists have made films and written books about the so-called man prints and man tracks found

BOX *2.2*

THE PALUXY RIVER FOOTPRINTS

Scientists have explored the region around the Paluxy River near Glen Rose, Texas, since the 1930s, finding hundreds of dinosaur tracks (Fig. 2.6). The geology and paleontology of the area are well known. Scientific creationists claim human tracks are found among the dinosaur tracks, which if true would challenge the interpretations of evolutionists. Contrary to television and comic book portrayals of "cave men" with dinosaur neighbors, humans evolved millions of years after dinosaurs became extinct, and remains of dinosaurs and humans are never found together.

What about the Paluxy River "man tracks," then? In some of the "man tracks" presented in creationist books, faint traces of side toes can be seen, suggesting that these footprints are really just eroded dinosaur tracks. These tracks show claw marks at the "heel" of the "human" print, another indication that the track is a misinterpreted dinosaur track. Also, in at least one footprint sequence, dinosaur tracks and human footprints alternate. Either people evolved very rapidly from dinosaurs and then back again, or the "human" tracks are just indistinct dinosaur tracks!

These dinosaur prints lack the anatomy of human footprints, although some creationists claim to be able to see "big toes," "balls," and "arches" in eroded holes in the eroded holes in the river bank. If the whole bank is surveyed, however, it can be seen that there are hundreds of erosion holes and washed-out places. The irregular

shapes are like inkblot tests: one can imagine all kinds of figures. The "human" prints imagined from these erosional features are carefully selected examples that are best described as wishful projections of the hopes of scientific creationists to see what they want to see.
SOURCE: Scott 1984.

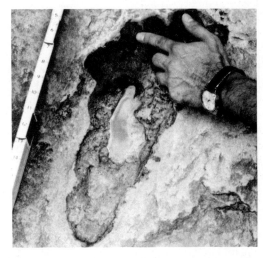

FIGURE *2.6*

PALUXY RIVER "FOOTPRINTS"
Creationists have long regarded this as a human footprint inside a brontosaurus footprint. It is neither one nor the other, but a purely natural erosional feature.

in the Paluxy River near Glen Rose, Texas (Morris 1986; Taylor 1985), which allegedly prove that humans and dinosaurs (and all other extinct forms of life) coexisted before the flood. These man prints and man tracks are the imaginative results of wishful thinking (see Box 2.2). As a result of field inspections carried out by a team of anthropologists (Cole and Godfrey 1985), the widely distributed creationist film, "Footprints in Stone," was withdrawn from circulation (Taylor 1985). It is now admitted that "certain of the prints once labeled human are taking on a completely different character"—that is, the character of dinosaur, not human, footprints (Morris 1986:ii).

Scientific creationists propose that before the flood, everyone spoke the same language; afterward each group suddenly began to speak in mutually unintelligible languages. This unintelligiblility in turn caused people to emigrate from their homeland to distant parts of the globe. But there is no evidence to support such an event, and in fact it is contradicted by all that is known about the history of languages. As we shall see (p. 129), the science of historical linguistics has patiently reconstructed the ancestral forms of the major linguistic families of the globe. The languages we speak today evolved gradually from these ancestral protolanguages. The evolution of new languages did not provoke the migration and separation of ancient populations; rather, it was the migrations and separations of ancient populations that led to the evolution of new languages.

Creationists claim that the Old Stone Age lasted not the 2 million years (or more) that archaeologists contend (see p. 136), but only 3000 years, from the dispersal caused by the Tower of Babel to the reappearance of advanced civilizations outside the Middle East. Their reasoning goes like this: If the Old Stone Age had lasted for a million years, the population of the earth would be much greater than it is today. But as we shall see (p. 222), a substantial anthropological literature demonstrates that prehistoric peoples maintained very low rates of population increase by means of abstinence, abortion, prolonged nursing, and direct and indirect forms of infanticide.

Furthermore, the creationist theory that all civilizations can be traced back to the Middle East ignores the most important archaeological discoveries of the twentieth century—that pre-Columbian state societies in Mexico and Peru evolved from a hunter-gatherer base independently of significant Old World influences. Archaeologists have found step-by-step evidence for the processes by which native American plants and animals unknown in the Old World—such as llamas, alpacas, guinea pigs, potatoes, manioc, maize, and amaranth—were domesticated and integrated into prehistoric native American cultures. These plants and animals furnished the food-energy base for the evolution of bands into villages, villages into chiefdoms, chiefdoms into states, and states into empires in pre-Columbian America (Weatherford 1988).

At the close of the nineteenth century, leading philosophers, theologians, and scientists succeeded in bringing about a truce between science and religion that had raged ever since Giordano Bruno was burned at the stake in A.D. 1600 for saying that the earth was not the center of the universe. Scientists and theologians of many faiths came to accept the idea that there was no need for conflict between them as long as religious beliefs that science could not empirically test were not said to be scientific theories. People of deep religious conviction have ever since found it perfectly compatible with their beliefs in God, Christ, Krishna, Allah, heaven, and immortality to accept basic scientific theories about the origin and evolution of the earth, life, humankind, and culture. And scientists, some of whom embrace the same faiths, have found it equally compatible with their research

to let the empirically nontestable essence of modern-day world religions stand entirely free of scientific attack. But if creationists insist on attacking the evolutionary core of modern science, modern science has no choice but to strike back against the religious core of creationism (Berra 1990; Spuhler 1985).

The next three chapters will set forth the sequence of evolutionary transformations that resulted in the emergence of human species, from other "kinds" of animals.

SUMMARY

Organic evolution is a consequence of the interaction of reproductive and evolutionary processes. Reproductive processes depend on the replication of genetic information encoded by the DNA molecules found on the chromosomes. In human and other sexually reproducing organisms, chromosomes and genes are randomly shuffled according to the law of independent assortment (genes on non-homologous chromosones are inherited separately) and the law of segregation (father-derived alleles and mother-derived alleles on homologous chromatids are separated from each other during reduction division and end up in different sex cells).

The actual assemblage of genes on an organism's chromosomes is its genotype; its phenotype is its appearance as a result of the suppression of recessive alleles and the interaction of the genotype with the environment. Biological evolution begins with changes in the frequency of genes found in a given population. Four major forces account for gene frequency changes: drift, migration, mutation, and natural selection. Of these, natural selection is the most powerful, since it accounts for the adaptedness of species. Phyletic gradualism and punctuated equilibrium are alternative views of the rates of speciation. Both conform to Darwin's view that speciation results from natural processes.

The theories of scientific creationism are not acceptable alternatives to evolutionism. They are either untestable or contradicted by the available evidence. Evolutionary theories have been rigorously tested and found to be compatible with the available evidence. If creationism is presented as untestable religious belief, then there can be no quarrel between creationism and evolutionism. But scientists are obliged to criticize creationism if it is set forth as an alternative scientific theory.

The Human Pedigree and Human Nature

This chapter sets out to define human nature from a biological point of view. It begins by describing the anatomical and behavioral traits that we share with our most distant relatives in the animal kingdom such as fish and mammals. Then it focuses on the anatomical and behavioral traits that we share with a particular group of mammals known as primates. We then see, from the many anatomical similarities and the use of techniques that actually measure the amount of genetic material possessed in common, that it is with the great apes rather than monkeys or other primates that our species shares the closest common ancestor. Finally, we zero in on the traits that distinguish human beings from apes. Those of you who feel uncomfortable about sharing ancestry with gorillas and chimpanzees may find the final part of this chapter reassuring: It shows how, despite our close genetic resemblance, we differ from apes in many profound ways, including how we move about, chew, stand up, reproduce, and, above all, communicate.

FROM EARLY ANIMALS TO PRIMATES

Biologists use Latin terms to classify organisms by means of a standard set of increasingly inclusive categories ranging upward from species to kingdom. They call the various types of organisms within each category *taxa* (singular, *taxon*). The objective of such categorization is to group in the same taxon all organisms having a common ancestor. So if one is interested in the question "What is human nature?" part of the answer surely lies in learning about the taxa to which our ancestors belong. All of these taxa have contributed something to human nature.

Table 3.1 defines our species, *Homo sapiens,* in terms of the standard major taxonomic categories used by biologists to identify taxa within the animal kingdom.

Human beings are Animalia: mobile, multi-celled organisms that get their energy by eating other organisms. Animals are radically different from members of other kingdoms, such as plants, bacteria, one-celled creatures, and fungi.

TABLE *3.1*

CATEGORIES AND TAXONS RELEVANT TO HUMAN ANCESTRY

Category	Taxon	Common description
Kingdom	Animalia	Animals
Phylum	Chordata	Animals with notochords
Subphylum	Vertebrata	Animals with backbones
Superclass	Tetrapoda	Four-footed vertebrates
Class	Mammalia	Vertebrates with body hair and mammary glands
Subclass	Theria	Mammals bearing fetal young
Infraclass	Eutheria	Mammals that nourish young in womb
Order	Primates*	Primates
Suborder	Anthropoidea*	All monkeys, apes, and humans
Superfamily	Hominoidea*	Apes and humans
Family	Hominidae*	Humans and their immediate ancestors
Genus	*Homo*	Human species living and extinct
Species	*Homo sapiens*	Modern human species
Subspecies	*Homo sapiens sapiens*	All contemporary human beings

*The English words *primate, anthropoid, hominoid,* and *hominid* are often used as informal substitutes for Primates, Anthropoidea, Hominoidea, and Hominidae, respectively. Some categories used by biologists (e.g., "cohort" and "tribe") are not needed to define our ancestry. Disagreement exists about mammalian subclasses and infraclasses.

We are also Chordata, the animal phylum, all of whose members possess (1) a *notochord,* a rodlike structure that provides internal support for the body; (2) *gill pouches,* lateral slits on the throat; and (3) a hollow nerve chord ending in a brain. (We display the first two of these features only when we are embryos.) The Chordata contrast radically with some 24 different animal phyla such as the sponges, the stinging jellyfish, the flatworms, the roundworms, the mollusks, and the arthropods (insects, crustaceans, millipedes, and spiders).

Human beings are also Vertebrata, uniquely distinguished from other subphyla of the Chordata by two features: (1) In all adult Vertebrata the notochord is surrounded or replaced by a column of cartilaginous or bony disks (the vertebrae); and (2) the brain is encased within a bony covering (the skull, or *cranium*).

Among the Vertebrata we belong in the superclass Tetrapoda, which means literally "four-footed," as distinguished from Pisces, the superclass of the fish. The Tetrapoda are divided into four classes: Amphibia, Reptilia, Aves (birds), and Mammalia. Our class, Mammalia, is distinguished from the others by (1) milk-secreting mammary glands; (2) hair; and (3) incisor, canine, and molar teeth for cutting, tearing, and grinding, respectively. In addition, mammals share with birds the capacity to maintain their bodies at a constant temperature.

The Mammalia are usually divided into two subclasses: Theria, mammals like us that do not lay eggs; and Prototheria (also called monotremes), egg-laying mammals, of which the spiny anteater and the duckbill platypus are the best-known and the only surviving representative genera (Fig. 3.1).

The subclass Theria, which does not lay eggs, is divided into two living infraclasses: Metatheria, or *marsupials;* and our own infraclass, Eutheria. The principal characteristic of Eutheria is the presence of the *placenta,* a unique nutrient- and waste-exchanging structure that enhances fetal development within the mother's body. Metatheria lack part or all of the placental structure. Instead, many, though not all, have an external pouch in which the tiny newborn young complete their fetal development (Fig. 3.2). Besides familiar marsupials, such as the kangaroo and the opossum, the metatherians occur in a dazzling variety of forms. Many live an arboreal life, feeding on insects and fruits; others are predators; others dig tunnels; others are aquatic; and still others are jumpers and gliders. There are marsupials that resemble mice and others that evoke comparisons with foxes, minks, wolves, and squirrels (Fig. 3.3). These resemblances are of great theoretical in-

FIGURE *3.1*

EGG-LAYING MAMMALS
(A) The *Echidna,* or spiny anteater, and **(B)** the *Ornithorhyncus,* or duckbill platypus, are representatives of the mammalian subclass Prototheria (also known as monotremes). The platypus has mammary glands but no teats, so its young lick the milk from their mother's fur instead of suckling. Both the platypus and the spiny anteater have but one body opening that serves for elimination, mating, and birth—hence the name monotreme (from *mono,* meaning one, and *treme,* meaning hole).

(A)

(B)

terest because they are not caused by descent from a common ancestor but by adaptations to similar ecological conditions. Closely related taxa that undergo a similar series of adaptations are said to have undergone parallel evolution (Fig. 3.4).

Our infraclass, Eutheria, contains 16 orders, including, for example, insectivores, carnivores, and

FIGURE *3.2*

A WALLABY MOTHER AND CHILD
Among the metatherians, the tiny newborn
young complete their fetal development inside
the mother's pouch.

rodents. The order we belong to is called *Primates*
(pronounced "primahtees"), a taxon that includes
monkeys, apes, tarsiers, lemurs, and other close relatives. We shall use the informal term *primates* to designate this order (see footnote, Table 3.1).

THE PRIMATE ORDER

As compared with the earliest mammals, primates
have (1) distinctive hands, feet, toes, toenails, and fingernails; (2) specialized forelimbs; (3) acute vision;
(4) a small number of offspring per birth; (5) prolonged pregnancies and infancies; (6) complex social
behavior; and (7) large brains (Schwartz et al. 1978).

*1. Distinctive hands, feet, toes, and
nails* Primates have prehensile hands and feet,
meaning that they have flexible fingers and toes that

are adept at grasping and clutching. In many primate
species, the big toe and the thumb are *opposable*—
the tips can be made to lie against the tips of the
other digits (Fig. 3.5). Closely associated with prehensility is the absence or reduction of the claws used by
several other mammalian orders for climbing, predation, and defense. Instead, most primates have flat
nails, which protect and reinforce the tips of their
fingers and toes without interfering with prehensility
(Fig. 3.6).

2. Specialized forelimbs Primates have a
highly developed ability to rotate, flex, and extend
their forelimbs. This capability accounts for the
distinction between arms and legs. Arms in conjunction with a prehensile hand are well suited
for exploring the space under leaves and between
branches and twigs, and for clutching and drawing
in fruits and berries, as well as for catching small animals and insects.

3. Acute vision Primate eyes are large proportionate to facial surface and are typically located toward the front of the head instead of at the sides (Fig.
3.7). This arrangement helps to produce stereoscopic
vision and the ability to gauge distances. Most primates also have color vision. But in contrast to their
well-developed sense of sight, primates have a relatively poor sense of smell. Many other mammals get
most of their information by sniffing the environment,
and have eyes located behind their snouts. Dogs, for
example, lack stereoscopic vision and see only in
black and white tones. They are literally led by their
noses. The positioning of primate eyes is related to
prehensility and to the mobility of the forelimbs. Typical primate feeding involves a grasping action that
brings objects close to the mouth, where they are ex-
amined by the eyes before being swallowed. Snouted
mammals, on the other hand, examine what they eat
primarily by the sense of smell.

4. Small number of offspring per birth Primates tend to give birth to no more than two or three
infants at a time, and a single offspring per birth is
the rule among many primate species. In keeping
with this characteristic, primates have only two mammary glands (unlike dogs, cats and other mammals
that have to nurse seven or eight infants at a time).

5. Prolonged pregnancies and infancies Most
mammalian orders that rely on large numbers of offspring per birth for reproductive success have short
pregnancies followed by rapid onset of sexual maturity and adulthood. Mammals that have large litters depend on numbers to compensate for defective
births. A high proportion of the individuals in the
litter are either stillborn or weeded out shortly after
birth as a result of the competition among the litter-

FIGURE *3.3*

METATHERIA OF AUSTRALIA
(A) Numbat. **(B)** Koala. **(C)** Quoll. **(D)** Tasmanian devil. These marsupials resemble
Eutherian mammals but have had a distinct evolutionary history.

(A)

(C)

(B)

(D)

mates for the mother's milk and for her protection and care. In contrast, primates concentrate on one infant at a time and provide high-quality care for that one infant until it is large enough to fend for itself. Compared with the rest of the animal kingdom, primate mothers pamper their babies (Fig. 3.8). This does not mean, however, that infanticide and child abuse are absent or rare in primate social life (Reite and Caine 1983).

6. Complex social behavior A further consequence of not having large litters is that primate patterns of behavior are highly social. This arises from the prolonged mother-child relationship and the in-

tense care given to each offspring. Manual dexterity also adds to social interdependence, since it permits primates to groom each other's hair. Most primates spend their lives as members of groups (although not necessarily the group they are born into), and these groups cooperate in finding food and in defending themselves against predators. Group life is facilitated among primates by relatively complex communication systems consisting of signals that indicate the presence of food, danger, sexual interest, and other vital matters. Primates need social companionship not only to survive physically but to mature emotionally. Many studies have shown that

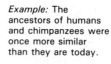

FIGURE *3.4*

THREE KINDS OF EVOLUTION

Divergent: Closely related taxa become increasingly dissimilar.

Example: The ancestors of humans and chimpanzees were once more similar than they are today.

Convergent: Distantly related taxa become more alike than their ancestors as a result of adaptations to similar environments.

Example: Penguins and seals are distantly related yet both have developed flippers—seals from front feet and penguins from wings—as a result of adapting to an aquatic mode of life.

Parallel: Closely related taxa undergo a similar series of adaptations.

Example: Australian marsupials evolved into into many species that resemble Eutherian mammals.

---

monkeys brought up in isolation display severe neurotic symptoms, such as excessive timidity or aggressiveness (Harlow et al. 1966).

7. Large brains Most primates have a high ratio of brain weight to body weight. This "brainyness" relates to the complexity of primate social life. The prolonged dependency of the primate infant; the large amount of auditory, visual, and tactile information passed between mother and offspring; the intense play among juveniles; and the mutual grooming among adults all presuppose a heightened ability to acquire, store, and recall information. Human beings, the brainiest of the primates, are also the most social of the primates. Our intelligence is above all an evolutionary consequence of our dependence on each other for almost everything that we do.

Primates and Life in the Trees

Most living and fossil primates are found in tropical forest habitats. Several of the traits that distinguish the primates from other mammals probably were selected for their advantages in an *arboreal*—tree-dwelling—way of life in these forests: prehensile

hands and feet for moving up and down trunks and branches; forelimbs for exploring between leaves, plucking fruits and berries, and capturing and picking up small insects and reptiles; keen vision as a compensation for not being able to follow scents from branch to branch or tree to tree; and small numbers of offspring per birth as an adaption to the difficulty and dangers to both mother and offspring of having a litter cling to her as she runs and jumps high above the ground.

But life in the trees by itself is not sufficient to account for the earliest phases of primate evolution. Squirrels, for example, have claws and nonprehensile forelimbs, and lack stereoscopic vision, yet they are accomplished aerial acrobats. It seems likely that the grasping functions of primate hands and feet evolved primarily to facilitate cautious, well-controlled movements in pursuit of small animals and insects amid the lower branches and leaves. The stereoscopic vision of the primates resembles that of predator cats and birds, which also evolved in relation to predation practiced against small animals and insects (Cartmill 1974).

FIGURE *3.5*
GIBBON FOOT
The big toe is prehensile and opposable.

FIGURE *3.6*
PRIMATE GRIPS
All primates have prehensile hands. Humans, however, have the most prehensile and dexterous hands of all.

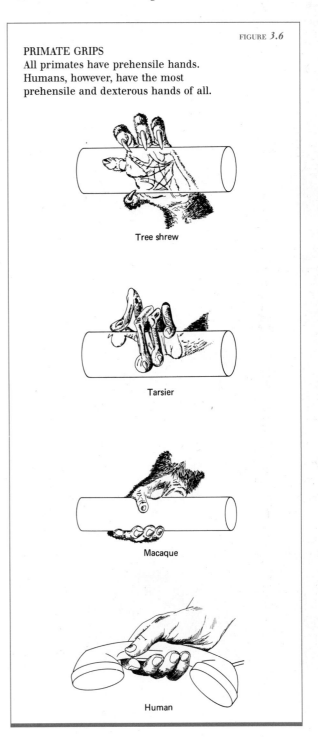

Tree shrew

Tarsier

Macaque

Human

It seems certain that at least some of our most remote ancestors lived in the trees. But as in the case of many other primates species (e.g., baboons) our more recent ancestors went on to adopt a *terrestrial*—ground-dwelling—way of life at some point in the past. The time of this transition will be discussed below.

Suborder Anthropoidea Versus Suborder Prosimii

The order Primates contains two suborders: Anthropoidea and Prosimii. All monkeys, great apes, and human beings are Anthropoidea. The Prosimii consist of lemurs, lorises, tarsiers, and galagos (Fig. 3.9). These less familiar cousins of ours are found in Africa, Madagascar, India, and Southeast Asia.

The Anthropoidea are sometimes called the "higher primates." They have relatively larger and rounder skull cases, flatter faces, and mobile upper and lower lips detached from the gums. This last feature is important for making facial expressions, which ability in turn relates to the intensity of the social life of monkeys and apes, since facial expres-

sions assist in communicating feelings and intentions. In contrast, lorises and lemurs (but not tarsiers) have their upper lip attached externally to their nose by a moist strip of skin called a *rhinarium,* which can also be seen on the snouts of cats and dogs. We humans boast a dry nose and a dry, hairy upper lip. But the two vertical ridges under our nose suggest that someone in our family tree once had a rhinarium.

FIGURE *3.7*

VISUAL ACUITY
(A) A prosimian, the tarsier is a nocturnal arboreal insect- and fruit-eating primate. It has binocular stereoscopic vision, disklike adhesive pads on its digits, elongated hind legs, and a long tail. These characteristics are all suited to hopping along tree limbs. (B) Like the tarsier, the chimpanzee has stereoscopic vision and depends greatly on the sense of sight.

(A)

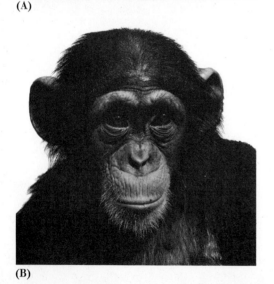

(B)

THE ANTHROPOIDEAN SUPERFAMILIES

The suborder Anthropoidea is made up of three superfamilies: (1) the Ceboidea, or New World monkeys; (2) the Cercopithecoidea, or Old World monkeys; and (3) the Hominoidea, which include all fossil and contemporary species of both apes and human beings.* Old and New World monkeys have different dental patterns that indicate an ancient divergence from a common primate or prosimian ancestor. Old World

*Some taxonomists distinguish two infraorders within the Anthropoidea—Catarrhini and Platyrrhini—with the superfamilies Cercopithecoidea and Ceboidea, respectively placed within the former and the latter.

FIGURE *3.8*

RHESUS MOTHER AND CHILD
A typical agile, alert, dexterous, and highly sociable monkey.

FIGURE *3.9*

PROSIMIANS
(A) Galagos are African Prosimians.
(B) The ancestors of the primates may
have looked like this tree shrew. (C) A
ring-tailed lemur, which locomotes in
a distinctive manner called "vertical
leaping and clinging."

(A)

(C)

(B)

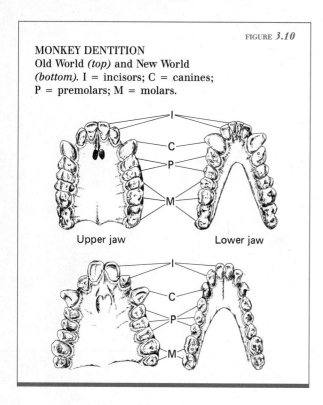

FIGURE *3.10*

MONKEY DENTITION
Old World *(top)* and New World
(bottom). I = incisors; C = canines;
P = premolars; M = molars.

Upper jaw   Lower jaw

monkeys have what is known as the cercopithecoid dental formula: 2.1.2.3 (Fig. 3.10). The numbers denote from left to right the number of incisors, canines, premolars, and molars in one quadrant (quarter) of the jaw. The total number of teeth equals the number in one quadrant times 4 (provided that as in the present instance all quadrants have the same pattern). All New World anthropoids, on the other hand, have either 2.1.3.3 or 2.1.3.2 patterns. If your wisdom teeth have erupted, you may discover for yourself that humans share a 2.1.2.3 pattern with the Old World monkeys and apes.

CHARACTERISTICS OF THE HOMINOIDEA

The hominoids consist of apes and humans. There are two families of living apes: the Hylobatidae, which consist of siamangs and gibbons (the *lesser apes*); and the Pongidae, which consist of chimpanzees, gorillas, and orangutans (the *great apes*).

In general, the Hominoidea are larger than other Anthropoidea and have developed distinctive postures and modes of locomotion. Unlike most monkeys, three of the living Hominoidea—*H. sapiens,* the gibbon, and the siamang—seldom move on all fours.

The gibbon and siamang are primarily *brachiators*—they swing from branch to branch with legs tucked up close to their bodies, propelled through graceful trajectories by extraordinarily long and powerful arms (Fig. 3.11).

Although the chimpanzee, gorilla, and orangutan also have long arms, they are too big and heavy as adults to brachiate energetically. Their long arms, however, are put to good use while they practice *suspensory feeding*—hanging by a combination of arms and prehensile feet and reaching out to pluck off fruity morsels from slender branches that cannot bear their weight (Fig. 3.12). In addition, the great apes have developed special forms of walking on the ground. This is especially true of the chimpanzee and gorilla, who spend the majority of their lives during the day on the ground. In this they are similar to ground-dwelling monkeys such as the baboons. But whereas baboons maintain the basic four-footed gait by walking on the palms of their hands, gorillas and chimpanzees practice *knuckle walking:* Their long arms lock at the elbow into a rigid straight line, and their forward weight rests on their knuckles (Fig. 3.13). Orangutans usually walk on the sides of their fists during their fairly frequent visits to the ground (Galdikas-Brindamour 1975; Napier 1970; Tuttle 1969).

The long, mobile arms of all the living pongids suggest that they all have ancestors who were vigorous brachiators and suspensory feeders.

H. sapiens also probably had ancestors who were brachiators and suspensory feeders, since we too have mobile arms that are quite long in comparison with the length of our trunks. In our case, however, the capacity for brachiation was almost entirely given up in favor of *bipedalism* (two-leggedness). This resulted in the lengthening of our legs to a degree that is unique among the hominoids (Fig. 3.14).

Perhaps I should also add that the Hominoidea are probably more intelligent than the other primates, as our recent experiences with teaching chimps and gorillas to communicate suggest (see Chapter 8).

Commmon Ancestry of Apes and Humans

In recent years, methods have been developed for measuring the degree of relatedness between living species based on biochemical analyses (Pilbeam 1985). Species show tell-tale differences in the degree to which they possess the same DNA molecules. These differences can be measured directly by analyzing the sequence of bases (see p. 31) in their DNA, or indirectly by comparing the sequence of amino

FIGURE *3.11*

GIBBONS

These Hominoidea are assigned to the family Hylobatidae. Their entire anatomy reflects the influence of brachiation. Note especially the huge arms, long fingers, short legs, and short thumbs.

(A)

(B)

FIGURE *3.12*

SUSPENSORY FEEDING

Orangutan reaching out to pluck leaves from small vines and branches.

acids in certain proteins that they possess in common. The currently preferred method for comparing the "genetic distance" (degree of similarity) between two species is called *DNA hybridization* (see Box 3.1). All of the biochemical tests used thus far point to the same conclusion: Among the anthropoidia, it is the sequences of base pairs on the DNA of gorillas and chimpanzees that are most like the base pair sequence of human DNA. However, the question of whether it is the gorilla or the chimpanzee that is genetically more similar to humans remains undecided (Caccone and Powell 1989; Goodman et al. 1990; Marks 1991; Sibley, Comstock, and Ahlquist 1990). In any event, the difference between human DNA and its two closest great ape cousins is about the same as the difference between the DNA of a domestic cat and

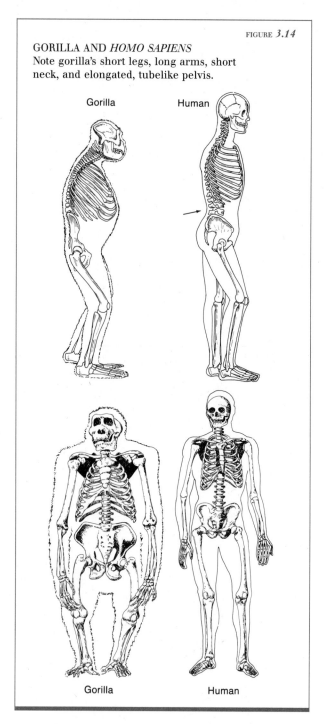

FIGURE *3.13*

ADULT MALE GORILLA
Knuckle-walking involves anatomical
modifications in the elbows as well as
in the wrists and fingers.

FIGURE *3.14*

GORILLA AND *HOMO SAPIENS*
Note gorilla's short legs, long arms, short
neck, and elongated, tubelike pelvis.

Gorilla   Human

Gorilla   Human

the DNA of a lion (Sarich 1974:31; Pilbeam 1986:307).
Much greater "genetic distances" separate the chimp
and gorilla from the orangutan and the gibbon (see
Fig. 3.15).

    An intriguing aspect of the DNA hybridization
method is that it provides a measure not only of
the genetic distance between two taxa, but also of
the time that has elapsed since the taxa branched
off from their nearest common ancestor (see next
chapter).

FAMILY HOMINIDAE VERSUS FAMILY PONGIDAE AND FAMILY HYLOBATIDAE

As we have just seen, the superfamily Hominoidea
contains three families: (1) the Hominidae—all varieties of hominids, of which *H. sapiens* is the sole surviving representative; (2) the Pongidae—all contemporary and extinct varieties of great apes; and (3) the
Hylobatidae—all contemporary and extinct varieties
of the gibbon and siamang.

    What distinguishes humans from apes? Setting
aside for the moment behavioral traits associated
with the evolution of culture, the most conspicuous

anatomical differences all relate to the development
of bipedalism in hominids. As we shall see in greater
detail in the next chapter, the hominids gave up
suspensory feeding and brachiation in the trees in
favor of life spent mostly on the ground in a habitat

BOX *3.1*

DNA HYBRIDIZATION

1. Take tissues from two different taxa, A and B.

2. Extract DNA from the cells of A and B.

3. Separate the double strands of A's DNA by applying heat. (Remember that DNA is normally two-stranded—the double helix.)

4. Repeat Step 3 for B's DNA.

5. Mix single strands of A's DNA with single strands of B's DNA.

6. The single strands "find" the closest "complementary strands" (strands on which the sequences of bases are most nearly similar) and bind together, forming hybrid double strands of DNA, not found in nature.

7. Apply heat to separate the hybrid double strands.

8. Compare the amount of heat needed to separate the hybrid double-stranded DNA with the amount that was needed to separate the normal double-stranded DNA. (Less heat will be needed for the hybrid because the sequences of base pairs do not match as well in the hybrid and hence less energy is needed to drive them apart.)

9. The difference between the energy needed for Step 3 and the energy needed for Step 8 is a measure of the degree to which the base sequences in A differ from those in B.

---

that was relatively open or savannahlike. From this basic change of habitat and gait there arose a series of anatomical and behavioral adaptations that set the hominids off from the great apes. To understand who we are, we must begin from the ground up.

1. The foot Lifting power from our calf muscles raises the heel bone. Then a forward and upward spring is imparted by leverage against the big toe. Arches extending from front to rear and side to side keep the action springy. The big toe of the human foot, unlike the pongid toe, is lined up with the rest of the toes and has lost practically all its opposability. Whereas the pongid foot can be used to touch and grasp objects, the human foot is specialized for standing, walking, and running (Fig. 3.16).

2. Arms and hands The great advantage of hominid bipedalism is that it frees the arms and hands to carry, throw, and pick up objects without impeding the ability to stand, walk, or run. The gorilla, the chimpanzee, and the orangutan depend on their arms either for brachiation or for semierect walking. Hominids are the only animals that can comfortably travel long distances on the ground while carrying heavy objects in their hands. Moreover, the dexterity of the hominid hand is unsurpassed; in the gibbon and the orangutan the requirements of climbing and of brachiation interfere with the size and dexterity of their thumb. The chimpanzee and the gorilla are

---

FIGURE *3.15*

BRANCHING OF MONKEY, APE, AND HUMAN DESCENT BASED ON DNA HYBRIDIZATION
The numbers indicate the difference between the temperature (in degrees Centigrade) needed to separate a certain percentage of the hybrid double-stranded DNA and the temperature needed to separate the same percentage of normal double-stranded DNA. (From Caccone and Powell 1989:931.)

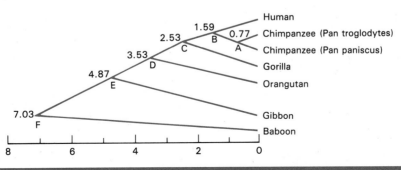

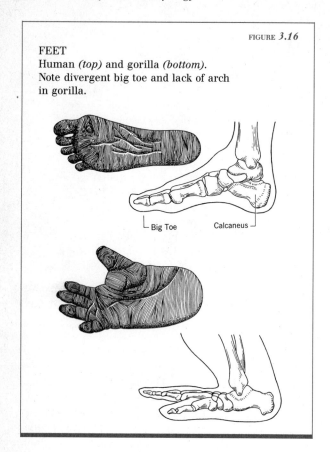

FIGURE *3.16*

FEET
Human *(top)* and gorilla *(bottom)*.
Note divergent big toe and lack of arch
in gorilla.

Big Toe   Calcaneus

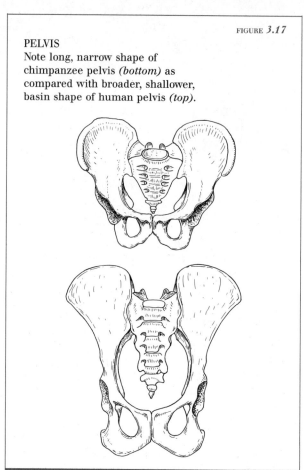

FIGURE *3.17*

PELVIS
Note long, narrow shape of
chimpanzee pelvis *(bottom)* as
compared with broader, shallower,
basin shape of human pelvis *(top)*.

quite dexterous, but our thumb is larger, more heavily muscled, and more supple. The length and strength of the human thumb give us a uniquely precise grip, powerful yet delicate (see Fig. 3.5). This grip, almost as much a hallmark of humanity as bipedalism and braininess, has helped to make us the supreme artisans of the animal kingdom.

3. The lower limbs Human legs relative to trunk length are the longest among the Hominoidea (see Fig. 3.14a). The large calf of our lower leg is distinctive; the great apes lack prominent calf muscles. Even more dramatically human is the massive gluteal musculature, which, when we are not sitting on it, provides much of the force for walking uphill, straightening up after bending, and running and jumping.

4. The pelvic girdle In four-footed mammals the pelvis has the contour of a narrow tube to which the rear legs are attached at nearly a right angle. About one-half of the weight of an animal that moves on all fours is transmitted through the pelvis to the rear legs. Among the Pongidae the rear legs bear a higher percentage of the total body weight. The chimpanzee pelvis, for example, shows some flattening and strengthening as a result of its increased weight-bearing function. But in hominids the pelvis is basinlike, and the body's center of gravity passes directly through it (Fig. 3.17). The basinlike character of the human pelvis is completed by inward-turning vertebrae and their ligaments at the base of the spine (a vestigial tail), which close off the bottom portion of the pelvic cavity. A main function of the pelvis is to provide attachments for the powerful muscles that control the legs. The basin or ring shape of the human pelvis with its two broad-bladed hip bones increases the effective force of all the musculature involved in bipedalism. Muscles attached to the hip bones and to other portions of the pelvis provide much of the power for moving the lower limbs.

5. The vertebral column To allow for upright posture, the human vertebral column has developed extra vertebrae that form a unique curve in the lum-

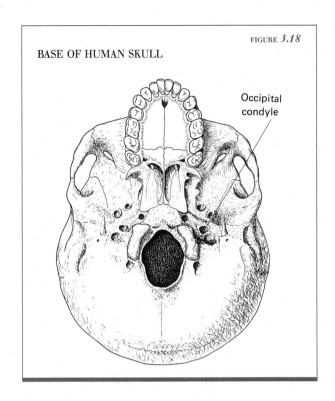

FIGURE *3.18*

BASE OF HUMAN SKULL

Occipital condyle

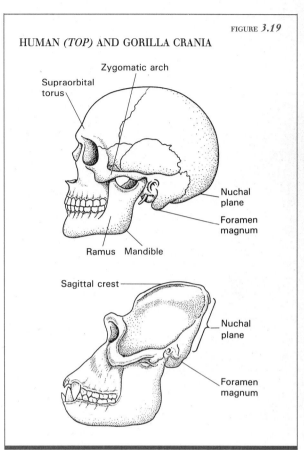

FIGURE *3.19*

HUMAN *(TOP)* AND GORILLA CRANIA

Zygomatic arch
Supraorbital torus
Nuchal plane
Foramen magnum
Ramus   Mandible
Sagittal crest
Nuchal plane
Foramen magnum

bar region (see Fig. 3.13). Here the column bends forward over the center of the pelvis, and on meeting the pelvis reverses itself to form a "sickle" with the handle above. Without this curve, people would have a tendency to topple over backward. Although capable of supporting 700 pounds or more, our vertebral column is subject to malfunction. The intense pressures on the cartilaginous disks between the vertebrae lead to their rupture and misalignment, and to characteristically human "pains in the back." At its upper end (the cervical region), the human spinal column curves forward, then upward and slightly to the rear, meeting our skull at a point close to its center of gravity. The human neck vertebrae lack the long spiny rearward extensions that anchor the gorilla's large neck muscles (Birdsell 1981:223 ff.; Harrison and Montagna 1969).

6. The neck The head pivots atop the vertebral column on a pair of bony knobs found at the base of our skulls. These knobs are called *occipital condyles* (Fig. 3.18). In pongids the main weight of the head is well forward of the pivot points. The powerful neck muscles needed for stability completely obscure the skeletal contour of the gorilla's cervical region. Modern hominids are different; our occipital condyles are very close to the head's center of gravity. Our head almost balances by itself at the top of the cervical

curve, so we need only relatively small neck muscles and have a distinctively long, thin neck.

7. The cranium The rear portion of the skull to which the neck muscles are attached is called the nuchal plane (see Fig. 3.19). Among the pongids this area is very large and rises to form an abrupt angle with the rest of the head at the nuchal crest. In *H. sapiens* the nuchal crest is absent, the area of the nuchal plane is smaller, and its position is underneath rather than at the rear of the skull. This gives a smooth, spherical contour to the rear of the human skull. The roundedness continues into the forehead region and is clearly related to the fact that our brain is the largest and heaviest of primate brains. Viewed from the rear, our skull is distinguished by steeply rising side walls. Its maximum width is above rather than below the ears. A gorilla's head is more massive than ours, but a much smaller space is available inside. Much of its skull is taken up by the thick bones and prominent crests, which serve as attachments for muscles and as structural reinforcements.

Such crests, as we shall see in the next chapter, are also found in certain extinct hominids.

8. The face and upper jaw   Among pongids the face extends well beyond the plane of the forehead. The forward thrust is continued by the upper jaw, resulting in a shape known as *prognathism* (see Fig. 3.19). In contrast, the modern human upper jaw is orthognathic; it is aligned vertically with the forehead, directly under the eye sockets. Among gorillas there is a large bar over the eyes known as the supraorbital torus. This structure protects the upper face from the gorilla's massive jaws and powerful chewing muscles. With the exception of certain extinct species, hominids in contrast have smaller jaws, less powerful chewing muscles, and a smaller supraorbital torus. The introduction of cooked foods, which do not have to be chewed as vigorously as raw foods, may be responsible for the reduced size of the *H. sapiens* jaw.

9. Jaws and teeth   Our chewing equipment is one of our most important and distinctive features. Fossilized fragments of jaws and even of single teeth are relied on for tracing hominid ancestry and for distinguishing between hominid and pongid taxa. Seen from above, the teeth of modern pongids form a distinctive arc in which long parallel rows of molars and premolars are joined by a U-shaped curve of canines and incisors. In contrast, the hominid dental arc is parabolic and greatly compressed to conform to the orthognathism of the hominid face. Pongids have incisors and canines that are larger than their molars and quite massive compared with hominid incisors and canines. Unlike pongids, hominids have smaller incisors and canines than their molars (Fig. 3.20).

These differences imply fundamentally different feeding adaptations. The massive size of the pongid's front teeth probably relate to the use of incisors and canines to cut and rip the outer covering of woody shoots (such as bamboo and wild celery), and the tough skin of forest fruits. The hominid's small incisors and canines relative to its large molars suggests a different diet, based on substances that are easily processed into bite-size portions by the front teeth but that thereafter must be subjected to a considerable amount of grinding and milling before they can be swallowed. The importance of teeth for milling and grinding in the adaptation of our ancestors is also suggested by the flexible way in which our lower jaw is hinged, enabling both back-to-front and side-to-side rotary motions as we chew.

Another feature suggestive of grinding and milling is the delayed eruption of the hominid molars, so that as the front molars are worn down they are replaced by fresh molars to the rear. A final aspect of this pattern is that hominid molars are higher

FIGURE 3.20

JAWS
Gorilla jaw *(top)* and human jaw *(bottom)*. Note the large incisors and canines of the gorilla.

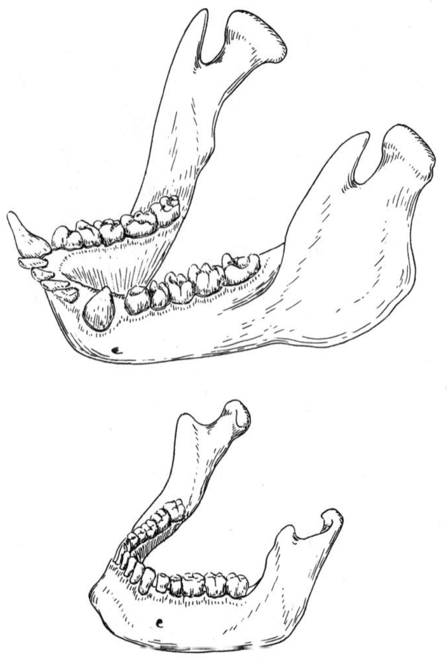

than they are either broad or long. This is another feature that would provide a selective advantage in resisting the attrition produced by prolonged milling action (Simons 1968; Simons and Ettel 1970).

Another important feature of hominid dentition is that our canines project only slightly or not at all above the level of the adjacent teeth. In contrast, pongid canines, especially the upper canines, are so large that they need spaces in the lower jaw to enable its mouth to shut tightly. Canines are especially conspicuous among male pongids. In addition to ripping woody stalks and opening hard-covered fruits, they are used to threaten predators, females, and junior males. Since we have neither large canines nor other large teeth, our jaws have lost the defensive or offensive capacity that jaws serve in so many other animals (Sheets and Gavan 1977).

The basic pattern of hominid dentition weighs heavily against the popular stereotype that our ancestors were bloodthirsty "killer apes." In fact, just the opposite seems to be true (see p. 58). Deprived of canines, and equipped with fingernails and toenails instead of claws, we humans are anatomically curiously harmless creatures. Naked, without weapons or a knowledge of judo or karate, we would find it virtually impossible to kill any large, healthy animal, including our own adult fellow humans, matched for size. (Fists, so prominent in fictional American fighting, are too fragile to do lethal damage, and barefooted kickers break their toes.) This does not mean that our ancestors were vegetarians; on the contrary, as we shall see, they were undoubtedly both meat and plant eaters, or omnivores.

HOMINID SEXUALITY

Among almost all living primates, the frequency of copulatory behavior is closely controlled by the female's ovulatory cycle. At the time of ovulation, when the mature ovum is ready to be fertilized, female primates signal that they are in a heightened state of sexual receptivity called *estrus* ("in heat") in a variety of ways. They may display colorful swellings of their skin, especially in the anal-genital region, emit sexually exciting odors, and exhibit behavioral changes such as actively presenting their rump to males or becoming more aggressive. Sexual receptivity in chimpanzees, for example, is signaled by a bright pink swelling in the anal-genital skin, and during this period as many as 20 male chimpanzees have been observed copulating with a single female (van Lawick-Goodall 1965). What estrus accomplishes is that it makes certain that when a female's egg is ready to be fertilized, male sperm will be there to fertilize it.

Although the menstrual cycle of the human female is similar in many respects to that of the pongids and other primates, humans do not have an estrus cycle. There are no external signs indicating the period during which viable ova can be fertilized by sperm. This period is remarkably short: the ovum remains fertile for about 24 hours, while the sperm can live in the uterine mucosa for three days (Djerassi 1990:106l). Most women cannot tell when they are ovulating. Instead of estrus, humans have evolved a unique system for making certain that during the brief interval when the ovum is ready to be fertilized, sperm will be present to do the job. This system involves keeping both males and females sexually active during a high percentage of days, weeks, and months throughout the year. In this sense, humans are unusually "sexy" animals.

Why did our ancestors lose the estrus cycle and come to rely on extreme sexiness as the means of ensuring the presence of sperm at the time of ovulation? Since this pattern of mating calls for a much larger expenditure of energy than estrus would, it seems likely that it had compensating advantages.

The most likely explanation is that the loss of estrus was selected for because it contributed to the development of intense cooperative bonds between human males and females. The frequent satisfaction of mutual sexual needs provides a basis for the unique extent to which human males and females cooperate in the care and feeding of their offspring and of each other. This heightened degree of cooperation assures human males and females a high degree of reproductive success despite the waste of energy involved in not synchronizing peak rates of copulation with ovulation.

PYGMY CHIMPANZEE SEXUALITY

Among primates, the closest approach to the human pattern of using sexuality to create social and economic bonds has been found among pygmy chimpanzees (*Pan paniscus*) (Fig. 3.21). Because of the close genetic relationship between chimpanzees and hominids, the pygmy chimpanzee pattern of sexuality may provide a model of the pattern that prevailed among the earliest hominids.

Although the pygmy chimp, like the common chimp (*Pan troglodytes*), exhibits increasing and decreasing anal-genital swelling during the ovulatory cycle, the swellings remain conspicuous most of the time and there is a high rate of sexual activity involving both female homosexual and heterosexual copu-

FIGURE *3.21*

BONOBOS (PYGMY CHIMPS) MATING
These "sexy" apes adopt face-to-face positions once thought to be distinctive of human lovemaking.

lation on a daily basis throughout the month and year. Not only are these chimps extraordinarily "sexy," but the males appear to share food with females and juveniles more than among any other nonhuman primate. Most impressive is the fact that the females have been observed to initiate food sharing with both males and females by engaging in copulatory behavior. This phenomenon lends support to the hypothesis that there is a link between hypersexuality and the degree of social interdependence in the evolution of a distinctive human nature (Badrian and Badrian 1984; Kano 1990. See Box 3.2).

LANGUAGE AND CULTURE

Many animals possess learned traditions that are passed on from one generation to the next and that constitute a rudimentary form of culture. As we shall see in the next chapter, chimpanzees and other primates make and use tools as a result of such learning. However, it is only among the hominids that culture has become a primary source of adaptive behavior, more important than biological evolution based on changes in gene frequencies. Able to stand and walk erect, their hands freed entirely from locomotor and support functions, the earliest hominids probably manufactured, transported, and made effective use of tools as a primary means of subsistence. Apes, on the other hand, survive nicely with only the barest inventory of such tools. Hominids, ancient or modern, have probably always depended on some form of culture for their very existence.

Closely linked with the capacity for cultural adaptations is the uniquely human capacity for language and for language-assisted systems of thought. While other primates use complex signal systems to facilitate social life, human languages are qualitatively different from all other animal communication systems. The unique features of human languages— to be discussed in Chapter 8—undoubtedly arise from genetic adaptations related to the increasing dependence of the earliest hominids on social cooperation and on culturally acquired modes of subsistence. Human infants are born with the kind of neural circuitry that makes learning to talk as natural for them as learning to walk (Bickerton 1990). This circuitry in turn represents the kind of mental "wiring" useful for a creature that needs to acquire and transmit large amounts of new information during its lifetime.

SUMMARY

H. sapiens shares some traits with all animals. The animals with which we share the most traits are the Chordata, Vertebrata, Tetrapoda, Mammalia, Theria, Eutheria, Primates, Anthropoidea, and Hominoidea. The ancestors of each of these taxons were also our ancestors. Our closest evolutionary relatives are other

---

BOX *3.2*

SEX AND SHARING AMONG PYGMY CHIMPANZEES

While both common and pygmy chimp females obtain prized foods by begging with their outstretched arm (see p. 59) pygmy females do something seldom observed among any nonhuman species. They precede their begging, or dispense with it entirely, by copulating with the individual who possesses the desired food. Sueshi Karoda of the Laboratory of Physical Anthropology of Kyoto University gives these examples: "A young female approached a male, who was eating sugar cane. They copulated in short order, whereupon she took one of the two canes held by him and left. In another case a young female persistently presented to a male possessor, who ignored her at first, but then copulated with her and shared his sugar cane" (Karoda 1984:317).

Pygmy chimp females do not restrict themselves to exchanging sex for food with males. Nearly half of all food-sharing incidents observed between females were preceded by face to face, genital-to-genital rubbing episodes.

Heterosexual copulation also frequently takes place in the face-to-face position (contrary to the long-held belief that only humans copulate in this manner). Copulation does not take place until both sexes have indicated their readiness by facial and vocal signals. They stare into each other's eyes for 15 minutes prior to copulation and maintain eye contact while copulating (Thompson-Handler et al. 1984:355; Badrian and Badrian 1984.)

members of the Primates order, especially members of the anthropoidean suborder. We share the following traits with other primates: (1) prehensile hands, (2) legs and extremely mobile arms specialized for different functions, (3) stereoscopic color vision, (4) one or two babies per birth episode, (5) long pregnancies and a long period of infant dependency, (6) intense social life, (7) large brains relative to body size. Most of these traits reflect an actual or ancestral adaptation to an arboreal way of life in tropical forest habitats.

With Old World monkeys we also share the cercopithecoid dental formula, and with the great apes we share large body size and a high degree of intelligence.

The anthropoidean suborder includes monkeys, apes, and human beings, all of whom are descended from a common primate ancestor. Among the pongids, gorillas and chimpanzees bear the closest resemblance to hominids, as confirmed by the analysis of various biochemical tests. Like the pongids, the hominids probably had an ancestor who brachiated and practiced suspensory feeding but who subsequently developed additional specialized modes of walking on the ground.

Living hominids are distinguished from pongids by (1) feet specialized for walking; (2) extremely dexterous hands; (3) long legs relative to trunk length; (4) basinlike pelvis; (5) lumbar curve; (6) head balanced on top of spine; (7) smooth, spherical, enlarged cranium; (8) small jaws; (9) reduced canines, parabolic dental arcade, and orthognathic face.

Among living representatives at least, hominid females do not have seasonal or monthly periods of sexual receptivity, nor do modern hominid females have sexual swellings and other sexual signals synchonized with ovulation. This implies a high rate of sexual activity selected for its advantages as a means of establishing cooperative bonds between hominid males and females. Pygmy chimpanzees, whose DNA sequences closely resemble our own, have an extremely active daily, monthly, and yearly sex life even though they have sexual swellings that are at a maximum at ovulation. As in hominids, this hypersexuality is associated with a high degree of food sharing between males and females and adults and juveniles.

The most distinctive behavioral features of the hominids, however, relate to a uniquely expanded dependence on social learning, tool use, language, and culture.

Chapter 4

The First Hominids

Would you like to know who the first human beings were? What they looked like? Where they lived? Whether they were fierce, carnivorous "killer apes," bold scavengers, or mild-mannered vegetarians? Did they make tools? Did they live on the ground or in the trees? These questions are what this chapter is about. It provides a review of the fossil evidence for the evolution of the earliest hominids. (Fossils are rocklike relics formed by the substitution of minerals for bone and tissue that preserve the shape of long-dead organisms.) While much is known, the pace of discovery of new fossils that bear on these questions quickens from year to year. As a result, only tentative answers can be given to some of these questions, and you must be prepared to cope with conflicting interpretations offered by different experts.

THE EVOLUTIONARY ROAD

Life probably began about 3 or 4 billion years ago. The first microorganisms were not fossilized and disappeared without leaving a trace, but a variety of complex soft-bodied organisms left their imprints in rocks that are over 1 billion years old (Grey 1985). It was not until 600 mya (million years ago) that large hard-bodied animals became abundant. As shown in Figure 4.1, the phylum Chordata, subphylum Vertebrata, and superclass Tetrapoda were present about 400 to 350 mya. Mammals appeared between 225 and 180 mya, during the Mesozoic era. There were primates toward the end of the Mesozoic or the beginning of the Cenozoic era, 70 to 60 mya. Between 38 and 25 mya during the Oligocene epoch, the Anthropoidea became abundant. In the next epoch, the Miocene, the Hominoidea became widespread. The earliest unmistakable hominids did not appear until the Pliocene epoch, about 7 to 4 mya. The genus *Homo* appeared close to the Pliocene-Pleistocene transition, and our own species, *H. sapiens,* near the end of the Pleistocene (Box 4.1).

If the evolutionary road that life has traveled is reduced to the scale of 1 mile, then the distance traveled since the appearance of the first humans is 32 inches.

FROM PROSIMIANS TO HOMINOIDS

The earliest of the Primates lived during the Paleocene and Eocene eras. They resembled the Prosimii and were probably the ancestors of today's lemurs and tarsiers.

During the Eocene, the Prosimians underwent several *adaptive radiations*—that is, they rapidly filled out new ecological niches with new species and genera. These adaptive radiations were followed by widespread extinctions of prosimiam taxa, possibly as a result of competition with arboreal rodents, bats, and the newly emerging ancestors of the modern anthropoids.

Another adaptive radiation took place during the Oligocene, when the ancestors of today's apes and monkeys appear in the fossil record for the first time.

Fossils that show the divergence of Old World monkeys and apes from a common ancestor have not yet been identified. Fossils found in Oligocene strata at Fayum, Egypt, and previously identified as "apes" are now regarded as representative of primitive catarrhine anthropoids antecedent to the monkey-ape divergence. No direct linkage can be drawn between Fayum fossil anthropoids such as *Aegyptopithecus* (Fig. 4.2) or *Propliopithecus* (Fig. 4.3) and the Cercopithecoid monkeys and apes that inhabited East Africa in the late Miocene (Fleagle et al. 1987:1247). "At present, we have virtually no evidence of anthropoid evolution between 30 and 20 million years ago, the time of a major adaptive radiation of catarrhines and probably the phyletic divergence of monkeys and apes" (ibid.; Ciochon 1985; Klein 1989; Simons 1985).

During the early Miocene, various kinds of apes evolved in widely separated parts of the Old World (but none in the New World). (See Fig. 4.4 for a map of major sites of human evolution.) Not until the middle to late Miocene did apes appear that markedly resemble modern hominoids. The earliest of these is the African ape, *Kenyapithecus*, which lived about 14 mya (Fig. 4.5).

There are three other groups of middle to late Miocene apes: pliopiths, dryopiths, and sivapiths (Klein 1989:87). The pliopiths and dryopiths ("forest

FIGURE *4.1*

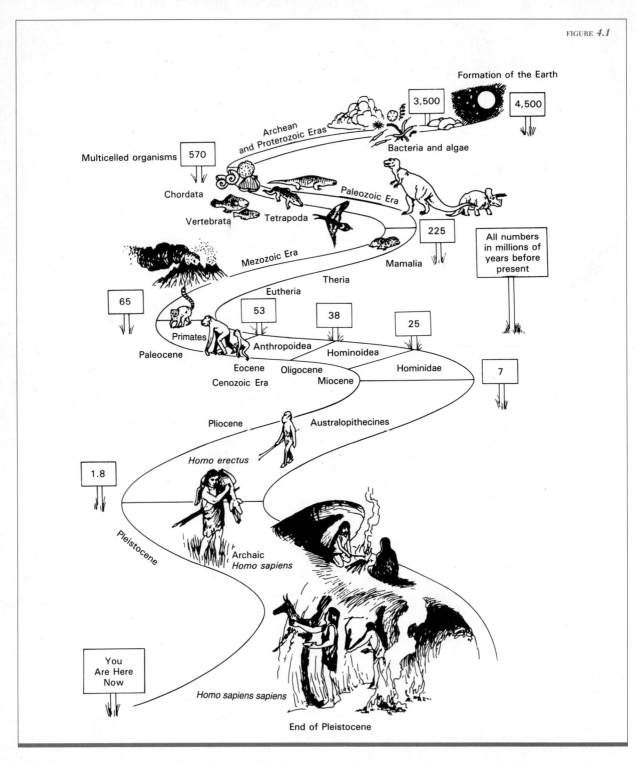

apes"; see Fig. 4.6) are found mainly in Europe, while the sivapiths (named after the Hindu god, Siva) are found in both Europe and Asia.

The dryopiths were chimpanzee-sized apes that became extinct about 8 mya. Their contribution to the ancestry of the modern Hominoidea is unknown.

While the pliopiths were gibbonlike in some features, they seem to have died out without contributing to modern hominoid ancestry. However, most experts now consider the sivapiths to be on or near the line leading to the modern orangutan (ibid.:92).

One of the most interesting fossil apes is *Gi-*

BOX *4.1*

HOW FOSSILS ARE DATED

CARBON FOURTEEN (^{14}C)

A certain percentage of the carbon in every organism's body consists of the isotope ^{14}C. This isotope decays at a constant rate into an isotope of nitrogen. But the ratio of ^{14}C to ^{12}C is kept constant as long as the organism takes in fresh supplies of ^{14}C through eating and breathing. When it dies, however, the ratio of ^{14}C to ^{12}C begins to fall at a constant rate—namely, by one-half every 5,730 years. Knowing the ratio of ^{14}C to ^{12}C, one can calculate the year that the organism died. This method is unreliable beyond 70,000 years and thus is used mainly in archaeology, not in paleontology.

POTASSIUM-ARGON (^{10}K − ^{40}AR)

During volcanic eruptions a bed of lava containing the isotope of potassium, ^{40}K, is laid down. This isotope decays into the isotope of argon, ^{40}Ar, at the rate of one-half every 1.31 billion years. Fossils found below or above dated beds of volcanic ash can thus be assigned upper or lower dates. This method is reliable from about 200,000 to up to several billion years ago, but fossils are not always conveniently sandwiched between layers of volcanic ash (Fleming 1977).

FISSION TRACK DATING

The most abundant isotope of uranium, ^{238}U, makes microscopic tracks as it spontaneously fissions in glassy substances associated with volcanic activity. The older the specimen, the larger the number of tracks. Since the rate of fissioning is constant, all one need know is the amount of ^{238}U that was originally present in the specimen. This is determined by laboratory techniques involving neutron bombardment. Depending on the richness of the specimen in ^{238}U, this method can supply accurate dates ranging from a few hundred years to 3 billion years ago (Macdougall 1976).

GEOMAGNETIC DATING

During the history of the earth, the magnetic poles have altered their position from time to time. The dates of these "magnetic events" have been calculated by various isotope decay methods. The minerals in sedimentary strata respond to magnetic fields and point toward the position of the magnetic poles when they were deposited and solidified. They thus contain a record of the dated magnetic events that took place during their formation.

THERMOLUMINESCENCE

This technique depends upon the fact that electrons get trapped in crystalline substances (such as flint or ceramics) that are exposed to the naturally occurring background radiation of uranium, thorium, and radioactive potassium. Heating these substances permits these electrons to escape with an accompanying and proportionate quantity of photons (light). On the assumption that the older the sample, the more electrons trapped and the greater the emission of light, one can estimate the time that has elapsed since the sample was last heated. Best applications are for dates in the 10,000- to 200,000-year range.

gantopithecus, an Asian genus whose jaws, teeth, and body were almost four times as massive as in a modern human (Fig. 4.7). Except for its size, *Gigantopithecus* could be classified as a member of the sivapith group. It flourished during the Pliocene and survived well into the Pleistocene, becoming extinct only about 0.5 mya.

DNA hybridization and other molecular techniques cannot be applied to fossils that are millions of years old. Hence, the position of the known Miocene fossil apes on the family tree of the modern Hominoidea cannot yet be ascertained biochemically.

Which of the available fossil apes, if any, were the ancestors of the modern gibbons, orangutan, gorilla, chimpanzees, and hominids must be determined by anatomical comparison of available fossils. The solution to the tantalizing mystery of the origin of the hominoids must await the discovery of new fossil apes, especially those that lived during the late Miocene and early Pliocene. However, the gaps in the fossil record do not prevent the use of molecular techniques to determine the order and time of branching of the common ancestors of the living species of apes and humans.

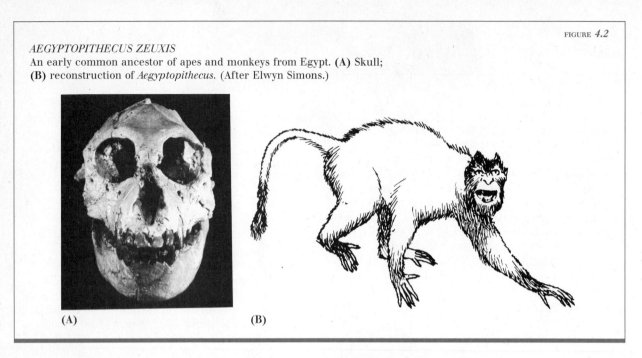

FIGURE 4.2

AEGYPTOPITHECUS ZEUXIS
An early common ancestor of apes and monkeys from Egypt. **(A)** Skull;
(B) reconstruction of *Aegyptopithecus*. (After Elwyn Simons.)

(A)   **(B)**

On the basis of DNA hybridization studies (Box 3.1 on page 33) it appears that the ancestor of the gibbon was the first of the surviving apes to branch off from the hominid *clade* (a group of organisms that are descended from a single common ancestor and that share a distinctive set of features not found in any other taxon). According to the molecular clock (Box 4.2), this took place 16 to 23 mya during the Miocene ape radiation. But there is no consensus concerning the identity of the ancestral fossil. The next to diverge—12 to 17 mya—was the orangutan, to which it is generally agreed that the Asian sivapiths bear a striking resemblance. Much later came the separation of the gorilla and the chimpanzee. As mentioned earlier, which of these branched first has yet to be definitely decided, but some hybrid DNA studies place the branching of humans from chimp ancestors as recently as 5.5 mya (see Fig. 4.8).

FROM HOMINOIDS TO THE FIRST HOMINIDS

The earliest fossil hominids that we know about are members of the genus *Australopithecus* (it means "southern ape"—because they were first discovered in South Africa). Four species of *Australopithecus* have been identified (see Fig. 4.9):

A. afarensis
A. africanus
A. robustus
A. boisei

Informally, they are collectively known as the "australopithecines."

Afarensis is the oldest. Most of its remains have been found at Hadar in the Afar region of northern Ethiopia (hence the "afar" in afarensis). But they have also been found at Omo in southern Ethiopia; around the shores of Lake Turkana at Koobi Fora, and West Turkana, Kenya; and at Laetoli and Olduvai Gorge in Tanzania (see Figs. 4.10 and 4.11).

Afarensis lived from about 4 mya, surviving until about 2.9 mya, when it probably gave rise to one

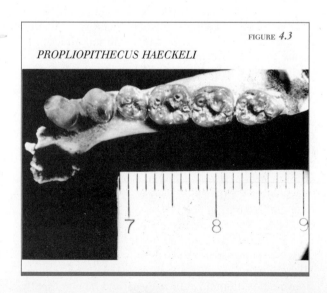

FIGURE 4.3

PROPLIOPITHECUS HAECKELI

FIGURE *4.4*

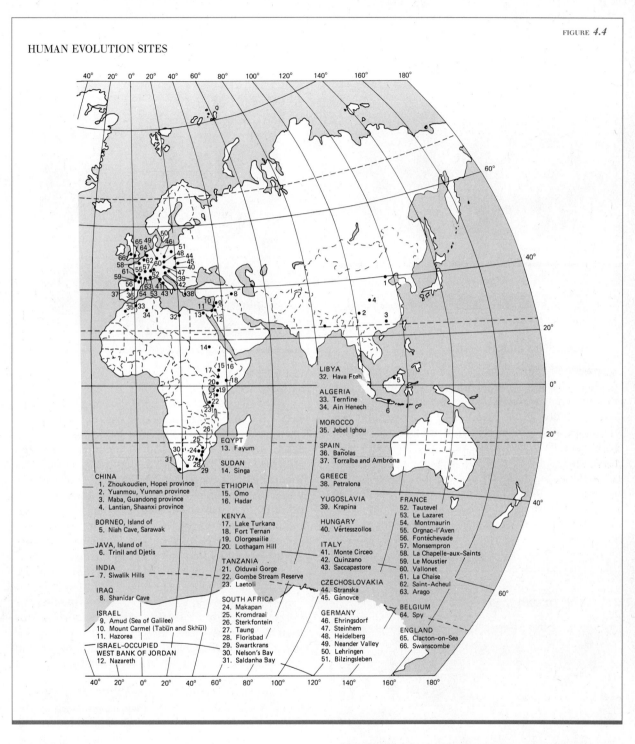

HUMAN EVOLUTION SITES

CHINA
1. Zhoukoudien, Hopei province
2. Yuanmou, Yunnan province
3. Maba, Guandong province
4. Lantian, Shaanxi province

BORNEO, Island of
5. Niah Cave, Sarawak

JAVA, Island of
6. Trinil and Djetis

INDIA
7. Siwalik Hills

IRAQ
8. Shanidar Cave

ISRAEL
9. Amud (Sea of Galilee)
10. Mount Carmel (Tabūn and Skhūl)
11. Hazorea

ISRAEL-OCCUPIED
WEST BANK OF JORDAN
12. Nazareth

EQYPT
13. Fayum

SUDAN
14. Singa

ETHIOPIA
15. Omo
16. Hadar

KENYA
17. Lake Turkana
18. Fort Ternan
19. Olorgesailie
20. Lothagam Hill

TANZANIA
21. Olduvai Gorge
22. Gombe Stream Reserve
23. Laetoli

SOUTH AFRICA
24. Makapan
25. Kromdraai
26. Sterkfontein
27. Taung
28. Florisbad
29. Swartkrans
30. Nelson's Bay
31. Saldanha Bay

LIBYA
32. Hava Fteh

ALGERIA
33. Ternfine
34. Ain Henech

MOROCCO
35. Jebel Ighou

SPAIN
36. Bañolas
37. Torralba and Ambrona

GREECE
38. Petralona

YUGOSLAVIA
39. Krapina

HUNGARY
40. Vértesszollos

ITALY
41. Monte Circeo
42. Quinzano
43. Saccapastore

CZECHOSLOVAKIA
44. Stranska
45. Gánovce

GERMANY
46. Ehringsdorf
47. Steinhem
48. Heidelberg
49. Neander Valley
50. Lehringen
51. Bilzingsleben

FRANCE
52. Tautevel
53. Le Lazaret
54. Montmaurin
55. Orgnac-l'Aven
56. Fontéchevade
57. Monsempron
58. La Chapelle-aux-Saints
59. Le Moustier
60. Vallonet
61. La Chaise
62. Saint-Acheul
63. Arago

BELGIUM
64. Spy

ENGLAND
65. Clacton-on-Sea
66. Swanscombe

or two successor hominid species (see p. 47). The most famous of the *afarensis* fossils is a small female known as Lucy. Approximately 40 percent of her skeleton is preserved, including pelvic, arm, and leg bones (Fig. 4.12). Lucy was 105 centimeters tall (3 feet 5 inches) and weighed about 60

pounds. But other remains at Hadar—fragments of at least 36 hominid individuals have been found there—and the remains at additional *afarensis* sites indicate that *afarensis* males were a foot and a half taller and considerably heavier (see Table 4.1). Some authorities however, argue that the larger specimens are

FIGURE *4.5*

KENYAPITHECUS MANDIBLE
An early Sivapith from Kenya,
possible ancestor of the orangutan.

FIGURE *4.7*

GIGANTOPITHECUS
Molar teeth (*right*), compared with
modern human teeth (*left*).

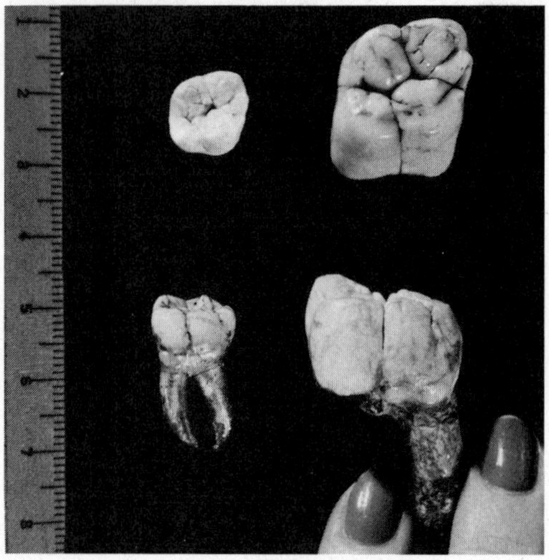

not males but members of a more robust species
(Zihlman and Lowenstein 1985).

Bipedalism and *Afarensis*

Analysis of the pelvis, leg bones, and foot bones found
at Hadar and other *afarensis* sites leaves no room for
doubting that *afarensis* was a bipedal hominid. In
addition, there is the evidence of a remarkable 75-
foot-long trail of footprints found at Laetoli, Tanzania
(M. Leakey 1979; Charteris, Wall, and Nottrodt 1982).
These footprints (Fig. 4.13) preserved in volcanic
ash, date to 3.5 mya. They were laid down by two
or three hominids who ranged from 4 to 5 feet in
height, as determined by the ratio of foot length to
stride length. They resemble the footprints of con-

FIGURE *4.6*

A DRYOPITH (*DRYOPITHECUS FONTANI*)

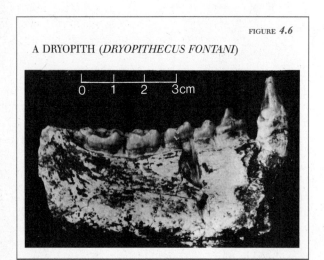

temporary humans in having a well-shaped heel, a
strong arch, and a well defined ball, plus a big toe
that is straight in line and does not stick out to the
side (see Fig. 3.16 on p. 34), as do the big toes of apes
(Johanson and Edey 1981:250; White and Suwa 1987).

Examination of the toe bones of *afarensis* indicates that they retained very little of the grasping ability characteristic of the feet of tree-climbing pongids
(Latimer and Lovejoy 1990). But like pongids, *afarensis* had forelimbs that were longer in relation to its
legs, which may have made them somewhat more
adept at tree-climbing than modern humans.

While *afarensis*'s feet are very un-apelike, the
volume of its brain case (its *cranial capacity*), was
about 415 cc (cubic centimeters), providing room for
only a very small, apelike brain. Chimpanzees and
gorillas average about 400 to 500 cc, while modern
humans average about 1350 cc (Klein 1989:101).

A distinctly hominid feature associated with upright posture is the position of the opening where the
vertebral column meets the skull. In *afarensis* as in
modern humans it is well forward and underneath
the skull (see p. 35).

Afarensis's teeth have several primitive apelike
features. The incisors are broader and more protu-
berant than in modern humans. And while the canines are smaller than in apes, they still protrude into

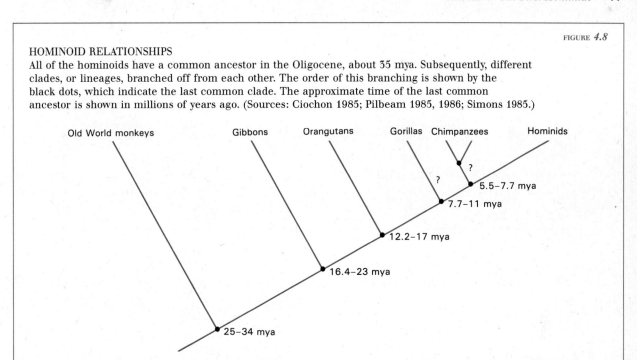

FIGURE *4.8*

HOMINOID RELATIONSHIPS
All of the hominoids have a common ancestor in the Oligocene, about 35 mya. Subsequently, different clades, or lineages, branched off from each other. The order of this branching is shown by the black dots, which indicate the last common clade. The approximate time of the last common ancestor is shown in millions of years ago. (Sources: Ciochon 1985; Pilbeam 1985, 1986; Simons 1985.)

special gaps in the tooth rows. Overall, however, there is little resemblance to the jaws and teeth of the modern apes.

Other Australopithecines

Africanus was the first of the australopithecines to be discovered (by Raymond Dart in 1924). With females slightly taller than Lucy and with less *sexual dimorphism* (difference in size, height, and body mass between one sex and the other), *africanus* lived in South Africa from about 3.0 mya to 2.4 mya.

Robustus, despite what the name implies, was about the same height as *afarensis* and *africanus*. (Table 4.1). It differed from them, however, in having pronounced chimpanzeelike crests and flanges on its skull to which massive chewing muscles were attached. These features together with its large molar teeth suggest that it was adapted to feeding on seeds and other tough plant food. *Robustus* flourished in South Africa from about 1.86 mya to 1.62 mya.

Boisei is the East African robust species. It was about the same size as *robustus* but its powerful jaw muscles were attached to huge gorillalike crests and flanges on its skull. As with robustus, its strong jaws and large molar teeth suggest a seed and plant-eating

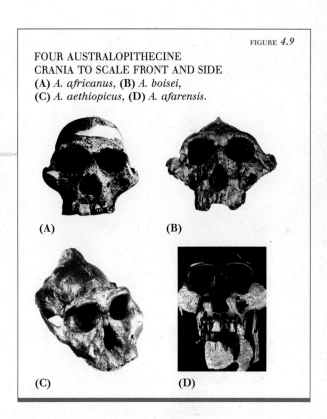

FIGURE *4.9*

FOUR AUSTRALOPITHECINE
CRANIA TO SCALE FRONT AND SIDE
(A) *A. africanus,* (B) *A. boisei,*
(C) *A. aethiopicus,* (D) *A. afarensis.*

(A)　(B)

(C)　(D)

FIGURE *4.10*

IMPORTANT FOSSIL SITES IN EAST AND SOUTH AFRICA

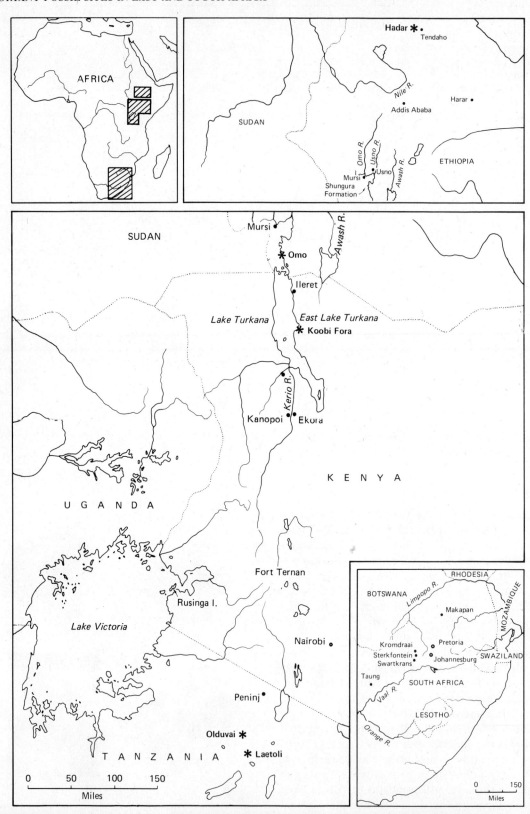

FIGURE *4.11*

AFRICAN ARCHAEOLOGICAL SITES
(A) Laetoli, a Tanzanian site at which some of the oldest hominid remains have been found. **(B)** Hadar, an Ethiopian site at which have been found the remains of the putative ancestor of the australopithecines and of the earliest human beings. **(C)** Olduvai Gorge, one of the principal sites in Tanzania (Mary Leakey in the foreground).

(A)

(B)

(C)

way of life. *Boisei* first appears in the fossil record at about 2.0 mya and disappears at 1.3 mya, making it the last australopithecine to become extinct (Delson 1986; Grine 1988; Klein 1989; McHenry 1991a:154; 1991b; Walker et al. 1986).

One other australopithecine must be mentioned. Its skull was discovered in 1985 and cataloged in the Kenya National Museum as West Turkana specimen number 17,000—KNM-WT 17000 for short. It displays a mix of features that lead some authorities

BOX *4.2*

DATING DESCENT WITH MOLECULAR CLOCKS

It has been established that most of the base-pair sequences in an organism's DNA do not code for specific traits that are acted on by natural selection. Instead, the majority of base-pair sequences are adaptively neutral and accumulate as the result of genetic drift (see p. 15). Over many thousands of years, the rate of change of the nonadaptive base pairs is thought to be more or less constant. (The rate of adaptive changes, on the other hand, is inherently irregular.)

The greater the difference between the genomes of two species as estimated through DNA hybridization (p. 31) and other biochemical techniques, therefore, the longer the time since the two species diverged from a common ancestor.

If one knows through other dating techniques (see Box 4.1) how many thousands of years ago two species had a common ancestor, and one knows as well the percent by which their base pairs differ, then the molecular clock can be "set" to show average rates of change per thousand years (Sibley, Comstock, and Almquist 1990; Diamond 1989; Goodman et al. 1990).

Basic to the accuracy of the molecular clock is the assumption that the rate of accumulation of neutral base-pair mutations is constant for all species. This assumption, however, has to be corrected to take into account the different rates at which new generations mature in different species, since the accumulation of neutral base-pair mutations and their spread by drift through a population depend on the rate of breeding. Rodents, for example, with their extremely short generation time, accumulate DNA changes 10 times faster than humans (Sibley and Almquist 1987:112).

FIGURE *4.12*

"LUCY"
Found by Don Johanson and Tom Gray at Hadar; proposed as the ancestor of the genus *Homo.* To convey the surreal effect of his reunion with this remarkably complete 3.2-million-year-old ancestress, Johanson named her Lucy, evoking the popular Beatles song "Lucy in the Sky with Diamonds," itself a cryptogram for mind-blowing LSD.

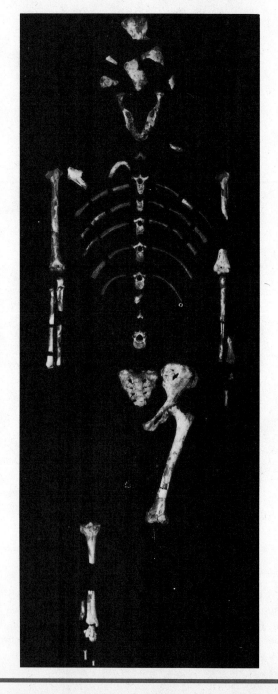

FIGURE *4.13*
EARLIEST HOMINID FOOTPRINTS
These footprints were discovered at Laetoli by Mary Leakey. Human foot is shown for comparison.

TABLE *4.1*
STATURE AND WEIGHT OF EARLY HOMINIDS

	Body weight (kg)		Stature (cm)	
	Male	Female	Male	Female
A. afarensis	45	29	151	105
A. africanus	41	30	138	115
A. robustus	40	32	132	110
A. boisei	49	34	137	124
H. habilis	52	32	157	125
H. erectus (African)	68		180	160

SOURCE: McHenry 1992:18.

FIGURE *4.14*
KNM-WT 17000
Found in Kenya by Alan Walker in 1985. (*Source:* Johanson and Shreeve 1989:127.)

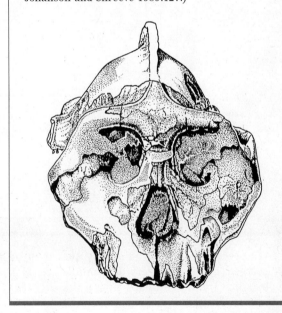

to regard it as an early *boisei* and others as a separate robust species to which they have given the name *A. aethiopicus* (Fig. 4.14). The importance of KNM-WT 17000 is its early date—about 2.5 mya (Feibel et al. 1989:610)—which weakens the previously favored theory that *boisei* and *robustus* were the descendants of *africanus*. As shown in Fig. 4.15, KNM-WT 17000 makes it difficult to decide among at least four different phylogenetic scenarios for the australopithecines.

HOMO HABILIS

About 2 million years separate the appearance of the first australopithecines and the emergence of the genus *Homo*. The earliest species in this genus is called *H. habilis,* which literally means "handy person," in recognition of the putative association between *habilis* and the beginning of stone tool manufacturing (Fig. 4.16). *Habilis* remains have been found at Olduvai Gorge in Tanzania; Koobi Fora in Kenya; and Hadar in Ethiopia. Their earliest date is close to 2.0 mya. *Habilis*'s cranial capacity ranged from 509 to 752 cc, with an average of 630 cc.

To everyone's amazement, the discovery of the limb bones of a female *habilis* in 1986 at Olduvai Gorge indicated that despite her bigger brain, she was about the same size as *afarensis* females (Johanson et al. 1987).

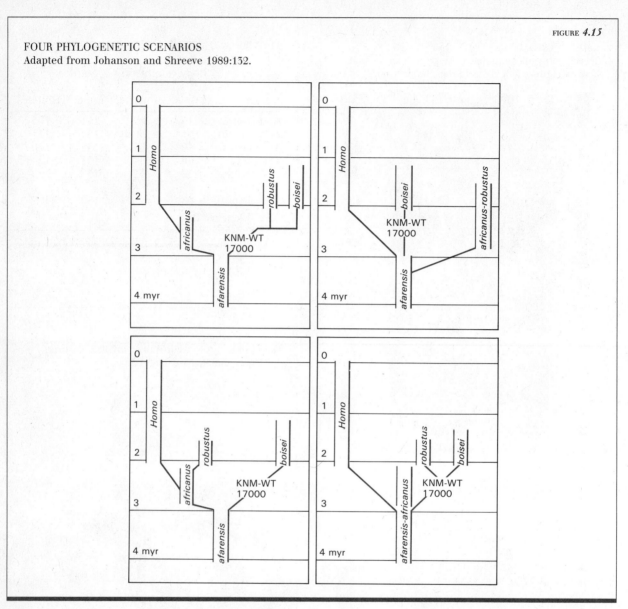

FIGURE *4.15*

FOUR PHYLOGENETIC SCENARIOS
Adapted from Johanson and Shreeve 1989:132.

Whatever scenario is ultimately shown to be most correct (by the discovery of additional fossils), it is clear that the first humans shared the earth for hundreds of thousands of years with at least two or three different kinds of australopithecines. Moreover, it seems likely that the extinction of these australopithecines was a direct result of pressures placed on them by the evolution of the genus *Homo* (Fig. 4.15).

WERE THE AUSTRALOPITHECINES MAKERS AND USERS OF TOOLS?

Both australopithecine and *habilis* fossil remains have been found near a variety of flakes, "choppers," scrap-

ers, and hammerstones, known as Oldowan tools (Fig. 4.18). Wherever such tools show up, it has generally been assumed that they are the handiwork of *Homo* rather than of *australopithecus*. It remains an open question, however, as to whether the australopithecines themselves made and used at least some of the stone tools found in east and south Africa. The extent to which they manufactured and used other kinds of tools made from more perishable materials, such as bone and especially wood, also remains in doubt.

The earliest known stone tools are from East and West Gona, sites near Hadar in Ethiopia. Conservatively, based on the potassium-argon dating method, these tools were manufactured 2.5 mya but

FIGURE *4.16*

HOMO HABILIS (KNM-ER 1470)
This skull may be 2.0 myr old, and its
volume is greater than that of the
australopithecines living at the same
time. Front view (*left*); side view (*right*).

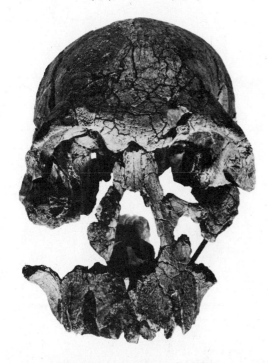
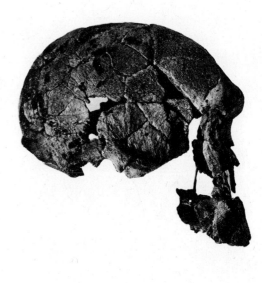

FIGURE *4.17*

TIME AND PLACE OF EARLY AFRICAN HOMINIDS
Source: Fleagle 1988:416.

Millions of Years

	4.5	4.0	3.5	3.0	2.5	2.0	1.5	1.0
Hadar		*A. afarensis*						
Omo				*A. afarensis* / *A. boisei*	*H. habilis*	*H. erectus*		
Lake Turkana			*A. aethiopicus*	*A. boisei*	*H. erectus*	*H. habilis*		
Olduvai					*H. habilis* / *A. boisei*	*H. erectus*		
Laetoli	*A. afarensis*							
South Africa			*A. africanus*	*A. robustus*		*H. erectus*		

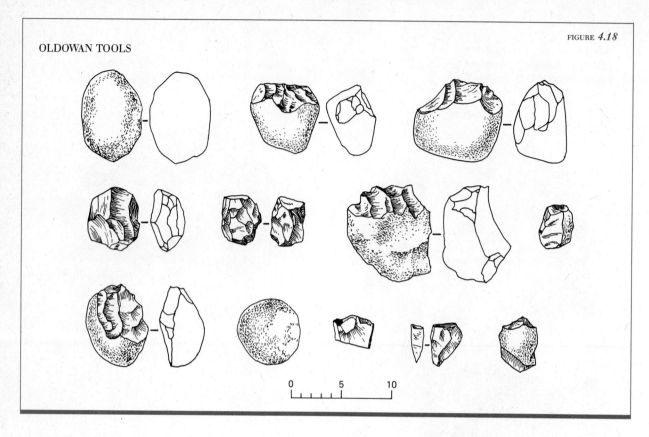

OLDOWAN TOOLS

FIGURE 4.18

0   5   10

possibly as early as 3.1 mya. Another set of very early tools (Fig. 4.19) has been found in the Omo Valley, Ethiopia, with potassium-argon dates of approximately 2.4 mya (J. W. K. Harris 1983; Toth and Schick 1986:22). These dates are considerably older than the dates for the earliest *habilis* (which in any event is anatomically not all that different from *afarensis*). Moreover, there are a number of sites in both east and south Africa where stone tools have been discovered and where either *robustus* or *boisei* were the only hominids known to have been present (Susman 1989:472). Recent analysis of the thumb, finger, and hand bones of *robustus* indicates that these australopithecines had a precision grip (see p. 27) at least as refined as that in *habilis* or even in modern humans (ibid.). There is a distinct probability, therefore, that habilis was not the first hominid to make and use stone tools. This could help to account for the development of bipedal terrestrial locomotion among the australopithecines. Greater tool-using ability is one of the advantages of having forelimbs that are not needed for walking and running.

But would a creature as small-brained as *afarensis* have the intellectual capacity to manufacture and use tools?

TOOL USE AMONG CONTEMPORARY MONKEYS AND APES

Paleontological and archaeological data do not prove definitely that all the australopithecines used tools, but studies of modern-day animals favor the conclusion that the australopithecines as well as *habilis* made and used tools.

A tool is an object that is not part of the user's body, that the user holds or carries during or just prior to use, and that is used to alter the form or location of a second object with which it was previously unconnected (Beck 1975). By this definition, a chimpanzee banging a fruit against a rock is not using a tool, but a chimpanzee that bangs a rock or a stick against the fruit is using a tool (Whitesides 1985).

Experimental approaches to behavior show that most birds and mammals and especially primates are "intelligent" enough to learn to make and use simple tools under laboratory conditions. Under natural free-ranging conditions, however, the capacity to make and use tools is expressed less frequently, because most animals can get along quite effectively without having to resort to artificial aids. Natural selection has adapted them to their particular habitat by providing

FIGURE *4.19*

OMO TOOLS
These tools, found at Omo in Ethiopia, may have been manufactured as long as 2 mya.

FIGURE *4.20*

JANE GOODALL
Making friends with a young chimpanzee in Gombe National Park, Tanzania.

body parts such as snouts, claws, teeth, hooves, and fangs. Thus, while primates are intelligent enough to make and use tools, their anatomy and normal mode of existence disincline them to develop extensive tool-using repertoires. Among monkeys and apes the use of the hand for tool use is especially inhibited by the importance of the forelimbs in walking, running, and climbing. That is probably why the most common tool-using behavior among many different species of monkeys and apes is the repelling of intruders with a barrage of nuts, pinecones, branches, fruits, feces, or stones. Throwing such objects requires only a momentary loss of the ability to run or climb away if danger threatens.

Among free-ranging primates the most accomplished tool user is the chimpanzee. Over a period of many years, Jane van Lawick-Goodall and her associates have studied the behavior of a single population of free-ranging common chimpanzees in the Gombe National Park in Tanzania (Fig. 4.20). One of their most remarkable discoveries is that the chimpanzees "fish" for ants and termites (Fig. 4.21). "Termiting" involves first breaking off a twig or a vine, stripping it of leaves and side branches, and then locating a suitable termite nest. Such a nest is as hard as concrete and impenetrable except for certain thinly covered tunnel entrances. The chimpanzee scratches away the thin covering and inserts the twig. The termites inside bite the end of the twig, and the chimpanzee pulls it out and licks off the termites clinging to it. Especially impressive is the fact that the chimpanzees will prepare the twig first and then carry it in their mouths from nest to nest while looking for a suitable tunnel entrance (van Lawick-Goodall 1986).

"Anting" provides an interesting variation on this theme. The Gombe chimps "fish" for a species of aggressive nomadic driver ant that can inflict a painful bite. On finding the temporary subterranean nest of these ants, the chimps make a tool out of a green twig and insert it into the nest entrance. Hundreds of fierce ants swarm up the twig to repel the invader:

> *The chimpanzee watches their progress and when the ants have almost reached its hand, the tool is quickly withdrawn. In a split second the opposite hand rapidly sweeps the length of the tool . . . catching the ants in a jumbled mass between thumb and forefinger. These are then popped into the open, waiting mouth in one bite and chewed furiously.* [McGrew 1979:278]

Additionally, chimpanzees can manufacture "sponges" for sopping up water from an inaccessible

FIGURE *4.21*

CHIMPANZEE TERMITING
A stick carefully stripped of leaves is inserted into the nest. The chimpanzee licks off the termites that cling to the stick when it is withdrawn.

hollow in a tree. They strip a handful of leaves from a twig, put the leaves in their mouth, chew briefly, put the mass of leaves in the water, let them soak, put the leaves to their mouths, and suck the water off. A similar sponge is employed to dry their fur, to wipe off sticky substances, and to clean the bottoms of chimpanzee babies. Gombe chimpanzees also use sticks as levers and digging tools to pry ant nests off trees and to widen the entrance of subterranean beehives.

Observers in other parts of Africa report similar types of behavior—variants of fishing for ants, dipping for termites, and digging up insect nests or prying them loose. Chimpanzees in Tanzania collect the honey of a stingless species of bee by inserting a stick into the nest and licking off the honey that adheres to it. Elsewhere, observers have watched chimpanzees pound or hammer tough-skinned fruit, seeds, and nuts with sticks and stones. The chimps of the Tai forest of the Ivory Coast open the hard shells of the panda nut with rocks that serve as hammers. They search the forest floor for a suitable hammerstone, which may weigh anywhere from 1 to 40 pounds. Then they bring the stones back in the crook of their arm, hobbling on three legs, from as far as 600 feet. They place the nuts on thick tree roots or exposed

rock that serve as anvils, and pound away (Boesch and Boesch 1984; 1991; Whitesides 1985). In West Senegal chimps use stone hammers to pound open the fruits of the baobab tree (Bermejo et al. 1989).

Chimpanzees appear to go further than other primates in using weapons and projectiles. They hurl stones, feces, and sticks with considerable accuracy. One Gombe chimp threw a large stone at an adult bush pig, hitting it and driving it off long enough for another chimp to rush in and capture the piglet that the pig had been guarding (Teleki 1981:336).

Under semicontrolled conditions, chimpanzees have been observed to wield long clubs with deadly aim. One investigator (Kortlandt 1967) built a stuffed leopard whose head and tail could be moved mechanically. He set the leopard down in open country and when the chimpanzees came into view he animated the leopard's parts. The chimpanzees attacked the leopard with heavy sticks, tore it apart, and dragged the remnants off into the bush.

It has long been known that chimpanzees in zoos and laboratories readily develop complex patterns of behavior involving tool use. Belle, a female chimpanzee at the Delta Regional Primate Station, cleaned her companion's teeth with a pencillike object manufactured from a twig (McGrew and Tutin 1973). Other captive chimpanzees have learned how to shine a flashlight into their mouth in order to clean their throat and teeth with their fingers while watching their reflection in a mirror (Menzel et al. 1985). Provided with a box on which to stand, sticks that fit together, and bananas out of reach, chimps quickly learn to push the box under the bananas, put the sticks together, stand on the box, and knock down the bananas. Captive chimpanzees will also spontaneously employ sticks to pry open boxes and doors and to break the mesh on their cages. At the Delta Regional Primate center, they broke big sticks into little sticks, then crammed the little sticks into small crevices in the 20-foot wall and, using the little sticks as hand and foot holds escaped over the top.

The kinds of tool-using behavior that captive primates exhibit outside their native habitat are perhaps even more significant than what they normally do in their natural setting. In order for tool use to become an integral part of an animal's behavior, it must contribute to the solution of everyday problems that the animal cannot solve as efficiently by relying on its own body parts. The ease with which chimpanzees and other primates expand their tool-using repertory outside their normal habitat is thus extremely significant for assessing the potential for tool use among the early small-brained hominids. It seems likely that no radical enlargement or reorganization of the brain was needed for the first hominids to expand their tool-making and tool-using behavior (see p. 54). The australopithecines need not have been "smarter" than the average chimpanzee in order to make more regular use of clubs and projectiles to repel predators, stones to smash bones and cut hides, and sticks to dig for roots and tubers (Kitahara-Frisch 1980; Kortlandt 1984). Indeed, Nicholas Toth of the University of Indiana has been teaching a chimpanzee named Kanzi how to make stone tools (Gibbons 1991) (Fig. 4.22). Ultimately Toth hopes that Kanzi will teach his fellow chimps to do the same. (See p. 121 for more about Kanzi.)

NONHUMAN CULTURE AND THE EVOLUTION OF THE HOMINIDS

The great evolutionary novelty represented by culture is that the capabilities and habits of culture-bearing animals are acquired through social heredity rather than through the more ancient process of biological heredity (see p. 104). By *social heredity* is meant the shaping of a social animal's behavior in conformity with information stored in the brains of other members of its social community. Such information is not stored in the organism's genes. (It must be stressed, though, that actual cultural responses always depend in part on genetically predetermined capacities and predispositions.)

There appears to be no specific genetic information that is responsible for chimpanzee termiting and anting. True, in order for this behavior to occur, genetically determined capacities for learning, for manipulating objects, and for omnivorous eating must be present in the young chimpanzee. But these general biological capacities and predispositions cannot explain termiting and anting. Given nothing but groups of young chimpanzees, twigs, and termite nests, termiting and anting are unlikely to occur. The missing ingredient is the information about termiting and anting that is stored in the brains of the adult chimpanzees. This information is displayed to the young chimpanzees by their mothers. Among the Gombe chimpanzees, the young do not begin termiting until they are 18 to 22 months old. At first their behavior is clumsy and inefficient, and they do not become proficient until they are about 3 years old. Van Lawick-Goodall witnessed many instances of infants watching intently as the adults termited. Novices often retrieved discarded termiting sticks and attempted to use them on their own. Anting, with its risk of being bitten, takes longer to learn. The youngest chimp to achieve proficiency was

FIGURE *4.22*

HANDY CHIMP
Pygmy chimp Kanzi fashions a stone tool.

about 4 years old (McGrew 1977:282). The conclusion that anting is a cultural trait is strengthened by the fact that chimps at other sites do not exploit driver ants even though the species is widely distributed throughout Africa. At the same time, other groups of chimps do exploit other species of ants and in ways that differ from the Gombe tradition. For example, chimps in the Mahali mountains 170 km south of Gombe insert twigs and bark into the nests of tree-dwelling ants, which are ignored by the Gombe chimps (Nishida 1973).

The most extensive studies of nonhuman culture have been carried out with Japanese macaques. Primatologists of the Primate Research Institute of Kyoto University have found among local monkey troops a wide variety of customs and institutions based on social learning. The males of certain troops, for example, take turns looking after the infants while the infants' mothers are feeding. Such baby-sitting is characteristic only of the troops at Takasaki-yama and Takahashi. Other cultural differences have been noted too. When the monkeys of Takasaki-yama eat the fruit of the muku tree, they either throw away the hard stone inside or swallow it and excrete it in their feces. But the monkeys of Arashi-yama break the stone with their teeth and eat the pulpy interior. Some troops eat shellfish; others do not. Cultural differences have also been noted with respect to the characteristic distance from each other that the animals maintain during feeding, and with respect to the order of males, females, and juveniles in line of march when certain troops move through the forest.

The scientists at the Primate Research Institute have been able to observe the actual process by which behavioral innovations spread from individual to individual and become part of a troop's culture independently of genetic transmission. To attract monkeys near the shore for easier observation, sweet potatoes were set on the beach. One day a young female began to wash the sand from the sweet potatoes by plunging them in a small brook that ran through the beach. This washing behavior spread throughout the group and gradually replaced the former rubbing habit. Nine years later, 80 to 90 percent of the animals were washing their sweet potatoes, some in the brook, others in the sea (Fig. 4.23). When wheat was spread on the beach, the monkeys of Koshima at first had a hard time separating the kernels from the sand. Soon, however, one of them invented a process for removing sand from the wheat, and this behavior was taken over by others. The solution was to plunge the wheat into the water (Fig. 4.24). The wheat sinks more slowly than the sand (Itani 1961; Itani and Nishimura 1973; Miyadi 1967).

Given the presence of rudimentary cultures among contemporary monkeys and apes, there seems little reason to deny that the australopithecines possessed extensive repertoires of socially learned behavior.

HUNTING AND THE FIRST HOMINIDS

Playwright Robert Ardrey wrote a best-seller entitled *African Genesis* on the theme that the australopithecines, unlike all previous "apes," were killers armed with lethal weapons. According to Ardrey, we are a "predator whose natural instinct is to kill with a weapon" (1961:316). It should be noted, however, that an emphasis on hunting among the australopithecines or *habilis* need not have produced a nature any more fierce or bloodthirsty than that of contemporary apes and monkeys, most of whom readily take to diets that include meat (Fig. 4.25).

FIGURE *4.23*

JAPANESE MONKEY CULTURE
A female monkey of Koshima troop washing a sweet potato.

Chimpanzees, as well as baboons and other primates, frequently attack and eat small terrestrial animals (Hamilton 1987; McGrew et al. 1979). During a year of observation near Gilgil, Kenya, Robert Harding (1975) observed 47 small vertebrates being killed and eaten by baboons. Their most common prey were infant gazelles and antelopes. Over the course of a decade, chimpanzees of the Gombe National Park are known to have eaten 95 small animals—mostly infant baboons, monkeys, and bush pigs (Teleki 1973). About 10 percent of a chimpanzee's total time devoted to feeding is taken up by predation on mammals (Teleki 1981:327). According to recent estimates of the amount of meat consumed by Gombe chimps over a 13-year period, males ate upwards of 25 kg (55 lb) of meat per year, which falls within the lower range of meat consumption for some modern-day human hunting-and-gathering societies (Wrangham and Riss 1990).

FIGURE *4.24*

JAPANESE MONKEYS WASHING WHEAT
(A) Members of Koshima troop separating wheat from sand by placing mixture
n water. **(B)** Central figure carrying the mixture in its left hand. Two monkeys
in foreground are floating the wheat and picking it up.

(A)

(B)

Much of the hunting carried out by chimpanzees is done cooperatively, and the eating of the prey animals involves an unusual amount of sharing and intense social interaction. Gombe chimpanzees pursue various prey species in a coordinated manner, positioning and repositioning themselves repeatedly to maintain an enclosure. They do this sometimes for an hour or more, effectively anticipating and cutting off all potential escape routes of the prey (Teleki 1981:332). In the Tai forest of the Ivory Coast, 92 percent of 200 hunts for monkeys were carried out by groups of between three and six chimpanzees (Boesch and Boesch 1991:56).

Both males and females chimps hunt and consume meat. In Gombe during an 8-year period from 1974 to 1981, females were seen to capture or steal, and then eat, at least part of 44 prey animals, not counting another 21 prey that they attacked or seized but were unable to hold onto (van Lawick-Goodall 1986:304–305). Males, however, hunted more than females and consumed more meat. The social behavior surrounding meat consumption is marked by sharing and much excitement, unlike plant-eating occasions. Chimpanzees at Gombe occasionally share some plant foods, but meat is always shared unless the prey is captured by a solitary chimpanzee in the forest (ibid. 372). Meat-sharing often results from persistent "begging." This involves holding an outstretched hand under the meat possessor's mouth, or parting the lips of a meat-chewing companion. Failure to obtain meat by begging can lead to whimpering and other signs of extreme frustration (see Box 4.3).

Chimpanzees are also known to scavenge dead animals (Hasegawa et al. 1983). Further, chimpanzee meat-eating and terrestrial hunting have been observed in both forested and semiforested habitats (Suzuki 1975). It is virtually certain, therefore, that the first hominids were, like our closest ape cousins, to some degree hunters and scavengers. But the extent and nature of this hunting and scavenging remains very much in doubt, as does its significance for the evolution of the hominids.

FIGURE *4.25*

CHIMPANZEES EATING MEAT
(A) Two males devouring a bushbuck. Male on right is threatening female, whose arm appears in upper right **(B)**, begging for a morsel.

(A)

(B)

Early Hominid Meat-Eating

While meat seems to occupy an important place in the diet of many anthropoids, none of the anthropoids, including the australopithecines, exhibit the kind of dental patterns that would identify them as specialized carnivores (i.e., exclusively or mainly meat-eaters). Mammals that consume large quantities of meat (from large animals as opposed to insects) have an unmistakable dental pattern: large canine teeth for puncturing and ripping; enlarged premolars shaped like long, narrow blades for shearing and cutting; and small, narrow molars. Inspection of a convenient domestic cat will reveal only one small molar in each quadrant. Nothing could be more ill-suited to the needs of a "killer ape" than the set of 12 massive, high-crowned, flat "grinders" possessed by both *habilis* and australopithecines, and to a lesser extent by modern humans (Isaac and Crader 1981:40).

It is generally agreed that the australopithecines and *habilis,* like most primates, were omnivores (i.e., they ate both plant and animal foods). Exactly what portion of their diet consisted of meat is at present unknown (Stahl 1984), but several new kinds of tests are being used to answer this question (see Box 4.4).

The most convincing direct evidence to date of significant meat-eating concerns the hominids who lived about 2 mya at Olduvai Gorge. The evidence consists of sharp stone flakes in close association with tens of thousands of herbivore bones; microscopic inspection of many of these bones—especially the ones that would have had a lot of meat on them, like the "ham" bones and the bones of the upper forelimbs—reveals fine parallel incised lines (Fig. 4.26). Experimental dismemberment and defleshing of similar animals by using similar stone flakes has shown that similar incised lines are regularly produced when meat is cut close to the bone (Bunn and Kroll 1986).

IN THE BEGINNING WAS THE FOOT

By analogy with chimpanzee behavior, it is reasonable to suppose that the Miocene ancestors of the australopithecines were forest-dwelling apes who derived the majority of their subsistence from plant foods but who also consumed significant amounts of insects and small animals. It is known that during the Pliocene, climatic changes reduced the forested area available for arboreal foraging. At the same time, the area of nearby savannas, covered with ant and termite nests, abounding in subsurface tubers, and teeming with grazing and browsing animals, became more extensive. Selection for apes that were able to exploit this habitat may underlie the selection for bipedalism (Lewin 1987). A simple digging stick carried as a tool for prying open the insect nests and getting at

BOX *4.3*

WORZLE THROWS A TANTRUM

There are occasions when the solicitations of begging chimpanzees make it all but impossible for the possessor to feed; at the very least, they are a source of irritation. If he dispenses pieces of meat, the recipients usually move off, sometimes followed by others. Even if the possessor only relinquishes chewed leaf-meat wedges, social harmony will temporarily be restored and he will be able to eat a few mouthfuls in peace.

Quite often a supplicant may be allowed to share the carcass with the possessor, or to break off a portion. Leaf-meat wedges are frequently deposited in the outstretched hand of a begging individual or are transferred directly from mouth to mouth, usually after the meat-eater has extracted all he wants, but sometimes after only a few chews. Occasionally the possessor breaks off a portion of meat and places it in the outstretched hand of a supplicant. Once in a while possessors gave meat to individuals close by who were not overtly begging, although their intense interest in the food was obvious. This happened most often at the end of long meat-eating sessions when a male sometimes handed over the entire remains of the carcass to the individual closest to him. Frequently this was a female.

Sometimes after a lengthy and unrewarded session of begging, the supplicant starts to whimper or (especially an infant or juvenile) throws a tantrum. Once, when Goliath (in 1968) had the freshly caught body of a baboon infant, Mr. Worzle begged persistently, following the possessor from branch to branch, hand outstretched and whimpering. When Goliath pushed Worzle's hand away for the eleventh time, the lower-ranking male threw a violent tantrum: he hurled himself backward off the branch, screaming and hitting wildly at the surrounding vegetation. Goliath looked at him and then, with a great effort (using hands, teeth, and one foot), tore his prey in two and handed the entire hindquarters to Worzle.

SOURCE: van Lawick-Goodall 1986:373–374.

---

the underground tubers would also have been useful for chasing away vultures and other small scavengers from carcasses that had been abandoned by feline predators but still offered some juicy tidbits. By throwing sticks and stones, *afarensis* might even have been a match for the big predators and scavengers such as saber-toothed tigers, giant hyenas, packs of wild hogs, and giant panthers. Successful exploitation of the savannas would also have been related to the ability to avoid these competitors by running off with morsels of scavenged meat to a nearby stand of trees and perhaps climbing into the branches. In this connection, note that chimpanzees are not able to move rapidly while carrying bulky items. Once selection had begun to modify the foot, pelvis, and vertebral column in the direction of bipedalism, added advantages would be derived from greater tool use. While the australopithecines never became mighty hunters, they probably did improve their ability to compete as scavengers. Lacking their own sharp claws or fangs, they had to wait for the teeth of better endowed species to rip open the tough hides of the larger carcasses. But some time between 3.0 and 2.5 mya they discovered how to make sharp cutting tools out of pieces of smashed rock and how to use them to cut through

BOX *4.4*

HOW MUCH MEAT DID THE EARLY HOMINIDS CONSUME?

The following kinds of tests are being used to answer this question:

1. Microscopic examination of the earliest tools to reveal distinctive patterns of wear on edges and surfaces caused by cutting bones and meat.
2. Microscopic examination of early hominid teeth to reveal distinctive patterns of wear caused by meat-eating.
3. Microscopic examination of fossil animal bones to show distinctive breakage and cut marks caused by the use of tools.
4. Chemical analysis of the ratio of ^{15}N: ^{14}N in fossil bones, which is known to reflect the proportion of animal to plant food consumed while living.
5. The analysis of coprolites (fossilized feces) found at Plio-Pleistocene hominid sites.

SOURCE: Toth and Schick 1986:64–71.

FIGURE *4.26*

EVIDENCE OF MEAT-EATING
Antelope leg bone from Olduvai. Note
dismembering cut marks in close-up.

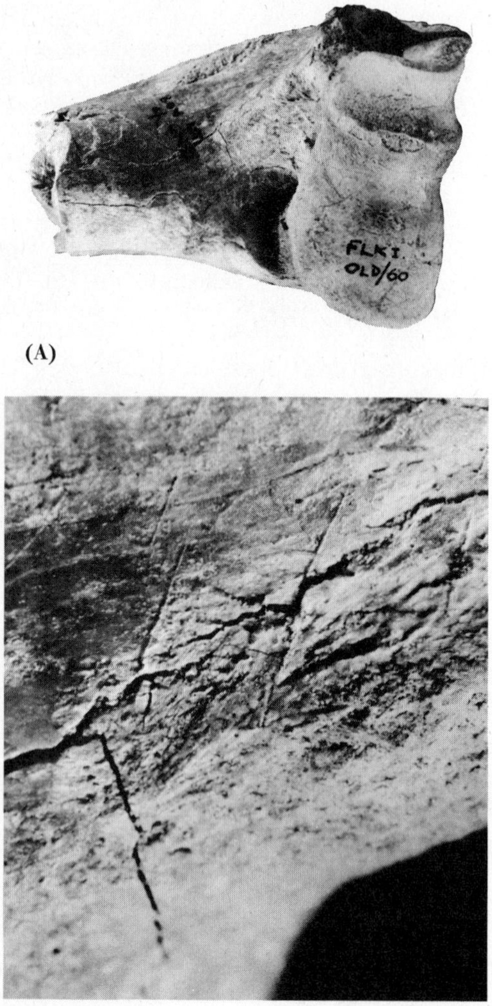

(A)

(B)

the thickest hides and to dismember the choice parts.
The brain of a chimpanzee is all that one needs to do
these things, given a radically transformed vertebral
column, pelvis, and foot (Lewin 1984; Shipman 1986).

THE MEAT AND BASE CAMP SCENARIO

While almost all anthropologists reject the killer-ape
scenario for the australopithecines, the provisioning
of meat, even in small quantities, seems to offer an
important clue to the origins of human social life. Regardless of whether the australopithecines obtained

meat through hunting or scavenging, meat would
have encouraged the development of sharing, especially between males and females. Sharing of meat
would have made advantageous long-term bonding
and joint provisioning of offspring.

Sharing of meat further implies that individuals
carried tools and possibly containers over long distances, returning with diverse products of their daily
foraging expeditions to a "home base". A final implication of this scenario is that there was selection for
improved communication and symbolizing abilities to
facilitate the production and exchange of food and the
manufacture of tools and other artifacts.

It seems likely that the portability and high food
value of meat helped establish an adaptive complex
that involved the transport and sharing of food obtained by the complementary endeavor of different
members of the same social group (Isaac and Crader
1981:95).

A word of caution: The evidence for the use of
a home base by the early hominids consists of dense
concentrations of Oldowan tools in association with
large numbers of fossil animal bones. But alternative
explanations can be given for these concentrations of
animal bones and tools (Fig. 4.27). For example, it is
possible that the "home bases" were protected sites
at which were stored stone tools or the stones from
which they were made, and to which the early hominids carried or dragged hunted and/or scavenged
carcasses away from dangerous animal carnivores
and scavengers. Over several years of use, such sites
would accumulate dense concentrations of bones and
tools without at any time serving as true home bases
where hominids slept, exchanged food, ate, and returned every day.

A weakness of the home-base scenario is that
large carnivores and predators would have been
strongly attracted to a place where animal carcasses
and meat-bearing bones were present. Minimizing
the time spent at such sites would have been more
adaptive than staying put and inviting an attack (Potts
1984:158). Given the probable lack of fire and heavy-
duty projectiles, australopithecine home bases would
seem to have been an idea whose time had not yet
come.

Another word of caution: Although in all
modern-day hunting-and-gathering societies men
specialize in hunting and women specialize in gathering, we cannot conclude that this was the case
among the Plio-Pleistocene hominids. To the extent that limited hunting was practiced by *habilis*,
both males and females could have engaged in it. As
we have seen (p. 59), both male and female chimpanzees hunt. And there is no reason to suppose that

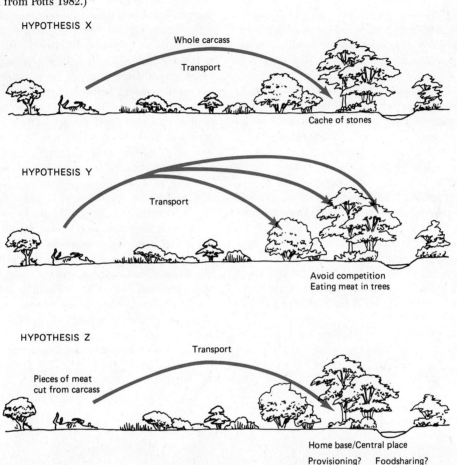

FIGURE *4.27*

THREE RIVAL HYPOTHESES
These account for the formation of artifacts plus broken-up animal bones. All
involve active hominid transport of both the stones and the bones, but only one (Z)
involves a central-place foraging (home base) pattern. (Sources: Isaac 1984:67;
Hypothesis X from Potts 1982.)

HYPOTHESIS X

Whole carcass

Transport

Cache of stones

HYPOTHESIS Y

Transport

Avoid competition
Eating meat in trees

HYPOTHESIS Z

Transport

Pieces of meat
cut from carcass

Home base/Central place

Provisioning?   Foodsharing?

female *habilis* could not have scavenged for meat as
effectively as the males (Tanner 1983).

SUMMARY

This chapter deals with the evolution of the hominoids and hominids from the Oligocene epoch (about
38 to 23 mya) to Plio-Pleistocene times (about 5 to
1.75 mya). Although the first "apes" and Old World
monkeys appeared during the Oligocene and perhaps
as early as the Eocene, it is not possible to identify
the hominid clade until much later. By middle to late
Miocene times (about 15 to 8 mya), there were three

main groups of apes: the dryopithys, pliopiths, and
sivapiths. Except for the sivapiths, which appear to be
the ancestors of the modern orangutan, the relationship between these hominoids and the first pongids
and first hominids is not known as yet.

DNA hybridization shows that the order of
branching of the ancestors of the living apes from
the human clade was gibbon first followed by orang;
the sequence with regard to gorilla and chimpanzee
is less clear, although they both branched off much
later than the orang.

The earliest definite hominids belong to the
genus *Australopthicus*. Four species are generally
recognized: *afarensis* and *boisei*, mainly found in East

Africa, and *africanus* and *robustus* mainly found in South Africa. *Afarensis* dates to more than 4 mya and is the oldest. *Boisei* and *robustus* have large head crests, powerful jaws, and large molar teeth, but they were not much taller than *afarensis* or *africanus*.

Several different hypothetical scenarios linking *afarensis* with the other australopithecines have been proposed. It seems likely that some variety of *afarensis* was the ancestor of *Homo habilis,* the first member of the genus *Homo.* This transition probably took place between 2.5 and 2.0 mya.

All of these early hominids were fully bipedal, lived in savanna habitats, were equipped with large molar teeth and relatively small canines, and probably consumed both plant and animal foods. Long arms relative to legs in *afarensis* and *habilis* suggest a continued adaptation to emergency tree climbing. *Boisei* and *robustus* may have depended more on seeds and other tough plant foods that required much milling and grinding, for which their large molars were adapted.

On the basis of analogies with tool use by contemporary monkeys and apes, it is probable that the australopithecines as well as *habilis* made and used some kinds of tools. The earliest known stone tools date to the period just prior to the appearance of *habilis* at about 2.0 mya.

Also on the basis of analogies with modern primates, it is probable that the australopithecines as well as *habilis* had acquired rudimentary social traditions or cultures. However, *habilis,* with its enlarged cranial capacity, probably had advanced further than the other hominids toward culturally patterned means of subsistence and social life, with a consequent decrease in dependence on genetically programmed or instinctual patterns of behavior.

Again on the basis of analogies with modern chimpanzees, it seems likely that the increased reliance on culture arose primarily from the advantages to be gained from sharing food, especially meat, between males and females, leading to the joint provisioning of children by adults of both sexes. But there is nothing in the fossil record to indicate that it is human nature to be a "killer ape." Rather, it is human nature to be the animal that is most dependent on social traditions for its survival and well-being.

Knowing exactly how much meat was consumed and whether it was hunted or scavenged awaits further research. Similarly, it is not known whether the early hominids operated from a home base.

The greatest difference between the early hominids and their hominoid ancestors is related to the bipedal mode of walking and running. Bipedalism enabled the hominids to increase their reliance on tools; to make better tools; to carry tools, food, and other objects over longer distances; to escape predators by running; and hence to exploit their savanna habitat more effectively than their forest-dwelling ancestors.

Chapter 5

The Origins of *Homo Sapiens*

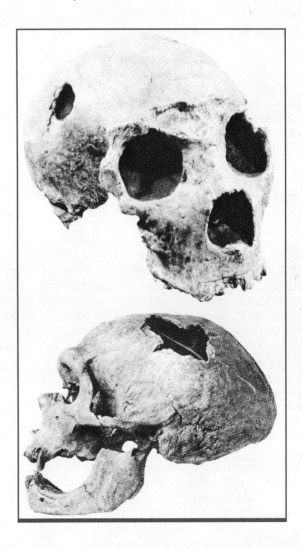

This chapter continues the story of hominid evolution, from Homo habilis *to our own species. We learn first about the life and times of* H. erectus, *the species that replaced* habilis *and held sway over a large part of the Old World for almost the next 1.5 million years. Then we explore the question of the rudimentary and relatively unchanging nature of* erectus's *tools. Why did* erectus's *brain expand so slowly? Did they hunt large animals? Did they have fire? Soon, the first or archaic* sapiens *begin to appear, among whom the Neandertals are best known. Did these humans possess developed powers of speech? Were they the first to have religious beliefs? Finally we come to the question of where the first fully modern* sapiens *originated: Was it in Africa? Or was it in several different regions at more or less the same time? And did they intermarry with the Neandertals? Or did they simply use their more advanced capacity for language and culture to wipe out all vestiges of earlier* sapiens *types?*

HOMO ERECTUS

As we have seen (p. 73), by about 2.0 mya, *habilis,* characterized by an enlarged brain and developed tool-making traditions, had evolved out of the smaller-brained *afarensis* line. Within another scant 0.3 my, *habilis* in turn evolved into a much bigger-brained species called *Homo erectus,* whose cranial volume ranged between 727 and 1067 cc, overlapping at the lower end with *habilis* and on the upper end with *H. sapiens* (Miller 1991:397–398). The average was about 1000 cc (Rightmire 1990:173, 175). (See Fig. 5.1 for a comparison of *erectus* and more recent hominids.)

The earliest *erectus* remains (Fig. 5.2a) have been found at Koobi Fora, Kenya, with an approximate date of 1.78 mya (Feibel et al. 1989:612). Additional early African specimens with dates of about 1.2 to 1.1 mya have been found at Olduvai Gorge; and at sites in Morocco and Algiers in North Africa, with dates from 1.0 to 0.6 mya (Hublin 1985:284). It is now generally accepted that *habilis* and the australopithecines never ventured outside Africa. *Erectus,* originating in Africa, was the first hominid to spread from there to Asia, Indonesia, and Europe. The crucial site for evidence of this dispersal is Ubeidiya in the Jordan Valley, Israel, where there are Acheulean artifacts (see p. 68) associated with *erectus* and dating to at least 1.0 mya.

As evidence from a growing number of sites in China and Java shows, *erectus* (Fig. 5.2b and 5.2c) had reached the Far East and Indonesia by about 0.9 mya (Pope 1988:55; Rightmire 1990; Wu and Lin 1985). The oldest *erectus* in China is the Gongwangling cranium from Lantian, dating to 0.85 mya (Pope 1988:55); the earliest in Java are those found in the Sangiran-Trinil area of central Java, with an approximately similar date (Klein 1989:193).

Erectus was the contemporary of the *boisie* australopithecines for more than a million years. Altogether, *erectus* may have inhabited the world for more than 1.5 million years. As we shall see in the following section, it changed remarkably little during this great expanse of time.

HOMO ERECTUS IN EUROPE?

Archaeologists have found what some claim are simple quartz tools at Saint-Eble in south-central France with a well-established date of 2.4 mya. However, they do not agree that the Oldowan-like objects are really artifacts (Ackerman 1989). Other objects that were definitely artifacts with dates of as much as 1.0 mya have been found in many parts of Europe, thereby establishing the existence of some form of early hominid, but there is no unquestionable fossil evidence that it was *erectus* who made these tools.

The earliest hominid fossils found in Europe are all probably younger than 0.5 my. Some experts classify these fossils as late *erectus* while others see them as "archaic" or early *H. sapiens.* The features that these fossils share with *erectus* and with *sapiens* will be discussed on page 72.

Homo Erectus Cultures

To judge from its enlarged brain, *erectus* possessed a greater capacity for cultural behavior than the australopithecines or *habilis.* The extinction of the australopithecines suggests that the early African hominids were subject to intense selection for this ca-

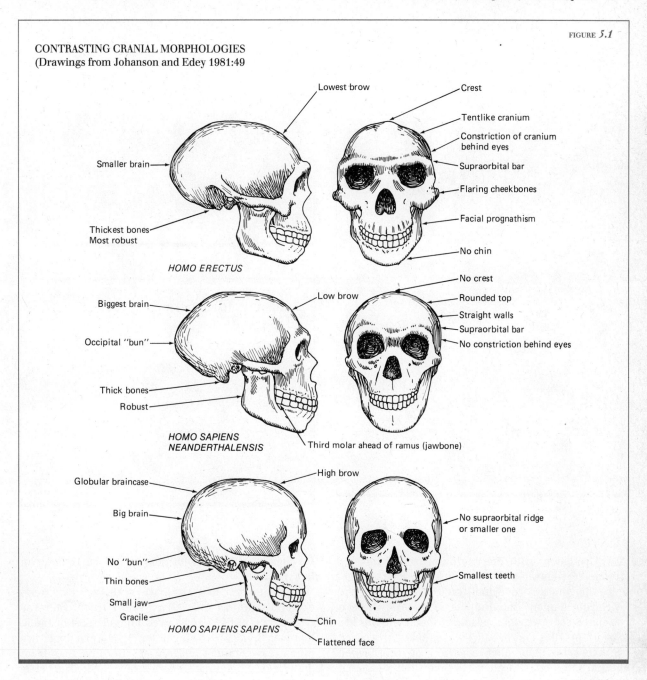

FIGURE *5.1*

CONTRASTING CRANIAL MORPHOLOGIES
(Drawings from Johanson and Edey 1981:49

Lowest brow
Crest
Tentlike cranium
Constriction of cranium behind eyes
Smaller brain
Supraorbital bar
Flaring cheekbones
Facial prognathism
Thickest bones Most robust
No chin
HOMO ERECTUS

Biggest brain
Low brow
No crest
Rounded top
Straight walls
Occipital "bun"
Supraorbital bar
No constriction behind eyes
Thick bones
Robust
HOMO SAPIENS NEANDERTHALENSIS
Third molar ahead of ramus (jawbone)

Globular braincase
High brow
Big brain
No supraorbital ridge or smaller one
No "bun"
Thin bones
Smallest teeth
Small jaw
Gracile
Chin
HOMO SAPIENS SAPIENS
Flattened face

pacity. *Erectus* tool kits were more complex and efficient than the tool kits of its australopithecine contemporaries, and its socially acquired subsistence practices were probably more highly evolved in terms of cooperation, division of labor, and food sharing and other forms of economic exchange.

As we saw (pp. 53–54), the oldest geological beds at Olduvai contain an assortment of flakes, choppers, scrapers, hammerstones, and other tools mixed with numerous animal bones. The set of tools is called the Oldowan tool industry (Fig. 5.3). Presumably, *habilis* was the manufacturer of most of these tools, yet for reasons previously discussed, the possibility should not be dismissed that robust australopithecines who lived at the same time also made some of them.

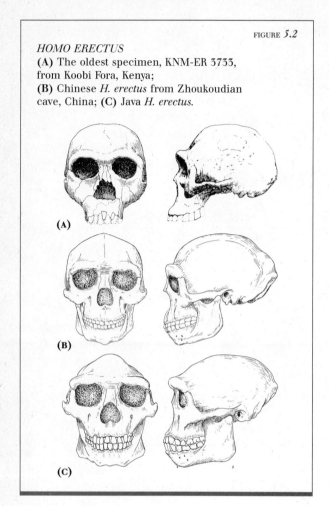

FIGURE *5.2*

HOMO ERECTUS
(A) The oldest specimen, KNM-ER 3733, from Koobi Fora, Kenya;
(B) Chinese *H. erectus* from Zhoukoudian cave, China; **(C)** Java *H. erectus.*

(A)

(B)

(C)

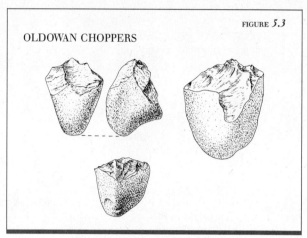

FIGURE *5.3*

OLDOWAN CHOPPERS

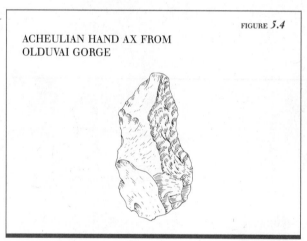

FIGURE *5.4*

ACHEULIAN HAND AX FROM OLDUVAI GORGE

Coincident with the transition from *habilis* to *erectus* at Olduvai and elsewhere in East Africa, there appears a second tool tradition known as the *Acheulean,* named after the site in France where it was first discovered. Its characteristic implements are *bifaces*—pebbles and/or large flakes that are worked on both sides to produce a variety of well-formed cutting, scraping, and piercing edges and points. Of these, the most typical is the hand ax (Fig. 5.4), a multipurpose instrument that probably evolved out of the Oldowan choppers. Hand axes probably served to break soil and roots, to hack off branches, and to dismember game.

The *erectus* tool kit usually also included smaller flake implements for trimming wood, cutting meat and sinew, and scraping hides. Such flakes are the natural by-products of the manufacture of biface tools (Fig. 5.5). Thousands of such flakes, useful for cutting meat and hides, have been found at *erec-*

tus sites (see Table 5.1 for possible uses of Acheulean tools).

Acheulean tool kits have been found in western and southern Asia, Africa, and Europe wherever *erectus* and early *sapiens* lived. In Asia, east of India, however, hand axes and other Acheulean tools are much less common and are absent altogether from many early hominid sites. Instead, East Asian *erectus* is associated with a separate stone tool tradition known as the chopper-chopping tradition (Fig. 5.6). But the geographical distribution of the Acheulean and chopper-chopping traditions are not as exclusive as was formerly supposed, for it is now clear that tools of the chopper-chopping tradition occur in Europe as well as in East Asia, and that numerous hand axes were made in East Asia as well as in Europe during early and mid-Pleistocene times (Yi and Clark 1983). For example, at Vertesszollos in Hungary there are thousands of chopper cores and flakes but

FIGURE *5.5*

BIFACE MANUFACTURE
Core is held in one hand and blows 1, 2, and 3 are delivered with hammerstone
held in other. Core is turned over and blows 4 and 5 are delivered, creating cutting
edge. Acheulian hand ax *(bottom)* was made in this manner. Flakes (not shown)
may also have been used as tools.

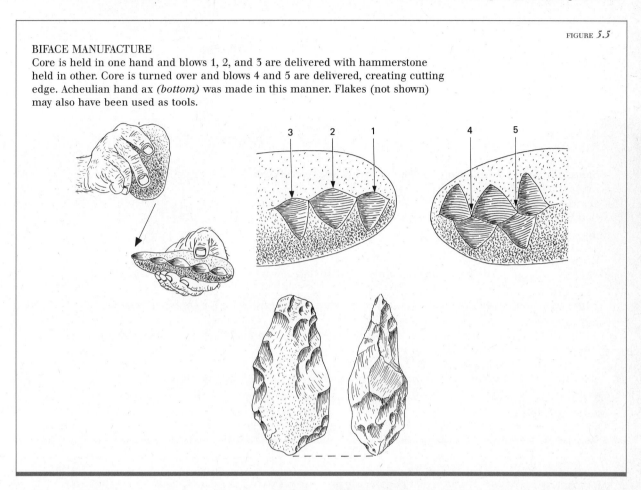

no hand axes, while at Chon-Cok-Ni in Korea, 50 hand axes and Acheulean-type cleavers have been found (Yi and Clark 1983:183). Nonetheless, the relative infrequency of *erectus*-associated hand axes in East and Southeast Asia calls for an explanation.

One promising theory is based on the fact that the geographical distribution of the chopper-chopping tradition corresponds closely to the geographical distribution of bamboo. A rich variety of cutting and scraping tools made from bamboo might have played the same technological role that stone tools played in other regions. The assumption is that these carefully crafted artifacts have not been preserved, creating the incorrect impression that East Asian *erectus* and early Asian *sapiens* possessed a relatively impoverished tool kit (Pope 1988:65).

HUNTING VERSUS SCAVENGING AGAIN

Some archaeologists insist that despite the abundance of stone tools found in association with animal bones at *erectus* sites, *erectus* remained a timid scavenger rather than a bold hunter to the end of his or her days (Binford and Stone 1986). But the arguments in favor of regarding *habilis* and even the gracile australopithecines as significantly involved in predation as well as scavenging (pp. 60–61) apply with greater force to *erectus*. Nonetheless, the balance between hunting and scavenging remains unclear. At sites such as Olorgesailie in Kenya, Terra Amata in France, and Torralba and Ambrona in Spain (Fig. 5.7) accumulations of the bones of animals belonging to a single species in association with Acheulean tools have been interpreted as evidence that *erectus* was using drives and surrounds to trap big game in swamps and along lake shores. However, the accumulated animal remains can also be interpreted as animals that were scavenged by *erectus* after they were trapped and killed by other predators (Klein 1989:221).

FIRE?

Evidence for the use of fire by *erectus* is equally inconclusive. There are concentrated patches of discol-

TABLE *5.1*

FEASIBILITY OF USING ACHEULIAN TOOLS TO PERFORM VARIOUS TASKS BASED ON EXPERIMENTAL TRIALS

	Severing a branch	Wood shaping	Hide slitting	Dismembering small animal	Dismembering large animal	Meat division
Smallish flakes and flake fragments	0	2	1	1	1–2	1

Summary: Very useful for *all* cutting and whittling operations; not useful for heavy-duty wood hacking.

Flake scrapers	0	1	2	2	2	—

Summary: The best form for wood shaping-whittling.

Choppers and related forms (> 300 g)	2	Var.	0	0	Var.	—

Summary: Moderately useful for hacking off branches; not very good for cutting up carcasses.

Core-scrapers	2	1	0	0	Var.	—

Summary: Hollow sectors good for shaving wooden shafts (also true for some choppers).

Handaxes	3	Var.	3	3	1	—

Summary: Good butchery tools for large animals. Serviceable also for branch severing and hide splitting.

Cleavers	1	2?	2	3	1	—

Summary: The best form for branch severing and excellent large-animal butchery tools.

NOTE: 0 = no use; 1 = best; 2 = useful but not optimal; 3 = possible but difficult; Var. = varies with individual tool.

SOURCE: Isaac 1984:12.

FIGURE *5.6*

IMPLEMENTS FROM *HOMO ERECTUS* LEVELS OF ZHOUKOUDIAN CAVE, CHINA

  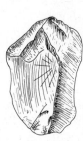   

Choppers   Flakes

Cleaver

FIGURE 5.7

AMBRONA (SPAIN)
Early Acheulian human occupation site, with tusks and other parts of several carcasses of elephants.

ored soils at Koobi Fora and Chesowanja, Kenya, burnt bones at Swartkrans in South Africa (Brain 1990), burnt flints at Terra Amata in Spain, and dispersed charcoal at several other European sites. All of these phenomena could easily be interpreted as the consequence of natural fires or other soil-discoloring processes. Similar problems exist with the association between fire and *erectus* in Zhoukoudian Cave near Beijing, China, based on the occurrence of concentrated layers of charcoal dating to 0.3 mya. Some anthropologists regard these deposits of charcoal to be the accumulated product of cave-dwelling *erectus* "hearths." Others maintain that the layers of charcoal are too widely dispersed to serve as evidence of warming and cooking hearths and that they merely point to the occurrence of fires within the cave. It is a long way from these data to the conclusion that *erectus* regularly warmed themselves and cooked with these fires or could ignite and extinguish them at will (Binford and Stone 1986; Gargett 1989a and 1989b; James 1989; Lanpo 1989). The earliest date for an unambiguous hearth in Europe is 0.2 mya (Straus 1989), but that is long after *erectus* had passed from the scene.

GRADUAL VERSUS PUNCTUATED MODELS

The origin of humankind's incredibly complex and intelligent brain is one of the remaining great mysteries of nature. Anthropologists and other scientists generally believe that the evolution of this amaz-

ing organ was favored by positive feedback (see p. 313) among increased intelligence, tool manufacture, social communication, and coordination—all slowly leading to more effective satisfaction of basic biological drives and needs (food, sex, security against predators, shelter, etc.), and hence to greater reproductive success of bigger-brained and smarter human individuals and groups. This corresponds to the gradualist model of evolution (see p. 16).

As more data have accumulated about the evolutionary history of *erectus,* the alternative "punctuated" model has become more plausible. Between *africanus* and *erectus,* a span of only 300,000 to 400,000 years, brain size doubled. But during the next 1.4 million years, *erectus* brain size increased very little if at all (Rightmire 1991:196–197; see Fig. 5.8). In addition, as we shall see (p. 136), the basic *erectus* Achuelean tool kit also changed remarkably little, considering the vast amount of time during which *erectus* lived on earth. During the past 35,000 years culture has evolved at least a hundred times faster than when *erectus* was alive. Indeed, the slow rate of cultural change associated with *erectus* strongly suggests that their brains were organized quite differently from the brains of modern *sapiens* and that they lacked a fully evolved, distinctively human capacity for acquiring and changing cultural patterns of thought and behavior.

Could it be that the size of the *erectus* brain relative to the australopithecine brain was selected not so much for advanced cognitive capabilities but for

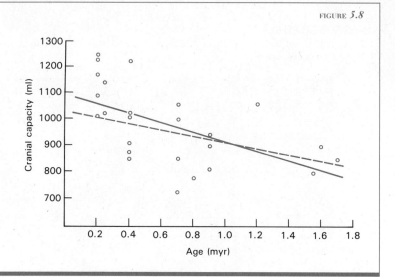

FIGURE *5.8*

ERECTUS BRAIN SIZE
Erectus cranial capacity plotted against age of *erectus* fossil crania indicated by open circles. Dashed line shows slope when doubtful Ndangdong (Solo Man) specimen is removed. Neither line has a slope that is signifigantly different from zero. (*Source:* Adapted from Rightmire 1990:196.)

some other adaptive function? One interesting theory about what the other adaptive function might have been is that bigger brains could have made it possible for *erectus* to hunt in the midday sun—at a time of day when other predators sought shade and water, and refrained from the pursuit of game (Fiałkowski 1986, 1990; cf. Eckhardt 1987). This theory is based on the assumption that by having extra brain cells, the brain of *erectus* was less likely to break down under heat stress. Such stress, to which brain cells are more susceptible than the cells of other organs, can lead to convulsions, failure of cognition (e.g., inability to track prey), stroke, and death.

A basic principle of information theory holds that in an information system that has elements prone to breakdown (such as the human brain), the reliability of the system can be increased by increasing the number of elements that perform the same function and by increasing the number of connections between them. The size of *erectus*'s brain may therefore reflect a large amount of neural redundancy selected for as a means of achieving fail-safe operation under stressful conditions generated by running down prey animals through relentless pursuit under extremes of daytime heat and intense tropical solar radiation.

This theory is especially interesting because several other aspects of human anatomy dovetail with its emphasis upon the importance of heat dispersal. For example, humans possess 2–5 million sweat glands that cool by evaporation—more than any other animal. Humans also have an absence of furlike body hair that might impair the evaporative efficiency of the sweat glands. Also to be considered is that while

many four-legged animals can run faster than two-legged hominids for short distances, by running erect on two legs, humans expose much less of their body surface to the overhead rays of the tropical sun. Note also that thick body hair remains on the head as insulation and that there are few sweat glands on top of the head, but lots on our hairless brows.

Another line of argument supporting the theory that *erectus*'s brain was enlarged first as a consequence of its effects on running rather than its effects on thinking is that *erectus* tool kits lack stone projectile points that could be used to bring down fleeing game at a distance. But such points would not be needed if animals were pursued until they became exhausted and could be killed at close quarters with wooden lances and clubs. If modern humans don't owe our distinctive cultural capabilities to *erectus,* we can still praise them for giving us our unmatched potential for running marathons (Carrier 1984; Devine 1985; and Fig. 5.9).

ARCHAIC *HOMO SAPIENS*

Most authorities agree that *erectus* evolved into and was replaced by larger-brained but still low-browed and big-boned forms of hominids known as archaic (or early) *H. sapiens.* When and where and how many times this transition took place is a matter of continuing debate. In Europe the transition to archaic *sapiens* seems to have been completed before 0.25 mya. At Zhoukoudien, near Beijing in China, and at Ngang-dong in Java, remains that have been dated from 0.35

FIGURE *5.9*

LO, THE ALL-DAY RUNNER!
As the increasing popularity of marathon races demonstrates, humans have an extraordinary, innate physiological capacity to run all day, which probably harks back to our *H. erectus* ancestors.

Archaic *Sapiens* in Europe

There are several fossils in Europe that seem to be intermediate between *erectus* and *sapiens,* dating to between 0.5 and 0.2 mya. These include, among others, Mauer, Swanscombe, and Steinheim (Fig. 5.10). These finds have cranial capacities within the *sapiens* range, but their cranial vaulting and the thickness of their bones suggest a status intermediate between *H. erectus* and *H. sapiens.* Indeed, they could just as properly be classified as late *erectus* as early *sapiens.*

Many additional archaic *sapiens* have been found in Spain, Germany, Italy, France, Greece, and Yugoslavia for the time period between 0.2 mya and 0.1 mya. Some or all of these later archaic European *sapiens* were probably the ancestors of the much-discussed archaic *sapiens* fossils known as the Neandertals (see below).

Archaic *Sapiens* in Africa

In Africa from the Sahara to the Cape of Good Hope, *erectus* began to be replaced by archaic *sapiens* at about the same time as in Europe. The oldest archaic sapiens in Africa have been found in Ethiopia, South Africa, Olduvai Gorge, and Zambia with dates ranging between about 0.4 to 0.3 mya (Fig. 5.11). However, in contrast to what happened in Europe, late archaic *sapiens* in Africa were not succeeded by Neandertals, but by much more anatomically modern *sapiens* populations. We will discuss the significance of this finding on p. 78.

Archaic *Sapiens* in Asia

In Asia, *erectus* seems to have persisted longer than in Europe or Africa. The earliest contender for archaic *sapiens* status are the fossils found at Ngangdong ("Solo Man"), Java, which date to about 0.35 mya (Fig. 5.12a). Many authorities, however, prefer to regard Ngangdong as a late *erectus.* Several archaic *sapiens* are known from China. So far, the Dali skull (Fig. 5.12b) is the most complete fossil from China for the interval between *erectus* and modern *sapiens.* It has a cranial volume of 1120 cc; a long, low cranial vault; and moderately thick bones; it dates to about 0.2 mya. Maba from Guangdong was another big-brained, low-browed individual who lived about 0.13 mya (Fig. 5.12c).

to 0.24 mya have been variously interpreted as *erectus,* archaic *sapiens,* or transitional *erectus-sapiens* form (Klein 1989:194; Pope 1988:62).

The features that archaic sapiens share with erectus are

1. large brow ridges
2. flat, receding brow
3. skull widest at base
4. thick cranial walls
5. massive, chinless jaws
6. large teeth

The features that distinguish archaic sapiens from erectus are

1. cranial capacity well within modern range
2. rounded back of head (occipital bone)
3. wider brows
4. brow ridges that form two distinct arches rather than a continuous bar or shelf

THE ORIGIN AND FATE OF THE NEANDERTALS

In Europe, anatomically modern *sapiens* (known formally as *H. sapiens sapiens*) did not evolve directly

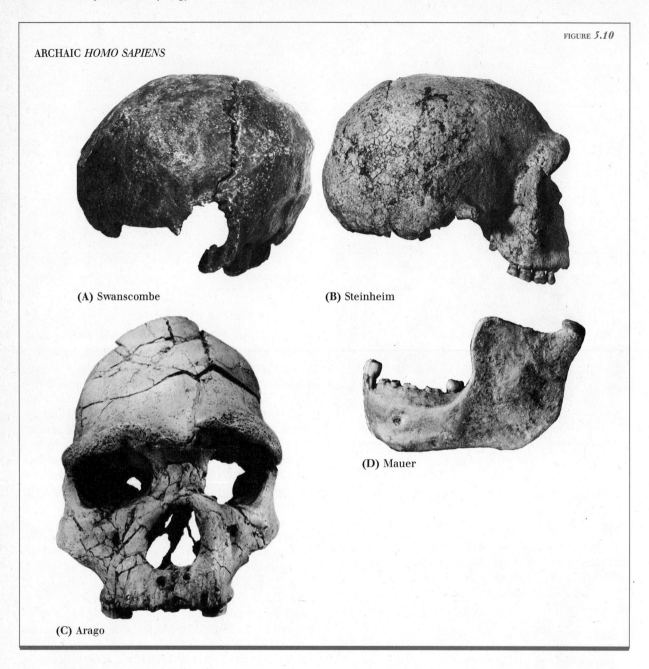

FIGURE *5.10*

ARCHAIC *HOMO SAPIENS*

(A) Swanscombe

(B) Steinheim

(C) Arago

(D) Mauer

from the earlier archaic *sapiens*. Instead, there emerged at about 130,000 B.P. (before the present) a robust, chinless, low-browed subspecies known as *H. sapiens neandertalensis* (Fig. 5.13). This variety of *sapiens*, whose robust appearance was combined with a cranial capacity of 1600 cc—larger than that of modern humans—lived in Europe and nearby parts of Southwest Asia from about 130,000 to about 35,000 B.P. (See Figure 5.1 for a comparison of the Neandertals with *erectus* and anatomically modern *sapiens*.)

This time period coincides roughly with the last major Eurasian glaciation, and many anatomical features of the Neandertals are believed to represent the effects of selection for living in extremely cold climates close to the continental glaciers. For example, the Neandertal's massive large front teeth may have been adapted to the chewing of heavy animal skins as a means of softening such materials for use as blankets and clothing, as evidenced by their worn-down appearance even in young individuals. The same kind

FIGURE *5.11*

ARCHAIC AFRICAN *HOMO SAPIENS*
(A) Bodo—from Ethiopia; ca. 0.4 mya. **(B)** "Rhodesian Man"
from Broken Hill, Zimbabwe; ca. 0.25 mya.

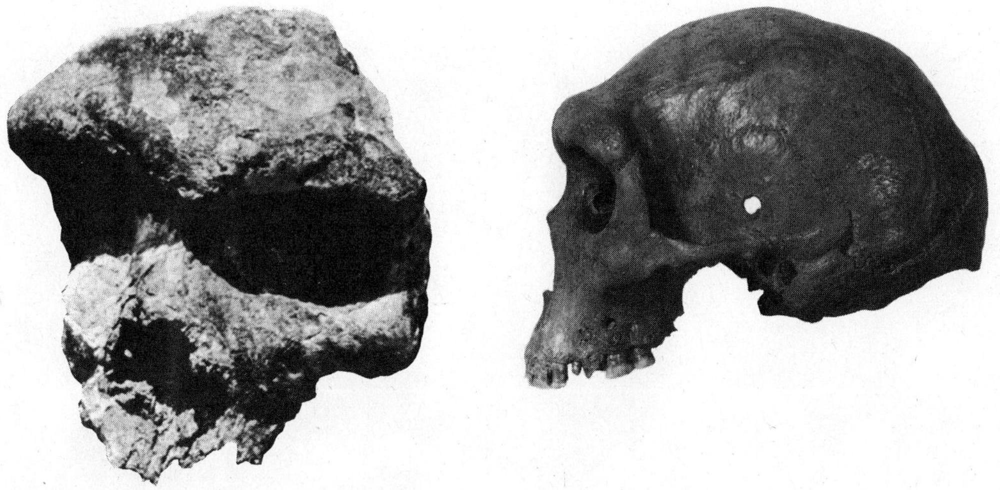

(A)   **(B)**

of adaptation may be reflected in the forward displacement of Neandertal's teeth, resulting in a gap between the edge of the upward slanting part of the ramus (jaw bone) and the third molar. The heavy supraorbital torus (eyebrow ridge) can also be interpreted as part of the same complex. It may have served as a reinforcement of the upper face against the powerful thrust generated by the robust jaw and large front teeth. Finally, relative to modern *sapiens,* Neandertal's lower arms are unusually short in comparison with their upper arms, and their lower legs are unusually small in comparison with their upper legs (Jacobs 1985; P. Smith, 1983; Trinkhaus 1983).

This is a relationship that conserves body heat and is associated with cold-adapted mammals (see p. 92).

DID NEANDERTAL HAVE A HUMAN TYPE OF LANGUAGE?

One of the most provocative ideas about the Neandertals is that they did not yet possess the distinctive modern human capacity for language. The modern human vocal tract has a unique ability to produce certain vowel and consonant sounds as a function of the enlarged size of our pharynx—the sound-resonating

FIGURE *5.12*

ASIAN ARCHAIC *HOMO SAPIENS*
(A) Solo skull cap from Ngandong, Java.
(B) Dali skull, Shaanxi, China; ca. 0.3 to 0.2 mya.
(C) Maba skull cap, Guangdong, China; ca. 0.125 mya.

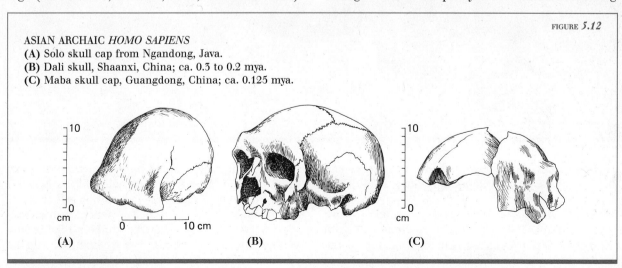

(A)   **(B)**   **(C)**

FIGURE *5.13*

EUROPEAN *HOMO SAPIENS NEANDERTALENSIS*
(A) Saccopastore, Italy; ca. 120,000 B.P. **(B)** La Chapelle aux Saints, France; ca. 45,000 B.P.; cranial capacity 1625 cc. (The hole is thought to have been made by a spear.)

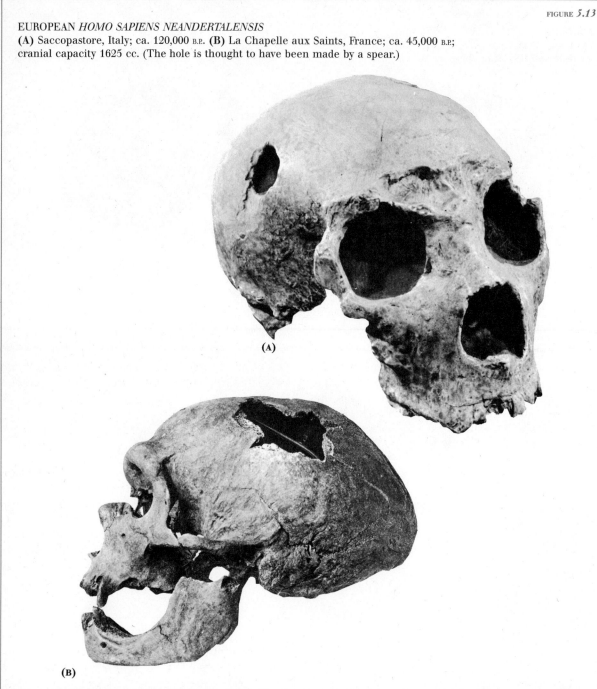

(A)

(B)

portion of our throats between the vocal cords and the back of the mouth (Lieberman 1985a, 1985b). The comparatively small size of the chimpanzee's pharynx, for example (Fig. 5.14), seems to explain why we have been able to teach them to communicate with us in the medium of sign language but not in the medium of spoken words (see p. 118). Chimpanzees cannot make sounds such as [i], [u], or [a], which are essential components in all human languages. When did the hominids achieve this ability? This is a difficult question to answer because the soft parts of the mouth and throat are not preserved in the fossil record. There appears, however, to be a relationship between the angularity of the base of the skull and the presence of an enlarged pharynx (Fig. 5.15). By measuring the angles involved, some experts have con-

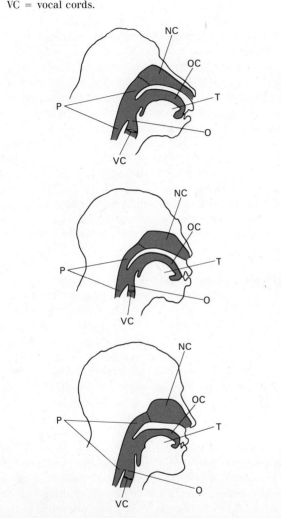

FIGURE *5.14*

AIR PASSAGES
Chimp *(top)*, neandertal *(middle)*, and human *(bottom)*. P = pharynx; NC = nasal cavity; T = tongue; O = opening of larynx in pharynx; VC = vocal cords.

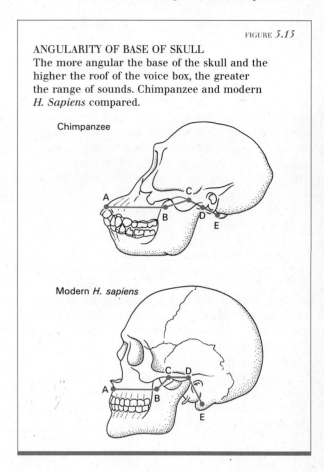

FIGURE *5.15*

ANGULARITY OF BASE OF SKULL
The more angular the base of the skull and the higher the roof of the voice box, the greater the range of sounds. Chimpanzee and modern *H. Sapiens* compared.

Chimpanzee

Modern *H. sapiens*

cluded that Neandertal was unlikely to have been able to use the full range of human sounds and that if they spoke, it was in a slow and faltering manner (Laitman 1985a, 1985b; Lieberman 1984, 1985). Others, however, insist that Neandertal possessed an essentially modern vocal tract. New evidence consisting of a Neandertal hyoid bone (the bone that moves up and down with the Adam's apple) that belonged to a 65,000-year-old Neandertal from Kabera Cave in Israel has not resolved the controversy (Gibbons 1992; Arensburg et al. 1990).

NEANDERTAL RELIGION?

There is other evidence that the Neandertals lacked a fully modern human form of communication and cognition: Virtually no personal adornments (such as beads and pendants) or artistic products (such as decorative incisions on their artifacts, paintings, or sculpture) have been found in their habitation sites. There is general agreement that the Neandertals did occasionally bury their dead in shallow graves, and that they placed the deceased in a fetal-like position with legs drawn up to the chest. Recently, however, skepticism has increased concerning the evidence that Neandertals provided the dead with grave goods such as finely worked tools and joints of meat, or that they colored the body with red dye, or surrounded it with bear skulls or blocks of stone, and placed bouquets of flowers on it. To the extent that these phenomena have been accurately reported, they can almost always be attributed to cave-ins, post-burial disturbances by hyenas, and other accidents or natural processes rather than to religious symbolism stemming from a belief in an afterlife. As for the burials themselves, they may simply have been a practical solution to a desire to stay close to and to protect the bodies of life-long companions. The absence of shovels, picks, and other efficient digging implements would then lead to placing the body in a fetal position simply to avoid the extra effort that would be required to accommodate an outstretched figure (Chase and Dibble 1987; Clark and Lindly 1989; Gargett 1989a, 1989b; Lindly and Clark 1990; Stiner 1991; White and Toth 1991; but see Marshack 1989).

Small groups of Neandertals lingered on in Europe (for example, at Saint Cesaire, France) until about 35,000 B.P., after which they were completely replaced by anatomically modern Europeans.

There are two major theories regarding the fate of the Neandertals and the origins of modern *sapiens.* One is that the Neandertals were more or less abruptly replaced by migrating groups of modern *sapiens* who came from Africa via the Middle East. The other is that the Neandertals independently evolved into modern *sapiens* in Europe at approximately the same time that other late archaic *sapiens* populations were evolving into modern *sapiens* in Africa and Asia. We shall review some of the evidence for these theories in a moment.

THE SAPIENIZATION PROCESS

The evolution of more gracile modern *sapiens* from one or more of the various rugged forms of early archaic *sapiens* can be explained in terms of selection for an increased biological capacity to use culture as a means of enhancing reproductive success. Cultural improvements in knives, scrapers, and other tools and an increased dependence on cooking lessened the adaptive value of large front teeth, heavy brow ridges, and powerful jaw muscles. The entire face could become smaller and recede further under the skull. As the lower jaw became less prognathic (see p. 36), it left behind a remnant of its earlier robusticity in the form of a chin, one of the most diagnostic features of modern *sapiens* anatomy. Freed from the restraints and structural stresses of large jaws and powerful chewing muscles, the cranium could assume a more globular shape, since a sphere is the most efficient form for packing lots of brains in a small space. Reliance on brains rather than brawn would then feed back to reductions in the robusticity of the rest of the body (see J. D. Clark 1983:7–8; Trinkhaus 1986:198).

THE ORIGIN OF *H. SAPIENS SAPIENS:* THE SINGLE ORIGIN THEORY

While European archaic *sapiens* were adapting to the frigid conditions of the last glaciation and becoming more robust in the process, their counterparts in Africa were becoming more gracile and evolving more rapidly in the direction of modern *sapiens.* The analysis of fossils found at Klasies Cave, South Africa; Border Cave, South Africa; Singa, in the Sudan; and several other sites strongly indicates the presence of populations that were anatomically much closer to modern *sapiens* than the Neandertals who were living in Europe during the same period—about 130,000 to 35,000 B.P. (Brauer 1984; Klein 1989:353; Rightmire 1984; Singer and Wymer 1982; Stringer 1985:294). The dating of these fossils has led to the theory that modern sapiens arose first in Africa and then spread to Europe, Asia, and Oceania via the Middle East, resulting in the extinction of the Neandertals in Europe and of all other Eurasian archaic *sapiens* forms (Fig. 5.16).

This theory, which can be called "the single origin theory," has received support from DNA sequence-mapping techniques applied to the DNA that is found inside the mitochondria of human cells. Since the mitochondrial DNA is transmitted only through mothers, attempts have been made to trace all living populations to an original female ancestress—a so-called "Eve." (Popular accounts fail to indicate that such an ancestress would be an Eve only for mitochondrial genes and not for the rest of the human genome). Preliminary applications of this technique have led some researchers to conclude that a mitochondrial Eve lived in Africa about 200,000 years ago (Cann et al. 1987; Stoneking and Cann 1989; Vigilant et al. 1991). If this were true, then all archaic moderns outside of Africa (including Neandertal) would be excluded from being ancestral to modern *sapiens.* However, the validity of the techniques involved and the conclusions drawn have been the object of intense criticism (Barinaga 1992; Hedges et al. 1991; Lovejoy et al. 1992; Templeton 1991).

Remains of both Neandertals and anatomically modern *sapiens* had been found in many sites in the Middle East, but never at the same site together. It had generally been assumed that as in Europe, the Neandertal sites were older than the modern *sapiens* sites. But support for the "single origin" idea has been provided by new estimates that reverse this sequence in the Middle East. In Israel at Jebel Qafzeh Cave near Nazareth and at Tabun Cave on Mt. Carmel,

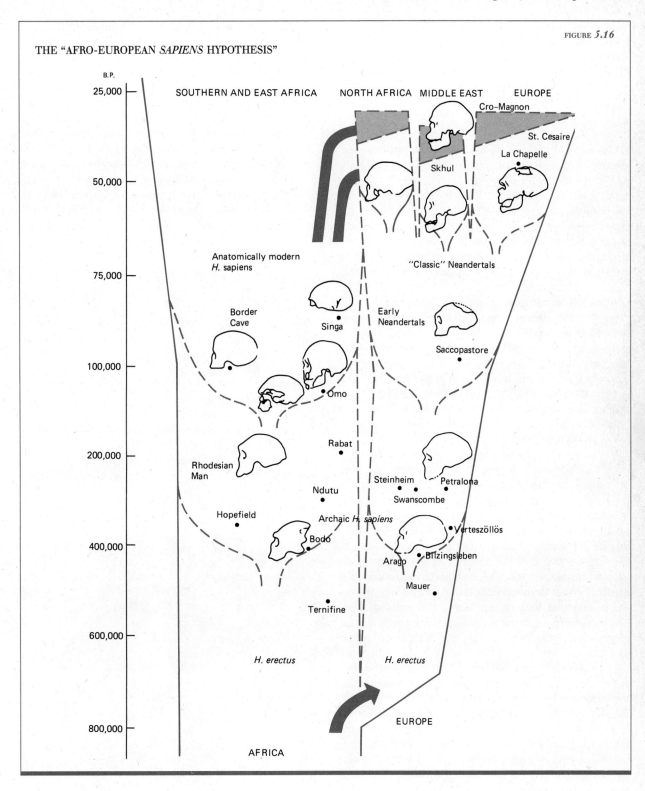

FIGURE *5.16*

THE "AFRO-EUROPEAN *SAPIENS* HYPOTHESIS"

burnt flints were found in association with Neandertal (Tabun) and modern *sapiens* (Qafzeh). Thermoluminescence (see Box 4.1, p. 43) dates Jebel Qafzeh to 92,000 B.P. and Tabun to only 60,000 B.P.

THE ORIGIN OF *H. SAPIENS SAPIENS:* THE MULTIPLE ORIGIN THEORY

Proponents of the second or "multiple origin theory" regard all archaic *sapiens,* including the Neandertals, as phases or "grades" in the widespread "sapienization" process described above that led to the parallel evolution (see p. 26) of *erectus* into modern *sapiens* throughout most of the Old World. The fact that some groups like the European Neandertals crossed the threshold to modern *sapiens* slightly later than others is to be expected in a process that was unfolding across such a vast expanse of the earth and under so many different local conditions.

Multiple origin proponents reject the mitochondrial DNA evidence on a variety of technical grounds such as the postulated mutation rate, the assumption that there was no gene flow, and the adequacy of the samples used to establish African ancestry (Clark and Lindly 1989:976; Wolpoff 1989). They also challenge the accuracy of the thermoluminescent technique as applied to the Jebel Qafzeh and Tabun remains (Clark and Lindly 1989:978).

Another point made by the advocates of the multiple origin theory is that the first modern *sapiens* to appear in Asia, Indonesia, and Australia do not possess any physical traits that can be described as notably "African" in appearance. Instead, they possess certain distinctive physical traits that occur only among the archaic and modern populations found in their respective regions. Thus in East Asia, unlike in Africa, the incisor teeth of both archaic and modern *sapiens* have a distinctive flattened form which makes them look like shovels. Similarly, the earliest modern *sapiens* in Australia have distinctive rugged brow ridges that are absent in modern Africans (Thorne and Wolpoff 1992).

Moreover, they ask, regarding the finding that Jebel Qafzeh moderns preceded Tabun Neandertals by 30,000 years and were already present in the Middle East 90,000 B.P.: Why did it take the moderns until 35,000 B.P. to appear in Europe? The most probable answer is that they lacked any decisive cultural advantages over the Neandertals because they were really not a more advanced species but a racial variant of the same species.

This leads to the most compelling criticism of the single origin theory, namely, that there is virtually no difference between the cultural remains of the moderns and Neandertals in the Middle East (Mellars 1989:7–8). Both exhibited the same variety of Middle Stone Age industry (the Mousterian—see p. 138) that is also associated with the Neandertals of Europe. Indeed, none of the cultural remains associated with African modern *sapiens* prior to 40,000 B.P. shows evidence of any kind of disjunction or leap forward as far as cultural behavior is concerned. None of the African early modern sites has thus far yielded evidence of increased aesthetic and symbolic behavior in the form of art and rituals (Lindley and Clark 1989:238–239). It is clear therefore that the decisive neural reorganization of the human brain that led to cultural "take-off" (see p. 141) after 40,000 B.P. cannot be detected from an examination of the external anatomy of the modern *sapiens* skull.

ONE SPECIES

Regardless of which of these theories is eventually verified, there is agreement that by about 40,000 to 30,000 B.P. a single fully modern *sapiens* species occupied all of the inhabited areas of the old world. Cro-magnon (Fig. 5.17) is one of the most famous of these modern *sapiens sapiens.* During approximately the same time period other *sapiens sapiens* appeared in China and Indonesia. Even remote Australia shows signs of being populated by *sapiens sapiens* by 35,000 B.P. (Rhys Jones 1989; Kramer 1991). But, as we shall see in Chapter 11, the possibility that modern *sapiens*

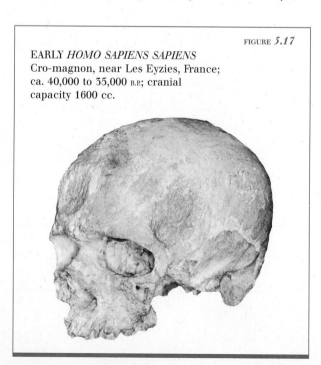

FIGURE *5.17*

EARLY *HOMO SAPIENS SAPIENS*
Cro-magnon, near Les Eyzies, France; ca. 40,000 to 35,000 B.P.; cranial capacity 1600 cc.

had penetrated to the New World at about the same time remains undecided.

We will discuss the evidence for a rather sudden cultural "takeoff" as a defining characteristic of this most recent phase of hominid evolution in Chapter 9. But this is a good place to note that for the past 35,000 years there has been only one hominid genus, one hominid species, and one hominid subspecies in the world—*H. sapiens sapiens.* And further, in no part of the world, however remote, are there hominids whose nature is less human than the rest.

SUMMARY

Erectus, the successor to *habilis,* originated in Africa about 1.8 mya and came to inhabit a large part of the Old World, including China and Indonesia. In Africa and western Asia, *erectus* is associated with Acheulean cultures characterized by hand axes and other biface tools. The scarcity of Acheulean artifacts in China and Indonesia may result from the substitution of bamboo for stone as the basic raw material for tool manufacture. There is considerable evidence that *erectus* was a proficient hunter who possessed some degree of control over fire.

As it has become clear that *erectus* endured for almost 1.5 myr, the gradualist model of hominid evolution has been subject to criticism. A punctuated model appears to fit the insignificant growth in the size of *erectus*'s brain and the virtual stasis of its Acheulean tool kit. The doubling in cranial capacity between *africanus* and *erectus,* followed by the absence of significant growth thereafter until the appearance of archaic *sapiens,* suggest that *erectus*'s brain size may have been selected for some function other than an enhanced potential for cultural evolution. One possibility is that brain size expanded to provide fail-safe neural redundancies against heat stress, thereby enabling *erectus* to run down game in the heat of the day. This theory helps to explain the lack of thick body hair and the abundance of sweat glands and other heat-dispersing features of human physiology.

Erectus began to be replaced by rugged, chinless, but large-brained forms known loosely as early archaic *sapiens* during the period of 0.4 mya to 0.2 mya. In Europe between about 130,000 and 75,000 B.P. the early archaic *sapiens* were followed by the more robust, big-brained, cold-adapted subspecies known as the Neandertals. Considerable uncertainty surrounds the question of the linguistic, cognitive, and cultural capacities of the Neandertals.

According to the single origin theory, a process of sapienization, involving selection for more gracile features, smaller teeth, rounded skulls, and greater reliance on culture, began first in Africa, possibly as early as 125,000 B.P. Evidence from mitochondrial DNA studies supports the single origin theory. In this view, modern *sapiens* originated in Africa and migrated to Europe and the rest of the Old World, everywhere replacing the preexisting local and regional archaic *sapiens* populations. This view is opposed by the proponents of the multiple origin theory, according to whom the regional archaic *sapiens,* including Neandertal, underwent a parallel process of sapienization at only slightly different rates. A crucial part of the debate about the origins of modern *sapiens* is that there are no significant differences between the tool kits and other cultural practices of the Neandertals and the early modern *sapiens.* One implication is that the early moderns—prior to 40,000 to 30,000 B.P.—were no more advanced than the Neandertals in their capacity for fully human language and culture.

Regardless of the details of the evolutionary process, the crucial fact is that after 35,000 B.P., there was only one hominid species in all the world, "our kind"—*Homo sapiens sapiens.*

Chapter 6

Race, Human Variation, and the Forces of Evolution

This chapter completes our inquiry into the origin of the human species. It deals with the processes that are responsible for biological variations found in and among human populations, especially in relation to the concept of race. No subject is more widely misunderstood. What is a race, anyway? How many races are there? How old are they? Are there any pure races? What is the significance of skin color? What was the original color of human skin? What accounts for the extremely light skin of northern Europeans and the extremely dark skin of central Africans and of their respective descendants? What about blood types and other racial characteristics? And finally, do the races really differ in intelligence? I hope you read this chapter with extra care, for misapprehensions about race are a major threat to the survival and well-being of our species.

RACES AS POPULATIONS

In biological taxonomies, a *race* denotes a large, geographically isolated population within a species that has had little or no gene flow (p. 15) with other populations for a long time. There is no evidence that any large subdivisions of *Homo sapiens* are encountering increasing biological difficulties in interbreeding with any other large subdivision. Hence, there is no basis for viewing any contemporary subgroups as being on the verge of speciation, and consequently, one could scientifically do without using the term *race* in referring to human groups. The impulse to do without the term *race* is further strengthened by an additional host of conceptual errors associated with popular taxonomies of race as exemplified in such terms as *black, brown, yellow,* and *white;* or *negroid, mongoloid,* and *caucasoid;* or *African, Asian,* and *European.* Indeed, the discrepancy between popular ideas about race and modern scientific principles of taxonomy and genetics is so great that many anthropologists want to eliminate the word *race* from anthropology textbooks altogether (Fried 1968; Littlefield, Lieberman, and Reynolds 1982; Montagu 1974) and to use the term *population* instead.

A human population is simply any group of people whose members interbreed and who exhibit distinctive gene frequencies when compared with neighboring groups of people. The word *race* and its popular meanings, however, are too important to be ignored. The position adopted in this book is that expressed by Wenda Trevathan: "To sidestep race, treat it as though it did not exist as a valid or invalid concept in physical anthropology, is to take the ostrich approach at best, unethical at worst" (1982:652). We shall therefore continue to use the term *race* as we try to expose the conceptual errors that are often implied when it is used in popular contexts.

TRADITIONAL RACIAL TAXONOMIES

The definition of race as a population in which one or more genes occur with a distinctive frequency contradicts popular notions about the racial divisions of modern *H. sapiens.* In the popular view, *H. sapiens* is divided into a small and fixed number of racial groups whose members possess a set of race-defining hereditary traits.

These traits are readily noticeable external features. Each race is thought to possess a particular "bundle" of such readily noticeable features. Thus, caucasoids (Box 6.1) are thought of as having pale

---

BOX *6.1*

WHY CAUCASOID?

The term *caucasoid* was introduced in the eighteenth century by Johann Blumenbach, a biologist who had a collection of human skulls. One skull from the Caucasus region of Europe appeared to him to be more beautiful than the other skulls from Europe. Thereafter, Europeans and persons of European ancestry have been called, for no better reason, Caucasoids (or Caucasians).

SOURCE: Montagu 1972:75.

skin, straight or wavy hair, large amounts of body hair, noses of narrow to medium width, and medium to tall stature. Negroids are thought of as having black or dark brown skin, wiry hair, medium body hair, and thick noses and lips. And Mongoloids are thought of as having pale to light brown skin, straight black hair, dark brown eyes with epicanthic folds (flaps over the eyes, giving them a "slanted" look), short to medium stature, and relatively hairless faces and bodies.

The first problem with this concept of race is that the features in the bundles do not stay together in space or time. Instead, each feature can be independently assorted and genetically segregated (see p. 12) and is subject to the evolutionary forces of mutation, drift, and selection. As a result, at least one-half of the population of the world today displays bundles of readily visible features not anticipated in popular racial stereotypes. For example, millions of people with thin lips, thin noses, and wavy hair, but brown to dark brown skin live in northeast Africa. The native inhabitants of southern Africa have epicanthic eye folds, light brown to brown skin, and tightly spiraled hair. India has millions of people with straight or wavy hair, dark brown skin, thin lips, and thin noses. On the steppes of central Asia, epicanthic eye folds combine with wavy hair, light eyes, considerable body and facial hair, and pale skins. In Indonesia, there is a high frequency of epicanthic folds, light to dark brown skin, wavy hair, thick noses, and thick lips. Varied combinations of brown to dark brown skin with contrastive forms and quantities of hair and facial features are found among the inhabitants of the islands of Oceania. One of the most interesting bundles of features occurs among the Ainu of northern Japan, who have light skins and thick brow ridges

and are among the hairiest people in the world. Finally, in Australia, pale to dark brown skin color and wavy blond to brown hair are found (see Fig. 6.1).

The error of trying to cram all of these populations into the mold of three or four racial categories is well illustrated by the system of racial identity currently employed in the United States. In the American folk taxonomy, if one parent is "black" and the other is "white," the child is "black" despite the fact that by the laws of genetics, half of the child's genes are from the black parent and half from the white. The practice of cramming people into racial pigeonholes becomes absurd when black ancestry is reduced to a single grandparent or great-grandparent. This produces the phenomenon of the "white" who is socially classified as "black." The arbitrary nature of this practice extends to many ostensibly scientific studies of "blacks" and "whites." Most American blacks have received a significant portion of their genes from recent European ancestors. When samples of American blacks are studied (see p. 93), the assumption that they genetically represent Africans is incorrect.

Both scientists and laymen would do well to emulate the Brazilians (Fig. 6.2), who identify racial types not by three or four terms but by 300 or 400 (Harris 1970; Meintel 1978; Stephens 1989).

PUREBLOODS

Another popular misconception about race is that there are "pure-blooded" individuals who are more representative than others of a race's "essential" features or "archetype." For example, curly-haired, thick-lipped, dark-skinned individuals are regarded

WHAT RACES DO THESE PEOPLE BELONG TO?

FIGURE *6.1*

(A)   (B)   (C)   (D)   (E)

(A) Egyptian; (B) Laplander; (C) Fijian; (D) Australian aborigine; (E) Ainu.

FIGURE *6.2*

BRAZILIAN PORTRAITS
The great variety of facial types in Brazil suggests that it is futile to think about human beings in terms of a small number of fixed sharply distinct races.

as less essentially caucasoid than light-skinned, light-eyed individuals. But every individual whose genes are part of a population's gene pool is as much a member of that population as anyone else. When speaking of European caucasoids as having straight to wavy hair, one must not forget that many Europeans have curly hair. Similarly, a small percentage of Europeans have epicanthic folds. Europeans who are shorter than 5 feet are no less European caucasoids than those who are 7 feet tall. Similarly, both the $4\frac{1}{2}$-foot Ituri Mbuti and the 7-foot Watusi are negroids. If one ignores individuals who do not conform to what a "typical" African is supposed to look like, one violates the concept of race as a population. The genes of everyone in the population's gene pool count equally in determining the population's gene frequencies.

Physical anthropologists sometimes divide Europeans into Baltics, Nordics, Alpines, Dinarics, and Mediterraneans. Adding similar subgroups around the world yields classifications that have tens or even hundreds of groupings. But within all such subgroups, traits such as hair form, skin color, and stature continue to vary widely. Even if one takes each of the 2000 or so "tribes" known to ethnographers and declares each a "race," no individuals could be found who would represent the true or pure type of their groups (Hiernaux 1969).

CLINES

Popular notions of race envision races as occupying sharply bounded "homelands." But in reality, the genes responsible for differences in skin color, hair form, and the other traits popularly used to define racial categories usually occur with gradually increasing or decreasing frequency from one region to another. Such distributions are called *clines*. For example, the frequency of the genes responsible for dark skin color gradually increases as one moves from Mediterranean Europe south along the Nile or across the Sahara and into central Africa. There are no sharp breaks anywhere along the way. Similarly, the incidence of epicanthic folds gradually increases from west to east across Asia, whereas the frequency of wavy hair gradually increases in the reverse direction (Fig. 6.3).

Clines result from two evolutionary processes: gene flow and selection. One can expect a gradual change in gene frequencies with distance as a result of the gradual flow of genes through adjacent populations. A similar pattern will result if there is an adaptive advantage for a gene and if that advantage

varies with latitude, longitude, or altitude. Skin color, for example, has a clinal pattern from lower to higher latitudes related to the gradually changing intensity of the sun's rays from equatorial to Arctic regions (see below).

The existence of clines casts doubt on the notion that the races are associated with fixed, age-old homelands. Gene flow, mutation, and selection are constantly at work shifting the frequencies of genes and the boundaries of populations. Hence, there is no starting point when all of the modern-day races were purebreeds and lived only in their homelands.

BLOOD GROUPS AND RACE

There is another problem with defining races by using the traditional bundle of traits. To the degree that one adds additional traits to the original bundle, especially traits that are not readily visible, the boundaries of the races change. This can be seen in the case of the alleles that determine the immunological properties of blood (and hence the outcome of blood transfusions between one human and another).

The best-known blood groups are controlled by three alleles called A, B, and O. These alleles give rise to four phenotypes: A, B, AB, and O. The relationship between the alleles and phenotypes is as follows:

Allele genotype	Blood group phenotype
OO	O
AO	A
AA	A
BO	B
BB	B
AB	AB

All humans have one of the four blood group phenotypes. (There are also subtypes that we need not discuss here.) Type O has the widest distribution, occurring on all continents and crosscutting all major racial divisions (see Fig. 6.4). It occurs with a frequency of 70–80 percent in Scotland, central Africa, Siberia, and Australia. Type A is equally unmindful of major racial boundaries: Africa, India, and southern and northern China all have 10–20 percent frequencies, while Japan, Scotland, and much of aboriginal Australia are in the 20–29 percent bracket. Asians have frequencies of type B ranging from 10 to 30 percent, yet the native Americans, whose ancestors were Asians, are in the 0–5 percent range, a frequency shared by the Australian aborigines. West Africa and eastern Europe both show type B frequencies of about

15–20 percent. Similar racially nonconforming distributions are characteristic of other blood systems, such as MNS and Rh (Hulse 1973; Kelso 1974), although some degree of match-up can be achieved by using the statistical technique known as multivariate analysis (Bodmer and Cavalli-Sforza 1976; Stern 1973:319).

RACE AND POLYMORPHISMS

Blood group variations are an example of genetic polymorphisms (*poly* = several, *morphisms* = shapes) that result when a gene has one or more alleles. As many as 30 percent of all human genes are estimated to have one or more alleles (Nelson and Jurmain 1988:142). Traditional ideas about race make very small contributions toward understanding why these polymorphisms occur and why they are distributed unevenly from one population to the next.

Several multivariate analyses have been carried out to measure the amount of variation in polymorphic traits that occurs within the major races versus the amount of genetic variation of polymorphic traits that occurs within local groups (such as tribes and small ethnic communities). It turns out that 85 percent of the genetic differences occur *within* local groups *within* the major races (Lewontin 1972). This means that one could take any tribe or small ethnic group at random and expect to find 85 percent of all the genetic variation in the human species represented in its gene pool (Silk and Boyd 1989: Chap. 9:8).

The failure of the idea of racial archetypes to explain the distribution of polymorphisms accounts in large measure for the declining interest that physical anthropologists have shown in using the concept of race (Livingstone 1982). Physical anthropologists have found it much more productive to approach the problem of genetic polymorphisms from a dynamic evolutionary viewpoint and to study the role of natural selection and other evolutionary forces in bringing about variations in gene frequencies.

For example, there is considerable evidence linking the ABO series with different resistances to diseases that may affect reproductive success, such as smallpox, bubonic plague, and food poisoning by toxic bacteria. (There are also linkages with duodenal ulcers and stomach cancer, but these may occur too late in life to affect reproductive success.) Hence, the explanations for blood type polymorphisms may have to be sought primarily in the history of transient exposures of different populations to different diseases rather than in racial ancestry.

SICKLE CELL AND RELATED POLYMORPHISMS

One of the most interesting cases of polymorphism are the alleles responsible for the disease known as sickle-cell anemia. The red blood cells of persons afflicted with this congenital defect are sickle-shaped instead of round and are incapable of transporting normal amounts of oxygen (Fig. 6.5). An individual falls victim to this potentially lethal defect only when both parents carry the allele for sickling. Individuals who have inherited the allele from one parent show only mild symptoms.

Several sickling alleles appear to have originated in Africa and to have spread to the Mediterranean region and India. Another independently evolved sickling allele is found in Southeast Asia. All of the regions in which these alleles occur are noted for the high incidence of malaria. It was found that in the presence of the sickling alleles the malarial parasite was unable to reproduce and that individuals who have the allele in a heterozygous form possess much greater resistance to this disease than individuals who are homozygous for normal red blood cells. While homozygotes for sickling tend to die off, the heterozygotes prosper. Since the heterozygotes outnumber the homozygotes in a ratio of 2:1 (see p. 15), the sickling allele is never eliminated as long as malaria remains endemic. Alleles that remain balanced in this way are called *balanced polymorphisms*.

A similar form of balanced polymorphism appears to account for the persistence of the disease known as *thalessemia*. This disease is a form of anemia that results from impairment of the ability to produce sufficient numbers of red blood cells, not from a defect in the cells. In the homozygous state, the thalessemia allele is often fatal; in the heterozygous state, it seems to have no deleterious effect. Like the sickle cell allele, the thalessemia allele is found in regions that are now or recently were infested by malaria, especially in countries bordering on the Mediterranean Sea and southern India. Why is there a difference between the blood polymorphisms that protect against malaria in the Mediterranean as compared with Africa? The answer is not known, but one point seems clear. Mutations have probably produced thousands of red blood cell abnormalities, most of which are useless for protecting against malaria. A handful however, did prove to be effective antimalarials and were recurrently selected for by natural selection. Their overall similarity as antimalarials constitutes a remarkable example of convergent evolution (see p. 26) at the molecular level (Diamond 1989).

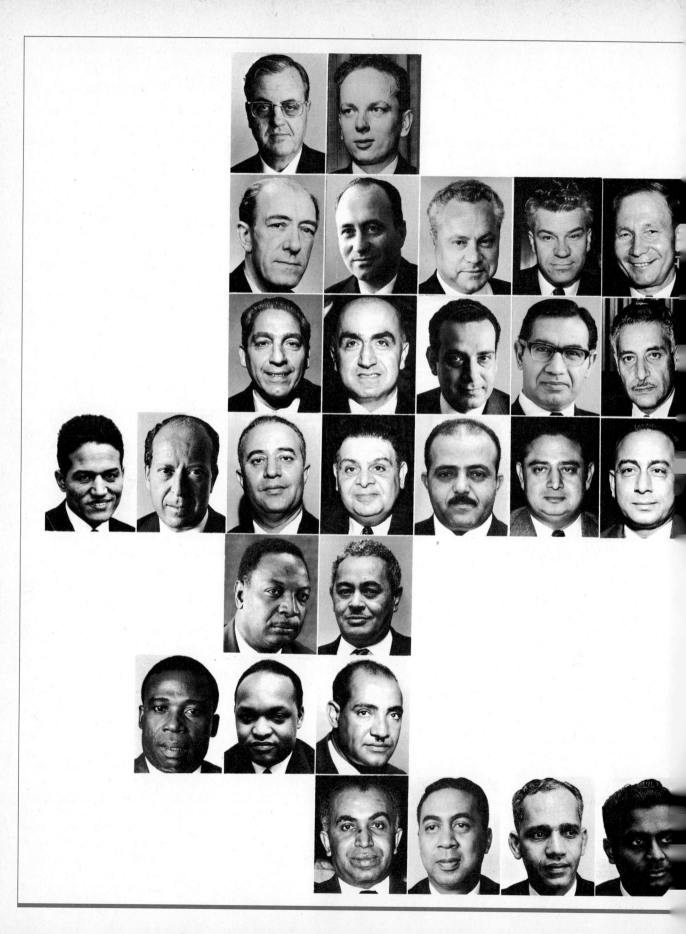

FIGURE 6.3

UNITY OF HUMANKIND
There are sharp breaks in the distribution of racial types across Africa and Eurasia.
(Only men are shown because of the difficulty of obtaining a comparable set of photos
of women all dressed alike and having similar hairdos. This difficulty
results from the domination by men of U.N. missions and consular posts.)

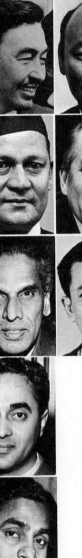

1 Mauritania
2 Tunisia
3 Eq. Guinea
4 Sweden
5 Denmark
6 Italy
7 Libya
8 Niger
9 Burundi
10 Finland
11 Hungary
12 Greece
13 Egypt
14 Sudan
15 Ethiopia
16 Zanzibar
17 Ukraine
18 Iraq
19 Yemen
20 Madagascar
21 USSR
22 Iran
23 Pakistan
24 Mauritius
25 USSR
26 Afghanistan
27 Pakistan
28 Maldive Is.
29 Tuva (USSR)
30 Nepal
31 India
32 India
33 India
34 Mongolia
35 China
36 Burma
37 Laos
38 Malaysia
39 Japan
40 Philippines
41 Indonesia
42 Ponape
43 Fiji

FIGURE *6.4*

DISTRIBUTION OF ALLELES
OF THE ABO BLOOD GROUP SYSTEM

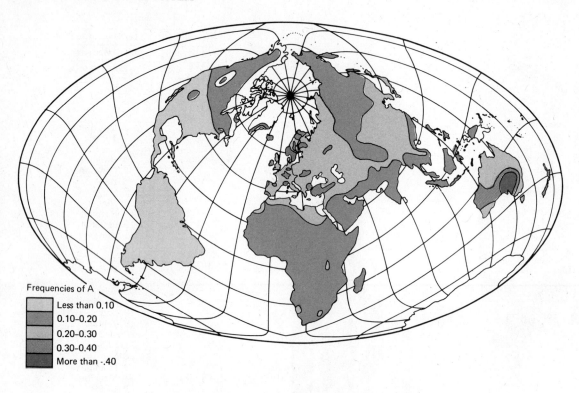

Frequencies of A

- Less than 0.10
- 0.10–0.20
- 0.20–0.30
- 0.30–0.40
- More than -.40

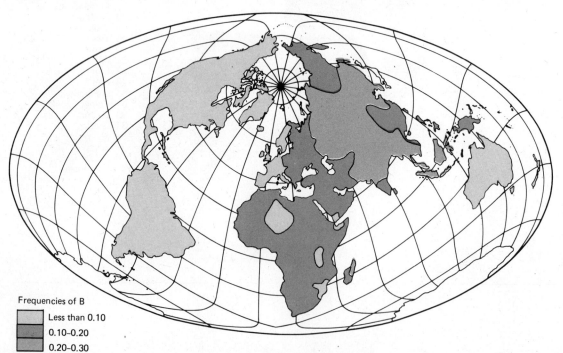

Frequencies of B

- Less than 0.10
- 0.10–0.20
- 0.20–0.30

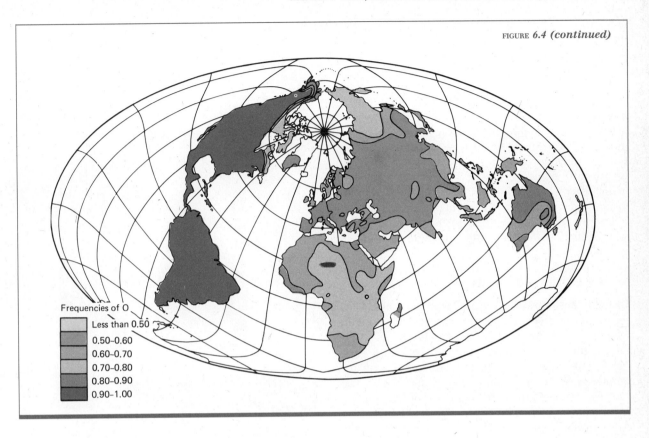

FIGURE **6.4** *(continued)*

Frequencies of O
- Less than 0.50
- 0.50–0.60
- 0.60–0.70
- 0.70–0.80
- 0.80–0.90
- 0.90–1.00

FIGURE **6.5**

RED BLOOD CELLS
Micrographs of **(A)** normal and **(B)** sickled cells. (Normal cells magnified × 1200; sickled cells × 8000.)

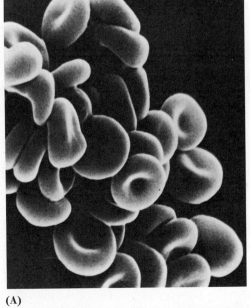

(A)   **(B)**

Another interesting polymorphism is the ability to taste the bitter substance phenylthiocarbamide, or PTC. Tasters have the dominant allele T, whereas nontasters are homozygous for the recessive allele t. The frequency of t ranges from 60 percent among Asian Indians to 10 percent among native Americans. A possible explanation may lie in the fact that goiter, produced by a malfunction of the thyroid gland, is more common among nontasters than among tasters. PTC chemically resembles certain substances found in mustard plants, cabbage, and brussels sprouts, which, if overconsumed, can cause the thyroid gland to malfunction. Hence, the ability to taste PTC as a bitter substance may be related to the ability to detect plants that adversely affect thyroid functions.

NOSES AND BODY BUILD

Distributions of traits associated with the major races have been studied for clues concerning their possible adaptive value (contribution to reproductive success). Results thus far have been inconclusive, but a number of interesting suggestions relate certain traits to temperature, humidity, and other climatological factors. For example, the high frequency of long narrow noses among Europeans may have resulted from the need to raise extremely cold, damp air to body temperature before it reached the lungs. The generally rounded squat form of the Innuit can be viewed as another type of adaptation to cold. A spherical shape presents a maximum of body mass to a minimum of body surface. This links maximum heat production to maximum heat conservation (i.e., the greater the biomass, the more heat generated; the smaller the surface area, the less heat that is lost). A tall, thin body form, on the other hand, combines a minimum of body mass with a maximum of body surface leading to maximum heat loss (Fig. 6.6). This may explain the characteristics of the tall, thin Nilotic Africans who inhabit regions of intense arid heat (Coon 1965:112).

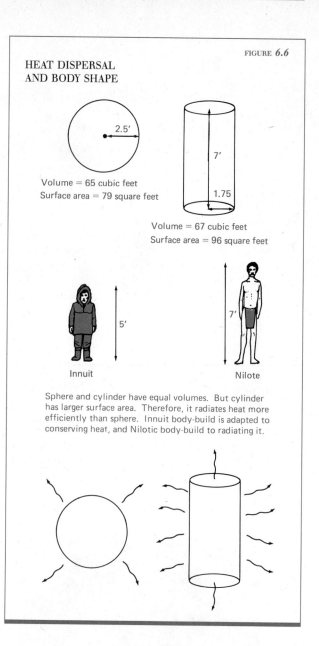

FIGURE 6.6

HEAT DISPERSAL AND BODY SHAPE

2.5'

Volume = 65 cubic feet
Surface area = 79 square feet

7'

1.75

Volume = 67 cubic feet
Surface area = 96 square feet

5'   Innuit

7'   Nilote

Sphere and cylinder have equal volumes. But cylinder has larger surface area. Therefore, it radiates heat more efficiently than sphere. Innuit body-build is adapted to conserving heat, and Nilotic body-build to radiating it.

LACTASE DEFICIENCY

Lactase deficiency is still another polymorphism. The ability to digest milk depends on the body's ability to produce the enzyme lactase, which breaks down the complex milk sugar, lactose, into the simpler sugars glucose and galactose. Most adult mammals, including most *sapiens,* lose the ability to produce lactase as juveniles or adults and thereafter suffer severe forms of indigestion when they consume large quantities of unfermented milk. This presumably has an adaptive value since it prevents competition between mature individuals and infants for mother's milk. However, in populations whose subsistence depends on drinking large quantities of milk from dairy animals, there is a higher incidence of the allele that enables adults to produce lactase. Where fluid milk was the principal source of calcium because other dietary sources of calcium were in short supply (see p. 95), as was the case for prehistoric northern Europeans, selection for lactase-sufficient adults was especially intense (Harris 1985; Harrison 1975; Paige and Bayless 1978; Simoons 1982). This then accounts for the unusual ability of northern Europeans and their descendants to drink copious quantities of unfermented milk. (Lactase-insufficient individuals can consume fermented milk and milk products such as cheese without adverse effects because fermentation transforms the lactose into simpler sugars.)

ADAPTATION AND RACIAL ANTIQUITY

Because of the operation of evolutionary forces—mutation, selection, drift, and gene flow—and the principles of independent assortment and genetic segregation, the traits that are used to define races today and in the recent past may not have existed as part of the same bundle of traits in more remote times. No one knows what bundle of traits characterized populations 25,000 or more years ago. This is especially true of the soft parts of the body and of skin color, since these traits are not preserved in the fossil record. Modern-day images of racial types therefore cannot be projected onto populations that lived tens of thousands of years ago, since our remote ancestors probably had entirely different bundles of polymorphisms and bore little resemblance to negroids, caucasoids, or mongoloids as we know them today.

The belief that today's races represent ancient breeding isolates is further contradicted by the adaptive effects of selection. As we have just seen, human polymorphisms may result from selection for advantageous alleles. If traits used for racial classification are strongly adaptive, they cannot be used as evidence of ancient common biological descent. For example, suppose a group with a low-sickling frequency moves into an area of endemic malaria inhabited by an unrelated people who have a high frequency of sickling alleles. After a number of generations (predictable by genetic equations), the frequency of sickling will increase among the immigrants even if there is no intergroup mating, and after a relatively short time the natives and the immigrants will become indistinguishable with respect to the sickling trait.

As we shall see in the next section, there is a strong possibility that skin color—one of the most popular diagnostics of human racial groupings—is an adaptive trait and is therefore not a reliable indication of common ancestry.

SKIN COLOR

Most human beings are neither very fair nor very dark, but brown. The extremely fair skin of northern Europeans and their descendants, and the very dark skin of central Africans and their descendants are probably special adaptations. Brown-skinned ancestors may have been shared by modern-day blacks and whites as recently as 15,000 to 10,000 B.P.

Human skin owes its color to the presence of particles known as melanin, the same substance that allows lizards to change their color and that makes octopus ink black. In humans the primary function of melanin is to protect the upper levels of the skin from being damaged by the ultraviolet wavelength of sunlight that penetrates the atmosphere. This radiation poses a critical problem for our species because we lack the dense coat of hair that acts as a sunscreen for most mammals. Hairlessness, as we have seen (p. 72), has its advantages: It allows abundant sweat glands to cool our bodies through evaporation, thereby bestowing on our species the unique ability to pursue and run down swift game animals over long distances during the midday heat. But hairlessness has its price. It exposes us to two kinds of radiation hazards: ordinary sunburn with its blisters, rashes, and risk of infection; and skin cancers, including malignant melanoma, one of the deadliest diseases known. Melanin is the body's first line of defense against these afflictions. The more melanin particles, the darker the skin and the lower the risk of sunburn and all forms of skin cancer (Malkenson and Keane 1983).

Malignant melanoma is primarily a disease of light-skinned individuals of northern European parentage with a history of exposure to intense solar radiation. One of the highest rates of all forms of skin cancer is found in Australia, where the white population is primarily of northern European descent. Solar radiation is implicated for two reasons: The rate of melanoma occurrence quadrupled coincident with an increase in outdoor sports and the wearing of scanty attire, and the rate varies with the amount and intensity of solar radiation from the temperate to the tropical latitudes (Ariel 1981).

If exposure to solar radiation had nothing but harmful effects, natural selection would have favored inky black as the color for all human populations. But the sun's rays do not present an unmitigated threat. As it falls on the skin, sunshine converts a fatty substance in the epidermis into vitamin D. The blood carries vitamin D from the skin to the intestines (technically making it a hormone rather than a vitamin), where it plays a vital role in the absorption of calcium. In turn, calcium is vital for the growth and strength of every bone in the body. Without it, bones become soft and grotesquely deformed, and people fall victim to the crippling diseases rickets and osteomalacia (Figs. 6.7 and 6.8). In women, calcium deficiencies can manifest themselves in deformed birth canals,

FIGURE *6.7*

MULLEN'S ALLEY, 1888
Lacking both sunlight and dietary sources of
vitamin D, the children of the urban industrial slums
fell victim to rickets, despite their light skin color.

FIGURE *6.8*

RICKETS
A young victim.

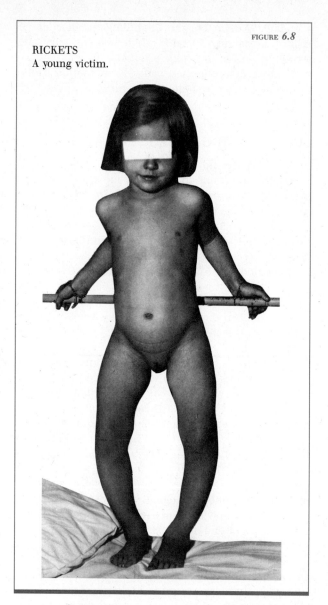

which make childbirth lethal for both mother and fetus (Malkenson and Keane 1983; Molnar 1983:162 ff.).

While vitamin D can be obtained from a few
foods, primarily the oils and livers of marine fish, in-
land populations must rely on the sun's rays and their
own skins for the supply of this crucial substance. The
particular color of a human population's skin therefore represents in large degree a trade-off between
the hazards of too much versus too little solar radiation: acute sunburn and skin cancer on one hand,
and rickets and osteomalacia on the other. It is this
trade-off that largely accounts for the preponderance
of brown people in the world and for the general tendency for skin color to be darkest among equatorial
populations and lightest among populations dwelling
at higher latitudes.

At middle latitudes, the skin follows a strategy of changing its colors with the seasons. Around
the Mediterranean basin, for example, exposure to
the summer sun brings high risk for cancer but low
risk for rickets; more melanin is produced and people

grow darker (i.e., they get suntans). Winter reduces
the risk of sunburn and cancer; less melanin is produced and the tan wears off.

The correlation between skin color and latitude is not perfect because other factors—such as
the availability of foods containing vitamin D and
calcium, regional cloud cover during the winter,
amount of clothing worn, and cultural preferences—
may work for or against the predicted relationship.
Arctic dwelling Innuits, for example, are not as light-
skinned as expected, but their habitat affords them a
diet that is exceptionally rich in both vitamin D and
calcium.

The Origin of White Skin

The Mediterranean farming and dairying people who settled northern Europe about 6000 years ago (see p. 166) must have been acutely endangered by rickets. As they migrated northward they had to cover themselves with heavy garments for protection against the long, cold, cloudy winters. But unlike the Innuit and the mesolithic (preagricultural—see p. 150) peoples of northern Europe, their farming and dairying economy did not provide them with marine fish rich in vitamin D. Fair-skinned, nontanning individuals who could utilize the weakest and briefest doses of sunlight to synthesize vitamin D would have been strongly favored by natural selection. During the frigid winters, only a small circle of a child's face could be left to peek out at the sun through the heavy clothing, thereby favoring the survival of individuals with translucent patches of pink on their cheeks characteristic of many northern Europeans.

Depigmentation went a long way toward solving the problem of producing vitamin D in the skins of these displaced Mediterraneans. But vitamin D by itself will not prevent rickets. There also has to be an adequate intake of calcium. The dairy animals that the migrants had with them were a splendid resource in this regard. Not only is milk rich in calcium but it has been discovered that the sugar in milk—lactose—also facilitates the absorption of calcium (Simoons 1982). But in order to take advantage of the antiricketic properties of milk, another genetic obstacle had to be overcome: The migrants had to acquire the ability to digest lactose in adulthood as well as childhood. As we have just seen (p. 92), lactase insufficiency leads to general digestive problems, a condition adverse to the absorption of calcium. It is therefore no accident that northern Europeans have both distinctively fair skins and an unusual ability to digest copious quantities of fresh fluid milk.

If light-skinned individuals on the average had only 2 percent more children per generation, the changeover in their skin-color gene frequencies could have begun 6000 years ago and reached present levels well before the beginning of the Christian era (Cavalli-Sforza 1972). But natural selection need not have acted alone; cultural selection may also have played a role. It seems likely that whenever the northern farmers consciously or unconsciously had to decide which infants to nourish and which to neglect, the advantage would go to those with lighter skin, experience having shown that such individuals tended to grow up to be taller, stronger, and healthier than their darker siblings, despite their inability to tan. Adults would also favor lighter skinned individuals as mates. One might say that white came to be regarded as beautiful because whiter individuals were healthier and had more children.

The Origin of Black Skin

To account for the evolution of very dark skin in equatorial latitudes, one has merely to reverse the combined effects of natural and cultural selection. With the sun directly overhead most of the year, and clothing a hindrance to work and survival, vitamin D was never in short supply. Moreover, calcium was easily obtained from vegetables. Rickets and osteomalacia were rare. Skin cancer was the main problem, and what nature started, culture amplified. Darker infants were favored by parents because experience showed that they grew up to be freer of disfiguring and lethal malignancies. And experience also showed that darker-colored mates lived longer and had more children. Thus black came to be regarded as beautiful and was both culturally and biologically selected for. (It is interesting to note that Africans were repulsed by their first glimpse of Europeans, because white for them was the color they associated with death and the devil.)

THE IQ CONTROVERSY

Despite the evidence that the vast majority of sociocultural differences and similarities cannot be explained by genetic differences and similarities (see Appendix), racial explanations continue to find favor on a popular level and in certain scientific circles. Many people remain convinced that some racial groups are naturally smarter, more musical, more athletic, more spirtual, or more sexy than others. These stereotypes arise from a common methodological problem: the failure to control for the effects of cultural influences on the behavior of the groups in question.

In recent times the question of the significance of racial differences has centered on the issue of whether some races are more intelligent than others. A vast amount of research has been devoted especially to the testing and comparison of the IQs of American whites and blacks. It has long been known that nationwide, whites score an average of 15 points higher than blacks. This gap persists even when samples of blacks and whites are matched for socioeconomic status—income, job type, and years of schooling (McGurk 1975; Shuey 1966).

During the early years of the IQ controversy, intelligence was regarded as a completely inherited trait that could not be affected by any kind of environmental influence. Later it was admitted that environment and culture could have some effect on how well an individual performed on an IQ test. Much effort has since been expended on trying to measure how much of a test score can be attributed to environmental and cultural influences and how much to heredity.

HERITABILITY

Certain psychologists (Eysenck 1973; Herrnstein 1973; Jensen 1969) contend that intelligence has a "heritability" factor of 80 percent—that is, 80 percent of the variance (statistical dispersal around the mean) is due to heredity and 20 percent to environment. This would mean that only 20 percent of the difference between white and black IQ scores could ever be eliminated by adjusting cultural and environmental variables (through Head Start and other special educational programs, for example). Two kinds of objections have been raised against this conclusion. First, the concept of heritability is fatally flawed when applied to human beings. And second, empirical evidence indicates that the difference between the IQs of whites and blacks can in fact be completely eliminated by changing their environments.

How was the heritability figure of 80 percent arrived at? To measure "heritability," one must be able to observe the development of samples of individuals who have similar genotypes (see p. 12), but who are reared in dissimilar environments. The closest one can get to the controlled conditions suitable for calculating heritability in humans is to see what happens when identical twins (twins born of the same ovum and same sperm), and non-identical twins (different ova, different sperm), are given to foster parents and reared apart in different families. The degree of similarity of the IQs of these adoptees provides a measure of the heritability of IQ.

Heritability, however, is a valid predictor of IQ or any other trait only under a given set of environmental conditions. Heritability says nothing about what IQ scores or other heritable traits will be like under a different set of environmental conditions. And heritability does not define the limits of change. Even if IQ heritability is as high as the hereditarians claim it to be under present conditions, unknowably large changes in IQ scores could still be produced by altering the environment of low-IQ children (Bouchard et al. 1991; Kamin 1974; Lochlin and Nichols 1976 see Osborne 1978).

The greater the amount of cultural difference between populations, the more trivial and futile the heritability measurements. Thus, the highest recorded IQ gains in controlled studies are reported from populations with the greatest cultural contrasts. In Israel, for example, Jewish immigrants from Arab countries show a 20-point gain in one year (Bereiter and Engelmann 1966:55–56). There is no evidence that similar gains could not be achieved by American blacks if they were to experience a sudden and pervasive shift in their cultural milieu. (If this seems unlikely, it is not because of the heritability of IQ, but because of the political and ideological factors that keep blacks in a subordinate position—see p. 455).

When psychologists first began to recognize that the Stanford-Binet IQ test was "culture-bound," they attempted to develop substitutes that would be "culture-free" or "culture-fair" (Cattell 1940). It is a contradiction in terms, however, to suppose that any human being can be approached in such a way as to overcome or cancel out the effects of culture (see Lynn 1978; Warren 1980). In the words of Paul Bohannan:

There is no possibility of any "intelligence" test not being culturally biased. The content of an intelligence test must have something to do with the ideas or with the muscle habits or with habitual modes of perception and action of the people who take the test. All these things are culturally mediated or influenced in human beings.... This is not a dictum or a definition—it is a recognition of the way in which cultural experience permeates everything human beings perceive and do. [1973:115]

THE MINORITY FACTOR

The fact that a 15-point gap in IQ persists when whites and blacks are matched for socioeconomic status, therefore, does not confirm the innateness of the difference between black and white IQs; rather it points to the inadequacy of the socioeconomic factors being used to control for environmental and cultural differences. Chief among the factors that such studies fail to control for is the effect on test performance of being a member of a group that is demeaned, segregated, and discriminated against and that has never been able to develop a strong tradition of honoring scholastic and intellectual achievement. In order to control for these factors, we would have to place a sample of black infant twins for adoption, one from each pair in a white household and the other in a black household. Then we would do the same for a sample of white infant twins—half in white households and half in black households. And even then we would have to change the color of the white children to black and the black children to white to control for the possible effects of social rejection of transracial fostering. Needless to say, various ethical and practical considerations make it impossible to carry out this experiment. Small wonder that behavior geneticist Jerry Hirsch (1981:36) reached the conclusion that the attempt to measure racial differences in intelligence is "impossible and therefore worthless."

Nonetheless, there is one study that has approximated some of the conditions that are needed to control for the effects on IQ of being brought up in a white versus a black household. This study compared the IQ scores of black children who had been adopted by affluent white parents with the IQ scores of white children who had been adopted and brought up by the *same* parents as the black children (Scarr and Weinberg 1976). The results, shown in Figure 6.9, follow:

1. Both black and white adopted children had higher scores than the general population.
2. There was no difference between the IQs of the black and white adopted children.
3. Natural children of the white parents had higher test scores than their adopted siblings.

The last point can be explained as an effect that some aspect(s) of the adoption processs had on the ability of the adopted children to obtain the full benefit of being brought up in advantaged households. One could alternatively argue that the adoptive parents had extrahigh IQs, which gave their natural children an hereditary advantage over their adopted siblings—or some combination of these two.

Another experiment that sought to overcome the minority factor made use of the fact that blacks in the United States are a socially defined group whose gene pool has been established by gene flow between recent white and black ancestors (see above, p. 84). This has resulted in varying degrees of genetic proximity to African ancestors. If low IQ is correlated with race, then lowest IQs should be found among individuals who have the greatest percent of African ancestry, and the highest among those with the greatest percent of white ancestry. No such correlations were found (Scarr et al. 1977).

RACE AND INDUSTRIALIZATION

In the nineteenth century the failure of blacks and other races to compete successfully against white nations in manufacturing, commerce, and war was taken as incontrovertible evidence that whites were a superior race. Had not whites from Europe and their descendants in North America gained political and economic control over almost the entire human species? Eager to justify their imperial expansion, Europeans and North Americans failed to see the hollowness of this argument. They conveniently forgot that history is full of tales of empires brought to their knees by peoples who were at one time considered to be unalterably backward, such as the "barbarians" who conquered Rome and China (see Box 6.2).

Today, despite this record of supposedly inferior "races" gaining ascendancy over their erstwhile superiors, many people continue to think that black

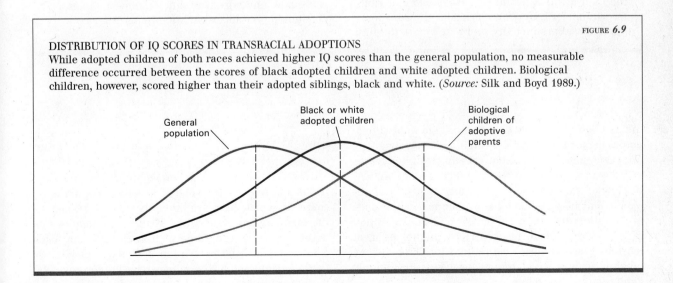

FIGURE *6.9*

DISTRIBUTION OF IQ SCORES IN TRANSRACIAL ADOPTIONS
While adopted children of both races achieved higher IQ scores than the general population, no measurable difference occurred between the scores of black adopted children and white adopted children. Biological children, however, scored higher than their adopted siblings, black and white. (*Source:* Silk and Boyd 1989.)

General population

Black or white adopted children

Biological children of adoptive parents

BOX *6.2*

THE WAGES OF RACISM

Alfred Kroeber, founder of the Department of Anthropology at the University of California at Berkeley, succinctly conveyed the irony of Rome's collapse at the hands of despised barbarian races in these words:

Had Julius Caesar or one of his contemporaries been asked whether by any sane stretch of fantasy he could imagine the Britons and the Germans as inherently the equals of Romans and Greeks, he would probably have replied that if these north-erners possessed the ability of the Mediterraneans they would long since have given vent to it, in-stead of continuing to live in disorganization, poverty, ignorance, rudeness, and without great men or products of the spirit.

As for China's racial arrogance, nothing tells it better than Emperor Ch'ien-Lung's 1792 rejection of a "red-faced barbarian" delegation's request to open up trading relationships. England, the Emperor said, had nothing China wanted. "As your ambassador can see for himself, we possess all things." There was a lot of truth in Ch'ien-Lung's observation. Almost to the end of the eighteenth century, China's technology was as advanced as England's. The Chinese excelled at making porcelain ("chinaware"), silk cloth, and bronze castings. They had invented gunpowder, the first computer (the abacus), the canal lock gate, the iron-chain suspension bridge, the first true mechanical crank, the stern-post rudder, the man-lifting kite, and the escapement, a vital forerunner of European clockwork. In transport, agricultural productivity, and population, the tiny

nations of Europe scarcely merited comparison. Ch'ien-Lung's empire stretched from the Arctic Circle to the Indian Ocean and 3,000 miles in-land. It had a population of 300 million, all under the control of a single, centralized bureaucracy. It was the biggest and most powerful empire the world had ever seen. Yet in fewer than fifty years after Ch'ien-Lung's arrogant verdict, Chinese im-perial power was destroyed, its armies humiliated by a handful of European troops, its seaports con-trolled by English, French, German, and Amer-ican merchants, its peasant masses gripped by famine and pestilence.

Much of the humiliation suffered by U.S. in-dustry and commerce at the hands of Japanese competitors stems from racial arrogance. In the 1930s, Americans knew the Japanese only as makers of cheap toys, paper fans, and watches with mainsprings that broke at the first wind-ing. American engineers soberly declaimed that no matter how hard the Japanese might try, they could never catch up with the industrial super-powers, especially with the United States. They didn't have that special inborn quality that Amer-icans called "Yankee ingenuity." How earnestly the Julius Caesars of American industry argued that Japan could only imitate! By no "sane stretch of fantasy" could they imagine that in fifty years Japanese auto imports would bring Detroit to its knees and that Japanese microscopes, cameras, digital watches, calculators, television sets, video-recorders, and dozens of other made-in-Japan consumer products would dominate America's market.

Africa is doomed by its genetic heritage to be a per-petual laggard in a world of high-tech industrialism. Are the genetic aptitudes for creating a United States or a Japan somehow in short supply in black Africa? In view of the frequency with which the roles of su-perior and inferior have been upended in the past, racial differences do not merit serious consideration as an explanation of black Africa's predicament, at least not until the historical reasons for black Africa's lagging pace of development have been thoroughly explored (see Box 6.3).

SUMMARY

Modern *H. sapiens* is a polymorphic species consist-ing of many partially isolated breeding populations, some of which have traditionally been assigned to the taxonomic category *race*. With its implications of a subspecies on the verge of branching off to form a new species, the term race is strictly speaking a taxonomically inappropriate designation for any con-temporary human population.

BOX *6.3*

WHY AFRICA LAGS

In A.D. 500, the feudal kingdoms in West Africa— Ghana, Mali, Sanghay—strongly resembled the feudal kingdoms of Europe except for the fact that the Africans were cut off by the Sahara from the heritage of technology and engineering that Rome had bequeathed to Europe. Subsequently, the great desert inhibited the southward flow of Arabic influences that did so much to revitalize European science and commerce. While the people who lived in the Mediterranean basin carried out their trade and warfare on ships and became maritime powers, their dark-skinned counterparts south of the Sahara were mainly concerned with crossing the desert and lacked any motivation for maritime adventures. So when the first Portuguese ships arrived off the Guinea coast in the fifteenth century, they were able to seize control of the ports and seal the fate of Africa for the next 500 years. After exhausting their gold mines, the Africans settled down to hunting slaves to exchange for European cloth and firearms. This led to increased amounts of warfare, rebellion, and the breakup of the indigenous feudal states, cutting short the trajectory of Africa's political development and turning vast portions of the interior into a no-man's-land whose chief product was a human crop bred for export to the sugar, cotton, and tobacco plantations on the other side of the Atlantic.

With the end of the slave trade, the Europeans forced the Africans to farm and mine for them.

Meanwhile, colonial authorities made every effort to keep Africa subservient and backward by encouraging tribal wars, by limiting African education to the most rudimentary level possible, and, above all, by preventing colonies from developing an industrial infrastructure that might have made it possible for them to compete on the world market after they achieved political independence. With such a history, Africans will have to be considered not as racial inferiors but as superhumans if they succeed in creating a single advanced industrial society of their own before the middle of the next century.

If you doubt that colonialism could have such long-lasting consequences, just think of Indonesia and Japan. In the sixteenth century these two island civilizations shared many features of agrarian feudal states. Indonesia became a Dutch colony, while Japan shut its doors to European traders and missionaries, accepting nothing but books as imports from the West, especially technical books that told how to make munitions, build railways, and produce chemicals. After 300 years of close contact with their European masters, Indonesia emerged into the twentieth century an underdeveloped, overpopulated, pauperized basket case, while the Japanese were ready to take their place as the most advanced industrial power in the Far East. Of course, there are other factors to be considered in this story, but race isn't one of them.

Modern concepts of populations and genetic processes cannot be reconciled with the traditional division of the species into three or four major races. In the traditional view, these races were like archetypes whose essence was expressed by "pureblooded" individuals and whose distinctiveness was as old as the species. As populations, however, groups such as Europeans, East Asians, and Africans possess no such attributes. First of all, there is no individual who can be considered a "pureblood" and who is more representative of a population than others of "mixed blood." To have any scientific validity, the characterization of a population must refer to frequencies of genes, but individuals do not have frequencies of genes. Second, the traditional racial taxons cannot be reconciled with the existence of genetic clines associated with intermediate or transitional gene frequencies. There is no justification for regarding these clines as the product of hybridization between hypothetical pure races that once existed in the past. Instead, the clines point to the existence of constantly shifting gene frequencies resulting from natural selection, mutation, drift, and gene flow. Finally, the traditional racial divisions are based on a bundle of traits that do not vary coordinately with the gene frequencies of other genes, such as those involved in the ABO blood groups. Such nonconforming distributions are predictable from Mendel's law of independent assortment and segregation. By setting aside the traditional concept of race, physical anthropologists can place the study of human polymorphisms on a sound genetic and evolutionary basis. The ABO blood groupings, sickle-cell anemia, and PTC tasting are examples of polymorphisms whose genetic mechanisms are best understood in terms of adaptive processes. With additional research it may eventually be possible to explain the distribution of the alleles responsible for these traits in terms of natural selection in relation to medical and nutritional factors. The implication of such factors in the explanation of many polymorphisms casts additional doubt on the antiquity of present-day races. Selection can rapidly alter the frequency of an allele either in a convergent direction among populations that have been genetically isolated or in divergent directions in populations that have high rates of gene flow. The extent to which features such as stature, hair form, nose shape, and epicanthic folding can be explained by adaptive processes remains to be seen. Heat and cold stress have been viewed as possible sources of selection pressure for these traits. A complex set of adaptive processes involving melanin, solar radiation, skin cancer, lactose malabsorption, and vitamin D deficiency have been implicated in the correlation between pale skin and northern habitats, and between dark skin and tropical habitats.

Despite persistent efforts by racial determinists to prove that IQ test scores measure inherited differences in intelligence, no method exists for fully separating the influence on test score performance of culture and environment from the influence of heredity. It has been demonstrated, however, that very large changes in test scores can be achieved by altering the environment and culture. All correlations between race and IQ scores are spurious because it is impossible to control for the environmental and cultural differences to which different racial groups are exposed. The effects of minority status cannot be controlled for by any simple matching of socioeconomic indicators. There are no culture-free tests. Attempts to control for the minority factor by using transracial adoptions show no difference in the IQs of black versus white children. The degree of African or European ancestry shows no correlation with IQ.

Efforts to rank human races as inferior or superior based on technological, commercial, or military prowess are negated by the many historical examples of underdogs becoming topdogs, as in ancient Rome, China, and modern Japan. Racialist explanations of black Africa's underdevelopment must be rejected in favor of explanations that take into account the crippling effects of colonialism and the slave trade.

CULTURE
AND LANGUAGE

*P*art II is short. But its two chapters bring us face to face with the most unique and important characteristics of human existence: our dependence on culture as a means of interacting with people and the natural world; and our dependence on language as a means of constructing and transmitting our cultural universe. These two chapters occupy a strategic position within the text. Behind lies the story of our physical evolution. Ahead lies the story of our cultural evolution. Part II bridges the gap.

Chapter 7

The Nature of Culture

This chapter expands on the definition of culture, relates the concept of culture to that of society, and identifies certain general processes that must be considered in explaining why customs, traditions, and behavior are both similar and different around the world. We embark on the difficult but necessary task of deciding what are the principal parts of the system of behaviors and thoughts that constitute the realm of human social life, and discuss the alternative perspectives in which they can be viewed. I try to set forth as simply as possible the particular theoretical viewpoint that has guided my own work as an anthropologist and that underlies the organization of this textbook. It is tempting to spare you such brain-busting concepts as emics and etics or infrastructure, structure, and superstructure, but I think that would greatly diminish the scope and coherence of the explanations offered in the chapters to come.

DEFINITIONS OF CULTURE

As we have seen, culture refers to the learned, socially acquired traditions that appear in rudimentary form among mammals, especially primates. When anthropologists speak of a human culture, they usually mean the total socially acquired life-style of a group of people including patterned, repetitive ways of thinking, feeling, and acting. Note that they do not just mean the literary and artistic achievements and standards of "cultured" elites. For anthropologists, plumbers and farmers are as "cultured" as art collectors and opera-goers. And studying the lives of ordinary people is just as important as studying the lives of famous and influential people.

The definition of culture as consisting of patterns of acting (behavior) as well as patterns of thought and feeling follows the precedent set by Sir Edward Burnett Tylor, the founder of academic anthropology in the English-speaking world and author of the first general anthropology textbook:

> *Culture ... taken in its wide ethnographic sense is that complex whole which includes knowledge, belief, art, morals, law, custom, and any other capabilities and habits acquired by man as a member of society. The condition of culture among the various societies of mankind, in so far as it is capable of being investigated on general principles, is a subject apt for the study of laws of human thought and action.* [1871:1]

Many anthropologists, however, prefer to view culture as a purely mental phenomenon consisting of the ideas that people share concerning how one should think and act. As such, culture has been compared to a computer program—to a kind of "software" that tells people what to do under various circum-

stances. It is implicit in this view that ideas guide and cause behavior. But the relationship between ideas and behavior is much more complex. Behavior can also guide and cause ideas. This can be seen in times when cultures change rapidly, as is happening today in most of the world. For example, prior to the 1970s, women who had husbands and school-age children in the United States believed that wives should depend on their husbands for family income. Driven by rising prices and a desire to maintain or raise their standard of living, increasing numbers of married women with school-age children violated this "program" and went to work anyway. Today, the majority of married women are in the labor force, with the highest participation rates found among women with school-age children, and it is generally regarded as fitting and proper for women to do this (see Chapter 26 for a more detailed look at how and why the program governing marriage and the family in the United States changed).

Another drawback of viewing culture as a mental program rather than as having both mental and behavioral aspects is that many of the most pressing social problems of our times are not programmed at all. Traffic jams, for example (see below), are a highly patterned cultural phenomenon that occur in spite of the programming that drivers receive to keep moving. Poverty is another example of a whole complex of activities that people are programmed not to do (see below).

SOCIETY, SUBCULTURE, AND SOCIOCULTURAL SYSTEM

As used in this book, the term *society* means an organized group of people who share a habitat and who depend on each other for their survival and well-being. Each human society has an overall culture, but all societies contain groups of people who have lifestyles that are not shared by the rest of the society. In referring to patterns of culture characteristic of such groups, anthropologists often use the term *subculture*. Even small societies have subcultures associated with such groups as males and females, or children and adults. In larger and more complex societies, one encounters subcultures associated with groups based on ethnic, religious, and class distinctions.

Finally, the term *sociocultural* should be noted. This term is short for "social and cultural" and is useful as a reminder that society and culture form a complex system of interacting parts (more about the components of sociocultural systems in a moment).

ENCULTURATION AND CULTURAL RELATIVISM

The culture of a society tends to be similar in many respects from one generation to the next. In part this continuity in life-ways is maintained by the process known as *enculturation*. Enculturation is a partially conscious and partially unconscious learning experience whereby the older generation invites, induces, and compels the younger generation to adopt traditional ways of thinking and behaving. Thus, Chinese children use chopsticks (Fig. 7.1) instead of forks, speak a tonal language, and learn to worship their ancestors because they have been enculturated into Chinese culture rather than into the culture of the United States. Enculturation is primarily based on

FIGURE *7.1*

HOW, WHAT, AND WHEN WE EAT: CULTURE AT WORK
(A) Midday meal, Rangoon, Myanmar. Food is good to touch as well as to eat. **(B)** Fast food, America's most notable contribution to world cuisine. **(C)** The correct way to eat in China.

(A)

(B)

(C)

the control that the older generation exercises over the means of rewarding and punishing children. Each generation is programmed not only to replicate the behavior of the previous generation but also to reward behavior that conforms to the patterns of its own enculturation experience and to punish, or at least not to reward, behavior that does not so conform (Fig. 7.2).

The concept of enculturation (despite its limitations, as discussed below) occupies a central position in the distinctive outlook of modern anthropology. Failure to comprehend the role of enculturation in the maintenance of each group's patterns of behavior and thought lies at the heart of the phenomenon known as *ethnocentrism*. Ethnocentrism is the belief that one's own patterns of behavior are always natural, good, beautiful, or important, and that strangers, to the extent that they live differently, live by savage, inhuman, disgusting, or irrational standards. People who are intolerant of cultural differences usually ignore the following fact: Had they been enculturated within another group, all those supposedly savage, inhuman, disgusting, and irrational life-styles would now be their own. Recognizing the fallacy of ethnocentrism leads to tolerance for and curiosity about cultural differences.

FIGURE *7.2*

PASSING CULTURE ON
(A) In Bali a man reads to his grandchildren from a script on narrow bamboo strips. **(B)** In India, a Sikh father teaches his daughter how to wrap a turban. **(C)** In Mission Viejo, California, young people learn the culturally approved manner of eating artichokes. **(D)** Navajo rug makers are made, not born.

(A)

(B)

(C)

(D)

The Self-Adorning Species

One of the most important indications of cultural takeoff in the archaeological record is the sudden abundance of traces of body paint and pendants, necklaces, and other adornments made out of bone, ivory, and shells at the beginning of the Upper Paleolithic. Self-adornment continues to be a major preoccupation of cultures around the world. This photo essay presents only a small sample of the almost infinite variety of materials, pigments, and fabrics that contemporary cultures employ to modify and decorate the human form. At all levels of sociocultural evolution, self-adornment is an element in the celebration of important events in the life cycle.

Samburu youth, Kenya. (© 1989 Champlong, The Image Bank.)

New Yorker in adornment-conscious Greenwich Village. In most modern cultures, women adorn themselves more than do men. (Smith/The Image Works.)

Masai youth, Kenya. (©1985, Faint, The Image Bank.)

Tatoo. The word derives from Polynesian languages. Here we see a champion canoeist in Honolulu. His paddle is decorated with traditional designs; his body, with a mixture of the old and the new. (© 1988 Place, The Image Bank.)

Body painting. The body is the canvas among the Masai. (© Arthus, Peter Arnold.)

Beard dyeing—a Dallas Cowboys fan at a game. (Woo, Stock, Boston.)

(A) | (B)

(A) High school prom, Irvine, California—the closest Americans come to a ritual signifying the end of adolescence. **(B)** At the same prom, girls dance together. (© Grant, Monkmeyer Press Photo.)

A Masai "prom," a ceremony marking the transition to adulthood. (© Arthus-Bertrand, Peter Arnold.)

Apache girl's puberty ceremony. The old life of the child is washed away. (Stephen Trimble.)

Kikuyu dancers in Kenya. Here elaborately adorned men dance with men. (© Cooper, Peter Arnold.)

American wedding. Men's adornments are muted, but the neckties indicate that this is a special occasion. (© Goodwin, Monkmeyer Press Photo.)

Anthropologists place great emphasis on the viewpoint known as *cultural relativism*, which means that they are committed to trying to understand how the world looks to people in different cultures without letting their own preferences and beliefs get in the way. This does not mean that anthropologists are equally tolerant of all cultures and subcultures. Like everybody else, anthropologists make ethical judgments about the value of different kinds of cultural patterns. One need not regard cannibalism, warfare, human sacrifice, and poverty as worthy cultural achievements in order to carry out an objective study of these phenomena. Nor is there anything wrong with setting out to study certain cultural patterns because one wants to change them. Scientific objectivity does not arise from having no biases—everyone is biased—but from taking care not to let one's biases influence the result of research (Jorgensen 1971).

LIMITATIONS OF THE ENCULTURATION CONCEPT

Under present world conditions it is easy to see that enculturation cannot account for a considerable portion of the life-styles of existing social groups. Clearly, replication of cultural patterns from one generation to the next is never complete (Fig. 7.3). Old patterns are not always faithfully repeated in successive generations, and new patterns are continually being added (Fig. 7.4). Recently, the rate of innovation and nonreplication in the industrial societies has reached proportions alarming to adults who were programmed to expect that their children's behavior would duplicate their own. This lack of cross-generational continuity has been called the *generation gap.* As explained by Margaret Mead:

Today, nowhere in the world are there elders who know what the children know; no matter how remote and simple the societies are in which the children live. In the past there were always some elders who knew more than any children in terms of their experience of having grown up within a cultural system. Today there are none. It is not only that parents are no longer guides, but that there are no guides, whether one seeks them in one's own country or abroad. There are no elders who know what those who have been reared within the last twenty years know about the world into which they were born. [1970:77–78]

Enculturation, in other words, can account for the continuity of culture but it cannot account for the evolution of culture.

FIGURE 7.3

CULTURE, PEOPLE, AND THE SUN
The relationship between people and the sun is mediated by culture. Sunbathing **(A)** is a modern invention. On the beach at Villerville in 1908 **(B)**, only "mad dogs and Englishmen went out in the midday sun" without their parasols. As the rising incidence of skin cancer attests, sunbathing can indeed be hazardous to your health.

(A)

(B)

Even with respect to the continuity of culture, enculturation has important limitations. As indicated above, every replicated cultural pattern is not the result of the programming that one generation experiences at the hands of another. Many patterns are replicated because successive generations adjust to similar conditions in social life in similar ways. Sometimes the programming received may even be at vari-

FIGURE *7.4*

THE LIMITATIONS OF ENCULTURATION
(A) Michael Jackson's generation cannot be said to have been musically enculturated by (B) Frank Sinatra's.

(A) (B)

ance with actual patterns; people may be enculturated to behave in one way but be obliged by conditions beyond their control to behave in another way. For example, enculturation is responsible for replicating the patterns of behavior associated with driving a car. Another replicated pattern consists of stalled traffic. Are automobile drivers programmed to make traffic jams? On the contrary, they are programmed to keep moving and to go around obstacles, yet traffic jams are a highly patterned cultural phenomenon (Fig. 7.5).

Poverty requires a similar analysis, as we will see in a later chapter (Chapter 19). Many poor people find themselves living in houses, eating food, working at jobs, and raising families according to patterns that replicate their parents' subculture, not because their parents trained them to follow these patterns, but because poor children confront educational, political, and economic conditions that perpetuate their poverty.

DIFFUSION

Whereas enculturation refers to the passing of cultural traits from one generation to the next, *diffusion* refers to the passing of cultural traits from one culture and society to another (Fig. 7.6). This process is so common that the majority of traits found in any society can be said to have originated in some other society. One can say, for example, that much of the government, religion, law, diet, and language of the United States was "borrowed" or diffused from other cultures. Thus the Judeo-Christian religions come from the Middle East; parliamentary democracy comes from Western Europe; the food grains in the American diet—rice, wheat, maize— come from Asian, Middle Eastern, and Native American civilizations, respectively; and the English language comes from the amalgam of several different European tongues (see p. 130).

FIGURE 7.5

TRAFFIC JAMS
(A) New York, (B) Mexico City.

(A)

(B)

Early in this century (see Appendix), diffusion was regarded by many anthropologists as the most powerful explanation for sociocultural differences and similarities. The lingering effects of this approach can still be seen in popular attempts to explain the similarities among major civilizations as the result of the derivation of one from another—Polynesia from Peru, or vice versa; lowland Mesoamerica from highland Mesoamerica (Mesoamerica is Mexico plus Central America), or vice versa; China from Europe, or vice versa; the New World (the Americas) from the Old, and so forth.

In recent years, however, diffusion has lost ground as an explanatory principle. It is true that, in general, the closer two societies are to each other, the greater will be the cultural resemblance between them. But these resemblances cannot simply be attributed to some automatic tendency for traits to diffuse. It must be kept in mind that societies close together in space are likely to occupy similar environments; hence, the similarities between them may be caused by the effects of similar environmental conditions (Harner 1970). Moreover, there are numerous cases of societies in close contact for hundreds of years that maintain radically different ways of life. For example, the Incas of Peru (see p. 316) had an imperial government, while the nearby forest societies lacked centralized leadership of any kind. Other well-known cases are the African Ituri forest hunters and their Bantu agriculturalist neighbors, and the "apartment house" Pueblos and their marauding, nomadic Apache neighbors in the southwest United States. Resistance to diffusion, in other words, is as common as acceptance. If this were not the case, there would be no struggle between Catholics and Protestants in Northern Ireland; Mexicans would speak English (or U.S. citizens Spanish), and Jews would accept the divinity of Jesus Christ (or Christians would reject it).

Furthermore, even if one accepts diffusion as an explanation, there still remains the question of why the diffused item originated in the first place. Finally, diffusion cannot account for many remarkable instances in which people who are known never to have had any contact with each other invented similar tools and techniques and developed remarkably similar forms of marriage and religious beliefs. The most dramatic examples of such independent inventions consist of discoveries and inventions that not only occur independently but at approximately the same time (see Box 7.1).

In sum, diffusion is no more satisfactory than enculturation as a mode of explanation for cultural differences and similarities. If nothing but diffusion and enculturation were involved in determining hu-

FIGURE 7.6

DIFFUSION
Can you reconstruct the diffusionary history of the objects and activities shown in these scenes?
(A) Headman in Arnhem, Australia, summoning his clanspeople to a meeting with a portable transmitter;
(B) Mongolian metropolis; **(C)** Brazilian woodsman.

(A)

(B)

(C)

BOX *7.1*

SIMULTANEOUS INDEPENDENT INVENTIONS

When the culture process has reached a point where an invention or discovery becomes possible, that invention or discovery becomes inevitable....

The discovery of sun spots was made independently by at least four men in a single year: by Galileo, Fabricius, Scheiner, and Harriott, in 1611. The parallax of a star was first measured by Bessel, Struve, and Henderson, working independently, in 1838. Oxygen was discovered independently by Scheele and Priestly in 1774. The invention of the self-exciting dynamo was claimed by Hjorth, Varley, Siemens, Wheatstone, and Ladd in 1866–67, and by Wilde between 1863–67. The solution of the problem of respiration was made independently by Priestly, Scheele, Lavoisier, Spallanzani, and Davy, in a single year: 1777. Invention of the telescope and the thermometer each is claimed by eight or nine persons independently and at approximately the same time.

"Even the southpole, never before trodden by the foot of human beings, was at last reached twice in one summer." The great work of Mendel in genetics lay unnoticed for many years. But when it was eventually re-discovered, it was done not by one man but by three—de Vries, Correns, and Tschermak—and in a single year, 1900. One could go on indefinitely. When the growing, interactive culture process reaches a certain point, an invention or discovery takes place.

The simultaneity of multiple inventions or discoveries is sometimes striking and remarkable. Accusations of plagiarism are not infrequent; bitter rivalries are waged over priorities. "The right to the monopoly of the manufacture of the telephone was long in litigation; the ultimate decision rested on an interval of hours between the recording of concurrent descriptions by Alexander Bell and Elisha Gray."

SOURCE: White 1949:208–210.

---

man social life, then we should expect all cultures to be the same and to stay the same; this is clearly not the case.

It must not be concluded, however, that diffusion plays no role in sociocultural evolution. The nearness of one culture to another often does influence the rate and direction of change as well as shape the specific details of sociocultural life, even if it does not shape the general features of the two cultures. For example, tobacco smoking originated among the native peoples of the Western Hemisphere and after 1492 spread to the remotest regions of the globe. This could not have happened if the Americas had remained cut off from the other continents (the tobacco plant did not grow outside of the Americas). Yet contact alone obviously does not tell the whole story, since hundreds of other native American practices such as living in wigwams or living in matrilocal households (see p. 281) did not diffuse even to the colonists who lived next door to native American peoples.

MENTAL AND BEHAVIORAL ASPECTS OF CULTURE

By talking with people, anthropologists learn about a vast inner mental world of thought and feeling.

This inner world exists on different levels of consciousness. First, there are patterns that exist far below consciousness. The rules of grammar are an example of such "deep structures." Second, there are patterns that exist closer to consciousness and that are readily formulated when the appropriate questions are asked. People can usually formulate values and norms, and proper codes of conduct for activities such as weaning babies, courting a mate, choosing a leader, treating a disease, entertaining a guest, categorizing kin, worshiping God, and thousands of additional commonplace behaviors. But such rules, plans, and values may not ordinarily be formalized or completely conscious. Third, there are equally numerous, fully conscious, explicit, and formal rules of conduct and statements of values, plans, goals, and aspirations that may be discussed during the course of ordinary conversations, written in law codes, or announced at public gatherings (e.g., rules about littering, making bank deposits, playing football, trespassing, and so on). Finally, to make matters more complex, cultures have rules not only for behavior but for breaking rules for behavior—as when one parks in front of a sign that says "No Parking" and gambles on not getting a ticket (Fig. 7.7).

But conversations are not the only source of anthropological knowledge about culture. In addition,

FIGURE *7.7*

RULES FOR BREAKING RULES
Cultural behavior cannot be predicted from a knowledge of a simple set of rules. In **(B)**, a handicapped driver is taking down the license number of a car that has parked against the rule.

(A)

(C)

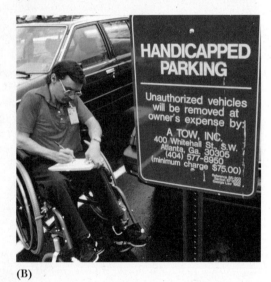

(B)

(D)

anthropologists observe, measure, photograph, and take notes about what people do during their daily, weekly, or annual rounds of activities. They watch births take place, attend funerals, go along on hunting expeditions, watch marriage ceremonies, and attend hundreds of other events and activities as they actually unfold. These actual events and activities constitute the behavioral aspect of culture.

EMIC AND ETIC ASPECTS OF CULTURE

The distinction between mental and behavioral events does not resolve the question of what constitutes an adequate description of a culture as a whole. The problem is that both the thoughts and behavior of the participants can be viewed from two different perspectives: that of the participants themselves, and that of the observers. In both instances, scientific, objective accounts of the mental and behavioral fields are possible. In the first instance the observers employ concepts and distinctions that are meaningful and appropriate to the participants; in the second instance they employ concepts and distinctions that are meaningful and appropriate to the observers. The first way of studying culture is called *emics*—pronounced ee-miks—and the second way is called *etics*—pronounced et-iks (see Chapter 8 for the derivation of these terms from the linguistic concepts "phonemics" and "phonetics").

The test of the adequacy of emic descriptions is whether they correspond with a view of the world that natives accept as real, meaningful, or appropriate. In carrying out emic research, anthropologists attempt to acquire a knowledge of the categories and rules one must know in order to think and act as a native. They attempt to learn, for example, what rule lies behind the use of the same kin term for mother and mother's sister among the Bathonga, or when it is appropriate to shame house guests among the Kwakiutl, or when to ask a boy or a girl out for a date among U.S. teenagers.

The test of the adequacy of etic descriptions, however, is simply their ability to generate scientific theories about the causes of sociocultural differences and similarities. Rather than employ concepts that are necessarily real, meaningful, and appropriate from the native point of view, the anthropologist now uses categories and rules derived from the vocabulary of science—categories and rules that are often unfamiliar to the native. Thus etic studies may involve the measurement and juxtaposition of activities and events that native informants find inappropriate or meaningless (Headland, Pike, and Harris 1990).

EMICS, ETICS, AND CATTLE SEX RATIOS

The following example demonstrates the importance of distinguishing between emics and etics when trying to describe and explain cultural differences and similarities. In the Trivandrum district of the state of Kerala in southern India, farmers insist that they never deliberately shorten the life of one of their animals—that they never kill it or starve it to death—thereby affirming the standard Hindu prohibition against the slaughter of cattle. Yet among Kerala farmers the mortality rate of male calves is almost twice as high as the mortality rate of female calves. In fact, male cattle 0–1 year of age are outnumbered by female cattle of the same group in a ra-

tio of 67:100. The farmers themselves are aware that male calves are more likely to die than female calves, but they attribute the difference to the relative "weakness" of the males. "The males get sick more often," they say. When asked to explain why male calves get sick more often, some farmers suggest that the males eat less than the females. Finally, some farmers even admit that the male calves eat less because they are not allowed to stay at the mother's teats for more than a few seconds. But none say that since there is little demand for traction animals in Kerala, male cattle are culled and female cattle are reared. The emics of the situation are that every calf has the "right to live" regardless of its sex. But the etics of the situation are that cattle sex ratios are systematically adjusted to the needs of the local ecology and economy through preferential male "bovicide." Although the unwanted calves are not slaughtered, many are more or less starved to death. Of course, emic and etic descriptions need not always be so different from each other. And even in this case, if one gets to know Indian farmers very well, some of them may reluctantly discuss the need they feel to cull animals of the unwanted sex. But only an etic perspective can lead one to explain why in Northern India, where different ecological and economic conditions prevail, etic "bovicide" is practiced more against female than male cattle, resulting in some states in an adult cattle sex ratio of over 200 oxen for every 100 cows (see Chapter 23 for more discussion on the emics and etics of cattle in India).

The comparison of etic and emic versions of culture gives rise to some of the most important and intriguing problems in anthropology.

THE UNIVERSAL PATTERN

In order to compare one culture with another, the anthropologist has to collect and organize cultural data in relation to cross-culturally recurrent aspects or parts of the sociocultural system. The total inventory of these recurrent aspects or parts is called the *universal pattern*.

Anthropologists agree that every human society has provisions for behavior and thoughts related to making a living from the environment, having children, organizing the exchange of goods and labor, living in domestic groups and larger communities, and the creative, expressive, playful, aesthetic, moral, and intellectual aspects of human life. However, there is no agreement on how many subdivisions of these categories should be recognized or on what priority they should be given when it comes

BOX *7.2*

THE ETIC AND BEHAVIORAL COMPONENTS OF THE UNIVERSAL PATTERN

INFRASTRUCTURE

Mode of production The technology and the practices employed for expanding or limiting basic subsistence production, especially the production of food and other forms of energy, given the restrictions and opportunities provided by a specific technology interacting with a specific habitat.

Technology of subsistence
Techno-environmental relationships
Ecosystems
Work patterns

Mode of reproduction The technology and the practices employed for expanding, limiting, and maintaining population size.

Demography
Mating patterns
Fertility, natality, mortality
Nurturance of infants
Medical control of demographic patterns
Contraception, abortion, infanticide

STRUCTURE

Domestic economy The organization of reproduction and basic production, exchange, and consumption within camps, houses, apartments, or other domestic settings.

Family structure
Domestic division of labor
Domestic socialization, enculturation, education
Age and sex roles
Domestic discipline hierarchies, sanctions

Political economy The organization of reproduction, production, exchange, and consumption within and between bands, villages, chiefdoms, states, and empires.

Political organizations, factions, clubs, associations, corporations
Division of labor, taxation, tribute
Political socialization, enculturation, education
Class, caste, urban, rural hierarchies
Discipline, police/military control
War

SUPERSTRUCTURE

Art, music, dance, literature, advertising, values
Religious rituals and beliefs
Sports, games, hobbies
Science

---

to doing research. A universal pattern consisting of three major divisions—*infrastructure, structure,* and *superstructure*—will be used in this book (Box 7.2).

1. Infrastructure. Consists of the technologies and productive and reproductive activities that bear directly on the provision of food and shelter, protection against illness, and the satisfaction of sexual and other basic human needs and drives. Infrastructure also embraces the limitations and opportunities placed on production and reproduction by a society's natural habitat, as well as the means employed to increase or decrease population growth. For example, a sketch of the infrastructure of modern-day Japan might refer to items such as Japan's electronic computerized and robotized information and manufacturing economy, its dependence on imported raw materials, the effectiveness of its public health system, its reliance on abortions as a means of population regulation, and the extensive damage that has been done to the natural habitat by various forms of industrial pollution and economic growth.

2. Structure. Consists of the groups and organizations present in every society that allocate, regulate, and exchange goods, labor, and information. The primary focus of some groups is on kinship and family relations; others provide the political and economic organization for the whole society; still others provide the organization for religious rituals and various intellectual activities. To continue to use Japan as an example, structural features would include a domestic economy based on small, male wage-earner, urban-dwelling nuclear families (see p. 258) and a political

economy that is characterized by global corporations regulated and assisted by the state, and a moderately democratic parliament. It would also include organizations such as universities, Buddhist temples, and art museums.

Obviously the focus of a given social group may overlap with the focus of another. Multinational corporations, for example, do more than produce and sell commodities—they also foster or create beliefs about free trade and consumerism. Governments may contribute to the regulation of every aspect of social life; established churches may regulate sexual and reproductive behavior as well as spread religious beliefs. But in order for us to study these connections, we must begin with some preliminary map of a society's structure based on the primary focus of its most important groups.

3. Superstructure. Consists of behavior and thought devoted to artistic, playful, religious, and intellectual endeavors plus all the mental and emic aspects of a culture's infrastructure and structure. This would include in the case of Japan such features as the Shinto and Buddhist religions; distinctive forms of Japanese painting, theater, and poetry; a penchant for baseball and wrestling; and a belief in teamwork as a source of competitive advantage.

THE DIVERSITY OF ANTHROPOLOGICAL THEORIES

The kinds of research that anthropologists carry out and the kinds of conclusions they stress are greatly influenced by the basic assumptions they make about the causes of cultural evolution. Basic assumptions made by anthropologists of different theoretical persuasions are called *research strategies,* or *paradigms.*

No textbook can conceivably be written so as to represent all the current research strategies with bias toward none and equal coverage for all. In the chapters to come I have made a conscious effort to include alternative viewpoints on controversial issues. Inevitably, however, my own research strategy dominates the presentation. The point of view followed throughout is known as *cultural materialism.* This research strategy holds that the primary task of cultural anthropology is to give scientific causal explanations for the differences and similarities in thought and behavior found among human groups. Cultural materialism makes the assumption that this task can best be carried out by studying the material constraints to which human existence is subjected. These constraints arise from the need to produce food, shelter, tools, and machines and to reproduce human populations within limits set by biology and the environment. They are called *material constraints* or *conditions* in order to distinguish them from constraints or conditions imposed by ideas and other mental or spiritual aspects of a society's superstructure, such as values, religion, and art. For cultural materialists, the most likely causes of variation in the mental or spiritual aspects of human life are the variations in a society's infrastructure.

Thus, infrastructure, structure, and superstructure are not equally effective in determining the retention or extinction of sociocultural innovations. When innovations originate on the infrastructural level (industrial robots, for example), they are likely to be selected for if they enhance the efficiency with which infrastructure satisfies basic human biopsychological needs and drives. Moreover, such infrastructural changes are likely to be selected for, even if there is a marked incompatibility between the innovation and preexisting structural and superstructural components (unionized, labor-intensive assembly lines; fear that robots will cause unemployment). In other words, the resolution of any deep incompatibility between an adaptive infrastructural innovation and the structural and superstructural components will usually consist of substantial changes in the other components. In contrast, innovations that arise in the structural or superstructural sectors (for example, new religions) are likely to be selected against if there is any deep incompatibility between them and infrastructure (if they substantially impede the system's ability to satisfy basic human needs and drives).

This does not mean that the mental and spiritual aspects of cultures are regarded as being somehow less significant or less important than production, reproduction, and ecology. Moral values, religious beliefs, and aesthetic standards are in one sense the most significant and most distinctively human of all our attributes. Their importance is not an issue. What is an issue is how we can best explain—if we can explain at all—why a particular human population has one set of values, beliefs, and aesthetic standards while others have different sets of values, beliefs, and aesthetic standards. (See the Appendix for a discussion of alternative approaches in anthropology.)

SUMMARY

A culture consists of the socially acquired ways of thinking, feeling, and acting of the members of a particular society. Cultures maintain their continuity by means of the process of enculturation. In studying cultural differences, it is important to guard against the habit of mind called ethnocentrism, which arises from a failure to appreciate the far-reaching effects of enculturation on human life. Enculturation, however, cannot explain how and why cultures change. Moreover, not all cultural recurrences in different generations result from enculturation. Some result from reactions to similar conditions or situations.

Whereas enculturation denotes the process by which culture is transmitted from one generation to the next, diffusion denotes the process by which culture is transmitted from one society to another. Diffusion, like enculturation, is not automatic and cannot stand alone as an explanatory principle. Neighboring societies can have both highly similar as well as highly dissimilar cultures.

Culture, as defined in this book, consists of thoughts that take place inside of people's heads plus the behavior that people engage in. Unlike other social animals, which possess only rudimentary cultures, human beings can describe their thoughts and behavior from their own point of view. In studying human cultures, therefore, one must make explicit whether it is the native participant's point of view or the observer's point of view that is being expressed. These are the emic and etic points of view, respectively. Both mental and behavioral aspects of culture can be approached from either the emic or etic point of view. Emic and etic versions of reality often differ markedly. However, there is usually some degree of correspondence between them. In addition to emic, etic, mental, and behavioral aspects, all cultures share a universal pattern. The universal pattern as defined in this book consists of three main components: infrastructure, structure, and superstructure. These in turn consist respectively of the modes of production and reproduction; domestic and political economy; and the creative, expressive, aesthetic, and intellectual aspects of human life. The definition of these categories is essential for the organization of research, and differs according to the research strategy one adopts.

Within anthropology there are many alternative research strategies; the one followed in this book is cultural materialism. The aim of this strategy is to discover the causes of the differences and similarities in thought and behavior that characterize particular human populations. Cultural materialists regard infrastructure as the key to understanding the evolution of sociocultural systems. This does not mean that structure and superstructure are less important or less essential for human social life.

Language

This chapter contains a brief introduction to anthropological linguistics. It begins with mention of the contribution of language to the beginning of cultural takeoff. Then we explore the fascinating experiments that probe the limits of communication between humans and apes. We go on to define the unique features of human language. Then the basic analytic concepts that are employed in formal linguistics are introduced and defined. We move on rapidly to such questions as the relative value of different languages, the effect of language on culture, the relationship between language and gender discrimination, and the processes that account for the evolution of different languages from a common parent language. A remarkable feature of languages is that they have a structure that maintains its coherence through centuries of change without native speakers being aware of the changes taking place. Many other aspects of human social life exhibit the same discontinuity between consciousness and change.

CULTURAL TAKEOFF

At about 45,000 years ago, culture entered a period of "takeoff." Prior to this time, cultural and biological evolution occurred at comparable rates, and cultural and biological changes were closely tied together. After cultural takeoff, the rate of cultural evolution increased dramatically without any concurrent increase in the rate of human biological evolution. The occurrence of cultural takeoff justifies the contention of most anthropologists that to understand the last 45,000 years of the evolution of culture, primary emphasis must be given to cultural rather than biological processes. Natural selection and organic evolution lie at the base of culture, but once the capacity for culture became fully developed, a vast number of cultural differences and similarities could arise and disappear entirely independently of changes in genotypes. We will return to this important issue in Chapter 9.

LANGUAGE AND CULTURAL TAKEOFF

Closely linked with cultural takeoff is the development of a uniquely human capacity for language and for language-assisted systems of thought. While other primates use complex signal systems to facilitate social life, human languages are qualitatively different from all other animal communication systems. The unique features of human languages undoubtedly arose from genetic changes related to the in-

creasing dependence of the earliest hominids on traditions of tool use and other social activities that are facilitated by exchanging and pooling information.

One way to sum up the special characteristics of human language is to say that we have achieved "semantic universality" (Greenberg 1968). A communication system that has semantic universality can convey information about aspects, domains, properties, places, or events in the past, present, or future, whether actual or possible, real or imaginary, near or far.

APES AND LANGUAGE

In recent years, a revolutionary series of experiments has revealed that the gap between human and ape language capacities is not as great as had previously been supposed. Yet these same experiments have shown that innate species-specific factors prevent this gap from being closed. Many futile attempts had been made to teach chimpanzees to speak in human fashion. But after six years of intensive training, the chimpanzee Viki learned to say only "mama," "papa," and "cup." When it was found that the vocal tract of apes cannot make the sounds necessary for human speech, attention shifted toward trying to teach apes to use sign languages and to read and write (Fig. 8.1).

Washoe, a female chimpanzee, learned 160 different standard signs of Ameslan (American Sign Language). Washoe used these signs *productively,* that is, she combined them in novel ways to send

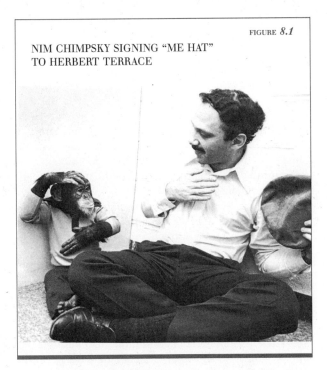

FIGURE *8.1*

NIM CHIMPSKY SIGNING "ME HAT"
TO HERBERT TERRACE

FIGURE *8.2*

LANA USING YERKISH TO COMMUNICATE WITH A
COMPUTER
She can read and "write" 71 cards.

many different messages (see p. 120). She first learned the sign for "open" with a particular door and later spontaneously extended its use beyond the initial training context to all closed doors, then to closed containers such as the refrigerator, cupboards, drawers, briefcases, boxes, and jars. When Susan, a research assistant, stepped on Washoe's doll, Washoe had many ways to tell her what was on her mind: "Up Susan; Susan up; mine please up; gimme baby; please shoe; more mine; up please; please up; more up; baby down; shoe up; baby up; please move up" (Gardner and Gardner 1971, 1975).

David Premack (1971, 1976) used a set of plastic chips to teach a chimpanzee named Sarah the meaning of a set of 130 symbols that they could use to communicate with each other. Premack could ask Sarah rather abstract questions, such as "What is an apple the same as?" Sarah could respond by selecting the chips that stood for "red," "round," "stem," and "less desirable than grapes." Premack made a special effort to incorporate certain rudimentary grammatical rules into his human-chimp language. Sarah could respond appropriately to the plastic-chip command: "Sarah put the banana in the pail and the apple in the dish." Sarah herself, however, did not make such complex demands of Premack.

Another approach, with a $3\frac{1}{2}$-year-old chimpanzee named Lana, utilized a keyboard controlled by a computer and a written language known as Yerkish (Fig. 8.2). Lana could read and write such sen-

tences as "Please machine make the window open," correctly distinguishing between sentences that begin appropriately and inappropriately and that have permitted and prohibited combinations of Yerkish words in permitted and prohibited sequence (Rambaugh 1977).

Both Washoe and Lucy, a chimpanzee raised by Roger Fouts, learned to generalize the sign for "dirty" from the sign for "feces." Lucy applied it to Fouts when he refused her requests! Lucy also invented the combinations "cry hurt food" to name radishes and "candy fruit" for watermelon.

Koko, a female gorilla trained by Francine Patterson, has acquired a vocabulary of 300 Ameslan words (Fig. 8.3). Koko signed "finger bracelet" for ring, "white tiger" for zebra, and "eye hat" for mask. Koko has also begun to talk about her inner feelings, signaling happiness, sadness, fear, and shame (Hill 1978:98–99).

A remarkable achievement of more recent studies is their demonstration that signing chimpanzees can pass on their signing skills as a cultural tradition to nonsigning chimpanzees without human mediation. Loulis, a 10-month-old chimp whose mother

FIGURE *8.3*

KOKO
Koko is giving the sign "pour-drink" to her teacher, Francine Patterson.

had been incapacited by a medical experiment, was presented to Washoe, whose baby had died. Washoe adopted the infant and promptly began to sign to him. By 36 months, Loulis was using 28 signs that he had learned from Washoe. After about 5 years of learning to sign from Washoe and two other signing chimps, but not from humans, Loulis had acquired the use of 55 signs. Washoe, Loulis, and other signing chimps regularly used their sign language to communicate with each other even when humans were not present. These "conversations," as recorded on remote videotape, occurred from 118 to 659 times a month (Fouts and Fouts 1985; 1989: 301).

All of the chimpanzees mentioned thus far have belonged to the common species (*P. troglodytes*). Only in the last few years has it become possible to study the acquisition of symbolic languages by representatives of the pygmy species (*P. paniscus*). In their communicative skills, as in other aspects of social life (see p. 57), pygmy chimps appear to come closer to the human condition than any other primate. Pygmy chimps seem to acquire the practice of symbolic communication with less training and in an easier and more natural manner than the common chimp (although new approaches to the training of the common chimp may alter this conclusion). They do use symbols not merely to make requests of their human guardians, but also to make comments and statements. Moreover, it has been found that at 6 years of age, a pygmy chimp prodigy named Kanzi had

spontaneously, without training, developed a true comprehension of 150 spoken English words (see Fig. 4.22, p. 57). Like human children, Kanzi acquired his comprehension of spoken words merely by listening to the conversations that surrounded him from infancy on (Rambaugh et al. 1990:247ff.). With the help of a keyboard and voice synthesizer, Kanzi can carry on extensive conversations in English. Every precaution has been taken in testing Kanzi's comprehension of symbols to make sure that no unconscious prompting or scoring bias has been introduced by his guardian teachers (see Box 8.1).

It is clear, however, that a vast gap still remains between the language performances of humans and apes. Despite all the effort being expended on teaching apes to communicate, none has acquired the linguistic skills we take for granted in 3-year-old children (Terrace 1979). What all these experiments have shown is that it is entirely plausible to conceive of natural selection giving rise to the human capacity for semantic universality by selecting for intellectual skills already present in rudimentary form among our apelike hominid ancestors (Lieberman 1991; Parker 1985:622; Savage-Rumbaugh 1987; Snowdon 1990).

PRODUCTIVITY

Human languages achieve semantic universality in part by possessing the feature known as productivity (Hockett and Ascher 1964). To every message that we send, we can always add another whose meaning cannot be predicted from the information in previous messages.

Nonhuman languages have only limited powers of productivity. C. R. Carpenter's (1940) classic study of gibbon language shows the limits of the productivity of nonhuman primate languages in natural settings. Carpenter found that gibbons have nine major types of calls. These calls convey socially useful information such as: "I am here," "I am angry," "Follow me," "Here is food," "Danger!" and "I am hurt." Because each call can be repeated at different volumes and durations, the gibbon system possesses a small amount of productivity. For example, the gibbon can say "Danger!" with different degrees of emphasis roughly equivalent to the series "Danger!" "Danger! Danger!" "Danger! Danger! Danger!" and so on. But this series exhibits little productivity because the amount of information conveyed does not increase at the same rate that the length of the message increases. A "danger" call repeated 20 times in succession is informationally not much different from "danger" repeated 19 times. In contrast, the productivity

BOX *8.1*

KANZI'S ACCOMPLISHMENTS

Kanzi's comprehension of spoken English has led to a variety of tests of his understanding of vocabulary and syntax. In a vocabulary test, Kanzi listened to words presented over earphones and had to pick one of three lexigrams presented to him. The person testing him could neither hear the word nor see the lexigrams that were presented. He responded correctly at 75% or better performance to 149 of the 194 words presented with natural speech and 103 of 150 words produced by a speech synthesizer that had no intonation. When 24 pairs of similarly sounding words were presented (Orange-Onion or Shot-Shirt) Kanzi correctly discriminated among 21 of the pairs.... In a recent comprehension test,

Kanzi was presented with more than 700 novel commands asking him to do things with objects or people in a way he had never done before. These novel sentences were presented by an experimenter who was out of sight, and the responses were evaluated by observers wearing headphones playing music so that they could not hear the commands. Kanzi responded correctly on more than 90% of these trials, indicating an ability to understand the symbolic referents of the words and the way in which the relationship between words was encoded by syntax. Because each sentence was novel, there is no possibility of rote learning accounting for the results.

SOURCE: Snowden 1990:221–222.

of human language is extremely efficient. In order to convey more and more specific information in a particular domain, our messages do not have to keep getting longer. We can say: "Be careful, there's a strange movement over there," "I think I see a leopard," and "It's in that tree." Moreover, these unique powers of productivity are not constrained to the small set of subjects that gibbons and other primates "talk about." Rather, we are capable of producing an infinite number of messages about an infinite number of subjects.

DISPLACEMENT

Another component of semantic universality is the feature known as displacement (Hockett and Ascher 1964). A message is displaced when either the sender or the receiver has no immediate direct sensory contact with the conditions or events to which the message refers. We have no difficulty, for example, in telling each other about events like football games after they are over or about events like meetings and appointments before they take place. Human language is capable of communicating an infinity of details about an infinity of displaced domains. This contrasts with all nonhuman communication systems. Among primates, for example, usually only the listener exhibits some degree of displacement, as when a "danger" message is understood at a distance. But the sender must be in sensory contact with the source

of danger in order to give an appropriate warning. A gibbon does not say, "Danger! There may be a leopard on the other side of this hill." On the other hand, in human communication both sender and receiver are frequently displaced. We talk routinely about people, places, and things seen, heard, or felt in the past or future; or that others have told us about; or that enjoy a completely imaginary existence.

Displacement is the feature we usually have in mind when we refer to human language as having the capacity to convey "abstract information." Some of the greatest glories of human life, such as poetry, literature, and science, depend on displacement, but so too do some of our species's most shameful achievements such as lies and false promises. As St. James put it: "But the tongue can no man tame; it is an unruly evil, full of deadly poison.... Out of the same mouth proceedeth blessing and cursing" (James 3:6–11).

Actually, humans are not the only liars. Birds, for example, often lead predators away from nests by feigning broken wings, and many animals "play dead." Some birds give the alarm call that warns against attacking hawks when no such threat exists. This false alarm enables them to consume the cherries on a tree without having to share with unwanted neighbors. And chimpanzees hide their facial expressions to prevent competing chimpanzees from detecting their fear (de Waal 1983). Nonetheless, with our unlimited capacity for displacement, humans are certainly the world's most accomplished liars.

ARBITRARINESS

Another feature that contributes to semantic universality is that human languages are constructed out of sounds whose physical shape and meaning have not been programmed in our genes. Most nonhuman communication systems consist of genetically stereotyped signals whose meaning depends on genetically stereotyped decoding behavior. For example, in communicating its sexual receptivity, a female dog emits chemical signals whose interpretation is genetically programmed into all sexually mature male dogs. Primate call patterns, like those of Carpenter's gibbons, are somewhat less tied to specific genetic programs and are known to vary among local groups of the same species. But the basic signal repertory of primate communication systems is species-specific. The facial expressions, hand gestures, cries, whimpers, and shrieks of chimpanzees constitute a genetically controlled repertory that is shared by all chimpanzees.

This is not the case with human languages. True enough, the general capacity to speak like a human is also species-specific; that is, the ability to acquire semantic universality is genetically determined. Nonetheless, the actual constituents of human languages are virtually free of genetic constraints (not counting such things as the physiology of the ear and of the vocal tract). Take as an example the languages of England and France. There are no genes that make the English say "water," "dog," or "house." These words are arbitrary because (1) they do not occur in the language behavior of most human beings; (2) neighboring populations in France, with whom there is considerable gene flow, utilize "eau," "chien," and "maison" to convey similar meanings; and (3) all normal human infants drawn from any population will acquire these English or French words with equal facility depending on whether they are enculturated (see p. 103) in England or in France.

There is another important sense in which human language is arbitrary. Human language elements lack any physically regular relationship to the events and properties that they signify. That is, there is no inherent physical reason why "water" designates water. Many nonhuman communication systems, on the other hand, are based on elements that resemble, are part of, or are analogous to the items they denote. Bees, for example, trace the location of sources of nectar by smelling the pollen grains that cling to the feet of their hive mates. Chimpanzees communicate threats of violence by breaking off branches and waving or throwing them. Although we humans also frequently communicate by means of similar icono-graphic symbols—like shaking our fists or pointing to a desired object—the overwhelming majority of the elements in spoken language do not bear any resemblance to specific objects or sounds. Even words that imitate natural sounds are arbitrary. "Ding-dong" may sound like a bell to speakers of English but not to Germans, for whom bells say "bimbam."

DUALITY OF PATTERNING

Human semantic universality is achieved by means of a remarkably small number of arbitrary sounds called *phonemes*. Phonemes are sounds that native speakers perceive as being distinct—that is, as contrasting with other sounds. Phonemes are meaningless in isolation, but when combined into prescribed sequences, they convey a definite meaning. The contrastive sounds in the utterance "cat" by themselves mean nothing but combined, they signify a small animal. In reverse order the same sounds signify a small nail or a sailing maneuver. Thus the basic elements in human language have duality of patterning: The same contrastive sounds combine and recombine to form different messages.

Theoretically, semantic universality could be achieved by a code that has duality of patterning based on only two distinctive elements. This is actually the case in the dots and dashes of Morse Code and the binary 0 and 1 of digital computers. But a natural language having only two phonemes would require a much longer string of phonemes per average message than one having several phonemes. The smallest number of phonemes known in a natural language is 13, in Hawaiian. English has between 35 and 40 (depending on which authority is cited). Once there are more than 10 or so phonemes, there is no need to produce exceptionally long strings per message. A repertory of 10 phonemes, for example, can be combined to produce 10,000 different words consisting of 4 phonemes each. Let us now take a closer look at how phonemes can be identified and at how they are combined to form meaningful utterances.

PHONEMIC SYSTEMS

Phonemes consist of etic sounds called *phones*. In order to convey information effectively, the phones of a language must be clearly distinguishable, or contrastive with respect to each other. But all sounds share some elements. Therefore, no two phones "naturally" contrast with each other. If we are able to distinguish one phoneme from another it is only because as native speakers we have learned to accept and recognize certain phones and not others as being clearly distinguishable and contrastive. For example, the [t] in "ten" and the [d] in "den" are automatically regarded by speakers of English as contrastive sounds. (A symbol between brackets denotes a phone.) Yet these two sounds actually have many acoustical phonetic features in common. It is culture, not nature, that makes them significantly different.

What is the critical difference between [t] and [d] for speakers of English? Let us examine the articulatory features—that is, the manner in which they are produced by the vocal tract (Fig. 8.4). Notice that when you produce either sound, the tip of your tongue presses against the alveolar ridge just behind the top of your teeth. Notice also that when either sound is made, the flow of the column of air coming from the lungs is momentarily interrupted and then released. In what way, then, are they different? The major articulatory difference between [t] and [d] consists of the way the column of air passes through the vocal chords. The vibration of the vocal chords produces a voiced effect in the case of [d] but not in the case of [t]. Both [t] and [d] are described phonetically as alveolar stops, but [d] is a voiced alveolar stop, whereas [t] is an unvoiced alveolar stop. The use of a voiced and unvoiced alveolar stop to distinguish utterances such as "ten"-"den," "tock"-"dock," "to"-"do," or "train"-"drain" is an entirely arbitrary device that is characteristic of English but is absent in many other languages. The phonemic system of a given language thus consists of sets of phones that are arbitrarily

and unconsciously perceived by the speakers as contrastive.

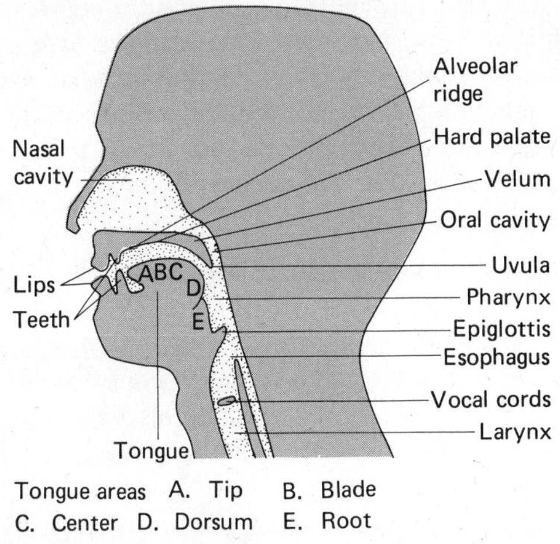

The structure of a given language's phonemic system—its system of sound contrasts—is discovered by testing observed phonetic variations within the context of pairs of words that sound alike in all but one respect. The testing consists in part of asking native speakers whether they detect a change in meaning. That is what is achieved in the comparison between "ten" and "den." By asking native speakers to compare similar pairs of words, we can detect most of the phonemic contrasts in English. For example, another instance in which voicing sets up a phonemic contrast is found in "bat"-"pat." Here the initial sounds are also stops, but this time they are made by pressing both lips together, and are called bilabial stops. Again one of the stops, [b], is voiced, whereas the other, [p], is unvoiced. It is only the fact that these phones are contrastive from the native speaker's point of view that validates the classification of these two sounds as different phonemes. It is this fact that is generalized when the terms *emic* from phonemic and *etic* from phonetic are applied to other domains of culture (see p. 113).

To the linguist's trained ear, many sound differences that escape the notice of the native speaker will appear as possible contenders for phonemic status. For example, the removal of the labial obstruction in the utterance "pat" is accompanied by a slight puff of air that is not found in the word "spat." This phonetic feature is known as aspiration and can easily be detected by placing your hand close to your lips and pronouncing first "pat" and then "spat" several times in succession. A more precise phonetic description of the [p] in "pat," therefore, is that it is an aspirated bilabial unvoiced stop, for which the phonetic symbol is [ph].

Do [p] and [ph] constitute separate phonemes in English? The answer is no, because there are no meaningful English utterances in which the substitution of [p] for [ph], or vice versa, alters the meaning of the utterance. Instead, [p] and [ph] are in complementary distribution; that is, they occur regularly in different sound environments so that they never contrast with each other. Closely resemblant but nondistinctive sounds like [p] and [ph] are called allophones. In a sense, every specific instance of any given phoneme is an allophone, since no two utterances are ever exactly the same in either articulation or acoustic effect. A given phoneme, then, designates a range or class of allophones.

Phones that regularly occur in one language may not occur at all in another. Furthermore, when the same phone does occur in two languages, it may

FIGURE *8.4*

PARTS OF ORAL PASSAGE

Alveolar ridge
Hard palate
Velum
Oral cavity
Uvula
Pharynx
Epiglottis
Esophagus
Vocal cords
Larynx

Nasal cavity
Lips
Teeth
Tongue

Tongue areas A. Tip B. Blade
C. Center D. Dorsum E. Root

be phonemic in one but not the other. And when similar phones are phonemic in two languages, they may have a different set of allophones.

In Chinese, for example, the nonphonemic aspirated and nonaspirated [t] of English "tick" and "stick" are phonemic. Also, Chinese uses "sing-song" tonal differences for phonemic contrasts in ways that English does not. On the other hand, in English the initial sound difference in "luck" and "rot" is phonemic, whereas in Chinese it is not (in an initial position). Hence "rots of ruck" sounds the same as "lots of luck" to a Chinese learning English.

MORPHEMES

The smallest units of language that have a definite meaning are called morphemes. Like each phoneme, each morpheme designates a class of basic units. In this case the constituents of the class are called *morphs*. Hence, just as phonemes are a class of allophones, so morphemes are a class of allomorphs. For example, the prefix "in-" as in "insane" and the prefix "un-" as in "unsafe" are morphs that belong to a morpheme meaning "not."

Morphemes may consist of single phonemes or of strings of phonemes in many different combinations and permutations. Some morphemes can occur as isolates, whereas some can occur only in conjunction with other morphemes. "Hello," "stop," and "sheep" are free morphemes because they can constitute the entirety of a well-formed message. ("Are those goats or sheep?" "Sheep.") But the past-forming /-ed/ of "talked" or "looked" and the /-er/ of "speaker" or "singer" are bound morphemes because they can never constitute well-formed messages on their own. Languages vary widely in their reliance on free or bound morphemes. Chinese, for example, has many free morphemes, while Turkish has many bound morphemes. Words are free morphemes or combinations of morphemes that can constitute well-formed messages. ("The" by this definition is not a word but a bound morpheme.)

GRAMMAR: RULES GOVERNING THE CONSTRUCTION OF MORPHEMES

Grammar consists of sets of unconscious rules for combining phonemes into morphemes and morphemes into appropriate sentences. Some linguists also include as part of grammar the rules for interpreting the meaning of words and the rules for

speaking in ways that are appropriate in particular contexts. The existence of rules governing the formation of permitted sequences of phonemes can be seen in the reaction of speakers of English to common names in Polish such as Zbigniew Brzezinski. English, unlike Polish, does not permit sound combinations such as "zb." Similarly, speakers of English know by unconscious rule that the words "btop" and "ndak" cannot exist in English, since they involve prohibited sound combinations.

GRAMMAR: SYNTAX

Similar unconscious rules govern the combination of morphemes into sentences. This branch of grammar is called *syntax*. Native speakers can distinguish between grammatical and nongrammatical sentences even when they have never heard particular combinations before. Here is a classic example:

a. Colorless green ideas sleep furiously.
b. Furiously sleep ideas green colorless.

Most speakers of English will recognize sentence (a) as a grammatical utterance but reject (b) as ungrammatical even when both seem equally nonsensical.

Native speakers can seldom state the rules governing the production of grammatical utterances. Even the difference between singular and plural nouns is hard to formulate as a conscious rule. Adding an *s* converts "cat" into "cats," "slap" into "slaps," and "fat" into "fats"; but something else happens in "house"-"houses," "rose"-"roses," "nose"-"noses"; and something else again in "crag"-"crags," "flag"-"flags," and "hand"-"hands." What is happening here? Three different allomorphs—/-s/, /-ez/, and /-z/—are employed according to a complex rule that most native speakers of English cannot put into words.

The set of unconscious structural rules and the sharing of these rules by the members of a speech community make it possible for human beings to produce and interpret a potentially infinite number of messages, none of which need precisely replicate any other previous message. Noam Chomsky described this behavior as follows:

Normal linguistic behavior... as speaker or reader or hearer, is quite generally with novel utterances, with utterances that have no physical or formal similarity to any of the utterances that have ever been produced in the past experience of the hearer or, for that matter, in the history of the language, as far as anyone knows. [1973:118]

DEEP STRUCTURE

How is it possible for us to create so many different messages and still be understood? No one is quite sure of the answer to this question. One of the most popular theories is that proposed by Chomsky. According to Chomsky, every utterance has a surface structure and a deep structure. Surface structures may appear dissimilar, yet deep structure may be identical. For example, "Meat and gravy are loved by lions" is superficially dissimilar to the sentence "Lions love meat and gravy." Yet both sentences take as their model a third sentence: "Lions love meat and lions love gravy." This third sentence more closely reflects the "deep structure," which can be transformed into various superficially different variations.

An essential feature of Chomsky's notion of grammar is that at the deepest levels, all human languages share an inborn species-specific structure. It is the existence of this inborn structure that makes it possible for children to learn to speak at an early age and that makes it possible to translate any human language into any other human language. Other authorities, however, doubt the existence of inborn grammar and attribute the acquisition of language skills by children to ordinary learning processes.

ARE THERE SUPERIOR AND INFERIOR LANGUAGES?

Linguists of the nineteenth century were convinced that the languages of the world could be arranged in a hierarchical order. Europeans invariably awarded the prize for efficiency, elegance, and beauty to Latin, the mastery of whose grammar was long a precondition for scholarly success in the West.

Beginning with the study of American Indian languages, however, anthropological linguists, led by Franz Boas, showed that the belief in the superiority of "civilized" grammars was untenable. It was found that grammatical rules run the full gamut from simple to complex systems among peoples on all levels of technological and political development. The conclusion of the great anthropological linguist Edward Sapir (1921: 234) stands unchallenged: "When it comes to linguistic form, Plato walks with the Macedonian swineherd, Confucius with the headhunting savages of Assam."

Other kinds of language differences are often cited as evidence that one language is more "primitive" than another. For example, there are numerous words for different types of parrots in native Brazil-ian Tupi languages, and yet no term for parrots in general. This has been attributed to an alleged primitive linguistic capacity. On the other hand, some languages seem to lack specific terms. For example, there are languages that have no specific words for numbers higher than five. Larger quantities are simply referred to as "many." This has also been attributed to an alleged linguistic deficiency.

These evaluations fail to take into account the fact that the extent to which discourse is specific or general reflects the culturally defined need to be specific or general, not the capacity of one's language to transmit messages about specific or general phenomena. A Brazilian Indian has little need to distinguish parrots in general from other birds, but must be able to distinguish one parrot from another, since each type is valued for its plumage. The ordinary individual in a small-scale society can name and identify 500 to 1000 separate plant species, but the ordinary modern urbanite can usually name only 50 to 100 such species. Paradoxically, urbanites usually have a more complex set of general terms, such as plant, tree, shrub, and vine, than band and village peoples, for whom such generalities are of little practical use (Witowski and Brown 1978:445– 446). English, which has terms for many special vehicles—cart, stretcher, auto, sled, snowmobile—lacks a general term for wheeled vehicles. Yet this does not prevent one from communicating about wheeled vehicles as distinguished from sleds and helicopters when the need arises. Similarly, the absence of higher-number terms usually means that there are few occasions in which it is useful to specify precisely large quantities. When these occasions become more common, any language can cope with the problem of numeration by repeating the largest term or by inventing new ones.

It has been found that small-scale societies tend to have languages with fewer color terms than more complex societies. Some languages have separate terms only for brightness contrasts, such as those designated by black and white. With the evolution of more complex societies, languages tend to add color distinctions in a regular sequence: red → green or blue → brown → pink, orange, purple. The emergence of these distinct color terms is probably linked with increasing technological control over dyes and paints (Witowski and Brown 1978). Similarly, many languages use one term to designate "hand" and "arm" and one term for "leg" and "foot." It has been found that this lack of distinction correlates with languages spoken by peoples who live in the tropics and wear little clothing. Among peoples who live in colder climates and who wear special garments (gloves, boots, sleeves, pants, etc.) for different parts of the body, the parts of the limbs tend to be designated by distinctive terms (Witowski and Brown 1985).

These differences, in any event, are necessarily superficial. Semantic productivity is infinite in all known languages. When the social need arises, terms appropriate to industrial civilization can be developed by any language. This can be done either through the direct borrowing of the words of one language by another (*sputnik, blitzkrieg, garage*) or by the creation of new words based on new combinations of the existing stock of morphemes (*radiometric, railroad, newspaper*). No culture is ever at a loss for words—not for long, that is.

LANGUAGE, SOCIAL CLASS, AND ETHNICITY

Another manifestation of the claim for language superiority is associated with the dialect variations characteristic of stratified societies (see p. 331). One hears of the "substandard" grammar or "substandard" pronunciation of a particular ethnic group or social class. Such allegations have no basis in linguistic science except insofar as one is willing to accept all contemporary languages as corrupt and "substandard" versions of earlier languages.

When the dialect variant of a segment of a larger speech community is labeled "substandard," what is usually being dealt with is a political rather than a linguistic phenomenon (Hertzler 1965; Southworth 1974). The demotion of dialects to inferior status can be understood only as part of the general process by which ruling groups attempt to maintain their superordinate position (see Chapter 19). Linguistically, the phonology and grammar of the poor and uneducated classes are as efficient as those of the rich, educated, and powerful classes.

This point should not be confused with the problem of functional vocabulary differences. Exploited and deprived groups often lack key specialized and technical words and concepts as a result of their limited educational experience. This constitutes a real handicap in competing for jobs, but has nothing to do with the question of the adequacy of the phonological and grammatical systems of working-class and ethnic dialects (Fig. 8.5).

Well-intentioned educators often claim that the poor and ghetto children are reared in a "linguistically deprived" environment. In a detailed study of the actual speech behavior of blacks in northern ghettos, William Labov (1972) has shown that this belief

FIGURE *8.5*

CLASS AND ACCENT
The language spoken by these youths in London **(A)** is as distinct from that spoken by the royal guests at the Ascot horse races **(B)** as the clothes worn by each class.

(A)

(B)

reflects the ethnocentric prejudices of middle-class teachers and researchers rather than any deficit in the grammar or logical structure of the ghetto dialect. The nonstandard English of the black ghetto, black vernacular English, contains certain forms that are unacceptable in white, middle-class settings. Among the most common are negative inversion ("don't nobody know"), negative concord ("you ain't goin' to no heaven"), invariant "be" ("when they be sayin"), dummy "it" instead of "there" ("it ain't no heaven"), and copula deletion ("if you bad"). Yet the use of these forms in no way prevents or inhibits the expression of complex thoughts in concise and logically consistent patterns (Box 8.2).

BOX *8.2*

BLACK ENGLISH

Soon as you die, your spirit leaves you. (And where does the spirit go?) Well, it all depends. (On what?) You know, like some people say if you're good an' shit, your spirit goin' t'heaven …'m' if you bad, your spirit goin' to hell. Well, bullshit! Your spirit goin' to hell anyway, good or bad. (Why?) Why? I'll tell you why. 'Cause, you see, doesn' no body really know that it's a God, y'know, 'cause, I mean I have seen black gods, pink gods, white gods, all color gods, and don't nobody know it's really a God. An' when they be saying if you good, you goin' t'heaven, tha's bullshit, 'cause you ain't goin' to no heaven. 'Cause it ain't no heaven for you to go to.

SOURCE: Labov 1972:214–215.

BOX *8.3*

LANGUAGE AND LOGIC

Whatever problems working-class children may have in handling logical operations are not to be blamed on the structure of their language. There is nothing in the vernacular which will interfere with the development of logical thought, for the logic of standard English cannot be distinguished from the logic of any other dialect of English by any test that we can find.

SOURCE: Labov 1972:229.

The grammatical properties of nonstandard language are not haphazard and arbitrary variations. On the contrary, they conform to rules that produce regular differences with respect to the standard grammar. All the dialects of English possess equivalent means for expressing the same logical content (see Box 8.3).

LANGUAGE, THOUGHT, AND CAUSALITY

A question that has been investigated by linguists for many years is the extent to which different word cat-

egories and grammars produce habitually incompatible modes of thought among peoples who belong to different language communities (Hymes 1971; Kay and Kempton 1984). At the center of this controversy is the comparison made by the anthropological linguist Benjamin Whorf between native American languages and the Indo-European family of languages, a group that includes English, many of the languages of Europe, Hindi, Persian, and others (see p. 129). According to Whorf, when two language systems have radically different vocabularies and grammars, their respective speakers live in wholly different thoughtworlds. Even such fundamental categories as space and time are said to be experienced differently as a result of the linguistic "molds" that constrain thought (Box 8.4).

According to Whorf, English sentences are constructed in such a way as to indicate that some substance or matter is part of an event that is located at a definite time and place. Both time and space can be measured and divided into units. In Hopi sentences, however, events are not located with reference to time but, rather, to the categories of "being" as opposed to "becoming" (Fig. 8.6). English encourages one to think of time as a divisible rod that starts in the past, passes through the present, and continues into the future—hence, the English language's past, present, and future tenses. Hopi grammar, however,

BOX *8.4*

WHORF'S HYPOTHESIS

The forms of a person's thoughts are controlled by inexorable laws of pattern of which he is unconscious. These patterns are the unperceived intricate systematizations of his own language—shown readily enough by a candid comparison and contrast with other languages, especially those of a different linguistic family. His thinking itself is in a language—in English, in Sanskrit, in Chinese. And every language is a vast pattern-system, different from others, in which are culturally ordained the forms and categories by which the personality not only communicates, but also analyzes nature, notices or neglects types of relationship and phenomena, channels his reasoning, and builds the house of his consciousness.

SOURCE: Whorf 1956:252.

FIGURE 8.6

A HOPI INDIAN CARING FOR YOUNG CORN

merely distinguishes all events that have already become manifest from all those still in the process of becoming manifest; it has no equivalent of past, present, and future tenses. Does this mean that a Hopi cannot indicate that an event happened last month or that it is happening right now or that it will happen tomorrow? Of course not. But Whorf's point is that the English tense system makes it easier to measure time, and he postulated some type of connection between the tense system of Indo-European languages and the inclination of Euro-Americans to read timetables, make time payments, and punch time clocks.

In rebuttal, other linguists have pointed out that the three-tense system that is supposed to color thinking about time really does not exist in English. First, there is no specific verb form indicating the future tense in English; one uses auxiliaries like *will* and *shall*. Second, English speakers frequently use the present tense and even the past tense to talk about the future: "I'm eating at six this evening"; "If I told you, would you do anything?" This means that the use of tenses in English is a good deal more relaxed and ambiguous than high school grammars indicate. If one needed an opportunity to become confused about time, English provides no unusual obstacles (Haugen 1975).

A more important objection to Whorf's point of view is that it implicitly distorts the fundamental causal relationships between language and culture. No one would deny that the absence of calendars, clocks, and timetables must have given preindustrial

societies like the Hopi an orientation to time very different from that of industrial-age societies. But there is no evidence to support the view that industrialization is in any way facilitated or caused by having one kind of grammar rather than another.

An interest in calendars and other time-reckoning devices is a recurrent feature of social and political development associated with peoples whose languages are as diverse as those of the Egyptians and the Mayans. Indeed, the Chinese contributed as much to the invention of modern mechanical clocks as did the Europeans. On the other hand, a lack of concern with counting time is a characteristic of preindustrial peoples in general, from Patagonia to Baffin Land and from New Guinea to the Kalahari desert, among peoples who speak a thousand different tongues.

As it is with time reckoning, so it is with other aspects of culture. The Aztecs, whose powerful state marks the high point of political development in aboriginal North America, spoke a language closely related to that of the hunting and food-gathering Utes. Religions as different as Hinduism, Christianity, and Buddhism have flourished among peoples who speak closely related Indo-European languages. Malayo-Polynesian, Bantu, and Arabic have served equally well as media for the spread of Islam, whereas Chinese, Russian, and Spanish have served equally well for the spread of Marxism. Industrial capitalism in Japan shares much with that in the United States, although the Japanese and English languages show few resemblances.

OBLIGATORY ELITISM AND SEXISM

Languages differ in having certain obligatory categories built into their grammatical rules. English requires us to specify number. Speakers of the Romance languages must indicate the sex (gender) of all nouns. Certain American Indian languages (for example, Kwakiutl) must indicate whether an object is near or far from the speaker and whether it is visible or invisible. These obligatory categories in all probability do not indicate any active psychological tendency to be obsessed with numbers, sex, or the location of people or objects. It should not be concluded, however, that grammatical conventions are always trivial.

Certain obligatory categories in standard English seem to reflect a pervasive social bias in favor of male-centered viewpoints and activities. Many nouns and pronouns that refer to human beings lack gender—*child, everybody, everyone, person, citizen,*

American, human, and so on. Teachers of standard English used to prescribe masculine rather than feminine pronouns to refer to these words. Thus it was considered "correct" to say: "Everyone must remember to brush his teeth," even though the group being addressed consists of both males and females. Newspaper columnists were fond of writing: "The average American is in love with *his* car." And high school grammars used to insist that one must say: "All the boys and girls were puzzled but no one was willing to raise *his* hand" (Roberts 1964:382). Obviously a perfectly intelligible and sexually unbiased substitute is readily available in the plural possessive pronoun *their.* In fact, nowadays almost everybody uses *their* in their [sic] everyday conversation (Newmeyer 1978). The male-centered conventions of the English language may not be as benign and trivial as some male anthropologists once believed them to be (Lakoff 1973; Philips 1980:531). It seems likely, for example, that the use of *him* and *he* as pronouns for God reflects the fact that men are the traditional priests of Judaism and Christianity.

LINGUISTIC CHANGE

Like all other parts of culture, language is constantly undergoing change. These changes result from slight phonological, morphemic, or grammatical variations. They are often identifiable at first as "dialect" differences, such as those that distinguish the speech of American Southerners from the speech of New Englanders or the speech of Londoners. If groups of Southerners, New Englanders, and Londoners were to move off to separate islands and lose all linguistic contact with each other and their homelands, their speech would eventually cease to be mutually intelligible. The longer the separation, the less resemblance there would probably be among them. The process of dialect formation and geographical isolation is responsible for much of the great diversity of languages. Many mutually unintelligible languages of today are "daughter" languages of a common "parent" language. This can be seen by the regular resemblances that languages display in their phonological features. For example, English /t/ corresponds to German /z/, as in the following pairs of words (after Sturtevant 1964:64–66):

tail	*Zagel*	tin	*Zinn*
tame	*zahm*	to	*zu*
tap	*zapfen*	toe	*Zehe*
ten	*zehn*	tooth	*Zahn*

These correspondences result from the fact that both English and German are daughter languages of a common parent language known as Proto-West Germanic.

In the 2000 years that have elapsed since the Roman conquest of Western Europe, Latin has evolved into an entire family of languages, of which French, Italian, Portuguese, Rumanian, and Spanish are the principal representatives. If linguists did not know of the existence of Latin through the historical records, they would be obliged to postulate its existence on the basis of the sound correspondences among the Romance languages. It is obvious that every contemporary spoken language is nothing but a transformed version of a dialect of an earlier language, and even in the absence of written records, languages can be grouped together on the basis of their "descent" from a common ancestor. Thus, in a more remote period, Proto-West Germanic was undifferentiated from a large number of languages, including the ancestral forms of Latin, Hindi, Persian, Greek, Russian, and Gaelic members of the Indo-European family of languages. Inferences based on the similarities among the Indo-European languages have led linguists to reconstruct the sound system of the parent language from which they all ultimately derive. This language is called Proto-Indo-European (Fig. 8.7).

Many non-Indo-European languages spoken in Asia, Africa, and the Americas have also been shown to belong to linguistic superfamilies that originated in a single language thousands of years ago. The question that is now being debated among linguists is whether these protolanguages can in turn be traced back to a small number of still more ancient tongues—perhaps even to just one—the orignal language of the first anatomically modern humans (Ross 1991).

Languages may also change without any geographical separation of different portions of a speech community. For example, within 1000 years, English changed from Old English to its modern form as a result of shifts in pronunciation and the borrowing of words from other languages. The two languages today are mutually unintelligible (see Box 8.5). As these changes illustrate, Modern English can be regarded as a "corruption" of Old English. Indeed, all modern languages are "corruptions" of older ones. This does not prevent people from forming committees to save the "King's English" or to protect the "purity" of French.

Indeed, the expectation of linguistic change is so great that linguists have developed a technique for dating the separation of one language from another, called *glottochronology.* This technique is based on the assumption that due to borrowing and internal changes, about 14 percent of the most basic words in a language's vocabulary will be replaced every 1000 years.

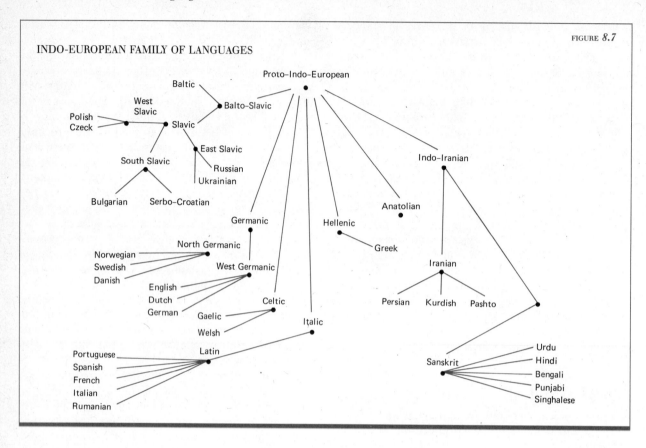

FIGURE *8.7*

INDO-EUROPEAN FAMILY OF LANGUAGES

LANGUAGE AND CONSCIOUSNESS

Language and language change illustrate the remarkable forms that can emerge in human culture without the conscious design of the participants. As pointed out by Alfred Kroeber:

> *The unceasing processes of change in language are mainly unconscious or covert, or at least implicit. The results of the change may come to be recognized by speakers of the changing languages; the gradual act of change, and especially the causes, mostly happen without the speaker being aware of them.... When a change has begun to creep in, it may be tacitly accepted or it may be observed and consciously resisted on the ground of being incorrect or vulgar or foreign. But the underlying motives of the objectors and the impulses of the innovator are likely to be equally unknown to themselves.* [1948:245]

This aspect of language change can be generalized to changes in all of the other sectors of sociocultural systems. As stated long ago by Adam Fergusson, a great eighteenth-century Scottish philosopher, the forms of society "even in what are termed enlightened ages are made with equal blindness toward the future." Cultural systems are "indeed the result of human action, but not the execution of any human design."

It is true that we are the only animals capable of talking about ourselves and of consciously analyzing our problems. We alone have conscious self-awareness, which many people regard as the most important attribute of human nature (Smith 1985). Yet something is usually overlooked when consciousness is celebrated as our species's crowning glory. What is often forgotten is that our minds are subject to restraints that do not affect the mental life of other organisms. Since we live by culture, our minds are shaped and channeled by culture. Hence, the gift of semantic universality has many strings attached to it. Language does not necessarily give us freedom of thought; on the contrary, it often traps us into delusions and myths. Because we live by culture and

BOX *8.5*

THE KING'S ENGLISH A.D. 1066

On bissum eare....be he cyning waes, he for ut mid scrip-here to eanes Willelme; and ba hwile com Tosti eorl into Humbran mid 60 scripum. Eadwine eorl com mid land-fierde and darf hine ut; and ba butse-carlas hine forsocon, and he for to Scotlande mid 12 snaccum, and hine emette Harald se Norrena cyning mid 300 scipum, and Totsi him tobeag. And man cyode Harolde cyning hu hit waes baer edon and ewor-den, and he com mid miclum here Engliscra manna and emette hine aet Staengfordes brycge and hine of slog, and bone eorl Tosti, and eallne bone here ehtlice ofercom.

In this year when he [Harold] was king, he went out with a fleet against William; and meanwhile Earl Tosti came into the Humber with sixty ships. Earl Edwin came with a land force and drove him out; and then the sailors forsook him [Tosti], and he went to Scotland with twelve small boats, and Harald, the Norwegian king, met him with three hundred ships, and Tosti submitted to him. And they told King Harold (Fig. 8.8) what had been done and had befallen there, and he came with a large army of Englishmen and met him [the Norwegian king] at Starnford Bridge and slew him and Earl Tosti, and courageously over-came the whole army.

SOURCE: The Anglo-Saxon Chronicle.

because our minds are molded by culture, we have more to become aware of than other creatures. We alone must struggle to understand how culture controls what goes on inside our heads. Without this additional level of awareness, the human mind cannot be said to be fully conscious.

SUMMARY

The period of cultural takeoff began about 45,000 years ago. The rate of cultural change increased while the rate of biological change remained the same. Vast cultural transformations began to occur without corresponding changes in the human biogram.

A vital ingredient in this takeoff was the development of the human capacity for semantic universality. As shown by numerous experiments, chimpanzees and gorillas can be taught to use several hundred signs. Compared with 3-year-old human infants, however, apes have only rudimentary capacities for grammatical communication. Human language is unique in possessing semantic universality, or the capacity to produce unlimited numbers of novel messages without loss of informational efficiency. In contrast to gibbon calls, for example, human language has unrestricted powers of productivity. One of the most important means of achieving this productivity is the arbitrariness of the elements that convey the information. Despite the importance of the genetic heritage for acquiring speech, the actual languages spoken depend entirely on enculturation; moreover, words in general lack any physical or iconographic resemblance to their referents.

Another important component in the achievement of semantic universality is duality of patterning. This refers to the use of arbitrary code elements in different combinations to produce different messages. The basic code elements of human languages are the phonemes, or classes of contrastive phones. A phoneme consists of a class of allophones that are contrastive with respect to the allophones of other phonemes. Different languages have widely different repertories of phones, phonemes, and allophones. None of these elements carries meaning in itself.

Duality of patterning is further exemplified by the combination of phonemes into morphemes, which are the minimal units of meaningful sound. Morphemes are classes of phonemes and contain variant forms called *allomorphs*. Morphemes are either free or bound, depending on whether they can occur alone and constitute well-formed utterances.

The ability to send and receive messages in a human language depends on the sharing of rules for combining phonemes into morphemes and morphemes into sentences. These rules are part of a language's grammar, and they are usually held unconsciously. On the phonemic level they specify the permitted and prohibited combinations of phonemes; on the morphemic level they specify the sequences of morphemes and allomorphs required for well-formed utterances. Such rules are called *syntax*. Knowledge of the rules of syntax makes it possible to produce completely novel utterances and yet be understood. A theory that accounts for this property of syntax states that there is a deep structure to which various superficially dissimilar utterances can be reduced. Novel

sentences are transformations of these deep structures and can be understood by tracing them back to their underlying components.

All human languages are mutually translatable, and there is no evidence that some languages have more efficient grammars than others. Categories and vocabularies differ widely, but these differences do not indicate any inherent defect in a language or any intellectual inferiority on the part of the speakers. General and specific categorizations—as with numbers, plant classifications, and color terms—reflect the practical need for making general or specific distinctions under particular cultural and natural conditions.

The view that certain dialects of standard languages are "inferior" forms of speech reflects class and ethnic biases. Dialects such as black vernacular English do not in and of themselves inhibit clear and logical thought.

Attempts to show that differences in grammar determine how people think and behave in different cultures have not been successful. There are very few, if any, correlations other than vocabulary that can be shown between language and the major forms of demographic, technological, economic, ecological, domestic, political, and religious aspects of sociocultural systems.

Obligatory linguistic categories such as those concerned with sex, age, and class differences may play a role in the maintenance of various forms of hierarchical relationships.

Languages, like all other aspects of culture, are constantly being changed as a result of both internal and external processes. All languages are "corruptions" of earlier parent languages. Glottochronology is based on the premise that not only do all languages change but they change at a predictable rate.

The study of language change, as well as the study of the other aspects of linguistics, shows the importance of unconscious factors in sociocultural life. Although semantic universality is a great and uniquely human gift, it does not automatically bestow on us full consciousness and genuine freedom of thought. To become fully conscious, we must strive to understand how culture controls what we think and do.

PART III

ARCHAEOLOGY AND PREHISTORY

*P*art III provides a sketch of the principal lines of cultural evolution as seen through the findings of archaeology. Two chapters describe the evolution of cultures in the Old World (Europe, Asia, Africa and Oceania), while one chapter deals with the main lines of development in the New World (North and South America). Our coverage begins with the earliest artifacts and forms of social life and ends with the appearance of preindustrial states in the Old and New worlds. As this million-year-old story unfolds, we shall attempt to identify the causes of its major transition points in the hope of understanding why human cultures have evolved along parallel and convergent as well as divergent paths.

The Old World Paleolithic

The study of cultural evolution begins with the facts and inferences of prehistoric archaeology. Archaeology is to anthropology as paleontology is to biology. Without archaeology, anthropologists could neither describe nor explain the course of cultural evolution. As a result of the great sweep of time and space studied by archaeologists, anthropology enjoys a unique position among the social sciences because it can observe the operation of long-range trends and can formulate and test causal theories of cultural evolution. This chapter traces the evolution of Old World cultures (European, Asian, and African) from the earliest known artifacts indicative of gathering, hunting, and scavenging modes of production up to the threshold of the domestication of plants and animals.

PREHISTORIC PERIODS

Stone implements provide most of the evidence about the earliest phases of cultural evolution. Hence, archaeologists divide the entire period of early prehistory into lithic ("stone") ages. Three such ages are recognized in the cultural evolution of Europe: Paleolithic (old stone age), Mesolithic (middle stone age), and Neolithic (new stone age). These ages were of drastically different lengths: The Paleolithic lasted over 2 million years (longer in Africa and Asia), while the Mesolithic and Neolithic combined did not last more than 10,000 years. Paleolithic cultures were based on hunting, fishing, and gathering rather than on farming or stock raising. Groups were small, the total population of the world was only a few million, and the groups were widely dispersed. To make efficient use of available plant and animal resources, the Paleolithic hunter-gatherers ranged over a wide territory and usually did not settle at any one campsite, cave, or shelter for more than a few weeks or months at a time.

Three Paleolithic subdivisions are generally recognized: (1) the long Lower Paleolithic, dominated by simple Oldowan tools, core biface tools, and simple flake tools; (2) the brief Middle Paleolithic, characterized by an enlarged and refined repertory of core tools, flake points, and other flake tools; and (3) the still briefer Upper Paleolithic, characterized by an enlarged and refined repertory of blade tools (see p. 138) and by many specialized ivory, bone, and antler implements and artifacts.

In the same highly general perspective, one may characterize the Neolithic as the age of cultural systems based on domesticated plants and animals. Group size and total population were larger, and settlement was more nucleated. To make efficient use of the domesticated plants, permanent settlements or villages replaced the temporary camps of the Paleolithic hunters and gatherers (although in certain favored habitats, hunter-gatherers also lived in permanent settlements). The transition to Neolithic farming communities took place under a variety of conditions in various parts of the Old and New Worlds. The Mesolithic denotes this transitional age in Europe. (Ages transitional between hunting and gathering infrastructures and farming infrastructures in other parts of the world often have local or regional names.)

FROM LOWER TO MIDDLE PALEOLITHIC

As we have seen (Chapter 5), there is a rough correlation between the appearance of new hominid species in the fossil record and the appearance of new tool kits in the archaeological record. Thus, while the small-brained australopithecines were probably rudimentary tool-makers (p. 52), it was not until the time of *habilis* and *erectus* that large concentrations of well-made stone tools begin to be formed. These earliest stone tool traditions (in which tools were made to a definite pattern), the Oldowan and Acheulian, characterize the Lower Paleolithic and have already been described, along with their remarkably slow rate of change (p. 71). Important new stone tool traditions appear only after an interval of about 1.3 myr, coincident with the transition from erectus to archaic sapiens.

We shall resume our account of the archaeological evidence for the evolution of culture with the changes in tool types that begin to appear at the end

"Criminy! . . . It seems like every summer there's more
and more of these things around!"

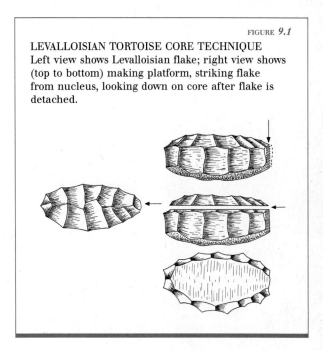

FIGURE *9.1*

LEVALLOISIAN TORTOISE CORE TECHNIQUE
Left view shows Levalloisian flake; right view shows
(top to bottom) making platform, striking flake
from nucleus, looking down on core after flake is
detached.

of the Lower Paleolithic. At this time, approximately
125,000 years ago, Acheulian tool kits in Europe and
Africa began to be supplemented with flake tools produced by an ingenious method known as the Levallois
technique (Fig. 9.1).

A tortoise-shaped core of flint was prepared as
if one were about to produce a thick hand ax, except that shaping proceeded on only one side of the
tortoise core. Next a transverse blow was struck at
one end of the core, creating a ledge, or striking
platform. Then, a longitudinal blow was administered
to the striking platform, detaching a thin elongated
flake with sharp, straight edges. Levalloisian cores
and flakes have been found throughout Africa and
Europe and usually mark the transition to Middle Paleolithic industries.

THE MIDDLE PALEOLITHIC

Euro-African Middle Paleolithic tool kits also contain varying percentages of hand axes and other
Acheulian-type implements. Points that might have
been attached to lances or spears make their appearance. They were fashioned from Levallois and
other kinds of flakes and were light enough and sharp
enough to have functioned as the tips of effective projectiles.

In many regions, Middle Paleolithic flake-tools
conform to the type of industry known as Mousterian. These tools consist of small flakes removed from
Levallois and other disk-shaped cores. They were
subjected to secondary flaking by being struck with
softer materials such as bone or antler or by being
subjected to pressure applied around their edges (Fig.
9.2).

Middle Paleolithic tool kits thus usually included a few hand axes and numerous flake tools such
as several varieties of points, scrapers, notched flakes
for shaving wood, and borers. A high degree of control had been achieved over the secondary flaking or
retouching of working edges, and special bone instruments presumed to have been employed for this purpose are found at many Middle Paleolithic sites. It has
been shown that excellent retouching and trimming
can also be achieved by biting the edge of a flake with
one's teeth (Gould, Koster, and Sontz 1971). There is
some evidence that Middle Paleolithic peoples had begun to wear personal adornments and craft ritual objects (Fig. 9.3).

The transition from Acheulian industries to
Middle Paleolithic Mousterian industries in Europe
and north Africa is correlated with the appearance
of the Neandertals. But recent evidence from the
cave at Jebel Qafzeh, Israel (see p. 78 and Fig. 10.1),
has complicated the linkage between the Neandertal

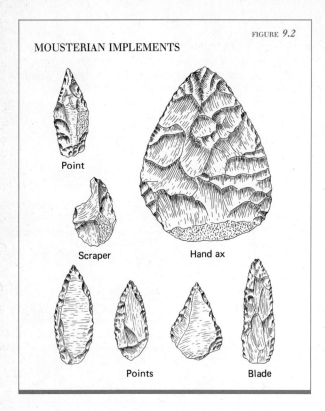

FIGURE *9.2*

MOUSTERIAN IMPLEMENTS

Point

Scraper

Hand ax

Points

Blade

FIGURE *9.3*

MOUSTERIAN JEWELRY AND RITUAL OBJECT

(A) Pendants from the site of La Quina, France, made from a reindeer phalange and the canine of a young fox (natural size). **(B)** Ritual object carved from the section of a mammoth's molar.

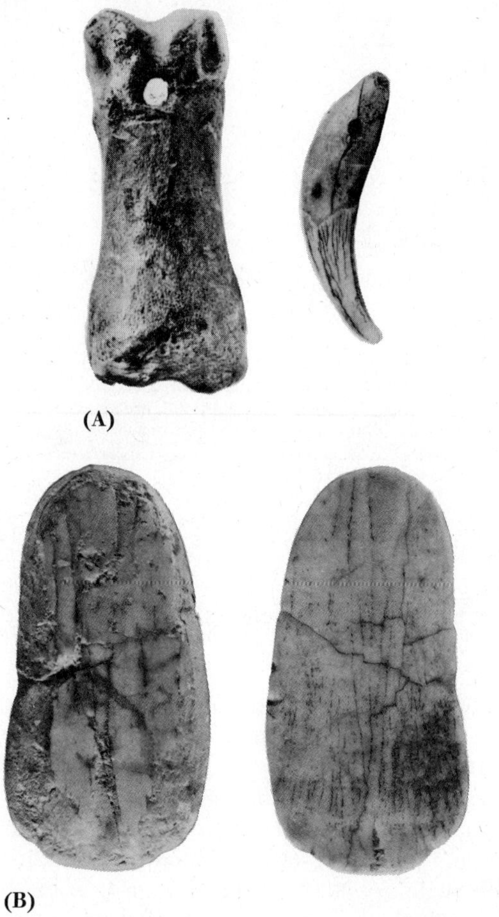

(A)

(B)

physical type and Mousterian cultural type. As previously stated, at Jebel Qafzeh, anatomically modern *sapiens* who antedated the appearance of local Neandertal types by 40,000 years are associated with Mousterian industries (Mellars 1989:7). At the other end of the Middle Paleolithic there are sites in Europe, notably at Saint-Cezaire, France (Fig. 9.4), dating to 37,000 B.P., where a late Neandertal population is associated with an Upper Paleolithic industry (ibid.:2).

THE UPPER PALEOLITHIC

The Upper Paleolithic is characterized by a marked increase in blade tools and by a great florescence of ivory, bone, and antler implements. Flakes that have parallel edges and that are twice as long as they are broad are known technically as *blades* (Fig. 9.5). Blade tools have been found at numerous Mousterian Middle Paleolithic sites and with Levallois tools at Lower Paleolithic sites in East Africa (Conrad 1990). A few blades have even been found in Oldowan assemblages. But the blade tools of these earlier ages occur with less frequency and do not display the high level of craft and virtuosity of the Upper Paleolithic blade tools (Fig 9.6).

Bone, ivory, and antler tools also occur earlier

than the Upper Paleolithic, but the variety, abundance, and craft of the Upper Paleolithic bone, ivory, and antler artifacts "is clearly on a scale and of a nature quite different from the possible instances of Mousterian bone working" (Straus 1982:185). The Mousterians *used* bones, antlers, and tusks but they did little to shape them into specific tools (Mellars 1989:343). Another distinctive feature of Upper Paleolithic technology is the development of composite tools (i.e., tools that have several parts), such as harpoons and hafted weapons and projectiles. Projectile points with special shoulders or tangs for attachment to spears, plus evidence for the use of traps, nets, and

FIGURE *9.4*

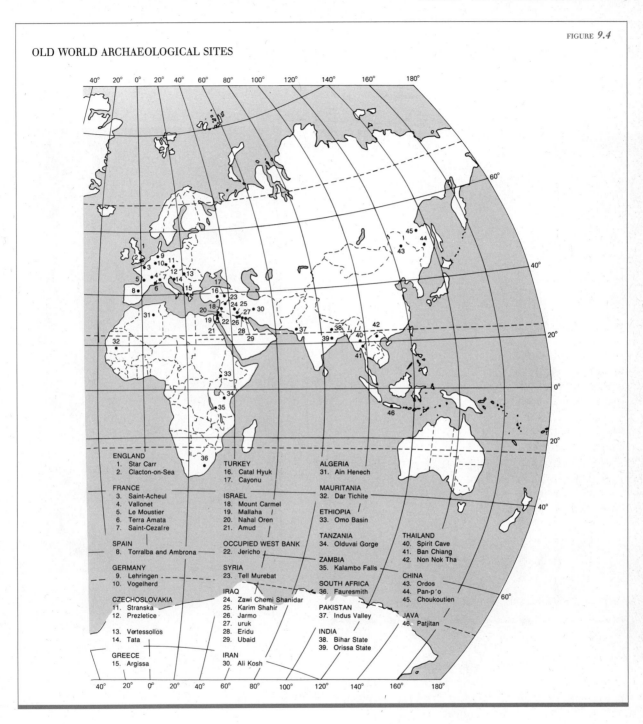

OLD WORLD ARCHAEOLOGICAL SITES

ENGLAND
1. Star Carr
2. Clacton-on-Sea

FRANCE
3. Saint-Acheul
4. Vallonet
5. Le Moustier
6. Terra Amata
7. Saint-Cezaire

SPAIN
8. Torralba and Ambrona

GERMANY
9. Lehringen
10. Vogelherd

CZECHOSLOVAKIA
11. Stranska
12. Prezletice
13. Vertessollos
14. Tata

GREECE
15. Argissa

TURKEY
16. Catal Hyuk
17. Cayonu

ISRAEL
18. Mount Carmel
19. Mallaha
20. Nahal Oren
21. Amud

OCCUPIED WEST BANK
22. Jericho

SYRIA
23. Tell Murebat

IRAQ
24. Zawi Chemi Shanidar
25. Karim Shahir
26. Jarmo
27. uruk
28. Eridu
29. Ubaid

IRAN
30. Ali Kosh

ALGERIA
31. Ain Henech

MAURITANIA
32. Dar Tichite

ETHIOPIA
33. Omo Basin

TANZANIA
34. Olduvai Gorge

ZAMBIA
35. Kalambo Falls

SOUTH AFRICA
36. Fauresmith

PAKISTAN
37. Indus Valley

INDIA
38. Bihar State
39. Orissa State

THAILAND
40. Spirit Cave
41. Ban Chiang
42. Non Nok Tha

CHINA
43. Ordos
44. Pan-p'o
45. Choukoutien

JAVA
46. Patjitan

weirs, "suggest the development of technologies far more complex and specialized than those of the middle Paleolithic" (Straus 1982:185).

Archaeologists divide the Upper Paleolithic in Western Europe into several overlapping "traditions" or cultures. The two earliest of these are known as the Chatelperronian and Aurignacian, with dates beginning between 40,000 and 35,000 B.P. Next, there is the Gravettian, beginning about 28,000 B.P.; then the Solutrean, at about 22,000 B.P.; and finally the Magdalenian, which began at about 17,000 B.P. and lasted to the end of the last glaciation at about 10,500 B.P.

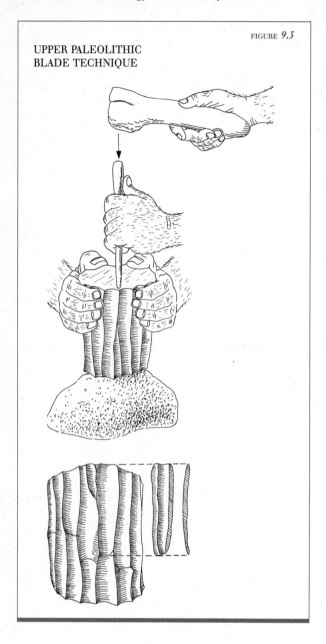

FIGURE *9.5*

UPPER PALEOLITHIC
BLADE TECHNIQUE

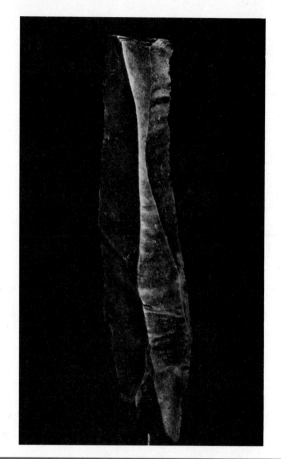

FIGURE *9.6*

UPPER PALEOLITHIC BLADE
Basic form of many Upper Paleolithic instruments. Specialized tools were made by retouching edges and ends. This blade is 4 inches long and only 1/4 inch thick.

The Chatelperronian is confined to a limited area in western and northern France and adjacent parts of northwestern Spain; it lasts for only three or four thousand years at most. It is distinguished by the occurrence of a mixture of Middle Paleolithic Mousterian artifacts including flake tools and even small hand axes, together with new forms of blade knives and projectile points that strongly resemble typical Upper Paleolithic blade tools. In contrast, the Aurignacian occurs over a much larger area than the Chatelperronian, embracing most of Europe from eastern Spain to the Black Sea (giving it the widest distribution among all Upper Paleolithic industries).

Moreover, the Aurignacian lasts longer and replaces the Chatelperronian wherever the latter had once been present (Fig. 9.7).

The Aurignacian is characterized by fine blades, knives, scrapers, and burins; bone awls, pierced antlers thought to have been used as arrow straighteners, and bone spearheads with a cleft base for hafting are also common (Fig. 9.7b). Beyond an advanced technology, the Aurignacian marks the beginning of a great surge in aesthetic and symbolic accomplishments (see Fig. 9.8 and Box 9.1), including the first appearance of extensively shaped bone, antler, and ivory adornments; marine shells; and other prized

FIGURE 9.7

UPPER PALEOLITHIC IMPLEMENTS
(A) Chatelperronian, (B) Aurignacian,
(C) Solutrean, (D) Magdalenian.

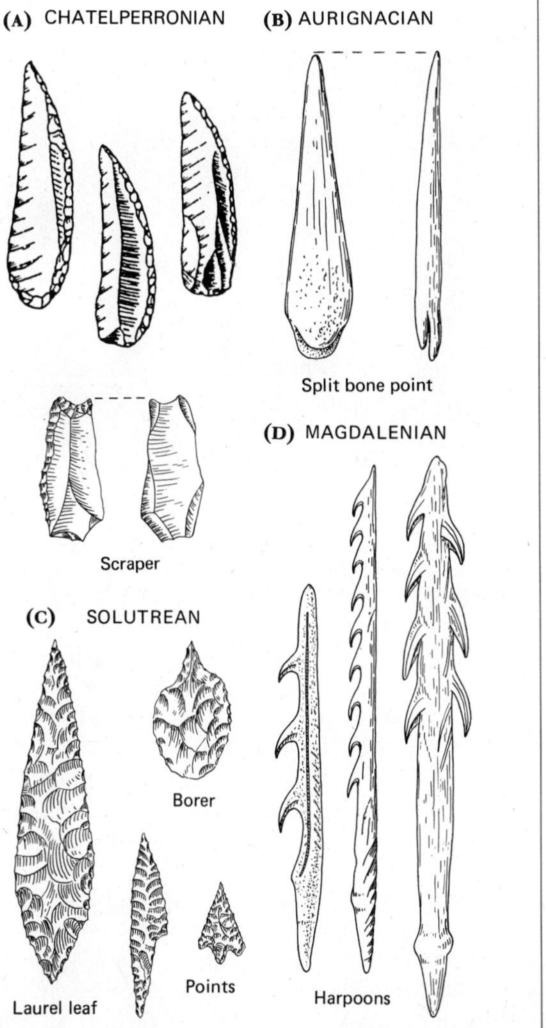

(A) CHATELPERRONIAN **(B) AURIGNACIAN**

Split bone point

(D) MAGDALENIAN

Scraper

(C) SOLUTREAN

Borer

Laurel leaf

Points

Harpoons

materials traded over long distances, and the first examples of representational art in the form of animal figurines. In addition, there is evidence for an increase in the size of local groups and regional population.

In other words, the whole spectrum of the archaeological evidence recovered from Aurignacian sites in Europe would appear to reflect a new element of complexity and innovation not only in technology but in several other spheres of behavior and organization. [Mellars 1989:374]

The relationship between the Chatelperronian and the Aurignacian is a crucial issue for understanding the evolution of culture and the origins of modern humans. On the one hand, the evidence can be interpreted to mean that there was a rapid transition from Mousterian industries and their associated Neandertal populations as a result of the intrusion of anatomically modern *sapiens* into Europe from the Middle East. In this view the mixture of Middle and Upper Paleolithic industries in the Chatelperronian would represent the acculturation of the Neandertal-Mousterians to the superior technology and symbol system of the *sapiens*-Aurignacian invaders. On the other hand, it can be argued that the mixture of tool traditions in the Chatelperronian actually represents an evolutionary transition taking place in Neandertal cultures in the absence of any intrusive populations. In this view, the Neandertals were not replaced by but evolved into modern *sapiens* (see p. 78 and Clark and Lindly 1989).

The Solutrean is found throughout much of France and Spain. The most famous Solutrean artifacts are magnificently flaked symmetrical daggers and spear points made in the shape of long, thin laurel leaves (Fig. 9.7c). The Solutreans also made finely worked stemmed and barbed points. Needles found at Solutrean sites indicate that skin clothing may have been sewn to form-fitting shapes.

The Magdalenian is the richest of the Upper Paleolithic traditions in terms of the diversity of artifacts and craft skills (Fig. 9.7d). Harpoons were added to the inventory of hunting weapons, their barbed points made of bones and antler. Fine bone needles attest to the probable importance of tailored clothing. For hunting, the early Magdalenians used the spear-thrower, a short rod or slat with a notch or hook at one end. The hook fits into the butt end of the spear (Fig. 9.9). The spear-thrower increases the force with which a spear can be hurled. Toward the end of the Magdalenian, the bow and arrow were probably in use, as depicted in some of the cave paintings of France and Spain. Magdalenian lance heads, harpoon points, and spear-throwers were often decorated with carvings of horses, ibex, birds, fish, and geometrical designs, some of which may be notations representing lunar cycles and seasonal changes (see below).

CENTRAL AND EASTERN EUROPEAN UPPER PALEOLITHIC

It should be emphasized that Upper Paleolithic cultures varied from region to region as well as chronologically (Gamble 1986). Much depended on regional and local climates, plant life, and the species of animals that inhabited particular environments. On the plains of Central Europe and Russia, for example, a distinct tradition known as Gravettian flourished

FIGURE *9.8*

AURIGNACIAN SIGNS AND
ORNAMENTS
Source: Hahn 1972.

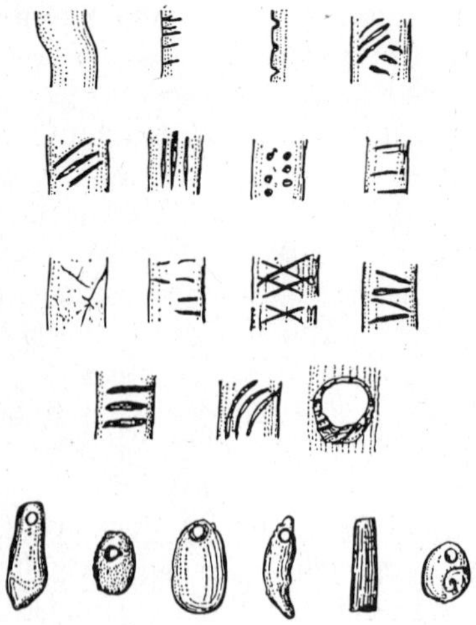

FIGURE *9.9*

MAGDALENIAN SPEAR-THROWER FRAGMENT
Weighted end engraved with bison
licking its side. Shaft which forms rest
of spear-thrower has been broken off
behind bison's head. Spear end was
laid in notch which is here shown
upside down. From Dordogne, France.

BOX *9.1*

AURIGNACIAN TAKEOFF

Some of the best-dated Aurignacian I levels are precisely those that have yielded the earliest known representational art, for example, the three dimensional ivory animal figures from Geissenklösterle, dated to well before 30,000 b.p.,...and a red-deer canine replicated in steatite from Castillo with accelerator dates...of 37,700–39,900 b.p. Most Aurignacian I assemblages in which organic materials have been preserved have yielded personal ornaments and/or decorated objects, not to mention items of bone and antler technology....

The appearance, in the Aurignacian, of substantial numbers of representational objects (after 2.5 million years in which they apparently did not exist) is a qualitative and revolutionary development with general evolutionary consequences...at least as profound as those of such landmarks in cultural evolution as the emergence of food production.

SOURCE: White 1990:251.

from about 25,000 B.P. It was distinguished by small blade knives whose backs have been blunted, perhaps to protect the user's fingers; bone awls; and various objects of personal adornment such as bone beads, bracelets, and pins. Many of the bone and ivory objects are decorated with incised geometric designs. Perhaps the most notable of the Gravettian artifacts are small female figurines, known as Venus statues, made out of stone, bone, ivory, and clay. About 120 examples have been recovered at sites all the way from Siberia to France. About half of the figurines depict women with enlarged breasts and buttocks (Fig. 9.10). As Sarah Nelson (1990) points out, there has been a tendency to pay attention only to the "abnormal" figurines. Perhaps they possessed some ritual significance associated with the fertility of women and animals. Alternatively, those with enlarged buttocks and breasts may have represented the desire of people to be fat as a sign of well-being. Unfortunately that leaves us without an interpretation for the thin Venuses (Fig. 9.11).

As indicated by refuse bones, the Gravettians hunted mammoth, horse, reindeer, bison, and other large herd animals. They made their camps both in the open and at the mouths of caves and rock shelters. In Czechoslovakia, the Gravettians lived in round animal-skin dwellings reminiscent of American Indian tepees or wigwams.

In southern Russia, archaeologists have identified the remains of a Gravettian mammoth-hunter's

FIGURE *9.10*

FAT VENUS STATUE
Reconstructed from fragments, showing typical enlargement of breasts and buttocks.

FIGURE *9.11*

SLENDER VENUSES
Source: Soffer 1987:336.

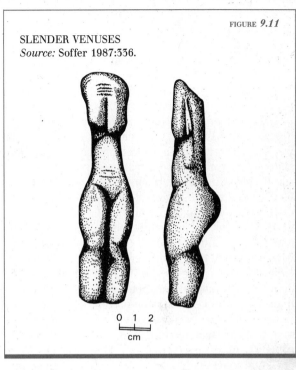

0 1 2
cm

animal-skin dwelling set in a shallow pit 40 feet long and 12 feet wide. Further out on the treeless Central Russian plain, Upper Paleolithic dwellings were constructed almost entirely out of mammoth tusks and bones, and mammoth bones were the principal cooking fuel (Fig. 9.12). Another interesting aspect of these mammoth hunters is their fondness for jewelry. From a burial containing two children and an adult dating to 24,000 B.P., Soviet archaeologists have removed over 10,000 beads made of bone and ivory (Soffer 1985:457).

UPPER PALEOLITHIC ART

The control achieved by Upper Paleolithic peoples over the techniques of tool manufacture in stone, bone, ivory, antler, and wood was reflected in their mastery of several art forms. In addition to the Venus statues, they produced thousands of engravings on antler and bone. Some cave sites contain large numbers of engraved stone tablets. Animals were the

FIGURE *9.12*

RECONSTRUCTED UPPER PALEOLITHIC DWELLING, CENTRAL RUSSIA
Mammoth bones substituted for wood frames in a treeless habitat. Skins presumably were laid over the bones. In this reconstruction wooden supports are used, but they probably were not part of the original dwelling.

favorite subjects depicted in these portable engravings, but remarkable depictions of human faces also occur (Fig. 9.13).

The most spectacular examples of Upper Paleolithic art are found on the walls and ceilings of deep caves in Spain and France. In hidden galleries far from the light of day, Upper Paleolithic peoples painted and engraved pictures of the animals they hunted. An occasional human figure—sometimes wearing a mask—outlines of hands, pictographs, and geometric symbols also occur, but the vast majority of the paintings and engravings depict horses, bison, mammoths, reindeer, ibex, wild boars, wild cattle, woolly rhinoceros, and other big-game animals. In spite of the magnificent economy of line and color, so much admired today, Upper Paleolithic cave art must be considered at least as much an expression of culturally established ritual as of individual or cultural aesthetic impulses. The animals were often painted one on top of another even though unused surfaces were available, indicating that they were done first and foremost as rituals rather than as art (Fig. 9.14). Their placement in dark and inaccessible caves is certainly not compat-

ible with modern notions of how to exhibit a Rembrandt or Picasso—but it is compatible with an interpretation of the paintings as one element in recurrent, complex religious-theatrical performances. The use of music is attested to by about 20 flutes made of bird or cave bear bones found at different sites (Pfeiffer 1982:180). That there were dancers wearing masks and costumes is strongly suggested by some of the cave paintings themselves (Fig. 9.15). No one knows the precise meaning of each of the elements in the performance, but it seems likely that the caves were the scenes of dramatic communal events similar to the kinds of ceremonies that are commonly performed today by the members of preliterate societies to intensify their sense of social identity, to educate and conduct young people into adulthood, and to ensure the continuity of their traditions (see Chapter 21). In Australia, for example, music, dance, masking, body decoration, use of ritual objects, and painting remote walls of cliffs are combined into dramatic performances that serve complex educational, social, aesthetic, and religious functions (Figs. 9.16 and 9.17).

This interpretation of cave art as an element in communal ritual implies that in the Upper Paleolithic, local groups of hunters and gatherers had developed a relationship of possessive control over hunting territories and that the caves were sacred places at the centers of these territories. The emphasis on group identity and territory in turn suggests that Upper Paleolithic peoples were experiencing a considerable amount of population pressure and intergroup competition for favorable hunting territories. In this connection it is interesting to note that the occurrence of cave art is largely confined to southwestern France and Spain (although eastern France and other parts of Europe do not lack for caves). Southwestern France and Spain were warm-climate refuge areas as a result of the absence of ice and proximity to the ocean, into which animals and their human predators crowded during the peak periods of glacial advance (Jochim 1983; Mellars 1985). This raises the possibility that some of the most favored prey animals may have become scarce or actually entirely absent from certain localities, and that the cave paintings and rituals were intended in part to restore their numbers. The evidence in favor of this interpretation is that there is a mismatch between the frequency with which prey animals are painted on the walls and the frequency with which they turn up in the faunal remains associated with a particular cave. For example, horses are the most frequently depicted but least frequently consumed prey species in several of the best-studied caves in southwestern France and northern Spain

FIGURE *9.13*

MAGDALENIAN FACES
Three portraits copied from original engraved plaques recovered from a Magdalenian site at La Marche, France. The site has yielded over 1500 engraved stone plaques. Examples are drawn to scale. (Champion et al. 1984:79.)

FIGURE *9.14*

PALEOLITHIC MASTERPIECES
It is as if Picasso were to paint on canvas already used by Rembrandt.
(A) Altamira, Spain; **(B)** La Caverne de Font de Gaume, France.

(A)

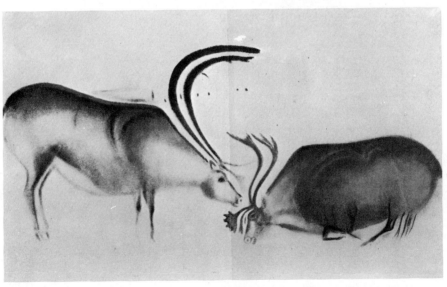

(B)

FIGURE *9.15*

MASKED DANCER?
Note human feet and hands. From Trois Frères, France.

FIGURE *9.16*

AUSTRALIAN ROCK PAINTINGS
The ritual activities of many modern hunter-gatherers include painting on rock surfaces.
From rock shelter in Northern Kimberly.

(Altuna 1983). However, on a regional basis, there is a good correlation between animals hunted and animals painted (Rice and Patterson 1986).

AN UPPER PALEOLITHIC CALENDAR?

Upper Paleolithic art in all of its forms suggests that a new phase in the process of cultural takeoff had been reached. Never before had humans become so deeply and inextricably enmeshed in a world of culturally created symbols. The kind of shared symbols implicit in cave paintings, engraved lines, or figurines is different from the symbolism that is implicit in the manufacture of a hand ax. A Paleolithic youth could learn the meaning of a hand ax by watching one being made and used, but he or she would have to be told about the meaning of an engraved zigzag line, a cave painting, or a Venus statue.

As we have already noted, the beginning of the Upper Paleolithic is also marked by a great increase in the use of pendants, beads, and other bodily adornments carefully crafted from ivory, bone, animal teeth, and shells. These artifacts can be interpreted as evidence of a growing consciousness of individual statuses—the more beads, the higher the status. They also reinforce the interpretation of cave art as a symbolic intensification of group identity since the styles of ornaments vary from place to place, much more than the basic tool traditions. (White 1989:385).

A number of attempts have been made to interpret various painted and incised geometric designs— dots, grids, scratches, lines—on Upper Paleolithic cave walls and on antler and bone implements. The

FIGURE *9.17*

PEACE-MAKING CEREMONY, AUSTRALIA
Group ceremonies include body painting, dancing, singing, shouting-chanting, and percussion sound.

theory that the holes and lines found on certain antler and bone plaques and "batons" were records of the passage of days and phases of the moon (Marshack 1985) has been cast into doubt (D'Errico 1989). Nonetheless it seems likely that the artists responsible for the amazingly realistic scenes on the cave walls were aware of the phases of the moon and other celestial events, thereby preparing the way for the future development of calendars and the science of astronomy.

THE PALEOLITHIC IN OTHER REGIONS

Sequences of Paleolithic industries similar to those in Europe also occur in Africa and Asia. For example, Levallois techniques and Mousterian industries succeed Acheulian traditions throughout Africa. There is even a Mousterian-like flake industry in North China. By 40,000 to 30,000 B.P., bone, flake, and blade tools were being made in Siberia and there is evidence that similar tool complexes may have appeared in the Americas shortly thereafter (see p.174). For the period 20,000 to 10,000 B.P. it is impossible to say that any particular region had achieved decisive technological or symbol-using advantages over the others. To be sure, there was great variation in the specific content of the tool kits of the Eurasian mammoth hunters, the Southeast Asian forest-dwellers, and the Australian hunters of marsupials, but this variation probably reflected local adaptation more than different levels of technological progress (Bricker 1976).

In the realm of artistic achievements, representational art probably began as early in Africa as in Europe. Such art is known from Namibia dating to 27,000 B.P. Even earlier rock paintings may have been made in Tanzania (Annati 1986). In Australia, which may have been occupied by modern *sapiens* about 40,000 B.P., some artwork deep inside caves and on exposed rock surfaces has been dated to 30,000 B.P. (Jones 1989: 771).

THE END OF THE PALEOLITHIC

Despite the many technological triumphs of the Paleolithic, the basic mode of subsistence remained essentially what it had been since Acheulian times. All human groups continued to have some variety of a hunting-gathering-fishing mode of production. To be sure, neither the environmental opportunities for hunting and gathering nor the technological inventory available for exploiting the natural environment had remained constant. Throughout the hundreds of thousands of years of glacial advances and retreats, climatic zones underwent drastic changes. These changes in turn brought about a constantly changing succession of plant and animal life. With each advance of the glaciers, warm-weather species of animals were driven south, tundras replaced plains, plains replaced forests, forests turned to deserts, and elsewhere, deserts bloomed. The quality and nutritive value of the Paleolithic diet was determined as much by the local abundance of plants and animals as by technology. Inefficient technology yielded a high standard of living when there was a great abundance of plants and animals, whereas even the most efficient hunting and collecting technologies and techniques did not stave off hunger and extinction when game and plant resources became scarce. Human well-being was thus directly related to the response of animals and plants to natural conditions. But Paleolithic groups were not entirely without the means to influence these conditions. Forest could be burned to increase grassland areas, which supported more game; some plants could be left unharvested to assure that there would be more for the picking in another year, and certain endangered animals and plants could be protected by tabooing their consumption for certain members of the group. But much of the influence Paleolithic groups could exert was negative, leading to overkill and uncontrolled gathering.

THE MESOLITHIC

The limitations of hunting-and-gathering modes of production are well illustrated in the transition from the Upper Paleolithic to the Mesolithic cultures of northern and western Europe. Toward the end of the last glaciation, the region south of the glaciers received a flow of meltwater favoring the growth of grassy plains on which herds of horses, bison, mammoths, and reindeer grazed. As the glaciers retreated, these animals spread into the grassy plains, followed by their human predators. Both animal and human populations prospered, but unbeknown to either, their mutual way of life was doomed. The Eurasian grasslands were merely a temporary ecological phase. At about 12,000 B.P. trees began to invade the grasslands. Underneath the leafy forest canopy, no grass could grow. By 10,000 B.P. much of the so-called Pleistocene megafauna (*mega* = extra big; *fauna* = animals) had become extinct in Europe. Gone were the woolly mammoth and rhino, steppe bison, giant elk, and wild ass (Fig. 9.18). No doubt the marvelously skilled Upper Paleolithic hunters themselves contributed to this ecological catastrophe, just as New World hunters probably played a role in the extinction of the Pleistocene megafauna in the New World (see p. 177). Elephants, rhinos, and other genera had survived numerous prior advances and retreats of grasslands and forests throughout the Pleistocene. What was new in the situation may have been the unprecedented efficiency of Upper Paleolithic technology (Martin 1984).

In Europe the Mesolithic was a time of intense local ecological change. Forests of birch and pine spread over the land, and the hunters made their camps in clearings along riverbanks and at lakesides, estuaries, and the seashore. The forests sheltered game such as moose, red deer, roe deer, wild cattle (aurochs), and wild pigs. But to locate these animals, new tracking skills were needed. Forest-dwelling animals would disappear from view unless the kill was prompt and silent. Part of the solution was to enlist the help of a species whose sense of smell suited it for hunting in deep forest. Thus it was during the Mesolithic that dogs for the first time became the companions and helpers of human hunters, with a date of about 9500 B.P. at Star Carr in England (Champion et al. 1984:96). (Dogs may have been domesticated in the Middle East at a still earlier date to assist in herding sheep and goats— see page 160.) In the forest the dog's sense of smell directed the hunter to within bowshot of evasive prey. But hunting under forested conditions, even with improved bows and hound dogs, could not yield the quantities of meat that were formerly obtained from herds of reindeer and bison. Thus, the Mesolithic people turned increasingly to a broad spectrum of plant foods and fish, mollusks, and other riverine and maritime sources of food. Some coastal regions of Northern Europe, however, were particularly rich in fish and sea mammals. In such favored habitats, Mesolithic people lived in large, permanent villages

FIGURE *9.18*

WOOLLY MAMMOTHS
Artist's rendering of one of the species of big-game animals that became extinct
in Europe at the end of the last glaciation.

similar perhaps to those found among the Native American peoples of the Pacific Northwest in the United States (Price 1991). Elsewhere along the seacoast the heaped-up debris of centuries of Mesolithic shellfish eating formed mounds called kitchen middens. Although clams, oysters, and mussels are good sources of protein, it took a lot of eating for a hungry person to fill up on such food.

The Mesolithic also marks the end of the great cave paintings. The distinctive art form of this period consisted of geometric designs and symbols incised on tools, weapons, and painted pebbles (Fig. 9.19). Clearly this shift in aesthetic concerns mirrors the disappearance of the big-game animals that had been the basis of subsistence during the Paleolithic.

THE END OF THE PALEOLITHIC IN WORLD PERSPECTIVE

The European Mesolithic was a regional manifestation of a trend toward broad-spectrum modes of production that took place within a range of about 6000 years (about 13,000 to 7,000 B.P.) in several different parts of the world. This trend was marked by the exploitation of mollusks, marine mammals, fish, birds, seeds, nuts, and other dispersed and therefore relatively costly food sources. In the Near East, for example, about 12,000 B.P., a people called the Natufians hunted gazelle and deer, harvested wild varieties of wheat, and fished with nets, harpoons, and fishhooks (for more on the Natufians, see the next

FIGURE *9.19*

PAINTED PEBBLES
Typical Mesolithic artifacts whose function and meaning remain a mystery.

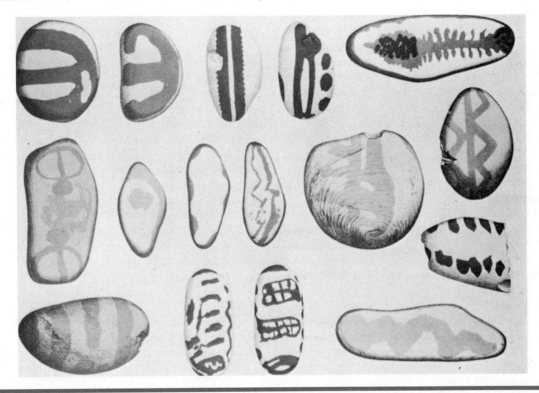

BOX *9.2*

MESOLITHIC ACHIEVEMENTS

Technology develops toward greater efficiency in transport, in tools, and in subsistence procurement. Subsistence equipment, both implements and facilities, becomes more diverse in form, more specialized in function, and more abundant in number. An incredible range of fishing gear, including nets, weirs, leisters, hooks, and harpoons, is known. Ground stone artifacts appear for the first time as axes, celts, plant-processing equipment, and other tools. Large canoes and snow sleds...are known from this period in northern Europe. Projectile weapons are armed with a vast array of specialized tips, made of bone, wood, antler, and stone....Other chipped stone implements begin to take a secondary role in many activities, becoming tools to make tools of wood, bone, and antler that are used directly in food procurement.

Settlements are larger, of longer duration, and more differentiated, both in terms of the internal organization of the settlement and in the number and variety of sites and locales in use. Large co-resident groups and permanent occupation are hallmarks of Mesolithic settlement in several areas.

SOURCE: Price 1983:770.

chapter). A similar complex can be found in Nubia and Upper Egypt along the margins of the Nile Valley, where the broad spectrum included wild grains, birds, fish, and some larger animals (Krzyzaniak 1981). A broad-spectrum mode of production provided the basis for a "fullfledged Mesolithic village" located on a lakeshore in the state of Uttar Pradesh in India and dating to about 10,300 B.P. (Jacobson 1979:481). Comparable developments can be discerned in China in the lake region of Yunnan Province and in Japan, where shellfish middens (refuse heaps) resembling European Mesolithic middens date to 9000 B.P. Finally, as will be seen in our discussion of New World prehistory (Chapter 11), broad-spectrum modes of production also occur at the end of the Pleistocene at sites in Mexico, the Peruvian coast, and the Mississippi Valley.

It is difficult to avoid the conclusion that this recurrent trend appears to reflect such factors as environmental changes induced by the recession and melting of the continental glaciers, the consequent rise in sea level, and the extinction of the Pleistocene megafauna (Clark 1981; Cohen 1977, 1987; Harris 1987; Yessner 1987).

In some respects, the Mesolithic may have been a time of deteriorating standards of living. Life expectancy, for example, seems to have declined (Cohen 1987). Yet paradoxically, the Mesolithic was also a time of rapid technological change, proving perhaps that necessity is the mother of invention (see Box 9.2).

SUMMARY

The longest and most ancient age of hominid prehistory is called the Paleolithic. This age began over 2 mya with the Oldowan and Acheulean and it lasted until about 10,000 years ago. The mode of production practiced throughout that entire span of time was scavenging, hunting, gathering, and fishing. There were no domesticated plants or animals except dogs, which appeared at the very end of the Paleolithic. Three divisions of unequal length within the Paleolithic are distinguished: Lower, Middle, and Upper.

It was only at the transition between the Lower and Middle Paleolithic, about 125,000 B.P., that fundamental changes in tool technology began to occur. The best-known innovation is the Levallois tortoise-core method for the preparation of flake tools. The European Middle Paleolithic is closely associated with the Neandertals and with Mousterian tools. Elsewhere, the Middle Paleolithic is associated with other archaic *H. sapiens,* but in the Middle East it is also associated with anatomically modern *sapiens.*

Much of the tool manufacture during the Middle Paleolithic involved soft-hammer techniques and secondary flaking, retouching, and trimming. Points suitable for spears appeared. But there is little evidence for the development of the aesthetic and symbolic aspects of culture. The question of whether Neandertals buried their dead has not been settled and there is little evidence of personal adornments, art, or complex ideologies.

The Upper Paleolithic began between 40 to 35 thousand years ago with the Chatelperronian and the Aurignacian traditions. The former was a mixture of Mousterian Middle Paleolithic with Upper Paleolithic tool types and is associated with the last of the Neandertals. The Aurignacian replaced the Chatelperronian at about the same time that modern *sapiens* replaced the Neandertals. One interpretation is that the cultural mixture is actually evidence of an evolutionary transition from the Mousterian to the Aurignacian and of Neandertal to modern *sapiens.* Another interpretation is that the *sapiens* were an intrusive population who brought with them their Aurignacian culture, which surviving pockets of Neandertals tried to adopt before disappearing from the scene.

In either event, the Aurignacian is characterized by a great increase in the production of ivory, bone, and antler implements and there was an explosive growth in personal adornments, representational paintings and figurines, and incised symbols, all suggesting a quantum leap in the use of symbols.

During subsequent phases of the Upper Paleolithic, such as the Soloutrean and Magdelenian, blades and other stone tools became highly specialized and beautifully crafted. Needles suggest the use of skin clothing in northern latitudes. Harpoons, spear throwers, fish hooks, and bows and arrows were invented and/or perfected.

Upper Paleolithic cave art was an element in complex religious-theatrical performances involving music, dancing, masking, body adornment, and ritual objects. One hypothesis about cave art, with its depiction of game animals, was that it was intended to restore big game species that had become scarce in certain regions. Whatever the precise meaning of the paintings, it is clear that cultural takeoff was well under way during the Upper Paleolithic.

Considerable regional variation prevailed throughout the Upper Paleolithic. In southern

Russia for example, the Gravettian cultures specialized in hunting mammoths, eating mammoth flesh, making houses out of mammoth tusks, and keeping warm by burning mammoth bones.

In Europe, the Upper Paleolithic peoples preyed on the big game that roamed the lush grasslands along the southern edges of the continental glaciers. After 10,000 years B.P., reforestation, aided to an unknown degree by human hunting, destroyed this megafauna. Hence, the European Mesolithic is characterized by cultures adapted to coastal, riverine, and forest habitats. The dog was domesticated to aid in forest hunting. Many other basic technological inventions were introduced, suitable for exploiting a broad spectrum of plants and animals that lived in coastal, riverine, and forest habitats. Similar patterns of broad-spectrum adaptations occur widely at the end of the Pleistocene in both the Old World and the New World in the period of 13,000 to 7,000 B.P.

It seems likely that the end of the Paleolithic represented relatively "hard times" for many of the descendants of the Upper Paleolithic big-game hunters. In Europe the new infrastructure also had rather drastic effects on art. Both the herd animals and the ritual art depicting them disappeared at about the same time. The aesthetic component in Mesolithic rituals expressed itself in geometric designs and symbols incised on tools and weapons and painted on pebbles.

Despite the disappearance of cave art, the Mesolithic was a time of cultural innovation. The domestication of the dog was an achievement no less significant than cave paintings. To meet the challenge and the opportunity provided by the great abundance of trees, new techniques were developed for making and hafting woodworking tools. For the first time, axes were produced by grinding rather than by flaking processes. Fishhooks, fish spears, and harpoons were perfected; fish nets and bark floats, boats and paddles, sleds and skis were also either invented or improved upon. As local groups camped for longer periods near renewable resources such as shellfish beds or fishing streams, population density increased and new opportunities for cultural evolution were opened up.

Chapter 10

The Neolithic and the Rise of States

This chapter describes the further evolution of cultures in the Old World from the end of the Mesolithic to the rise of cities and states. We shall see that between 12,000 and 2,000 B.P., as a result of the domestication of plants and animals, more changes of a fundamental nature were introduced into Old World cultural beliefs and practices than in the previous million years of cultural evolution. How, when, and where did domestication first take place? Was it population growth and environmental depletions that forced people to adopt new modes of production? Whatever the cause, we shall see that Neolithic villages evolved into urban centers and the first city states with surprising rapidity. Where did this happen first, and why? And even more crucially, did the Neolithic spread from one center of domestication to all the others? Or was domestication invented again and again? And did the fateful transition to the state also occur independently in Europe, Asia, and Africa?

THE NEOLITHIC

Neolithic literally means "new stone age." When the term was first introduced in the nineteenth century, it gave recognition to the appearance of tool kits dominated by stone implements that had been prepared by the techniques of grinding and polishing. Today the term *Neolithic* is used to designate not new stone-working methods but new methods of food production. During the Neolithic, greater control over the reproduction of plants and animals was achieved by the development of farming and stock raising. This in turn provided the material basis for high-density, sedentary settlements and for rapid population increase. Farming and stock raising also set the stage for profound alterations in domestic and political economy, centering on access to land, water, and other basic resources, and for the emergence of differences in wealth and power. Without agriculture, the development of large towns, cities, states, and empires could not have occurred.

DOMESTICATION

Domestication involves a complex symbiotic relationship between human populations—the domesticators and certain favored plants and animals—the domesticates. The domesticators destroy or clear away undesirable flora and fauna from the domesticates' habitats. They adjust the supply of space, water, sunlight, and nutrients, and they interfere in the reproductive activity of the domesticates to ensure maximum favorable use of available resources. Domestication usually involves genetic changes. For example, a key difference between wild and domesticated varieties of wheat, barley, and other cereals is that wild grains break off upon ripening and fall to the ground on their own, whereas ripe domesticated grains remain intact even when roughly handled. Indeed, the ripe domesticated grains must be pulled or beaten off if they are to be made available for human consumption. In the case of American Indian maize, the ripe kernels do not fall off at all, and the plant is incapable of reproducing itself without human assistance. Other instances of this phenomenon are found in the banana plant and date palm. The final step in domestication occurs when the domesticate is removed from its natural habitat to an area that is markedly different, or when, as a result of cultivation, its original habitat is markedly transformed (Barrau 1967).

Domestication must be distinguished from cultivation. Domestication of plants is a process of genetic change that begins with cultivation—the planting and harvesting of wild varieties of seeds and tubers (Blumler and Byrne 1991). Similarly, the domestication of animals is a process that begins with animal husbandry—the penning, coralling, or milking of wild animals—and that ends with genetically altered tame varieties. It is relatively easy to identify the earliest domesticates in the archaeological record because of the changes in shape, size, or other characteristics of seeds or bones; but the beginnings of cultivation and animal husbandry are less distinct.

THE NEOLITHIC IN THE MIDDLE EAST

One of the earliest archaeologically known transitions from hunting and gathering to a Neolithic mode of production took place in the Middle East (Fig. 10.1). (Archaeologists refer to this region as the Near East. Almost everyone else, including the news media, refers to it as the Middle East.) Domesticated barley, wheat, goats, and sheep dating between 10,300 and 8,000 B.P., have been identified at a number of sites in this region (Bar-Yosef 1992). The sites are concentrated in the Jordan Valley, northward to southern Turkey, eastward to the headwaters of the Tigris and Euphrates rivers in Syria and Iraq, and southward along both flanks of the Zagros Mountains (Fig. 10.2), which form the border between Iraq and Iran. There is some evidence that the area of earliest domestication, especially of cattle, pigs, and goats, extended as far west as Greece (Protsch and Berger 1973; cf. Bokonyi, Braidwood, and Reed 1973). Also, it seems likely that leguminous plants including peas, lentils, broad beans, and chickpeas were domesticated almost at the same time as the basic grain crops (Zohary and Hopf 1988).

The areas in which the Middle Eastern Neolithic transformation occurred correspond roughly to the regions in which wheat, barley, peas, lentils, goats, and sheep occur naturally in a wild state (Harlan 1978; Zohary and Hopf 1988). At the end of the Pleistocene, Middle Eastern peoples incorporated these plants and animals into their food supply through hunting and gathering techniques, cultivation, and animal husbandry. The culture of these preagricultural peoples was a local form of the terminal Paleolithic (or a Middle Eastern version of the Mesolithic). Much of the big game had become extinct as early as 20,000 B.P. (Cohen 1977:132). Like the European Mesolithic peoples, the terminal Pleistocene Middle Easteners had tool kits containing barbed harpoons, bone needles, and fishhooks. They exploited a broad spectrum of food resources: small game, fish, turtles, seasonal waterfowl, terrestrial and marine snails, mussels, and crabs, as well as legumes, nuts, fruits, and other plant foods. One critical difference, however, was that the Middle Easterners made increasing use of grass seeds, including the wild ancestors of wheat and barley. The absence of these wild grasses from the broad spectrum of resources that could be exploited in western Europe perhaps explains why the Neolithic transformation did not

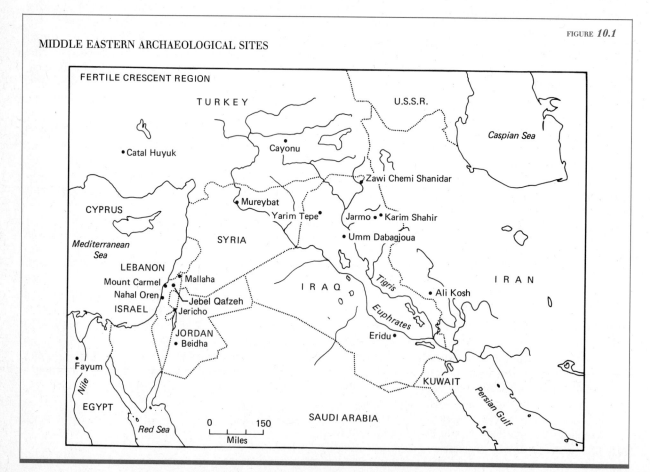

FIGURE *10.1*

MIDDLE EASTERN ARCHAEOLOGICAL SITES

FIGURE *10.2*

HILLY FLANKS, NORTHERN IRAQ
Several early Neolithic sites are located in this region. The Zagros Mountains are
in the background.

originate directly from the western European Mesolithic base.

The contribution grains (i.e., the seeds of cereal grasses) made to the food supply was at first
relatively minor. Their use was limited by a number of technical problems. First, the ripening of wild
wheat and barley occurs during three weeks in the
late spring. Stands of wild wheat still grow thick
enough in Turkey and other parts of the Middle East
for an individual using a flint-blade sickle to harvest
a kilogram of grain per hour—enough for a family of
experienced plant collectors working over a three-
week period to gather more grain than they could
possibly consume in a whole year (Harlan 1978:280).
This implies that waterproof storage facilities would
be needed to protect the grain. Moreover, to make
use of such a harvest, a considerable amount of additional labor was needed to process the grains. The
processing technology was in itself quite complex
since wild wheat and barley, unlike later domesticated varieties, had to be either soaked or roasted in
order to remove the husk. Then the seeds had to be
winnowed, ground, and cooked. Carrying around the
heavy stones needed for grinding would be especially
troublesome for groups with a nomadic hunting-and-

gathering mode of production. The obvious solution
to these difficulties was to settle in relatively permanent dwellings where the grain could be stored
and the heavy grinding and roasting equipment left
in place. Thus, Middle Eastern groups began to settle down in permanent villages 2000 years before
domesticated varieties of wheat and barley were in
use (Flannery 1973; Harris and Hillman 1989, Henry
1985).

The Natufians

Perhaps the earliest people to cultivate wild cereals
were the Natufians, who lived in the southern part
of the Levant at the end of the Pleistocene (Bar-Yosef
and Belfer-Cohen 1991). Near Mt. Carmel in Israel,
the Natufians carved out basin-shaped depressions at
the front of their rock shelters, laid courses of stone
pavement, and built rings of stone around what appear to be permanent hearths. In the Jordan River
Valley, at the 12,000 B.P. Natufian site of Mallaha, stone
foundations of round houses with plastered storage
pits have been excavated.

The strongest evidence that the Natufians were
cultivating cereals derives from the microscopic
study of the sheen and striations on the stone-bladed

sickles (Fig. 10.3) that occur in great abundance at Natufian sites. By matching the effects produced by ten thousand swings of freshly made experimental sickles against each of several different species of plants with the sheen on the ancient sickles, one can determine what kinds of plants were being harvested by the Natufians. Cereals fit the pattern best. Further experiments reveal that the striations are deepest and most frequent when the harvest has been carried out on plants rooted in loose soils (more grit). Many Natufian sickles have these deep striations, suggesting that the harvest had been carried out in soils loosened to receive deliberately planted seeds (Unger-Hamilton 1989). There is a strong likelihood that the earliest domestication of wheat and barley took place in the southern Levant as an outgrowth of Natufian cultivation practices (Bar-Yosef and Valla 1990).

Other areas of the Middle East, though, should not be ruled out as the initiators of agriculture. Early evidence of preagricultural grain-harvesting, grain-roasting, and grain-storing village life has also been found at Zawi Chemi Shanidar in Iraq (Fig. 10.4) at the upper drainage of the Tigris River, and at Karim Shahir on the flanks of the Zagros Mountains, both dating from 12,000 to 10,000 B.P. (Solecki 1981). Evidence of preagricultural village life dating to 12,000 B.P. has also been discovered at Tell Mureybat on the headwaters of the Euphrates River in Syria (Fig. 10.5). Here, clay-walled houses, grinding stones, and roasting pits have been found, together with 18 different types of wild seeds including wild wheat and barley.

Preagricultural Sedentism

The discovery of preagricultural sedentary villages has revolutionized previous theories concerning the origin of agriculture. Prior to 1960 it was generally believed that settled village life must have come after, not before, the development of domesticates. As

FIGURE *10.4*

SITE OF ZAWI CHEMI SHANIDAR
An early preagricultural village in Iraq. Mortars in foreground attest to the importance of cereals in the diet.

noted for the European Mesolithic (page 149), it is now recognized that hunters and gatherers can live in relatively dense and sedentary settlements if the resources they exploit are concentrated in restricted areas—for example, mollusk beds, fish that migrate upstream to spawn, and fields of wild grasses.

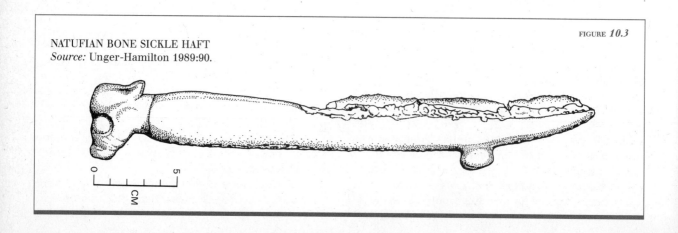

NATUFIAN BONE SICKLE HAFT
Source: Unger-Hamilton 1989:90.

FIGURE *10.3*

0   5
CM

FIGURE *10.5*

TELL MUREYBAT
Large preagricultural village in Syria.

THE ORIGINS OF AGRICULTURE

Thus, the preagricultural villages in the Middle East were adapted to the need to store wild grain, process it into flour, and convert it into flat cakes or porridge. The construction of houses, walls, roasters, grinders, and storage pits represented an investment that people would be very reluctant to give up in order to move to another site.

In order for their system of wild grain collection to remain viable for any length of time, the collectors had to refrain from harvesting all the stalks in a particular field. Selective harvesting of this sort is still practiced by many contemporary hunting-and-gathering peoples to ensure future harvests from the same wild stands. Thus, with selective grain harvests supplemented by hunting and other collecting activities, villages were able to feed themselves without having to move their dwellings.

But selective grain harvesting is not as efficient as agriculture proper. The trouble is that in their wild state, wheat and barley have heads that con-sist of a brittle axis to which the seed husks are affixed. When it is ripe, the axis (called a rachis) shatters easily (Fig. 10.6). Harvesters may move through a field of wild grains, cutting off the entire ear or stripping the husk-encased seeds with their fingers. Either way, their activity shatters the most brittle heads (if the wind has not already done so), and these are the ones that reseed themselves. What the harvesters need are plants whose ripened seeds will not be dislodged by next year's winds before the harvesters can get to them—yet these are the ones they take home to eat. And so the harvesters would seem to be unconsciously selecting against the very feature that is most essential for the breeding of domesticated grains.

How was this selection reversed? One theory is that when sheaths of tough-rachis grain were brought to the village to be threshed and winnowed, tough-rachis seeds would accidentally be scattered in the area around the houses where human waste and garbage provided ideal growing conditions. The next step would be deliberate planting of these tough-rachis seeds in an attempt to increase the area from

FIGURE *10.6*

EMMER WHEAT RACHIS

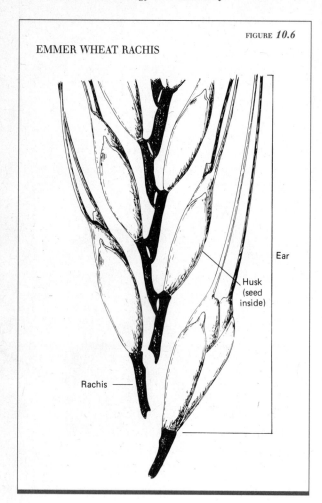

Ear

Husk
(seed
inside)

Rachis

THE DOMESTICATION OF ANIMALS

Which came first—the domestication of sheep and goats or the domestication of wheat and barley? Some archaeologists believe that the peoples of the southern Levant pioneered in the domestication of plants while the people of the more northerly and easterly hilly flanks of the Zagros and Anatolia pioneered in the domestication of sheep and goats (Hole 1984, 1987). Others view the domestication of both plants and animals as part of a single process. As humans began to obtain their food in a new way, plants and animals were forced into new relationships with each other. The wild grasses, including the ancestors of wheat and barley, had been a major food source for wild sheep and goats. As permanent villages more and more often came to be located in the middle of dense fields of grain, herds of wild sheep and goats were forced into closer contact with people. With the aid of dogs, people began to control the movements of these herds, keeping the sheep and goats permanently on the margins of the grainfields, allowing them to eat the stubble but keeping them away from the ripe grain. Hunting, in other words, became greatly simplified. The hunters no longer had to go to the animals; instead, the animals, finding the lush fields of concentrated grasses irresistible, came to the hunters. This would have resulted in a temporary increase in meat production. The spread of agriculture, however, leads to the depletion and eventual extinction of regional game resources because wild species find their natural range lands greatly diminished, and the hunters find it easier to locate their quarry. The domestication of animals, therefore, can be viewed as a prehistoric attempt to preserve endangered species. Feeding sheep and goats, and slaughtering only males while protecting the females kept these animals off the growing list of valuable species that became extinct at the end of the Pleistocene.

Like many modern-day hunter-gatherers, Paleolithic and Mesolithic peoples were thoroughly familiar with the habits and characteristics of the animals they hunted (Russell 1988). Indeed, there is evidence from the sex and age distribution of prey animal bones that as early as 15,000 B.P. pre-Neolithic Middle Eastern hunter-collectors were exerting a considerable amount of control over the wild fauna in their habitat. For several thousand years prior to their actual domestication, it is inferred that species such as wild sheep and goat were occasionally herded, penned, and even fed (Moore 1985). (Modern hunter-gatherers keep the young of prey species as pets.) It was not lack of knowledge, therefore, that prevented prehistoric hunter-gatherers from raising ani-

which grains could be harvested. Finally, it would be recognized that sowing seeds from a few plants with good harvesting qualities produced whole fields of tough-rachis plants.

Another change may have involved selection for husks that did not adhere firmly to the seeds and that could easily be detached during threshing. In the wild varieties the husks had to be heated or soaked in order to get at the grain. This may explain the presence of roasting pits and subterranean earth ovens in the earliest villages (see above). Other desirable genetic changes, leading to larger ears with multiple rows of seeds, were easily achieved by following one simple rule: Don't eat the seeds from plants that have the most desirable features; plant them. Thus, as indicated above, the cultivation of cereal grains led to the genetic changes characteristic of the domesticates.

mals and making use of them for food and other functions. Rather, the problem was that hunter-collectors would soon run out of food for themselves if they had to share it with animals (see p. 215). But the beginning of agriculture opened new possibilities: Sheep and goats thrive on stubble and other portions of domesticated crops that humans cannot digest. Now animals could be penned, fed on stubble, milked, and slaughtered selectively. Breeding for desirable features, unlike the initial phases of plant domestication, would have been quite straightforward. Animals that were too aggressive, grew too slowly, or were too delicate were eaten before they reached reproductive age.

THE CAUSES OF THE NEOLITHIC

There is considerable evidence that Middle Easterners, especially those in the southern Levant, confronted a deteriorating ecological situation at the end of the Pleistocene caused by the onset of prolonged hot dry summers—even hotter and dryer than summers characteristic of modern-day Mediterranean climates. An important consequence of this change was that it favored the spread of annual grasses such as the wild ancestors of wheat and barley. (Annual grasses put their energy into seeds that lie dormant until the winter rains, at which point they sprout and grow rapidly to maturity. Thus, unlike perennial plants, they cannot be killed off by a prolonged dry season.) Another important consequence of the arid climate was that lakes and streams dried up, making it essential to live near permanent sources of water, which had the effect of creating larger concentrations of dwellings and people.

With increasing summer aridity and the shrinking of the lakes, people faced seasonal shortages of critical resources. By responding to these shortages through storage and sedentism, people increased the pressure on local environments and began to deplete them. Rather than move, perhaps because other sedentary populations had likewise depleted nearby locations, people intensified their efforts to harvest...annual seeds. [McCorriston and Hole 1991:59]

The broad-spectrum mode of hunting and collecting can itself be interpreted as a response to a decline in the availability of larger game animals and calorie-rich plants (see p. 211 for interpretation of broad-spectrum diets in terms of "optimal foraging theory"). Indeed, there is some justification for interpreting the time of the broad-spectrum modes of production in Europe, the Middle East, and other regions just before the development of agriculture as a pre-

historic "crisis" in food production (Binford 1983:210–212; Cohen 1977, 1987; Young et al. 1983). The Neolithic can be viewed as a response to this "crisis."

Some archaeologists reject the idea that agriculture started as a result of food shortages or hard times. Rather, they see the domestication of plants as resulting from an increased interest in innovative forms of food production (Adams 1983; Voigt 1986). One intriguing suggestion is that what got early Neolithic peoples "hooked" on growing grains was that they discovered that the liquid portion of porridges left overnight under certain conditions turned into alcohol (Katz and Voigt 1986).

DEMOGRAPHIC CONSEQUENCES OF THE NEOLITHIC

Everyone agrees, however, that once agriculture was adopted, for whatever immediate motive, there were profound consequences for population growth. Agriculture lessens the cost of rearing children. Among mobile hunters and gatherers, additional children are costly because infants must be carried over long distances, and male children do not become effective hunters until they are adolescents. But with agriculture, the more children, the more plants and animals that can be taken care of. Children can be put to work at an early age in a number of simple tasks connected with planting, weeding, and herding and can easily "pay" for themselves—at least as long as there is plenty of land available (or game, where there are no domesticated animals; see p. 228). Moreover, with agriculture, women are freed from much of the burden of having to carry infants over long distances each day. In permanent village situations there is less need for long-distance travel and hence less of a penalty associated with shortening the span of years between the rearing of one infant and another. This reduction in "cost" per child per woman (see p. 225) must be included among the factors that were responsible for the initial concentration on seed gathering even before plants and animals were domesticated (Dumond 1975; Lee 1979:312ff; Sengel 1973; Sussman 1972).

Thus, the Neolithic was associated with a rapid increase in population. Starting with 100,000 people in 10,000 B.P., the population of the Middle East probably reached 3.2 million shortly before 6000 B.P.—a 30-fold increase in 4000 years (Carneiro and Hilse 1966; Hassan 1978). While there may have been an improvement in the standard of living at the beginning of this period, evidence of increasing rates of disease, physical stress, and shortened life expectancy have been detected for the later phases (Cohen 1987).

NEOLITHIC DEVELOPMENTS

At Zawi Chemi Shanidar, one of the earliest villages in Iraq, domesticated sheep appeared shortly after 11,000 B.P. The earliest domesticated goats have been found at Ali Kosh in Iran, dating to 9500 B.P., along with domesticated wheat and barley. At Jericho in Jordan, there were domesticated varieties of wheat, barley, and goats by 9000 B.P., and the same complex is found at Jarmo (Fig. 10.7) in Iraq by 8800 B.P. (Herre and Rohrs 1978; Harlan 1978; Braidwood and Braidwood 1986; Braidwood et al. 1983). Many other early Neolithic sites have been excavated, and new ones are being brought to light every year.

Life in early Neolithic times used to be depicted by archaeologists as peaceful, secure, highly egalitarian, self-sufficient, and slow-changing. While this picture may be accurate for some of the earliest villages, recent findings have led to a different interpretation. As the threshold to the Neolithic was being crossed, new domesticates, tools, productive techniques, and forms of social life appeared with explosive rapidity. It is now clear that large towns had become commonplace as far back as 10,000 B.P. The best-known of these is Jericho in Jordan, which covered 10 acres and had about 2000 inhabitants (Hamblin 1973; Kenyon 1981). Situated in an oasis, Jericho was surrounded by a moat and walls, which may have served to protect the settlement against floods and mudflows rather than enemy attacks. But there was also a tower set in the walls (Fig. 10.8), whose function was more likely military defense (cf. Bar-Yosef 1986:161). Other early Neolithic towns, such as Maghzaliyah in Iraq, were surrounded by walls that were more certainly defensive in nature. The image of peaceful villages is also difficult to reconcile with the discovery at Çayönü, in southern Turkey, of several hundred skulls next to a stone slab that had once been stained with blood (Mellaart 1975).

By 8000 B.P., at least one Neolithic town, Çatal Hüyük, covered 32 acres and was inhabited by 6000 people (Mellaart 1975). Located in southern Turkey not far from Çayönü, Çatal Hüyük contains a dazzling array of art objects, woven cloth, murals, and wall sculpture (Fig. 10.9). The people of Çatal Hüyük grew barley and three varieties of wheat. They kept sheep, cattle, goats, and dogs. The people lived in adjoining rectangular one-story, sun-dried brick houses opening on courtyards. There were no doors; entrance was gained through holes in the flat roofs. Initially there was considerable hunting of wild species, especially of aurochs (wild cattle). By about 8000 B.P., the wild cattle were replaced by smaller domesticated cattle (Todd 1978).

FIGURE *10.7*

EXCAVATION AT JARMO
An early Neolithic village in northeast Iraq, where barley, wheat, goats, sheep, and dogs were all in use by 8500 B.P.

FIGURE *10.8*

TOWER OF JERICHO
Rubble of habitation rose above top of the tower, built in 10,000 B.P. Tower is hollow and contains a central stairway.

FIGURE *10.9*

ÇATAL HÜYÜK
(A) View of rooms and walls; **(B)** bull's head wall sculpture; **(C)** painting of bull. Cattle played a prominent role in the economy and in religious and artistic life.

(A)

(B)

(C)

The prosperity of towns like Jericho and Çatal Hüyük may have been based on control of trade. It seems likely that Çatal Hüyük was a center for the domestication, breeding, and export of cattle, for which it received a variety of imported artifacts and raw materials, including 35 different kinds of minerals (Sherratt 1982:14). Çatal Hüyük's wall paintings (Fig. 10.9c)—the earliest known paintings on a house wall—depict a large bull, 6 feet long, other animals being hunted, dancing men, and vultures attacking human bodies. Colors include red, pink, mauve, black, and yellow.

The degree of specialization both within and between Neolithic settlements appears to have been much greater than archaeologists once believed was possible so long ago. At Beidha, in Jordan, there were workshops divided into separate areas devoted to bone tool making, arrowhead manufacture, and bead making. This suggests that different individuals concentrated on producing a surplus of artifacts that were exchanged with other households or with other communities. At Çayönü a group of houses specialized in making beads. At Umm Dabaghiyah in northern Iraq, the whole settlement seems to have been devoted to tanning animal skins, while the inhabitants of Yarim Tepe and Tell-es-Sawwan specialized in the mass production of pottery (Voigt 1990).

Specialization and mass production implies that there was trade between widely separated communities. One of the principal objects in early Neolithic trade was obsidian, a volcanic glass that was the principal raw material for the manufacture of blade tools. Pottery has also been traced over long distances at a slightly later date.

For reasons to be discussed in Chapter 18, long-distance warfare and trade frequently form part of a widespread complex of institutions that also includes distinctions of rank and the redistribution of valuables involving high-ranking warrior-chiefs. Evidence for distinctions of rank and redistribution in the early Neolithic has been found at Bouqras in Syria, where a storage structure adjoins a house that was larger than others, and at Çatal Hüyük and Tell-es-Sawwan, Iraq, where burial chambers differ in size or in the amount of grave goods interred with different individuals (Voigt 1990). As we shall see in Chapter 18, there is a strong resemblance between these newly reinterpreted Neolithic societies and the "chiefdoms" that are known to precede the appearance of the state in other parts of the world.

THE URBAN REVOLUTION

Once cattle were domesticated, a whole series of additional technological and environmental innovations and interactions followed. Harnessed to plows, which were invented by 5500 B.P. or earlier, cattle made it possible to extend farming to new zones and to intensify farming in old zones. As population increased, village settlements spread out over the fertile but rainless southern portion of the Tigris-Euphrates Valley. Confined at first to the margins of the natural watercourses, dense clusters of villages and towns came increasingly to rely on artificial irrigation to water their fields of wheat and barley. By 6350 B.P., monumental mud-brick temples called ziggurats (Fig. 10.10) reared up from the center of major towns. Finally, at Uruk (Fig. 10.11) between 5800 and 5200 B.P., there appeared the first cities, whose streets, houses, temples, palaces, and fortifications covered hundreds of acres and were surrounded by thousands of acres of irrigated fields.

The list of technological achievements now included spinning and weaving (which were earlier Neolithic inventions), as well as ceramics, smelting and casting of bronze, baked brick, arched masonry, the potter's wheel, sailing ships, wheeled vehicles, writing, calendrical time-reckoning, weights and measures, and the beginnings of mathematics. Here for the first time, human communities became divided

FIGURE *10.10*

ZIGGURAT OF UR
Characteristic of Mesopotamian monumental architecture; located in southern Iraq. Construction began in 5000 B.P. The Tower of Babylon was a ziggurat, estimated to have been 300 feet high.

FIGURE *10.11*

URUK—THE FIRST CITY?
Excavations are in progress. Structures date to 5800 B.P.

into rulers and ruled, rich and poor, literate and illiterate, townspeople and peasants, artists, warriors, priests, and kings.

THE RISE OF THE STATE

Briefly considered, the process of state formation in Mesopotamia (the area between the Tigris and Euphrates rivers) seems to have involved a number of factors that recurred in other regions where cities and states developed after the appearance of chiefdoms (see p. 309). Mesopotamian soils were extremely fertile, but because of the deficiency of rainfall, irrigation was needed to expand and intensify agricultural production. As population density increased, competition within and between local settlements for access to and control over the water needed for irrigation also increased. Mesopotamia was also deficient in stone, ores, wood, and many other raw materials. These deficits were made up by extensive trade with other regions, and the need to organize and control trading activities blended with the need to organize and control the waterworks and to regulate the distribution of grain harvests. The task of organizing production, distribution, trade, and defense was gradually taken over by a political-religious-military hierarchy, which formed the nucleus of the first state bureaucracies.

These elite groups provided services in the form of record-keeping, calendrical calculations, provision of emergency rations, support of artisan specialists, and religious ceremonials. They eventually developed into exploitative classes whose despotic power rested on a monopoly of police-military force. By imposing various forms of taxation, the first dynastic ruling classes succeeded in diverting a substantial portion of the farming population's harvests into state enterprises, thereby preventing the peasant food producers from slackening their productive efforts or from enjoying the leisure or security that are intuitively but erroneously associated with the adoption of advanced technologies (see p. 253). More and more intensive irrigation provided additional means of consolidating and intensifying the ruling elite's power over people and nature. Life expectancy (for commoners) was lower than it was during the Neolithic, which in turn, as mentioned above, was lower than it was during the Upper Paleolithic (Cohen 1987). We shall take a closer look at the processes responsible for the rise of class-stratified state societies and some alternative theories of state formation in Chapter 18 (cf. Adams 1966, 1972; Areshian 1990; Braidwood and Willey 1962; Carneiro 1970; Childe 1952; Cohen and Service 1978; Hass 1982; Johnson and Earle 1987; Mitchell 1973; Webster 1990; Wenke 1990; Wittfogel 1957; Young et al. 1983).

THE NEOLITHIC SPREAD

Through a combination of diffusion and independent invention (see Chapter 7), Neolithic modes of production spread from the Middle East into Europe. In some instances, as in Greece, animals and plants that were present locally seem to have been domesticated almost at the same time as in the Middle East. In other instances, as in central and northern Europe, plants and animals spread by diffusion, sometimes as a result of actual movements of Neolithic peoples and sometimes merely by contact between Mesolithic and Neolithic cultures. By 8000 B.P., farming communities in Thessaly (northern Greece) were raising wheat, barley, cattle, pigs, and sheep. Cattle and pigs were previously available, but sheep and goats were imports.

Regional variants of the Neolithic appeared along the middle Danube river by 7300 B.P., Holland by 6800 B.P., England by 6300 B.P., southeast and central Europe and southern France by 6000 B.P., and Scandinavia by 5500 B.P. (Fagan 1989:297 ff.).

The spread of the Neolithic from Eastern to Northern Europe involved the rapid migration of farming communities and their livestock. Although the initial interaction between the farmers and the indigenous mesolithic hunters and gatherers may have been peaceful, the discovery of elaborately fortified 6000-year-old villages in Belgium suggests that the Mesolithic peoples soon did try to gain access to the farmers' stored grains and livestock (Keeley and Ca-

hen 1989). Between 5000 and 4000 B.P., population increased and settlements became more permanent, leading to considerable deforestation. These changes set the stage for more intensive forms of mixed farming involving ox-drawn plows and the keeping of animals for wool and milk. In southern Europe agriculture was intensified through the use of tree crops such as olives, the planting of vineyards, and irrigation. After 6000 B.P., monumental constructions called megaliths begin to appear over wide areas of Europe. By 4000 B.P., the size of megalithic constructions suggests that the people who built them must have been organized into chiefdoms whose leaders were capable of coordinating the quarrying, transportation, and erection of huge stones by levers and ropes. Stonehenge (Fig. 10.12), the most famous megalithic monument, was begun about 4800 B.P. and completed about 3100 B.P. (Daniel 1980:87). Another well-known megalithic construction is Carnac, in Brittany, France (Fig. 10.13).

It was in southern Europe, however, that the transition to state forms of political economy took place first. Copper and bronze metallurgy spread rapidly (during the so-called Copper and Bronze Ages), and trade in these metals increased as the tools and weapons made from them became an important factor in the development of bellicose chiefdoms. Incipient European city-states appeared in Crete and southern Greece at about 4000 B.P. (At this time, the Great Pyramids of Egypt had already been standing for 1300 years.) Not until the "barbarian" chiefdoms of northern Europe found themselves in a death struggle with the Roman Empire, however, did states form in northern Europe. We shall return to a discussion of this point in Chapter 18 (Champion et al. 1984; Daniel 1980; Dennell 1983; Renfrew 1973; Whittle 1985; Webster 1990).

THE EAST ASIAN NEOLITHIC

The Neolithic reached Afghanistan and Pakistan by about 5000 B.P. and the Indus Valley in India by 4500 B.P. (Vishnu-Mittre 1975). The role of independent invention and diffusion in this spread remains obscure. But there is mounting evidence that China and Southeast Asia were the centers of one or more Neolithic food-producing "revolutions" based on a complex of plant and animal domesticates different from those of the Middle East and largely or entirely independent of Middle Eastern influences.

Recent radiometric datings have pushed the beginnings of sedentary village life in China back before 6000 B.P. One of the earliest sites is at Pan-p'o (Fig. 10.14) in the semiarid highlands bordering the

FIGURE *10.12*

STONEHENGE
Neolithic ceremonial center of Salisbury Plain, Wiltshire, England. Megalithic structure implies the existence of large, coordinated labor supply, a considerable degree of centralized planning, and an agricultural mode of production.

upper reaches of the Yellow River. Here, there were village settlements employing a form of field agriculture involving domesticated millet and domesticated pigs and dogs. The well-patterned graveyards, painted pottery, and prototypes of the characters used

FIGURE *10.13*

CARNAC
There are 2934 megaliths at this neolithic center in Brittany, France.

in the Chinese form of writing indicate that still earlier Neolithic sites remain to be discovered. Indeed, in Kiangsi province some sites with pottery, polished stone implements, and evidence of agriculture have been radiocarbon-dated to over 10,000 B.P. (Chang 1984b:572).

The major varieties of millet found at Pan-p'o have wild ancestors that grew both in China and Europe. While domesticated millet has been found at Argissa, Greece, with a date of 7500 B.P., there may not have been any connection between the onsets of European and Chinese millet farming. It is also possible that the domestication of the pig in the West had nothing to do with its domestication in the Far East. The pig was a relatively marginal component in the agricultural complex of the Middle East, but in China the pig has always been more important than cattle, sheep, or goats as a source of animal food.

Millet apparently provided the energy basis for the first Chinese cities, which were located along the central floodplains of the great bend of the Yellow River, dating to about 4000 B.P. Eventually, in the period 3300 to 3000 B.P., wheat and barley reached China and were incorporated into the agricultural system. But by that time two additional important crops, rice and soybeans—unknown in Europe and the Middle East—were also being used. The Middle Eastern plow and oxen arrived even later—2200 B.P.

All this indicates that the early North China system of field agriculture and stock raising had developed independently of the Middle Eastern Neolithic (Chang 1973, 1983, 1984a, 1984b, 1986; Harlan 1978;

FIGURE *10.14*

PAN P'O
The Chinese have built a museum to protect the site of their earliest village.

Ho 1975). Moreover, there is increasing evidence that there was a second independent transition to the Neolithic in southern China. People who lived in the Lower Yangtze and Huai river plains were using domesticated rice, gourds, water buffalo, dogs, and pigs by 7000 B.P. (Chang 1986). These people were already expert potters and skilled farmers who must have been preceded by still earlier Neolithic populations.

The earliest archaeologically known dynastic state in China is Shang, dated to about 3700 B.P. (Chinese tradition refers to a still earlier civilization called Hsia). Shang was centered in the lower Yellow River (Huang He) Basin in Henan (Honan) province and was based on irrigated rice, wheat, and millet farming. The Shang possessed wheeled vehicles, horses, cattle, a system of writing, and an advanced knowledge of bronze metallurgy (Fig. 10.15). Their capital near Anyang was enclosed by a huge earthen wall and had residential districts inhabited by craft specialists and royal tombs displaying evidence of human sacrifice. Life in this dynasty, despite the basically independent origins of Chinese civilization, was remarkably similar to early dynastic life in the Middle East (Chang 1980; Keightly 1983; Young 1982).

THE NEOLITHIC IN SOUTHEAST ASIA

The Neolithic in North China and the Middle East was based on the domestication of grains whose wild an-

cestors were adapted to semiarid temperate upland habitats. The possibility must be kept open that the transition to settled Neolithic village life was also independently achieved in humid semitropical habitats of Southeast Asia through the domestication of root crops, especially yams and taro (Harlan 1978; D. Harris 1976; Hutterer 1976; Meacham 1977). Remains of such crops decompose more readily than grains and are difficult to recover archaeologically. But there is no doubt that a concern with broad-spectrum plant gathering extends about as far back in time in Southeast Asia as in the Middle East. At Spirit Cave in northwest Thailand, 11,500-year-old remains of almonds, candle nuts, betel nuts, peppers, gourds, phaseolus beans, peas, cucumbers, and other edible plants have been identified. Some of these plants may have been domesticated, but expert opinion is divided (Gorman 1969, 1978; Solheim 1970; Vishnu-Mittre 1975; Yen 1977).

The role of rice in the development of a distinctive Southeast Asian Neolithic is still poorly understood. Species of wild rice occurred in almost all the riverine deltas and estuaries of southern and southeastern Asia. It seemed likely, therefore, that the domesticated varieties of rice arose from the selective harvesting of wild varieties. Until recently this supposition was challenged by the fact that the two earliest sites with domesticated rice were in northeast Thailand, far from rivers and estuaries. However, still earlier evidence for rice cultivation in Southeast Asia

FIGURE *10.15*

SHANG BRONZE METALLURGY
(A) Rhinoceros container, Eastern Zhou, 475-221 B.C.; **(B)** bird-shaped wine vessel,
Shang dynasty, thirteenth to eleventh century B.C.

(A)

(B)

has been found at Kok Phanom Di close to the sea in southern Thailand, with a date of about 7000 B.P. (Higham 1988). Since this site is quite large, one can assume that, as in the case of the earliest Chinese Neolithic villages, there are still earlier Neolithic sites yet to be discovered in southeast Asia. Just as in the Middle East, environmental changes at the end of the Pleistocene may have contributed to the transition from hunting and gathering to agriculture in southern China and Southeast Asia. The melting of the polar ice caps and continental glaciers raised the level of the sea. This resulted in the inundation of half of the land area of Southeast Asia, confronting the region's broad-spectrum hunters and gatherers with a food crisis similar to the hypothesized food crisis of the Natufians (Cohen 1977).

THE AFRICAN NEOLITHIC

The transition to agriculture began in the Nile Valley somewhat later than in Mesopotamia. As in the Levant, the first domesticates in Egypt—barley and cattle—have been found in the arid lands that border the river valley. They date to about 8000 B.P. The climate grew dryer after that date, obliging the incipient farmers to concentrate in the Valley itself at about 7000 B.P. The earliest Neolithic settlements date to between 6300 and 5300 B.P. (Hassan 1981, but see Krzyzaniak 1981; Wendorf and Schild 1981). In all likelihood still earlier settlements were buried under sediments borne by the Nile during one of its frequent rampages. Domesticated cattle, sheep, goat, wheat, barley, and date palms may have been present by 7800 B.P. As in Mesopotamia, the intensification of agriculture through flood control and irrigation accompanied the rise of the earliest Egyptian states at about 5500 B.P. (Price 1992). In the upper Nile Valley and in regions to the west, cattle herding without agriculture appeared surprisingly early, at about 8000 B.P. These pastoralists spread westward across the Sahara at a time when there was sufficient rainfall to support herds of elephants, wild oxen, and buffaloes, and lakes full of fish, mollusks, and hippopotami. By 6000 B.P., herds consisting of over 100 domesticated cattle were depicted in rock paintings found in southern Algeria (Fig. 10.16). After about 4500 B.P., full desert conditions set in and the Sahara became largely uninhabited.

Agriculture was late in developing outside the Nile Valley. There is no direct archaeological evidence for the use of domesticated plants in West Africa until after 4000 B.P. (Phillipson 1985; Sowunmi 1985). The earliest domesticated plants found in the dry areas of West Africa are millet and sorghum. After

FIGURE *10.16*

ROCK PAINTINGS SHOWING DOMESTICATED CATTLE; SOUTHERN ALGERIA
The area is too arid today even for camels.

3500 B.P. there was considerable local experimentation with several other domesticates, such as groundnuts, cowpeas, yams, and oil palms (McIntosh and McIntosh 1983). Recent evidence indicates that chiefdoms arose in West Africa independent of outside influences. "These were followed by highly intensified societies with power and wealth concentrated in the hands of god-like kings. By A.D. 1000, large areas of West Africa were organized into empires...replete with armies, cities, craft industries and organized trade" (ibid.:245).

SUMMARY

The domestication of plants and animals and the development of the first Old World agricultural modes of production took place during the archaeological period known as the Neolithic. In addition to the transition to the Neolithic in the Middle East, similar transitions probably occurred independently in China and Southeast Asia. The evidence is not yet complete enough to rule out the possibility that these or other regions crossed the threshold to the Neolithic as early as the Middle East.

The transition in the Middle East and Egypt was preceded by a broad-spectrum hunting-and-gathering economy that resembled the western European Mesolithic, except for the increasing importance of wild grains. These wild grains made sedentary village life possible some 2000 years before plants and animals were domesticated. Climatic changes leading to prolonged dry summers selected for annual grasses. Dependence on these grasses, the wild progenitors of wheat and barley, encouraged sedentism. Cultivation of the wild grains and husbandry of the wild animals attracted to the grains gradually emerged from the commitment to sedentary settlements. The tough-rachis varieties of barley and wheat received favored treatment and gradually replaced the brittle varieties, while sheep and goats were fed on stubble and selected for useful behavioral and physical traits.

The completion of the transition to farming and stock raising brought greater production per capita of proteins and carbohydrates, thus relieving temporarily the food crisis associated with the period of broad-spectrum hunting and gathering. However, one of the consequences of sedentism is that it reduces the need for women to carry infants and children over long distances, thereby permitting women to shorten the interval between births. This led to additional population growth, which raised the density of human settlements and forced the spread of Middle Eastern Neolithic populations into regions deficient in rainfall as well as other natural resources. These deficits were overcome by irrigation agriculture and by trade. With population density on the rise, competition for access to irrigable lands and trade goods increased the incidence of warfare and led to the emergence of chiefdoms. With further population growth, the need to organize irrigation works, control trade, and coordinate military and police activities gave rise to incipient bureaucracies and the division of society into rulers and ruled.

The Neolithic complex spread from southeastern to northwestern Europe during the period 8000 to 6000 B.P. Both independent invention and diffusion were responsible for the spread. Diffusion involved both the migration of Neolithic villagers and the passing of Neolithic traits from one group to another.

In China, the earliest domesticates were millets and pigs. This suggests an independent origin for the transition from the East Asian Upper Paleolithic to the Neolithic and the subsequent development of cities and states in North China. A second independent center of domestication involving rice and water buffalo may have existed in the Lower Yangtse near the South China coast.

In Southeast Asia, there may also have been an independent Neolithic transition involving root crops, legumes, and rice. Broad-spectrum hunting and gathering involving many wild progenitors of domesticated crops was being practiced in northwest Thailand possibly as early as 11,500 B.P. However, the earliest archaeological evidence for domesticated rice in a Neolithic setting has been found in southern Thailand close to the sea. It seems likely that the transition to the Neolithic in South China and Southeast Asia as in the Middle East was a response to a food crisis brought on by an environmental change—in this case, the inundation of half the region caused by the the rise in sea level that accompanied the end of the last Ice Age.

In Africa, the earliest evidence for the transition to farming and stockraising comes from the arid lands bordering the Nile Valley, shortly after similar occurrences in the Levant. The evidence for the first full-scale Neolithic villages in the Valley itself is probably buried under the soil deposited by the Nile floods. The full Neolithic was slow to spread to other parts of Africa. Instead, there was a rapid spread of pastoral modes of production into regions to the south and west of the Nile Valley. Cattle herders were present between 8000 and 6000 B.P. in the middle of what became the Sahara Desert. There is no direct evidence for agriculture in West Africa prior to 4000 B.P. Thereafter, local grains, root crops, and tree crops were domesticated and provided the basis for the emergence of chiefdoms and states.

Chapter 11

The Second Earth

This chapter outlines the main archaeological evidence for the evolution of cultures in North and South America. We begin with the question of who really discovered America and how and when they did it. Then we trace the development of New World village life, the domestication of plants and animals, and the appearance of cities and states in the Mississippi Valley, Mexico, and the Andes, the greatest of which was the Inca empire. We shall see that there are significant differences in the way cultures evolved in the New and Old Worlds. But the similarities, such as the invention of writing, calendars, metallurgy, and hundreds of other traits, are astonishing. Most important, we shall see that in the main, cultural evolution in the New World did not depend on what happened in the Old and that the comparison of the two hemispheres therefore provides us with a veritable "second Earth"—a wonderful testing ground for theories that seek to explain evolutionary processes.

WHEN WAS AMERICA DISCOVERED?

The ancestors of the American "Indians" reached *Homo sapiens* status in the Old World. No apes, australopithecines, or *erectus* fossils have been found in the Americas, nor does anyone expect them to be found. The dental formula of the New World monkeys indicates that they diverged from the Old World hominoid line tens of millions of years ago (see p. 30). Nonetheless, controversy surrounds the question of how long humans have been living in the New World.

The most likely origin of the first Americans was Asia. This seems probable, first of all, because native Americans of today phenotypically resemble Asians. Like East Asians, they have straight black hair, epicanthic folds, very little body hair, distinctive "shovel-shaped" incisors, and other distinctive dental features (Greenberg, Turner, and Zegura 1986). It seems unlikely that these features could be derived from either European or African ancestors. Asia is also indicated as their place of origin if we consider how the first Americans could have gotten to the New World.

The migrations probably began during the late Pleistocene-Upper Paleolithic. This was long before the invention of ocean-going craft, so it is extremely improbable that the first Americans crossed either the Atlantic or the Pacific oceans. On the other hand, they could easily have entered the New World across the Bering Strait, where one can, on a clear day, see Alaska from Siberia. Actually, at the maximum of the last continental glaciation, there was no water at all between Siberia and Alaska because an amount of moisture sufficient to reduce the level of the oceans by about 300 feet was held on land in the form of ice. Since the Bering Strait is less than 300 feet deep, the earliest migrants had neither to swim nor hop from one iceberg to another in order to enter the Western Hemisphere. The first unsung "discoverers of America" could easily have walked across on dry land. When the sea was down only 150 feet, they could have walked across on a "bridge" between 100 to 200 miles wide. At its maximum, Beringia, as this now submerged land is called, was 1000 miles wide.

Even without the land bridge, the Bering Strait would not have been much of a barrier. From time to time the straits still freeze over solid enough for people and animals to walk across on the ice.

At various intervals during the period 60,000 to 18,000 B.P., Beringia was above water. Once the migrants had walked across the land bridge, however, they would have come up against walls of ice blocking the path to the east and south. Yet even at these times, a narrow ice-free corridor offering a route south existed behind the mountain ranges (Fig. 11.1). By 12,000 B.P., with the retreat of the glaciers, conditions were optimum for crossing on dry land and for southward movements of both hunters and prey. But at no time during the past 60,000 years was human migration into North America made impossible by environmental obstacles (Fladmark 1986).

THE NEW WORLD PALEOLITHIC

Considerable uncertainty surrounds the question of the kinds of equipment and modes of production the first Americans brought with them on their journey (or journeys) from Asia. Disagreement exists concerning the identity and antiquity of the earliest artifacts that have been found on both sides of Beringia.

FIGURE *11.1*

NORTH AMERICA DURING
THE LAST GLACIATION
Beringia was over 1000 miles wide.

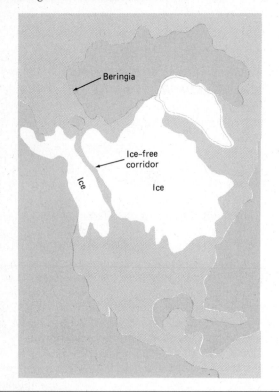

FIGURE *11.2*

CORES FROM WHICH BLADES HAVE BEEN
STRUCK
(A) Mongolian People's Republic, (B) Alaska and
Northwest Territories.

(A)

(B)

Claims have been made by archaeologists that core
and flake tools found in Siberia represent Middle
or even Lower Paleolithic tool kits. These controversial findings are matched by crude stone and bone
tools purportedly dating to 80,000 or more years ago
at sites in the Yukon, California, and Mexico (Irving
1985:542–549). Many Soviet and U.S. archaeologists,
however, regard these "tools" as geofacts (made by
natural geological forces); others deny that the dating is correct (Yi and Clark 1983).

In addition to crude core tools, sophisticated
Levallois-like microcore and blade tools have also
been found in Siberia. Some Russian archaeologists
date these tools to 35,000 B.P., while others place them
close to the end of the last glaciation, at 20,000 to
15,000 B.P. Levallois-like microcores and blades have
also been found in both Mongolia and Alaska (Fig.
11.2).

No one disputes that humans were hunting
mastodons, horse, bison, and other large game at
or after 11,500 B.P. on the great plains of North

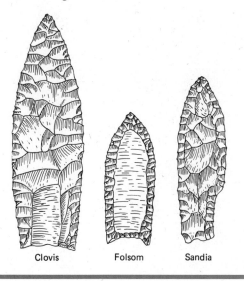

FIGURE *11.3*

NEW WORLD PALEOLITHIC PROJECTILE POINTS
Clovis is about 4 inches long. Fluting and channel-
ing of Clovis and Folsom enhanced hafting to spear
shafts. "Tang" on Sandia point suggests alternative
mode of hafting.

Clovis   Folsom   Sandia

FIGURE *11.4*

HYPOTHETICAL HAFTING OF CLOVIS POINTS
This modern replica of a Clovis point hafted to a
spear as shown proved to be capable of fatally pene-
trating the hide of modern-day elephants during an
attempt to relieve overcrowding in Hwange National
Park, Zimbabwe.

America. The glitch in this scenario is that the favored
weapons employed by the Paleo-Indian hunters were
distinctive fluted stone points known as Clovis points
(Fig. 11.3 and Fig. 11.4), which bear no resemblance
to the grooved caribou antlers inset with micro-
blades that were the favored projectile points of the
hunters on the Siberian side of Beringia. It should be
noted, however, that a small number of finely crafted
stone points have been found with the Siberian antler
points, and a few antler points have been found alongside North American Clovis points. It is possible,
therefore, that as the Siberian hunters traveled south
out of the zone inhabited by caribou, they rapidly
adapted their technology in favor of Clovis points
(Guthrie 1983:277).

Efforts to prove that the Americas were penetrated by Asian hunter-gatherers before 35,000 B.P.
have not been substantiated. Evidence of early bone
artifacts found at old Crow Flats in Alaska (Morlan
1978; see Fig. 11.5) can only be regarded as inconclusive (cf. Irving 1985). Several claims for great antiquity, such as for 70,000-year-old flints and 50,000-
year-old skeletal remains from southern California,
have been discredited as a result of refinements in
carbon 14 dating methods (Bada 1985). The oldest
reliably dated human skeleton is from Montana, with
an age of 10,600 years B.P. (Taylor et al. 1985:138).

The most impressive evidence for a human
presence in the Americas prior to 11,500 B.P. has been
found at the Meadowcroft Rock Shelter near Pittsburgh, Pennsylvania (Fig. 11.6). Here, six radiocarbon dates firmly associated with cultural artifacts indicate that humans were present between 14,000 to
14,500 B.P. Claims that the samples tested were contaminated by particles of coal have been vigorously
refuted (Adovasio, Donahue, and Stuckenrath 1990;
1992). For the moment at least, there is no compelling
reason to doubt the Meadowcroft dates.

There are many other sites for which an antiquity greater than 11,500 years has been claimed. At
Taima-taima, Venezuela, a quartzite projectile point

FIGURE *11.5*

NEW WORLD ARCHAEOLOGICAL SITES

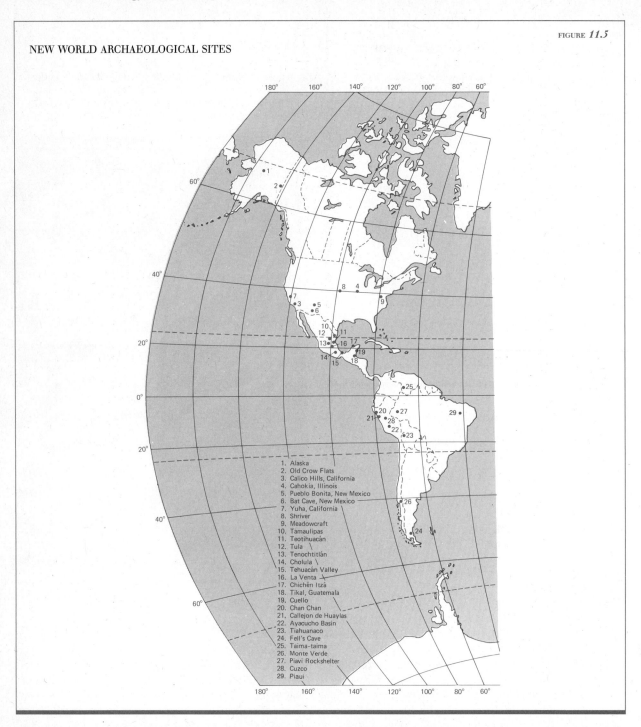

1. Alaska
2. Old Crow Flats
3. Calico Hills, California
4. Cahokia, Illinois
5. Pueblo Bonita, New Mexico
6. Bat Cave, New Mexico
7. Yuha, California
8. Shriver
9. Meadowcraft
10. Tamaulipas
11. Teotihuacán
12. Tula
13. Tenochtitlán
14. Cholula
15. Tehuacán Valley
16. La Venta
17. Chichén Itzá
18. Tikal, Guatemala
19. Cuello
20. Chan Chan
21. Callejon de Huaylas
22. Ayacucho Basin
23. Tiahuanaco
24. Fell's Cave
25. Taima-taima
26. Monte Verde
27. Piaví Rockshelter
28. Cuzco
29. Piaui

was recovered inside the pelvic bone of a juvenile mastodon that is said to have been killed at least 13,000 and possibly more than 14,000 years ago. Other tools found at Taima-taima include a knife, scrapers, and rough stones used as choppers or pounders (Bryan 1987; Bryan et al. 1978). Monte Verde, a well-preserved settlement—almost a village—has been found in the forests of southern Chile and dated radiometrically to between 13,000 and 12,500 B.P. (Dillehay 1984). Claims for still earlier manifestations of human activity continue to be made. Tools and hearths in highland Peru are said to be between 20,000 to 15,000 years old (MacNeish 1978). Continuing excavation at Monte Verde has led to the discovery of

hammerstones and crude flaked tools 2 meters below the settlement, with dates of 33,000 B.P. (Dillehay and Collins 1988; but see Lynch 1990 for a negative opinion). Another site with a very early date is a rock shelter in Piaui, northeastern Brazil, where hearths and crude quartz tools appear to have been made 31,500 years ago (Guidon and Delibrias 1986; but see Lynch 1990). Since similar claims for the great antiquity of the peopling of the Americas have often been discredited, it is best to withhold judgment until these latest finds have been scrutinized by skeptical experts (see Box 11.1). Of course, if these early dates are verified for South America, the time of the crossing of the Bering Strait will have to be pushed back even earlier to allow for the southward migration of the first arrivals.

PALEO-INDIAN TRADITIONS

Although some Clovis points have been found in the eastern United States, Clovis hunters mainly preyed on the big game that roamed the high plains of Oklahoma, Colorado, New Mexico, and southern Arizona. While they would occasionally take smaller animals, they appear to have specialized in the hunting of mammoths. Clovis cultures ceased to flourish after 11,000 B.P., perhaps as a result of the dimished supply of their favorite prey species as a result of overkill.

The Clovis mammoth hunters were succeeded by other big game hunters equipped with several different varieties of finely worked but smaller points.

FIGURE *11.7*

FOLSOM POINT EMBEDDED IN RIBS
OF AN EXTINCT BISON
An historic discovery, altering the conception
of the antiquity of the American Indian presence
in the New World.

One variety called Folsom was used to kill now-extinct species of bison on the Central Plains from Montana to Texas (Fig. 11.7).

Separate but possibly related regional big-game hunting traditions of comparable age have also been found in the Valley of Mexico, in the Andes from Argentina to Chile, and in Venezuela. One of the most interesting assemblages is that of Fell's Cave near the Strait of Magellan. Here, stone tools, including fluted points, were found with the remains of extinct ground sloths and American horses, revealing that the ancestors of the American "Indians" had already spread out from Alaska to the tip of South America 11,000 years ago.

From the tools and the associated remains of slaughtered animals, it seems clear that the Paleo-Indian mode of production was the specialized hunting of large game, closely paralleling the terminal Upper Paleolithic in the Old World. "Only occasional, and often questionable, pieces of grinding equipment occur with these sites; actual plant remains are almost never found; and fish, shellfish, and fishing equipment are scarce or absent" (Cohen 1977:130).

ARCHAIC TRADITIONS

Only after 10,000 to 9,000 B.P. do sites with numerous milling stones suggest a significant concentration on seeds and other plant foods. As in the European Mesolithic, many forest, coastal, and riverine habitats now became populated, and increased attention was paid to fish, shellfish, and other aquatic resources. Although not all archaeologists agree, there is much to be said in favor of viewing North and South American modes of production from 10,000 B.P. on as native American versions of the broad-spectrum hunting-and-gathering systems that characterized European and Middle Eastern Mesolithic and incipient agricultural times in China and Southeast Asia (Lynch 1983:125).

As in the Old World, a basic cause of the shift to broad-spectrum food production may have been the extinction of many species of large animals that had flourished during Pleistocene times. In the New World these extinctions involved considerably more species than in the Old World. Thirty-one genera died out, including mastodons, mammoths, big-horn bison, camels, tapirs, horses, pigs, several kinds of goats and sheep, musk ox, varieties of antelopes, oxen, yaks, giant beavers, giant armadillos, giant ground sloths, giant rodents, saber-toothed tigers, and species of bears, wolves, and coyotes. As we have seen (p. 161), the relative importance of human overkill and of natural factors associated with the retreat of the last glaciation in these extinctions is the subject of considerable debate (Martin 1984). The people who were equipped with Clovis and Folsom weaponry were undoubtedly extremely efficient hunters. Indeed, one could reasonably interpret their advanced stoneworking skills as both a response to and a cause of the increasing scarcity of big game brought about initially by environmental changes. It seems likely that they heightened the stress experienced by the Pleistocene fauna. At the very least, one can say that they did not prevent the extinction of many valuable species and, as we shall see, this was to have dire consequences in later times.

THE NEW WORLD "NEOLITHIC"

The discovery and explanation of the origins of New World agriculture constitutes an outstanding scientific achievement. Many details remain unknown, but there is one basic fact: The domestication of plants and animals by Americans did not depend on the diffusion of farming or stock raising from any of the Old World centers of domestication. This means that diffusion is also unlikely to account for the other remarkable similarities between the Old and the New World, such as the development of sedentary village life, cities, states, empires, monumental architecture, writing, and metallurgy. The independent origins of New World agriculture lend weight to the view that there is a tendency for human cultures to evolve with probabilities considerably higher in some directions than in others. It further suggests that explanations for both differences and similarities in prehistory and history must be sought in the study of processes that tend to produce similar sociocultural consequences under similar conditions.

There had always been strong circumstantial evidence for postulating an independent native American development of agriculture. The inventory of New World crops consists almost entirely of domesticates whose wild prototypes grew only in North and South America. At the time of contact with the first Europeans, this inventory was as diverse and nutritionally satisfactory as that of the combined Middle Eastern and Southeast Asian plant complex (Box 11.2) A variety of agricultural systems ranging from slash-and-burn (see p. 96) to irrigation were used to raise these crops (Matheny and Gurr 1983). Some of the effects of the European encounter with New World agriculture are discussed in Box 11.3.

Until the 1960s many anthropologists were unwilling to concede that the native Americans had been able to domesticate these important plants without help from the Old World. This view persisted because of the apparent chronological priority of plant domestication in the Middle East, China, and Southeast Asia. Thus, it was suggested that a boatload of post-Neolithic migrants from across the Atlantic or

---

BOX *11.2*

NEW WORLD PLANT DOMESTICATES

Grains such as maize, amaranth, and quinoa.
Legumes like black beans, string beans, and lima beans.
Other important vegetables like squash, melons, and tomatoes.
Root crops like manioc, potatoes, and sweet potatoes.
Peanuts.
Condiments such as chili peppers, cacao, and vanilla.
Narcotics and stimulants such as coca and tobacco.
Useful fiber-yielding plants such as henequen, maguey, cotton, and sisal. (Cotton was independently domesticated in the Old World and the New World.)

BOX *11.3*

HOW NEW WORLD CROPS CHANGED THE COURSE OF HISTORY

The joining of native American domesticates with those of the Old World after 1492 had important consequences all over the world (Weatherford 1988). For example, sugar combined with cacao yielded chocolate. Sugar cane, which had been domesticated first in Southeast Asia, was then planted in Brazil and the Caribbean islands to make sugar for chocolate and to sweeten coffee and tea. It was the attempt to find cheap labor for the sugar plantations that led to the development of the slave trade and to the transport of tens of millions of African blacks to the New World (Mintz 1985). Maize was taken to China, where it provided extra calories for a population explosion in the sixteenth century. Manioc became a staple food crop of tropical populations throughout Africa. The potato was taken to Ireland, where it sustained a population explosion followed by crop failures, a famine, and a mass exodus to America. Tobacco was taken to Europe, then sent back to Virginia, where it provided the impetus for the development of plantation slavery in the United States.
SOURCE: Wolf 1982.

Pacific had washed up in Mexico, Brazil, or Peru, bringing with them the idea of plant domestication. Some archaeologists even argued that the voyagers must have brought maize with them (Godfrey and Cole 1979; cf. Schneider 1977).

Diffusionist theories of New World agricultural origins have been decisively refuted by the identification of ancestral forms of maize and the sequence of modifications that these forms underwent in the arid highlands of Mexico (Macneish 1978). Maize was domesticated from the grass called *teosinte,* which still grows wild in highland Mexico. Teosinte has been crossed with modern maize, and the results are extremely similar to the earliest corn cobs (Fig. 11.8). Like modern popcorn, teosinte can be popped by being heated; it can also be cracked, ground, or softened up for eating by soaking in water (Beadle 1981; Flannery 1973). Domestication of maize may have taken place as early as 7000 B.P. (Benz and Iltis 1990). Between 5000 and 3000 B.P. the primitive varieties of maize were improved by selection and cross-breeding, lost their ability to seed themselves, and acquired the more numerous rows of kernels found in modern varieties. These modern varieties of maize, like many other domesticated plants (see p. 155), depend on humans for continued propagation, since

their kernels will not come off without being pulled off (even after boiling, there is still "corn on the cob"!).

Thus, native Americans on their own not only domesticated maize, but they also subjected it to a great amount of selection and morphological change and adapted it to as wide a geographical range as any major food plant (Flannery 1973). In this process Euro-Asian or African "ideas" about other crops could not have played a significant role (Pickersgill and Heiser 1975).

DEVELOPMENTS IN LOWLAND MESOAMERICA

At some point between 5000 and 4000 B.P. maize was brought down from its native highland habitat and adopted by lowland tropical forest peoples in Vera Cruz and Guatemala. Unlike the highland people, the lowlanders had already settled down to a form of village life based on the exploitation of a broad spectrum of riverine and coastal flora and fauna by 4900 B.P., and perhaps as early as 7300 B.P., prior to the arrival of maize. Along the Gulf Coast of Vera Cruz and Tabasco, these early maritime, sedentary, and pre-agricultural villages formed the basis for the development of the first chiefdoms and incipient states of North America. (As discussed below, lowland pre-agricultural maritime villages along the coast of Peru were the basis for the growth of the earliest chiefdoms and incipient states in South America.) Being sedentary, these villages were "preadapted" to agriculture. They easily added the exploitation of crops such as squash and peppers to their broad-spectrum mode of production. With the diffusion of maize from the highlands, they began to concentrate on agriculture, their population grew more dense, and their political organization more complex.

The earliest chiefdoms and incipient states in Vera Cruz and Tabasco were created by a people known as the Olmec. Olmec sites are marked by carved stone monuments and earthen platforms. At the best-known Olmec site, La Venta, there is an earth-fill pyramid shaped like a volcano with gullied slopes. It is 105 feet in height and 420 feet in diameter (Fig. 11.9). Construction was underway by 3000 B.P. As at several other Olmec localities, 9-foot-high round-faced stone heads (Fig 11.10), stone altars, tombs, and stelae (monolithic carved columns) also occur. Basalt rocks for these constructions had to be transported from quarries over 50 miles away (Coe 1968; Sharer and Grove 1989). The Olmec sites appear to be associated with natural levees produced by meandering rivers on

FIGURE *11.8*

EARLY MAIZE
Modern corn cob on the right.

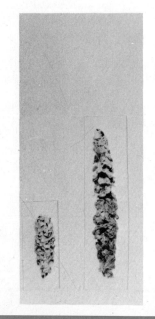

FIGURE *11.9*

LA VENTA PYRAMID
Landing strip and oil refinery were not built by the Olmec.

FIGURE *11.10*

OLMEC HEAD, SAN LORENZO, MEXICO
The massiveness and abundance of Olmec monuments suggest the existence of state-level institutions.

which intensive forms of maize agriculture were practiced. This was combined with fishing, shellfishing, turtling, and some terrestrial hunting. The levee land was the best-suited for growing maize, but its area was limited. It appears likely that the building of the monuments and the development of the chiefdoms were related to the control of these productive lands by a ruling elite to meet the needs of an increasing population. Olmec rulers also probably controlled extensive trade networks. The Olmec subsistence base, however, was not ample enough to support the kinds of dense populations associated with fully developed states; by 2400 B.P., the Olmec heartland was no longer a flourishing part of Mesoamerica (Sharer and Grove 1989).

THE RISE AND FALL OF THE MAYA

Developments somewhat similar to those characteristic of the Olmec took place in the Yucatan peninsula among the Maya but about 500 years later. It is not known exactly when village farmers first moved into the Maya area. Between 3000 and 2300 B.P., more complex chiefdoms with temple platforms began to appear as at Nakbe in lowland Guatemala (Hansen 1991) and the Cuello site (Fig 11.11) in Belize (Andrews and Hammond 1990). At this time the area was heavily forested and agriculture was based on the slash-and-burn method (see p. 213). During the next several hundred years, the forest cover was greatly reduced, possibly as the result of repeated burning at shorter and shorter intervals. By about 2000 B.P. the Maya were practicing a more intensive form of maize agriculture—the raised-field method—involving the drainage and mounding of low-lying swampy areas, plus the cultivation of fruit trees mulched with household wastes. By A.D. 300 this new mode of production had given rise to a rapid increase in population, the development of ruling elites, the construction of hundreds of ceremonial centers, and the emergence of numerous chiefdoms followed by states (Hammond and Miksicek 1981; Turner and Harrison 1981).

Although the precise nature of the Maya states remains a matter of controversy, it is clear that the Maya achieved a high degree of political centralization and urbanization, as well as great sophistication

FIGURE *11.11*

CUELLO SITE
An early Maya ceremonial structure.

in learning, architecture, and sculpture. The Maya maintained far-flung trade networks into the highlands, and it is likely that their development was stimulated by trade with the more powerful states that arose in the highlands at roughly the same time as the Maya states began to flourish.

There was a time when archaeologists portrayed the Maya states as peace-loving theocracies dedicated to astronomical lore and mathematics. More recently however, it has become clear that warfare played a crucial role in the evolution of the Maya's civilization. Celebrated in murals and written in stone on commemorative stelae, the Maya elites reveled in battle, and in the capture, humiliation, and ritual sacrifice of their prisoners of war (Fig. 11.12).

Between A.D. 300 and 900, Maya ceremonial centers were at their maximum. Elaborately ornamented, multiroom buildings were constructed on top of supporting platforms and grouped symmetrically around plazas. Ball courts for ceremonial games, stelae and altars incised with calendrical and historical hieroglyphics, and massive statuary were also part of the plaza complexes. Towering over all were great, truncated pyramids (Fig. 11.13) with stone facing and flights of steps leading to temples at their crests (Coe 1977; Henderson 1981). In addition there were scores of medium-sized but still imposing centers, plus several hundred smaller ones. Tens of thousands of hamlets housed a total population of several million people.

Most of the ceremonial centers are located within 1 kilometer of seasonally wet, swampy lands on high grounds near permanent sources of water, and the largest ones are remarkably evenly spaced at about a day's walk (26 kilometers) apart (Harrison 1982).

FIGURE *11.12*

BONAMPAK MURALS, CHIAPAS, MEXICO
Maya rulers, warriors, and captives.

FIGURE *11.13*

MAYA TEMPLE, PALENQUE, CHIAPAS, MEXICO
This structure covers a tomb that was reached by an interior stairway.

It has been estimated that at Tikal (Fig. 11.14), the largest of the Maya centers, there was a population of 45,000 people in an area of 123 square kilometers (Haviland 1970). Most of these people lived on small farms an hour's walk from the main civic centers. The number of rulers, priests, bureaucrats, and artisans who resided at the centers was much smaller. Based on analogies with modern-day descendants of the Maya, some of the civic and ceremonial centers may have been relatively empty most of the year, filling up with people only on ceremonial occasions, when they also probably served as market centers for the dispersed populations (Vogt 1969).

Although the lowland Maya area is heavily forested, it is subject to an annual dry season. Moreover, because the bedrock forming the Yucatan Peninsula is limestone, almost all surface water sinks into the ground and disappears during the dry spell. All the lowland Maya civic centers are, therefore, located in the vicinity of natural waterholes or are associated with artificial reservoirs (Matheny 1982). Thus, it is possible that the Maya rulers controlled access to sources of drinking water, which were critical for survival during years of drought (Scarborough and Gallopin 1991).

The need for locating settlements adjacent to artificial or natural sources of drinking water and areas suitable for raised-field cultivation restricted the mobility of Maya farmers and obliged them to utilize more concentrated and labor-intensive methods of production. Permanent or short-fallow fields were created by mounding wet soil dug from networks of drainage canals, which were probably also exploited for their aquatic flora and fauna (Dickson 1981; Hammond 1978; Harrison and Turner 1978; Matheny 1976; Scarborough 1983; Turner 1974, 1990:191).

The relative lack of potential for expansion of the lowland rainfall agricultural modes of production is probably related to the collapse of Maya

FIGURE *11.14*

TIKAL
The largest of the Maya centers.

civilization after A.D. 800. Not only were the major ceremonial centers abandoned, but the Peten region, which contained the largest sites, became virtually uninhabited and to this day has yet to recover its former glory. (There was a postclassic form of Maya state at Chichen Itza and Mayapan in northern Yucatan, but these are generally recognized as being colonial dominions of a highland-based empire known as the Toltecs—see p. 187.)

A theory that accounts for most of the relevant facts is that as the population increased, the rulers attempted to intensify agricultural production by stepping up tax and labor demands on the commoner farmers. The farmers responded by intensifying their agricultural efforts, progressively shortening fallow periods until infestations of weeds and grass, soil erosion, and soil exhaustion made it impossible to sustain high yields. At Tikal there is evidence that the hillsides lost their topsoil, which collected in basins, drainage-ways, and alluvial flats, creating conditions adverse for raised-field agriculture. Alteration in patterns of rainfall caused by excessive forest clearing may also be implicated. Additional crises may have been produced by the silting up of drinking water reservoirs (Adams, Brown, and Culbert 1981; Cook 1972; Cowgill 1964; Culbert 1988; Flannery 1982; Hamblin and Pitcher 1980; Lentz 1991; Marcus 1983; Olson 1978; Sanders 1972; Turner 1990; Webster 1985; Willey 1977; Willey and Shimkin 1971). These ecological changes would have increased competition between the various centers and increased popular discontent. Wars, peasant revolts, and the disruption of trade routes would then have brought the final ruination of the classical Maya world.

This explanation of the Maya collapse is related to another puzzling feature of Maya civilization. Despite the constant warfare between Maya centers, no center appears to have been able to gain control of any other center, so that Maya political systems stopped well short of becoming empires, in contrast to highland Mexican developments. The explanation for this may lie in the less productive and more open resources of the Maya habitat. Thus, the Maya elites may not have been able to push their peasant producers hard enough to sustain massive wars of conquest. Indeed, it has been suggested that the collapse of Mayan civilization was brought about by one last unsuccessful attempt on the part of the major centers to establish control over each other (Friedel 1986:108; Sanders and Webster 1978:295).

DEVELOPMENTS IN HIGHLAND MEXICO

The Mexican highlands were occupied at 11,000 B.P. by hunting-and-gathering peoples whose way of life was probably similar to that of Clovis and Folsom big-game hunters. By 9000 B.P., most of the Pleistocene megafauna had become extinct and broad-spectrum modes of production began to predominate. Grinding stones for processing wild seeds appear, along with remains of animals such as deer, rabbits, gophers, rats, turtles, and birds, plus a wide variety of plants, including the ancestors of domesticated squash, avocados, maize, and beans.

Between 9000 and 7000 B.P., seed and fruit pit planting gradually emerged as part of a careful scheduling of movements from one ecological zone to another as the seasons changed. Between 7000 and 5000 B.P., small amounts of domesticated maize, beans, squash, amaranth, chili peppers, and avocados were being planted. Seminomadism continued. Population density increased.

Between 5000 and 3500 B.P., reliance upon plant domesticates increased and the first small villages appeared. Thereafter, maize became the predominant staple, population increased, and agricultural production was intensified through the use of various systems of irrigation (Farnsworth et al. 1985; Flannery 1973; Macneish 1978). Chiefdoms, cities, and states began to appear in the Mexican highlands starting about 3000 B.P. As in the Middle East, the appearance of these chiefdoms and states is closely associated with increased trade, grain production, warfare, and population increase (see p. 312).

THE DEVELOPMENT OF STATES IN HIGHLAND MESOAMERICA

In the Mexican highlands a fundamentally different potential for growth existed than in the lowlands. Here, the developmental sequence of cultures culminated in native American political systems of genuinely imperial dimensions.

The first agriculturalists entered the southern and southwestern parts of the basin of Mexico in the central Mexican highlands at the comparatively late date of 3400 to 3200 B.P., apparently only after adjacent regions more favorable to agriculture had already been utilized for several centuries. They practiced a form of slash-and-burn (see p. 213) agriculture on the hillsides, at middle altitudes above the basin floor where they could obtain a balance between maximum amounts of rainfall and minimum amounts of crop-limiting frosts. Between 2900 and 2200 B.P., the less favored central part of the basin filled with settlements. With continuing population growth, settlements gradually moved on to the still less favorable northern fringe where rainfall was lowest (500–600 millimeters annually). It was here, in the valley of Teotihuacán some 25 miles northeast of modern-day Mexico City, that the first great imperial city of the New World was founded.

Because of the scarcity and irregularity of rainfall in this part of the valley, the villages near Teotihuacán made increasing use of the set of large permanent springs. By using this water for irrigation, they overcame the limitations imposed by frost and rainfall. But to make use of it, they had to invest much more labor to build and maintain the dams, canals, and drainage works. Between 2200 B.P. and A.D. 100, there were three large villages and about 25 hamlets in the Teotihuacán Valley, most of which still probably depended on rainfall agriculture. Toward the end of this period these dispersed settlements were replaced by a single focus of population around the springs. Teotihuacán thereafter grew at an explosive rate and by A.D. 500 it covered an area of 20 square kilometers (7.7 square miles) and had a population of over 100,000 people. Control over strategic trade routes also undoubtedly played a role in this expansion (Charlton 1978; Kurtz 1987). There was formal planning of the city's residential and civic precincts, as indicated by the grid pattern of the avenues and alleys, markets in various districts, and exclusive quarters allotted to craft specialists (Millon 1970; cf. Nichols 1982; Santley 1987). In the middle of Teotihuacán there is a complex of public buildings and monuments that, by comparison, dwarf even those of Tikal and render the Olmec sites puny. The central monument is the so-called Pyramid of the Sun (Fig. 11.15), still among the world's largest artificial structures. Measuring 67.0 meters (214 feet) in height and over 213.3 meters (700 feet) on a side, this edifice contains 840,000 cubic meters of fill. A sec-

ond, smaller pyramid contains 210,000 cubic meters, which still makes it about twice as big as the Olmec pyramid at La Venta (Fig. 11.16). The civic buildings of Tikal cover only a small fraction of the area of Teotihuacán's ceremonial complex (Millon 1973; Sanders and Price 1968). At the height of its power, Teotihuacán dominated trade between the highlands and the lowlands, and its influence extended to such contemporary highland centers as Monte Alban and Kaminaljuyu, 700 miles to the south.

At about A.D. 750 Teotihuacán was burned and abandoned. Once again there is reason to suspect that overintensive use and depletion of natural resources played a role, in combination with internal and external unrest and wars. Deforestation in the hillsides surrounding Teotihuacán may have changed the pattern of rainfall runoff and diminished the flow of irrigation water for the network of spring-fed canals (Nichols 1982; Sanders, Santley, and Parsons 1979).

The basin of Mexico, however, unlike the Maya homeland in the Peten, did not become depopulated. A succession of neighboring highland imperial centers took Teotihuacán's place. The first of these was located at Cholula, where there is an unexcavated pyramid even bigger than the Pyramid of the Sun. Then from A.D. 968 to 1156 the reigning empire was that of a people called the Toltecs, whose capital was at Tula (Fig. 11.17). Their influence extended as far as Chichen Itza in the Yucatán.

The final and biggest of the native American empires in North America was that of the Aztecs. Tenochtitlán, the Aztec capital, contained well over 100,000 inhabitants when Cortez's disbelieving eyes first glimpsed its gardens, causeways, markets, pyramids, and temples (Coe 1977; Fagan 1984; Vaillant 1966; Wolf 1959). Aztec agriculture involved an even more intensive mode of production than Teotihuacán. It was based on massive flood control, desalinization, and drainage works, which made it possible to raise crops year round on misnamed "floating gardens," or *chinampas* (Fig. 11.18). These were actually raised mounds built up out of the mud and debris of lakeside lands, interconnected for drainage and transportation by a complex network of canals (Carasco 1978).

The continued operation and maintenance of the entire Chinampa system was possible only through a massive system of dams, sluice gates, gates and canals that regulated the water level within narrow limits.... This critical water control system was so large, complex, and interconnected that it almost certainly was managed directly by the Aztec state. [Parsons 1976:253]

FIGURE *11.15*

TEOTIHUACÁN
(A) Pyramid of the Sun; (B) closeup of the Pyramid of the Sun. Compare this with Figure 11.14.

(A)

(B)

FIGURE *11.16*

TEOTIHUACÁN, TIKAL, and LA VENTA
Comparison of principal pyramids.
(Adapted from Saunders and Price 1968:138.)

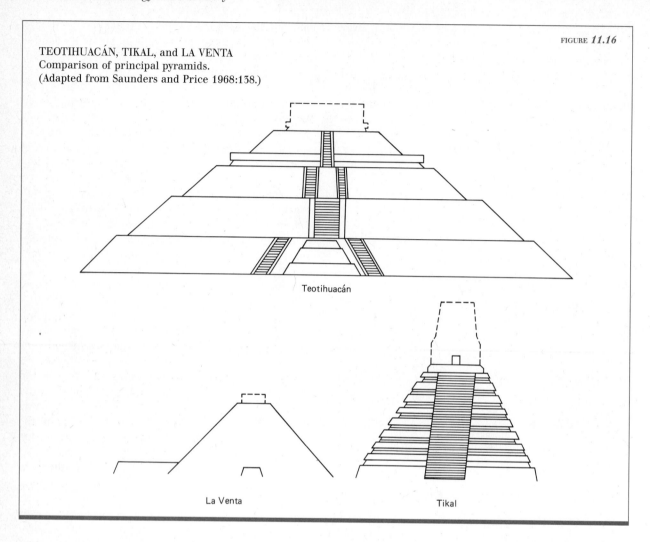

Teotihuacán

La Venta   Tikal

FIGURE *11.17*

RUINS OF TULA, HIDALGO, MEXICO
This was the capital city of the pre-Aztec people known as the Toltecs.
It was destroyed by invaders in A.D. 1160.

FIGURE *11.18*

CHINAMPAS OF XOCHIMILCO
The gardens obviously do not float, as can be seen from the trees growing on them.
Note corn growing in fields.

Despite the enormous productivity of *chinampas* agriculture, there is evidence that the swift growth of population and the continuing depletion of natural resources during Aztec times had created a politically and ecologically unbalanced situation (B. Williams 1989). The problem of procuring an adequate supply of animal fat and protein was especially acute, and the practice of cannibalism on a large scale under the auspices of the Aztec state religion may have been a compensation for the shortage of meat (see p. 396) (Harner 1977; Harris 1987). The Aztecs, however, met a fate different from all previous New World civilizations. In A.D. 1519 they were conquered by invaders who arrived from another world, equipped with steel weapons and mounted on horses, animals that had not been seen in Mexico for 10,000 years.

THE ROLE OF ANIMAL DOMESTICATES

A major difference between the period of early agriculture in the Middle East and highland Mesoamerica was that the Americans retained their seminomadic way of life for a long time after they had begun to domesticate their basic food crops. Sizable highland Mesoamerican villages that predate 5000 B.P. have not yet been found. The ecological basis for this difference seems clear. In the Middle East, sedentary villages could have their plants and their animal fat and protein too, since both plants and animals were domesticated at about the same time. However, because of the more extensive range of extinctions affecting the New World Pleistocene fauna, opportunities for animal domestication were limited by a lack of suitable wild species. The only domesticated New World animal at all comparable to sheep, goats, or cattle is the llama. But the ancestors of this small if useful beast did not survive in Mesoamerica. Although the ancient Peruvians domesticated the llama, there was no chance for the Mesoamericans to do so. The same is true of the guinea pig, which became an important source of meat in the Andes but never in Mexico.

The Mexicans ultimately did domesticate the turkey, the muscovy duck, the honeybee, and hairless dogs bred for meat, but these species were of no significance in the incipient agricultural phase and never did amount to much in later periods. One can only speculate why the Mesoamericans did not domesticate species such as tapirs, peccaries, and antelopes (Hunn 1982). Suffice it to say they did not, nor has anyone else.

In the Middle East, sedentary village life was based on the domestication of both plants and animals. Sedentism increased the productivity of the plant domesticates, which increased the productivity of animal domesticates, which increased the productivity of sedentary village life, and so on. In highland Mexico, however, the need to retain animal food in the diet worked against the abandonment of hunting. Hence, compared with the Middle East, the development of village sedentism in highland Mesoamerica did not precede the first phases of cultivation but followed it after a lapse of several thousand years. This difference in animal domestication probably accounts for the lag in the development of New World empires as compared with those of Europe and Asia, and explains why it was the Old World that conquered the New and not vice versa.

DEVELOPMENTS NORTH OF MEXICO

Just as the Neolithic spread from the earliest centers of domestication into Europe, India, and parts of Africa, so too, in the New World, the basic Mesoamerican farming complex gradually affected the life-styles of people living in remote parts of North America. And again, as in the Old World, as the farming complex spread, it encountered diverse environments and was adapted and readapted by hundreds of different local cultures.

The first people north of Mexico to practice intensive maize agriculture probably lived in the lower Mississippi Valley. Maize, however, was not the earliest plant domesticate in what is now the United States. In the Ohio River Valley, for example, broad-spectrum foragers were experimenting with gourds, squash, sunflower seeds, pigweed, and other native plants at 2800 B.P. (Watson 1977), before they began to plant maize.

The two main phases of cultural traditions in the Ohio and Mississippi valleys—known as Adena-Hopewell, and Mississippian—were marked by the construction of thousands of earth mounds, some containing burials and others serving as platforms for temples or residences. Dense, maize-eating populations, appeared during the Mississippian phase, giving rise to urban nucleations and elaborate temple-priest-idol cults that exhibited strong Mesoamerican

influences. The greatest expression of this trend toward monumentality, urbanism, and state formation occurred at Cahokia, near East St. Louis, between A.D. 900 and 1100 (Emerson and Lewis 1986). Here, fortified with energy and nutrients derived from the Mexican plant food "trinity"—maize, squash, and beans—the Mississippians built a mound that was 100 feet high and covered 15 acres. Numerous additional large and small mounds, supporting houses and temples, surrounded the main structure. It is clear that the Mississippians had reached the incipient stages of state formation, although there are theoretical reasons to suppose that their potential for growth was very restricted. These reasons will be discussed in Chapter 18 (Stoltman 1978).

The effects of the introduction of maize agriculture were less spectacular in the eastern woodlands, where ancestors of peoples like the Iroquois and Cherokee continued to live in small villages and to rely on hunting and gathering as a major source of their food supply.

West of the Mississippi, the principal region of intensive agriculture and advanced chiefdoms was the southwest of what is now the United States. Maize was introduced there from Mexico at about 2500 B.P. (Berry 1985; but see Simmons 1986). Its introduction was followed rather rapidly by the appearance of three major cultural traditions: Mogollon, Hohokam, and Anasazi.

Mogollon peoples lived in permanent villages consisting of small clusters of pit houses in the valleys of the Mogollon Mountain Range in New Mexico starting at about 2300 B.P., but continued to rely heavily on hunting and gathering.

Hohokam soon appeared in the valleys of the Salt and Gila rivers in southern Arizona. The Hohokam peoples built extensive irrigation systems fed by canals 10 miles long, and constructed pyramidal mounds and Mexican-style ball courts (Cordell 1984; Jennings 1974).

Anasazi peoples at first lived in rock shelters; later, in round houses set deeply into the earth; and still later in dwellings built above ground that had large numbers of contiguous rooms. With the beginning of intensive maize agriculture at about A.D. 400, the earlier pit houses were placed entirely underground and evolved into ceremonial structures known as kivas (Fig. 11.19), while adobe dwellings were constructed above ground. By A.D. 900, large clusters of multistoried adobe houses had become the famed pueblos of Arizona, New Mexico, Utah, and Colorado, in which lived the ancestors of modern day Hopi and Zuni. At Pueblo Bonito (Fig. 11.20), long before the coming of the first Europeans, people lived

FIGURE *11.19*

ANASAZI KIVAS
Ritual centers of prehistoric pueblo Indians.

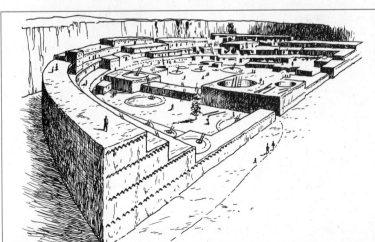

FIGURE *11.20*

PUEBLO BONITO
Artist's rendering of probable appearance, about A.D. 1050. (Adapted from Jennings 1974:306.) Compare with Çatal Hüyük, Figure 10.9.

in apartment houses five stories tall, containing 800 rooms. Pueblo houses were typically entered by ladders through small holes in the roof (note the resemblance to Catal Hüyük [p. 162].) Their architecture served as a defense against nonagricultural marauders who attacked the pueblos to get at the rich harvests of grain stored within the houses. This defensive posture culminated with the construction of pueblo villages on the sides of cliffs, sheltered under huge overhangs and accessible from the top of the cliff only via secret foot holes carved in the rock (Fig. 11.21).

Development of pueblo political organization was limited by the unreliability of rainfall and the intermittent nature of the streams and rivers in the southwest (Cordell 1984). It is believed that the Anasazi were forced to abandon many of their pueblos by a long drought that gripped the southwest during the thirteenth century (Jennings 1974).

AGRICULTURE REJECTED

Elsewhere in North America there were vast regions into which agriculture never penetrated. The peoples of the entire Pacific Coast from California to Alaska, for example, never abandoned their reliance on broad-spectrum hunting, wild-seed gathering, fishing, and shellfish collecting. One can only conclude that intensive farming offered no conspicuous advantages over the existing subsistence practices in these regions. This is especially true of the northwest Pacific Coast, where, by exploiting annual upstream migrations of fish, people were able to live in large plankhouses in permanent villages (see Chapter 14).

THE DEVELOPMENT OF STATES IN SOUTH AMERICA

The Andean region of South America was the center of an independently developed complex of domesticated animals and plants. This complex provided the basis for the rise of additional native American chiefdoms and states and for the largest of the New World empires.

The phase of big-game hunting in South America was followed, as in the rest of the hemisphere, by expansion of broad-spectrum modes of produc-

FIGURE *11.21*

MESA VERDE CLIFF DWELLINGS
The location was clearly intended to discourage attacks by enemies.

tion into variegated habitats, but especially into high-altitude and riverine and coastal regions. Although maize eventually became the principal crop of the Inca Empire and although the Andean region shared many other domesticates with Mesoamerica, several important New World plants and animals were specialties of the Andes. Chief among these are high-altitude tubers like the potato and high-altitude grains like quinoa. The discovery of two kinds of domesticated beans at Callejon de Huaylas, Peru, dating between 10,500 and 7,500 B.P., suggests that plant domestication was under way at least as early in the Andes as in Mesoamerica (Kaplan, Lynch, and Smith 1973). However, claims for maize earlier than 3000 B.P. remain to be substantiated (Bird 1990 vs. Bonavia and Grobman 1989). As for animals, it was only in the Andes that large herbivores—the llama and alpaca—were domesticated, possibly by 6000 B.P. (Browman 1976:469).

As in Mesoamerica, the earliest sedentary villages appear in coastal locales and precede the introduction of the first animal and plant food domesticates, which presumably originated elsewhere (Moseley 1983).

Along the coast of Peru the earliest chiefdoms were probably based on an infrastructure of maritime resources with virtually no contribution from domesticated food plants. The people who built the first large coastal platform mounds and masonry monuments at about 4000 B.P. may have been nourished primarily by catches of a small fish, the anchovetta, which schools in vast numbers off the coast of Peru. Supplementary marine resources also included large fish, mollusks, and water birds.

Viewed as a complex, these marine resources are concentrated along the shoreline and in the near-shore waters. They are extremely abundant ... and available throughout the year. The maritime interpretation holds that this resource complex underwrote the rise of large sedentary populations and supplied the foundation for the coastal civilization. [Ibid.:205]

Michael Mosely (1992) has shown that by using small-meshed nets, the preagricultural societies of coastal Peru could have harvested enough anchovetta to feed millions of people.

While complex chiefdoms may have arisen on the Peruvian coast without benefit of agriculture, it was only after an agricultural infrastructure was created in the coastal river valleys that states developed. After 1000 B.P., settlements inhabited by as many as 3000 to 4000 people grew up in the floodplains of the Peruvian coastal rivers. Before and after the introduction of irrigation and maize, the coastal popula-

tion underwent rapid growth. Canal systems extending across whole valleys were constructed, and the first small states made their appearance at about 2350 B.P. Thereafter, a series of wars and conquests led to the emergence of larger states, which united adjacent coastal valleys into single political systems. Chimor (or Chimu) was the largest of the coastal states. It controlled 12 major river valleys along the coastal plain, linking them together with canals that ran for 20 miles. Its walled capital, Chan Chan (Fig. 11.22), covered 4 square miles (10.3 square kilometers).

Meanwhile comparable series of developments unfolded in the high valleys of the Andes. One of the earliest of the highland states grew up around the shores of Lake Titicaca, again with intensive irrigation agriculture as its mode of production (Kolata 1986). This kingdom, known as Tiahuanaco, reached its apogee at about A.D. 900 (Fig. 11.23).

The greatest Andean state, the Inca, emerged when control over both the high valleys and coastal rivers was vested in one system. The Inca, whose capital, Cuzco, was in the highlands, conquered the Chimu and created an empire in A.D. 1438 that stretched for 2000 miles along the highland valleys and up and down the Pacific coast (Hyslop 1984; Isbell and Schreiber 1978; Jennings 1983). We discuss the organization of the Inca Empire in Chapter 18.

THE MEANING OF THE "SECOND EARTH"

Until the Spanish conquest, technology in the New World had been evolving along lines remarkably parallel to the Middle Eastern sequence. Nonetheless, native American technological change was definitely proceeding at a slower rate. Much of the "lag" can be attributed to the differential natural endowments of the Middle Eastern and nuclear American regions. As discussed above, the extinction of potential animal domesticates among the Pleistocene megafauna made native America vulnerable to military conquest by Europeans mounted on horseback. The same megafauna extinction also deprived the Americas of potential animal domesticates that might have served to provide traction for plows and for wheeled vehicles. (The Inca actually did have a form of plow that people pushed and pulled.) The preconquest Mesoamericans understood the principle of the wheel at least to the extent of putting wheels on children's toys. No one knows whether these inventions and their applications would have been improved upon and extended if the Americas had been left alone.

Lack of steel tools also placed the native Americans at a great disadvantage during the European invasions. But the development of American

FIGURE *11.22*

CHAN CHAN
Capital of the Chimu Empire.

FIGURE *11.23*

TIAHUANACO
Ruins of the pre-Inca civilization near Lake Titicaca, Bolivia.

FIGURE *11.24*

PRE-COLUMBIAN METALLURGY
Silver alpaca, llama, and figurine.

metallurgical techniques had already passed beyond the hammering of sheet copper to the smelting and casting of copper, gold, silver, and several alloys (Fig. 11.24). Just before the Conquest, bronze mace heads and bronze knives were being made. Had the Americans not been conquered, would they have eventually discovered the superior qualities of iron and steel? It seems likely that they would have done so since they had already independently accomplished so many other technological achievements. For example, like their Old World counterparts, native American priests and rulers were concerned with the regulation of agricultural production. Under state and temple auspices, astronomical observations were carried out, which led to the development of calendars. Indeed, the Maya calendar was more accurate than its Egyptian counterpart. To keep calendrical records, as well as records of agricultural production, taxes, and other state affairs, hieroglyphic writing systems were invented by several Mesoamerican peoples (Fig. 11.25). Of special interest is the Maya system of vigesimal numeration (numbers with the base of 20), which incorporated the principle of the zero. The zero was absent in the Middle Eastern, Greek, and Roman number systems. Without the concept of a zero quantity to mark the absence of the base number or its exponents, it is extremely difficult to perform arithmetical operations involving large numbers. In this respect, at least, the native Americans appear to have been ahead of their Old World counterparts.

Given the fact that the ecosystems of the Old World and the Americas were initially quite different, precise parallels leading toward urban and imperial societies in the two hemispheres should not be expected. Again and again, however, the peoples of the two hemispheres independently achieved convergent solutions to similar problems when the underlying technological, environmental, and demographic conditions were approximately similar (Box 11.4).

After landing in Vera Cruz in 1519, Cortez marched to the Aztec capital, Tenochtitlan (today Mexico City), thereby ending the biological and cul-

FIGURE *11.25*

MAYA GLYPHS
Source: Bulletin of the Society for American Archaeology(6), 1988:2.

"was born"   "accession to the throne"   "seated in office"   "battle"   "bloodletting or autosacrifice"   "death"

"received the manikin scepter"   "marriage"   "was captured"   "interment"   "deceased"   "ritual apotheosis"

BOX *11.4*

OLD AND NEW WORLD SIMILARITIES

All items listed were present in both Old and New Worlds prior to 1492.

TECHNOLOGY

Textiles
  Purple dye
    Prepared from coastal mollusk
    Elite connotation of purple
  Scarlet dye (cochineal/kermes)
    Prepared from plant louse
  Resist dyeing
  Loom
  Cotton
  Clothing
    Turban
    "Nightcap"
    Pointed-toe shoes
    Long robes
    Sash, mantle, sandals, loin-cloth
Weapons, armor
  Kettle-shaped helmet
  Sling
  Thickened textile armor
Metallurgy
  Lost-wax casting
  Smelting, alloying, forging, hammering, gilding, etc.
Ceramics highly developed
Paper
  Lime sizing of writing surface

ARCHITECTURE

Colonnade, aqueduct, canal, cement-lined reservoir, highway
Corbelled arch
True arch
Walled city
Fired brick
Pyramids

MATHEMATICS

Place value notation
Zero concept
Zero sign

ASTROLOGY

Day names with associations like Eurasian constellations

WRITING

Hieroglyph system (ca. 750 signs; use of ideographs, rebus, affixes)

ASTRONOMY

Articulated lunar, solar, stellar calendar counts
360-day calendar plus 5 extra

tural isolation of the Earth's two worlds. Despite the fact that they had gone their separate ways for 20,000 years, Spain and Mexico were remarkably similar in many respects:

He passed through cities, towns, villages, markets and irrigated fields; he saw slavery, poverty, potentates, farmers, judges, churches, massive pyramids, roads, boats, pottery and textiles; in short he encountered a world whose almost every aspect he could understand in terms of his own experience as an urban Spaniard of the sixteenth century. [Wenke 1980:555–556]

The meaning of the "second earth," therefore, is that sociocultural systems are subject to determining forces that select innovations and shape the course of cultural evolution. This does not mean that all cultures must pass through the same stages of evolution, any more than the principle of natural selection means that all organisms must pass through the same stages of evolution. The causality that governs sociocultural systems produces both similar and dissimilar trajectories of evolutionary transformation. It does this because the conditions under which the interaction between culture and nature takes place are enormously diverse. But what the geological time perspective of archaeology teaches is that even when cultures diverge, their differences can usually be understood in terms of orderly, scientifically intelligible processes.

ASTRONOMY (CONTINUED)

BOX 11.4, *continued*

Cycle of 7 days
Day measured sunset to sunset
Observatories
Eclipse records

SOCIAL ORGANIZATION

Merchant class or caste
Organized trade, "caravans"
Corvée labor
Kingship complex
  King concept
  Divine mandate
  Throne
  Canopy
  Umbrella, parasol, sign of dignity, rank
  Sceptre
  Crown or diadem
  Tomb in elevated structure with or without
    temple atop
  Burial chamber with hidden entry
  "Royal tombs" (conspicuous display)
  Dedicatory sacrifice, subfoundation burial of
    children
  Gold necklace, sign of office
  Heraldic devices
  Litter
  Deference of bowing, downcast eyes

RELIGION AND RITUAL

Paradise concept
Underworld, "hell" concept

Dualism (strongly manifest)
Earth, air, fire, water as basic elements
Deluge motif
  Produced by rain
  A few persons saved in a vessel
  Bird sent forth to check drying
Pyramid tower built for safety against deluge
  Destroyed by being blown down by wind
Sacrifice complex
  Animals slain
  Offerings burned
  On altar in ceremonial area
  Communion sense in consumation of part of
    the sacrifice
  Accompanied by incense
    Incense mixed with cereal one type of
      offering
  Parched grain or meal as offering
  Blood offered as sacrifice
  Blood scattered over area and participants
Snake symbolism
  Signifying wisdom, knowledge
  Signifying healing
  Signifying fertility
Incense and incense furniture
  Strong emphasis on, accompanying most
    rituals
  For purification
  For offering to gods, sweet, attractive
  Symbolizing prayer
  As route for ascent of soul

SOURCE: Adapted from Riley et al. 1971

SUMMARY

Homo sapiens was the first hominid in the New World. The precise date of the "discovery of America" is not known. It definitely occurred by 11,000 B.P. and possibly before 25,000 B.P. The discoverers were undoubtedly groups of Siberian hunters who walked across the Bering Straits when it was frozen or when Beringia was above water. Some of the earliest American tools were produced from discoidal microcores that are found on both sides of Beringia. Claims that humans were present as long ago as 80,000 to 65,000 years continue to be made, but as yet none of these claims has withstood retesting and close scrutiny. Recently, dates from 31,000 to 14,000 B.P. have been claimed for sites in Chile and Brazil. The Meadowcroft Rock Shelter in Pennsylvania, dated to 14,500 B.P., is the best-authenticated case of human presence in the Americas during the Pleistocene.

No one doubts, however, that by about 11,000 B.P. distinctive Paleo-Indian tool traditions had appeared in North America. These were characterized by the finely crafted fluted points of the Clovis and Folsom assemblages, which are associated with large animal kills. Lack of stone grinders suggests that Clovis and Folsom tools were used by specialist big-game hunters for whom plant gathering was of secondary significance. There were similar Paleo-Indian adaptations in South America.

Traditions known as the Archaic appear about 10,000 B.P. They are characterized by broad-spectrum hunting, gathering, and fishing economies adapted to forested, riverine, and coastal habitats. This shift to broad-spectrum modes of production coincided, as in the Old World Mesolithic, with extinctions of megafauna. It is likely that both post-Pleistocene climate changes and intensive predation by efficient hunters contributed to the loss of numerous genera and species. As in the Old World, the broad-spectrum modes of production were practiced in diverse habitats, some of which contained plant and animal species suitable for domestication. New World domesticates covered a broad range of grains, root crops, legumes, and vegetables. Only a rather narrow range of animals was domesticated, however, as a result of the extent of the megafauna extinctions. The spread of New World crops, such as maize, cacao, manioc, and potatoes, has had an enormous impact on the history of the entire world since 1492. The fact that the major New World plant domesticates were unknown in the Old World strongly suggests an independent origin for New World agriculture. Recent discoveries of the gradual steps in the improvement of maize make this a virtual certainty.

Broad-spectrum modes of production preceded the development of intensive maize agriculture in the Mexican highlands. After the megafauna extinctions, small animals, birds, and a wide variety of plants including many of the later domesticates were the main source of subsistence for small hunter-gatherer bands. After 9000 B.P. grinding tools were prominent and meat began to lose its importance as a source of calories. In order to take advantage of the seasonal availability of wild plant foods in different ecozones, careful scheduling of band movements was necessary. The periodic return to fields of wild grains, squash, and other plants led to seed and fruit pit planting as a means of guaranteeing a regular harvest. Squash, amaranth, chili peppers, and avocados were the earliest domesticates. Maize became the dominant staple after 3500 B.P.

Sedentary villages were first built in Mesoamerica not by the incipient agriculturalists but by broad-spectrum hunter-gatherers living in lush coastal and riverine habitats. It seems likely that the delay in reaching sedentism in the highlands was related to the absence of animal domesticates and the reliance on wild species as a source of animal fats and proteins.

As in the Old World, agricultural modes of production laid the basis for the emergence of native American cities, states, and empires. Different regions, however, had different limits of growth. In the Mesoamerican lowlands, the Olmec and, to a greater degree, the Maya, supplemented slash-and-burn techniques with raised-field and other intensive forms of agriculture. Warfare, soil depletion, and other effects of intensification probably caused the collapse of the great Maya ceremonial centers and the depopulation of the Peten area. In the highlands, the use of spring-fed canal irrigation at Teotihuacán and *chinampas* near the Aztec capital of Tenochtitlan, together with extensive trade networks, encouraged the growth of larger and more powerful state systems.

North of Mexico, agriculture was practiced with local domesticates as part of broad-spectrum modes of production long before the introduction of maize. As in Mesoamerica, even the planting of maize did not necessarily lead to sedentary village life. However, as maize spread up the Mississippi Valley, it did eventually give rise to populous chiefdoms, the largest of which—Cahokia—was located on the Mississippi River. Large maize-growing chiefdoms also evolved in the Southwest. Multistoried pueblos and cliff-dwellings that only the residents knew how to climb down to probably served defensive functions. But agriculture was never adopted in many parts of North and South America. Regions rich in aquatic resources found little advantage in utilizing agricultural modes of production, and under especially favorable conditions, sedentary villages and chiefdoms evolved on the basis of foraging economies.

The largest New World states and empires developed in the Andes region of South America, including the adjacent Pacific Coast. Again, the distinctiveness of many Andean animal and plant domesticates points to a largely independent transition from large anchovetta-fishing villages along the coast to large agricultural communities in the irrigated river valleys. With a full range of grains, tubers, and vegetables, plus llamas and guinea pigs, the potential for growth of the Andean states was greater than that of Mesoamerica and was epitomized by the Inca Empire, which developed shortly before the Spanish conquest.

The independent origin of cities, states, and empires in the New World lends support to research strategies that are concerned with cultural evolutionary processes.

PART IV

INFRASTRUCTURE

Cultural evolution has given rise to a great variety of sociocultural systems. In Part III we viewed some of the principal varieties of these systems from the perspective of the archaeological record. Now in Part IV we will examine sociocultural systems primarily from the perspective of enthnography and cultural anthropology. To organize our survey, and to provide a coherent framework for explaining the causes of the differences and similarities we shall encounter, we focus first on the principal varieties of infrastructures. For it is in the interaction among the technological, economic, demographic, and ecological aspects of human social life that the basic sources of both diversity and similarity are to be found.

Production

In this chapter we will be considering primarily the aspects of infrastructure that make up a society's mode of production. (Modes of reproduction are taken up in the next chapter). The focus is on different modes of food production such as hunting and gathering, pastoralism, and preindustrial and industrial forms of agriculture. There are, of course, many kinds of production besides food production (e.g., handicrafts, mining, manufacturing, etc.), but food production systems were the main focus of productive effort throughout history and prehistory. Using energy as a measure of input and output, we will take a close look at how the environment sets limits on the amount of food that can be produced by a given technology. However, diminishing rates of return for productive effort can lead to new and more productive technologies. What, then, is the long-range result of technological innovation? The answer may surprise you.

EVOLUTION OF ENERGY PRODUCTION

Production is a consequence of the application of human labor and technology to natural resources. The most fundamental kind of production is that of energy. Human life and culture cannot exist unless societies appropriate and transform the energy available in the environment. The amount of energy produced and the method of production depend in turn on an interaction between the energy-producing technology that a culture possesses at a given time and the exploitable features of the habitat, such as sunlight, soils, forests, rainfall, or mineral deposits, to which the culture has access. Since neither technology nor the features of the environment can be changed rapidly or limitlessly, a culture's mode of energy production exerts a powerful constraining force on a people's entire way of life.

The interaction between technology and environment during the process of energy production is also basic for an understanding of human ecology (sometimes called cultural ecology): the study of how human populations and their activities are affected by the inorganic and organic features of their environments, and of how these inorganic and organic characteristics are in turn affected by human populations and their activities (Moran 1982).

During the time of the earliest hominids, all the energy utilized for the conduct of social life stemmed from food. Exactly when fire began to be used is not known. Partial control over fire may have been achieved by *erectus*, but full control may not have been achieved before the appearance of *sapiens* (see p. 79). Certainly by the time of cultural takeoff 40,000 years ago, fire was being used for cooking, warmth, protection against carnivores, driving game animals over cliffs or into ambushes, and possibly for favoring the growth of desired plant species. By 10,000 years ago, animals began to provide energy in the form of muscle power harnessed to plows, sleds, and wheeled vehicles. At about the same time, considerable wood and charcoal fuel was expended to produce pottery. With the rise of states, wind energy for sailing ships and wood energy for melting and casting metals began to be used. The energy in falling water was not tapped extensively until the medieval period in Europe. It was only in the last 200 or 300 years that the fossil fuels—coal, oil, and gas—began to dominate human ecosystems.

New sources of energy have followed each other in a logical progression, with the mastery of later forms dependent on the mastery of earlier ones. For example, in both the Old World and the New World, the sequence of inventions that led to metallurgy depended on the prior achievement of high-temperature wood-fire ovens and furnaces for baking ceramics, and the development of this technique depended on learning how to make and control wood fires in cooking. Low-temperature metallurgical experience with copper and tin almost of necessity had to precede the use of iron and steel. Mastery of iron and steel in turn had to precede the development of the mining machines that made the use of coal, oil, and gas possible. Finally, the use of these fossil fuels spawned the Industrial Revolution, from which the technology for today's nuclear energy derives (Fig. 12.1).

These technological advances have steadily increased the average amount of energy available per human being from Paleolithic times to the present.

FIGURE *12.1*

CHERNOBYL NUCLEAR EXPLOSION
Explosion of reactor near Kiev contaminated meat
and milk as far away as Sweden. Nuclear energy
may yet turn out to be the least efficient mode of
energy production ever created.

unsuited for agriculture: the lands close to the Arctic
Circle or deserts like the interior of Australia. Most
of these hunter-gatherers are organized into small
groups called bands, numbering from about 20 to 50
people. Bands consist of individual families who make
camp together for periods ranging from a few days to
several years before moving on to other campsites.
Band life is essentially migratory; shelters are temporary and possessions are few.

One must be careful, however, not to overgen-
eralize, since even in recent times, some hunter-
gatherers lived in lush environments and necessarily had sociocultural systems that were more
complex than those who inhabited less bountiful regions (Box 12.1). As we have previously indicated, the
hunter-gatherers who inhabited the coastal zones of
the Pacific Northwest, an environment rich in fish,
wild plants, and sea mammals, lived in permanent
villages. Moreover, as previously shown, during the
Mesolithic–Neolithic transitions (Ch. 10) in both the
Old and New Worlds, sedentism based on broad-
spectrum hunting and gathering preceded the appearance of agriculture and stock raising (pp. 157,
180). Certainly no claim can be made that recent
band-organized hunter-gatherers are representative
of all of the hunter-gatherers of the Upper Paleolithic
when there were no agriculturalists or pastoralists
anywhere, and every kind of habitat, dry or wet, cold
or hot, bountiful or sparse, was occupied by hunter-
gatherers.

Agriculture

Agricultural peoples tend to live in more permanent
settlements than hunter-gatherers. But again, not all
agricultural societies are alike. Many groups depend
on a mixture of hunting and gathering and farming or
stock raising. And, of course, there are many different
kinds of farming and stock raising, each with its own
ecological and cultural implications. *Rainfall agriculture*, for example, utilizes naturally occurring show-
ers as a source of moisture; *irrigation agriculture* depends on artificially constructed dams and ditches to
bring water to the fields. Several varieties of rainfall
agriculture and irrigation agriculture, each with its
own ecological and cultural implications, must also
be distinguished.

If rainfall agriculture is to be practiced, the
problem of replenishing the nutrients taken from the
soil by successive crops must be solved.

One of the most ancient methods for solving this
problem, still widely practiced to this day, is known as
slash-and-burn. A patch of forest is cut down and left
to dry. Then the slash is set on fire and later the ashes,
which contain a rich supply of nutrients, are spread

But the rise in energy does not necessarily mean that
humankind's ability to control nature has grown proportionately. Nor does increased use of energy per
capita necessarily bring a higher standard of living
or less work per capita. Also, a distinction must be
made between total amount of energy available and
the efficiency with which that energy is produced and
put to use.

MODES OF FOOD PRODUCTION

Hunting and Gathering

As we have seen (p. 136), hunting and gathering was
the only mode of food production during the Paleolithic. Most of the living hunter-gatherers who have
been studied by anthropologists or who are known
through historical documents occupy regions that are

BOX *12.1*

NOT ALL HUNTER-GATHERERS ARE ALIKE

There are two main varieties of hunter-gatherer societies: simple and complex. The !Kung are an example of the simple variety and the Kwakiutl (see p. 243) are an example of the complex variety. Complex hunter-gatherers share many features in common with sedentary agricultural peoples. The major differences between the two varieties of hunter-gatherers are:

SIMPLE	COMPLEX
Low-population density	High-population density
Not dependent on stored foods	Dependent on stored foods
Live in temporary camps most of the year	Live in villages most of the year
Weak distinctions of rank	Strong distinctions of rank

SOURCE: Keely 1988; Testart 1982; Woodburn 1982a and b.

over the area to be planted (Fig. 12.2). In regions of heavy rainfall, a slash-and-burn garden cannot be re-planted for more than two or three seasons before the nutrients in the ashes become depleted. A new patch of forest is then cleared and burned. Slash-and-burn thus requires large amounts of land in fallow awaiting the regrowth of vegetation suitable for burning.

A totally different solution to the problem of maintaining soil fertility is to raise animals as well as crops and to use their manure as fertilizer. This is known as *mixed farming*, and was once characteristic of the European and American small family farm.

With the advent of the industrial era, soil fertility came to depend primarily on chemical fertilizers, eliminating the need for raising animals and crops on the same farm (but intoducing a whole new set of problems associated with the toxicity for humans of the chemicals employed).

In irrigation agriculture, soil fertility is a lesser problem, since the irrigation water often contains silt and nutrients that are automatically deposited on the fields. But irrigation agriculture varies greatly in type and in scale (Hunt 1988; D. Price 1992). Some irrigation systems are confined to terraces on the walls of mountain valleys, as in the Philippines; others embrace the floodplains of great rivers such as the Nile and the Yellow River (Fig. 12.3). One form of irrigation involves *mounding:* Mud is scooped from shallow lakes and piled up to form ridges in which crops are planted, as in the chinampas of Mexico (see p. 187). In the Middle East, huge underground aqueducts called *qats* conduct water from mountain streams to distant desert farmlands (Fig. 12.4). Throughout much of In-

FIGURE *12.2*

PLANTING IN A SWIDDEN
(A SLASH-AND-BURN GARDEN)
This Amahuaca woman is using
a digging stick to plant corn
in a recently burned garden.

dia, irrigation water is pulled up by ox power from deep brick-lined wells. More recently, it is pumped up electrically through drilled pipes.

FIGURE *12.3*

IRRIGATION AGRICULTURE

There are many different types of this form of agriculture, each with a special influence on social life. **(A)** Massive Chinese water works. **(B)** Terraces cover much of Javanese croplands. **(C)** Ifuago, Philippines, where terraces are constructed on steep mountain slopes and are among the engineering wonders of the world.

(A)

(B)

(C)

FIGURE *12.4*

MIDDLE EASTERN QAT
Drawing water from an underground
aqueduct.

THE INFLUENCE OF THE ENVIRONMENT

Any item of technology must interact with factors present in a particular environment. Similar kinds of technologies in different environments may lead to different energy flows and different sociocultural systems. For example, the productivity of irrigation farming varies according to the size and dependability of the water supply, the availability of flat terrain, and the amount of minerals in the water. Similarly, the productivity of slash-and-burn agriculture varies in relation to how much forest is available for burning and how quickly the forest can regenerate itself. Thus, it is really not possible to speak of technology in the abstract; rather, we must always refer to the interaction between technology and the conditions characteristic of a specific natural environment.

In industrial societies, the influence of environment often appears to be subordinate to the influence exerted by technology. But it is incorrect to believe that industrial societies have liberated themselves from the influence of the environment or that our species now dominates or controls the environment. It is true that replicas of American suburbs have been built in the deserts of Saudi Arabia and the snowfields of Alaska and that they can also be constructed on the

moon. But the energy and material involved in such achievements derive from the interactions between technology and environment carried out in mines, factories, and on farms in various parts of the world, all of which are depleting irreplaceable reserves of oil, water, soil, forests, and metallic ores. Similarly, at all sites where modern technology extracts or processes natural resources or where any form of industrial construction or production takes place, the problem of disposing of industrial wastes, pollutants, and other biologically significant by-products arises (Fig. 12.5). Efforts are now under way in many industrial nations to reduce air and water pollution and to prevent the depletion and poisoning of the environment. The costs of these efforts testify to the continuing importance of the interaction between technology and environment. These costs will continue to mount, for this is only the very beginning of the industrial era. In the centuries to come, the inhabitants of specific regions may pay for industrialization in ways as yet uncalculated.

CARRYING CAPACITY AND THE LAW OF DIMINISHING RETURNS

Factors such as abundance of game, quality of soils, amounts of rainfall, and extent of forests available for energy production set an upper limit on the amount of energy that can be extracted from a given environment by means of a given technology of energy production. The upper limit of energy production in turn sets a constraint on the number of human beings who can live in that environment. This upper limit on population is called the environment's *carrying capacity*.

Carrying capacity is difficult to measure (Glassow 1978; Street 1969). Many puzzling features of food production result from adjustments to recurrent but infrequent ecological crises, such as droughts, floods, frosts, hurricanes, and epidemics of animal and plant diseases that require long periods of observation. Moreover, a basic principle of ecological analysis states that communities of organisms adjust to the minimum life-sustaining conditions in their habitats rather than to the average conditions. One formulation of this principle is known as *Liebig's law of the minimum*. This law states that growth is limited by the minimum availability of one necessary factor rather than by the abundance of all necessary factors. The short-time observer of human ecosystems is likely to see the average condition, not the extremes, and is likely to overlook the limiting factor.

Nonetheless, there is some evidence that food production among preindustrial peoples is often only

FIGURE *12.5*

(A)

THE HIDDEN COSTS
OF THE INDUSTRIAL MODE
OF PRODUCTION
(A) Abandoned hazardous waste dump. Pit is 5 feet
deep and covers 34,000 square feet. **(B)** Times
Beach, Missouri. Floodwaters spread soil con-
taminated with dioxin, prevoiusly concentrated
near highways, all over residential neighborhoods.
Cleanup crews collect samples for analysis.

(B)

about one-third of what it might be if full advantage
were taken of the environment's carrying capacity
by means of the existing technology (Sahlins 1972).
In order to understand why this "underproduction"
occurs, we must distinguish between the effect of exceeding carrying capacity and the effect of exceeding the *point of diminishing returns* (Fig. 12.6). When
carrying capacity is exceeded, production will begin
to decline as a result of damage to the environment.
The depletion of soils is an example of the consequence of exceeding carrying capacity. When the
point of diminishing returns is exceeded, however,
production may hold steady or may even continue to
increase, even though there is less produced per unit
of effort as a result of the growing scarcity or impov-
erishment of one or more environmental factors. The

present condition of the ocean fisheries of the world
is an example of exceeding the point of diminishing
returns. The rate of return per unit of effort has declined by almost half, yet the total catch of fish has
held steady (Brown 1978; Brown et al. 1991). A similar situation exists with respect to world agriculture and in the production of oil and gas (see Expansion, Intensification, and Technological Change,
page 210.)

Except when they are under some form of political pressure, people will attempt to keep output below the point of diminishing returns by limiting the
expansion of their production efforts; no one willingly
wants to work more for less. Thus, people may feel the
need to change their routines and to institute cultural
innovations long before carrying capacity is reached.

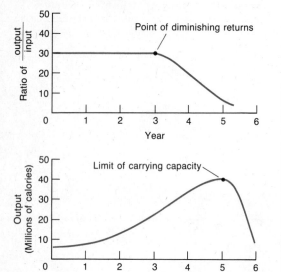

FIGURE *12.6*

PRODUCTION, CARRYING CAPACITY, AND DIMINISHING RETURNS
Point of diminishing returns is reached in year 3, but limit of carrying capacity is reached in year 5. Production is intensified and continues to increase until year 5, then crashes.

EXPANSION, INTENSIFICATION, AND TECHNOLOGICAL CHANGE

If technology is held constant, production can be increased by putting more people to work or by having them work longer or faster. If this increase in input occurs without enlarging the area in which food production is taking place, *intensification* has occurred. If, however, there is a proportionate increase in the area throughout which food production takes place so that the input per hectare remains the same, then the system is *expanding* or growing but not being intensified.

Since all modes of production (indeed, all modes of activity of any sort) depend on finite resources, expansion cannot continue forever. Sooner or later any further increase in production will have to depend on intensification. And intensification, more or less rapidly, must lead to the point of diminishing returns caused by the depletion of resources and a drop in efficiency. If the intensification is sustained, sooner or later production will collapse and fall to zero.

The all-important condition in this scenario, however, is that the technology is held constant.

Among humans, a common response to diminishing returns is to change the technology. Thus, as suggested in the work of Ester Boserup (1965), when hunters and gatherers deplete their environments and pass the point of diminishing returns, they are likely to begin to adopt an agricultural mode of production; when slash-and-burn peoples pass the point of diminishing returns, they may begin to cultivate permanent fields using animal fertilizer; and when rainfall agriculturalists using permanent fields deplete their soils, they may shift to irrigation agriculture. The shift from preindustrial to industrial and petrochemical forms of agriculture can also be seen as a response to depletion and declining yield per unit of effort (Harris 1977).

HUNTER-GATHERER ECOLOGY

The !Kung San (the ! designates a sound that is not used in English, called a click) are a hunter-gatherer people who live in the Kalahari Desert on both sides of the border between Botswana and Namibia in southern Africa (Lee 1979). They may be taken to represent the "simple," band-organized, mobile hunter-gatherers identified in Box 12.1. Like most hunter-gatherers who inhabit sparse environments, the !Kung San move about a great deal from one camp to another in search of water, game, and wild plant foods. They build only temporary shelters and have a minimum of possessions, yet they are well nourished and moderately long-lived. As occurs almost universally (see p. 252), the !Kung San men specialize in hunting while the !Kung San women specialize in gathering, although on occasion women will bring a small animal back to camp and men will help in carrying heavy loads of nuts (Fig. 12.7).

The number of people in a !Kung camp varies from 23 to 40, with an average camp size of 31 (20 adults and 11 children). During a four-week study period, Richard Lee calculated that 20 adults put in an average 2.4 days per week in hunting and gathering. On any particular day, the number of people hunting or gathering varied from zero to 16. About 71 percent of the calories consumed by a !Kung camp are provided by women's gathering activities. Women range widely throughout the countryside, walking about 2 to 12 miles a day round-trip for a total of about 1500 miles a year each. On an average trip, each woman brings back a load of from 15 to 33 pounds of nuts, berries, fruits, leafy greens, and roots, whose proportions vary from season to season.

Men hunt on the average only every three or four days and are successful only about 23 percent of the time they hunt. Hunting is therefore not an efficient source of energy for the !Kung. For every calo-

FIGURE *12.7*

!KUNG WOMEN RETURNING TO CAMP
They have been out gathering wild vegetables
and are carrying digging sticks.

rie (above basal metabolism) expended on hunting, only about 3 calories' worth of meat was produced. Of the average total of about 2355 calories consumed per person per day, meat provides about 29 percent, nuts and vegetables the rest. One nut in particular, the mongongo, alone accounts for about 58 percent of the !Kung caloric intake and a large share of protein as well.

Studies of the !Kung and like band-organized hunter-gatherers have dispelled the notion that the hunting-gathering way of life, even in adverse environments, necessarily condemns people to a miserable hand-to-mouth existence, with starvation avoided only by dint of unremitting daily effort. About 10 percent of the !Kung are over 60 years of age (as compared with 5 percent in agricultural countries such as Brazil and India), and medical examination shows them to be in good health.

Judged by the large quantity of meat and other sources of protein in their diet, their sound physical condition, and their abundant leisure, the !Kung San have a high standard of living. The key to this situation is that their population is low in relation to the resources they exploit. There is less than one person per square mile in their land and their production effort remains far below carrying capacity, with no appreciable intensification (except where they have become involved in raising livestock).

OPTIMAL FORAGING THEORY

Despite their dependence on wild plants and animals, hunters and gatherers do not eat every edible species in their habitat. They pass up many edible plants and animals even when they encounter them while searching for food. Of some 262 species of animals known to the !Kung San, for example, only about 80 are eaten (Lee 1979:226). This pickiness also occurs among animals that, like human hunter-gatherers, must *forage* (i.e., search) for their food.

To account for this selective behavior, ecologists have developed a set of principles known as *optimal foraging theory* (Box 12.2). This theory predicts that hunters or collectors will pursue or harvest only those species that maximize the rate of caloric return for the time spent foraging. There will always be at least one species that will be taken on encounter, namely, the one with the highest rate of caloric return for each hour of "handling time"—time spent in pursuing, killing, collecting, carrying, preparing, and cooking the species after it is encountered. The foragers will take a second, third, or fourth species when they encounter it only if by doing so it raises the rate of caloric return for their total effort (Charnov 1976; E. A. Smith 1983). Of course, foragers do not actually measure how many calories they expend or obtain. But through repeated trial and error, they achieve a rather precise knowledge of whether it is worth their while to take a particular species. (If lions and wolves can develop this selective behavior, so can humans!)

To illustrate, suppose that there are only three animal species in a particular forest: wild pigs, anteaters, and bats. Suppose further that in 4 hours of searching through this forest, a forager can expect to

BOX *12.2*

AN INTUITIVE EXPLANATION OF OPTIMAL FORAGING

Imagine that you are in a forest in which some trees have a $1 bill and other trees have a $20 bill hanging from the topmost branches. Should you climb every money tree you come across or should you climb only the $20 trees? The answer depends on how many $20 money trees there are. If there are a lot of them, it would be a mistake to climb $1 trees. On the other hand, no matter how scarce $20 trees might be, if you happened to find one, you would always stop to climb it.

encounter one wild pig, and that the handling (pursuit, killing, cooking) of a wild pig costs 2 hours, while its caloric value is 20,000 calories. If the handling time for an anteater is also 2 hours, but its caloric return is only 10,000 calories, will the hunter stop to catch an anteater when he encounters one or will he hold out for a wild pig? In four hours of searching, if he takes wild pig and nothing but wild pig, the hunter's rate of caloric return will be:

$$\frac{20,000 \text{ cal}}{4 \text{ hr} + 2 \text{ hr}} = \frac{20,000 \text{ cal}}{6 \text{ hr}}$$

$$= \frac{3,333 \text{ cal}}{1 \text{ hr}}$$

If he also stops to take an anteater, his rate of return will be:

$$\frac{20,000 \text{ cal} + 10,000 \text{ cal}}{4 \text{ hr} + 2 \text{ hr} + 2 \text{ hr}} = \frac{30,000 \text{ cal}}{8 \text{ hr}}$$

$$= \frac{3,750 \text{ cal}}{1 \text{ hr}}$$

He should not pass up anteaters, since 3,750 is greater than 3,333. What about bats? Suppose that for bats, handling time is also 2 hours but caloric return is only 500 calories. Will he stop for a bat?

$$\frac{20,000 \text{ cal} + 10,000 \text{ cal} + 500 \text{ cal}}{4 \text{ hr} + 2 \text{ hr} + 2 \text{ hr} + 2 \text{ hr}}$$

$$= \frac{30,500 \text{ cal}}{10 \text{ hr}} = \frac{3,050 \text{ cal}}{1 \text{ hr}}$$

If he stopped for a bat instead of holding out for an anteater or a wild pig, he would be "wasting energy," since 3,750 is greater than 3,050.

In other words, optimal foraging theory predicts that foragers will continue to add items to their diets only as long as each new item increases (or does not diminish) the overall efficiency of their foraging activities. This prediction is especially interesting with regard to the question of how the abundance of a food item—such as an insect species—influences its position on or off the optimal diet list. Items that lower the overall rate of caloric return will not be added to the list no matter how abundant they become. Only the abundance of the higher-ranked items influences the breadth of the list. As a high-ranking item becomes scarce, items previously too inefficient to be on the list get added. The reason for this is that since more time must be spent before the high-ranking item is encountered, the average rate of return for the whole list shifts downward so that it is no longer a waste of energy to stop for items that have a lower rate of caloric return.

In a study of the actual rates of caloric return among the Aché Indians of eastern Paraguay (Fig. 12.8), Kristen Hawkes and her associates found that only 16 species were taken on encounter during foraging expeditions (Hawkes, Hill, and O'Connell 1982). The average rate of return after encounter of the 16 resources ranged from 65,000 calories per hour for collared peccaries to 946 calories per hour for a species of palm fruit. As predicted, despite the fact that each item was decreasingly efficient measured in postencounter calories per hour, its inclusion in the diet raised the overall efficiency of the Aché foraging system. For example, if the Aché were to take only the top two species—collared peccaries and deer—their overall foraging efficiency would be only 148 calories per hour, since despite their high caloric return, these species are scarce and seldom encountered. By adding the third- and fourth-ranked items—pacas and coatis—overall foraging efficiency increases to 405 calories per hour. As each of the remaining less valuable species is added, the overall average rate of return continues to rise, but in smaller and smaller increments. The list ends at a species of palm fruit that yields 946 calories per hour. Presumably, the Aché do not include additional species because they have found by trial and error that there are none available that would not lower their overall foraging efficiency (about 872 calories per hour for all 16 items).

Optimal foraging theory therefore offers an explanation for what must otherwise seem to be a capricious indifference on the part of many human societies to thousands of edible species of plants and animals in their habitats. It also presents a predictive framework for possible past and future changes in the list of products consumed by foragers based on fluctuations in the abundance of the more efficient food sources. If, for example, collared peccaries and deer were to become increasingly abundant, the Aché would soon find it to be a waste of energy to gather palm fruits; eventually, they would give up eating palm larvae, and if encounter rates with deer and collared peccaries rose to a point where stopping to take anything else lowered the overall rate of return, they would take nothing but deer and collared peccaries. Going the other way, if deer and collared peccaries became decreasingly abundant, the Aché would never cease to capture them on encounter, but they would no longer find it wasteful to stop and harvest resources—including certain kinds of insects—that they now spurn.

Optimal foraging theory helps to explain why people on skimpy diets may nonetheless pass up items that are very abundant in their habitats, such as insects and earthworms. It is not the commonness or

FIGURE *12.8*

ACHÉ HUNTERS
(A) Drawing bow. (B) Returning from hunt
with slain peccary.

(A)

(B)

rarity of a food item that predicts whether it will be
in the diet, but its contribution to the overall efficiency of food production. A word of caution is useful
here, though: It should not be concluded that energetic efficiency is the only factor determining the diet
of human hunter-gatherers. Many other factors, such
as protein, fat, mineral, and vitamin composition of
foods, may also determine which species are favored.
But energetic efficiency is always an important consideration and is the factor that has thus far been
measured most successfully by anthropologists.

SLASH-AND-BURN FOOD ENERGY SYSTEMS

Roy Rappaport (1968, 1984) has made a careful study
of the food energy system of the Tsembaga Maring, a
clan living in semipermanent villages on the northern slopes of the central highlands of New Guinea.
The Tsembaga, who number about 204, plant taro,
yams, sweet potatoes, manioc, sugar cane, and several
other crops in small gardens cleared and fertilized
by the slash-and-burn method (Fig. 12.9). Slash and
burn is a more efficient method of meeting caloric
needs than hunting, yielding 18 calories of output for
every 1 calorie of input. Thus, the Tsembaga are able

FIGURE *12.9*

"COOKING" THE GARDEN
A Tsembaga Maring woman during
the burning phase of swidden cycle.

to satisfy their caloric needs with a remarkably small investment of working time—only 380 hours per year per food producer spent on raising crops. At the same time, the Tsembaga manage to feed almost ten times as many people as the !Kung and to live in semipermanent houses.

But tropical slash-and-burn modes of production are constrained by environmental problems. First, there is the problem of forest regeneration. Because of leaching by heavy rains and because of the invasion of insects and weeds, the productivity of slash-and-burn gardens drops rapidly after two or three years of use, and additional land must be cleared to avoid a sharp reduction in labor efficiency and output (Clark 1976; Janzen 1973). Optimum productivity is achieved when gardens are cleared from a substantial secondary growth of large trees. If gardens are cleared when the secondary growth is very immature, only a small amount of wood-ash fertilizer will be produced by burning. On the other hand, if the trees revert to climax-forest size, they will be very difficult to cut down. Optimum regeneration may take anywhere from 10 to 20 years or more, depending on local soils and climates.

Thus, in the long run, slash-and-burn ecosystems use up a considerable amount of forest per capita, but in any particular year, only 5 percent of the total territory may actually be in production (Boserup 1965:31). The Tsembaga, for example, plant only 42 acres in a given year. Nonetheless, about 864 acres in their territory have been gardened. This is about the amount of forest that the Tsembaga will need if their population remains at about 200 people and if they burn secondary-growth garden sites every 20 years. Rappaport estimates that the Tsembaga had at their disposal an amount of forest land sufficient to support another 84 people without permanently damaging the regenerative capacities of the trees. However, the bulk of this land lies above or below the optimum altitude levels for their major crops and thus would probably somewhat diminish efficiency if put into use. All slash-and-burn peoples confront the ultimate specter of "eating up their forest" (Condominas 1977) by shortening the fallow period to a point where grasses and weeds replace trees. At least this is what has happened to other New Guinea peoples not so far from the Tsembaga (Sorenson 1972; Sorenson and Kenmore 1974). Nonetheless, there are situations, such as in the Amazon jungle, where vast untapped reserves of trees remain and where population densities are so low that the supply of burnable trees cannot be the factor limiting carrying capacity or determining the point of diminishing returns.

THE PROBLEM OF ANIMAL FOOD

Another problem with tropical slash-and-burn modes of production is the depletion of animal species. This problem is especially acute where the main staples are protein-deficient root crops such as sweet potatoes, plantains, yams, manioc, and taro. Natural tropical forests produce a vast amount of *plant biomass* per acre, but they are very poor producers of *animal biomass* as compared, for example, with grasslands and marine ecosystems (Richards 1973). The animals that inhabit tropical forests tend to be small, furtive, and arboreal. As human population density rises, these animals quickly become very scarce and hard to find. The total animal biomass—the weight of all the spiders, insects, worms, snakes, mammals, and so on—in a hectare of central Amazon rain forest is 45 kilograms. This compares with 304 kilograms in a dry East Africa thorn forest. In East African savannah grasslands, 627 kilograms of large herbivores are found per hectare, far outweighing all the large and small animals found per hectare in the Amazon (Fittkau and Klinge 1973:8). Although plant foods can provide nutritionally adequate diets if eaten in variety and in large quantities, meat is a more efficient source of essential nutrients than plant food, kilo for kilo. Hence, one of the most important limiting factors in the growth of slash-and-burn energy systems is thought to be the availability of animal food (Gross 1975, 1981; Harris 1984). Whatever etic ecological and nutritional reason there may be for it, there is no doubt that the Tsembaga, like virtually every other human group, highly prize animal food, especially in the form of fatty meat (vegetarians who abstain from meat usually prize animal foods in the form of milk and yogurt). The Tsembaga, whose population density is 67 persons per square mile, compared with less than 1 per square mile among the !Kung San, have depleted the wild animals in their territory. Among the Tsembaga, the flesh eaten on the majority of days ranges from nothing at all to less than 1 ounce. Fruits and vegetables constitute approximately 99 percent by weight of the usual daily intake. These figures do not include the sometimes considerable amount of meat that the Tsembaga consume on special festive occasions (Rappaport 1984:448).

The Tsembaga have compensated for the scarcity of game animals by stocking their land with a domesticated animal—the pig. The Tsembaga's pigs root for themselves during the day but come home to a meal of sweet potatoes and food scraps in the evening. An average Tsembaga pig weighs as much as an average Tsembaga human, and Rappaport estimates that each pig consumes almost as much garden produce as each person. When the Tsembaga pig herd is at its maximum, almost as much time and energy are devoted to feeding pigs as to feeding people. Like many New Guinea cultures, the Tsembaga allow their pig population to increase over a number of years, slaughtering pigs only on ceremonial occasions (Watson 1977). When the effort needed to care for the pigs becomes excessive, a pig feast is held, resulting in a sharp decline in the pig population (Fig. 12.10). This feast may be related to the cycle of reforestation in the Tsembaga's gardens and the regulation of war and peace between the Tsembaga and their neighbors (Morren 1984:173).

IRRIGATION AGRICULTURE

Under favorable conditions, irrigation agriculture yields more calories per calorie of effort than any other preindustrial mode of food production. And among irrigation farmers, the Chinese have excelled for thousands of years.

A detailed study of the labor inputs and weight yield of agricultural production in pre-Communist times was carried out by the anthropologists Fei Hsiao-t'ung and Chang Chih-I (1947) in the village of Luts'un, Yunnan Province. Over 50 calories were obtained for each calorie of effort in the fields. The principal crops were rice (which accounted for 75 percent of the total), soybeans, corn, manioc, and potatoes. Because of the high productivity of their agriculture, the 700 people of Luts'un produced five times more food than they consumed. What happened to the *surplus*? It was diverted from the village to towns and cities; it was exchanged via markets and money for nonfarm goods and services; it was taxed away by the local, provincial, and central governments; it went into rent as payment for use of land; and it was used

FIGURE *12.10*

DISPATCHING A PIG
Pigs have a great ritual significance throughout New Guinea and Melanesia.
The people in this scene are Fungai Maring, neighbors of the Tsembaga Maring.

to raise large numbers of children and to sustain a high rate of population increase.

The high population density of parts of China and of other societies that practice irrigation agriculture results from the fact that if the amount of water fed to the fields is expanded, increasing amounts of labor can be invested in production without substantial losses in the output–input ratio. Thus, instead of using the labor-saving potential of their technology to work less, irrigation agriculturalists opt for intensifying their effort and increasing their output.

ENERGY AND PASTORAL NOMADISM

Grains (such as wheat, barley, and maize) convert about 0.4 percent of photosynthetically active sunlight into human edible matter. If one feeds this grain to animals rather than to people and then eats the meat, 90 percent, on the average, of the energy available in the grains will be lost (National Research Council 1974). The loss in efficiency associated with the processing of plant food through the gut of domesticated animals accounts for the relatively infrequent occurrence of cultures whose mode of food production is that called *pastoral nomadism* (Fig. 12.11). Full pastoral nomads are peoples who raise domesticated animals and who do not depend on hunting, gathering, or the planting of their own crops for a significant portion of their diets. Pastoral nomads typically occupy arid grasslands and steppes in which precipitation is too sparse or irregular to support rainfall agriculture, and that cannot be irrigated because they are too high or too far from major river valleys. By specializing in animal husbandry, pastoral nomads can move their herds about over long distances and take advantage of the best pastures.

However, pastoral peoples must obtain grain supplements to their diet of milk, cheese, blood, and meat (the last always being a relatively small part of the daily fare). The productivity of herding alone is not adequate to support dense populations. Grains are usually obtained through trade with agricultural neighbors, who are eager to obtain hides, cheese, milk, and other animal products that are in short supply wherever preindustrial agricultural systems support dense populations. Pastoralists frequently attempt to improve their bargaining position by raiding the sedentary villagers and carrying off the grain harvest without paying for it. They can often do this with impunity, since their possession of animals such as camels and horses makes them highly mobile and militarily effective. Continued success in raiding may force the farming population to acknowledge the pastoralists as their overlords. Repeatedly in the history of the Old World, relatively small groups of pastoral nomads—the Mongols and the Arabs being the two most famous examples–have succeeded in gaining control of large civilizations based on irrigation agriculture. The inevitable outcome of these conquests, however, was that the conquerors were absorbed by the agricultural system as they attempted to feed the huge populations that had fallen under their control (Khazanov 1984; Lattimore 1962; Lees and Bates 1974; Salzman 1971; for varieties of pastoral nomadic systems, see Galaty and Johnson 1990).

FIGURE *12.11*

PASTORAL NOMADISM
The huts of these inhabitants of Turkomenia (formerly of the U.S.S.R.) are made of camel skins, felt, and cane, and are easily disassembled and transported to a new camp.

TABLE *12.1*

PER CAPITA ENERGY FROM AGRICULTURE			
	Total output in calories (in thousands)	Population	Per capita output in calories (in thousands)
!Kung	23,400	35	670
Tsembaga	150,000	204	735
Luts'un	3,790,000	700	5,411

ENERGY AND THE EVOLUTION OF CULTURE

According to Leslie White (1949:368–369), a basic law governs the evolution of cultures: "Other factors remaining constant, culture evolves as the amount of energy harnessed per year is increased, or as the efficiency of the means of putting energy to work is increased." The first part of this law seems to be supported by the per capita output of Chinese irrigation agriculture and the per capita output of the !Kung and Tsembaga, as Table 12.1 shows.

The second part of White's law is not so clear. It is true that if one considers only human labor inputs, the ratio of output to input rises from 11:1 for the !Kung to 18:1 for the Tsembaga to 54:1 for Luts'un (Harris 1971:204ff). But these figures do not include the energy that the Tsembaga use in the combustion of trees to make their gardens, nor the considerable amount of energy that the Tsembaga "waste" in converting vegetable foods to pork. Nor do the figures for Luts'un include the considerable energetic cost of milling and cooking rice. As Timothy Bayliss-Smith (1977) has shown in an attempt to test White's law, South Sea communities drawn into participating in aspects of modern industrial modes of production produce much more food energy per capita, but their efficiency shows no clear upward trend. In fact, if we consider the total energy outputs and inputs of food production in fully industrial societies, the trend in efficiency of putting energy to work runs counter to White's prediction.

INDUSTRIAL FOOD ENERGY SYSTEMS

It is difficult to estimate the output–input ratio of industrial agriculture because the amount of indirect labor put into food production exceeds the amount of direct labor (Fig. 12.12). An Iowa corn farmer, for example, puts in 9 hours of work per acre, which

FIGURE *12.12*

INDUSTRIAL FARMING
Rice harvest near Yuba City, California. Are these farmers or engineers?

yield 81 bushels of corn with an energy equivalent of 8,164,800 calories (Pimentel et al. 1973). This gives a nominal ratio of 5000 calories of output for every calorie of input! But this is a misleading figure. First, three-quarters of all the croplands in the United States are devoted to the production of animal feeds, with a consequent 90 percent reduction in humanly consumable calories. Indeed, the livestock population of the United States consumes enough food calories to feed 1.3 billion people (Cloud 1973). Second, enormous amounts of human labor are embodied in the tractors, trucks, combines, oil and gas, pesticides, herbicides, and fertilizers used by the Iowa corn farmer.

A misunderstood aspect of industrial food energy systems is the difference between higher yields per acre and the ratio of energy input to output. As a result of more and more intensive modes of production, involving genetically improved crops and higher dosages of chemical fertilizers and pesticides, yields per acre have steadily improved (N. Jensen 1978). But this improvement has been made possible only as a result of a steady increase in the amount of fuel energy invested for each calorie of food energy produced. In the United States, 15 tons of machinery, 22 gallons of gasoline, 203 pounds of fertilizer, and 2 pounds of chemical insecticides and pesticides are invested per acre per year. This represents a cost of 2,890,000 calories of nonfood energy per acre per year (Pimentel et al. 1975), a cost that has increased steadily since the beginning of the century. Before 1910, more calories were obtained from agriculture than were invested in it. By 1970, it took 8 calories in the form of fossil fuels to produce 1 calorie of food. Today, vast quantities of energy are used simply to process and package food (Box 12.3). If the people of India were to emulate the U.S. system of food production, their entire energy budget would have to be devoted to nothing but agriculture (Steinhart and Steinhart 1974). In the words of Howard Odum:

BOX *12.3*

ENERGY INPUT IN PACKAGING AND PROCESSING INDUSTRIAL FOOD

ENERGY REQUIRED TO PRODUCE VARIOUS FOOD PACKAGES

Package	kcal
Wooden berry basket	69
Styrofoam tray (size 6)	215
Molded paper tray (size 6)	384
Polyethylene pouch (16 oz, or 455 g)	559
Steel can, aluminum top (12 oz)	568
Small paper set-up box	722
Steel can, steel top (16 oz)	1,006
Glass jar (16 oz)	1,023
Coca-Cola bottle, nonreturnable (16 oz)	1,471
Aluminum TV-dinner container	1,496
Aluminum can, pop-top (12 oz)	1,643
Plastic milk container, disposable (½ gal)	2,159
Coca-Cola bottle, returnable (16 oz)	2,451
Polyethylene bottle (1 qt)	2,494
Polypropylene bottle (1 qt)	2,752
Glass milk container, returnable (½ gal)	4,455

ENERGY INPUTS FOR PROCESSING VARIOUS PRODUCTS

Package	kcal/kg
Instant coffee	18,948
Chocolate	18,591
Breakfast cereals	15,675
Beet sugar (assumes 17% sugar in beets)	5,660
Dehydrated foods (freeze-dried)	3,542
Cane sugar (assumes 20% sugar in cane)	3,380
Fruit and vegetables (frozen)	1,815
Fish (frozen)	1,815
Baked goods	1,485
Meat	1,206
Ice cream	880
Fruit and vegetables (canned)	575
Flour (includes blending of flour)	484
Milk	354

SOURCE: Adapted from Pimentel and Pimentel 1985: 38–39.

A whole generation of citizens thought that the carrying capacity of the earth was proportional to the amount of land under cultivation and higher efficiencies in using the energy of the sun had arrived. This is a sad hoax, for industrial man no longer eats potatoes made from solar energy; now he eats potatoes made of oil. (1970:15)

SUMMARY

The comparative study of modes of production involves consideration of the quantitative and qualitative aspects of energy production and of ecological relationships. Most of the energy flowing through preindustrial energy systems consists of food energy. The technology of energy production cannot be altered by whim. It has evolved through successive stages of technical competence, in which the mastery of one set of tools and machines has been built on the mastery of an earlier set. Through technological advance, the energy available per capita has steadily increased. However, technology never exists in the abstract, but only in the particular instances where it interacts with a specific environment. There is no such thing as technology dominating or controlling the natural environment. Even in the most advanced industrial ecosystems, depletion and pollution of habitats add unavoidable costs to energy production and consumption. Technology interacting with environment determines carrying capacity, which is the upper limit of production, and hence the limit of the human population density possible without depletion and permanent damage.

When carrying capacity is exceeded, production will decline precipitously. The fact that a food energy system is operating as much as two-thirds below carrying capacity does not mean that ecological restraints are absent. Energy systems tend to stop growing before reaching the point of diminishing returns, which is defined as the point at which the ratio of output to input begins to fall, holding technology constant. A distinction must also be made between the effects of growth and the effects of intensification. Growth may continue for a long time without leading to a decline in the ratio of output to input. However, intensification, which is defined as increased input in a fixed area, may lead to critical depletions, diminishing returns, and irreversible damage to the habitat's carrying capacity. All the factors in production must be approached from the perspective of Liebig's law, which states that extremes, not averages, set the limits for carrying capacity.

A common human cultural response to declining efficiency brought about by intensification is to alter technology and thereby adopt new modes of production.

Hunting and gathering was the universal mode of food production until the end of the Paleolithic. Depending on the kind of technology and the environmental conditions, different types of hunter-gatherer can be distinguished. The !Kung San are an example of the simple, band-organized, mobile variety found in less favored habitats. Their output-to-input efficiency is low, especially for the male-dominated activity of hunting. However, by maintaining low population densities and avoiding intensification, they enjoy a relatively high standard of living (i.e., good diets, unpolluted environments, and lots of leisure time).

Energetic efficiency plays an important role in the selection of the species that hunter-gatherers use for food. According to optimal foraging theory, foragers stop to take only those species whose handling adds to or does not decrease the overall efficiency of their foraging effort.

Slash-and-burn agriculturalists such as the Tsembaga Maring produce their caloric needs with greater efficiency than the !Kung San, but they have depleted the game animals in their habitat and must rely on costly domesticated pigs for their animal proteins and fats. By using irrigation agriculture, the people of Luts'un produce a large surplus. Their output–input ratio for human effort is three times higher than the output–input ratio of the Tsembaga.

Pastoralism, another preindustrial mode of food production, is practiced only in areas unsuitable for agriculture, because feeding plant food to domesticated animals rather than consuming crops directly results in a 90 percent reduction in the efficiency of conversion of sunlight to human food.

As Leslie White predicted, there has been a steady increase in the amount of energy harnessed per capita as cultures have evolved. Energy efficiency has also increased as measured by the return for human labor input. But when other sources of energy are included in the calculation of efficiency, advances in technology are shown to have resulted in a decrease in the efficiency of food production, as demonstrated by the enormous energy inputs that characterize industrial agricultural systems.

Reproduction

We will now focus on the reproductive aspect of infrastructure. Given the potential that human beings have to increase population, how is population brought into balance with modes of production and the carrying capacity of the environment? We will see that preindustrial societies have employed a variety of means to regulate population growth, including infanticide and prolonged nursing. But, have you ever wondered why people in poverty-stricken parts of the world persist in having large families while people in rich industrial countries have fewer and fewer children? We will see that the key to answering this question and to understanding rates of population growth is not the possession of contraceptives or abortificants, but what the costs and benefits of raising children are under different modes of production. What are the implications of this approach for the abortion debate? If people regulate reproduction not only before but after birth, when does human life really begin?

THE RELATION BETWEEN PRODUCTION AND REPRODUCTION

Reproduction is a form of production—the "product" being new human beings. Under optimal conditions, human females can have between 20 and 25 live births during their fertile years (which last roughly from age 15 to 45). In all human societies, women on the average have far fewer children than that. The record, 8.97 children per woman, is held by the Hutterites, a communitarian sect in western Canada (Lang and Göhlen 1985). If all children born live to reproduce, any number of births greater than 2 per woman would potentially result in population increase (holding death rates constant). Even small rates of increase can result in enormous populations in a few generations. The !Kung, for example, have a growth rate of 0.5 percent per year. If the world had started 10,000 years ago with a population of 2, and if that population had grown at 0.5 percent per year, the world population would now be 604,436,000,000,000,000,000,000. No such growth has occurred because, through various combinations of cultural and natural factors, reproduction has been kept within limits imposed by systems of production.

Much controversy surrounds the nature of the relationship between production and reproduction. Followers of Thomas Malthus, the founder of the science of demography (i.e., the science of population phenomena), have long held the view that the level of population is determined by the amount of food produced. According to the Malthusians, population would always rise to the limit of production; in fact, it would tend to rise faster than any conceivable rise in productivity, thereby dooming a large portion of humanity to perpetual poverty, hunger, and misery. However, from the evidence showing that many preindustrial societies maintain their levels of production well below carrying capacity (see Chapter 12), it is clear that Malthus was wrong in at least one crucial respect. It is possible, moreover, to turn Malthus upside down and see the amount of food produced as being determined by the level of population growth. In this view, which has been advocated most forcefully by Ester Boserup (see p. 210), food production tends to rise to the level demanded by population growth. As population expands, production is intensified and new modes of production evolve to satisfy the increased demand for food.

In light of modern anthropological research, the position that seems most correct is that production and reproduction are equally important in shaping the course of sociocultural evolution, and that to an equal extent, each is the cause of the other. Reproduction generates *population pressure* (i.e., physiological and psychological costs such as malnutrition and illness). Population pressure often leads to intensification, diminishing returns, and irreversible environmental depletions. Depletions often lead, in turn, to new technologies and to new modes of production.

POPULATION PRESSURE

Note that population pressure and population growth are not the same thing. Under favorable environmental conditions, population size and density can increase, at least temporarily, without lowering a people's standard of living. During the nineteenth century, for example, the settling of the American West was accompanied by high fertility rates (see Fig. 15.6), rapidly rising populations, and a rising standard of living among pioneer farm families.

Moreover, population pressures may exist even if population is not growing. To prevent the erosion of their standard of living, people often limit population growth by using physically and emotionally costly means of reproductive controls, such as infanticide and nonmedical abortion (see below). For example, Arctic hunter-gatherers had very low population densities and virtually zero rates of population growth. Yet they experienced population pressure because their standard of living was maintained only by practicing a considerable amount of infanticide. It might even be argued that population pressure can exist among people who are experiencing a population decline. Many Native American peoples who live in the Amazon, for example, are declining in numbers at the same time that they find it increasingly difficult to maintain their standards of health and well-being (Turner 1991).

Perhaps the best way to envision population pressure is to regard it as present with varying intensity among virtually all societies. Even in high-tech industrial countries where completed fertility rates have fallen below replacement levels (see p. 464) largely through the use of modern anti-reproductive technologies, population pressure has a role to play in phenomena such as unemployment, crime, homelessness, child abuse, and pollution. While each of these problems is partly the result of the inequitable distribution of wealth, each is also made worse by the increase in human numbers. This is certainly clear in the case of energy consumption and pollution. "At any given level of per capita pollution, more people means more pollution" (Brown 1991:16). There is a limit to the ability of the earth's rivers, oceans, forests, and atmosphere to absorb industrial waste. Similarly, given the finite nature of our capacity to produce energy, population growth can only drive up the price of energy and the goods and services energy makes possible. At best, population pressure is a destabilizing force. It interacts with natural sources of instability, such as changes in ocean currents and advances and retreats of continental glaciers, to bring about large-scale shifts in modes of production. As we have seen, it was this combination of natural and cultural pressures and opportunities that may account for the transition from Paleolithic to Neolithic modes of production (Ch. 10).

Thus, while production sets limits to population growth, population pressure provides the motivation

to overcome such limits (Johnson and Earle 1987; Keeley 1988).

PREINDUSTRIAL POPULATION-REGULATING PRACTICES

Contrary to the Malthusian view, much evidence supports the conclusion that preindustrial cultures regulated the sizes of their families so as to minimize the costs and maximize the benefits of reproduction. In an age that lacked condoms, diaphragms, pills, spermicides, or knowledge of the human ovulatory cycle, how could such regulation occur? Four categories of practice that had the effect of regulating population growth were relied on: (1) care and treatment of fetuses, infants, and children; (2) care and treatment of girls and women (and to a lesser extent of boys and men); (3) intensity and duration of lactation (i.e., the period of breast feeding); and (4) variations in the frequency of coital intercourse. To say that they were relied on does not mean that they were relied on consciously, but that they formed part of etic behavioral practice, sometimes in direct opposition to emic rules.

Treatment of Fetuses and Children

Maltreatment of fetuses, infants, and young children is a common means of lowering reproductive costs. A subtle gradation leads from active attempts to *avoid* fetal death (abortion), infant death, and child death to active efforts to *promote* fetal death, infant death, and child death. Full support of the fetus involves supplementing the diets of pregnant women and reducing their work loads (MacCormack 1982:8). Indirect abortion begins when heavy work loads and meager diets are imposed on pregnant women. Direct abortion occurs with starvation diets for pregnant women and often involves trauma caused by squeezing the mother's abdomen with tight bands, jumping on her, or having her ingest toxic substances. In a study of 350 preindustrial societies, George Devereux (1967:98) found that direct abortion was "an absolutely universal phenomenon."

Some forms of infanticide are as widely practiced as abortion. Again, there is a subtle gradation from indirect to direct methods. Full support of the life of a newborn infant requires that it be fed to gain weight rapidly and that it be protected against extremes of temperature and from falls, burns, and other accidents. Indirect infanticide begins with inadequate feeding and careless and indifferent handling, especially when the infant is sick. Direct infanticide involves more-or-less rapid starvation, dehydration, exposure to the elements, suffocation, or blows to the head (S. Scrimshaw 1983). Often there is no sharp distinction between abortion and infanticide. The Yanomamö (see p. 301), for example, induce labor during the sixth or seventh month of pregnancy and kill the fetus if it shows signs of life after expulsion. Similarly, there is often no clear distinction between infanticide and the direct or indirect removal of unwanted children 2 or 3 years old by more or less rapid starvation and neglect during illness. In this connection, it should be pointed·out that many cultures do not regard children as human until certain ceremonies, such as naming or hair cutting, are performed. Infanticide and the induced death of small children seldom take place *after* such ceremonies have been performed (Minturn and Stashak 1982). Hence, in the emic perspective, such deaths are rarely seen as homicides.

Treatment of Women

The treatment of women can raise or lower the age at which women begin to be capable of bearing children and the age at which they can no longer conceive. It can also affect the total number of pregnancies they are capable of sustaining. Women who are nutritionally deprived are not as fertile as women whose diets are adequate, although considerable controversy exists as to how severe the deprivations must be before significant declines in fertility occur (see Box 13.1). It is known that severe, famine-level nutritional deprivation can reduce fertility by 50 percent (Bongaarts 1980:568). Rose Frisch (1984:184), however, maintains that a 10 to 15 percent weight loss is sufficient to delay menarche and to disrupt the menstrual cycle. It should be kept in mind that this dispute concerns the effects of malnutrition on fertility. The effects of nutritional stress on mother, fetus, and infant are well established. Poor maternal nutrition increases the risk of premature births and of low birth weights, both of which increase fetal and infant mortality; poor maternal nutrition also diminishes the quantity if not the quality of breast milk, thus lowering the chances of infant survival still further (Hamilton et al. 1984:388). In turn, women who become pregnant and who recurrently provide mother's milk from a nutritionally depleted body also have elevated mortality rates (Fredrick and Adelstein 1973; Jelliffe and Jelliffe 1978; Trussell and Pebly 1984). These nutritional effects will all vary in interaction with the amount of psychological and physical stress imposed on pregnant and lactating women. In addition, female

---

BOX *13.1*

SOME BASIC DEMOGRAPHIC CONCEPTS

Crude Birth Rate The number of births per thousand people, in a given year.

Crude Death Rate The number of deaths per thousand people, in a given year.

Fertility Rate The number of live births per thousand women ages 15 to 44, in a given year.

Completed Fertility Rate The average number of children born to women who have completed their reproductive years.

Fecundity The physiological capacity to produce a live child.

Mortality Death as a factor in population stability or change.

---

life expectancy can be affected by exposure to toxic, body-shock techniques of abortion, again in interaction with general nutritional status.

Extreme malnutrition and physical and mental stress can also affect male fecundity (see Box 13.1) by reducing libido (sexual desire) and sperm count. However, the abundance of sperm as compared with the ova and the female's birthing and nursing physiology renders the treatment of females far more important than the treatment of males in regulating reproduction. High sickness and mortality rates among males are readily counterbalanced by the widespread practice of polygyny (one husband with several wives—see p. 261) and by the fact that one male can impregnate dozens of females.

Lactation

Amenorrhea (disruption of the menstrual cycle) is a typical accompaniment of breast feeding. The effect is associated with the production of *prolactin*, a hormone that regulates mammary activity. Prolactin, in turn, inhibits the production of the hormones that regulate the ovulatory cycle. Several biocultural factors appear to control the duration of lactation amenorrhea. To begin with, there is the state of the mother's health and her diet. Additional variables include the intensity of suckling as determined by the age at which the infant is fed supplemental soft foods and by the scheduling of suckling episodes. While the relative importance of these factors remains controversial

(Bongaarts 1980, 1982; Frisch 1984), it is clear that under favorable conditions, prolonged nursing can result in birth-spacing intervals of 3 or more years, with a degree of reliability comparable to that of modern mechanical and chemical contraceptives (Short 1984:36). But one must be on guard against the notion that any social group is free to adjust its fertility rate upward or downward merely by intensifying and prolonging lactation (Fig. 13.1). Prolonged lactation cannot take place without suitably nourished mothers. Moreover, because human breast milk is deficient in iron, its use as the sole source of nourishment much beyond the age of 6 months will cause anemia in the infant.

Coital Frequency and Scheduling

Coital abstinence can be sustained long enough to reduce pregnancies, and delays in the onset of coital behavior can shorten the female's reproductive span (Nag 1983). The effects of lactational amenorrhea can

FIGURE *13.1*

BREASTFEEDING OLDER CHILDREN
San women breastfeed their children for 4 or 5 years per child.

be reinforced by coital abstinence while the mother continues to nurse her child. And various forms of nonreproductive sex can influence fertility rates: Homosexuality, masturbation, coitus interruptus (withdrawal before ejaculation), and noncoital heterosexual techniques for achieving orgasm can all play a role in regulating fertility. Age of marriage is another important population-regulating variable, but its significance depends on the existence of a taboo on extramarital sex and unwed motherhood. As we shall see (p. 267), many societies do not regard couples who have not had children as being married. In such cases, age of marriage cannot influence the number of children a woman will have (Wilmsen 1982:4).

Type of marriage is also relevant to fertility. Polygyny, for example, assures that almost all females will engage in reproductive sex (in the absence of contraception). But polygyny is also effective in prolonging female sexual abstinence and the latter's reinforcing effect on lactational amenorrhea. In addition, polygyny probably results in lower rates of coital intercourse per wife as husbands grow older (Bongaarts et al. 1984:521–522).

It is clear from this summary that preindustrial societies have never lacked means for regulating their reproductive rates in response to the limits and possibilities of their modes of production.

THE INFLUENCE OF DISEASE AND OTHER NATURAL FACTORS

Most of the great lethal epidemic diseases—smallpox, typhoid fever, influenza, bubonic plague, and cholera—are primarily associated with dense urbanized populations rather than with dispersed hunter-gatherers or small village cultures. Even diseases like malaria and yellow fever were probably less important among low-density populations that could avoid swampy mosquito breeding grounds. (Knowledge of the association between swamps and disease is very ancient, even though mosquitoes were not recognized as disease carriers.) Other diseases such as dysentery, measles, tuberculosis, whooping cough, scarlet fever, and the common cold were also probably less significant among hunter-gatherers and early farmers (Armelagos and McArdle 1975; Black 1975; Cockburn 1971; Wood 1975). The ability to recuperate from these infections is closely related to the general level of bodily health, which in turn is heavily influenced by diet, especially by balanced protein levels (N. Scrimshaw 1977). The role of disease as a long-term regulator of human population is thus to some extent a consequence of the success or failure of other population-regulating mechanisms. Only if these alternatives are ineffective and population density rises, productive efficiency drops, and diet deteriorates will some diseases figure as an important check on population growth (Post 1985).

There is some evidence to indicate that Paleolithic hunter-gatherers were healthier than late Neolithic agriculturalists and the peasant farmers of preindustrial state societies. Exactly when and where a deterioration occurred is the focus of much continuing research (Cohen 1987; Cohen and Armelagos 1984). It seems likely that for much of the Upper Paleolithic, at least, "artificial" population controls rather than sickness were the principal factors governing rates of population growth (Handwerker 1983:20).

Obviously, it cannot be denied that a component in human birth and death rates reflects "natural" causes over which cultural practices have little influence. In addition to lethal diseases, natural catastrophes such as droughts, floods, and earthquakes may raise death rates and lower birth rates in a manner that leaves little room for cultural intervention. And there are, of course, biological constraints on the number of children a human female can have, as well as natural limitations on the length of human life. But to a surprising degree, cultural practices are relied on that modify the effects of natural factors.

THE COSTS AND BENEFITS OF REARING CHILDREN

"Population pressure" implies that people are sensitive to the costs and benefits entailed in the process of reproduction. Costs of rearing children include the extra food consumed during pregnancy, the work forgone by pregnant women, the expenses involved in providing mother's milk and other foods during infancy and childhood, the burden of carrying infants and children from one place to another, and, in more complex societies, expenditures for clothing, housing, medical care, and education. In addition, the birth process itself is dangerous and often places the life of the mother at risk.

Benefits of reproduction include the contributions that children make to food production, to family income in general, and to the care and economic security of their parents. Children are also widely valued for their role in marital exchanges and intergroup alliances (see pp. 267 and 271); that is, in many cultures, groups exchange sons and daughters in order to obtain husbands and wives. These exchanges are used to arrange alliances against aggressors. Hence, where chronic warfare exists, larger groups are safer than smaller ones; they have more alliances as well as greater military strength. All this,

---

BOX *13.2*

THE ECONOMY OF PARENTAL LOVE

Children fulfill a need for close, affectionate, emotional relationships with supportive, concerned, trustworthy, and approving beings. We need children because we need to be loved. In the support parents lavish on children there is a culturally instructed expectation that a balance will be struck with the love and affection that children can be so good at giving in return.

Even in their least giving mood, babies respond with warm, wet sucking and mouthing; they grasp your fingers and try to put their arms around you. Already you can anticipate the ardent hugs and kisses of early childhood, the tot who clings to your neck, the 4-year-old tucked in bed, whispering "I love you," the 6-year-old breathless at the door or running down the path as you come home from work. And with a little more imagination you can see all the way to a grateful son or daughter, dressed in cap and gown, saying, "Thanks, Mom and Dad. I owe it all to you."

The fact that many of the sentimental rewards of parenthood are delayed does not mean that dreams rule the economy of love. As in every other kind of exchange, mere expectation of a return flow will not sustain the bonds indefinitely. The family sanctuary is a fragile temple. People will not forever marry and have children no matter how far the actual experience departs from expectation.

SOURCE: Adapted from Harris 1989: 230 ff.

---

of course, is not to deny that people have children for sentimental reasons as well (see Box 13.2).

Humans may have a genetically controlled propensity, shared with other primates, to find infants emotionally appealing and to derive emotional satisfaction from holding and fondling them and from watching and helping them play and learn. As children grow older, their respect and love for their parents may also be highly valued. But it is clear that this appreciation of infants and children, if it is innate, can be modified by culture so completely as to allow most people to have fewer children than they are biologically capable of producing and to enable others, such as monks, priests, nuns, and even some modern-day "yuppies" to have none at all.

Much recent evidence suggests that the rate at which the parental generation has children is largely determined by the extent to which having each additional child results in a net gain of benefits over costs for the average couple (Caldwell 1982; Harris and Ross 1987; Nardi 1983). As we have seen (p. 161), among band-organized hunter-gatherers, the number of children is limited by the burden that infants present to mothers who must carry them hundreds of miles each year on their foraging expeditions. According to Richard Lee, !Kung San mothers try to avoid having one child close on another, in order to escape the burden of carrying two children at once. The benefits of additional children are further reduced among hunter-gatherers by the vulnerability of wild species of plants and animals to depletion. As band size increases, per capita food production tends to decline, since hunter-gatherers have no effective way of creating a concomitant increase in the population of the wild plants and animals they use for food. Finally, the children of hunter-gatherers do not produce more than they consume until relatively late in childhood. For these reasons, population densities among hunter-gatherers seldom rise above one person per square mile. If contemporary hunter-gatherers are at all representative of prehistoric times, *Homo sapiens* must have been a very rare creature during the Paleolithic. Perhaps there were only 5 million people in the entire world in those times (Dumond 1975; Hassan 1978:78), certainly no more than 15 million (Mark Cohen 1977:54), compared with 5 billion today. Whether one takes the upper or lower estimate, there is no doubt that for tens of thousands of years the rate of growth of the human population was very slow (see Table 13.1).

As we have seen (p. 161), with the advent of agriculture and domesticated animals the balance of reproductive costs and benefits shifted in favor of having more children. Children no longer had to be carried about over long distances; they could perform many useful economic chores at an early age; and since the rate of reproduction of domesticated plants and animals could be controlled, a considerable amount of intensification and hence population growth could be achieved without a decline in per capita output. After weaning, children in many agricultural societies rapidly begin to "pay for themselves." They contribute to the production of their own food, clothing, and housing, and under favorable conditions they may begin to produce surpluses above their own subsistence needs as early as 6 years of age. This transition is hastened with successive births, since senior siblings and other children assume much of the costs of grooming and caring for their juniors.

MEASURING THE COSTS AND BENEFITS OF REARING CHILDREN

A number of attempts have been made to measure the economic value of children in contemporary peasant communities. For example, in village Java, boys of 12 to 14 years contribute 33 hours of economically valuable work per week and girls 9 to 11 contribute about 38 hours a week of the same. Altogether, children contribute about half of all work performed by household members (Fig. 13.2). Much household labor involves making handicrafts, working in petty trade, and processing various foods for sale. Similar findings are reported for Nepal (Nag et al. 1978; White 1976).

Costs are more difficult to measure, but Javanese children themselves do most of the work needed to rear and maintain their siblings, freeing mothers for income-producing tasks. In any event, larger households are more efficient income-producing

		TABLE *13.1*
RATE OF GROWTH OF THE HUMAN POPULATION		
Period	World population at end of period	Percentage annual rate of growth during period
Paleolithic	5,000,000	0.0015
Mesolithic	8,500,000	0.0330
Neolithic	75,000,000	0.1000
Ancient empires	225,000,000	0.5000
SOURCES: Hassan 1978, 1971; Spengler 1974.		

FIGURE *13.2*

CHILD WORKER
A Javanese boy earning his keep.

village (Fig. 13.3). Cain describes his findings:

Male children become net producers at the latest by the age of 12. Furthermore, male children work long enough hours at high enough rates of productivity to compensate for consumption during their earlier periods of dependence by the age of 15. Therefore, in general...parents...realize a net economic return on male children for the period when they are subordinate members of the parental household.

Thus, contrary to the popular perception that people in less developed countries have large numbers of children simply because they do not know how to avoid conception, there is much evidence that more children and larger households mean a higher, not a lower, standard of living in the short run. In explaining why they did not wish to join any family-planning programs, the men of Manupur village in the Punjab explained: "Why pay 2,500 rupees for an extra hand? Why not have a son?" (Mamdani 1973:77). It should be emphasized that high fertility may simply give large families a more favorable standard of living relative to that of smaller families in a situation in which the average standard of living for the whole farming sector is stagnant or even deteriorating (Weil 1986).

With the expansion of urban, industrial, technical, and white-collar employment opportunities, the net return from child rearing can be increased by investing in fewer but better-educated offspring. In Rampur village, close to the Indian capital of New Delhi, the number of children per woman declined as wage opportunities increased outside the village (Das Gupta 1978). Tractors, tube wells, and pumps reduced the demand for child labor. In addition, parents wanted their children to get more education to prepare for higher-quality jobs in New Delhi. Similarly, in Sri Lanka (Tilakaratne 1978), employers of wage labor have come to prefer adult males rather than children who are able to work only part time as a result of having to attend school. More white-collar jobs are becoming available for which children are unsuited because they have not achieved the required levels of literacy and mathematical skills. Even families headed by manual workers desire to have children participate in white-collar, high-status jobs and to give them more schooling. Marriage to an educated and well-employed man or woman has become the ideal, and this can be done only by postponing marriage, which in turn decreases the number of children per woman.

In Indian villages located near the city of Bangalore, three factors accounted for the trend against child labor: (1) Land holdings had become fragmented and too small to absorb the labor of additional

units in rural Java because a smaller proportion of total labor time is required for maintenance. Given these conditions, women have about five births and four surviving children, which "seems an entirely appropriate response" (White 1982:605). (It is nonetheless a response that yields an alarming 2 percent per annum increase in Java's population.)

Meade Cain (1977:225) has quantified both benefits and costs for male children in a rural Bangladesh

FIGURE *13.3*

CHILD WORKERS, BANGLADESH

children in agriculture; (2) new nonfarm employment opportunities requiring arithmetic skills and literacy had opened up; and (3) educational facilities had been introduced or improved within the villages (Caldwell et al. 1983). Similarly, on returning to the village of Manupur in the Punjab (see p. 227), Nag and Kak (1984) found a sharp increase in the number of couples practicing contraception and a sharp reduction in the number of sons regarded as desirable (Fig. 13.4). These changes resulted from shifts in the mode of production, which lowered the demand for child labor. Shortening or eliminating fallow, for example, has led to the disappearance of grazing land within the village, so that young boys can no longer make themselves useful tending cattle. The loss of cattle and the increased reliance on chemical fuels and fertilizers have also done away with

the childhood task of collecting cow dung to be used for fertilizer and fuel (see p. 408); with the introduction of industrial herbicides, children are no longer needed for weeding. Furthermore, there has been a substantial rise in the proportion of Manupur workers employed in industrial, commercial, and government sectors. Meanwhile, the mechanization of farm operations, the expanded use of credit, and the need to keep account books have made Manupur parents consciously eager to expand their children's educational horizons. Secondary school enrollment increased in a decade from 63 percent to 81 percent for boys and from 29 percent to 63 percent for girls. Parents now want at least one son to have a white-collar job so that the family will not be entirely dependent on agriculture; many parents want both sons and daughters to attend college.

FIGURE *13.4*

MANUPUR, PUNJAB, INDIA
Collection of cow dung by children to make cow-dung cakes for use as cooking fuel is becoming less important as families become more prosperous and the land is farmed more intensively.

be confident that when the balance is adverse, some form of birth or death control will be activated at some point in the reproductive process. The kinds of birth- or death-control measures employed, however, vary from one culture to another. To a degree that is shocking to modern sensibilities, preindustrial and underdeveloped societies employ reproduction-regulating measures that achieve their effect *after* the birth of a child (see Box 13.3).

The existence of postpartum reproduction-regulating practices can be obscured by the failure to distinguish between emic and etic viewpoints. Yet the recognition of postpartum etic death-control practices is essential to understanding the controversy concerning contraception, abortion, and infanticide. Much evidence exists that if reproduction is not limited *before* or during pregnancy, then it will be limited *after* pregnancy by direct or indirect infanticide or pedicide (the killing of young children). Attempts to discourage contraception, medical abortion, and other modern prepartum reproductive controls may inadvertently increase reliance on postpartum homicidal practices. It is with this possibility in mind that the case of indirect infanticide in Northeast Brazil is presented in the next section.

THE CONTRACEPTION, ABORTION, AND INFANTICIDE DEBATE

An important implication of the existence of powerful cultural practices for raising or lowering fertility and mortality rates is that human reproduction is not an act that can be described as taking place at a specific moment, such as the moment of the union between an ovum and a sperm. Human reproduction is a social process that begins long before conception and that continues long after birth. For human reproduction to take place, prospective parents must have adequate material and psychological support, the pregnant woman and her fetus must be nourished and protected, the nursing mother and her infant must be fed and cared for, and a commitment must be made by the parents and many other individuals to find the resources necessary to rear the newborn from infancy and childhood to adulthood.

As we have just seen, the decision to make the social effort necessary to give birth to and rear children is heavily influenced by the balance of costs and benefits confronting prospective parents. We can

INDIRECT INFANTICIDE IN NORTHEAST BRAZIL

Northeast Brazil is a region subjected to periodic droughts, chronic malnutrition, and widespread poverty. Its infant mortality rate is about 200 deaths per 1000 births in the first year of life (compared with a rate of less than 10 in developed countries). A study carried out by Nancy Scheper-Hughes (1984) in this region reveals that at least some of the infant and child deaths reported by a sample of 72 women are best described as forms of indirect infanticide. Out of a total of 686 pregnancies (an average of 9.5 per woman!), 85 were terminated by induced or spontaneous abortions, and there were 16 stillbirths. Out of 588 live births, 251 died before 5 years of age, an average of 3.5 infant and child deaths per woman. These deaths were concentrated at the beginning and end of the women's fertile years, a pattern that Scheper-Hughes attributes to the inexperience of mothers with their firstborn and to their economic, physical, and psychological inability to cope with the needs of the last born. (A more likely explanation for the higher mortality of the firstborn is that they

BOX *13.3*

SEX SELECTION IN JAPAN

Japan's country folk were at one time the world's most efficient managers of human reproduction. During the nineteenth century, Japanese farm couples precisely fitted the size and sexual compostion of their broods to the size and fertility of their land holdings. The small-holder's ideal was two children; one boy and one girl; people with larger holdings aimed for two boys and one or two girls. But the Japanese did not stop there! As expressed in a still-popular saying, "first a girl, then a boy," they tried to rear a daughter first and a son second. According to G. William Skinner, this ideal reflected the practice of assigning much of the task of rearing firstborn sons to an older sister. It also reflected the expectation that the firstborn son would replace his father as the farm's manager at an age when the father was ready to retire, and the son was not yet so old as to have grown surly while waiting to take over. A further complexity was the age at which couples got married. An older man would not dare to delay having a son; and so, if the firstborn was a male, he would count himself fortunate. Since the parents had no way of telling the sex of a child before birth, they were able to achieve these precise reproductive goals only by practicing systematic infanticide.

SOURCES: Adapted from Harris 1989: 218; Skinner 1987.

539). Children with the opposite traits were not given medical assistance when they became ill, and they were not fed as well as their sisters and brothers. Mothers spoke of children who " 'wanted to die,' whose will and drive toward life was not sufficiently strong or developed" (ibid.). These unwanted children tend to die during one of the crises of childhood: infections of the umbilical cord, infant diarrhea, or teething. The women regard some childhood diseases as incurable, but the diagnostic symptoms of these diseases are so broad that almost any childhood disorder can be interpreted as a sign that the child is doomed to die: fits and convulsions, lethargy and passivity, retarded verbal or motor function, or a "ghost-like" or "animal-like" appearance (Fig. 13.5). Scheper-Hughes writes (ibid.:541):

I do not know what exactly prompts a folk diagnosis of this kind, but I suspect that its flexibility allows mothers a great deal of latitude in deciding which of their children are not favored for survival as "normal" children.

When a child marked with one of these fatal diseases dies, mothers do not display grief: They say there was no remedy, that even if you treat the disease, the child "will never be right," that it is "best to leave them to die," and that no one wants to take care of such a child. As Scheper-Hughes points out, the folk (emic) symptoms of fatal childhood diseases in Northeast Brazil correspond to (etic) symptoms of "malnutrition and parasitic infections interacting with physical and psychological neglect." To the extent that mothers practice indirect (or direct) infanticide through neglect, they are reacting to life-threatening conditions that are not of their own making: shortage of food, contaminated water supplies, unchecked infectious diseases, lack of day care for children of working mothers, absence of affordable medical care, and the other stigmas and penalties of extreme poverty. While recognizing that mothers hasten the deaths of their unwanted children by rationing infant and child care, we must not fall into the trap of "blaming the victims." These women do not have access to modern forms of contraception or to medical abortion, and they are themselves too poorly nourished to limit their pregnancies by prolonged lactation. Moreover, abstinence is difficult for them because of their need to attract male support and companionship. In Scheper-Hughes's words, because of the indignities and inhumanities forced on them, these women must at times "make choices and decisions that no woman and mother should have to make" (1984:541, 1992).

were conceived while their mothers were still in their teens and were therefore still growing, which increases the probability that their babies would be born underweight and vulnerable to disease [Frisancho, Matos, and Flegel 1983].) Some women indicated that the last born had been unwanted and that "It was a blessing that God decided to take them in their infancy" (Scheper-Hughes 1984:539).

More important than birth order in determining a mother's tendency to withdraw support from a particular infant was the mother's "perception of the child's innate constitution and temperament as they relate to 'readiness or fitness for life.' " Mothers expressed a preference for "quick, sharp, active, verbal, and developmentally precocious children" (ibid.:

FIGURE *13.5*

DOOMED INFANTS, NORTHEAST BRAZIL
(A) Mother says that her 16-month-old son has an "aversion" to life and will not live much longer. The color of his hair and lack of teeth show that he is suffering from advanced protein-calorie malnutrition. **(B)** Baby has anemia and is listless and malnourished. The mother says she is conforming to God's will that the child will soon be an angel.

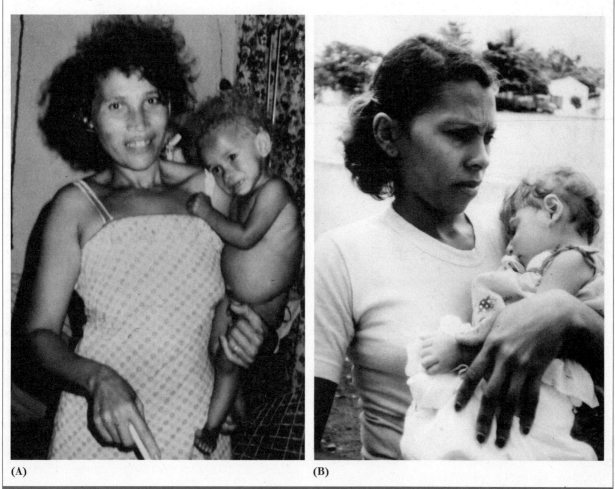

(A)   **(B)**

INDUSTRIAL MODES OF REPRODUCTION

Shifts in the costs and benefits of rearing children lie behind the "demographic transition" that took place in Europe, the United States, and Japan during the nineteenth century. This transition involved a drop in both birth rates and death rates and a slowing of the rate of population growth (Fig. 13.6).

With industrialization, the cost of rearing children rose rapidly, especially after the introduction of child-labor laws and compulsory education statutes. The skills required to earn a living took longer to ac-

quire; hence, parents had to wait longer before they could receive any economic benefits from their children. At the same time, the whole pattern of how people earned their livings changed. Work ceased to be something done by family members on the family farm or in the family shop. Rather, people earned wages as individuals in factories and offices. What the family did together was to consume; its only product was children. The return flow of benefits from rearing children came to hinge more and more on their willingness to help out in the medical and financial crises that beset older people. But longer life spans and

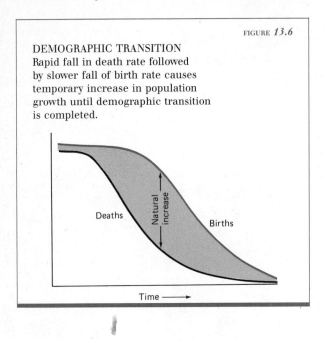

FIGURE *13.6*

DEMOGRAPHIC TRANSITION
Rapid fall in death rate followed
by slower fall of birth rate causes
temporary increase in population
growth until demographic transition
is completed.

spiraling medical costs make it increasingly unrealistic for parents to expect such help from their children. Thus, the industrial nations have been obliged to substitute old-age and medical insurance and old-age homes for the preindustrial system in which children took care of their aged parents.

To meet the rise in the cost of rearing children in industrial societies, wives as well as husbands must participate in the wage-earning labor force. As long as this situation continues, more and more men and women will decide to have only one child or none, and more and more individuals will find that the traditional forms of marriage, family, sex, and emotional togetherness are incompatible with the maintenance of middle-class status (Harris and Ross 1987). Further discussion of this process as it affects the United States is found in Chapter 26.

SUMMARY

Production sets limits to reproduction. Contrary to the position advocated by Thomas Malthus, populations do not normally rise to the maximum limit of production, nor are they usually checked by starvation and other catastrophes. Instead, they are usually maintained well below carrying capacity. Reproduction leads to population pressure, which leads to intensification, depletions, and changes in the modes of production. This can be seen in the sequence leading from Paleolithic big-game hunting to Neolithic agriculture.

Variations in reproductive rates cannot be explained by the universal desire to have children. Rather, reproductive rates reflect the variable costs and benefits of rearing children under different modes of production. Band-organized hunter-gatherer reproduction rates are influenced by the need for women to avoid carrying more than one infant at a time over long distances, as well as by the limited intensifiability of the hunter-gatherer mode of production. Sedentary agriculturalists rear more children because agriculture can be intensified, the burden of carrying infants and toddlers is reduced, children more rapidly "pay for themselves," and senior children can take care of juniors.

Findings from contemporary peasant societies lend support to the cost-benefit approach to reproductive rates. In Java, children contribute about half of all the wealth of household members. In Bangladesh, male children by age 12 produce more than they consume, and in 3 more years make up for all previous expenses incurred on their behalf. Moreover, contrary to the popular impression that the poorest peasant households have the most children, there is often a positive correlation between large numbers of children and wealthier families.

With the expansion of urban, industrial, technical, and white-collar employment, the benefits of raising fewer but "costlier" children outweigh the advantages of rearing many but "cheaper" children. In India and Sri Lanka, the number of children per woman has declined as children cease to have important roles in agriculture and as the offspring of peasants find advancement through white-collar jobs and business opportunities that require high levels of education. These shifts in the costs of rearing children in relation to new modes of production are similar to the shifts that brought about the "demographic transition" in nineteenth-century Europe and the United States.

Thus, again contrary to Malthusian theory, preindustrial cultures regulated the sizes of their families so as to minimize the costs and maximize the benefits of reproduction. While they lacked a modern technology of contraception or abortion, they were nonetheless never at a loss for means of controlling birth and death rates. Four principal categories of practices were used: care and treatment of fetuses, infants, and children; care and treatment of girls and women; intensity and duration of lactation; and variations in the frequency of heterosexual coitus. Subtle gradations exist among abortion, infanticide, and induced child mortality. While much controversy surrounds the question of whether poor nutrition reduces the ability of women to conceive, there is no doubt that poor nutrition jeopardizes the life of mother, fetus, and child. The amenorrhea associated with lactation is a more benign form of fertility regulation widely practiced by preindustrial people. Finally, various forms of nonreproductive sex and degree of sexual abstinence can raise or lower reproductive rates.

While there is a "natural" component in human death rates, the influence of natural variables is always conditioned to some extent by cultural practices. Moreover, the influence of disease on death rates in small-scale band and village societies should not be exaggerated. To a surprising extent, even when people are faced with epidemics, droughts, famine, and other natural catastrophes, cultural practices influence demographic outcomes. A vivid example of such practices can be seen in Northeast Brazil: Impoverished mothers who lack access to modern contraception or medical abortion contribute to the extremely high rates of infant and child mortality through the selective neglect and indirect infanticide of their unwanted offspring. Care must be taken not to "blame the victims": Lacking the means of rearing all their children, these mothers have no way to avoid a tragic choice.

The Everyday Life of the Yanomamö

The Yanomamö are a tropical forest horticultural and foraging people who inhabit the remote border region between Venezuela and Brazil near the headwaters of the Orinoco River. Although they have been depicted as extremely fierce and warlike, their life is a rich tapestry of activities devoted to making a living, maintaining peace and harmony within the village, and maintaining favorable relations with the spirit world. These are the aspects of their culture emphasized in the following photos.

*All of the photos were taken by ethnographer-anthropologist Kenneth R. Good, who has lived with the Yanomamö for over 12 years. He has told the story of how he fell in love and married Yarima, a beautiful Yanomamö woman, in an exciting book, **Into the Heart: One Man's Pursuit of Love and Knowledge Among the Yanomama**. The couple and their three children now live in New Jersey and return to visit Yarima's people from time to time.*

INFRASTRUCTURE

A young man uses a set of poles lashed around the peach palm tree with thick vines so that he can shimmy up the tree without touching the branchless trunk, which is covered with extremely sharp, long needles.

A man and his two young sons strip the peach palm fruit and store it in baskets to be boiled and distributed that day when a neighboring village arrives for a feast.

Women close in on the drugged fish in a nearby stream. Bark from a tree has been stripped and put in the water, causing the fish to become stupefied and float to the surface. This is done only once or twice during the dry season, when the streams are quite shallow. Large quantities of fish can be acquired, but this practice still does not change the relatively low importance of fish in the Yanomamö diet.

A young woman carries all the family possessions and her young child as she abandons her house and sets off on a trek in search of wild foods. This occurs when the gardens are exhausted and no foods are available near the communal house. The entire community participates in the trek. The man in the background is her husband and will carry only his bow and arrows so that they will be prepared to shoot animals encountered on the trail.

A boy learns from his father how to pluck feathers off a game bird.

The men of the village return from a five-day *heniyomou* hunt to get meat for a village funeral-feast ceremony. On this occasion, 30 men hunting from morning to night for five days did not acquire enough game for the feast and had to go out again to a different locale. This is not uncommon.

A visitor sits in his host's hammock, drinking plantain pap. He has walked for days through the forest to visit this community.

Grievances between villages can be resolved with a chest-pounding duel like this one. This event is more like a sporting contest and results in no further animosity unless someone is severely injured. Then emotions flare and more serious fights can ensue.

Aerial view of a Yanomamö *shapono*, or communal house. These are spaced throughout the forest, one or two days' walking distance apart. Although the house is communal, each family makes its section of the ring. If the leaves are woven tightly, the roof can last for five years. The village usually moves away before this time.

The ethnographer's wife, Yarima, decorates herself with parrot feathers and buzzard down in preparation for entrance and dance in the hosts' village.

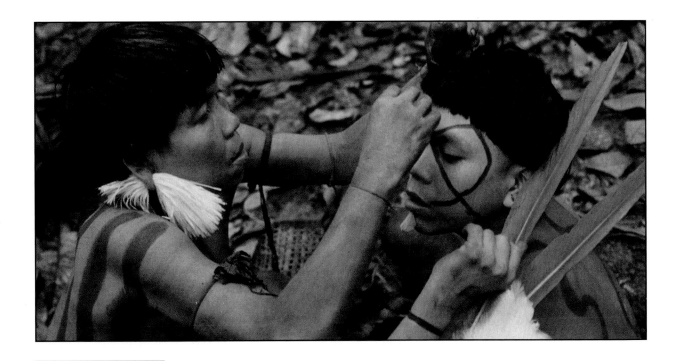

A mother paints her son with *onoto* in the gardens of their hosts before entering and dancing in the central plaza.

The headman of Hasupuweteri negotiates with his visitors in an early-morning trading session prior to their departure. Those villages with access to Western goods trade with more remote villages for Yanomamö goods such as hammocks, hunting dogs, and bows and arrows.

Women dance and sing at night while their men are on a five-day hunt far from the village. They believe that singing about different animals and even imitating their behavior will give the men success on their hunt.

The hallucinogenic drug called *epene* is taken at all shamanistic rituals. The fine powder is derived from the seeds of the spene tree and inhaled into the nostrils through a long tube.

STRUCTURE

In Part V we shall explore the organizational aspects of sociocultural systems. Specifically, Part V is concerned with how production and reproduction are organized through domestic and political groups. While the main source of data will continue to be ethnographic studies, an evolutionary perspective will also be used to explain many of the differences and similarities that characterize the structural features of sociocultural systems. We will be especially concerned to apply both viewpoints to the description and explanation of the structure of inequality as embodied in class, gender, and other types of hierarchical groups.

Economic Organization

In this chapter, our focus is no longer on types of subsistence practices or modes of regulating population growth but on the way in which various kinds of groups involved in production and reproduction organize productive and reproductive activities. We will be concerned mainly with the organization of production. Economies differ according to their characteristic modes of control over production and exchange. We identify the principal kinds of exchange and explore their relationship to infrastructural conditions. We will see that many societies organize their economic activities without the use of money, and that money itself comes in many specialized forms in addition to the all-purpose money with which we are familiar. This leads to the question of whether capitalist economies can be found among prestate societies. The chapter also takes up the question of why people work harder in industrial than in hunter-gatherer societies.

DEFINITION OF ECONOMY

In a narrow sense, *economy* refers to the kinds of decisions people make when they have only limited resources or wealth, and there are unlimited goods and services they would like to acquire or use. Most professional economists hold that in making such decisions, human beings in general tend to *economize,* that is, to maximize the achievement of ends while minimizing the expenditure of means (or to maximize benefits while minimizing costs). For most anthropologists, however, an economy refers to the activities people engage in to produce and obtain goods and services (setting aside the question of whether they are "economizing"):

An economy is a set of institutionalized activities which combine natural resources, human labor, and technology to acquire, produce, and distribute material goods and specialist services in a structured, repetitive fashion. (Dalton 1969:97)

These two definitions of economy are not incompatible. Anthropologists stress the fact that the specific motivations for producing, exchanging, and consuming goods and services are shaped by cultural traditions. Different cultures value different goods and services and tolerate or prohibit different kinds of relationships among the people who produce, exchange, and consume. As we will see in a moment, some cultures, for example, emphasize cooperation in the production and exchange of wealth, while others emphasize competition in the production and exchange of wealth. Some cultures emphasize communal property; others place great importance on private property. In other words, if "economizing"

takes place, it has different premises and different consequences in different cultural contexts.

INFRASTRUCTURAL VERSUS STRUCTURAL ASPECTS OF ECONOMIES

With respect to the broader definition of economy, it is useful to maintain a distinction between those aspects that have been treated as modes of production (Ch. 12) and hence as parts of infrastructure and those aspects that we can more conveniently examine as part of the structural level of sociocultural systems. As we have seen, modes of production are characterized by the way in which a given technology is applied to a specific environment to produce the energy on which social life depends. In this chapter, our concern is not with the type of production process, such as hunting and gathering, pastoralism, or industrial manufacturing, but with the way in which labor is organized and how access to resources, goods, and services is regulated or controlled.

What is the justification for distinguishing between economy as infrastructure and economy as structure? The answer is that many aspects of economic organization (as well as other structural features) have evolved in response to the opportunities and constraints presented by various types of infrastructures. By separating the infrastructural and structural aspects of economies, anthropologists can study the extent to which the organizational features of economy have evolved as a consequence of the evolution of particular kinds of infrastructures.

It is true that production and reproduction cannot proceed without the organizational components of the economy. It is also true that these organizational components in turn impose limits on production and reproduction. As we shall see, however, major transformations in the economic organization of social life do not occur randomly, but in response to infrastructural conditions characteristic of particular modes of production and reproduction. While there are feedbacks (see p. 313) between infrastructure and structure, much evidence supports the viewpoint that the structural features of sociocultural systems generally and in the long run are selected for or against depending primarily on their ability to maximize the benefits and minimize the costs of a given mode of production and reproduction. For example, as we shall see in a moment, various types of systems of exchange are the consequence of certain infrastructural conditions. This relationship cannot plausibly be reversed to make the infrastructural conditions the consequence of certain modes of exchange. Another prime example of how this principle works is the convergence toward a mixture of welfare and market economies among the members of the former Soviet bloc and the advanced industrial nations of the West (see p. 250).

EXCHANGE

Most of what is produced by human labor is distributed by means of *exchange.* (The exceptions consist of instances of direct consumption by the producers themselves.) Exchange refers to the practice of giving and receiving valued objects and services. This practice is more highly developed in our species than in any other. Human beings could not survive infancy without receiving valuable objects and services from their parents. However, patterns of exchange differ markedly from one culture to another. Following the work of the economist Karl Polanyi, anthropologists have come to distinguish three main types of exchange: *reciprocal, redistributive,* and *market.*

RECIPROCAL EXCHANGE

One of the most striking features of the economic life of hunter-gatherers and small-scale agricultural societies is the prominence of exchanges that are conducted according to the principle known as *reciprocity.* In reciprocal exchanges, the flow of products and services is not contingent on any definite counterflow. The partners in the exchange take according to need and give back according to no set rules of time or quantity (Fig. 14.1). (As we shall see [Ch. 18], reciprocity is characteristic of relatively egalitarian societies.)

FIGURE *14.1*
RECIPROCITY AT A YANOMAMÖ FUNERAL FEAST
Close relatives of the deceased are about to distribute a basketful of boiled plantains and smoked meats to the rest of the village.

Richard Lee has written a succinct description of reciprocity as it occurs among the !Kung. In the morning, anywhere from 1 to 16 of the 20 adults in the !Kung band leave camp to spend the day collecting or hunting. They return in the evening with whatever food they have managed to find. Everything brought back to camp is shared equally, regardless of whether the recipients have spent the day sleeping or hunting. Eventually all the adults will have gathered or hunted and given as well as received food. But wide discrepancies in the balance of giving and receiving may exist among individuals over a long period without becoming the subject of any special talk or action (see Box 14.1).

Some form of reciprocal exchange occurs in all cultures, especially among relatives and friends. In the United States and Canada, for example, husbands and wives, friends, and brothers, sisters, and other kin regulate and adjust their economic lives to a minor degree according to informal, uncalculated, give-and-take transactions. Teenagers do not pay cash for their meals at home or the use of the family car. Wives do not bill their husbands for cooking a meal. Friends give each other birthday gifts and Christmas presents. These exchanges, however, constitute only a small portion of the total acts of exchange among North Americans. The great majority of exchanges in modern cultures involve rigidly defined counterflows that must take place by a certain time.

RECIPROCITY AMONG THE !KUNG

Not only do families pool that day's production, but the entire camp—residents and visitors alike—shares equally in the total quantity of food available. The evening meal of any one family is made up of portions of food from each of the other families resident. Foodstuffs are distributed raw or are prepared by the collectors and then distributed. There is a constant flow of nuts, berries, roots and melons from one family fireplace to another until each person resident has received an equitable portion. The following morning a different combination of foragers moves out of camp and when they return late in the day, the distribution of foodstuffs is repeated.

SOURCE: Lee 1969:58.

RECIPROCITY AND THE FREELOADER

As we know from the experience of taking from parents or from giving a birthday or holiday gift and not receiving one in return, the failure of an individual to reciprocate in some degree will eventually lead to bad feelings, even between close relatives and friends or spouses. No one likes a "freeloader." In economies dominated by reciprocity, a grossly asymmetrical exchange does not go unnoticed. Some individuals will come to enjoy reputations as diligent gatherers or outstanding hunters, whereas others acquire reputations as shirkers or malingerers. No specific mechanisms exist for obliging the debtors to even up the score, yet there are subtle sanctions against becoming a complete freeloader. Such behavior generates a steady undercurrent of disapproval. Freeloaders are eventually subject to collective punishment. They may meet with violence because they are suspected of being bewitched or of bewitching others through the practice of sorcery (see p. 294).

What is distinctive about reciprocal exchange, therefore, is not that products and services are simply given away without any thought or expectation of return, but rather that there are (1) no immediate return, (2) no systematic calculation of the value of the services and products exchanged, and (3) an overt denial that a balance is being calculated or that the balance must come out even.

No culture can rely exclusively on purely altruistic sentiments to get its goods and services produced and distributed. But in simple band and prestate village societies, goods and services are produced and reciprocally exchanged in such a way as to avoid the notion of material balance, debt, or obligation. This is accomplished by expressing the necessity for reciprocal exchanges as kinship obligations. These kinship obligations (see Ch. 16) establish reciprocal expectations with respect to food, clothing, shelter, and other goods.

Kinship-embedded reciprocal exchanges constitute only a small portion of modern exchange systems, whereas among hunter-gatherers and small-scale agriculturalists, almost all exchanges take place among kin, for whom the giving, taking, and using of goods have sentimental and personal meaning.

RECIPROCITY AND TRADE

Even hunters and gatherers, however, want valuables such as salt, flint, obsidian, red ochre, reeds, and honey that are produced or controlled by groups with whom they have no kinship ties. Among band and village peoples, economic dealings among nonkin are based on the assumption that every "stranger" will try to get the best of an exchange through cheating or stealing. As a result, trading expeditions are likely to be hazardous in the extreme and to bear a resemblance to war parties.

One interesting mechanism for facilitating trade between distant groups is known as *silent trade*. The objects to be exchanged are set out in a clearing, and the first group retreats out of sight. The other group comes out of hiding, inspects the wares, lays down what it regards as a fair exchange of its own products, and retreats again. The first group returns and, if satisfied, removes the traded objects. If not, it leaves the wares untouched as a signal that the balance is not yet even. In this fashion, the Mbuti of the Ituri Forest trade meat for bananas with the Bantu agriculturalists, and the Vedda of Sri Lanka trade honey for iron tools with the Sinhalese. Sedentary villages are more likely to have open and regular forms of trade, but fear of treachery continues. In Malaita, one of the Solomon Islands, women regularly trade fish for pigs and vegetables under the armed guard of their menfolk (Fig. 14.2).

Among the Kapauku of western New Guinea (today, West Irian, Indonesia), full-fledged price markets involving shell and limited-purpose bead money (see p. 249) may have existed before the arrival of European or Indonesion merchants (Fig. 14.3). Generally speaking, however, trade based on marketing and

FIGURE *14.2*

NEW GUINEA MARKET
Man at left is giving yams in exchange for fish at right.

all-purpose money is associated with the evolution of the state (see Chapter 18) and with the use of soldiers and market police to enforce peaceful relations among buyers and sellers.

Perhaps the most common solution to the problem of trading with strangers in the absence of state-supervised markets is the establishment of special *trade partnerships*. In this arrangement, members of different bands or villages regard one another as metaphorical kin. The members of trading expeditions deal exclusively with their trade partners, who greet them as "brothers" and give them food and shelter. Trade partners try to deal with one another in conformity with the principle of reciprocity. They deny an interest in getting the best of the bargain, and offer wares as if they were gifts (Heider 1969).

FIGURE *14.3*

KAPAUKU OF WESTERN NEW GUINEA
The men (wearing penis sheaths) are
counting shell money.

THE KULA

A classic example of trade partnerships is described in Bronislaw Malinowski's *Argonauts of the Western Pacific.* The argonauts in question are the Trobriand Islanders, who trade with neighboring islands by means of daring canoe voyages across the open sea (Fig. 14.4). The entire complex associated with this trade is known as the *Kula.* According to the men who take these risky voyages, the purpose of the Kula trade is to exchange shell ornaments with their trade partners. The ornaments, known to the Trobrianders as *vaygu'a,* consist of armbands and necklaces. In trading with the Dobuans, who live to the southeast, the Trobrianders give armbands and receive necklaces. In trading with the people who live to the southwest, the Trobrianders give necklaces and receive armbands in return. The armbands and necklaces are then traded in opposite directions from island to island, finally passing through their points of origin

from the direction opposite to the one in which they were first traded.

Participation in the Kula trade is a major ambition of youth and a consuming passion of senior men. The *vaygu'a* have been compared with heirlooms or crown jewels. The older they are and the more complex their history, the more valuable they become in the eyes of the Trobrianders. Like many other examples of special-purpose exchange media (see p. 249), Kula valuables are seldom used to "buy" anything. They are, however, given as gifts in marriage and as rewards to canoe builders (Scoditti 1983). Most of the time the ornaments are simply used for the purpose of obtaining other armbands and necklaces. To trade *vaygu'a,* men establish more or less permanent partnerships with each other on distant islands. These partnerships are usually handed down from one kinsman to another, and young men are given a start in the Kula trade by inheriting or receiving an armband or a necklace from a relative.

When the expedition reaches shore, the trade partners greet one another and exchange preliminary gifts. Later, the Trobrianders deliver the precious ornaments, accompanied by ritual speeches and formal acts concerned with establishing the honorable, gift-like character of the exchange. As in the case of reciprocal transactions within the family, the trade partner may not immediately be able to provide a shell whose value is equivalent to the one just received. Although the voyager may have to return home empty-handed except for some preliminary gifts, he does not complain. He expects his trade partner to work hard to make up for the delay by presenting him with even more valuable shells at their next meeting.

Why all this effort in order to obtain a few baubles of sentimental or aesthetic value? As is often the case, the etic aspects of the Kula are different from the emic aspects. The boats that take part in the Kula expedition carry trade items of great practical value in the life of the various island peoples who participate in the Kula ring. While the trade partners fondle and admire their priceless heirlooms, members of the expedition trade for practical items: coconuts, sago palm flour, fish, yams, baskets, mats, wooden swords and clubs, green stone for tools, mussel shells for knives, creepers and lianas for lashings. These items can be bargained over with impunity. Although Trobrianders deny it, the *vaygu'a* are valuable not only for their qualities as heirlooms, but also for their truly priceless gift of trade (Irwin 1983:71ff; Scoditti 1983:265).

Kula is also better understood as part of the Trobriand and the neighboring island's system of achieving or validating political rank. Those who come into

FIGURE *14.4*

KULA CANOE
These large canoes are used by the Trobrianders for long-distance voyages.

possession of the most valuable shells are usually extremely able leaders who are accomplished navigators and, in former times, bold warriors (Campbell 1983:203). This accounts for the fact that in modern times, Kula has persisted even though the amount of practical items traded has declined.

Finally, why the clockwise and counterclockwise circulation of the shells? This feature accords with the notion that Kula is an institution for establishing peaceful interisland relationships to facilitate trade. By preventing partners from trading armbands for armbands or necklaces for necklaces, Kula assures the involvement of a large number of islands in the trade network. (Only limited numbers of long-distance canoe trips are possible.)

REDISTRIBUTIVE EXCHANGE

As we shall see in Chapter 18, the evolution of economic and political systems is in large degree a consequence of the development of coercive forms of exchange that supplement or almost entirely replace reciprocal exchange. Coercive forms of exchange did not appear in sudden full-blown opposition to reciprocal forms. Rather, they probably first arose through what seemed to be merely an extension of familiar reciprocal forms.

The exchange system known as *redistribution* can best be understood as such an extension. In redistribution exchange, the labor products of several different individuals are brought to a central place, sorted by type, counted, and then given away to producers and nonproducers alike. Considerable organizational effort is required if large quantities of goods are to be brought to the same place at the same time and given away in definite shares. This coordination is usually achieved by individuals who act as *redistributors*. Typically, redistributors consciously attempt to increase and to intensify production, for which they gain prestige in the eyes of their peers.

Egalitarian and stratified forms of redistribution must be distinguished. As an *egalitarian* system of exchange, redistribution is carried out by a redistributor who has worked harder than anyone else producing the items to be given away, who takes the smallest portion or none at all, and who, after it is all over, possesses no greater material wealth than anyone else. In its egalitarian form, therefore, redistribution appears to be merely an extreme example of reciprocity; the generous provider gives everything away and for the moment gets nothing in return, except the admiration of those who benefit from the transaction.

In the *stratified* form, however, the redistributor withholds his or her own labor from the production process, retains the largest share, and ends up with more material wealth than anyone else.

Redistributive exchange, like reciprocal exchange, is usually embedded in a complex set of kinship relations and rituals that may obscure the etic significance of the exchange behavior. Redistribution often involves a feast held to celebrate some important event such as a harvest, the end of a ritual taboo, the construction of a house, a death, a birth, or a marriage. A common feature of Melanesian redistributive feasts is that the guests gorge themselves with food, stagger off into the bush, stick their fingers down their throats, vomit, and then return to eating with renewed zest. Another common feature of redistributive feasting is the boastful and competitive attitude of the redistributors and their kin with respect to other individuals or groups who have given feasts. This contrasts markedly with reciprocal exchange. Let us take a closer look at this contrast.

FIGURE *14.5*

SEMAI HUNTER
Among the Semai, reciprocity prevails.

RECIPROCITY VERSUS REDISTRIBUTION

Boastfulness and acknowledgment of generosity are incompatible with the basic etiquette of reciprocal exchanges. Among the Semai of Central Malaya, no one even says "thank you" for the meat received from another hunter (Fig. 14.5). Having struggled all day to lug the carcass of a pig home through the jungle heat, the hunter allows his prize to be cut up into exactly equal portions, which are then given away to the entire group. As Robert Dentan explains, to express gratitude for the portion received indicates that you are the kind of ungenerous person who calculates how much you give and take:

In this context saying thank you is very rude, for it suggests first that one has calculated the amount of a gift and second, that one did not expect the donor to be so generous. (1968:491)

To call attention to one's generosity is to indicate that others are in debt to you and that you expect them to repay you. It is repugnant to many egalitarian peoples even to suggest that they have been treated generously.

Richard Lee tells how he learned about this aspect of reciprocity through a revealing incident. To please the !Kung with whom he was staying, he decided to buy a large ox and have it slaughtered as a Christmas present. He spent days searching the neighboring Bantu agricultural villages looking for the largest and fattest ox in the region. Finally, he bought what appeared to be a perfect specimen. But one !Kung after another took him aside and assured him that he had been duped into buying an absolutely worthless animal. "Of course, we will eat it," they said, "but it won't fill us up—we will eat and go home to bed with stomachs rumbling." Yet when Lee's ox was slaughtered, it turned out to be covered with a thick layer of fat. Lee eventually succeeded in getting his informants to explain why they had claimed that his gift was valueless, even though they certainly knew better than he did what lay under the animal's skin (see Box 14.2).

In flagrant violation of these prescriptions for modesty in reciprocal exchanges, redistributive exchange systems involve public proclamations that the host is a generous person and a great provider. This boasting is one of the most conspicuous features of

---

BOX *14.2*

MODEST PROVIDERS

Yes, when a young man kills much meat he comes to think of himself as a chief or a big man, and he thinks of the rest of us as his servants or inferiors. We can't accept this, we refuse one who boasts, for someday his pride will make him kill somebody. So we always speak of his meat as worthless. This way we cool his heart and make him gentle.

SOURCE: Richard Lee 1968:62.

FIGURE *14.6*

KWAKIUTL OF THE NORTHWEST
The signs over the doors read "Boston. He is the Head chief of Arweete. He is true Indian. Honest. He don't owe no trouble to white man" and "Cheap. He is one of the head chief of all tribes in this country. White man can get information." Photo was taken about 1901–1902.

BOX *14.3*

BOASTFUL PROVIDERS

I am the great chief who makes people
    ashamed.
I am the great chief who makes people
    ashamed.
Our chief brings shame to the faces.
Our chief brings jealousy to the faces.
Our chief makes people cover their faces
    by what he is continually doing in this
    world.
Giving again and again, [fish] oil feasts to
    all the tribes.
I am the only great tree, I the chief!
I am the only great tree, I the chief!
You are my subordinates, tribes.
You sit in the middle of the rear of the
    house, tribes.
I am the first to give you property, tribes.
I am your Eagle, tribes!
Bring your counter of property, tribes, that
    he may try in vain to count the property
    that is to be given away by the great cop-
    per maker, the chief.

SOURCE: Benedict 1934.

---

the *potlatches* (Jonaitas 1991) that were once engaged in by the native Americans who inhabit the northwest coast of the United States and Canada (Fig. 14.6). In descriptions made famous by Ruth Benedict in *Patterns of Culture*, the Kwakiutl redistributor seems like a virtual megalomaniac (See Box 14.3).

In the potlatch the guests behaved somewhat like Lee's !Kung. They grumbled and complained and were careful never to appear satisfied or impressed. Nonetheless, there was a careful public counting of all the gifts displayed and distributed (Fig. 14.7). Both hosts and guests believed that the only way to throw off the obligations incurred in accepting these gifts was to hold a counter potlatch in which the tables were reversed (Jonaitas 1991).

THE INFRASTRUCTURAL BASIS OF REDISTRIBUTION AND RECIPROCITY

Why do the !Kung esteem hunters who never draw attention to their own generosity, whereas the Kwak-

FIGURE 14.7

POTLATCH
Spokesman for Kwakiutl chief making speech next to blankets about to be given away.

iutl and other redistributor societies esteemed leaders who could boast about how much they gave away? One theory is that reciprocity reflects an adjustment to modes of production in which intensification would rapidly lead to diminishing returns and environmental depletions. Hunters and gatherers seldom have an opportunity to intensify production without rapidly reaching the point of diminishing returns. Intensification poses a grave threat to such peoples in the form of faunal overkills. To encourage the !Kung hunter to be boastful is to endanger the group's survival. In addition, reciprocity is advantageous for most hunter-gatherers because there is a great deal of chance variation in the success of individuals and families from one day to the next. As Richard Gould (1982:76) has observed, "The greater the degree of risk, the greater the extent of sharing."

Agricultural villages generally have greater leeway for increasing production by investing more la-

bor. They can raise their standards of consumption if they work harder, and yet not immediately jeopardize their energy efficiency by depleting their habitats. Additionally, agriculture is usually a more dependable, less risky mode of production than hunting and gathering.

The Kwakiutl were not agriculturalists; they derived most of their food from the annual upriver runs of salmon and candlefish. Using aboriginal dip nets, the Kwakiutl and their neighbors could not affect the overall rate of reproduction of these species. Hence, they relied on a highly intensifiable mode of production. Moreover, while there were fluctuations in the size of the annual migrations of these fish from one year to the next (Langdon 1979), there were few risks involved from day to day. Thus, it was ecologically feasible for the Kwakiutl to try to intensify production by using prestige and the privilege of boasting to reward those who worked harder or who got others to work harder (Isaac 1988; Mitchell and Donald 1988).

THE ORIGIN OF DESTRUCTIVE POTLATCHES

Potlatching came under scientific scrutiny long after the people of the Pacific Northwest had entered into trade and wage-labor relations with Russian, English, Canadian, and American nationals. Declining populations and a sudden influx of wealth had combined to make the potlatches increasingly competitive and destructive by the time Franz Boas began to study them in the 1880s (Rohner 1969). At this period, the entire tribe was in residence at the Fort Rupert trading station of the Hudson's Bay Company, and the attempt on the part of one potlatch giver to outdo another had become an all-consuming passion. Blankets, boxes of fish oil, and other valuables were deliberately being destroyed by burning or by throwing them into the sea. On one occasion, described in *Patterns of Culture* (Benedict 1934), an entire house burned to the ground when too much fish oil was poured on the fire. Potlatches that ended in this fashion were regarded as great victories for the potlatch givers.

It seems likely that before the coming of the Europeans, Kwakiutl potlatch feasts were less destructive and more like Melanesian feasts (see p. 308). Although rivalrous feasts are wasteful, the net increment in total production may exceed the loss due to gorging and spoilage. Moreover, after the visitors have eaten to their satisfaction, there still remains much food, which they carry back home with them.

The fact that guests come from distant villages leads to additional important ecological and economic advantages. It has been suggested that feasting rivalry between groups raises productivity throughout a region more than if each village feasts only its own producers. Second, as has been suggested for the Northwest Coast region, rivalrous intervillage redistributions may overcome the effects of localized, naturally induced production failures. Failure of the salmon runs at a particular stream could threaten the survival of certain villages, while neighbors on other streams continue to catch their usual quotas. Under such circumstances, the impoverished villagers would want to attend as many potlatches as they could and carry back as many vital supplies as they could get their hosts to part with by reminding them of how big their own potlatches had been in previous years. Intervillage potlatches thus may have been a form of savings in which the prestige acquired at one's own feast served as a tally. The tally was redeemed when the guests turned hosts. If a village was unable year after year to give its own potlatches, it lost its prestige credit (Piddocke 1965; Suttles 1960).

When an impoverished and unprestigious group could no longer hold its own potlatches, the people abandoned their defeated redistributor-chief and took up residence among relatives in more productive villages. Thus the boasting and the giving away and displaying of wealth led to the recruitment of additional labor power to the work force gathered about a particularly effective redistributor. This helps to explain why Northwest Coast peoples lavished so much effort on the production of their world-famous totem poles. These poles bore the redistributor-chief's "crests" in the guise of carved mythic figures; title to the crests was claimed on the basis of outstanding potlatch achievements. The larger the pole, the greater the potlatch power and the more the members of poor villages would be tempted to change their residence and gather around another chief.

With the coming of the Europeans, however, there was a shift toward more destructive forms of redistribution. The impact of European diseases had reduced the population of the Kwakiutl from about 10,000 in 1836 to about 2,000 by the end of the century. At the same time, the trading companies, canneries, lumber mills, and gold-mining camps pumped an unprecedented amount of wealth into the aboriginal economy. The percentage of people available to celebrate the glory of the potlatcher dropped. Many villages were abandoned; rivalry intensified for the allegiance of the survivors.

A final and perhaps the most important factor in the development of destructive potlatches was the change in the technology and intensity of warfare. The earliest contacts in the late eighteenth century between the Europeans and the native Americans of the Northwest Pacific Coast centered on the fur trade. In return for sea-otter skins, the Europeans gave guns to the Kwakiutl and to the Kwakiutl's traditional enemies. This had a double effect. On the one hand, warfare became more deadly; on the other hand, it forced local groups to fight one another for control of trade in order to get the ammunition on which success in warfare now depended. Small wonder, therefore, that as population declined, the potlatch chiefs were willing to throw away or destroy wealth that was militarily unimportant in order to attract manpower for warfare and fur trade (Ferguson 1984).

Stratified Redistribution

A subtle line separates *egalitarian* from *stratified* forms of redistribution. In the egalitarian form, contributions to the central pool are voluntary, and the workers either get back all or most of what they put into it or receive items of comparable value. In the stratified form, the workers must contribute to the central pool or suffer penalties, and they may not get back anything. Again, in the egalitarian form, the redistributor lacks the power to coerce followers to intensify production and must depend on their goodwill; in the stratified form, the redistributor has that power and the workers must depend on that person's goodwill. The processes responsible for the evolution of one form of redistribution to another will be discussed in Chapter 18. Here, we will only note that fully developed forms of stratified redistribution imply the existence of a class of rulers who have the power to compel others to do their bidding. The expression of this power in the realm of production and exchange results in the political subordination of the labor force and in its partial or total loss of control over access to natural resources, technology, and the place, time, and hours of work.

PRICE-MARKET EXCHANGE: BUYING AND SELLING

Marketplaces occur in rudimentary form wherever groups of strangers assemble and trade one item for another. Among hunter-gatherers and simple agriculturalists, marketplace trading usually involves the barter of one valuable consumable item for another: fish for yams, coconuts for axes, and so forth. In this type of market, before the development of all-purpose money (see the next section), only a limited range of goods or services is exchanged. The great bulk of exchange transactions takes place outside the marketplace and continues to involve various forms of reciprocity and redistribution. With the development of all-purpose money, however, *price-market* exchanges came to dominate all other forms of exchange. In a price market, the price of the goods and services exchanged is determined by buyers competing with buyers and sellers competing with sellers. Virtually everything that is produced or consumed soon comes to have a price, and buying and selling becomes a major cultural preoccupation or even an obsession (Fig. 14.8).

It is possible to engage in reciprocal exchange using money, as when a friend gives a loan and does not specify when it must be repaid. Redistributive exchange can also be carried out with money, as in the collection of taxes and the disbursement of welfare payments. Buying and selling on a price market, however, is a distinctive mode of exchange, since it involves the specification of the precise time, quantity, and type of payment. Furthermore, unlike either reciprocity or redistribution, once the money payment is concluded, no further obligation or responsibility exists between buyer and seller. They can walk away from each other and never meet again.

FIGURE *14.8*

HUNTING AND GATHERING IN THE U.S.

Price-market exchanges, therefore, are noteworthy for the anonymity and impersonality of the exchange process, and stand in contrast to the personal and kin-based exchanges of reciprocal and redistributive economies. Now let us take a closer look at the nature of that strange entity we call money.

MONEY

The use of certain objects to symbolize and measure the social value of other objects occurs almost universally. And such standard-of-value "stuffs" are widely exchanged for goods and services. Throughout much of East Africa, for example, cattle are a standard of value that can be used for measuring the value of a wife. A young man gives cattle to his father-in-law and gets a wife in return (see p. 266). In many parts of Melanesia, shells are exchanged for stone implements, pottery, and other valuable artifacts. Elsewhere, beads, feathers, shark teeth, dog teeth, or pig tusks are exchanged for other valuable items and are given as compensation for death or injury and for personal services rendered by magicians, canoe builders, and other specialists. While these standards of value possess some of the characteristics of modern coins or paper currency, they all lack one or more of the major characteristics of money found in societies that have price-market economies. In price-market economies money has the following characteristics:

1. *Portability.* It comes in sizes and shapes convenient for being carried about from one transaction to the next.
2. *Divisibility.* Its various forms and values are explicit multiples of each other.
3. *Convertibility.* A transaction completed by a higher-valued unit can be made as well by its lower-valued multiples.
4. *Generality.* Virtually all goods and services have a money value.
5. *Anonymity.* For most purchases, anyone with enough money to pay the market price can conclude a transaction.
6. *Legality.* The nature and quantity of money in circulation is controlled by a government.

Where reciprocity, egalitarian redistribution, and trade-partner relations are the dominant modes of exchange, modern dollar and cents types of money do not and cannot exist.

For example, cattle that are exchanged for wives are not the kind of currency you would want to take to the supermarket checkout counter, being neither very portable nor readily divisible. As employed in bride-price (see p. 268), cattle are frequently not convertible; that is, a large, beautiful, fat bull with a local reputation cannot readily be substituted for by two small and undistinguished animals. Furthermore, cattle lack generality, since only wives can be "purchased" with them, and they lack anonymity because any stranger who shows up with the right amount of cattle will find that he cannot simply leave the animals and take off with the bride. Cattle are exchanged for women only between kinship groups who have an interest in establishing or reinforcing preexisting social relationships. Finally, cattle are put into circulation by each individual household as a result of productive effort that is unregulated by any central authority.

Some prestate money stuffs bear a greater resemblance to modern currencies. A famous example is that of the shell money used by the inhabitants of Rossell Island, which lies off the east coast of New Guinea. The shells are classified into some 40 named units that rise from low to medium to high value. Shells of low value can be used to purchase food, pottery, tools, and other ordinary goods. However, these shells cannot be used for the important exchanges that accompany pig redistributions, weddings, and funerals. In order for such exchanges to take place, "payment" has to be made with the higher-ranking shells (Fig. 14.9). The most valuable shells are owned and traded by "big men" (see p. 308). No amount of low-value shells could buy a high-ranking one; that is, they are not convertible (see p. 348). Moreover, the high-ranking shells do not circulate. Instead, their owners take them back after the pig feast, marriage, or funeral and substitute a definite number of lower-ranking shells. While each higher-ranking shell is divisible in the sense of having a value that can be expressed in terms of lower-ranking shells, the lower-ranking shells are not acceptable for important exchanges. If Rossell Islanders who have only smaller-denomination shells want to hold a ceremony, they must appeal to a "big man" to bring out his higher-ranking shells to back up or validate the lower-ranking ones. This service enhances the big man's power and prestige (Lick 1983:511).

CAPITALISM

Price-market money exchange reaches its highest development when it is embedded in the form of political economy known as *capitalism*. In capitalist societies, buying and selling by means of all-purpose money extends to land, resources, and housing. Labor has a price called *wages,* and money itself has

FIGURE *14.9*
SHELL MONEY
Cowrie and Rongo shell money from the Solomon Islands.

a price called *interest*. Of course, there is no such thing as a completely free market in which price is set wholly by supply and demand and in which everything can be sold. By comparison with other forms of political economy, however, capitalism is aptly described as a political economy in which money can buy anything. This being so, everyone tries to acquire as much money as possible, and the object of production itself is not merely to provide valuable goods and services but to increase one's possession of money; that is, to make a profit and accumulate capital (Fig. 14.10). The rate of capitalist production depends on the rate at which profits can be made, and this in turn depends on the rate at which people purchase, use, wear out, and destroy goods and services. Hence, an enormous effort is expended on extolling the virtues and benefits of products in order to convince consumers that they should make additional purchases. Prestige is awarded not to the person who works hardest or gives away the greatest amount of wealth, but rather to the person who has the most possessions and who consumes at the highest rate. Capitalism inevitably leads to marked inequalities in wealth based on differential access to capital, technology, and

FIGURE 14.10

TOKYO STOCK EXCHANGE
The public sale and purchase of shares in companies and corporations is a fundamental feature of capitalist economies.

resources. As in all stratified political-economic systems, the rich use soldiers and police forces to prevent the poor from confiscating their wealth and privileges.

INDUSTRIAL INFRASTRUCTURE, COMMUNISM, AND CAPITALISM

Despite its many negative features, capitalism has emerged as a more efficient way of organizing the economy of advanced industrial countries than the former Soviet and East European centralized "communist" or "command" economies. As predicted by the principle that the infrastructural aspects of sociocultural systems influence the structural aspects more than the other way around, Russia and the other former members of the Soviet Union and the countries of Eastern Europe are converging toward a greater degree of reliance on price-market mechanisms, privatized investment, and more democratic forms of political organization.

It should not be forgotten, however, that the most advanced industrial countries have for a long time been converging toward economies in which market forces are subject to a substantial amount of state regulation and in which as much as 15 to 20 percent of the labor force is directly employed by government bureaucracies or state-supported industries. The massive convergence that appears to be taking place in response to the opportunities and constraints of advanced industrial modes of production is thus neither toward a market economy nor toward a command economy, but to a mixture of the two.

"PRIMITIVE CAPITALISM"? THE KAPAUKU CASE

In general, band and village societies lack the essential features of capitalism because, as we have seen, their exchange systems are based on reciprocal, and redistributive exchanges rather than on price-market exchanges. In some cases, however, egalitarian, reciprocal, and redistributive systems may have certain features strongly reminiscent of contemporary capitalism.

The Kapauku Papuans of West Irian, Indonesia, are a case in point (see Fig. 14.3). According to Leopold Pospisil (1963), the Kapauku have an economy that is best described as "primitive capitalism." All Kapauku agricultural land is said to be owned individually; money sales are the regular means of exchange; money in the form of shells and glass beads can be used to buy food, domesticated animals, crops, and land; money can also be used as payment for labor. Rent (see p. 328) for leased land and interest on loans are also said to occur.

A closer look at the land tenure situation, however, reveals fundamental differences between the political economy of Kapauku and capitalist peasant societies (see p. 329). To begin with, there is no landowning class. Instead, access to land is controlled by kinship groups known as *sublineages* (see p. 281). No individual is without membership in such a group. These sublineages control communal tracts of land, which Pospisil calls "territories."

It is only within sublineage territories that one may speak of private titles, and the economic significance of these titles is minimal on several counts: (1) The price of land is so cheap that all the gardens under production have a market value in shell money less than the value of ten female pigs. (2) Prohibition against trespass does not apply to sublineage kin. (3) Although even brothers will ask each other for land payments, credit is freely extended among all sublineage members. The most common form of credit with respect to land consists merely of giving land on loan and in expectation that the favor will shortly be returned. (4) Each sublineage is under the leadership of a *headman* (see Chapter 17) whose authority depends on his generosity, especially toward the members of his own sublineage. A rich headman does not refuse to lend his kinsmen whatever they need to gain access to the environment, since "a selfish individual who hoards money and fails to be generous never sees the time when his word is taken seriously and his advice and decisions followed, no matter how rich he may become" (Pospisil 1963:49).

Obviously, therefore, the wealth of the headman does not bestow the power associated with capitalist ownership. In Brazil or India, tenants or sharecroppers can be barred from access to land and water regardless of their landlord's "reputation." In the United States, under the rules of capitalist landownership, it is of no significance to the sheriff and the police officers when they evict farmers that the bank is being "selfish."

Pospisil states that differences in wealth are correlated with striking differences in consumption of food and that Kapauku children from poor homes are undernourished while neighbors are well fed. However, the neighbors are not members of the same sublineage: As Pospisil notes, sublineage kinsmen "exhibit mutual affection and a strong sense of belonging and unity" and "any kind of friction within the group is regarded as deplorable" (1963:39). It is true that certain sublineages are poorer than others. Sickness and misfortune of various sorts frequently lead to inequalities in physical well-being among kinship units, but such misfortunes do not lead to the formation of a poverty class as they do under capitalism. Without central political controls, marked economic inequalities cannot be perpetuated for long, because the rich cannot defend themselves against the demand of the poor that they be given credit, money, land, or whatever is necessary to end their poverty. Under aboriginal conditions, some Kapauku villagers might have starved while neighbors ate well, but it is extremely unlikely that those who starved did so because they lacked access to land, money, or credit.

A stingy egalitarian redistributor is a contradiction in terms, for the simple reason that there are no police to protect such people from the murderous intentions of those whom they refuse to help. As Pospisil tells it:

> Selfish and greedy individuals, who have amassed huge personal properties, but who have failed to comply with the Kapauku requirement of "generosity" toward their less fortunate tribesmen, may be, and actually frequently are, put to death. ...Even in regions such as the Kamu Valley, where such an execution is not a penalty for greediness, a nongenerous wealthy man is ostracized, reprimanded, and thereby finally induced to change his ways. (1963:49)

LANDOWNERSHIP

Ownership of land and resources is one of the most important aspects of political control. It is as much political as economic because unequal access to the environment implies some form of coercion applied by political superiors against political inferiors.

As we have just seen, certain forms of land and resource ownership do occur in egalitarian societies. Ownership of garden lands, for example, is often claimed by kin groups in village communities. Everybody belongs to such kin groups, and hence adults cannot be prevented from using the resources they need to make a living. Landownership by landlords, rulers, or the government, however, means that individuals who lack title or tenure may be barred from using land even if it leads to death through starvation.

As we will see in Chapter 18, ownership of land and resources results from infrastructural processes that select for more dense and more productive populations. In preindustrial and noncapitalist societies, control of land by a ruling class is a stimulus to production because it forces food producers to work longer and harder in order to pay rent for the opportunity to live or work on the owner's land. The food the landowner takes away as rent is not a *superfluous* quantity from the producers' standpoint. The producers usually can very well use the full amount of their output to ease the costs of rearing children or to raise their own standards of living. If they surrender their produce, it is usually because they lack the power to withhold it. In this sense, all rent is an aspect of politics, because without the power to enforce property titles, rent would seldom be paid. Thus, there is a close resemblance between rent and taxation: Both depend on the existence of coercive power in the form of police and weapons that can be called into action if the taxpayer or tenant refuses to pay.

In certain highly centralized societies, as in the ancient Inca Empire (see p. 316), there is no distinction between rent and taxes, since there is no landlord class. Instead, the government bureaucracy has a monopoly over the means of extracting wealth from commoner food producers. States and empires also exercise direct control over production by setting regional or community quotas for particular crops and by conscripting armies of commoners to work on construction projects. Compulsory labor conscription, known as *corvée,* is merely another form of taxation. As we will see in Chapter 18, all these coercive forms of extracting wealth from food producers probably arose from egalitarian forms of redistribution as a consequence of intensification and population pressure.

THE DIVISION OF LABOR

One of the most important organizational features of every economy is the assignment of different tasks to different people. This is called the *division of labor.* All economies, for example, assign different kinds of work to children and adults and to males and females. In most hunting and simple agricultural economies, men hunt large animals, fish, collect honey, and burn and clear forests. Women and children collect shellfish, plants, small animals; they weed, harvest, and process grains and tubers. Men do most of the craft work in hard materials such as stone, wood, and metals; women spin fibers, weave cloth, and make pottery and baskets. In more advanced economies, men usually do the plowing and the herding of large animals. In almost all societies, women do most of the cooking of plant foods, water carrying, cleaning, and other household chores, plus taking care of infants and small children. In general, in preindustrial societies, men perform the activities that require greater muscular effort and freedom of movement (Burton and White 1987; Murdock and Provost 1973).

It seems likely that the division between male and female tasks in hunter-gatherer and simple agricultural economies adds to the efficiency of food production. Because of their heavier musculature, men can bend stronger bows, hurl spears further, and wield bigger clubs (see p. 353). Training men rather than women in the use of these weapons has another advantage: Since the weapons of war are essentially the weapons of the hunt, investment in the training of men to be hunters simultaneously trains them to be warriors. In hunter-gatherer and simple agricultural societies, women are seldom trained to be warriors (see p. 353). It is consistent with this pattern, therefore, that men also specialize in craft production involving stone, metal, and wood, since these are the materials out of which the weapons of war and the hunt are fashioned (Murdock and Provost 1973).

While the muscle-strength differences between men and women can be reduced by training, the remaining advantage for males—20 to 30 percent—is sufficient to make the difference between life and death in certain kinds of economies. In India, for example, every ounce of human muscle power is needed to carry out plowing operations with oxen and crude plows. Males carry out the most physically demanding tasks not to keep women down but to keep production up (Maclachlan 1983).

The impact of various forms of the division of labor between males and females on sex and gender roles will be discussed in Chapter 20. Little of this explanation applies to the division of labor by gender in industrial societies, where the use of machines cancels out most of the muscular advantage that men have over women (see p. 356).

SPECIALIZATION

One of the most pronounced trends in cultural evolution is the increasing amount of *specialization* that accompanies the expansion of production and the growth of population. In hunter-gatherer and other small-scale societies, virtually every adult male does the same kind of work and virtually every adult female does the same kind of work. As per capita production increases, more and more adults become craft specialists, first parttime, then fulltime. Concomitant with the rise of the state, substantial numbers of people cease to work directly in food production but devote themselves full time to such crafts as pottery, weaving, metallurgy, canoe building, and trading. Others become scribes, priests, rulers, warriors, and servants. The tendency toward increasing specialization is even stronger in industrial societies. The U.S. Bureau of Labor Statistics, for example, keeps track of 80,000 different kinds of jobs. Clearly the process of specialization depends on high rates of production and reproduction. Of course, specialization itself increases the efficiency of production, but it cannot do so unless the basic mode of energy production is capable of being intensified. Only advanced forms of agriculture can support an economy organized around full-time specialists.

PATTERNS OF WORK

The flip side of the lack of specialization in hunter-gatherer and simple agricultural societies is that each adult performs many different tasks from day to day, in contrast to the standardized routines of factory or office employees. Moreover, the decision to switch from one task to another—from setting traps to making arrows or collecting honey, for example—is largely voluntary and arrived at either individually or by group consensus. Therefore, it would probably be correct to say that people in small-scale, prestate societies do not experience work as a tedious aspect of life. Indeed, recent experimental reforms of factory work patterns are designed to let workers do many jobs instead of just one and to include them in "quality circles" that make decisions about how tasks are performed. These experiments represent attempts to recapture some of the enviable characteristics of work in small-scale, unspecialized economies.

In societies with hunter-gatherer and simple agricultural infrastructures, people do not spend as much time at work as in intensive agriculture societies. The !Kung San, for example, put in an average of only about 20 hours per week in hunting. The basic reason for this is that their mode of production is not intensifiable. If they worked more hours per week, they would not only find it progressively more difficult to capture their prey, they would also run the risk of depleting the animal population below the point of recovery. In a sense, the !Kung San benefit from being at the mercy of the natural rates of increase of the plants and animals in their habitat; their mode of production obliges them to work less than intensive agriculturalists or modern factory workers.

In Table 14.1 the amount of time spent on work among the !Kung is compared with that in two other societies: the Machiguenga, slash-and-burn agriculturalists of the eastern Andes in Peru (Fig. 14.11), and Kali Loro, an irrigation rice-growing peasant village of Java. The average work time is considerably greater for both sexes in Kali Loro, the society that has the most advanced technology. The basic reason for this is that, as previously discussed, irrigation agriculture is highly intensifiable (p. 210). In addition, Kali Loro is part of a stratified state society in which there are political and economic controls such as taxation, rent, and price markets, which compel or induce people to work more hours than would be necessary if they could keep for their own use the value of all the goods and services they produce.

Work occupies an ever greater part of daily life among industrial wage earners. To the basic eight-hour day, add one hour for commuting, a half hour for shopping for food and other items (including transportation), a half hour for cooking, a half

	!Kung		Machiguenga		Kali Loro	
	Men	Women	Men	Women	Men	Women
Food production and preparation	3.09	1.80	4.60	4.20	5.49	4.70
Crafts	1.07	0.73	1.40	2.10	0.50	2.32
Trade/wage work	0.00	0.00	0.00	0.00	1.88	1.88
Housework/child care	2.20	3.20	0.00	1.10	0.50	2.07
Total	6.36	5.73	6.00	7.40	8.37	10.97

TABLE *14.1*

HOURS OF WORK PER DAY

SOURCES: Carlstein 1983; Johnson 1975; Lee 1979; White 1976.

FIGURE *14.11*

MACHIGUENGA AT WORK

As in most slash-and-burn economies, Machiguenga men do the heavy work of felling trees and clearing the forest for new plantings. Here, a Machiguenga uses the felled trees to build a house.

FIGURE *14.13*

LABOR-SAVING DEVICES THAT DON'T SAVE WORK

The first assembly line. Ford's Highland Park, Michigan, magneto assembly line saved 15 minutes per unit and initiated the era of mass production in 1913—but the workers worked harder than ever.

FIGURE *14.12*

ALL WORK AND NO PLAY IN A JAPANESE CAMERA FACTORY

Workers get 10 minutes per day for exercise and 10 minutes per day for a "tea break."

hour for housework and repairs, and a half hour for child care (including transportation of children and baby-sitters). These are minimal estimates; for many modern-day Americans, the time devoted to each activity could be more than doubled. (Gross 1984). The minimal total—11 hours—is on a par with the work time of the Javanese peasant women. (True, this schedule is kept only on workdays. But on the weekend, the time devoted to all the other forms of work greatly increases, and many people have second jobs, as well.) When labor leaders boast about how much progress has been made in obtaining leisure for the working class, they have in mind the standard established in nineteenth-century Europe, when factory workers put in 12 hours a day or more, rather than the standards observed by the Machiguenga or the !Kung (Figs. 14.12 and 14.13).

SUMMARY

All societies have an economy—a set of institutions that combines technology, labor, and natural resources to produce and distribute goods and services. The organizational aspects of economy are distinguished from its infrastructural aspects in order to explore the relationship between infrastructure and structure. The convergence toward mixed-market and command economies among advanced industrial societies, for example, is best understood as selection for an economic structure that increases the efficiency of the industrial mode of production. Similarly, selection for different modes of exchange reflects different degrees of intensifiability and population growth.

Exchange is an integral part of all economies, but there are several different ways of organizing the flow of goods and services from producers to consumers.

Modern-day price markets and buying and selling are not universal traits. The idea that money can buy everything (or almost everything) has been alien to most of the human beings who have ever lived. Two other modes of exchange—reciprocity and redistribution—once played a more important economic role than price markets.

In reciprocal exchange, the time and quantity of the counterflow is not specified. This kind of exchange can be effective only when it is embedded in kinship or close personal relationships. Daily food distribution among the !Kung San is an example of reciprocal exchange. Control over the counterflow in reciprocal exchange is achieved by communal pressure against freeloaders and shirkers. Reciprocity lingers on in price-market societies within kinship groups and is familiar to many of us as gift giving to relatives and friends.

In the absence of price markets and police-military supervision, trade poses a special problem to people accustomed to reciprocal exchange. Silent barter is one solution. Another is to create trading partners who treat each other as kin. The Kula is a classic example of how barter for necessities is carried out under the cloak of reciprocal exchanges.

Redistributive exchange involves the collection of goods in a central place and its disbursement by a redistributor to the producers. In the transition from egalitarian to stratified forms of redistribution, production and exchange cross the line separating voluntary from coerced forms of economic behavior. In its egalitarian form, the redistributor depends on the goodwill of the producers; in the stratified form, the producers depend on the goodwill of the redistributor.

Redistribution is characterized by the counting of shares contributed and shares disbursed. Unlike reciprocity, redistribution leads to boasting and overt competition for the prestigious status of great provider. The Kwakiutl potlatch is a classic example of the relationships between redistribution and bragging behavior. The predominance of redistribution over reciprocity is related to the intensifiability of various modes of production. Where production can be intensified without depletions, rivalrous redistributions may serve adaptive ecological functions, such as providing an extra margin of safety in lean years and equalizing regional production. The development of destructive potlatches among the Kwakiutl may have been caused by factors stemming from contact with Europeans, such as the intensification of warfare, trade for guns and ammunition, and depopulation.

Price-market exchange depends on the development of all-purpose money as defined by the criteria of portability, divisibility, convertibility, generality, anonymity, and legality. Although some of these features are possessed by limited-purpose standards of value, as in the case of Rossell Island shell money, all-purpose money and price markets imply the existence of state forms of control.

The highest development of the price-market mode of exchange is associated with the political economy of capitalism, in which virtually all goods and services can be bought and sold. Since capitalist production depends on consumerism, prestige is awarded to those who own or consume the greatest amount of goods and services. Price-market exchanges are embedded in a political economy of control made necessary by the inequalities in access to resources and the conflict between the poor and the wealthy. The Kapauku illustrate why price-market institutions and capitalism cannot exist in the absence of such controls.

The relationship between political forms of control and modes of production and exchange focuses in many societies on the question of landownership. Rent, corvée labor, and taxation all reflect differential access to nature and technology. Thus we see why the comparative study of economics must involve the study of the institutions in which economizing is embedded.

The division of labor is a hallmark of human social life. Gender and age are universally used to assign different economic tasks. In preindustrial societies, men carry out activities that require greater strength. Their monopoly over the weapons of the hunt is also probably related to their role as combatants in warfare. Women in preindustrial societies specialize in tasks centered on food gathering and child care. The infrastructural basis for this widespread sexual division of labor, however, ceases to exist in industrial societies.

Changes in infrastructure—higher energy outputs and bigger populations—are also responsible for changes in the numbers of full-time specialists in advanced agricultural and industrial economies as compared with hunter-gatherers and simple agriculturalists. Parallel with an increase in specialization, work becomes less voluntary, less spontaneous, and more coerced and routinized. Paradoxically, despite the greater amounts of energy harnessed per capita per year, most advanced agriculturalists and factory and office workers labor longer hours than people like the !Kung or the Machiguenga.

Domestic Life

In this chapter, we continue the comparative study of structural features, focusing on the variety of family groups and their relation to aspects of infrastructure. We catch our first glimpse of the astonishing variety of human family forms and of mating arrangements: monogamy, polygyny, and polyandry, secondary marriages and preferred-cousin marriages, to mention only a few. Although this chapter is primarily descriptive, some perennially interesting questions are taken up. Is the nuclear family universal? What is marriage? Can marriage take place between partners of the same sex? Are there marriages in which husband and wife never live together? Why do some types of marriages require a gift to the bride's family while others require a gift to the groom's family? Why is there a taboo against incest in every culture? Is the taboo based on instinctual sexual aversions or is it a cultural adaptation? One important conclusion: There is no single natural way to organize domestic life.

THE DOMESTIC SPHERE OF CULTURE

All societies have activities and thoughts that can usefully be lumped under the category of the *domestic sphere* of life. The focus of the domestic sphere is a dwelling space, shelter, residence, or domicile, in which certain universally recurrent activities take place. It is not possible to give a simple checklist of what these activities are (Netting, Wilk, and Arnould 1984). In many cultures, domestic activities include preparation and consumption of food; cleaning, grooming, teaching, and disciplining the young; sleeping; and adult sexual intercourse. However, there is no culture in which these activities are carried out exclusively within domestic settings. For example, sexual intercourse among band and village peoples more often takes place in the bush or forest than in the house where sleeping occurs. In other instances, sleeping itself takes place primarily away from the setting in which eating occurs, and in still other instances, domiciles may lack resident children, as when childless adults live alone or when children are sent off to school. The variety of combinations of activities that characterize human domestic life is so great that it is difficult to find any single underlying common denominator for all of them. This in itself, however, is an important fact, since no other species exhibits such an enormous range of different behaviors associated with patterns of eating, shelter, sleep, sex, and rearing of infants and children.

THE NUCLEAR FAMILY

Can a particular kind of group be found in all domestic settings? Many anthropologists believe there is such a group, and refer to it as the *nuclear family:* husband, wife, and children (Fig. 15.1). Ralph Linton held the view that father, mother, and child is the "bedrock underlying all other family structures," and he predicted that "the last man will spend his last hours searching for his wife and child" (1959:52). George Peter Murdock found the nuclear family in each of 250 societies. He concluded that it was universal. According to Murdock (1949), the nuclear family fulfills vital functions that cannot be carried out as efficiently by other groups. The functions identified by Murdock are:

1. *Sex.* The nuclear family satisfies sexual needs and diminishes the disruptive force of sexual competition.
2. *Reproduction.* The nuclear family guarantees the protection of the female during her long pregnancy and during the months and years of lactation.
3. *Education.* The nuclear family is essential for enculturation. Only the coresident adult man and woman possess knowledge adequate for the enculturation of children of both sexes.
4. *Subsistence.* Given the behavioral specialties imposed on the human female by her reproductive role, and given the anatomical and physiological differences between men and women, the sexual division of labor makes subsistence more efficient.

The nuclear family thus provides for heterosexual sex, reproduction, enculturation, and economic support more effectively than any other institution, according to this view.

FIGURE *15.1*

JAPANESE NUCLEAR FAMILES
All dressed up for a day at a shrine in the Meiji
area of Tokyo.

It is important to investigate the validity of these claims at some length. The idea that the nuclear family is universal or nearly universal lends support to the view that nonnuclear family domestic units are inferior, pathological, or contrary to human nature. In actuality, however, no one knows the limits within which human domestic arrangements must be confined in order to satisfy human needs and effectively carry out the functions listed above.

ALTERNATIVES TO THE NUCLEAR FAMILY

Even though nuclear families can be found in the overwhelming majority of human cultures, it has long been obvious that every culture has alternative forms of domestic organization and that these frequently are more important, involving a higher proportion of the population, than the nuclear family. Moreover, the four functions listed above, as already suggested, can readily be carried out in the context of alternative institutions that may lie entirely outside the domestic sphere.

In the case of the nuclear family in modern industrial cultures, this is evident with respect to enculturation and education. Enculturation and education in contemporary life are increasingly carried out in special nondomestic buildings—schools—under the auspices of specialist nonkinspeople—teachers.

Many village and band societies also separate their children and adolescents from the nuclear family and the entire domestic scene in order to teach them the lore and ritual of the ancestors, sexual competence, or the military arts. Among the Nyakyusa of southern Tanzania, for example, at age 6 or 7, boys begin to put up reed shelters or playhouses on the outskirts of their villages. These playhouses are gradually improved on and enlarged, eventually leading to the construction of a whole new village. Between the ages of 5 and 11, Nyakyusa boys sleep in their parents' house. But during adolescence, they are permitted to visit only during daylight hours and must sleep in the new village, although their mothers still handle cooking. The founding of a new village is complete when the young men take wives who cook for them and begin to give birth to the next generation (M. Wilson 1963).

Another famous variation on this pattern is found among the Masai of East Africa, where unmarried men of the same *age-set,* or ritually defined generation, establish special villages or camps from which they launch war parties and cattle-stealing raids. It is the mothers and sisters of these men who cook and keep house for them (Fig. 15.2).

The common English upper-class practice of sending sons aged 6 or older to boarding schools should also be noted. Like the Masai, the English aristocracy refused to let the burden of maintaining the continuity of their society rest on the educational resources of the nuclear household.

In many societies, married men spend a good deal of time in special *men's houses.* Food is handed

FIGURE *15.2*

MASAI AGE-SET
Masai warriors look fierce during an initiation ceremony.

in to them by wives and children, who are themselves forbidden to enter. Men also sleep and work in these "club-houses," although they may on occasion bed down with their wives and children.

Among the Fur of the Sudan, husbands usually sleep apart from their wives in houses of their own and take their meals at an exclusive men's mess. One of the most interesting cases of the separation of cooking and eating occurs among the Ashanti of West Africa. Ashanti men eat their meals with their sisters, mothers, and maternal nephews and nieces, not with their wives and children. But it is the wives who do the cooking. Every evening in Ashanti land there is a steady traffic of children taking their mother's cooking to their father's sister's house (see Barnes 1960; Bender 1967).

Finally, there is at least one famous case—the Nayar of Kerala—in which "husband" and "wife" do not live together at all. Many Nayar women "married" ritual husbands and then stayed with their brothers and sisters (Fig. 15.3). Their mates were men who visited overnight but continued to spend much of their time at their sister's house. Children born of these matings were brought up in households dominated by their mother's brother and never knew their father. We will return for a closer look at the Nayar in a moment.

POLYGAMY AND THE NUCLEAR FAMILY

Next we must consider whether the combination father-mother-child has the same functional significance where either father or mother is married to and is living with more than one spouse at a time. This is an important question because plural marriage—*polygamy*—occurs to some extent in at least 90 percent of all cultures (see Box 15.1).

In one form, called *polygyny* (Fig. 15.4), a husband is shared by several wives; in another, much less common form called *polyandry* (Fig. 15.5), a wife is shared by several husbands.

Is there a nuclear family when there are plural husbands or wives? C. P. Murdock suggested that nuclear families do exist in such situations. The man or woman simply belongs to more than one nuclear family at a time. But this overlooks the fact that plural marriages create domestic situations that are behaviorally and mentally very different from those created by *monogamous* (one husband, one wife) marriages.

Polygamous sexual arrangements, for example, are obviously quite different from those characteristic of monogamous marriages. The mode of reproduction is also different, especially with polygyny, because the spacing of births is easier to con-

FIGURE *15.3*

NAYAR OF KERALA
(A) Nayar villagers along the Kerala waterways.
(B) Nayar woman beating the outer shells of coconuts. The softened fibers will be woven into mats.

(A)

(B)

FIGURE *15.4*

POLYGYNY
(A) Polygynous household, Senegal. Islamic law permits this man to take one more wife to fill his quota of four, providing he can take good care of her. **(B)** Sitting Bull. This famous Sioux chief is shown with two of his wives and three of his children. Polygyny was widespread among native American peoples. This photo was taken in 1882 at Fort Randall, South Dakota.

(A)

(B)

BOX *15.1*

PRINCIPAL FORMS OF HUMAN MARRIAGE

Monogamy Marriage with one spouse exclusively and for life.

Serial Monogamy Marriage with one spouse at a time but with remarriage after death or divorce.

Polygamy Marriage with more than one spouse at a time.

Polygyny Marriage with more than one wife at a time.

Polyandry Marriage with more than one husband at a time.

FIGURE *15.5*

POLYANDRY
This Tibetan woman (wearing the veil) is being married to the two men on the left, who are brothers.

trol when husbands have several wives. Also, distinctive patterns of nursing and infant care arise when the mother sleeps alone with her children while the father sleeps with a different wife each night (see p. 374). From the point of view of child rearing, there are special psychological effects associated with a father who divides his time among several moth-

ers and who relates to his children through a hierarchy of wives. The monogamous U.S. or Canadian nuclear family places the focus of adult attention on a small group of full siblings. In a polygynous household, a dozen or more half-siblings must share the affection of the same man. Furthermore, the presence of co-wives or co-husbands changes the burden of child care a particular parent must bear. For example, industrial-age parents are troubled by the question of what to do with children when both parents go to work or visit friends. Polygynous families, however, have a built-in solution to the baby-sitting problem in the form of co-wives.

Turning finally to economic functions, the minimal polygamous economic unit often consists of the entire coresident production team and not each separate husband-wife pair. Domestic tasks such as nursing, grooming, cleaning, fetching water, cooking, and so on, often cannot be satisfactorily performed by a single wife. In polygynous societies, one of the main motivations for a man to take a second wife is to spread the work load and increase domestic output. It seems inappropriate, therefore, to equate nuclear families in monogamous households with husband-wife-child units in polygamous households.

THE EXTENDED FAMILY

In a majority of the societies studied by anthropologists, domestic life is dominated by groupings larger than simple nuclear or polygamous families. Some form of *extended family* is especially common. An extended family is a domestic group consisting of siblings, their spouses and their children, and/or parents and married children (Fig. 15.6). Extended families may also be polygynous. A common form of extended family in Africa, for example, consists of two or more brothers, each with two or three wives, living with their adult sons, each of whom has one or two wives. Among the Bathonga of southern Mozambique, domestic life fell under the control of the senior males of the polygynous extended family's senior generation. These prestigious and powerful men in effect formed a board of directors of a family-style corporation. They were responsible for making decisions about the domestic group's holdings in land, cattle, and buildings; they organized the subsistence effort of the coresident labor force—especially of the women and children—by assigning fields, crops, and seasonal work tasks. They tried to increase the size of their cattle herds and supplies of food and beer, obtain more wives, and increase the size and strength of the entire unit. The younger brothers, sons, and grandsons in Bathonga extended families could reach adulthood, marry, build a hut, carry out subsistence tasks, and have children only as members of the larger group, subject to the policies and priorities established by the senior males (Junod 1912). Within the Bathonga extended-family households, there really was no unit

equivalent to a nuclear family, and this is true, as previously indicated, of extended families in many other cultures, whether they are monogamous or polygamous.

In traditional Chinese extended families, for example, marriage is usually monogamous (Fig. 15.7). A senior couple manages the domestic labor force and arranges marriages. Women brought into the household as wives for the senior couple's sons are placed under the direct control of their mother-in-law. She supervises their cleaning, cooking, and raising of children. Where there are several daughters-in-law, cooking chores are often rotated, so that on any given day a maximum contingent of the domestic labor force can be sent to work in the family's fields (Myron Cohen 1976). The degree to which the nuclear family is submerged and effaced by these arrangements is brought out by a custom formerly found in certain Taiwanese households: "Adopt a daughter; marry a sister." In order to obtain control over their son's wife, the senior couple adopts a daughter. They bring the girl into the household at a very early age and train her to be hardworking and obedient. Later they oblige their son to marry this stepsister, thereby preventing the formation of an economically independent nuclear family within their midst, while at the same time conforming to the socially imposed incest prohibitions (Wolf 1968).

Among the Rajputs of northern India, extended families take similar stern measures to maintain the subordination of each married pair. A young man and his wife are even forbidden to talk to each other in the presence of senior persons, meaning in effect that they "may converse only surreptitiously at night" (Minturn and Hitchcock 1963:241). Here the husband is not supposed to show an open concern for his wife's welfare; if she is ill, that is a matter for her mother-in-law or father-in-law to take care of: "The mother feeds her son even after he is married...[and] runs the family as long as she wishes to assume the responsibility" (Minturn and Hitchcock 1963:241).

As a final brief example of how extended families modify the nuclear-family relations, there is Max Gluckman's (1955:60) wry comment on the Barotse of Zambia: "If a man becomes too devoted to his wife he is assumed to be the victim of witchcraft."

Why do so many societies have extended families? Probably because nuclear families frequently lack sufficient manpower and womanpower to carry out both domestic and subsistence tasks effectively. Extended families provide a larger labor pool and can carry out a greater variety of simultaneous activities (Pasternak, Ember, and Ember 1976).

FIGURE *15.6*

EXTENDED FAMILY, UNITED STATES
The demand for labor was high on this Minnesota farm in 1895.

FIGURE *15.7*

TAIWAN MARRIAGE
Groom's extended family assembled for wedding ceremony.

ONE-PARENT DOMESTIC GROUPS

Millions of children throughout the world are reared in domestic groups in which only one parent is present. This may result from divorce or death of one of the parents. But it also may result from inability or unwillingness to marry. The most common form of nonnuclear one-parent domestic arrangement is for the mother to be present and the father to be absent. Such households are called *matrifocal*. The mother accepts a series of men as mates, usually one at a time, but sometimes practices polyandry. The man and woman are usually coresident for brief periods, but over the years, there may be long intervals during which the mother does not have a resident mate.

At one extreme, associated with very rich or very poor women, mother and children may live alone. At the other extreme, mother and her children may live together with her sisters and her mother and constitute a large extended family in which adult males play only temporary roles as visitors or lovers.

Matrifocal households are best known from studies carried out in the West Indies (Blake 1961; Safa 1986; M. G. Smith 1966; R. T. Smith 1990), in Latin America (R. Adams 1968; O. Lewis 1961, 1964), and among U.S. inner-city African-Americans (Furstenberg et al. 1975; Gonzalez 1970; Stack 1974; Tanner 1974). But this form of household occurs throughout the world (Folbre 1991). Its incidence has been obscured by the tendency to regard such domestic units as aberrant or pathological (Moynihan 1965). In describing domestic groups, social scientists frequently concentrate on the emically preferred form and neglect etic and behavioral actualities. Mother-child domestic groups often result from poverty and hence are associated with many social ills and are regarded as undesirable. But there is no evidence that such domestic arrangements are inherently any more or less pathological, unstable, or contrary to "human nature" than the nuclear family.

WHAT IS MARRIAGE?

One of the problems with the proposition that the nuclear family is the basic building block of all domestic groups is that it rests on the assumption that widely different forms of matings can all be called "marriage." Yet in order to cover the extraordinary diversity of mating behavior characteristic of the human species, the definition of marriage has to be made so broad as to be confusing. Among the many ingenious attempts to define marriage as a universally occurring relationship, the definition proposed by Kathleen Gough (1968), who has studied the Nayar, merits special attention. But it must be read more than once! It makes the following points:

1. Marriage is a relationship established between a woman and one or more persons.
2. This relationship assures that a child born to the woman is accorded full birth rights common to normal members of his or her society, provided that
3. the child is conceived and born under certain approved circumstances.

According to Gough, for most if not all societies, this definition identifies a relationship "distinguished by the people themselves from all other kinds of relationships." Yet Gough's definition seems oddly at variance with English dictionary and native Western notions of marriage. First of all, it makes no reference to rights and duties of sexual access or to sexual performance. Moreover, it does not necessarily involve a relationship between men and women since it merely refers to a woman and "one or more" other persons of unspecified gender.

Gough does not mention sexual rights and duties because of the case of the Nayar. In order to bear children in a socially acceptable manner, pubescent Nayar girls had to go through a four-day ceremony that linked them with a "ritual husband." Completion of this ceremony was a necessary prerequisite for the beginning of a Nayar woman's sexual and reproductive career. Ideally, the Nayar strove to find a ritual husband among the men of the higher-ranking Namboodri Brahman caste. The males of this caste were interested in having sex with Nayar women, but they refused to regard the children of Nayar women as their heirs. So, after the ritual marriage, Nayar women stayed home with their sisters and brothers and were visited by both Namboodri Brahman and Nayar men. Gough regards the existence of the ritual husbands as proof of the universality of marriage (although not of the nuclear family), since only children born to ritually married Nayar women were "legitimate," even though the fathers were unknown.

But what can be the reason for defining marriage as a relationship between a woman and "persons" rather than between "women and men"? The answer is that among several African societies—the Dahomey case is best known—women "marry" women. This is accomplished by having a woman, who herself is usually already married to a man, pay bride-price (see p. 268) for a bride. The female bride-price payer becomes a "female husband." She starts a family of her own by letting her "wife" become pregnant through relationships with designated males. The offspring of these unions fall under the control of the "female father" rather than of the bio-logical *genitors* (see p. 275).

Wide as it is, Gough's definition ignores certain mating relationships that take place between males. For example, among the Kwakiutl, a man who desires to acquire the privileges associated with a particular chief can "marry" the chief's male heir. If the chief has no heirs, a man may "marry" the chief's right or left side, or a leg or an arm.

In Euramerican culture, enduring mating relationships between coresident homosexual men or between coresident homosexual women are also often spoken of as marriage. It has thus been suggested that all reference to the gender of the people involved in the relationship should be omitted in the definition of marriage in order to accommodate such cases (Dillingham and Isaac 1975).

The task of understanding varieties of domestic organization is made more difficult when all these different forms of mating are crammed into the single concept of marriage. Part of the problem is that when matings in Western culture are denied the designation "marriage," there is a tendency to regard them as less honorable or less authentic relationships. And so anthropologists are reluctant to stigmatize woman-woman or man-man matings, or Nayar or matrifocal visiting mate arrangements, by saying they are not marriages.

There is a simple way out of this dilemma. First, let us define marriage as the behavior, sentiments, and rules concerned with coresident heterosexual mating and reproduction in domestic contexts. Second, to avoid offending people by using *marriage* exclusively for coresident heterosexual domestic mates, let such other relationships be designated as *non-coresident marriages, man-man marriages, woman-woman marriages,* or by any other appropriate specific nomenclature. It is clear that these matings have different ecological, demographic, economic, and ideological implications, so nothing is to be gained by arguing about whether they are or are not "real" marriages.

LEGITIMACY

The essence of the marital relationship, according to some anthropologists, is embodied in that portion of Gough's definition dealing with the assignment of "birth rights" to children. As Bronislaw Malinowski put it, "Marriage is the licensing of parenthood."

It is true that women are universally discouraged from attempting to rear or dispose of their newborn infants according to their own whims, but most

societies have several different sets of rules defining permissible modes of conception and child rearing (Scheffler 1973:754–755). For example, among Brazilians living in small towns, there are four kinds of relationships between a man and a woman, all of which provide children with full birth rights: church marriage, civil marriage, simultaneous church and civil marriage, and consensual marriage. For a Brazilian woman, the most esteemed way to have children is through simultaneous church and civil marriage. This mode legally entitles her to a portion of her husband's property on his death. It also provides the added security of knowing that her husband cannot desert her and enter into a civil or religious marriage elsewhere. The least desirable mode is the consensual marriage, because the woman can make no property claims against her consort, nor can she readily prevent him from deserting her. Yet the children of a consensual arrangement can make property claims against both father and mother while suffering no deprivation of birth rights in the form of legal disadvantages or social disapproval as long as the father acknowledges paternity.

Among the Dahomey, Herskovits (1938) reported 13 different kinds of marriage, determined largely by bride-price arrangements. Children enjoyed different birth rights depending on the type of marriage. In some marriages, the child was placed under the control of the father's domestic group, and in others, under the control of a domestic group headed by a female "father" (see above). The point is not that a child is legitimate or illegitimate, but rather that there are specific types of rights, obligations, and groupings that emanate from different modes of sexual and reproductive relations. Most of the world's people are not concerned with the question of whether a child is legitimate, but with the question of who will have the right of controlling the child's destiny. No society grants women complete "freedom of conception," but the restrictions placed on motherhood and the occasions for punishment and disapproval vary enormously.

Where the domestic scene is dominated by large extended families and where there are no strong restrictions on premarital sex, the pregnancy of a young unmarried woman is rarely the occasion for much concern. Under certain circumstances, an "unwed mother" may even be congratulated rather than condemned. Among the Kadar of northern Nigeria, as reported by M. G. Smith (1968), most marriages result from infant betrothals. These matches are arranged by the fathers of the bride and groom when the girl is 3 to 6 years old. Ten years or more may elapse before the bride goes to live with her betrothed. During this time, a Kadar girl may become pregnant. This will disturb no one, even if the biological father is a man other than her future husband:

Kadar set no value on premarital chastity. It is fairly common for unmarried girls to be impregnated or to give birth to children by youths other than their betrothed. Offspring of such premarital pregnancies are members of the patrilineage . . . of the girl's betrothed and are welcomed as proof of the bride's fertility. (113)

In industrial countries today, the legal and moral basis for discriminating against unwed mothers and their children is giving way to a growing acceptance of a woman's right to control her reproductive destiny with or without being married. The causes of this change of values will be discussed in Chapter 26.

FUNCTIONS OF MARRIAGE

Every society has rules that define the conditions under which sexual relations, pregnancy, birth, and child rearing may take place, and that allocate privileges and duties in connection with these conditions. And every society has its own, sometimes unique combination of rules and rules for breaking rules in this domain. It would be futile to define marriage by any one ingredient in these rules—such as legitimation of children—even if such an ingredient could be shown to be universal. This point can be illustrated by enumerating some of the variable regulatory functions associated with institutions commonly identified as marriage. The following list incorporates suggestions made by Edmund Leach (1968). Marriage *sometimes:*

1. Establishes the legal father of a woman's children.
2. Establishes the legal mother of a man's children.
3. Gives the husband or his extended family control over the wife's sexual services.
4. Gives the wife or her extended family control over the husband's sexual services.
5. Gives the husband or his extended family control over the wife's labor power.
6. Gives the wife or her extended family control over the husband's labor power.
7. Gives the husband or his extended family control over the wife's property.
8. Gives the wife or her extended family control over the husband's property.
9. Establishes a joint fund of property for the benefit of children.
10. Establishes a socially significant relationship between the husband's and the wife's domestic groups.

As Leach remarks, this list could be greatly extended, but the point is "that in no single society can marriage serve to establish all these types of rights simultaneously, nor is there any one of these rights which is invariably established by marriage in every known society" (1968:76).

MARRIAGE IN EXTENDED FAMILIES

In extended families, marriage must be seen primarily in the context of group interests. Individuals serve the interest of the extended family. The larger domestic group never loses interest in or totally surrenders its rights to the productive, the reproductive, and the sexual functions of spouses and children. Marriage under these circumstances is aptly described as an "alliance" between groups. This alliance influences present and future matings involving other members of both groups.

Among most societies, the corporate significance of marriage is revealed by the exchange of personnel or of valuable goods between the respective domestic groups in which bride and groom were born. The simplest form of such transactions is called *sister exchange* and involves the reciprocal "giving away" of the groom's sisters in compensation for the loss of a woman from each group.

Among more than half of a sample of 1267 societies (Gaulin and Bostar 1990:994), corporate interests are expressed in the institution known as *bride-price* (Fig. 15.8) In bride-price, the wife-receivers give valuable items to the wife-givers. As stated earlier (p. 249), bride-price is not equivalent to the selling and buying of automobiles or refrigerators in modern industrial price-market societies. The wife-receivers do not "own" their woman in any total sense; they must take good care of her, or her family will demand that she be returned to them. The amount of bride-price is not fixed; it fluctuates from one marriage to another. (In much of Africa, the traditional measure of *bride-wealth* was cattle, although other valuables such as iron tools were also used. Nowadays, cash payments are the rule.) Among the Bathonga, a family that had many daughter-sisters was in a favorable position. By exchanging women for cattle, the family could exchange cattle back for women: the more cattle, the more mother-wives; the more mother-wives, the larger the reproductive and productive labor force and the greater the material welfare and influence of the corporate kin group.

FIGURE *15.8*

BRIDE-PRICE
Amoung the Kapauku, the bride-price
consists of shell money.

DOWRY

Bride-price and bride-service tend to occur where land is plentiful and the labor of additional women and children can result in additional wealth and well-being for the corporate group (Goody 1976). Where women's productive and reproductive powers are not valued because land is scarce and women's labor cannot be used to intensify production, wives may be regarded as an economic burden. Instead of paying bride-price to the family of the bride, the groom's family may demand a reverse payment, called *dowry* (Fig. 15.9). When this payment consists of money or movable property instead of land, it is usually associated with a low or oppressed status for women (Bossen 1988; Schlegel and Barry 1986:145; Schlegel and Eloul 1988). Dowry is much rarer than bride-price, occuring in only 3 percent of a sample of 1267 societies (Gaulin and Boster 1990:994). However, the

FIGURE *15.9*

DOWRY
This Arab bride is exhibiting her wealth.

Sometimes the transfer of wealth from one group to another is carried out in installments: so much on initial agreement, more when the woman goes to live with her husband, and another, usually final, payment when she has her first child. Failure to have a child often voids the marriage; the woman goes home to her brothers and father, and the husband's family gets its bride-price back.

A common alternative to bride-price is known as *bride-service* (sometimes called *suitor-service*). The groom or husband compensates his in-laws by working for them for several months or years before taking his bride away to live and work with him and his extended family. Bride-service may be involved in the conditions under which matrilocal residence tends to occur, as we will see in Chapter 16. If the suitor lingers on and never takes his bride home, he may be participating in an etic shift from patrilocal to matrilocal residence.

societies that have dowry are concentrated in the extremely populous states of Mediterranean Europe and southern Asia. Throughout this region, land is scarce and there is a form of intensive agriculture involving animal-drawn plows guided by men, while women's work is largely confined to the domestic scene. As we shall see (p. 352), dowry is closely associated in this region with the subordination of women and a marked preference for male children.

The opposite of bride-price is not dowry but *groom-price*, in which the groom goes to live and work with the bride's family and the bride's family compensates the groom's family for the loss of his productive and reproductive powers. This form of marriage compensation is extremely rare—only one well-documented case is known (Nash 1974).

DOMESTIC GROUPS AND THE AVOIDANCE OF INCEST

All these exchanges point to the existence of a profound paradox in the way human beings find mates. Marriage between members of the same domestic group is widely prohibited. Husband and wife must come from separate domestic groups. The members of the domestic group must "marry out"—that is, marry *exogamously;* they cannot "marry in"—that is, marry *endogamously.*

Certain forms of endogamy are universally prohibited. No culture tolerates father-daughter and mother-son marriages. Sister-brother marriage is also widely prohibited, but there are several important exceptions. It occurred among the ruling classes of highly stratified societies such as those of the Inca, ancient Egypt, ancient China, and Hawaii (Bixler 1982). While most of these royal marriages were between half-siblings, some were between full siblings. Moreover, in Egypt during Roman times (the first 300 years A.D.), commoners also practiced brother-sister marriage. Such marriages, according to historian Keith Hopkins (1980), were regarded as perfectly normal relationships, openly mentioned in documents concerning inheritance, business affairs, lawsuits, and petitions to officials.

In the emics of Western civilization, sister-brother, father-daughter, and mother-son sex relations and marriages are called *incest.* Why are these sex relations and marriages so widely prohibited? Explanations of nuclear-family incest prohibition fall into two major types: those that stress an instinctual component and those that emphasize the social and cultural advantages of exogamy.

Instinct

Advocates of genetic theories of incest avoidance long ago recognized that it was unlikely that genes contained definite instructions for shutting down sex drives in the presence of siblings, children, and parents. Following the lead of Edward Westermark (1894), they propose, instead, that there is an innate tendency for members of the opposite sex to find each other sexually uninspiring if they have been brought up in close physical proximity to each other during infancy and childhood (Shepher 1983; Spiro 1954). Westermark's principle is much in favor among sociobiologists because it provides a way out of the dilemma posed by the relatively high rates at which brother-sister incest may sometimes take place—for instance, it was quite common in ancient Egypt (Fig. 15.10). If the brother and sister were brought up apart from each other in different houses or by different nurses and caretakers, then, according to the Westermark principle, they might very well find each other sexually attractive enough to mate (Bixler 1982; Wilson 1978:38–39).

Behind the Westermark theory and other genetic explanations of incest avoidance is the assumption that close inbreeding results in an increased likelihood that individuals who carry defective genes will mate with each other and give birth to children who suffer from pathological conditions that lower their rate of reproduction. Another argument asserts that, simply by lowering the amount of genetic diversity in a population, inbreeding might have an adverse effect on the population's ability to adapt to new diseases or other novel environmental hazards. So, those individuals who find themselves "turned off" through the Westermark effect would have avoided inbreeding, reproduced at a higher rate, and gradually replaced those who were "turned on" by their close kin. (See Leavitt 1990 for a comprehensive critique of these issues.)

There are several soft spots in this part of the argument. It is true that in large modern populations, incest leads to a high rate of stillbirths and congenitally diseased and impaired children (Adams and Neil 1967; Stern 1973:497). But the same results need not occur from close inbreeding practiced in small preagricultural societies. Inbreeding in small preagricultural societies leads to the gradual elimination of harmful recessive genes because such societies have little tolerance for infants and children who are congenitally handicapped and impaired. Lack of support for such children eliminates the harmful genetic variations from future generations, and results in populations that

FIGURE *15.10*

CLEOPATRA
Product of 11 generations of brother-sister marriage.

carry a much smaller "load" of harmful gene variants than modern populations (Livingstone 1969, 1982).

To test the Westermark theory, one cannot point to the mere occurrence of incest avoidance. One has to show that sexual ardor cools when people grow up together, independent of any existing norms that call for incest avoidance. Since this cannot be done experimentally without controlling the lives of human subjects, advocates of the theory lean heavily on two famous case studies that allegedly demonstrate the predicted loss of sexual ardor. The first of these concerns Taiwanese adopt-a-daughter-marry-a-sister marriage (see page 262). Studies have shown that these marriages, in which husband and wife grow up together at close quarters, lead to fewer children, greater adultery, and higher divorce rates than normal marriages, in which future wives and husbands grow up in separate households (Wolf and Haung 1980). But these observations scarcely confirm Westermark's theory. The Taiwanese explicitly recognize that adopt a daughter marry a sister is an inferior, even humiliating, form of marriage. Normally, to seal a marriage bond, the families of the bride and groom exchange considerable wealth as a sign of their support for the newlyweds. But these exchanges are smaller or absent altogether in adopt a daughter marry a sister. This makes it impossible to prove that sexual disinterest rather than chagrin and disappointment over being treated like second-class citizens is the source of the couple's infertility.

The second case used to confirm Westermark's theory concerns an alleged lack of sexual interest displayed by boys and girls who attended the same classes from nursery school to age 6 in the Israeli cooperative community known as a kibbutz. Allegedly these boys and girls were so thoroughly "turned off" that among marriages contracted by people who were reared in a kibbutz, not one involved men or women who had been reared together from birth to age 6 (Shepher 1983). This seems impressive, but there is a fatal flaw. Out of a total of 2516 marriages, there were 200 in which both partners were reared in the same kibbutz, although they were not in the same class for six years. Given the fact that all kibbutz youth were inducted into the army and commingled with tens of thousands of potential mates from outside their kibbutz before they got married, the rate of 200 marriages from within the same kibbutz is far more than could be expected by chance. One must now ask, of the 200 marriages from within the same kibbutz, what was the chance that not a single one would be between a boy and a girl who had attended the same classes? Since girls were generally three years younger than the boys they married, only a very few marriages between people who were reared for six years in the same class could be expected. Actually, it turns out that five marriages did occur between boys and girls who had been reared together for part of the first six years of their lives (Fig. 15.11). Since Westermark's theory does not predict how long it takes for reared-together boys and girls to lose their interest in each other, these five marriages actually disconfirm the theory (Hartung 1985).

The proposal that there is an instinctual sexual aversion within the nuclear family is also con-

FIGURE *15.11*

KIBBUTZ BOYS AND GIRLS
Does childhood familiarity lead to sexual aviodance?

Fuck Freud

tradicted by evidence of strong sexual attraction between father and daughter and between mother and son. Freudian psychoanalysis indicates that children and parents of the opposite sex have a strong desire to have sexual encounters with each other. Indeed, in the case of the father-daughter relationship, at least, these wishes are acted on more frequently than is popularly believed. For example, social workers estimate that tens of thousands of cases of incest occur in the United States annually, of which the great majority involves fathers imposing on young daughters. (Cicchetti and Carlson 1989; Glaser and Frosh 1988).

Finally, the instinct theory of incest avoidance is hard to reconcile with the widespread occurrence of endogamous practices that are carried out simultaneously and in support of exogamic arrangements. Members of exogamous extended families, for example, frequently are involved in marriage systems that encourage them to mate with one kind of first cousin (*cross cousin*) but not another (*parallel cousin;* see p. 278). The difference between these two forms of inbreeding cannot be explained satisfactorily by natural selection (cf. Alexander 1977). Furthermore, the widespread preference for some form of cousin marriage itself weighs against the conclusion that exogamy expresses an instinct established by the harmful effects of inbreeding (Bittles et al. 1991).

The possibility that incest avoidance is genetically programmed in *Homo sapiens* has received some support from field studies of monkey and ape mating behavior. As among humans, father-daughter, mother-son, and brother-sister matings are uncommon among our nearest animal relatives, but they do occur. The avoidance of sex between these closely related pairs can be explained in terms of gender and age dominance patterns and sexual competition. In the wild, there are far more cases of group endogamy involving matings between closely related primates than there are exogamous matings and there is no experimental evidence suggesting an aversion to incest per se among monkeys and apes (Leavitt 1990). Moreover, even if such an instinctual aversion were found to exist among nonhuman primates, its significance for human nature would be dubious. After all, it is not only mates that get exchanged between human groups but a vast array of goods and services as well. Are we to believe that humans have an instinct that prevents us from not keeping food, tools, and labor within the nuclear family?

Social and Cultural Advantages of Exogamy

Nuclear family incest avoidance and other forms of exogamy among domestic groups can be explained quite effectively in terms of demographic, economic, and ecological advantages (Leavitt 1989). These advantages are not necessarily the same for all societies. For example, it is known that band societies rely on marriage exchanges to establish long-distance networks of kinspeople. Bands that formed a completely closed breeding unit would be denied the mobility and territorial flexibility essential to their subsistence strategy. Territorially restricted, endogamous bands of 20 to 30 people would also run a high risk of extinction as a result of gender imbalances caused by an unlucky run of male births and adult female deaths, which would place the burden for the group's reproduction on one or two aging females. Exogamy is thus essential for the effective utilization of a small population's productive and reproductive potential. Once a band begins to obtain mates from other bands, the prevalence of reciprocal economic relations leads to the expectation that the receivers will reciprocate. The taboos on mother-son, father-daughter, and brother-sister marriages can therefore be interpreted as a defense of these reciprocal exchange relationships against the ever-present temp-

tation for parents to keep their children for themselves, or for brothers and sisters to keep each other for themselves.

Another factor favoring nuclear family exogamy is the institution of marriage itself. Thus it is frequently overlooked that sexual encounters between father and daughter and mother and son constitute a form of adultery. Mother-son incest is an especially threatening variety of adultery in societies that have strong male supremacist institutions. Not only is the wife "double-dealing" against her husband, but the son is also "double-dealing" against his father. This may explain why the least common and emically most feared and abhorred form of incest is that between mother and son. It follows that father-daughter incest will be somewhat more common, since husbands enjoy double standards of sexual behavior more often than wives and are less vulnerable to punishment for adultery. Finally, the same consideration suggests an explanation for the relatively high frequency of brother-sister matings and their legitimizations as marriages in elite classes—they do not conflict with father-mother adultery rules.

After the evolution of the state, exogamic alliances between domestic groups continued to have important infrastructural consequences. Among peasants, exogamy also increases the total productive and reproductive strength of the intermarried groups. It permits the exploitation of resources over a larger area than the nuclear or extended families could manage on an individual basis, it facilitates trade, and it raises the upper limit of the size of groups that can be formed to carry out seasonal activities requiring large labor inputs (e.g., communal game drives, harvests, and so on). Furthermore, where intergroup warfare poses a threat to group survival, the ability to mobilize large numbers of warriors is decisive. Hence, in militaristic, highly male-centered village cultures, sisters and daughters are frequently used as pawns in the establishment of alliances. These alliances do not necessarily eliminate warfare between intermarrying groups, but they make it less common, as might be expected from the presence of sisters and daughters in the enemy's ranks (Kang 1979; Podolefsky 1984; Tefft 1975).

Among elite classes and castes, endogamy often combines with extended family exogamy to maintain wealth and power within the ruling stratum (see p. 326). But as already noted, even the nuclear family may become endogamous when there is an extreme concentration of political, economic, and military power. With the evolution of price-market forms of exchange, the extended family tends to be replaced by nuclear family domestic units. Domestic group alliances lose some of their previous adaptive importance and the traditional functions of incest avoidance must be reinterpreted. Incest has been decriminalized in Sweden, and there is an effort to do likewise in the United States (Y. Cohen 1978; De Mott 1980). Some anthropologists predict that nuclear family incest prohibitions will eventually disappear because there are so many alternative ways of establishing intergroup relationships in modern states, such as price markets, and compulsory universal public education (Leavitt 1989). Given the scientific knowledge that nuclear family incest is genetically risky in populations carrying a heavy load of harmful recessive genes, the complete repeal of anti-incest legislation seems unlikely and unwise (see Box 15.2).

PREFERENTIAL MARRIAGES

The widespread occurrence of exogamy implies that the corporate interests of domestic groups must be protected by rules that stipulate who is to marry whom. Having given a woman away in marriage, most groups expect either material wealth or women in exchange. Consider two domestic groups, A and B, each with a core of resident brothers. If A gives a woman to B, B may immediately reciprocate by giving a woman to A. This reciprocity is often achieved by a direct exchange of the groom's sister. But the reciprocity may take a more indirect form. B may return a daughter of the union between the B man and the A woman. The bride in such a marriage will be her husband's father's sister's daughter, and the groom will be his wife's mother's brother's son. (The same result would be achieved by a marriage between a man and his mother's brother's daughter.) Bride and groom are each other's cross cousins (see p. 278). If A and B have a rule that such marriages are to occur whenever possible, then they are said to have *preferential cross cousin marriage.*

Reciprocity in marriage is sometimes achieved by several intermarrying domestic groups that exchange women in cycles and are called *circulating connubia.* For example, A → B → C → A; or A → B and C → D in one generation and A → D and B → C in the next, and then back to A → B and C → D. These exchanges are enforced by preferential marriage with appropriate kinds of cousins, nephews, nieces, and other kin.

Another common manifestation of corporate domestic interest in marriage is the practice of supplying replacements for in-marrying women who die prematurely. To maintain reciprocity or to fulfill a marriage contract for which bride-price has been

---

BOX *15.2*

THE GREAT TABOO

With the evolution of money, of buying and selling, and of other price-market forms of exchange, the importance of incest avoidance as a means of establishing intergroup alliances is no longer as great as it was in previous epochs. Today, money buys everything (well, almost everything), including friends and allies. True, the right kind of marriage may still be the key to worldly success, but families nowadays need a good job or a fat annuity more than they need incest taboos to enjoy peace, security, and the good things in life.

... The Great Taboo, in other words, is greatly overrated. It is not just one thing but a set of sexual and mating preferences and avoidances that is selectively subject to change during the evolution of culture. In this age of sexual liberation and experiment, for example, brother-sister mating is probably on the verge of becoming just another "kinky" sexual preference of little interest to society, provided that incestuous siblings use contraceptive safeguards and seek genetic counseling.... Father-daughter, mother-son incest is another story, not only because they overlap with adultery but also because the age differences involved imply lack of informed consent, if not outright rape and child abuse.

SOURCE: Harris 1989:205.

paid, the brother of a deceased woman may permit the widower to marry one or more of the deceased wife's sisters. This custom is known as the *sororate* (i.e., a deceased woman is replaced in marriage by her sister). Closely related to this practice is the preferential marriage known as the *levirate,* in which the services of a man's widow are retained within the domestic unit by having her marry one of his brothers (i.e., a deceased husband is replaced in marriage by his brother). If the widows are old, the services rendered by the remarried widow may be minimal, and the levirate then functions to provide security for women who would otherwise not be able to remarry.

Thus, the organization of domestic life everywhere reflects the fact that husbands and wives usually originate in different domestic groups that continue to maintain a sentimental and practical interest in the marriage partners and their children.

SUMMARY

The structural level of sociocultural systems is made up in part of interrelated domestic groups. Such groups can usually be identified by their attachment to a living space or domicile in which activities such as eating, sleeping, marital sex, and nurturance and the discipline of the young take place. However, there is no single or minimal pattern of domestic activities. Similarly, the nuclear family cannot be regarded as the minimal building block of all domestic groups. While nuclear families occur in almost every society, they are not always the dominant domestic group, and their sexual, reproductive, and productive functions can readily be satisfied by alternative domestic and nondomestic institutions. In polygamous and extended families, the father-mother-child subset may not enjoy any practical existence apart from the set of other relatives and their multiple spouses. And there are many instances of domestic groups that lack a coresident husband-father. Although children need to be nurtured and protected, no one knows the limits within which human domestic arrangements must be confined in order to satisfy human nature. One of the most important facts about human domestic arrangements is that no single pattern can be shown to be more "natural" than any other.

Human mating patterns also exhibit an enormous degree of variation. While something similar to what is called marriage occurs all over the world, it is difficult to specify the mental and behavioral essence of the marital relationship. Man-man, woman-woman, female-father, and childless marriages make it difficult to give a minimal definition of marriage without offending someone. Even coresidence may not be essential, as the Nayar and other single-parent households demonstrate. And if we restrict the definition of marriage to coresident heterosexual matings that result in reproduction, there is a staggering variety of rights and duties associated with the sexual and reproductive functions of the marriage partners and their offspring.

In order to understand coresident heterosexual reproductive marriage in extended families, marriage must be seen as a relationship between corporate groups as much as between cohabiting mates. The divergent interests of these corporate groups are reconciled by means of reciprocal exchanges that take the form of sister exchange, bride-price, suitor-service, dowry, and groom-price. Except for dowry, the common principle underlying these exchanges is that in giving a man or woman away to another extended family, the domestic corporation does not renounce its interest in the offspring of the mated pair and expects compensation for the loss of a valuable worker.

Most domestic groups are exogamous. This can be seen as a result of instinctual programming or social and cultural adaptation. The discussion of exogamy necessarily centers on the incest prohibitions within the nuclear family. Father-daughter, sister-brother, and mother-son matings and marriages are almost universally forbidden. The chief exception is brother-sister marriages, which occur in several highly stratified societies among the ruling elites and among Egyptian commoners in Roman times. The instinct theory of incest avoidance stresses evidence from Taiwan and Israel which suggests that children reared together develop a sexual aversion to each other. This aversion is seen as genetically determined, since it reduces the risk of harmful genes. Other interpretations of the Taiwan and Israel studies can be made, however. A purely cultural theory of incest avoidance can be built out of the need for domestic groups to defend their capacity to engage in reciprocal marriage exchanges by preventing parents from keeping their children for themselves. In the future, the perpetuation of the incest taboos may be related exclusively to the increasing genetic dangers associated with close inbreeding in populations carrying a large load of harmful genes.

Exogamy and incest avoidance form only a small part of the spectrum of preferred and prohibited marriages that reflect the pervasive corporate interests of domestic groups. Preferences for certain kinds of marriage exchanges create circulating connubia in which reciprocity between domestic groups may be direct or indirect. Such preferences may be expressed as a rule requiring marriage with a particular kind of cousin. Preferential marriage rules such as the levirate and sororate also exemplify the corporate nature of the marriage bond.

Chapter 16

Kinship, Locality, and Descent

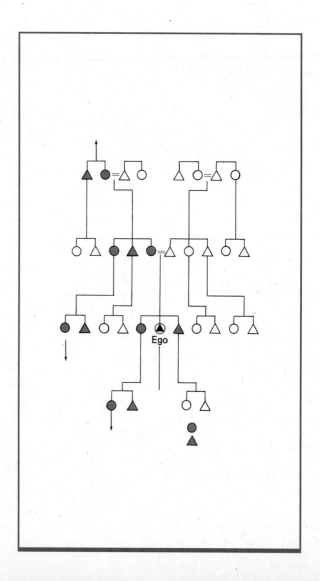

Herein we continue with domestic organization. We examine the principal mental and emic components of domestic groups, namely the concept of kinship through marriage and descent. Then we relate different varieties of kinship concepts to particular kinds of domestic groups and to the influence of infrastructural conditions. To top this off, there is a brief introduction to the wonders of kinship terminologies— systems for classifying relatives. Parts of this chapter may require an extra dose of concentration; but the study of varieties of kinship arrangements is one of the oldest interests of anthropology. Like language, kinship studies demonstrate the power of culture to form systems of thought and behavior on the level of groups rather than on the level of individuals. No one individual, for example, ever decided that our mother's sister and our father's sister should both be called by the single term "aunt" instead of two different terms as is true in other cultures. I hope you give this chapter a try. You may even enjoy it.

KINSHIP

The study of domestic life in hundreds of cultures all over the world has led anthropologists to conclude that two principles are expressed in the organization of domestic life everywhere. The first of these is the idea of *affinity,* or of relationships through marriage. The second is the idea of *descent,* or parentage. People who are related to each other through descent or a combination of affinity and descent are relatives, or kin. The domain of ideas constituted by the beliefs and expectations kin share about one another is called *kinship.* The study of kinship, therefore, must begin with the mental and emic components of domestic life.

DESCENT*

Kinship relations are often confused with biological relations. But the emic meaning of descent is not the biological meaning of descent. As we have discussed previously (p. 264), marriage may explicitly establish "parentage" with respect to children who are biologically unrelated to their culturally defined "father." Even where a culture insists that descent must be based on actual biological fatherhood, domestic arrangements may make it difficult to identify the biological father. For these reasons, anthropologists

---

*British social anthropologists restrict the term *descent* to relationships extending over more than two generations and use *filiation* to denote descent relationships within the nuclear family (Fortes 1969).

distinguish between the culturally defined "father" and the *genitor,* the actual biological father. A similar distinction is necessary in the case of "mother." Although the culturally defined mother is usually the genetrix, the widespread practice of adoption also creates many discrepancies between emic and etic motherhood.

Theories of reproduction and heredity vary from culture to culture, "but so far as we know, no human society is without such a theory" (Scheffler 1973:749). Descent, then, is the belief that certain persons play an important role in the creation, birth, and nurturance of certain children. As Daniel Craig (1979) has suggested, descent implies the preservation of some aspect of the substances or spirit of people in future generations and thus is a symbolic form of immortality. Perhaps that is why one form or another of parentage and descent is universally believed in.

In Western folk traditions, married pairs are linked to children on the basis of the belief that male and female make equally important contributions to the child's being. Blood, the most important life-sustaining and life-defining fluid, supposedly varies according to parentage. Each child's body is thought of as being filled with blood obtained from mother and father. As a result of this imagery, "blood relatives" are distinguished from relatives who are linked only through marriage. This led nineteenth-century anthropologists to use the ethnocentric term *consanguine* (of the same blood) to denote relations of descent. People persist in talking about "blood relatives" even though it is known that closely related individuals may have different blood types, distantly or unrelated individuals may have the same blood type, and the closeness of a relationship is measured by the proportion of shared DNA and not by shared blood.

Descent need not depend on the idea of blood inheritance, nor need it involve equal contributions from both father and mother. The Ashanti believe that blood is contributed only by the mother and that it determines only a child's physical characteristics, while a child's spiritual disposition and temperament are the product of the father's semen. The Alorese of Indonesia believe that the child is formed by a mixture of seminal and menstrual fluids, which accumulate for two months before beginning to solidify. Many other cultures share this idea of a slow growth of the fetus as a result of repeated additions of semen during pregnancy.

The Innuit believe that pregnancy results when a spirit child climbs up a woman's bootstraps and is nourished by semen. The Trobrianders contend that semen does not play any procreative role. Here also, a woman becomes pregnant when a spirit child enters her vagina. The only physical function of the Trobriand male is to widen the passageway into the womb. The Trobriand "father," nonetheless, has an essential social role, since no self-respecting spirit child would enter a Trobriand girl who was not married.

A similar denial of the male's procreative role occurs throughout Australia; among the Murngin, for example, there was the belief that the spirit children live deep below the surface of certain sacred waterholes. For conception to take place, one of these spirits appears in the future father's dreams. In the dream, the spirit child introduces itself and asks its father to point out the woman who is to become its mother. Later, when this woman passes near the sacred waterhole, the spirit child swims out in the form of a fish and enters her womb.

Despite the many different kinds of theories about the nature of procreative roles, there is worldwide acknowledgment of some special contributory action linking both husband and wife to the reproductive process, although they may be linked quite unevenly and with vastly different expectations concerning rights and obligations.

DESCENT RULES

By reckoning descent relationships, individuals are apportioned different duties, rights, and privileges with respect to other people and with regard to many different aspects of social life. A person's name, family, residence, rank, property, ethnic, and national status (see Fig. 16.1) may depend on ascriptions through

FIGURE *16.1*

AMERICAN KINDRED
Thanksgiving is an occasion for both siblings and cousins to get together.

descent independent of any achievements other than getting born and staying alive. (*Ascribed statuses* and *achieved statuses* are found in all cultures.)

Anthropologists distinguish two great classes of descent rules: the *cognatic* and the *unilineal*. Cognatic descent rules are those in which both male and female parentage are used to establish any of the above-mentioned duties, rights, and privileges. Unilineal descent rules, on the other hand, restrict parental links exclusively to males or exclusively to females. The most common form of cognatic rule is *bilateral descent*, the reckoning of kinship evenly and symmetrically along maternal and paternal lines in ascending and descending generations through individuals of both sexes (see Fig. 16.2 and Fig. 16.3).

The second main variety of cognatic rule is called *ambilineal descent* (Fig. 16.4). Here the descent lines traced by ego (Box 16.1) ignore the gender of the parental links, but the lines do not lead in all directions evenly. As in bilateral descent, ego traces descent through males and females, but the line twists back and forth, including some female ancestors or descendants but excluding others, and including some male ancestors or descendants and excluding others. In other words, ego does not reckon descent simultaneously and equally through mothers, fathers, and grandparents.

There are also two main varieties of unilineal descent: *patrilineality* and *matrilineality*. When descent is reckoned patrilineally, ego follows the ascending and descending genealogical lines through males only (Fig. 16.5). Note that this does not mean that the descent-related individuals are only males; in each generation there are relatives of both genders. However, in the passage from one generation to another, only the male links are relevant; children of females are dropped from the descent reckoning.

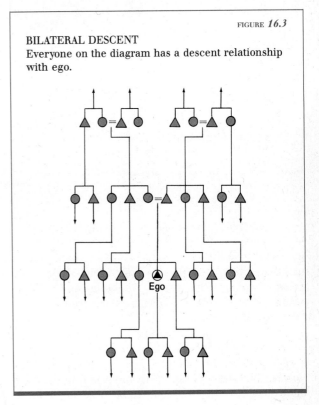

FIGURE *16.3*

BILATERAL DESCENT
Everyone on the diagram has a descent relationship with ego.

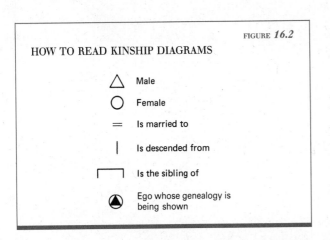

FIGURE *16.2*

HOW TO READ KINSHIP DIAGRAMS

△   Male

○   Female

=   Is married to

| Is descended from

⌐   Is the sibling of

◓   Ego whose genealogy is being shown

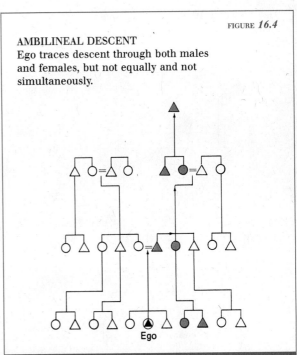

FIGURE *16.4*

AMBILINEAL DESCENT
Ego traces descent through both males and females, but not equally and not simultaneously.

EGO

Anthropologists employ the word *ego* to denote the "I" from whose point of view kinship relations are being reckoned. It is sometimes necessary to state whether the reference person is a male ego or a female ego.

When descent is reckoned matrilineally, ego follows the ascending and descending lines through females only (Fig. 16.6). Once again, it should be noted that males as well as females can be related matrilineally; it is only in the passage from one generation to another that the children of males are dropped from the descent reckoning.

One of the most important logical consequences of unilineal descent is that it segregates the children of siblings of the opposite sex into distinct categories. This effect is especially important in the case of cousins. Note that with patrilineal descent, ego's father's sister's son and daughter do not share common descent with ego, whereas ego's father's brother's son and daughter do share common descent with ego. In the case of matrilineal descent, the same kind of distinction results with respect to ego's "cousins" on the mother's side. Children whose parents are related to each other as brother and sister are known as *cross cousins;* children whose parents are related to each other as brother and brother or sister and sister are known as *parallel cousins* (Fig. 16.7).

Anthropologists distinguish an additional variety of descent rule called *double descent,* in which ego simultaneously reckons descent matrilineally through mother and patrilineally through father. This differs from unilineal descent, in which descent is reckoned only through males or only through females but not both together.

Many other combinations of these descent rules also may occur. For example, in all cultures there is some degree of bilateral descent in the reckoning of rights and obligations. If a society observes patrilineal descent in the grouping of people into landowning domestic groups, this does not mean that ego and mother's brother's daughter do not regard each other as having special rights and obligations. Modern Euramerican culture is strongly bilateral in kin-group

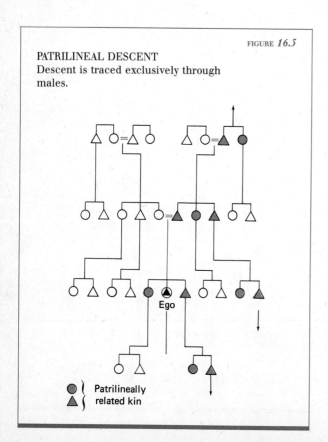

FIGURE *16.5*

PATRILINEAL DESCENT
Descent is traced exclusively through males.

Patrilineally related kin

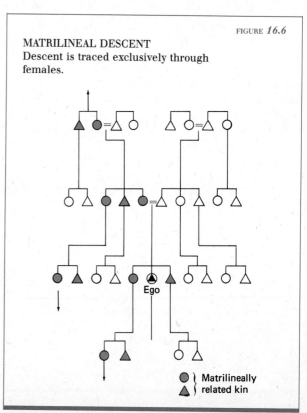

FIGURE *16.6*

MATRILINEAL DESCENT
Descent is traced exclusively through females.

Matrilineally related kin

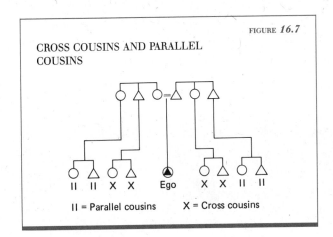

FIGURE *16.7*

CROSS COUSINS AND PARALLEL
COUSINS

|| = Parallel cousins   X = Cross cousins

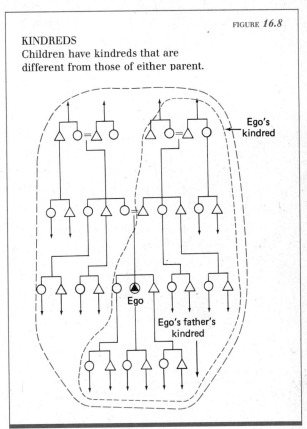

FIGURE *16.8*

KINDREDS
Children have kindreds that are
different from those of either parent.

composition and inheritance of wealth and property;
yet family names are *patronymic*—that is, they follow
patrilineal descent lines. The point is that several varieties of descent may occur simultaneously within
a given society if the descent rules are pertinent to
different spheres of thought and behavior.

Each of the above descent rules provides the
logical basis for mentally aligning people into emic
kinship groups. These groups exert great influence
on the way people think and behave in both domestic
and extradomestic situations. An important point to
bear in mind about kinship groups is that they need
not consist of coresident relatives; that is, they need
not be etic behavioral domestic groups. We proceed
now to a description of the principal varieties of kinship groups.

COGNATIC DESCENT GROUPS:
BILATERAL VARIETY

Bilateral descent applied to an indefinitely wide span
of kin and to an indefinite number of generations
leads to the concept of groups known as *kindreds* (Fig.
16.8). When modern-day Americans and Europeans
use the word *family* and have in mind more than just
their nuclear families, they are referring to their kindreds. The main characteristic of the kindred is that
the span and depth of bilateral reckoning are open-
ended. Relatives within ego's kindred can be judged
as "near" or "far," depending on the number of genealogical links that separate them; but there is no
definite or uniform principle for making such judgments or for terminating the extension of the kinship
circle. An important consequence of this feature, as
shown in Figure 16.8, is that egos and their siblings
are identified with a kindred whose membership
cannot be the same for any other persons (except for
ego's double cousins—cousins whose parents are two

brothers who have exchanged sisters). This means
that it is impossible for coresident domestic groups
to consist of kindreds and very difficult for kindreds
to maintain corporate interests in land and people.

COGNATIC DESCENT GROUPS:
AMBILINEAL VARIETY

The open-ended, ego-centered characteristics of the
bilateral kindred can be overcome by specifying one
or more ancestors from whom descent is traced
through males and/or females. The resultant group
logically has a membership that is the same regardless of which ego carries out the reckoning. This is
the *cognatic lineage* (the terms *ramage* and *sept* are
also used) (Fig. 16.9).

The cognatic lineage is based on the assumption that all members of the descent group are capable of specifying the precise genealogical links
relating them to the lineage founder. A common alternative, as in the ambilineal "clans" of Scotland, is
for the descent from the lineage founder to be *stipulated* rather than *demonstrated*. This can be done easily enough if the name of the founder gets passed on am-

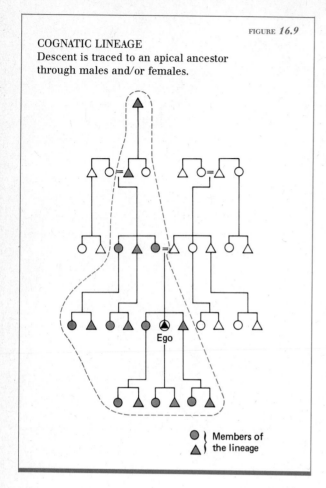

FIGURE *16.9*

COGNATIC LINEAGE
Descent is traced to an apical ancestor through males and/or females.

Ego

⬤ } Members of
▲ } the lineage

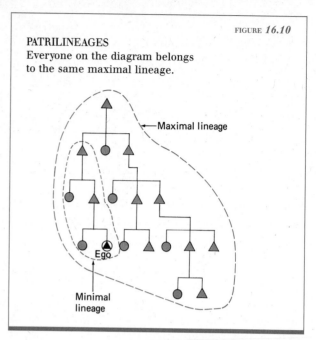

FIGURE *16.10*

PATRILINEAGES
Everyone on the diagram belongs to the same maximal lineage.

Maximal lineage

Ego

Minimal lineage

bilineally over many generations. After a while, many of the persons who carry the name will belong to the group simply by virtue of the name rather than because they can trace their genealogical relationship all the way back to the founding ancestor. An appropriate designation for such groups is *cognatic clan*. (In recent times, some members of Scots clans have different surnames as a result of patronymy and must demonstrate descent; see Neville 1979.)

UNILINEAL DESCENT GROUPS

When unilineal descent is systematically demonstrated with respect to a particular ancestor, the resultant kin group is called a *patrilineage* (Fig. 16.10) or a *matrilineage*. All lineages contain the same set of people regardless of the genealogical perspective from which they are viewed. This makes them ideally suited to be coresident domestic groups and to hold joint interests in persons and property. Because of exogamy, however, both sexes cannot remain coresident

beyond childhood. Some lineages include all the generations and collateral descendants of the first ancestor. These are *maximal lineages*. Lineages that contain only three generations are *minimal lineages* (see Fig. 16.10).

When unilineal descent from a specific ancestor is stipulated rather than demonstrated, the group that results is known as either a *patriclan* or a *matriclan* (the terms *patrisib* and *matrisib* are also in use). There are many borderline cases, however, in which it is difficult to decide whether one is dealing with a lineage or a clan.

POSTMARITAL LOCALITY PATTERNS

In order to understand the processes responsible for the evolution of different varieties of domestic groups and different ideologies of descent, we must discuss one additional aspect of domestic organization. There is considerable agreement among anthropologists that an important determinant of descent rules is the pattern of residence after marriage. The principal postmarital locality practices are described in Table 16.1.

Postmarital residence practices influence descent rules because they determine who will enter, leave, or stay in a domestic group (Murdock 1949; Naroll 1973). They thus provide domestic groups with distinctive cores of relatives that correspond to the inclusions and exclusions produced by the movements of married couples. These movements themselves are influenced by the demographic, technological, eco-

TABLE *16.1*

PRINCIPAL VARIETIES OF POSTMARITAL RESIDENCE

Name of pattern	Place where married couple resides
Neolocality	Apart from either husband's or wife's kin
Bilocality	Alternately shifting from husband's kin to wife's kin
Ambilocality	Some couples with husband's kin, others with wife's kin
Patrilocality	With husband's father
Matrilocality	With wife's mother
Avunculocality	With husband's mother's brother
Amitalocality	With wife's father's sister
Uxorilocality	With the wife's kin (several of the above may be combined with uxorilocality)
Virilocality	With the husband's kin (several of the above may be combined with virilocality)

nomic, and ecological conditions in which people find themselves. Thus, in many societies, descent rules and other kinship principles can be seen as organizing and justifying domestic group structures in relation to particular infrastructural conditions.

CAUSES OF BILATERAL DESCENT

Bilateral descent is associated with various combinations of neolocality, ambilocality, and bilocality (see Table 16.1 for definitions of locality patterns). These locality practices in turn usually reflect a high degree of mobility and flexibility among nuclear families. Mobility and flexibility, as we have seen (Ch. 12), are useful for hunters and gatherers, and are an intrinsic feature of band organization. The !Kung San, for example, are primarily bilateral, and this reflects in turn a predominant, bilocal, postmarital residence pattern. !Kung San camps contain a core of siblings of both sexes, plus their spouses and children and an assortment of more distant bilateral and affinal kin. Each year, in addition to much short-time visiting, about 13 percent of the population makes a more or less permanent residential shift from one camp to another, and about 35 percent divide their time equally among two or three different camps (Lee 1979:54). This mobility and flexibility is advantageous for people who must rely on hunting and gathering for their livelihood.

In industrial societies such as the United States and Canada, bilaterality is associated with a similar flexibility and mobility of nuclear families. Bilaterality in this case reflects a neolocal pattern that is advantageous with respect to wage-labor opportunities and the substitution of price-market money exchanges for kinship-mediated forms

of exchange. Whereas the !Kung San always live with relatives and depend on kindreds and extended families for their subsistence, industrial-age nuclear families often live far away from any relatives whatsoever and interact with their kindreds primarily at holidays, weddings, and funerals.

DETERMINANTS OF COGNATIC LINEAGES AND CLANS

Cognatic lineages and cognatic clans are associated with *ambilocality*. This is a form of postmarital residence in which the married couple elects to stay on a relatively permanent basis with the wife's or the husband's domestic group. Ambilocality differs from the neolocality of the U.S. and Canadian family, since residence is established with a definite group of kin. Ambilocality also differs from the bilocality of hunting-and-gathering societies in that the shifting from one domestic group to another occurs less frequently. This implies a relatively more sedentary form of village life and also a somewhat greater potential for developing exclusive "corporate" interests in people and property. Yet all cognatic descent groups, whether bilateral or ambilineal, have less potential for corporate unity than unilineal descent groups, a point to which we return in a moment.

One example of how cognatic lineages work has already been discussed. Such lineages occurred among the Pacific Northwest Coast potlatchers (see Chapter 14). The Kwakiutl potlatch chiefs sought to attract and to hold as large a labor force as they possibly could. (The more people a village put to work during a salmon run, the more fish they could catch.)

The core of each village consisted of a chieftain and his followers, usually demonstrably related to him through ambilineal descent and constituting a cognatic lineage known as a *numaym*. The chieftain claimed hereditary privileges and noble rank on the basis of ambilineal reckoning from his noble forebears. Validation of this status depended on his ability to recruit and hold an adequate following in the face of competition from like-minded neighbor chieftains. The importance placed on individual choice and the uncertainty surrounding the group's corporate estate are typical of cognatic lineages in other cultures as well.

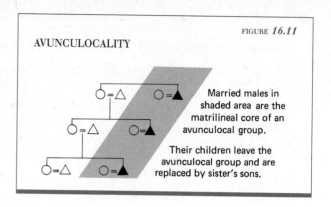

FIGURE *16.11*

AVUNCULOCALITY

Married males in shaded area are the matrilineal core of an avunculocal group.

Their children leave the avunculocal group and are replaced by sister's sons.

DETERMINANTS OF UNILINEAL LINEAGES AND CLANS

Although there is no basis for reviving nineteenth-century notions of universal stages in the evolution of kinship (see Appendix), certain well-substantiated, general evolutionary trends do exist. Hunting-and-gathering societies tend to have cognatic descent groups and/or bilocal residence because their basic ecological adjustment demands that local groups remain open, flexible, and nonterritorial. With the development of horticulture and more settled village life, the identification between domestic groups or villages and definite territories increased and became more exclusive. Population density increased and warfare became more intense, for reasons to be discussed (Ch. 17), contributing to the need for emphasizing exclusive group unity and solidarity (Ember, Ember, and Pasternak 1974). Under these conditions, unilineal descent groups with well-defined localized membership cores, a heightened sense of solidarity, and an ideology of exclusive rights over resources and people became the predominant form of kinship group. Using a sample of 797 agricultural societies, Michael Harner (1970) has shown that a very close statistical association exists between an increased reliance on agriculture as opposed to hunting and gathering and the replacement of cognatic descent groups by unilineal descent groups. Horticultural village societies that are organized unilineally outnumber those that are organized cognatically 380 to 111 in Harner's sample. Moreover, almost all the unilineal societies display signs of increased population pressure, as indicated by the depletion of wild plant and food resources.

Unilineal descent groups are closely associated with one or the other variety of unilocal residence—that is, patrilineality with patrilocality and matrilineality with matrilocality. In addition, there is a close correlation between avunculocality and matrilineality. With patrilineality,

fathers, brothers, and sons form the core of the domestic group; and with matrilocality, mothers, sisters, and daughters form the core of the domestic group. The connections between these locality practices and descent rules should be clear, although the reason for the connection between avunculocality and matrilineality is more complex. With avunculocality, mother's brothers and sister's sons form the core of the domestic unit. Sister's son is born in her husband's mother's brother's household, but as a juvenile or adult, sister's son leaves this household and takes up residence with his own mother's brother (Fig. 16.11). The way in which avunculocality works and the reason for its association with matrilineality will become clearer in a moment, as we examine the infrastructural causes of matrilocality and patrilocality.

CAUSES OF PATRILOCALITY

The overwhelming majority of known societies have male-centered residence and descent patterns. Seventy-one percent of 1179 societies classified by George Murdock (1967) are either patrilocal or virilocal (see Table 16.2); in the same sample, societies that have patrilineal kin groups outnumber societies that have matrilineal kin groups 588 to 164. Patrilocality and patrilineality are the statistically "normal" mode of domestic organization. They have been predominant not only, as was once thought, in societies that have plows and draft animals or that practice pastoral nomadism, but also in simple horticultural and slash-and-burn societies as well (Divale 1974).

It is difficult to escape the conclusion that the underlying reason for the prevalence of patrilocality among village societies is that cooperation among males is more often more crucial than cooperation among females. Specifically, men are more effective

TABLE *16.2*

RELATIONSHIP BETWEEN RESIDENCE AND DESCENT IN THE ETHNOGRAPHIC ATLAS

| | Postmarital residence | | | | |
Kin groups	Matrilocal or uxorilocal	Avunculocal	Patrilocal or virilocal	Other	Total
Patrilineal	1	0	563	25	588
Matrilineal	53	62	30	19	164

SOURCES: Divale and Harris 1976; Murdock 1967.

in hand-to-hand combat than women, and women are less mobile than men during pregnancy and when nursing infants. As a consequence, men generally monopolize the weapons of war and the hunt, leading to male control over trade and politics. The practice of intense small-scale warfare between neighboring villages may be a crucial factor in promoting a widespread complex of male-centered and male-dominated institutions (Divale and Harris 1976). We will return to the issue of sex and gender hierarchies in Chapter 20.

CAUSES OF MATRILOCALITY

It is generally agreed that matrilineal descent groups will not form independently—that is, in the absence of matrilineal neighbors—unless matrilocality is the postmarital residence practice. But why matrilocality? One theory holds that when women's role in food production became more important, as in horticultural societies, domestic groups tended to be structured around a core of females. This theory, however, must be rejected, because there is no greater association between horticulture and matrilocality than between horticulture and patrilocality (Divale 1974; Ember and Ember 1971). Moreover, it is difficult to see why field labor would require a degree of cooperation so high that only women from the same domestic groups could carry it out efficiently, nor why it would require all brothers and sons to be expelled from the natal domestic group (Burton and White 1987).

The question that we must ask concerning the origin of matrilocality is this: Under what conditions would the male specialties of warfare, hunting, and trade benefit from a shift to matrilocality (keeping in mind the clear advantage a shift from patrilocality to matrilocality offers to women)? The

most likely answer is that when warfare, hunting, and trade change from quick, short-distance forays to long-distance expeditions lasting several months, matrilocality is more advantageous than patrilocality. When patrilocal males leave a village for extended periods, they leave behind their patrilineal kin group's corporate interests in property and people to be looked after solely by their wives. The allegiance of their wives, however, is to another patrilineal kin group. A patrilocal group's women are drawn from different kin groups and have little basis for cooperating among themselves when they are unsupervised by the male managers of the corporate domestic units into which they have married. There is no one home, so to speak, "to mind the store." Matrilocality solves this problem because it structures the domestic unit around a permanent core of resident mothers, daughters, and sisters who have been trained to cooperate with each other from birth and who identify the "minding of the store" with their own material and sentimental interests. Thus, matrilocal domestic groups are less likely to be disrupted by the prolonged absence of their adult males.

The ability to launch and successfully complete long-distance expeditions implies that neighboring villages will not attack each other when the men are away. This is best assured by forming the expeditions around a core of males drawn from several neighboring villages or different households within a given village. Among patrilocal, patrilineal villages, the belligerent territorial teams consist of patrilineally related kin who constitute competitive "fraternal interest groups." These groups make shifting alliances with neighboring villages, exchange sisters, and raid each other. Most combat takes place between villages that are about a day's walk from each other. Matrilocal, matrilineal cultures, on the other hand, are bonded not by the exchange of women but by the inmarrying of males from different domestic groups.

Scattering fathers and brothers into several different households in different villages prevents the formation of competitive and disruptive fraternal interest groups.

Thus, matrilocal, matrilineal societies like the Iroquois of New York and the Huron of Ontario enjoy a high degree of internal peace. But most matrilineal societies, like the Iroquois and the Huron, have a history of intense warfare directed outward against powerful enemies (Gramby 1977; Trigger 1978). The matrilineal Nayar, to cite another example, were a soldier caste in the service of the kings of Malabar. Also among the matrilocal Mundurucu of the Amazon, conflict between villages was unheard of and interpersonal aggression was suppressed. But the Mundurucu launched raids against enemies hundreds of miles away, and unrelenting hostility and violence characterized their relations with the "outside world" (Murphy 1956). We will encounter other examples of warlike matrilineal societies in Chapter 18.

CAUSES OF AVUNCULOCALITY

In matrilocal, matrilineal societies, males are reluctant to relinquish control over their own sons to the members of their wives' kin groups, and they are not easily reconciled to the fact that it is their sons rather than their daughters who must move away from them at marriage. Because of this contradiction, matrilocal, matrilineal systems tend to revert to patrilocal, patrilineal systems as soon as the forces responsible for keeping males away from their natal villages and domestic groups are removed or moderated.

One way to solve this contradiction is to loosen the male's marital obligations (already weak in matrilocal societies) to the point where he need not live with his wife at all. This is the path followed by the Nayar. As we have seen, Nayar men had no home other than their natal domestic unit; they were untroubled by what happened to their children—whom they were scarcely able to identify—and they had no difficulty keeping their sisters and their nephews and nieces under proper fraternal and avuncular control.

But a more common solution to the tension between male interests and matrilineality is the development of avunculocal patterns of residence. It is a remarkable fact that there are more matrilineal descent groups that are *avunculocal* than matrilineal descent groups that are matrilocal (see Table 16.2).

Under avunculocality, a male eventually goes to live with his mother's brothers in their matrilineal domestic unit; his wife joins him there. At maturity, a male ego's son will in turn depart for ego's wife's brother's domestic unit (ego's daughter, however, may remain resident if she marries her father's sister's son). Thus, the male core of an avunculocal domestic unit consists of a group of brothers and their sister's sons. The function of this arrangement seems to be to maintain a male fraternal interest group in the residential core of the matrilineal descent group. Avunculocality thus provides the best of two worlds for males who aspire to military and political leadership. They can influence and draw on their sisters' sons and daughters and at the same time, they can influence the sons and daughters whom they reared from birth to marriage. Avunculocality is thus ideally suited for and correlated with the emergence of bellicose chiefdoms (Keegan and Maclachlan 1989).

The logical opposite of avunculocality—namely, *amitalocality* (*amita* = aunt)—exists if brother's daughters and father's sisters constitute the residential core of a patrilineal domestic unit. Most instances of amitalocality involve patrilocal, patrilineal descent groups that practice matrilateral cross cousin marriage. Such groups contain male ego's paternal aunts. These women will not constitute the residential core of the domestic unit, however, since it is they and not their husbands who depart from their natal domiciles to reside with their spouse (cf. Ottenheimer 1984).

A rather thin line separates avunculocality from patrilocality. If the resident group of brothers decides to permit one or more of its sons to remain with them after marriage, the residential core will begin to resemble an ambilocal domestic group. If more sons than nephews are retained in residence, the locality basis for a reassertion of patrilineal descent will be present.

After a society has adopted matrilocality and developed matrilineal descent groups, changes in the original conditions may lead to a restoration of the patrilocal, patrilineal pattern. At any given moment, many societies are probably in a transitional state between one form of residence and another and one form of kinship ideology and another. Since the changes in residence and descent may not proceed in perfect tandem at any particular moment—that is, descent changes may lag behind residence changes—one should expect to encounter combinations of residence with the "wrong" descent rule. For example, a few patrilocal societies and quite a large number of virilocal societies have matrilineal descent, and one or two uxorilocal societies have patrilineal descent (see Table 16.1). But there is evidence for a very powerful strain toward consistency in the alignment among domestic groups; their ecological, military, and economic adaptations; and their ideologies of descent.

KINSHIP TERMINOLOGIES

Another aspect of domestic ideology that participates in the same strain toward functional consistency is kinship terminology. Every culture has a special set of terms (such as *father, mother, cousin*) for designating types of kin. The terms plus the rules for using them constitute a culture's kin terminological system.

Lewis Henry Morgan was the first anthropologist to realize that despite the thousands of different languages over the face of the globe, and despite the immense number of different kinship terms in these languages, there are only a handful of basic types of kin terminological systems. These systems can best be defined by the way terms are applied to an abbreviated genealogical grid consisting of two generations, including ego's siblings of the same and opposite sex and ego's cross and parallel cousins. Here we will examine three well-known systems in order to illustrate the nature of the causal and functional relationships that link alternative kinship terminologies to the other aspects of domestic organizations. (It should be emphasized that these are basic terminological types. Actual instances often vary in details.)

Eskimo Terminology

The kind of kin terminological systems with which most North Americans are familiar is known as *Eskimo,* shown in Figure 16.12. Two important features of this system are these: First, none of the terms applied to ego's nuclear relatives—1, 2, 6, 5—is applied outside the nuclear family, and second, there is no distinction between maternal and paternal sides. This means that there is no distinction between cross and parallel cousins or between cross and parallel aunts or uncles. These features reflect the fact that societies using Eskimo terminology generally lack corporate descent groups. In the absence of such groups, the nuclear family tends to stand out as a separate and functionally dominant productive and reproductive unit. For this reason, its members are given a terminological identity separate from all other kin types. On the other hand, the lumping of all cousins under a single term (7) reflects the strength of bilateral as opposed to unilineal descent. The influence of bilateral descent is also reflected in the failure to distinguish terminologically between aunts and uncles on the mother's side and those on the father's side. The theoretical predictions concerning Eskimo terminology are strongly confirmed by the tabulations of Murdock's *Ethnographic Atlas* (1967). Of the 71 societies having Eskimo terminology, only 4 have large extended families and only 13 have unilineal descent groups. In 54 of the 71 Eskimo terminology societies descent groups are entirely absent or are represented only by kindreds.

As the name implies, "Eskimo" is frequently found among hunters and gatherers. This is because any factors that isolate the nuclear family increase the probability that an Eskimo terminology will occur. As we have seen, among hunting-and-gathering groups, the determining factors are low population densities and the need for maximum geographical mobility in relationship to fluctuations in the availability of game and other resources. In industrial societies, the same terminological pattern reflects the intrusion of price-market institutions into the domestic routine and the high level of wage-induced social and geographic mobility.

Hawaiian Terminology

Another common kin terminological system is known as *Hawaiian.* This is the easiest system to portray, since it has the fewest number of terms (Fig. 16.13). In some versions, even the distinction between the sexes is dropped, leaving one term for the members of ego's generation and another for the members of ego's parents' generation. The most remarkable feature of Hawaiian terminology, as compared with Eskimo, is the application of the same terms to people inside and outside the nuclear family. Hawaiian is thus compatible with situations where the nuclear family is submerged within a domestic context dominated by extended families and other corporate descent groups. In Murdock's *Ethnographic Atlas,* 21 percent of the Hawaiian terminology societies do indeed have large extended families. In addition, well over 50 percent of Hawaiian terminology societies have some form of corporate descent group other than extended families.

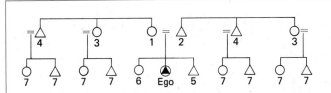

FIGURE *16.12*

ESKIMO TERMINOLOGY

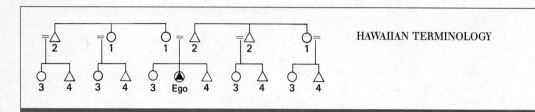

FIGURE **16.13**

HAWAIIAN TERMINOLOGY

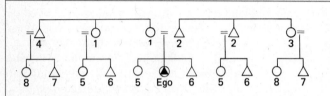

FIGURE **16.14**

IROQUOIS TERMINOLOGY

FIGURE **16.15**

FOR THE KINSHIP ENTHUSIAST: CROW TERMINOLOGY, MALE EGO
Many cultures have terminological systems in which the influence of lineality
overwhelms generational criteria. These systems occur in both matrilineal
and patrilineal versions. The matrilineal variety is known as *Crow*. Crow systems
involve the distinction between patrilateral and matrilateral cross cousins. Not only
are these cousins distinguished from each other, but the patrilateral cross cousins
are also equated with father and father's sister and brother. There is also the curious
fact that the matrilateral cross cousins are equated with ego's daughter and son.

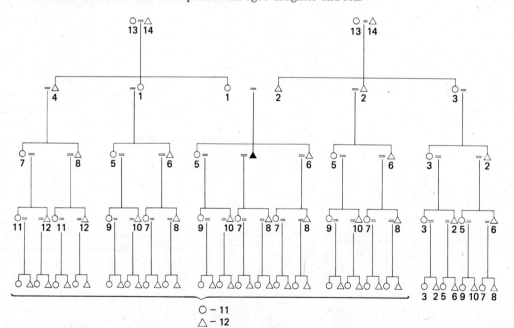

Theoretically, most of these descent groups should be cognatic rather than unilineal. The reason for this prediction is that the merging of relatives on the maternal side with those on the paternal side indicates an indifference toward unilineality, and an indifference toward unilineality is logically consistent with ambilineal or bilateral descent.

Data from Murdock's ethnographic sample only partially support this prediction: There are, indeed, many more Hawaiian terminology societies that have cognatic as opposed to unilineal descent, but there are many exceptions for which as yet no generally accepted explanation is available.

Iroquois Terminology

In the presence of unilineal kin groups, there is a worldwide tendency to distinguish parallel from cross cousins, as previously noted. This pattern is widely associated with a similar distinction in the first ascending generation, whereby father's brothers are distinguished from mother's brothers and father's sisters are distinguished from mother's sisters.

An *Iroquois* terminology exists where—in addition to these distinctions between cross and parallel cousins and cross and parallel aunts and uncles—mother's sister is terminologically merged with mother, father's brother is terminologically merged with father, and parallel cousins are terminologically merged with ego's brothers and sisters (Fig. 16.14).

This pattern of merging occurs in large part as a result of the shared membership of siblings in corporate unilineal descent groups and of the marriage alliances based on cross cousin marriage between such groups. In Murdock's ethnographic sample there are 166 societies having Iroquois terminology. Of these, 119 have some form of unilineal descent group (70 percent).

We have only skimmed the surface of a few of the many fascinating and important problems in the field of kinship terminology (Fig. 16.15). But perhaps enough has been said to establish at least one point: Kin terminological systems possess a remarkable logical coherence. Yet like so many other aspects of culture, kin terminological systems are never the planned product of any inventive genius. Most people are unaware that such systems even exist. Clearly, the major features of these systems represent recurrent unconscious adjustments to the prevailing conditions of domestic life. Yet there are many details of kin terminologies, as well as of other kinship phenomena, that are as yet not well understood.

SUMMARY

To study kinship is to study the ideologies that justify and normalize the corporate structure of domestic groups. The basis of kinship is the tracing of relationships through marriage and descent. Descent is the belief that certain persons play a special role in the conception, birth, or nurturance of certain children. Many different folk theories of descent exist, none of which corresponds precisely to modern-day scientific understandings of procreation and reproduction.

The principal varieties of cognatic descent rules are the bilateral and the ambilineal; these are associated, respectively, with kindreds on the one hand, and with cognatic lineages and clans on the other. The principal varieties of unilineal descent are matrilineality and patrilineality. These are associated, respectively, with patri- and matrilineages or patri- and matriclans.

An important key to understanding alternative modes of descent and domestic organization is the pattern of postmarital residence. Bilateral descent and bilateral descent groups are associated with neolocality, bilocality, and ambilocality. More specifically, the flexible and mobile forms of band organization are facilitated by bilocality, whereas the greater isolation of nuclear families in price-market economies gives rise to neolocality. Cognatic lineages and clans, on the other hand, give functional expression to ambilocality.

Unilineal domestic groups reflect unilocal patterns of residence. These in turn imply well-defined membership cores and an emphasis on exclusive rights over resources and people. There is a strong correlation between patrilocality and patrilineality on the one hand, and among matrilineality, matrilocality, and avunculocality on the other. Patrilocal and patrilineal groups are far more common than matrilineal or avunculocal groups. A reason for this is that warfare, hunting, and trading activities among village societies are monopolized by males. These activities, in turn, are facilitated by stressing the coresidence of fathers, brothers, and sons and the formation of fraternal interest groups. Under conditions of increasing population density and pressure on resources, local groups may find it adaptive to engage in long-distance war-trade-hunting expeditions. Such expeditions are facilitated by breaking up the fraternal interest groups and structuring domestic life around a residential core of mothers, sisters, and daughters or, in other words, by developing a matrilocal, matrilineal organization. Since males in matrilineal, matrilocal societies continue to dominate military and political institutions, they are inclined to reinject the patrilineal principle into domestic life and to moderate the effects of matrilocality on their control over their sons and daughters. This accounts for the fact that as many matrilineal societies are avunculocal as are matrilocal.

Thus, the principal function of alternative rules of descent may be described as the establishment and maintenance of networks of cooperative and interdependent kinspeople aggregated into ecologically effective and militarily secure domestic production and reproduction units. In order for such units to act effectively and reliably, they must share an organizational ideology that interprets and validates the structure of the group and the behavior of its members. This interpretation of kinship rules can also be applied to the principal varieties of kin terminological systems. Such systems tend to classify relatives in conformity with the major features of domestic organization, locality practices, and descent rules. Eskimo terminology, for example, is functionally associated with domestic organizations in which nuclear families tend to be mobile and isolated; Hawaiian terminology is functionally associated with cognatic lineages and cognatic clans; and Iroquois terminology, with its emphasis on the distinction between cross and parallel cousins, is functionally associated with unilinear descent groups.

Chapter 17

Law, Order, and War in Prestate Societies

As we continue with the structural aspect of sociocultural systems, the focus shifts from the structure of domestic groups to the regulation of interpersonal relationships and the maintenance of political cohesion and law and order within and between band and village societies. These societies enjoy a high degree of personal security without having written laws, police officers, jails, or any of the other parts of modern criminal justice systems. How do they do it? This is not to say that there is no violence in band and village societies. On the contrary, feuds and warfare do occur even among hunter-gatherers and small village societies that have very low population densities. Why do they do it? Some anthropologists argue that the propensity to engage in armed combat is part of human nature. Others, however, point to the fallacy of supposing that there are no scarce resources worth fighting over simply because population density is low. In one important case, at least, the scarce resource seems to be meat. War, then, is no more natural than peace.

LAW AND ORDER IN BAND AND VILLAGE SOCIETIES

People in every society have conflicting interests (Fig. 17.1). Even in band-level societies, old and young, sick and healthy, men and women do not want the same thing at the same time. Moreover, in every society people want something that others possess and are reluctant to give away. Every culture, therefore, must have structural provisions for resolving conflicts of interest in an orderly fashion and for preventing conflicts from escalating into disruptive confrontations. There are marked qualitative and quantitative differences, however, between the kinds of conflicting interests found in band and simple village societies and those found in more complex societies. There are also marked differences in the methods employed to prevent disruptive confrontations.

Simple hunter-gatherer societies such as the Innuit, the !Kung San of the Kalahari, and the native Australians enjoy a high degree of personal security without having any rulers or law and order specialists. They have no kings, queens, dictators, presidents, governors, or mayors; police forces, soldiers, sailors, or marines; CIA, FBI, treasury agents, or federal marshals. They have no written law codes and no formal law courts; no lawyers, bailiffs, judges, district attorneys, juries, or court clerks; and no patrol cars, paddy wagons, jails, or penitentiaries. This is also true of many village societies. How do people get along without law enforcement specialists and facilities, and why are modern societies so dependent on them?

The basic reasons for the differences are (1) the small size of simple band and simple village societies, (2) the central importance of domestic groups and kinship in their social organization, and (3) the absence of marked inequalities in access to technology and resources. Small size means that everyone knows everyone else personally; therefore, stingy, aggressive, and disruptive individuals can be identified by the group and exposed to the pressure of public opinion. The centrality of domestic group and kinship relations means that reciprocity can be the chief mode of exchange and that the collective interests of the domestic unit can be recognized by all its members. Finally, equality of access to technology and natural resources means that food and other forms of wealth cannot be withheld by a wealthy few while others endure shortages and hardships.

PRIMITIVE COMMUNISM?

Among simple band and village societies, all adults usually have open access to the rivers, lakes, beaches, oceans; to all the plants and animals; and to the soil and the subsoil. Insofar as these are basic to the extraction of life-sustaining energy and materials, they are communal property (Lee 1990).

Anthropologists have reported the existence of nuclear family and even individual ownership of hunting-and-gathering territories among native American band-level societies in Canada, but these ownership patterns were associated with the fur trade and did not exist aboriginally (Knight 1974; Leacock

FIGURE *17.1*

YANOMAMÖ CLUB FIGHT
Egalitarian people are not without problems of law and order.

1973). In other cases, reports of family territories fail to distinguish between ideological claims and actual behavior. The fact that a nuclear family regards a particular area as its "own" must be weighed against the conditions under which others can use the area and the consequences of trespass. If permission to use the area is always freely granted and if use without permission results merely in some muttering or name-calling, the modern notion of "ownership" may be the wrong concept to use.

Among the !Kung San, waterholes and hunting-and-gathering territories are emically "owned" by the residential core of particular bands. But since neighboring bands contain many intermarried kin, there is a great deal of sharing of access to resources as a result of mutual visiting. Neighbors who ask for permission to visit and exploit the resources of a particular camp are seldom refused. Even people who come from distant bands and who lack close kin ties with the hosts are usually given permission to stay, especially for short periods, since it is understood that the hosts may return the visit at some future date (Lee 1979:337).

The prevalence of communal ownership of land, however, does not mean that simple hunter-gatherers lack private property altogether. There is little support for the theory of "primitive communism," which holds that there was a universal stage in the development of culture marked by the complete absence of private property (Epstein 1968). Many material objects of band-level societies are effectively controlled ("owned") by specific individuals, especially items the user has produced. The members of even the most egalitarian societies usually believe that weapons, clothing, containers, ornaments, tools, and other "personal effects" ought not to be taken away or used without the consent of the "owner." However, the chance is remote that theft or misappropriation of such objects will lead to serious conflict (Woodburn 1982a). Why not?

First, the accumulation of material possessions is rigidly limited by the recurrent need to break camp and travel long distances on foot. In addition, most utilitarian items may be borrowed without difficulty when the owner is not using them. If there are not enough such items to go around (arrows, projectile points, nets, bark or gourd containers), easy access to the raw materials and mastery of the requisite skills provide the have-nots with the chance of making their own. Moreover, among societies having no more than a few hundred people, thieves cannot be anonymous. If stealing becomes habitual, a coalition of the injured parties will eventually take action. If you want something, better to ask for it openly. Most such requests are readily obliged, since reciprocity is the prevailing mode of exchange. Finally, it should be noted that, contrary to the experience of the successful modern bank robber, no one can make a living from stealing bows and arrows or feather headdresses, since there is no regular market at which such items can be exchanged for food (see Chapter 14).

MOBILIZING PUBLIC OPINION: SONG DUELS

The most important requirement for the control of disputes in band societies is the temporary insulation of the disputants from the corporate response of their respective kin groups. As long as the disputants feel they have the backing of their kin groups, they will continue to press their claims and counterclaims. The members of kin groups, however, never react mechanically. They are eager not to be caught in a situation in which they are opposed by a majority of people.

Public opinion, in other words, influences the support disputants can expect from their kin. What matters is not so much who is morally right or wrong, or who is lying or telling the truth; the important thing is to mobilize public opinion on one side or the other decisively enough to prevent the outbreak of large-scale feuding.

A classic example of how such mobilization can be achieved independently of abstract principles of justice is the *song contest* of the central and eastern Innuit (Fig. 17.2). Here, it frequently happens that one man claims that another man has stolen his wife. The counterclaim is that she was not stolen but left voluntarily because her husband "was not man enough" to take good care of her. The issue is settled at a large public meeting that might be likened to a court. But no testimony is taken in support of either of the two versions of why the wife has left her husband. Instead, the "disputants" take turns singing insulting songs at each other. The "court" responds to each performance with differential degrees of laughter. Eventually one of the singers gets flustered, and the hooting and hollering raised against him become total—even his relatives have a hard time not laughing (see Box 17.1).

The Innuit have no police-military specialists to see to it that the "decision" is enforced. Yet, chances are that the man who has lost the song duel will give in, since he can no longer count on anyone to back him up if he chooses to escalate the dispute. Nonetheless, the defeated man may decide to go it alone.

BOX *17.1*

INNUIT SONG

Something was whispered
Of a man and wife
Who could not agree
And what was it all about?
A wife who in rightful anger
Tore her husband's furs,
Took their boat
And rowed away with her son.
Ay-ay, all who listen,
What do you think of him
Who is great in his anger
But faint in strength,
Blubbering helplessly?
He got what he deserved
Though it was he who proudly
Started this quarrel with stupid words.

SOURCE: Adapted from Rasmussen 1929:231–232.

FIGURE *17.2*

SONG CONTEST
Innuit "disputants" in "court" in eastern Greenland.

Wife stealing does occasionally lead to murder. When this happens, the man who has lost public support may survive on the strength of his own vigilance and fighting skill. He will probably have to kill again, however, and with each transgression, the coalition against him becomes larger and more determined, until finally he falls victim to an ambush.

MOBILIZING PUBLIC OPINION: WITCHCRAFT ACCUSATIONS

Among band and simple village societies, part-time magico-religious specialists known as *shamans* frequently play an important role in mobilizing public opinion and in eliminating persistent sources of conflict. Most cultures reject the idea that misfortune can result from natural causes. If animals suddenly become scarce or if several people fall sick, it is assumed that somebody is practicing witchcraft. It is the shaman's job to identify the culprit. Normally this is done through the art of divination, or clairvoyance. Putting themselves into trances with the aid of drugs, tobacco smoke, or monotonous drumming, shamans discover the name of the culprit. The people demand vengeance, and the culprit is ambushed and murdered.

The chances are that the murdered individual never attempted to carry out any witchcraft at all! In other words, the witches are probably wholly "innocent" of the crime with which they have been charged. Nonetheless, the shaman's witchcraft accusations usually conserve rather than destroy the group's feeling of unity.

Consider the case reported by Gertrude Dole (1966) for the Kuikuru—an egalitarian village-dwelling group of Brazilian Indians (Fig. 17.3). Lightning had set fire to two houses. The shaman went into a trance and discovered that the lightning had been sent by a man who had left the village some years previously and had never returned. This man had only one male relative, who was also no longer living in the village. Before the accused witch left the village, he became engaged to a young girl. The shaman's brother had persuaded the girl's mother to break the betrothal and to permit him to marry the girl:

During the course of the divining ceremony, the shaman carried on dialogues with various interested members of the community. When he finally disclosed the identity of the culprit, it created considerable anxiety. One after another, several individuals stood apart in the plaza and spoke in long monologues.... In the heat of the excitement, the shaman's brother left with a few companions to kill the man suspected of witchcraft. [1966:761]

FIGURE *17.3*

KUIKURU SHAMAN
The shaman is leaving the village with his
assistants on the way to a nearby lake
to recover the lost soul of a patient lying ill
in the house seen in the background.
The shaman intends to dive to the bottom
of the lake and wrest the soul away from the evil
spirit who stole it from the patient, and then
implant it back into the patient's body.

The ethnographer points out that among the
Kuikuru a change of residence from one village to another usually indicates that there is trouble brewing
and that, in effect, the individual has been ostracized.
(The Kuikuru suspected Dole and her anthropologist
husband of having been "kicked out" of their own society.) Thus, the man accused of sorcery was not a
randomly chosen figure but one who fulfilled several
well-defined criteria: a history of disputes and quarrels within the village, a motivation for continuing to
do harm (the broken engagement), and a weak kinship backing.

The shaman's accusation was not based on
a spur-of-the-moment decision: There had been a
long incubation period during which the shaman, in
or out of trance, sounded out his fellow villagers on

their attitudes toward the accused. As Dole indicates,
the supernatural authority of the shaman allows him
to make public indictments. But shamans are not in
control, as in late-night movie versions of the sinis-
ter medicine man turning the "natives" against the
friendly European explorers. Rather, they are largely
constrained by public opinion. Although the act of divination appears to put the shaman in charge of the
judicial process, the shaman actually "deduces, for-
mulates, and expresses the will of the people" (Dole
1966:76).

Shamans abuse their supernatural gifts if they
accuse people who are well liked and who enjoy
strong kin-group support. If they persist in making
such mistakes, they themselves will be ostracized or
even murdered.

The peculiar thing about witchcraft as a means
of social control is that its practitioners, if they exist at
all, can seldom be detected. The number of persons
falsely accused of witchcraft probably far exceeds the
number who are justly accused. It is clear, therefore,
that nonpractice of witchcraft is no safeguard against
an accusation of witchcraft. How, then, do you protect
yourself from such false accusations? By acting in an
amiable, open, generous manner; by avoiding quarrels; and by doing everything possible not to lose the
support of your kin groups. The occasional killing of
a supposed sorcerer results in much more than the
mere elimination of a few actual or potential antisocial individuals. These violent incidents convince everyone of the importance of not being mistaken for
an evildoer. As a result, as among the Kuikuru, people are made more amiable, cordial, generous, and
willing to cooperate:

The norm of being amiable deters individuals from
accusing one another of delicts [crimes], hence in the
absence of effective political or kin-group control, in-
terpersonal relations have become a kind of game, in
which almost the only restrictive rule is not to show
hostility to one another for fear of being suspected of
witchcraft. [Dole 1966:741]

This system is not "fail-safe." Many cases are
known of witchcraft systems that seem to have broken down, involving the community in a series of destructive retaliatory accusations and murders. These
cases, however (especially in situations of intensive
colonial contact, as in Africa and Melanesia), must be
carefully related to the underlying conditions of communal life. In general, the incidence of witchcraft
accusations varies with the amount of community
dissension and frustration (Mair 1969; Nadel 1952).
When a traditional culture is upset by exposure to
new diseases, increased competition for land, and

recruitment for wage labor, an epoch of increased dissension and frustration can be expected. This period will also be characterized by frenzied activity among those who are skilled in tracking down and exposing the malevolent effects of witches, as in the case of the breakup of feudal society in Europe and the great witch craze of the fifteenth to seventeenth centuries.

HEADMANSHIP

To the extent that political leadership can be said to exist at all among band and simple village societies, it is exercised by *headmen* or, (far less commonly, headwomen). The headman, unlike such specialists as king, president, or dictator, is a relatively powerless figure incapable of compelling obedience. He lacks sufficient force to do so. When he gives a command, he is never certain of being able to punish physically those who disobey. (Hence, if he wants to stay in "office," he gives few direct commands.) In contrast, the political power of genuine rulers depends on their ability to expel or exterminate any readily foreseeable combination of nonconforming individuals and groups. Genuine rulers control access to basic resources and to the tools and weapons for hurting or killing people.

Among the Innuit, leadership is especially diffuse, being closely related to success in hunting. A group will follow an outstanding hunter and defer to his opinion with respect to choice of hunting spots. But in all other matters, the "leader's" opinion carries no more weight than any other man's.

Similarly, among the !Kung San, each band has its recognized "leaders," most of whom are males. Such leaders may speak out more than others and are listened to with a bit more deference than is usual, but they "have no formal authority" and "can only persuade, but never enforce their will on others" (Lee 1979:333–334;1982). When Richard Lee asked the !Kung San whether they had "headmen" in the sense of powerful chiefs, he was told: "Of course we have headmen! In fact we are all headmen...each one of us is headman over himself" (ibid.:348).

A similar pattern of leadership is reported for the Semai of Malaya. Despite recent attempts by outsiders to bolster the power of Semai leaders, the headman is merely the most prestigious figure among a group of peers. In the words of Robert Dentan, who carried out fieldwork among these egalitarian shifting horticulturalists:

[The headman] keeps the peace by conciliation rather than coercion. He must be personally respected.... Otherwise people will drift away from him or grad-

THE RIGHT STUFF
BOX *17.2*

The most significant qualifications for Mehinacu chieftainship are learned skills and personal attributes. The chief, for example, is expected to excel at public speaking. Each evening he should stand in the center of the plaza and exhort his fellow tribesmen to be good citizens. He must call upon them to work hard in their gardens, to take frequent baths, not to sleep during the day, not to be angry with each other, and not to have sexual relations too frequently.... In addition to being a skilled orator, the chief is expected to be a generous man. This means that when he returns from a successful fishing trip, he will bring most of his catch out to the men's houses where it is cooked and shared by the men of the tribe. His wife must be generous, bringing manioc cakes and pepper to the men whenever they call for it. Further, the chief must be willing to part with possessions. When one of the men catches a harpy eagle, for example, the chief must buy it from him with a valuable shell belt in the name of the entire tribe....A chief should also be a man who never becomes angry in public.... In his public speeches he should never criticize any of his fellow tribesmen, no matter how badly they may have affronted the chief or the tribe as a whole.

SOURCE: Gregor 1969:88–89.

ually stop paying attention to him. Moreover, the Semai recognize only two or three occasions on which he can assert his authority: dealing as a representative of his people with non-Semai; mediating a quarrel, if invited by the quarreling parties to do so but not otherwise; and...selecting and apportioning land for fields. Furthermore, most of the time a good headman gauges the general feeling about an issue and bases his decision on that, so that he is more a spokesman for public opinion than a molder of it. [1968:681]

Headmanship is likely to be a frustrating and irksome position. The cumulative impression given by descriptions of leadership among Brazilian Indian groups, such as the Mehinacu of Brazil's Xingu National Park (see Box 17.2), is that of a zealous scout-

FIGURE *17.4*

MEHINACU CHIEFTAINSHIP
In front of the men's house, the chief is redistributing presents given to him
by the ethnographer.

master on an overnight cookout. The first one up in the morning, the headman tries to rouse his companions by standing in the middle of the village plaza and shouting. The headman seems to cajole, harangue, and plead from morning to night. If a task needs to be done, it is the headman who starts doing it, and it is the headman who works at it harder than anyone else. Moreover, the headman must set an example not only for hard work but for generosity. After a fishing or hunting expedition, he is expected to give away more of the catch than anyone else; if trade goods are obtained, he must be careful not to keep the best pieces for himself (Fig. 17.4).

It is pertinent at this point to recall the plight of the ungenerous Kapauku headman (Ch. 14). Even the most generous headman in good standing cannot force obedience to his decisions:

If the principals are not willing to comply, the authority [headman] becomes emotional and starts to shout reproaches; he makes long speeches in which evidence, rules, decisions, and threats form inducements. Indeed, the authority may go as far as to start wainai *(the mad dance), or change his tactics suddenly and weep bitterly about the misconduct of the defendant and the fact that he refuses to obey. Some native authorities are so skilled in the art of persuasion that they can produce genuine tears which almost always break the resistance of the unwilling party.* [Pospisil 1968:221]

One wonders whether the Kapauku headman sheds tears more because he is frustrated than because he is skilled.

BLOOD FEUD

The ever-present danger confronting societies that lack genuine rulers is that their kinship groups tend to react as units to real or alleged aggression against one of their members. In this way, disputes involving individuals may escalate. The worst danger arises from disputes that lead to homicide. The members of most simple band and village societies believe that the only proper reaction to a murder is to kill the murderer or any convenient member of the murderer's kin group. Yet, the absence of centralized political authority does not mean that *blood feuds* cannot be brought under control.

BOX *17.3*

ORDERED ANARCHY

The lack of governmental organs among the Nuer, the absence of legal institutions of developed leadership, and generally, of organized political life is remarkable.... The ordered anarchy in which they live accords well with their character, for it is impossible to live among Nuer and conceive of rulers ruling over them.... The Nuer is a product of hard and egalitarian upbringing, is deeply democratic, and is easily roused to violence. This turbulent spirit finds any restraint irksome and no man recognizes a superior. Wealth makes no difference. A man with many cattle is envied but not treated differently from a man with few cattle. Birth makes no difference.... There is no master or servant in their society but only equals who regard themselves as God's noblest creation.... Among themselves even the suspicion of an order riles a man ...he will not submit to any authority which clashes with his own interest and he does not consider himself bound to anyone.

SOURCE: Evans-Pritchard 1940:181–182.

FIGURE *17.5*

LEOPARD SKIN CHIEF

Mechanisms for preventing homicide from flaring into a protracted feud include the transference of substantial amounts of prized possessions from the slayer's kin group to the victim's kin group. This practice is especially common and effective among pastoral peoples, whose animals are a concentrated form of material wealth and for whom bride-price is a regular aspect of kin-group exogamy.

For example, among the Nuer, a pastoral and farming people who live amid the marshy grasslands of the Upper Nile in the Sudan, there is no centralized political leadership (see Box 17.3). The Nuer settle their feuds (or at least deescalate them) by transferring 40 or more head of cattle to the victim's affines and kin. If a man has been killed, these animals will be used to "buy" a wife whose sons will fill the void left by his death. The dead man's closest kin are obliged to resist the offer of cattle, demanding instead a life for a life. However, more distant kin do their best to convince the others to accept the compensation. In this effort, they are aided by certain semi-sacred arbitration specialists. The latter, known as leopard skin chiefs (Fig. 17.5), are usually men whose kin groups are not represented locally and who can hence act more readily as neutral intermediaries.

The leopard skin chief is the only one who can ritually cleanse a murderer. If a homicide takes place, the killer flees at once to the leopard skin chief's house, which is a sanctuary respected by all Nuer. Nonetheless, the leopard skin chief lacks even the rudiments of political power; the most that he can do to the reluctant members of the slain man's relatives is to threaten them with various supernatural curses. Yet, the determination to prevent a feud is so great that the injured relatives eventually accept the cattle as compensation.

NONKIN ASSOCIATIONS: SODALITIES

Although relations of affinity and descent dominate the political life of band and simple village peoples, nonkin forms of political organization also occur to a limited extent. Such groups are called *sodalities*. A common form of sodality is the exclusive men's or women's association, or "club." These usually involve men and women drawn from different domestic groups who cooperate in secret ritual or craft performances. We will discuss these organizations in the chapter devoted to gender roles (Ch. 20).

Age-grade associations are another common form of sodality, already mentioned with respect to the Masai warrior camps (p. 259). Among the Samburu, another group of East African pastoralists, all men initiated into manhood over a span of about 12 to 14 years comprised an age set whose members had a special feeling of solidarity that cut across domestic and lineage kin groups. The age-set members advanced as a group from junior to senior status. As juniors, they were responsible for military combat and as seniors, they were responsible for initiating and training the upcoming age sets (Bernardi 1985; Kertzer 1978; Spencer 1965).

A classic case of sodality is the native North American military associations that developed on the Great Plains after the introduction of the horse. Among the Crow and the Cheyenne, these associations tried to outdo one another in acts of daring during combat and in horse-stealing expeditions. Although the members of each club did not fight as a unit, they met in their respective tepees to reminisce and sing about their exploits, and they wore distinctive insignia and clothing. Gretel and Pertti Pelto (1976:324) have aptly compared them to organizations like the Veterans of Foreign Wars and the American Legion because their main function was to celebrate military exploits and to uphold the honor and prestige of the "tribe." However, on the occasion of a long march to a new territory or on large-scale collective hunts, the military clubs took turns supervising and policing the general population. For example, they prevented overeager hunters from stampeding the buffalo herds, and they suppressed rowdy behavior at ceremonials by fining or banishing disruptive individuals. But these were only seasonal functions, since it was only during the spring and summer that large numbers of unrelated people could congregate.

WARFARE AMONG HUNTERS AND GATHERERS

War is defined as armed combat between groups of people who constitute separate territorial teams or political communities (Otterbein 1973). By this definition, feuds, "grudge fights," and "raids" constitute warfare. Some anthropologists hold that warfare is universally practiced, and that it occurred as far back in time as the Paleolithic (Lizot 1979:151). By excluding feuds and raids from their definitions of warfare, others hold that it was absent or uncommon until the advent of chiefdoms and states (Ferguson 1989a:197; Reyna 1989). Several hunter-gatherer societies—the Andaman Islanders, the Shoshoni, the Yahgan, and the Mission Indians of California (Lesser 1968; MacLeish 1972), and the Greenland Eskimo (Weyer 1932:109–110)—have been offered as exceptions to the claim that warfare is a universal feature of human social life. But the peacefulness of these groups may be a result of their having suffered defeat when they practiced warfare in earlier times. William Divale (1972) lists 37 hunting-and-gathering cultures in which warfare (feuds and raids included) is known to have been practiced. But some anthropologists attribute these cases to the shocks of contact with state societies. Archaeologists who have studied the pattern of broken and perforated bones suggest that warfare occurred among hunter-gatherers during periods of population increase and environmental stress (P. Walker 1988).

The archaeological evidence for warfare in the Paleolithic is inconclusive. Mutilated skulls found in Paleolithic caves have been interpreted as indicating prehistoric head-hunting and cannibalism. No one really knows how the individuals died. Even if cannibalism was practiced, the cannibalized individuals were not necessarily enemies. Eating the brains of deceased kin is a form of mortuary ritual (see p. 441).

The oldest archaeological evidence for cannibalism in conjunction with warfare is found in the Neolithic. At Fontbregoua Cave (6000–5000 B.P.) in southeastern France, the remains of at least six individuals were butchered and eaten in a manner that cannot be distinguished from the way in which the remains of animals were butchered and eaten (Villa et al. 1986).

Warfare probably increased in intensity during the Neolithic among village-organized farming cultures. As we have seen (Ch. 10), some of the earliest Neolithic towns in the Middle East contained watchtowers and fortification walls.

Among nonsedentary hunters and gatherers, warfare involved a higher degree of individualized combat directed toward the adjustment of real or imagined personal injuries and deprivations. Although the combat teams may have had temporary territorial bases, the organization of battle and the consequences of victory or defeat reflected the loose association between people and territory. The victors did not gain territory by routing their enemies. Warfare among village-dwelling cultivators, however, frequently involves a total team effort in which definite territories are fought over and in which defeat may result in the rout of a whole community from its fields, dwellings, and natural resources.

The slippery line between warfare and personal retribution among hunters and gatherers is well illustrated in the example of armed conflict among the Tiwi of Bathurst and Melville islands, northern Australia (Fig. 17.6). As recounted by C. W. Hart and Arnold Pilling (1960), a number of men from the Tiklauila and Rangwila bands developed personal grievances against a number of men who were residing with the Mandiimbula band. The aggrieved individuals, together with their relatives, put on the white paint of war, armed themselves, and set off, some 30 strong, to do battle with the Mandiimbula:

On arrival at the place where the latter, duly warned of its approach, had gathered, the war party an-

nounced its presence. Both sides then exchanged a few insults and agreed to meet formally in an open space where there was plenty of room. [1960:84]

During the night, individuals from both groups visited each other, renewing acquaintances. In the morning, the two armies lined up at the opposite sides of the battlefield. Hostilities were begun by elders shouting insults and accusations at particular individuals in the "enemy" ranks. Although some of the old men urged that a general attack be launched, their grievances turned out to be directed not at the Mandiimbula band but at one or at most two or three individuals: "Hence when spears began to be thrown, they were thrown by individuals for reasons based on individual disputes" (Hart and Pilling 1960:84). Marksmanship was poor because it was the old men who did most of the spear-throwing:

Not infrequently the person hit was some innocent noncombatant or one of the screaming old women who weaved through the fighting men, yelling obscenities at everybody, and whose reflexes for dodging spears were not as fast as those of the men....As soon as somebody was wounded...fighting stopped immediately until the implications of this new incident could be assessed by both sides. [ibid.]

Although hunters and gatherers seldom try to annihilate each other and often retire from the field after one or two casualties have occurred, the cumulative effect may be quite considerable. Remember that the average !Kung San band has only about 30 people in it. If such a band engages in war only twice in a generation, each time with the loss of only one adult male, casualties due to warfare would account for more than 10 percent of all adult male deaths. This is an extremely high figure when one realizes that less than 1 percent of all male deaths in Europe and the United States during the twentieth century have been battlefield casualties. In contrast, Lloyd Warner (1958) estimated that 28 percent of the adult male deaths among the Murngin, a hunter-gatherer society of northern Australia, were due to battlefield casualties.

WARFARE AMONG VILLAGE AGRICULTURALISTS

Although village peoples were not the first to practice warfare, they did expand the scale and ferocity of military engagements. Village houses, food-processing equipment, crops in the field, domestic animals, secondary-growth forests, and prime garden lands represent capital investments closely identified

FIGURE *17.6*

TIWI WARRIOR
Tiwi man dressed in traditional dance body paint and feathers.

with the arduous labor inputs of specific groups of individuals. The defense of this investment laid the basis for the development of stable, exclusive territorial identities. Villages often oppose each other as traditional enemies, repeatedly attack and plunder each other, and often expropriate each other's territories. Archaeologically, the onset of territoriality is suggested by the practice of burying deceased villagers beneath the houses they occupied during life (Flannery 1972). Ethnologically, the intensification of local identities is suggested by the development of unilineal systems of reckoning descent. The development of the concern with descent and inheritance, as Michael Harner (1970) has shown, is closely related to the degree to which agricultural populations cease to depend on hunting and gathering for their food supply.

Warfare among village cultivators is likely to be more costly in terms of battle casualties than among seminomadic hunters and gatherers. Among the Dani of West Irian, New Guinea, warfare has an open-field, ritualistic phase (which resembles the encounters described for the Tiwi) in which casualties are light. But there are also sneak attacks resulting in 100 fatalities at a time and in the destruction and expulsion of whole villages. Karl Heider (1972) estimates that the Dani lost about 5 percent of their population per year to warfare and that 29 percent of the men and 3 percent of the women died as a result of battle injuries incurred primarily in raids and ambushes. Among the Yanomamö (Fig. 17.7) of Brazil and Venezuela, who are reputed to have one of the world's "fiercest" and most warlike cultures, sneak raids and ambushes account for about 33 percent of adult male deaths from all causes and about 7 percent of adult female deaths from all causes (Chagnon 1974:160–161).

FIGURE *17.7*

YANOMAMÖ WARRIORS
Preparations for battle include body painting and "line-ups."

WHY WAR?

Because the population densities of band and simple village societies are generally very low, it often seems as if there is no infrastructural basis for warfare among such societies. The apparent absence of material motivations for warfare has given support to popular theories that attribute prestate warfare to an innate tendency for humans to be aggressive (Box 17.4). A variation on this theme is that band and village societies go to war not to gain any material advantage but because men regard it as an enjoyable sport. These theories are unsatisfactory. Although humans may have aggressive tendencies, there is no reason that such tendencies cannot be suppressed, controlled, or expressed in ways other than by armed combat. War is a particular form of organized activity that has developed during cultural evolution just as have other structural features, such as trade, the division of labor, and domestic groups. Just as there is no instinct for trade, for domestic organization, or for the division of labor, so there is no instinct for war. War is fought only to the extent that it is advantageous for some of the combatants.

The theory that warfare is engaged in because it is an enjoyable sport is contradicted by the fact that the most common reason cited by band and village warriors for going to war is to avenge deaths incurred in previous wars or deaths caused by enemy sorcerers. Combat is seldom entered into light-heartedly; the warriors need to "psych themselves up" with ritual dancing and singing, and often set out only after they have subdued their fears by taking psychotropic drugs. While some sports such as boxing and auto racing are also quite dangerous, they do not involve the same degree of mortal risk to which armed combatants expose themselves. Moreover, it is doubtful whether such dangerous sports would be practiced were it not for the substantial material rewards that await the winner.

As we have seen in Chapter 13, it is the adverse cost of rearing children that leads to low-population density and low rates of population growth among band and village societies. Therefore, the fact that population densities are low does not mean that band and village societies are not threatened by depletions of vital resources or by diminishing returns. Warfare in such societies almost always involves the prospect of safeguarding or improving a threatened standard of living by gaining access to vital resources, healthier habitats, or trade routes (Balee 1984; Biolsi 1984; Ferguson 1984, 1989a and b; Shankman 1991).

In his study of warfare among the Mae Enga of the western highlands of Papua, New Guinea, Mervyn

---

BOX *17.4*
AGGRESSION AND WAR

Our biological nature and evolutionary background may help us understand certain aspects of war. As a species, unquestionably we are capable of aggression on an unparalleled scale. But the capacity for collective violence does not explain the occurrence of war. Even if aggression is a universal trait, war is not. Warlike societies fight only occasionally, and many societies have no war at all. It is the circumstances of social life that explain this variation. But the image of humanity, warped by bloodlust, inevitably marching off to kill, is a powerful myth and an important prop of militarism in our society. Despite its lack of scientific credibility, there will remain those hardheaded "realists" who continue to believe in it, congratulating themselves for their "courage to face the truth," resolutely oblivious to the myth behind their reality.

SOURCE: Ferguson 1984:12.

Meggit estimates that aggressor groups succeeded in gaining significant amounts of enemy land in 75 percent of their wars. "Given that the initiation of warfare usually pays off for the aggressors, it is not surprising that the Mae count warfare as well worth the cost in human casualties" (1977:14–15). More general confirmation of this point has been supplied by Melvin and Carol Ember (1988), who have found in a study of a sample of 186 societies that preindustrial people mostly go to war to cushion or moderate the impact of unpredictable (rather than chronic) food shortages and that the victorious side almost always takes some resources from the losers.

Warfare is thus best understood as a deadly form of competition between autonomous groups for scarce resources (R. Cohen 1984a; Ferguson 1984).

GAME ANIMALS AND WARFARE: THE YANOMAMÖ

The Yanomamö provide an important test of the theory that warfare has an infrastructural basis even among band and village groups that have very low population densities. The Yanomamö, with a population density of less than one person per square mile, derive their main source of food calories, with little effort, from the plantains and banana trees that grow in their forest gardens. Like the Tsembaga Maring (p. 213), they burn the forest to get these gardens started, but bananas and plantains are perennials that provide high yields per unit of labor input for many consecutive years. Since the Yanomamö live in the midst of the world's greatest tropical forest, the little burning they do scarcely threatens to "eat up the trees." A typical Yanomamö village has fewer than 100 people in it, a population that could easily grow enough bananas or plantains in nearby garden sites without ever having to move (Fig. 17.8). Yet the Yanomamö villages constantly break up into factions that move off into new territories.

Despite the apparent abundance of resources, the high level of Yanomamö warfare is probably caused by resource depletion and population pressure. The resource in question is meat. The Yanomamö lack domesticated sources of meat and must obtain their animal foods from hunting and collecting. Moreover, unlike many other inhabitants of the Amazon Basin, the Yanomamö traditionally did not have access to big-river fish and other aquatic animals that elsewhere in the Amazon region provided high-quality animal foods sufficient to supply villages inhabited by over 1000 people.

Of course, it is possible for human beings to remain healthy on diets that lack animal foods; how-

FIGURE *17.8*

YANOMAMÖ VILLAGE
This scene is more representative of everyday life among the Yanomamö, despite their warlike reputation. Note the plantains, the staple food of the Yanomamö, hanging from the rafters. For more photos of the everyday life of the Yanomamö, see the photo essay following Chapter 18.

ever, meat, fish, and other animal products contain compact packages of proteins, fats, minerals, and vitamins that make them extremely valuable and efficient sources of nutrients throughout most of history and prehistory.

The theory relating meat to warfare among the Yanomamö is this: As Yanomamö villages grow, intensive hunting diminishes the availability of game nearby. Meat from large animals grows scarce and people eat more small animals, insects, and larvae—the familiar broad-spectrum response (see p. 152). The point of diminishing returns is reached (see p. 209). Increased tensions within and between villages lead to the breaking apart of villages before they permanently deplete the animal resources. Tensions also lead to the escalation of raiding, which disperses the Yanomamö villages over a wide territory, and also protects vital resources by creating no-man's-lands, which function as game preserves (Harris 1984).

Some anthropologists with firsthand knowledge of the Yanomamö have rejected this theory. They point to the fact that there are no clinical signs of protein deficiencies among the Yanomamö. Also, they have shown that in at least one village, whose population is 35, daily per capita overall protein intake was 75 grams per day per adult, which is far higher than the minimum 35 grams recommended by the Food and Agricultural Organization. They have also shown that Yanomamö villages with low levels of protein intake (36 grams) seem to engage in warfare just as frequently as those with high protein intake (75 grams) per adult. Finally, they point out that the other groups in the Amazon enjoy as much as 107 grams of animal protein per capita and still go to war frequently (Chagnon and Hames 1979; Lizot 1977, 1979). Kenneth Good (1987; 1989), however, has shown that obtaining adequate supplies of meat is a constant preoccupation among the Yanomamö, and that meat is actually consumed only once or twice a week on the average. This accords with the observation made by Eric Ross (1979) that the average daily amount of animal food consumed is a misleading figure. Because of fluctuations in the number and size of animals captured, there are actually many days during which there is little or no meat available for Amazonian villages. On days when a large animal such as a tapir is caught, the consumption rate may rise to 250 or more grams per adult; for weeks at a time, however, the consumption rate may not rise above 30 grams per adult per day.

The absence of clinical signs of protein deficiency is not an argument against the theory, but rather supports the general point that band and village peoples can enjoy high standards of health as long as they control population growth (see p. 211). The fact that villages with both high and low protein intake have the same level of warfare also does not test the theory, because warfare necessarily pits villages at different stages of growth against each other. Hence, Yanomamö groups with little immediate infrastructural basis to go to war may have no choice but to engage in counterraids against large groups that are depleting their game reserves and raiding their less populous neighbors in order to expand their hunting territory.

The preponderance of evidence strongly supports the view that Amazonian fauna are a fragile resource, readily depleted with consequent adverse costs and benefits and/or a decline in per capita meat consumption (Ferguson 1989a). Michael Baksh (1985), for example, has quantitatively documented the effect of the nucleation of dispersed Machiguenga homesteads (see p. 254) into a village of 250 people in eastern Peru. Baksh concludes that faunal resources in the vicinity of the village have been declining significantly in availability; that in the attempt to maintain previous levels of intake men are working harder; that there is more travel to distant hunting and fishing locations; and that faunal resources are limited in availability and encourage the existence of small, mobile groups. Men frequently arrive home empty-handed, or perhaps with a few grubs, some wild fruits, palm nuts, or manufacturing materials. A successful day-long or overnight trip might yield a small monkey or a few birds. One tapir and six peccary were obtained . . . over a 17-month period (Baksh 1985:150–151).

TREKKING

The desire to maintain or increase their level of meat consumption explains an important feature of Yanomamö life. Three or four times a year, the Yanomamö move out of their village as a group and go on a prolonged trek through the deep forest that lasts a month or more. Indeed, counting the time that the villagers also spend at distant campsites where they prepare new gardens, the Yanomamö spend almost half the year away from their communal house. It cannot be the desire for plant foods that provides the motive for going on a trek or planting new gardens since the Yanomamö could easily increase the size of their existing gardens and have enough bananas and plantains to feed themselves by staying at home. Although they gather wild fruits while trekking, meat remains their main preoccupation. Good has shown that while on the trek, the efficiency of hunting improves considerably and there is more meat available. Were it not for these long sojourns away from the village, game near the village would soon be completely wiped out (Good 1989).

While on their treks (or shorter hunting trips), the villagers are constantly on the lookout for places to plant their new gardens. Once these gardens begin to bear bananas and plantains, the old communal house is abandoned and a new one is built near the new gardens. Good makes two crucial points regarding this move. First, *plenty of forested land suitable for expanding the old gardens remains available near the old communal house.* Second, the new communal house and gardens are not located near the old house and gardens, *but several kilometers distant from the old communal house.* These facts make it clear that the gardens are not moved in order to increase the efficiency of plant production; nor is the site of the house moved because it has become insect infested, decayed, or surrounded by human excrement (cf. Ferguson 1989b:250). (Why not simply build the new house on the other side of the old gardens?) Rather, what moving accomplishes is to improve the accessibility of game animals that have been hunted out or frightened away from the old sites. Warfare among the Yanomamö therefore can be readily understood as a form of competition between autonomous villages for access to the best hunting territories. After all, since we have no difficulty in understanding why modern nations go to war to maintain access to oil, why, then, should we find it difficult to understand why the Yanomamö go to war to maintain access to game?

WARFARE AND THE REGULATION OF POPULATION GROWTH

In addition to providing victors with better access to crucial resources such as land and hunting territories, warfare among band and village people usually has a secondary effect that may help to explain why it is practiced so widely: It lowers the rate of growth of a region's population. It does this in several ways: first, by direct combat deaths; second, by the demoralization and economic and social breakdown of defeated villages to an extent that lowers their fertility rates; and third, by forcing defeated groups into ecologically marginal habitats where their numbers decline (Ferguson 1989b:257).

Among patrilocal groups such as the Yanomamö, still another mode of population regu-

SEX RATIOS AND WARFARE	TABLE *17.1*
	Young males per 100 females
Warfare present	128
Stopped 5–25 years before census	113
Stopped over 25 years before census	109
SOURCE: Divale and Harris, 1976.	

lation may result from warfare. William Divale has shown that there is a strong correlation between the practice of warfare and high levels of female mortality in the age group from birth through 14 years (Divale and Harris 1976; Divale et al. 1978; cf. Hirschfeld et al. 1978). This is revealed by the ratio of males to females in the 0–14 age bracket among band and village societies actively engaged in warfare when they were first censused (see Table 17.1).

It is generally accepted that slightly more boys than girls are born on a worldwide basis and that the average sex ratio at birth is about 105 males to 100 females. This imbalance, however, is much smaller than that found in the war-making societies. The discrepancy may be accounted for by a higher rate of death among female infants, children, and juveniles than among their male counterparts. This higher rate of female mortality probably reflects the practice of direct and indirect neglect and infanticide against females more often than against males. (See Chapter 13 for a discussion of indirect infanticide.) There is a strong correlation between societies that admit that they practice infanticide and those that were actively engaged in warfare when they were first censused; in these societies, at least, it is clear that female infanticide was more common than male infanticide.

A plausible reason for the killing and neglect of female children is that success in preindustrial warfare depends on the size of the male combat teams. When weapons are muscle-powered clubs, spears, and bows and arrows, victory will belong to the group that has the biggest and most aggressive males. Since there are ecological limits to the number of people who can be reared by band and village societies, war-making band and village societies tend to rear more males than females. The favoring of male over female children reduces the rate of growth of regional populations and this effect, whether or not consciously intended, may help to explain why warfare is so widely practiced by patrilocal prestate peoples who otherwise would find themselves with severely diminishing returns.

Although warfare seems cruel and wasteful, the preindustrial alternatives for keeping population below the point of diminishing returns were equally cruel and wasteful, if not more so—nonmedical abortion, malnutrition, and disease.

Needless to say, the theory that warfare was selected for because of its favorable cost/benefits is highly controversial. In the words of Brian Ferguson:

Assessment of available evidence indicates that people are not in a better relationship to their natural environment because of war. War may produce a fit between population and resources, but it is a bad fit. Life is worse for war. [1989b:258]

But if life is always the worse for war, why was war not selected against during the tens of thousands of years of history and prehistory?

SUMMARY

Orderly relationships between the individuals and domestic groups in band and village societies are maintained without governments and law enforcement specialists. This is possible because of small size, predominance of kinship and reciprocity, and egalitarian access to vital resources. Public opinion is the chief source of law and order in these societies.

There is an absence of individual or nuclear family ownership of land among hunting-and-gathering bands and most village peoples. However, even in the most egalitarian societies, there is private ownership of some items. The prevalence of the reciprocal mode of exchange and the absence of anonymous price markets render theft unnecessary and impractical.

The major threat to law and order among band and village societies stems from the tendency of domestic and kinship groups to escalate conflicts in support of real or imagined injuries to one of their members. Such support does not depend on abstract principles of right and wrong, but on the probable outcome of a particular course of action in the face of public opinion. The Eskimo song duel is an illustration of how public opinion can be tested and used to end conflicts between individuals who belong to different domestic and kinship groups.

Witchcraft accusations are another means of giving public opinion an opportunity to identify and punish persistent violators of the rules of reciprocity and other troublemakers. Shamans act as the mouthpiece of the community, but their position is precarious, and they themselves are frequently identified as the source of misfortune and conflict. As among the Kuikuru, the fear of being accused of witchcraft encourages people to be amiable and generous. However, under stressful conditions, witchcraft accusations may build to epidemic proportions and become a threat to the maintenance of law and order.

Headmanship reflects the pervasive egalitarian nature of the institutions of law and order in band and village societies. Headmen can do little more than harangue and plead with people for support. They lack physical or material means of enforcing their decisions. Their success rests on their ability to intuit public opinion. As exemplified by the Nuer, avoidance of blood feud can be facilitated by the payment of compensation and by appeal to ritual chiefs, who lack political and economic power.

Other instances of nonkin political organization take the form of voluntary associations or sodalities such as men's and women's clubs, secret societies, and age-grade sets. However, all these nonkin modes of political organization remain rather rudimentary and are overshadowed by the pervasive networks of kinship alliances based on marriage and descent, which constitute the "glue" of band and village societies.

Although both hunter-gatherers and village farmers engage in warfare, there is reason to believe that warfare was less frequent in the Paleolithic than in the Neolithic and that village farmers are more likely to attempt to rout each other.

Warfare cannot be explained as a consequence of aggression or as an enjoyable sport. Warfare is a particular form of organized activity and only one of the many ways in which cultures handle aggression. The causes of war in band and village societies are rooted in problems associated with production and reproduction, and almost always involve attempts to improve or preserve cost–benefit ratios and standards of living. Even where population densities are very low, as among the Yanomamö, problems of depletion and declining efficiency may exist. It cannot be said that the Yanomamö suffer from a shortage of protein, yet there is evidence that as their villages grow in size, the quality and quantity of animal resources decline and the cost of obtaining high-quality diets increases.

It also seems likely that warfare in some prestate contexts helped to restrain population growth and thus to protect resources from depletion. Among patrilocal band and village societies, warfare could have this effect through the encouragement of female infanticide and neglect. Evidence for this ecological interpretation of warfare consists of cross-cultural studies that correlate unbalanced sex ratios with active warfare. This theory is controversial, however.

Chapter 18

The Political Economy of Chiefdoms and States

In this chapter, we contrast the forms of political life characteristic of band and village societies with those of chiefdoms and states. How did the relatively egalitarian societies that once prevailed throughout the world give way to those that ranked people high and low and divided them into rulers and the ruled? How and why did the great transformations from bands and villages to chiefdoms and states take place? In seeking the answer, we shall look closely at both structural and infrastructural factors such as population density, territorial impaction, warfare, and the influence of redistributive modes of exchange. Turning to the state itself, we will discuss the role of coercive physical force and of more subtle forms of thought control in the maintenance of inequality and the status quo in ancient and modern times, including industrial democracies. Finally, we shall enquire into the tragic destiny of tribal peoples who have resisted incorporation into modern states.

BIGMANSHIP

As we have seen (p. 295), headmen often function as intensifiers of production and as redistributors. They get their relatives to work harder, and they collect and then give away the extra product. A village may have several headmen. Where technological and ecological conditions encourage intensification, headmen living in the same village may become rivals. They vie with one another to hold the most lavish feasts and to redistribute the greatest amount of valuables. Often, the most successful redistributors earn the reputation of being "big men."

Anthropologist Douglas Oliver (1955) carried out a classic study of "bigmanship" during his field-work among the Siuai on Bougainville in the Solomon Islands. Among the Siuai, a "big man" is called a *mumi* and to achieve mumi status is every youth's highest ambition (Fig. 18.1). A young man proves himself capable of becoming a mumi by working hard and by carefully restricting his consumption of meat and coconuts. Eventually, he impresses his wife, children, and near relatives with the seriousness of his intentions, and they vow to help him prepare for his first feast. If the feast is a success, his circle of supporters widens and he sets to work readying an even greater display of generosity. He aims next at the construction of a men's clubhouse in which his male followers can lounge about and in which guests can be entertained and fed. Another feast is held at the consecration of the clubhouse, and if this is also a success, the circle of people willing to work for him grows still larger and he will begin to be spoken of as a mumi. Larger and larger feasts mean that the

mumi's demands on his supporters become more irksome. Although they grumble about how hard they have to work, they remain loyal as long as their mumi continues to maintain or increase his renown as a "great provider."

Finally, the time comes for the new mumi to challenge the others who have risen before him. This is done at a *muminai* feast, where a tally is kept of all the pigs, coconut pies, and sago-almond puddings given away by the host mumi and his followers to the guest mumi and his followers. If the guest mumi cannot reciprocate in a year or so with a feast at least as lavish as that of his challengers, he suffers a great social humiliation and his fall from mumihood is immediate. In deciding on whom to challenge, a mumi must be very careful. He tries to choose a guest whose downfall will increase his own reputation, but he must avoid one whose capacity to retaliate exceeds his own.

At the end of a successful feast, the greatest of mumis still faces a lifetime of personal toil and dependence on the moods and inclinations of his followers. Mumihood does not confer the power to coerce others into doing one's bidding, nor does it elevate one's standard of living above anyone else's. In fact, since giving things away is the essence of mumihood, great mumis may even consume less meat and other delicacies than an ordinary, undistinguished Siuai. Among the Kaoka, another Solomon Island group reported on by H. Ian Hogbin (1964:66), there is the saying "The giver of the feast takes the bones and the stale cakes; the meat and the fat go to the others."

At one great feast attended by 1100 people, the host mumi, whose name was Soni, gave away 32 pigs plus a large quantity of sago-almond puddings. Soni

FIGURE *18.1*

SOLOMON ISLAND CHIEFS
They prefer to be called
chiefs rather than *mumis*,
as of old.

BOX *18.1*

BIG MAN AS WARRIOR

Thunderer, Earth-shaker
Maker of many feasts,
How empty of gong sounds will all the places
be when you leave us!
Warrior, Handsome Flower,
Killer of men and pigs,
Who will bring renown to our places
When you leave us?
SOURCE: Oliver 1955:399.

---

and his closest followers, however, went hungry. "We shall eat Soni's renown," his followers said.

BIG MEN AND WARFARE

Formerly, the mumis were as famous for their ability to get men to fight for them as they were for their ability to get men to work for them. Warfare had been suppressed by the colonial authorities long before Oliver carried out his study, but the memory of mumi war leaders was still vivid among the Siuai. As one old man put it:

In the olden times there were greater mumi than there are today. Then they were fierce and relentless war leaders. They laid waste to the countryside and their clubhouses were lined with the skulls of people they had slain. [Oliver 1955:411]

In singing praises of their mumis, the generation of pacified Siuai call them "warriors" and "killers of men and pigs" (see Box 18.1).

Oliver's informants told him that mumis had more authority in the days when warfare was still being practiced. Some mumi war leaders even kept one or two prisoners who were treated like slaves and forced to work in the mumi's family gardens; and people could not talk "loud and slanderously against their mumis without fear of punishment." This fits theoretical expectations, since the ability to redistribute meat and other valuables goes hand in hand with the ability to attract a following of warriors, equip them

for combat, and reward them with spoils of battle. Rivalry among Bougainville's war-making mumis appeared to have been leading toward an island-wide political organization when the first European voyagers arrived. According to Oliver (ibid.:420), "For certain periods of time many neighboring villages fought together so consistently that there emerged a pattern of war-making regions, each more or less internally peaceful and each containing one outstanding mumi whose war activities provided internal 'social cohesion.'" These mumis enjoyed regional fame, but their prerogatives remained rudimentary. This is shown by the fact that the mumis had to provide their warriors with prostitutes brought into the clubhouses and with gifts of pork and other delicacies. Said one old warrior:

If the mumi didn't furnish us with women we were angry....All night long we would copulate and still want more. It was the same with eating. The clubhouse used to be filled with food, and we ate and ate and never had enough. Those were wonderful times. [ibid.:415]

Furthermore, the mumi who wanted to lead a war party had to be prepared personally to pay an indemnity for any of his men who were killed in battle and to furnish a pig for each man's funeral feast.

CHIEFS AND CHIEFDOMS: TROBRIANDERS AND CHEROKEE

Headmen are the leaders of autonomous villages or bands. *Chiefs* are the leaders of more or less permanently allied groups of bands and villages called *chiefdoms*. The principal difference between autonomous bands and villages and chiefdoms is that chiefdoms consist of several communities or settlements.

Chiefs have more power than headmen, but headmen who are successful redistributors are hard to distinguish from the leaders of small chiefdoms. Whereas headmen must achieve and constantly validate their status by recurrent feasts, chiefs inherit their offices and hold them even if they are temporarily unable to provide their followers with generous redistributions. Chiefs tend to live better than commoners; unlike headmen, they do not always keep only "the bones and the stale cakes" for themselves. Yet, in the long run, chiefs, too, must validate their titles by waging successful war, obtaining trade goods, and giving away food and other valuables to their followers.

The Trobriand Islanders

The difference between headmen and chiefs can be illustrated with the case of the Trobriand Islanders. Trobriander society was divided into several matrilineal clans and subclans of unequal rank and privilege through which access to garden lands was inherited. Bronislaw Malinowski (1920) reported that the Trobrianders were keen on fighting and that they conducted systematic and relentless wars, venturing across the open ocean in their canoes to trade—or, if need be, to fight—with the people of islands over 100 miles away. Unlike the Siuai mumis, the Trobriand chiefs occupied hereditary offices and could be deposed only through defeat in war. One of these, whom Malinowski considered to be the "paramount chief" of all the Trobrianders, held sway over more than a dozen villages, containing several thousand people all told. Chieftainships were hereditary within the wealthiest and largest subclans, and the Trobrianders attributed these inequalities to wars of conquest carried out long ago. Only the chiefs could wear certain shell ornaments as the insignia of high rank, and it was forbidden for any commoner to stand or sit in a position that put a chief's head at a lower elevation than anyone else's. Malinowski (1920) tells of seeing all the people present in the village of Bwoytalu drop from their verandas as if blown down by a hurricane at the sound of a drawn-out cry announcing the arrival of an important chief.

The Trobriand chief's power rested ultimately on his ability to play the role of "great provider," which depended on customary and sentimental ties of kinship and marriage rather than on the control of weapons and resources. Residence among the Trobriand commoners was normally avunculocal (see p. 284). Adolescent boys lived in bachelor huts until they got married. They then took their brides to live in their mother's brother's household, where they jointly worked the garden lands of the husband's matrilineage.

In recognition of the existence of matrilineal descent, at harvest time, brothers acknowledged that a portion of the produce of the matrilineal lands was owed to their sisters and sent them presents of baskets filled with yams, their staple crop. The Trobriand chief relied on this custom to validate his title. He married the sisters of the headmen of a larger number of sublineages.

Some chiefs acquired several dozen wives, each of whom was entitled to an obligatory gift of yams from her brothers. These yams were delivered to the chief's village and displayed on special yam racks. Some of the yams were then distributed in elaborate feasts at which the chief validated his position as a "great provider"; the remainder were used to feed canoe-building specialists, artisans, magicians, and family servants who thereby became partially dependent on the chief's power.

In former times, the yam stores also furnished the base for launching long-distance Kula trading expeditions among friendly groups and raids against enemies (Brunton 1975; Geoffry 1983; Malinowski 1935).

The Cherokee

The political organization of the Cherokee of Tennessee (and of other southeastern woodland Native Americans) bears a striking resemblance to the Trobrianders' redistribution-warfare-trade-chief complex (Fig. 18.2). The Cherokee, like the Trobrianders, were matrilineal, and they waged external warfare over long distances. At the center of the principal settlements was a large, circular "council house" where the council of chiefs discussed issues involving several villages and where redistributive feasts were held. The council of chiefs had a supreme chief who was the central figure in the Cherokee redistributive network. At harvest time, a large crib, identified as the "chief's granary," was erected in each field. "To this each family carries and deposits a certain quantity according to his ability or inclination, or none at all if he so chooses." The chief's granaries functioned as "a public treasury... to fly to for succor" in the case of crop failure, as a source of food "to accommodate strangers, or travellers," and as a military store "when they go forth on hostile expeditions." Although every citizen enjoyed "the right of free and public access," commoners had to acknowledge that the store really belonged to the supreme chief who had "an exclusive right and ability... to distribute comfort and blessings to the necessitous" (Bartram 1958:326).

FIGURE *18.2*

CHEROKEE CHIEF
Black Coat, painted by George Catlin
at Fort Gibson in 1834.

FIGURE *18.3*

TIKOPIA CHIEF AND HIS "HONOR GUARD"
(A) Tikopia chief and **(B)** his hut. The two
men standing outside the hut are the chief's
"honor guard," but note the unpretentious
residence.

(A)

(B)

LIMITATIONS OF CHIEFLY POWER: THE TIKOPIA

Even though the Trobrianders feared and respected
their "great provider" war chiefs, they were still a
long way from a state society. Living on islands, the
Trobrianders were not free to spread out, and their
population density had risen in Malinowski's time to
60 persons per square mile. Nonetheless, the chiefs
could not control enough of the production system
to acquire great power. Perhaps one reason for this is
that Trobriand agriculture lacked cereal grains. Since
yams rot after four or five months (unlike rice or
maize), the Trobriand "great provider" could not manipulate people through dispensing food year-round,
nor could he support a permanent police-military
garrison out of his stores. Another important factor
was the open resources of the lagoons and ocean from
which the Trobrianders derived their protein supply.
The Trobriand chief could not cut off access to these
resources and hence could not exercise permanent
coercive political control over subordinates.

Another illustration of the constraints on the
power of chiefs is found on Tikopia, one of the smallest of the Solomon Islands (Fig. 18.3). Here the chiefs'
pretensions were even greater than those of the Trobriand chiefs, but their actual power was considerably less. The Tikopian chiefs claimed that they

"owned" all the land and sea resources, yet the size of the redistributive network and of the harvests under their control made such claims unenforceable. Tikopian chiefs enjoyed few privileges. Nominally, they claimed control of their cognatic kin group's gardens, but in practice they could not restrict their kin from any unused sites. Labor for their own gardens was in scarce supply, and they themselves worked like any "commoner" in the fields. To validate their positions, they were obliged to give large feasts, which in turn rested on the voluntary labor and food contributions of their kin. Ties of kinship tended to efface the abstract prerequisites and etiquette of higher rank. Raymond Firth describes how a man from a commoner family, who in the kin terminology of the Tikopians was classified as a "brother," could exchange bawdy insults with the island's highest-ranking chief (See Box 18.2).

The Cherokee chief had similar relations with commoners. Outside the council, "he associates with the people as a common man, converses with them, and they with him in perfect ease and familiarity" (Bartram 1958:325).

THE ORIGINS OF STATES

Under certain conditions, large chiefdoms evolved into *states*. The state is a form of politically centralized society whose governing elites have the power to compel subordinates to pay taxes, render services, and obey the law (Carneiro 1981:69). Three infrastructural conditions led to the transformation of chiefdoms into the first states, that is, the "pristine" cases.

1. Population increase. Villages grew to several thousand people and/or regional population densities rose in excess of 20 to 30 people per square mile.

2. Intensive agriculture. The staple was a grain such as rice, wheat, barley, or maize, which provided a surplus above immediate needs at harvest and could be stored for long periods at low cost without becoming inedible.

3. Circumscription. The emigration of dissatisfied factions was blocked by similarly developed chiefdoms in adjacent territories or by features of the environment that required emigrants to adopt a new and less efficient mode of production and to suffer a decline in their standards of living. Most of the earliest states were circumscribed by their dependence on modes of production associated with fertile river valleys surrounded by arid or semiarid plains or mountains. But circumscription can also be caused by the transformation of low-yielding into

---

BOX *18.2*

NOT SO MIGHTY CHIEF

On one occasion I was walking with the Ariki [chief] Kafika...when we passed the orchard of Pae Sao...all the principals present were "brothers" through various ties, and with one accord they fell upon each other with obscene chaff. Epithets of "Big testicles!" "You are the enormous testicles!" flew back and forth to the accompaniment of hilarious laughter. I was somewhat surprised at the vigor of the badinage for the Ariki Kafika, as the most respected chief of the island, has a great deal of sanctity attached to him.... However, this did not save him and he took it in good part.

SOURCE: Firth 1957:176–177.

---

higher-yielding habitats as a result of a long-term investment in the mounding, ditching, draining, and irrigating of a chiefdom's territory (Dickson 1987). The significance of circumscription, whatever its precise form, is that factions of discontented members of a chiefdom cannot escape from their elite overlords without suffering a sharp decline in their standard of living.

Given these infrastructural conditions, certain changes in a chiefdom's political and economic structure become likely. First, the larger and denser the population and the greater the harvest surplus, the greater the ability of the elites to support craft specialists, palace guards, and a standing professional army. Second, the more powerful the elite, the greater its ability to engage in long-distance warfare and trade, and to conquer, incorporate, and exploit new populations and territories. Third, the more powerful the elite, the more stratified its redistribution of trade wealth and harvest surplus (see Box 18.3). Fourth, the wider the territorial scope of political control and the larger the investment in the mode of production, the less opportunity there is to flee and the less there is to be gained. Soon, contributions to the central store cease to be voluntary—they become taxes; access to the farmlands and natural resources cease to be rights—they become dispensations; food producers cease being the chief's followers—they become peasants; redistributors cease being chiefs—they become kings; and chiefdoms cease being chiefdoms—they become states.

READINGS

1   2

12 → 214-7   →   217-9
14 → 242-7   →   247-55
16

CHAPT 17 → 295-305
        18 → 307-12   → 312-23
CHAPT 13
        20
        21
        23 → 396-409
        19
        ~~21~~
        24
        25
        26

BOX *18.3*

EGALITARIAN VERSUS HIERARCHICAL FORMS OF REDISTRIBUTION

The realization that there is a crucial difference between headmen and chiefs who generously give away as much as they get, and chiefs and kings who selfishly keep more than they give away has led some anthropologists to deny that kings or powerful chiefs engaged in redistribution. Robert Carneiro (1981:61), for example, writes that the chief who rewards his elite followers "through the shrewd and self-interested disbursement of taxes...is no longer a redistributor" but "an appropriator or a concentrator." The originators of the concept of redistribution, however, did not restrict its use to egalitarian exchanges. Furthermore, in the interest of conceptualizing the process by which political-economic-military power became concentrated in the hands of elites, it is important to stress the continuity between the egalitarian and hierarchical forms of exchange in order to show how the latter evolved out of the former. This is best achieved by recognizing a spectrum of redistributive systems ranging from the scrupulously egalitarian to the ruthlessly hierarchical.

As the governing elites compel subordinates to pay taxes and tribute, provide military or labor services, and obey laws, the entire process of intensification, expansion, conquest and stratification, and centralization of control is continuously increased or "amplified" through a form of change known as positive feedback (Box 18.4). Where modes of production could sustain sufficient numbers of peasants and warriors, this feedback process recurrently resulted in states conquering states and in the emergence of preindustrial empires involving vast territories inhabited by millions of people (Carneiro 1981; R. Cohen 1984a; Feinman and Neitzel 1984; Fried 1978; Haas 1982; Hommon 1986; Kirch 1984; MacLeish 1981; Service 1975; Upman 1990).

Once the first states came into existence, they themselves constituted barriers against the flight of people who sought to preserve egalitarian systems. Moreover, with states as neighbors, egalitarian peoples found themselves increasingly drawn into warfare and were compelled to increase production and to give their redistributor-war chiefs more and more power in order to prevail against the expansionist tendencies of their neighbors. Thus, most states of the world were produced by a great diversity of specific historical and ecological conditions (Fried 1967); once states come into existence, they tend to spread, engulf, and overwhelm nonstate peoples (Carneiro 1970; R. Cohen 1984a).

BOX *18.4*

TWO KINDS OF FEEDBACK

Negative: Changes are checked when certain limits are reached. Initial conditions tend to be restored. Example: Household temperature stays slightly above or slightly below the level set on a thermostat.

Positive: Changes are not checked. Each successive change increases or amplifies the tendency to change. Example: A microphone picks up the sound of its own loudspeaker and sends the signal back through its amplifier, which sends a stronger signal to the loudspeaker, resulting in a louder and louder sound.

HAWAII: ON THE THRESHOLD OF THE STATE

When visited by Captain James Cook in A.D. 1778, the Hawaiian Islands were divided into four intensely hierarchical polities, each containing between 10,000 and 100,000 persons and each on the threshold (if not past it) of becoming a full-fledged state. Each was divided into named districts containing populations that ranged from about 4,000 to 25,000 people. The districts were in turn divided into many elongated territorial units called *ahupua'a*, which extended inland from the coast to the higher elevations of the island's interior, and were each inhabited by an average of 200 persons. These inhabitants were of the commoner class, the *maka'ainana*—fishermen, farmers, and craftsworkers. Each *ahupua'a* was administered by officials of chiefly ranks, called *konohiki*, who were the local agents for the powerful district chiefs, called *ali'i*. These *ali'i* based their claims to high chiefly status on genealogies that extended upward for ten generations. (Such genealogies, however, were constantly adjusted and negotiated to accord with achieved political military status.) The chiefly class was topped off by a paramount figure called the *ali'i nui*, who was responsible for assigning privileges and administrative posts to the *ali'i*. In practice, the *ali'i* were in ceaseless turmoil over their relative rank, and the issue was decided by wars of conquest rather than genealogical reckoning. Up until the time of contact, no *ali'i nui* had managed to gain firm control over all of the districts on an island.

At the infrastructural level, the populous, incipient states of Hawaii were based on irrigation agriculture. Taro, sweet potatoes, and yams were the principal crops; both pigs and dogs were kept for meat. Hierarchical, taxlike forms of redistribution siphoned both food and craft items from the *maka'ainana* to the *ali'i*. It was the *konohiki's* main responsibility to see to it that the commoners in his charge produced enough to satisfy the demands of the *ali'i*. The *ali'i* in turn used these "gifts" to reward his warriors, priests, allies, and the *konohiki*.

Recent archaeological research demonstrates that the Hawaiian polities evolved out of an egalitarian system similar to that found in Tikopia, as a result of the positive feedback among population increase, environmental depletions (deforestation and soil erosion), intensification of production (irrigation and pig husbandry), increased trade, escalating warfare, and competition for elite status. Three phases to this process have been identified (Earle 1989; Hommon 1986; Kirch 1984)

Phase I: A.D. 500–1400. Initial colonization and population growth. Settlements are on best coastal sites. No irrigation is needed. Settlements are kinship-organized.

Phase II: 1400–1600. Expansion into less desirable island sites. Use of flood-water irrigation, mulching, and reduction of fallow periods.

Phase III: 1600–1778. Expansion of irrigation systems, use of marginal lands, deforestation, depletion of faunal resources, and soil erosion. Conquest, usurpation, and rebellion.

Would the Hawaiian polities have achieved a more stable and centralized state if their political history had not been interrupted by the landings of Europeans on their shores? (Actually, as a result of that contact, a unified Hawaiian kingdom was established in 1810, but this cannot be regarded as a pristine state.) According to the theory presented above, the answer is "no." All of the conditions for state formation were present, with one exception: The Hawaiian chiefs had no storageable grains. They did have storehouses that were used to sustain their followers. Indeed, David Malo, a nineteenth century Hawaiian chief, noted that the storehouses of the Hawaiian kings were designed as a means of keeping people contented, so that they would not desert him: "As the rat will not desert the pantry, so the people will not desert the king while they think there is food in his storehouse" (quoted in D'Altroy and Earle 1985:192). Lacking maize, rice, wheat, or any of the other staple grains that provided the nutritional and energetic basis for the emergence of pristine states everywhere else, the Hawaiian storehouses were unable to sustain large numbers of followers, especially during times of drought and warfare-induced food shortage. Thus, no *ali'i nui* was able to achieve an enduring advantage over his rivals.

AN AFRICAN KINGDOM: BUNYORO

The difference between a chiefdom and a state can be illustrated with the case of the Bunyoro, a kingdom located in Uganda and studied by John Beattie (1960). Bunyoro had a population of about 100,000 people and an area of 5,000 square miles. Supreme power over the Bunyoro territory and its inhabitants was vested in the Mukama, senior member of a royal lineage that reckoned its descent back to the beginning of time (Fig. 18.4). The use of all natural resources, especially of farming land, was a dispensation specifically granted by the Mukama to a dozen or more "chiefs" or to commoner peasants under their respective control. In return for these dispensations, quantities of food, handicrafts, and labor services were funneled up through the power hierarchy into the Mukama's headquarters. The Mukama in turn directed the use of these goods and services on behalf of state enterprises. Thus, the basic redistributive pattern was still plainly in evidence (see Box 18.5).

While the Mukama had a reputation for generosity, it is clear that he did not give away as much as he received. He certainly did not follow the Solomon Island mumis and keep only the stale cakes and bones for himself. Moreover, much of what he gave away did not flow back down to the peasant producers; instead, it remained in the hands of his genealogically close kin, who constituted a clearly demarcated aristocratic class. Part of what the Mukama took away from the peasants was bestowed on nonkin who performed extraordinary services on behalf of the state, especially

FIGURE *18.4*

MUKAMA OF BUNYORO
This is a king, not a chief.

THE GREAT PROVIDER

In the traditional system the king was seen both as the supreme receiver of goods and services, and as the supreme giver.... The great chiefs, who themselves received tribute from their dependents, were required to hand over to the Mukama a part of the produce of their estates in the form of crops, cattle, beer or women.... But everyone must give to the king, not only the chiefs.... The Mukama's role as giver was accordingly no less stressed. Many of his special names emphasize his magnanimity and he was traditionally expected to give extensively in the form both of feasts and of gifts to individuals.

SOURCE: Beattie 1960:34.

in connection with military exploits. Another part was used to support a permanent palace guard and resident staff who attended to the Mukama's personal needs and performed religious rites deemed essential for the welfare of the Mukama and the nation, such as custodian of spears, custodian of royal graves, custodian of the royal drums, custodian of royal crowns, "putters on" of the royal crowns, custodians of royal thrones (stools) and other regalia, cooks, bath attendants, herdsmen, potters, barkcloth makers, musicians, and others. Many of these officials had several assistants.

In addition, there was a loosely defined category of advisers, diviners, and other retainers who hung around the court, attached to the Mukama's household as dependents, in the hope of being appointed to a chieftainship. To this must be added the Mukama's extensive harem, his many children, and the polygynous households of his brothers and of other royal personages. To keep his power intact, the Mukama and portions of his court made frequent trips throughout Bunyoro land, staying at local palaces maintained at the expense of his chiefs and commoners.

FEUDALISM

As Beattie points out, there are many analogies between the Bunyoro state and the *feudal* system existing in England at the time of the Norman invasion

(1066). As in early medieval England, Bunyoro stratification involved a pledge of loyalty on the part of the district chiefs (lords) in return for grants of land and of the labor power of the peasants (serfs) who lived on these lands. The English king, like the Mukama, could call on these chiefs to furnish weapons, supplies, and warriors whenever an internal or external threat to the king's sovereignty arose. The survival of the English feudal royal lineage, as in Bunyoro, was made possible by the ability of the king to muster larger coalitions of lords and their military forces than could be achieved by any combination of disloyal lords. But there are important differences in demographic scale and in the ruler's role as redistributor that must also be noted. While redistribution was continued through a system of royal taxation and tribute, the police-military function of the English king was more important than among the Bunyoro. The English sovereign was not the "great provider." He was, instead, the "great protector."

With a population numbering over 1 million people and with agricultural and handicraft production organized on the basis of self-sustaining independent local estates, redistribution was wholly asymmetrical. It was not necessary for William the Conqueror (Fig. 18.5) to cultivate an image of generosity among the mass of peasants throughout his kingdom. Although he was careful to be generous to the lords who supported him, the display of generosity to the peasants was no longer important. A vast gulf had opened between the styles of life of peasants

FIGURE *18.5*

WILLIAM I (1027-1087), THE CONQUEROR
He invaded England from Normandy and conquered
the English in the Battle of Hastings in 1066.

and overlords. And the maintenance of these differences no longer rested mainly on the special contribution the overlords made to production, but largely on their ability to deprive the peasants of subsistence and of life itself.

In comparing African with European political development, we must remember that there were two periods of feudalism in Western and Northern Europe. The first, about which little is known, preceded the growth of the Roman Empire and was cut off by the Roman conquest. The second followed the collapse of the Roman Empire. Although the latter period provides the standard model of feudalism, the Bunyoro type of polity is actually a much more widely distributed form and probably closely resembles the political systems the Romans encountered and overran in their conquest of Western Europe (see Bloch 1964; Champion et al. 1984:315; Piggott 1965; Renfrew 1973).

Because of the influence of the Roman Empire, architecture, metallurgy, textiles, and armaments were far more advanced in feudal Europe. The product taxed away by the Bunyoro ruling class was small compared with what was taxed away by the English feudal aristocracy.

A NATIVE AMERICAN EMPIRE: THE INCA

In some regions, infrastructural factors favored the evolution of state systems that were larger and more centralized than those of medieval Europe. As we have seen (p. 179), independently in both the Old and New Worlds, there arose state systems in which scores of former small states were incorporated into highly centralized superstates or empires. In the New World, the largest and most powerful of these systems was the Inca Empire.

At its prime, the Inca Empire stretched 1500 miles from northern Chile to southern Colombia and contained possibly as many as 6 million inhabitants. Because of government intervention in the basic mode of production, agriculture was not organized in terms of feudal estates, but rather in terms of villages, districts, and provinces. Each such unit was under the supervision not of a feudal lord who had sworn loyalty to another lord slightly his superior and who was free to use his lands and peasants as he saw fit, but of appointed government officials responsible for planning public works and delivering government-established quotas of laborers, food, and other material (Morris 1976). Village lands were divided into three parts, the largest of which was probably the source of the workers' own subsistence; harvests from the second and third parts were turned over to religious and government agents, who stored them in granaries (D'Altroy and Earle 1985; D'Altroy 1988). The distribution of these supplies was entirely under the control of the central administration. Likewise, when labor power was needed to build roads, bridges, canals, fortresses, or other public works, government recruiters went directly into the villages.

Because of the size of the administrative network and the density of population, huge numbers of workers could be placed at the disposal of the Inca engineers. In the construction of Cuzco's fortress of Sacsahuaman (Fig. 18.6), probably the greatest masonry structure in the New World, 30,000 people were employed in cutting, quarrying, hauling, and erecting huge monoliths, some weighing as much as 200 tons. Labor contingents of this size were rare in medieval Europe but were common in ancient Egypt, the Middle East, and China.

Control over the entire empire was concentrated in the hands of the Inca. He was the firstborn of the firstborn, a descendant of the god of the sun and a celestial being of unparalleled holiness. This god-on-earth enjoyed power and luxury undreamed of by the poor Mehinacu chief in his plaintive daily quest for respect and obedience. Ordinary people could not approach the Inca face-to-face. His private audiences

FIGURE *18.6*

SACSAHUAMAN
The principal fortress of the Inca Empire, near
Cuzco, Peru.

were conducted from behind a screen, and all who
approached him did so with a burden on their backs.
When traveling, he reclined on an ornate palanquin
carried by special crews of bearers (Mason 1957:184).
A small army of sweepers, water carriers, woodcut-
ters, cooks, wardrobe men, treasurers, gardeners, and
hunters attended the domestic needs of the Inca in his
palace in Cuzco, the capital of the empire.

The Inca ate his meals from gold and silver
dishes in rooms whose walls were covered with precious metals. His clothing was made of the softest
vicuna wool, and he gave away each change of clothing to members of the royal family, never wearing the
same garment twice. The Inca enjoyed the services
of a large number of concubines who were method-
ically culled from the empire's most beautiful young
women. However, to conserve the holy line of descent
from the god of the sun, his wife had to be his own

full or half sister (see pp. 268, 316). When the Inca
died, his wife, concubines, and many other retainers
were strangled during a great drunken dance in order that he suffer no loss of comfort in the afterlife.
Each Inca's body was eviscerated, wrapped in cloth,
and mummified. Women with fans stood in constant
attendance on these mummies, ready to drive away
flies and to take care of the other things mummies
need to stay happy (Mason 1957).

THE STATE AND THE CONTROL OF THOUGHT

Large populations, anonymity, use of market money,
and vast differences in wealth make the maintenance
of law and order in state societies more difficult
to achieve than in bands, villages, and chiefdoms.
This accounts for the great elaboration of police and
paramilitary forces and the other state-level institutions and specialists concerned with crime and punishment (Fig. 18.7). Although every state ultimately
stands prepared to crush criminals and political sub-
versives by imprisoning, maiming, or killing them,
most of the daily burdens of maintaining law and order against discontented individuals and groups is
borne by institutions that seek to confuse, distract,
and demoralize potential troublemakers before they
have to be subdued by physical force. Therefore, every state, ancient and modern, has specialists who
perform ideological services in support of the status
quo. These services are often rendered in a manner
and in contexts that seem unrelated to economic or
political issues.

The main thought-control apparatus of preindustrial states consists of magico-religious institutions. The elaborate religions of the Inca, Aztecs, ancient Egyptians, and other preindustrial civilizations
sanctified the privileges and powers of the ruling
elite. They upheld the doctrine of the divine descent
of the Inca and the pharaoh, and taught that the entire balance and continuity of the universe required
the subordination of commoners to persons of noble and divine birth. Among the Aztecs, the priests
were convinced and sought to convince others that
the gods must be nourished with human blood, and
they personally pulled out the beating hearts of the
state's prisoners of war on top of Tenochtitlán's pyramids (see p. 396). In many states, religion has been
used to condition large masses of people to accept
relative deprivation as necessity, to look forward to
material rewards in the afterlife rather than in the
present one, and to be grateful for small favors from
superiors lest ingratitude call down a fiery retribution
in this life or in a hell to come. (Religion, of course,
has other functions, as we shall see in Chapter 23.)

FIGURE *18.7*

STRATIFICATION: THE KING
OF MOROCCO
Social inequality cannot endure without the use
or threat of force.

FIGURE *18.8*

THE GREAT PYRAMID OF KHUFU

To deliver messages of this sort and demonstrate the truths they are based on, state societies invest a large portion of national wealth in monumental architecture. From the pyramids of Egypt or Teotihuacán in Mexico to the Gothic cathedrals of medieval Europe, state-subsidized monumentality in religious structures makes the individual feel powerless and insignificant. Great public edifices—whether seeming to float, as in the case of the Gothic cathedral of Amiens, or to press down with the infinite heaviness of the pyramids of Khufu (Fig. 18.8)—teach the futility of discontent and the invincibility of those who rule, as well as the glory of heaven and the gods. (This is not to say that they teach nothing else.)

THOUGHT CONTROL IN MODERN STATES

A considerable amount of conformity is achieved not by frightening or threatening people, but by inviting them to identify with the governing elite and to enjoy vicariously the pomp of state occasions. Public spectacles such as religious processions, coronations, and victory parades work against the alienating effects of poverty and exploitation (Fig. 18.9). During Roman times, the masses were kept under control by encouraging them to watch gladiators killing each other, chariot races, circuses, and other mass spectator events. Today, the movies, television, and radio provide states with far more powerful means of thought control. Through modern media the consciousness of millions of listeners, readers, and watchers is often manipulated along rather precisely determined paths by censors and propaganda specialists. However, thought control via the mass media need not take the form of government-directed propaganda and censorship. More subtle forms of control arise from the voluntary filtering of news by reporters and commentators whose career advancements depend on avoiding objective coverage (Chomsky 1989; Herman and Chomsky 1988). "Entertainment" delivered through the air or by cable directly into the shanty-town house or tenement apartment is another form of thought control—perhaps the most effective "Roman circus" yet devised (Kottak 1990; Parenti 1986).

Compulsory universal education is another powerful modern means of thought control. Teachers and schools serve the instrumental needs of complex industrial civilizations by training each generation to provide the skills and services necessary for survival

FIGURE *18.9*

POMP AND CEREMONY
(A) General Schwarzkopf and Joint Chief of Staffs Colin Powell return home from the Gulf War to a hero's welcome. **(B)** The crowning of Queen Elizabeth II in England.

(A)

(B)

and well-being. But, schools also teach civics, history, citizenship, and social studies. These subjects are loaded with implicit or explicit assumptions about culture, people, and nature that favor the status quo.

The celebration in 1992 of the 500th anniversary of the voyage of Christopher Columbus to the New World is a good example of how interpretations of history that support the status quo become established through universal education. Generations of school children in the United States have been taught to regard Columbus as a hero whose daring voyage brought Christianity and "civilization" to the Americas. This view helps to sweep the question of Native American rights and welfare under the rug (Fig. 18.10). It overlooks and masks the fact that Columbus's voyage was a catastrophe for the people whose ancestors had already discovered the New World 15,000 or more years before Columbus was born. From the Native American point of view, Columbus's "discovery" initiated the greatest real estate swindle of all times and the decimation of the native population through slavery and the exposure to European diseases (D. Thomas 1989; 1991).

All modern states use universal education to instill loyalty through mass rituals. These include saluting the flag (Fig. 18.11a), pronouncing oaths of

FIGURE *18.10*

FIVE HUNDRED YEARS LATER
Native Americans protesting the stereotypes implicit in the use by baseball teams of names such as the Atlanta Braves and the Cleveland Indians.

FIGURE *18.11*

THOUGHT CONTROL IN TWO MODERN STATES
(A) American children; **(B)** Children in native costume at Expo 85, Tsukuba, Japan.

(A)

(B)

allegiance, singing patriotic songs, and staging patriotic assemblies, plays, and pageants (Fig. 18.11b) (Bowles and Gintis 1976; Ramirez and Meyer 1980).

In modern industrial as in ancient states, acceptance of extreme social and economic inequality depends on thought control more than on the exercise of naked repressive force. Children from economically deprived families are taught to believe that the main obstacle to achievement of wealth and power is their own intellectual merit, physical endurance, and will to compete. The poor are taught to blame themselves for being poor, and their resentment is directed primarily against themselves or against those with whom they must compete and who stand on the same rung of the ladder of upward mobility (De Mott 1990; Kleugel and Smith 1981).

THE STATE AND PHYSICAL COERCION

Although thought control can be an effective supplementary means of maintaining political control, there are limits to the lies and deceptions that governments can get away with. If people are experiencing stagnant or declining standards of living, no amount of propaganda and false promises can prevent them from becoming restless and dissatisfied. As discontent mounts, the ruling elites must either increase the use of direct force or make way for a restructuring of political economy. In China, popular dissatisfaction with the ruling class has been met in recent years by both more thought control and more direct physical repression (Fig. 18.12). The great upheavals in the Soviet Union and Eastern Europe during the 1980s and 1990s also illustrate dramatically what can happen when ruling classes fail to deliver on their promises of a better life (Fig. 18.13). No amount of thought control could hide the daily reality of long lines to buy food, the endless red tape, the shortages of housing and electricity, and the widespread industrial pollution characteristic of life behind the Iron Curtain.

The dominant classes of Western parliamentary democracies rely more on thought control than on physical coercion to maintain law and order, but in the final analysis they, too, depend on guns and jails to protect their privileges. Natural disasters such as Hurricane Hugo in 1990 and blackouts such as occurred in New York City in 1977 (Fig. 18.14a and b) quickly led to extensive looting and widespread disorder, proving that thought control is not enough and that large numbers of ordinary citizens do not believe in the system and are held in check only by the threat of physical punishment (Curvin and Porter 1978; Weisman 1978).

FIGURE *18.12*

FREE SPEECH VERSUS TANKS ON TIANANMEN SQUARE, BEIJING, CHINA
The tanks won.

FIGURE *18.13*

PEOPLE AGAINST DICTATORSHIP IN BUCHAREST
The people won.

THE FATE OF PRESTATE BANDS AND VILLAGES

The career of state-level societies has been characterized by continuous expansion into and encroachment on the lands and freedoms of prestate peoples.

FIGURE *18.14*

THE BREAKDOWN OF LAW AND ORDER
(A) Looting in the aftermath of New York City's blackout.
(B) National Guard troops patrol the streets of Charleston,
South Carolina, after Hurricane Hugo to prevent looting.

(A)

(B)

For advanced chiefdoms, the appearance of soldiers, traders, missionaries, and colonists often resulted in a successful transition to state-level organization. But over the vast regions of the globe inhabited by dispersed bands and villages, the spread of the state has resulted in the annihilation or total distortion of the ways of life of thousands of once free and proud peoples. These devastating changes have been aptly described as *genocide*—the extinction of whole populations—or as *ethnocide*—the systematic extinction of cultures.

The spread of European states into the Americas had a devastating effect on the inhabitants of the New World. Many methods were employed to rid the land of its original inhabitants in order to make room for the farms and industries needed to support Europe's overflowing population. Native American peoples were exterminated during unequal military engagements that pitted guns against arrows; others were killed off by new urban diseases brought by the colonists—smallpox, measles, and the common cold—against which people who lived in small, dispersed settlements lacked immunity (Crosby 1986:196ff; Dobyns 1983; Wirsing 1985). Against the cultures of the natives there were other weapons. Their modes of production were destroyed by slavery, debt peonage, and wage labor; their political lives were destroyed by the creation of chiefs and tribal councils who were puppets and conve-

nient means of control for state administrators (Fried 1975); and their religious beliefs and rituals were demeaned and suppressed by missionaries who were eager to save their souls but not their lands and freedom (Ribeiro 1971; D. Walker 1972).

These genocidal attacks were not confined to North and South America. They were also carried out in Australia, on the islands of the Pacific, and in Siberia. Nor are they merely events that took place a long time ago and about which nothing can now be done. For they are still going on in the remote vastness of the Amazon Basin and other regions of South America, where the last remaining New World free and independent band and village peoples have been cornered by the remorseless spread of colonists, traders, oil companies, teachers, ranchers, and missionaries (Bodley 1975; Davis 1977).

Most of the band and village peoples described in these pages are threatened with ethnocide. The Aché of eastern Paraguay (see p. 212), for example, have been systematically hunted, rounded up, and forced to live on small reservations in order to make room for ranchers and farmers. Their children were separated from their parents and sold to settlers as servants. The manhunters shot anyone who showed signs of resistance, raped the women, and sold the children. "Wild" Aché were captured and deliberately taken to a reservation, where it was known that an influenza epidemic was already raging (Munzel 1973).

The !Kung San (pp. 210, 240, 347) have become the target of immense statal forces that have changed their way of life and that threaten their physical survival. Many !Kung San men were lured into service for the South African army in its war against the guerillas who successfully fought to establish an independent state in Namibia. According to South African sources, the Sans' "acute sense of direction, tracking ability, knowledge of the bush, and far sight make them perfect guerilla fighters" (Lee and Hurlich 1982:338). South African patrols put the San out front to detect mines. Meanwhile, San women and children were rounded up and placed in military bush camps (see Box 18.6).

The forest habitat of the Yonomamö (pp. 301–304) on the Brazilian side of the Brazil-Venezuela border has been ravaged by a gold rush. Forty thousand miners have dug huge holes using high-power hoses. Mercury, used to separate the gold and soil from the excavations, has poisoned the streams where the Yanomamö fish; the road and airplane traffic has frightened off the game; and pools of

---

BOX *18.6*

THE FATE OF THE !KUNG SAN

Deep in the dense Caprivi bush a colony of Bushmen are being taught a new culture and a new way of life by the White man. More than a thousand Bushmen have already discarded the bow and arrow for the Rl rifle and their wives are making clothes out of cotton instead of skin. Gone are their days of hunting animals for food and living off the yield. They now have "braaiveis" and salads with salt and pepper while the men wear boots and their ladies dress in the latest fashions. Their children go to schools and sing in choirs.

A handful of South African soldiers started the Colony some time ago, attracting the children of the veld to a secret Army Base where they are teaching them the modern way of life. "The most difficult thing to teach them is to use a toilet," the Commander of the Base said. Money and trade is something completely new to them but they are fast learning the White man's way of bickering. In their small community they now have a store, hospital, school and various other training centres. The men are being trained as soldiers while their womenfolk learn how to knit, sew and cook.

SOURCE: Lee and Hurlich 1982:335–336.

BOX *18.7*

WE WILL NOT SEE THEIR LIKE AGAIN

The last of the tribal cultures are in serious jeopardy. When they are gone, we will not see their like again. The nonindustrialized statal cultures have joined forces with the industrialized states to eliminate them. The reason for this lies in the contrasting natures of statal and tribal cultures: the former are larger, more powerful, and expansionistic. Tribal cultures, representing an earlier cultural form, are denigrated as "savage" and viewed as an anachronism in the "modern world." The statal cultures have exercised their power by dividing all land on this planet among themselves.... This is as true for the Third World—where concerted efforts are made to destroy the last vestiges of tribalism as a threat to national unity—as it has been for the Western World.

SOURCE: Gerald Weiss 1977a:890.

---

stagnant water produced by the mining operations have provided perfect breeding conditions for malaria-bearing mosquitoes. In 3 years the population of the Brazilian Yanomamö fell by 20 percent as a result of malaria, other contagious diseases, and malnutrition (Turner 1991).

Can any of the prestate peoples survive much longer? Gerald Weiss observes (see Box 18.7):

No biologist would claim that evolution in the organic realm makes either necessary or desirable the disappearance of earlier forms, so no anthropologist should be content to remain a passive observer of the extinction of the Tribal World. [Weiss 1977a:891]

SUMMARY

Headmen, chiefs, and kings are found in three different forms of political organization: autonomous bands and villages, chiefdoms, and states, respectively. The "big man" is a rivalrous form of headmanship marked by competitive redistributions that expand and intensify production. As illustrated by the mumis of the Solomon Islands, bigmanship is a temporary status requiring constant validation through displays of generosity that leave the big man poor in possessions but rich in prestige and authority. Since they are highly respected, big men are well suited to act as leaders of war parties, long-distance trading expeditions, and other collective activities that require leadership among egalitarian peoples.

Chiefdoms consist of several more or less permanently allied communities. Like big men, chiefs also play the role of great provider, expand and intensify production, give feasts, and organize long-distance warfare and trading expeditions. However, as illustrated by the Trobriand, Cherokee, and Tikopian chiefdoms, chiefs enjoy hereditary status, tend to live somewhat better than the average commoner, and can be deposed only through defeat in warfare. The power of chiefs is limited by their ability to support a permanent group of police-military specialists and to deprive significant numbers of their followers of access to the means of making a living. In the transition from band and village organizations through chiefdoms to states, there is a continuous series of cumulative changes in the balance of power between elites and commoners that makes it difficult to say at exactly what point in the process we have chiefdoms rather than an alliance of villages, or states rather than a powerful chiefdom. The polities of the Hawaiian Islands illustrate the incipient phases of pristine state formation.

Dense populations, intensifiable modes of production, trade, storageable grains, circumscription, and intense warfare underly the emergence of pristine states. Secondary states, however, arose under a variety of conditions related to the spread of pristine states.

The difference between chiefdoms and states is illustrated by the case of the Bunyoro. The Mukama was a great provider for himself and his closest sup-porters but not for the majority of the Bunyoro peasants. Unlike the Trobriand chief, the Mukama maintained a permanent court of personal retainers and a palace guard. There are many resemblances between the Bunyoro and the feudal kingdoms of early medieval Europe, but the power of the early English kings was greater and depended less on the image of the great provider than on that of the great protector.

The most developed and highly stratified form of statehood is that of empire. As illustrated by the Inca of Peru, the leaders of ancient empires possessed vast amounts of power and were unapproachable by ordinary citizens. Production was supervised by a whole army of administrators and tax collectors. While the Inca was concerned with the welfare of his people, they viewed him as a god to whom they owed everything, rather than as a headman or chief who owed everything to them.

Since all state societies are based on marked inequalities between rich and poor and rulers and ruled, maintenance of law and order presents a critical challenge. In the final analysis, it is the police and the military, with their control over the means of physical coercion, that keep the poor and the exploited in line. However, all states find it more expedient to maintain law and order by controlling people's thoughts. This is done in a variety of ways, ranging from state religions to public rites and spectacles and universal education.

The plight of the remaining prestate band and village societies must not be overlooked. As in the case of the Aché, civilization and modernization often lead to slavery, disease, and poverty for such people. The continuing changes experienced by the !Kung San and Yanomamö illustrate the precarious future faced by the remaining prestate societies.

Chapter 19

Stratified Groups

Now we examine the principal varieties of stratified groups found in state-level societies. These include classes, castes, and ethnic, racial, and religious minorities. (The special case of gender hierarchies will be taken up in the next chapter.) We will see that people who live in state-level societies think and behave in ways that are determined to a great extent by their membership in stratified groups and by their position in a stratification hierarchy. The values and behavior of such groups are in turn often related to a struggle for access to the structural and infrastructural sources of wealth and power. In this regard, to what extent can subordinated groups be seen as the authors of their own fates? Does the underclass create its own misery? Does the jealousy of peasants—"the image of limited good"—prevent them from rising in the class hierarchy? Are the members of the urban underclass victims of their own subculture—the so called culture of poverty? Shall we blame the unemployed for being unemployed?

GENDER, AGE, AND HIERARCHY

Hierarchies based on gender are conventionally distinguished from classes and other types of state-society hierarchies. We will do the same and postpone the discussion of gender hierarchies to the next chapter (Chapter 20). This does not mean that the hierarchical relations between the sexes are less important than those between elites and other subordinated groups. Rather, it means that their significance is best appreciated in the wider context of gender roles (i.e., a general account of sociocultural relationships between males and females in all varieties of sociocultural systems).

Age groups within both state and prestate societies are also often associated with unequal distributions of power. Indeed, hierarchical differences between mature adults and juveniles and infants are virtually universal. Moreover, the treatment of children by adults sometimes involves highly exploitative and physically and mentally punitive practices. One might argue that age hierarchies are fundamentally different from other kinds of hierarchies because the maltreatment and exploitation of children is always "for their own good." Superordinate groups of all sorts, however, usually say this of the subordinate groups under their control. The fact that some degree of subordination of juveniles and infants is necessary for enculturation and population survival does not mean that such hierarchies are fundamentally different from other kinds of hierarchies. Brutal treatment of children can result in permanent damage to their health and well-being or even in their death.

Neglect and abuse of the old or infirm are also strong where old people constitute a despised and powerless group. In many societies, senior citizens are victims of punitive physical and psychological treatment comparable to that meted out to criminals and enemies of the state. Descriptions of hierarchical structures, therefore, must never lose sight of the differences in power and life-styles associated with gender and age groups within various other kinds of hierarchical groups such as classes.

CLASS AND POWER

All state societies are organized into a hierarchy of groups known as classes. A *class* is a group of people who have a similar relationship to the apparatus of control in state societies and who possess similar amounts of power (or lack of power) (Fig. 19.1). To be powerful in human affairs is to be able to get people to obey one's requests and demands. In practice, this kind of power depends on the ability to provide or take away essential goods and services, and this in turn ultimately depends on who controls access to energy, resources, and technology—especially the technology of armed coercion.

The power of particular human beings cannot be measured simply by adding up the amount of energy they regulate or channel. If that were the case, the most powerful people in the world would be the technicians who turn the switches at nuclear power plants, or airline pilots who control four engines, each of which has the power of 40,000 horses. Despite their

FIGURE *19.1*

POVERTY AND POWER
This man is not only poor, he has relatively little power.

we shall see, at their extreme, closed-class systems strongly resemble racial and ethnic minorities.

EMICS, ETICS, AND CLASS CONSCIOUSNESS

Class is an aspect of culture in which there are sharp differences between emic and etic points of view (Berreman 1981:18). Many social scientists accept class distinction as real and important only when it is consciously perceived and acted on by the people involved. They hold that in order for a group to be considered a class, its members must have a consciousness of their own identity, exhibit a common sense of solidarity, and engage in organized attempts to promote and protect collective interests (Fallers 1977; T. Parsons 1970). Moreover, some social scientists (see Bendix and Lipset 1966) believe that classes exist only when persons with similar forms and quantities of social power organize into collective organizations such as political parties or labor unions. Other social scientists, however, believe that the most important features of class hierarchies are the actual concentrations of power in certain groups and the powerlessness of others, regardless of any conscious or even unconscious awareness of these differences on the part of the people concerned, and regardless of the existence of collective organizations (Roberts and Brintnall 1982:195–217).

From an etic and behavioral viewpoint, a class can exist even when the members of the class deny that they constitute a class, and even when, instead of collective organizations, they have organizations that compete, such as rival business corporations or rival unions (De Mott 1990). The reason for this is that subordinate classes lacking class consciousness are obviously not exempt from the domination of ruling classes. Similarly, ruling classes containing antagonistic and competitive elements nonetheless dominate those who lack social power. Members of ruling classes need not form permanent, hereditary, monolithic, conspiratorial organizations in order to protect and enhance their own interests. A struggle for power within the ruling class does not necessarily result in a fundamentally altered balance of power between the classes. The struggle for political control waged by various factions within the ruling communist elites of China has left the hierarchy of classes in China more or less intact. Similarly, the competition among various corporations in the United States supports rather than subverts the the position of the executive class.

enormous capacity for killing and maiming, military field officers in the armed forces are not necessarily powerful people. The crucial question is who controls the technicians, pilots, and generals, and makes them turn their "switches" on or off?

All state societies necessarily have at least two classes arranged hierarchically: rulers and ruled. But where there are more than two classes, they are not necessarily all arranged hierarchically with respect to each other. For example, fishermen and neighboring farmers are usefully regarded as two separate classes because they relate to the ruling class in distinctive ways; have different patterns of ownership, rent, and taxation; and exploit entirely different sectors of the environment. Yet neither has a clear-cut power advantage or disadvantage with respect to the other. Similarly, anthropologists often speak of an urban as opposed to a rural lower class, although the quantitative power differentials between the two may be minimal.

One other feature of classes should be noted: They come in relatively *closed* or *open* systems. In open class systems, there is much mobility up and/or down the hierarchy. In closed-class systems, there is little mobility up and/or down the hierarchy. As

Of course, there is no disputing the importance of a people's belief about the shape and origin of their stratification system. Consciousness of a common plight among the members of a downtrodden and exploited class may very well lead to the outbreak of organized class warfare. Consciousness is thus an element in the struggle between classes, but it is not the cause of class differences.

ECONOMIC EXPLOITATION

The control over large amounts of power by one class relative to another permits the members of the more powerful class to exploit the members of the weaker class. There is no generally accepted meaning of the term *exploitation,* but the basic conditions responsible for economic exploitation can be identified by reference to the discussion of reciprocity and redistribution (Ch. 14). When balanced reciprocity prevails or when the redistributors keep only "the bones and stale cakes" for themselves, there is no economic exploitation (p. 308). But when there is unbalanced reciprocity or when the redistributors start keeping the "meat and fat" for themselves, exploitation may soon develop.

In the theories of Karl Marx, all wage laborers are exploited because the value of what they produce is always greater than what they are paid. Similarly, some anthropologists take the view that exploitation begins as soon as there is a structured flow of goods and services between two groups (Newcomer 1977; Ruyle 1973, 1975). Against this view it can be argued that the activities of employers and of stratified redistributors may result in an improvement in the well-being of the subordinate class, and that without entrepreneurial or ruling-class leadership, everyone would be worse off (Dalton 1972, 1974). One cannot say, therefore, that every inequality in power and in consumption standards necessarily involves exploitation. If as a result of the rewards given to or taken by the ruling class, the economic welfare of all classes steadily improves, it would seem inappropriate to speak of the people responsible for that improvement as exploiters.

Exploitation may be said to exist when the following four conditions exist: (1) The subordinate class experiences deprivations with respect to basic necessities such as food, water, air, sunlight, leisure, medical care, housing, and transport; (2) the ruling class enjoys an abundance of luxuries; (3) the luxuries enjoyed by the ruling class depend on the labor of the subordinate class; and (4) the deprivations experienced by the subordinate class are caused by the failure of the ruling class to apply its power to the production of necessities instead of luxuries and to redistribute these necessities to the subordinate class (Boulding 1973). These conditions constitute an etic and behavioral definition of exploitation.

Because of the relationship between exploitation and human suffering, the study of exploitation is an important responsibility of social scientists who are concerned with the survival and well-being of our species. We must see to it that the study of exploitation is conducted empirically and with due regard to mental and emic as well as to etic and behavioral components (P. Brown 1985).

PEASANT CLASSES

About 40 percent of the people in the world make a living from farming and are members of one kind of peasant class or another. Peasants are the subordinate food producers of state societies who use preindustrial technologies of food production and who pay rent in the form of services, crops, cash, or taxes. The kind of payments extracted from peasants defines the essential features of their structured inferiority. Many different types of payments are extracted from peasants, but "peasants of all times and places are structured inferiors" (Dalton 1972:406).

Each major type of peasant is the subject of a vast research literature. Anthropologists have studied peasants more than they have studied village peoples or hunters and gatherers (Pelto and Pelto 1973). Three major types of peasant classes can be distinguished.

1. Feudal peasants. These peasants are subject to the control of a decentralized hereditary ruling class whose members provide military assistance to one another but do not interfere in one another's territorial domains. Feudal peasants, or "serfs," inherit the opportunity to utilize a particular parcel of land; hence they are said to be "bound" to the land. For the privilege of raising their own food, feudal peasants render unto the lord rent in kind or in money. Rent may also take the form of labor service in the lord's kitchens, stables, or fields.

Some anthropologists, following the lead of historians of European feudalism, describe feudal relationships as a more or less fair exchange of mutual obligations, duties, privileges, and rights between lord and serf. George Dalton (1969:390-391), for example, lists the following services and benefits given by Europe's feudal lords to their peasants:

Granting peasants the right to use land for subsistence and cash crops.

Military protection (e.g., against invaders).

Police protection (e.g., against robbery).

Juridicial services to settle disputes.

Feasts to peasants at Christmas, Easter; also harvest gifts.

Food given to peasants on days when they work the lord's fields.

Emergency provision of food during disaster.

Dalton denies that feudal peasants are exploited, because it is not known whether "the peasant paid out to the lord much more than he received back." Other anthropologists point out that the reason feudal peasants are "structured inferiors" is that the feudal ruling class deprives them of access to the land and its life-sustaining resources, which is antithetical to the principle of reciprocity and egalitarian redistribution. The counterflow of goods and services listed by Dalton merely perpetuates the peasants' structured inferiority. The one gift that would alter that relationship—the gift of land, free of rent or taxes—is never given.

History suggests that the structured inferiority of feudal peasants is seldom acceptable to the peasants. Over and over again the world has been convulsed by revolutions in which peasants struggled in the hope of restoring free access to land (E. Wolf 1969).

Many feudal peasantries owe their existence to military conquest, and this further emphasizes the exploitative nature of the landlord-serf relationship. For example, the Spanish crown rewarded Cortez, Pizarro, and the other conquistadores with lordships over the inhabitants of large slices of the territories they had conquered in Mexico and Peru. The heavy tax and labor demands placed on the conquered Native Americans thereafter contributed to a precipitous decline in their numbers (Dobyns 1983; C. Smith 1970).

While feudalism and feudal peasants are fast disappearing from the world, a heritage of feudal class relations is an important component in the underdevelopment of many third-world countries.

This heritage remains strong in several Central and South American countries, especially in Guatemala, Salvador, Ecuador, and Peru. In these countries, land ownership continues to be concentrated in huge estates owned by small numbers of politically powerful families. The peasants who live on or near these estates are dependent on the big landownders for access to land, water, loans, and emergency assistance. The extreme disparity in land holdings and the semi-feudal relationships between the estate owners and the peasants lie behind the guerilla movements that are found throughout this region (S. Stern 1988).

2. Agromanagerial state peasantries. Where the state is strongly centralized, as in ancient Peru, Egypt, Mesopotamia, and China, peasants may be directly subject to state control in addition to, or in the absence of, control by a local landlord class. Unlike the feudal peasants, agromanagerial peasants are subject to frequent conscription for labor brigades drawn from villages throughout the realm to build roads, dams, irrigation canals, palaces, temples, and monuments (Yates 1990). In return, the state makes an effort to feed its peasants in case of food shortages caused by droughts or other calamities. The pervasive bureaucratic control over production and life-styles in the ancient agromanagerial states has often been compared to the treatment of peasants who until recently were under communist rule in China, Albania, and Cambodia. The state in these countries was all-powerful, setting production quotas, controlling prices, and extracting taxes in kind and in labor.

3. Capitalist peasants. In Africa, Latin America (Fig. 19.2), India, and Southeast Asia, feudal and

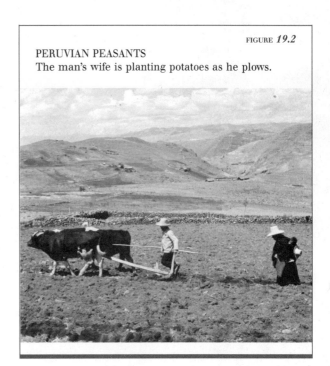

FIGURE *19.2*

PERUVIAN PEASANTS
The man's wife is planting potatoes as he plows.

agromanagerial types of peasantries have been replaced by peasants who enjoy increased opportunities to buy and sell land, labor, and food in competitive price markets. Most of the existing peasantries of the world now belong to this category. The varieties of structured inferiority within this group defy any simple taxonomy. Some capitalist peasants are subordinate to large landowners; others are subordinate to banks that hold mortgages and promissory notes. In more isolated or unproductive regions, holdings may be very small (Fig 19.3), giving rise to the phenomenon known as "penny capitalism" (that is, frequent buying and selling of small quantities of food and handicrafts).

FIGURE *19.3*

ECUADORIAN PEASANTS
Note the postage-stamp minifundia on the steep hillsides.

Capitalist peasants correspond to what Dalton calls "early modernized peasants." They display the following features:

Marketable land tenure
Predominance of production for cash sale; growing sensitivity to national commodity and labor price markets.
Beginnings of technological modernization.

Although many capitalist peasants own their own land, they do not escape payment of rent or its equivalent. Many communities of landowning peasants constitute labor reserves for larger and more heavily capitalized plantations and farmers. Penny-capitalists are frequently obliged to work for wages paid by these cash-crop enterprises. Penny capitalist peasants cannot obtain enough income to satisfy subsistence requirements from the sale of their products in the local market.

THE IMAGE OF LIMITED GOOD

A recurrent question concerning the plight of contemporary peasant communities is the extent to which they are victims of their own values (Kahn 1985; Peletz 1983). It has often been noted, for example, that peasants are very distrustful of innovations and cling to their old ways of doing things. Based on his study of the village of Tzintzuntzan, in the state of Michoacán, Mexico, George Foster (1967) has developed a general theory of peasant life based on the concept of the *image of limited good*. According to Foster, the people of Tzintzuntzan, like many peasants throughout the world, believe that life is a dreary struggle, that very few people can achieve "success," and that they can improve themselves only at the expense of other people. If someone tries something new and succeeds at it, the rest of the community resents it, becomes jealous, and snubs the "progressive" individual. Many peasants, therefore, are afraid to change their ways of life because they do not want to stir up the envy and hostility of friends and relatives.

Although there is no doubt that an image of limited good exists in many peasant villages in Mexico and elsewhere, the role it plays in preventing economic development is not clear. Foster provides much evidence for doubting the importance of the image of limited goods in Tzintzuntzan (Fig. 19.4). He tells the story of how a community development project sponsored by the United Nations achieved success initially, only to end in disasters that had little to do with the values held by the villagers. Also, most of the commu-

FIGURE *19.4*

IMAGE OF LIMITED GOOD
Peasant women of Tzintzuntzan with their
homemade pottery.

BOX *19.1*

A WORLD OF LIMITED GOOD

For the underlying, fundamental truth is
that in an economy like Tzintzuntzan's, hard
work and thrift are moral qualities of only the
slightest functional value. Because of the limitations on land and technology, additional hard
work does not produce a significant increment
in income. It is pointless to talk of thrift in a
subsistence economy, because usually there is
no surplus with which to be thrifty. Foresight,
with careful planning for the future, is also a
virtue of dubious value in a world in which the
best-laid plans must rest on a foundation of
chance and capriciousness.

SOURCE: Foster 1967:150–151.

nity's cash income was derived by working as migrant
laborers in the United States. To get across the border,
the migrants must bribe, scheme, and suffer great
hardships. Yet 50 percent of them had succeeded in
getting through, "many of them ten times or more"
(Foster 1967:277).

As Foster suggests, the image of limited good
is not a crippling illusion but rather a realistic appraisal of the facts of life in a society where economic
success or failure is capricious and hinged to forces
wholly beyond one's control or comprehension (see
Box 19.1).

James Acheson (1972), who studied a community near Tzintzuntzan, has argued that without realistic economic opportunities, development will not
occur. If opportunities present themselves, some individuals will always take advantage of them, regardless of the image of limited good: "It is one thing to
say that Tarascans [the people of the region of Tz-
intzuntzan] are suspicious, distrustful, and uncooperative; it is another to assume that this lack of cooperation precludes all possibility for positive economic
change" (Acheson 1972:1165; see Acheson 1974; Foster 1974).

CLASS AND LIFE-STYLE

Classes differ from one another not only in amount of
power per capita but also in broad areas of patterned
thought and behavior called *life-style.* Peasants, urban industrial wage workers, middle-class suburban-
ites, and upper-class industrialists have different life-
styles (Figs. 19.5 and 19.6). Cultural contrasts among
class-linked life-styles are as great as contrasts between life in an Eskimo igloo and life in an Mbuti
village of the Ituri forest. For example, the former
Mrs. Seward Prosser Mellon had a household budget
of $750,000 a year, plus a $20,000 item for the family
dog (Koskoff 1978:467).

Classes, in other words, have their own *subcultures* made up of distinctive work patterns, architecture, home furnishings, diet, dress, domestic routines,
sex and mating practices, magico-religious rituals,
art, and ideology. In many instances, different classes
even have accents that make it difficult for them to
talk to one another. Because of exposure of body parts
to sun, wind, and callus-producing friction, working-
class people tend to look different from their "superiors." Further distinctions are the result of dietary
specialties—the fat and the rich were once synony-
mous. (Today, in advanced capitalist societies, fatness
is a sign of a diet overloaded with fats and sugars, together with a lack of exercise, and is associated with
poverty rather than with wealth.) Throughout almost
the entire evolutionary career of stratified societies,
class identity has been as explicit and unambiguous as the distinction between male and female. The
Chinese Han dynasty peasant, the Inca commoner, or
the Russian serf could not expect to survive to maturity without knowing how to recognize members
of the "superior" classes. Doubt was removed in many

FIGURE *19.5*

CLASS AND LIFE-STYLE
South Bronx.

FIGURE *19.6*

CLASS AND LIFE-STYLE
Miami Beach.

FIGURE *19.7*

CARACAS SHANTYTOWN
Squatters in Latin American cities often enjoy the best views, since apartment houses were not built on hilltops because of lack of water. But this means that the squatters have to carry their water up the hill in cans.

cases by state-enforced standards of dress: Only the Chinese nobility could wear silk clothing; only the European feudal overlords could carry daggers and swords; and only the Inca rulers could wear gold ornaments. Violators were put to death. In the presence of their "superiors," commoners still perform definite rituals of subordination, among which lowering the head, removing the hat, averting the eyes, kneeling, bowing, crawling, or maintaining silence unless spoken to occur almost universally.

Throughout much of the world, class identity continues to be sharp and unambiguous. Among most contemporary nations, differences in class-linked life-styles show little prospect of diminishing or disappearing. Indeed, given the convergence in former communist countries toward market economies, ex-tremes of poverty and wealth may be on the rise. The contrast between the life-styles of the rich and powerful and those of people living in peasant villages or urban shantytowns (Fig. 19.7) may be greater than ever before. During the recent epochs of industrial advance, governing classes throughout the world have gone from palanquins to Mercedeses to private jets, while their subordinates find themselves without even a donkey or a pair of oxen. The elites now jet to the world's best medical centers to be treated with the most advanced medical technology, while vast numbers of less fortunate people have never even heard of the germ theory of disease and can't even afford the price of a bottle of aspirin. Elites attend the best universities, while over 1 billion of the world's adults remain illiterate (World Bank 1991:56).

"THE CULTURE OF POVERTY"

In studying the problems of people living in urban slums and shantytowns, Oscar Lewis thought he had found evidence for a distinct set of values and practices that he called the "culture of poverty." Although not exactly comparable point by point, the concepts of the culture of poverty and of the image of limited good resemble each other in many respects, and represent similar attempts to explain the perpetuation of poverty by focusing on the traditions and values of the underprivileged groups. And they are both wrong for similar reasons. Oscar Lewis (1966) pictures the poor in cities like Mexico City, New York, and Lima (Fig. 19.8) as tending to be fearful, suspicious, and apathetic toward the major institutions of the larger society; as hating the police and being mistrustful of government; and as "inclined to be cynical of the church." They also have "a strong present-time orientation with relatively little disposition to defer gratification and plan for the future." This implies that poor people are less willing to save money and are more interested in "getting mine now" in the form of stereos, color television, the latest-style clothing, and gaudy automobiles. It also implies that the poor "blow" their earnings by getting drunk or going on buying sprees. Like George Foster, Lewis recognizes that in some measure the culture of poverty is partly a rational response to the objective conditions of powerlessness and poverty: "an adaptation and a reaction of the poor to their marginal position in a class-stratified society" (1966:21). But he also states that once the culture of poverty comes into existence, it tends to perpetuate itself:

By the time slum children are six or seven they have usually absorbed the basic attitudes and values of their subculture. Thereafter they are psychologically unready to take full advantage of changing conditions or improving opportunities that may develop in their lifetime. (ibid.)

SQUATTERS IN LIMA
Life on a garbage heap.

FIGURE *19.8*

Lewis proposes that only 20 percent of the urban poor actually have the culture of poverty, implying that 80 percent fall into the category of those whose poverty results from infrastructural and structural conditions, rather than from the traditions and values of a culture of poverty. The concept of the culture of poverty has been criticized on the grounds that the poor have many values other than those stressed in the culture of poverty—values they share with other classes (Leeds 1970; see Parker and Kleiner 1970; Valentine 1970).

Although the poor may have some values that are different from those of members of other classes, such values cannot be shown to be harmful. Helen Icken Safa (1967) has demonstrated, for example, that developed patterns of neighborly cooperation frequently exist in established slums and shantytowns. And Oscar Lewis himself (1961, 1966) has shown in interviews transcribed from tape recordings that many individuals who are trapped in poverty nonetheless achieve great nobility of spirit.

Values said to be distinctive of the urban poor are actually shared equally by the middle class. For example, being suspicious of government, politicians, and organized religion is not an exclusive poverty-class trait; nor is the tendency to spend above one's means. There is little evidence that the middle class as a whole lives within its income more effectively than poor people do. But when the poor mismanage their incomes, the consequences are much more serious. If the male head of a poor family yields to the temptation to buy nonessential items, his children may go hungry or his wife may be deprived of medical attention. But these consequences result from being poor, not from any demonstrable difference in the capacity to defer gratification.

The stereotype of the improvident poor masks an implicit belief that the impoverished segments of society ought to be more thrifty and more patient than the members of the middle class. It is conscience saving to be able to attribute poverty to values for which the poor themselves can be held responsible (Piven and Cloward 1971).

"NOW WHOSE FAULT IS THAT?"

The tendency to blame the poor for being poor is not confined to relatively affluent members of the middle class. The poor or near-poor themselves are often the staunchest supporters of the view that people who really want to work can always find work. This attitude forms part of a larger world view in which there is little comprehension of the structural conditions that make poverty for some inevitable. What

must be seen as a system is viewed purely in terms of individual faults, individual motives, and individual choices. Hence, the poor turn against the poor and blame one another for their plight.

In a study of a Newfoundland community called Squid Cove, Cato Wadel (1973) has shown how a structural problem of unemployment caused by factors entirely beyond the control of the local community can be interpreted in such a way as to set neighbor against neighbor. The men of Squid Cove earn their living from logging, fishing, and construction (Fig. 19.9). Mechanization in logging, depletion of the fishing grounds, and upgrading of construction skills have left most of the men without steady, year-round means of making a living. A certain number of men, especially those who have large families and who are past their physical prime, place themselves on the able-bodied welfare rolls. In doing so, they must be prepared to wage a desperate struggle to preserve their self-esteem against the tendency of their

FIGURE *19.9*

NEWFOUNDLAND VILLAGE
Fishermen mending their nets. Hard work is a traditional part of life in this rugged habitat.

BOX *19.2*

WHOSE FAULT?

In explaining why he chose to study the plight of people on welfare, Cato Wadel writes "From what has been said so far, it should be clear that I am not much in doubt about 'whose fault it is'":

It is not the fault of the unemployed individual. If this study were summarized into a simple and clear statement, it would be that it is unemployment itself which produces behavior on the part of the unemployed which makes people blame the unemployment on the individual, and not the other way around: that a special attitude or personal defect produces unemployment.

SOURCE: Wadel 1973:127.

FIGURE *19.10*

POVERTY IN NAPLES
The infamous one-room hovels of the Bassi, usually without ventilation, running water, separate toilets, or heating, are home for tens of thousands of Neopolitan families.

neighbors to regard them as shirkers who "don't do nothin' for the money they get." What makes the plight of the Squid Cove welfare recipients especially poignant is that Newfoundlanders have long been noted for their intense work ethic. Many welfare recipients formerly worked at extremely arduous unskilled jobs. For example, Wadel's principal informant, George, was a logger for 29 years. George stopped logging because he injured a disk in his spine. The injury was sufficient to prevent him from competing for the better-paying unskilled jobs, but insufficient to place him on the welfare roles as a disabled worker. George says he is willing to work, provided it is not too heavy and does not require him to leave the house he owns in Squid Cove. "I'm willin' to work but there's no work around.... Now whose fault is that?" he asks. Others disagree. In Squid Cove, welfare is thought of as something "we," the taxpayers, give to "them," the unemployed. There is no generally accepted feeling that it is the responsibility of the government or the society to secure appropriate work; the responsibility for finding a job falls on the individual and no one else (see Box 19.2).

POVERTY IN NAPLES

Thomas Belmonte lived for a year in a slum neighborhood of Naples, Italy, a city that is known as the "Calcutta of Europe." Belmonte describes the neighborhood, Fontana del Re (see Fig. 19.10; Box 19.3), as being inhabited by a subproletariat, or underclass, who lacked steady employment and who produced so little that they could not even be said to be exploited because there was nothing to be taken away from them. There were people like Gabriele, who collected metal junk and broke it into pieces with the help of his four children, but who also ran a little store during the day and drove a taxi for prostitutes at night. Others were part-time sailors, waiters, bartenders, dockworkers, scavengers, and movers. Some groomed dogs, others were jacks-of-all-trades. Some were full-time smugglers, dope dealers, pickpockets, purse snatchers, and burglars. There were also dressmakers, flower vendors, beggars, and old women who added to their small pensions "by selling contraband cigarettes and condoms, and greasy sandwiches and wine so bad it burned a hole through your gut." The children of Fontana del Re did odd jobs that earned them about 33 cents an hour. Pepe, the 11-year-old son of a cobbler, had a job in a TV repair shop; his face and chest were scarred from defective tubes that blew up when he tested them. Several neighborhood children made daily forays to pry open the trunks of parked cars. Other children carried trays of espresso to offices and shops.

The people of Fontana del Re have many of Oscar Lewis's culture of poverty traits. But Belmonte

<table>
<tr><td>

BOX *19.3*

THE BROKEN FOUNTAIN

At Fontana del Re in a corner strewn now with rubble, beneath the bruised, shattered visage of a lion, the eroded figure of a sculpted stone sea shell recedes into a wall. "This was our fountain," they told me. "Oh you should have seen it, Tommaso. The water played night and day. In summer, the children scampered about in it. At night, falling asleep, you heard it, and it was like music." The young men told me it was they who had destroyed it. As children, many years before, with iron rods, they had gone every day to hammer and smash it, until they were satisfied and there was nothing left to break.

Thereafter, whenever I passed that ruined corner, I tried to imagine what the fountain had once been like, and thought and wondered and sorrowed the more as I understood how it came to be broken.

SOURCE: Belmonte 1979:144.

</td><td>

BOX *19.4*

CULTURE OR POVERTY?

The poor hesitate to plan for the future because they are hard-put to stay afloat in the present, and not because of a "present-time orientation." They have no trouble recalling the high and low points of their past. Their avoidance of banks relates to a realistic fear of inflation and a realistic mistrust of the literate officialdom. They do not patronize department stores because they prefer to cultivate their own, more personalized networks of local credit, marketing, and exchange. In direct contradiction to Lewis's formulation, the poor of Naples purchase vital supplies wisely and in bulk. They place numerous cultural controls on consumption, wasting nothing. They are habituated to delaying gratifications in terms of clothing, housing, plumbing, heating, travel, transportation, and entertainment. If in good times they allow themselves the one luxury of channeling surplus funds into good, abundant food, I think it ethnocentric to label them irrational or immature, since this is how they sublimate a historically inherited and confirmed terror of hunger.

Confronted by a scarcity of opportunities, they become resigned, to preserve their sanity, and do not think to transcend their condition so long as they remain in underdeveloped Naples.... They have a culture that is simultaneously against poverty, adapted to the stresses of poverty, and mangled by poverty. But they have a culture which is also fashioned out of a great Mediterranean tradition, in the crucible of a great Mediterranean city. Their culture reflects their various and ingenious strategies for survival and their low position in a hierarchy. In other words, it is a class culture as well as a regional one....

The Neapolitan urban poor are fashion-wise, street-wise, and urbane. They are not provincial. They live close to the gates of power in the wards of a great city, but unlike proletarians they are not integrated into the political and ideological currents of mass culture. They inhabit a world connected and apart from the main, a dense and crowded urban world, submerged; a crude, loud, pushy world where the moral order is exposed as a fraud which conceals the historical ascendancy of cunning and force.

SOURCE: Belmonte 1979:144.

</td></tr>
</table>

traces most of these traits to being penniless and lacking steady employment (Box 19.4).

MINORITIES AND MAJORITIES

In addition to classes, most state societies are also stratified into so-called racial and ethnic groups (R. Cohen 1978). These groups, often called *minorities* or *majorities,* differ from classes in three ways: (1) They have, or formerly had, cultural traditions characteristic of another society, (2) their members often belong to different classes, and (3) their members are conscious of their existence as a group set apart from the rest of the population.

The separation into racial or ethnic minorities is based on whether the criteria of group membership are primarily physical appearance, common origin in another country or region, or possession of a distinctive life-style. In reality, however, both criteria occur in a bewildering number of combinations. Racial and cultural differences and common ancestry are often claimed by or attributed to groups that lack them, giving rise to sharp discrepancies between emic and etic versions of group identity (Fig. 19.11).

FIGURE *19.11*

ETHNIC IDENTITY
All of these people identify themselves as Jews. **(A)** The man was born in Yemen
and **(B)** the girl in India. **(C)** The young woman was born in Morocco, and
(D) both boys in Israel.

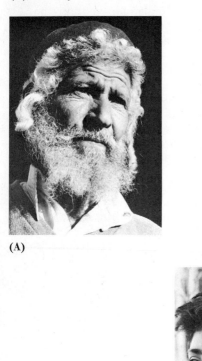

(A)

(B)

(C)

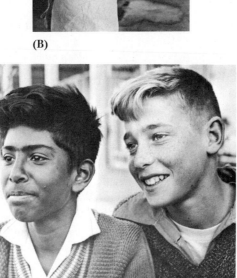

(D)

Racial and ethnic minorities are groups that are subordinate or whose position is vulnerable to subordination. The term majority refers to the higher-ranking and more secure racial or ethnic groups that control access to power, wealth, and prestige. The two terms are unsatisfactory because "majorities" like the whites in South Africa are sometimes vastly outnumbered by the "minorities" whom they oppress and exploit (Fig. 19.12). No satisfactory substitute for these terms has been devised, however (Simpson and Yinger 1972).

The most important point to bear in mind about minorities and majorities is that they are invariably locked into a more or less open form of political, social, and economic struggle to protect or raise their positions in the stratification system (Despres 1975; Jiobu 1988; Olzak and Nagel 1986; Schermerhorn 1970; Wagley and Harris 1958). Depending on their respective numbers, their special cultural strengths and weaknesses, and their initial advantages or disadvantages during the formation of the stratification system, their status as a group may rise

FIGURE *19.12*

THE LONG ROAD TO FREEDOM
Nelson Mandela emerges from 27 years of imprisonment to continue the struggle against apartheid in South Africa.

or fall in the hierarchy. Thus, although many minorities are subject to excruciating forms of discrimination, segregation, and exploitation, others may actually enjoy fairly high, although not dominant, positions.

ASSIMILATION VERSUS PLURALISM

The disappearance of an ethnic or racial group through its absorbtion by a majority is called *assimilation.* The resurgence in recent times of an emphasis on ethnic and racial identity has made it clear that assimilation is a rather rare outcome of minority-majority interaction. Some form of multiethnic and multiracial *pluralism* seems to be far more common. But it is important to distinguish the perpetuation of multiethnic and multiracial social groups from the preservation of their cultures. Minorities may adopt the language of the majority, lose their old ethnic traditions, and become culturally similar to the majority and yet remain unassimilated. (The change need not be one-sided—the majority may in turn adopt minority traditions such as ethnic foods and holidays, like pizza and St. Patrick's Day.) Even extensive intermarriage need not lead to assimilation. This appears to be true of the European immigrant groups in the United States such as Scots, Germans, Jews, English, French, and Italians, whose rates of exogamy range as high as 30 or 40 percent (Alba 1990). These groups maintain their identity through a principal of ambilineal descent (see page 279) whereby children of mixed marriages shift from one ethnic identity to another as they see fit.

An emphasis on differences in language, religion, and other aspects of life-styles can increase a minority's sense of solidarity and may help its members to compete in impersonalized, class-structured, competitive societies. Jewish, Chinese, Japanese, Greek, Syrian, Hindu, or Muslim merchants and businesspeople, for example, frequently enjoy important commercial advantages in highly competitive situations. Based on his study of the relations between African-Americans and Hindus in Guyana, Leo Despres (1975) suggests that ethnic, cultural, and racial identities confer competitive advantages with respect to environmental resources. The Hindu segment of Guyana society, for example, has a firmer grip on the land than the black segment. Ethnic groups thus exhibit a wide variety of adaptations to different niches in the natural and cultural environments (Abruzzi 1982; Barth 1974).

The problem is that strong minority solidarity carries with it the danger of overexposure and overreaction. In maintaining and increasing their own solidarity, minorities run the risk of increasing the majorities' resentment and hence of becoming the scapegoats of genocidal policies. The fate of the Jews in Germany and Poland, the Hindu Indians in east and southern Africa, the Chinese in Indonesia, and the Muslims and Sikhs in India are some of the better-known examples of "successful" minority adaptations that were followed by mass slaughter and/or expulsion.

Moreover, it is well to keep in mind that minorities are themselves stratified and that the upper classes and elites within the minority may therefore stand to gain more than the average member from the perpetuation of the minority. One important reason for the perpetuation of pluralist aims and symbols is that the wealthier and more powerful segments of both the minority and majority often derive economic and political strength from the maintenance of a separate identity for their subordinates. Roger Sanjek (1972, 1977) studied the relationships among 23 different "tribal" groups who live in the city of Accra, Ghana, and found that in terms of language, behavior, dress, residence, and facial markings, there was little to distinguish one group from another. Nonetheless, politicians relied heavily on their "tribal" identities in competing for political office. Similarly, the tragic history of Lebanon cannot be understood apart from the private fortunes that both Christian and Muslim elites have been able to amass as a result of drawn-out communal strife (Joseph 1978).

CASTES IN INDIA

Indian castes are closed, endogamous, and stratified descent groups. They bear many resemblances to both endogamous classes and racial, ethnic, and cultural minorities. No sharp line can be drawn between the castes of India and such groups as the Jews or blacks in the United States or the Inca elite. However, some features of the Indian caste hierarchy are unique and deserve special attention.

The unique features of Indian castes have to do with the fact that the caste hierarchy is an integral part of Hinduism, the religion of most of the people of India. (This does not mean that one must be a Hindu in order to belong to a caste. There are also Muslim and Christian castes in India.) It is a matter of religious conviction in India that all people are not spiritually equal and that the gods have established a hierarchy of groups. This hierarchy consists of the four major *varnas,* or grades of being. According to the earliest traditions (e.g., the Hymns of Rigveda), the four varnas correspond to the physical parts of Manu, who gave rise to the human race through dismemberment. His head became the Brahmans (priests), his arms the Kshatriyas (warriors), his thighs the Vaishyas (merchants and craftsmen), and his feet the Shudras (menial workers). According to Hindu scripture, an individual's varna is determined by a descent rule; that is, it corresponds to the varna of one's parents and is unalterable during one's lifetime.

The basis of all Hindu morality is the idea that each varna has its appropriate rules of behavior, or "path of duty" (*dharma*). At the death of the body, the soul meets its fate in the form of a transmigration into a higher or lower being (*karma*). Those who follow their dharma will be rewarded with a higher point on Manu's body during their next life. Deviation from the dharma will result in reincarnation in the body of an outcaste or even an animal (Long 1987).

One of the most important aspects of the dharma is the practice of certain taboos regarding marriage, eating, and physical proximity. Marriage below one's varna is generally regarded as a defilement and pollution, acceptance of food cooked or handled by persons below one's varna is also a defilement and pollution, and any bodily contact between Brahman and Shudra is forbidden (Fig. 19.13). In parts of India there were castes that were not only untouchable but also were unseeable, and who therefore could come out only at night. The worst of these restrictions became illegal after India gained its independence at mid-century.

Although the general outlines of this system are agreed on throughout Hindu India (Long 1987; Maloney 1987a, b), there are enormous regional and local differences in the finer details of the ideology and

FIGURE *19.13*

UNTOUCHABLES
Caste in India must be seen from the bottom up to be understood.

practice of caste relationships. The principal source of these complications is the fact that it is not the varna but thousands of internally stratified subdivisions known as *jatis* (or subcastes) that constitute the real functional endogamous units. Moreover, even jatis of the same name (e.g., "washermen," "shoemakers," "herders," and so on) further divide into local endogamous subgroups and exogamous lineages (Klass 1979).

CASTE FROM THE TOP DOWN AND BOTTOM UP

There are two very different views of the Hindu caste system. The view that predominates among Westerners is that which conforms largely to the emics of the top-ranking Brahman caste. According to this view, each caste and subcaste has a hereditary occupation that guarantees its members basic subsistence and job security. The lower castes render vital services to the upper castes. Hence, the upper castes know they cannot get along without the lower castes and do not abuse them. In times of crisis, the upper castes will extend emergency assistance in the form of food or loans. Moreover, since the Hindu religion gives everyone a convincing explanation of why some are inferior and others superior, members of lower castes do not resent being regarded as a source of pollution and defilement and have no interest in changing the status of their caste in the local or regional hierarchy (Dumont 1970).

The other view—the view from the bottom up—makes the Indian caste system hard to distinguish from the racial, ethnic, and cultural minorities with which Westerners are familiar. Critics of the top-down view point out that whites in the United States once insisted that the Bible justified slavery and that blacks were well treated, contented with their lot in life, and not interested in changing their status. According to Joan Mencher, who has worked and lived among the untouchable castes of southern India, the error in the top-down view is just as great in India as in the United States. Mencher reports that the lowest castes are not satisfied with their station in life and do not believe they are treated fairly by their caste superiors. As for the security allegedly provided by the monopoly over such professions as smiths, washermen, barbers, potters, and so on, such occupations taken together never engaged more than 10 to 15 percent of the total Hindu population. Caste professions never provided basic subsistence for the majority of the members of most castes. Among the Chamars, for example, who are known as leatherworkers, only a small portion of the caste engages in leatherwork. In the countryside, almost all Chamars are a source of cheap agricultural labor. When questioned about their low station in life, many of Mencher's low-caste informants explained that they had to be dependent on the other castes since they had no land of their own. Did landowners in times of extreme need or crisis actually give free food and assistance to their low-caste dependents? "To my informants, both young and old, this sounds like a fairytale" (Mencher 1974b).

Anthropological studies of actual village life in India have yielded a picture of caste relationships drastically opposed to the ideals posited in Hindu theology (Carroll 1977). One of the most important discoveries is that local jatis recurrently try to raise their ritual status. Such attempts usually take place

as part of a general process by which local ritual status is adjusted to actual local economic and political power. There may be low-ranking subcastes that passively accept their lot in life as a result of their karma assignment; such groups, however, tend to be wholly lacking in the potential for economic and political mobility. "But let opportunities for political and economic advance appear barely possible and such resignation is likely to vanish more quickly than one might imagine" (Orans 1968:878).

One of the symptoms of this underlying propensity for jatis to redefine their ritual position to conform with their political and economic potential is a widespread lack of agreement over the shape of local ritual hierarchies as seen by inhabitants of the same village, town, or region. This is true of even the lowest "untouchables" (Khare 1984).

The study of caste "dissensus" has long been a central concern of village Indian researchers (Barber 1968). Kathleen Gough (1959) indicates that in villages of South India, the middle reaches of the caste hierarchy may have as many as 15 castes whose positions in the caste hierarchy are ambiguous or in dispute. Different individuals and families even in the same caste give different versions of the rank order of these groups. Elsewhere, even the claims of Brahman subcastes to ritual superiority are openly contested (Srinivas 1955). The conflict among jatis concerning their ritual position may involve prolonged litigation in the local courts and if not resolved may lead to violence and bloodshed (see Berreman 1975; Cohn 1955).

Contrary to the view that these features of caste are a response to the recent "modernization" of India, Karen Leonard (1978) has shown that similarly fluid and flexible individual, family, and subcaste strategies date back at least to the eighteenth century. According to Leonard, the internal organization and external relationships of the Kayastks, originally a caste of scribes and record keepers, shifted continuously to adapt to changing economic, political, and demographic circumstances. Kayastks attempted to better their lot in life as individuals, as families, and as subcastes according to changing opportunities. Marriage patterns and descent rules were constantly modified to provide maximum advantages with respect to government and commercial employment, and even the rule of endogamy was broken when alliances with other subcastes became useful: "Adaptability, rather than conformity to accepted Brahmanical or scholarly notions about caste, has always characterized the Kayastk marriage networks and kin groups" (Leonard 1978:294).

Another way in which Hindu castes resemble ethnic and racial minorities around the world is in their having distinctive cultural traditions. Subcastes may speak different languages or dialects, follow different kinds of descent and locality rules, have different forms of marriage, worship different gods, eat different foods, and altogether present as great a contrast in life-styles as that which exists between New Yorkers and the Zuni Indians. Moreover, many castes of India are associated with racial differences comparable to the contrast between whites and blacks in the United States.

The stratification system of India is noteworthy not merely for the presence of endogamous descent groups possessing real or imagined racial and cultural specialties: Every state-level society has such groups. It is, rather, the extraordinary profusion of such groups that merits our attention. Nonetheless, the caste system of India is fundamentally similar to that of other countries that have closed classes and numerous ethnic and racial minorities. Like the blacks in the United States or the Catholics in Northern Ireland, low castes in India resist the status accorded them, with its concomitant disabilities and discrimination, and strive for higher accorded status and its attendant advantages. High castes attempt to prevent such striving and the implied threat to their positions. In this conflict of interests lies the explosive potential of all caste societies (Berreman 1966:318).

SUMMARY

All state societies are organized into stratified groups such as classes, minorities, and castes. Stratified groups consist of people who relate to the apparatus of control in similar ways and who possess similar amounts of power over the allocation of wealth, privileges, resources, and technology. In this context, power means the ability to move and shape people and things. All state societies have at least two classes: rulers and ruled. Classes come in open and closed varieties. When closed, they resemble castes and minorities.

Gender and age hierarchies are also important forms of stratification, but they are not confined to state societies. Class differences involve both differential access to power and profound differences in life-styles. The understanding of class and all other forms of social stratification is made difficult by the failure to separate emic and etic versions of stratification hierarchies. From an etic and behavioral point

of view, classes can exist even if there is no emic recognition of their existence and even if segments of the same class compete. Ruling classes need not form permanent, hereditary, monolithic, conspiratorial organizations. Their membership can change rapidly and they may actively deny that they constitute a ruling class. Similarly, subordinate classes need not be conscious of their identity and may exist only in an etic and behavioral sense.

The understanding of the phenomenon of exploitation also depends on the distinction between emic and etic perspectives. It cannot be maintained that the mere existence of differential power, wealth, and privilege guarantees the existence of exploitation, nor that exploitation exists only when or as soon as people feel exploited. Etic criteria for exploitation focus on the acquisition of luxuries among elites based on the deprivation of necessities among commoners and perpetuation or intensification of misery and poverty.

About 40 percent of the people in the world today are members of peasant classes. Peasants are structured inferiors who farm with preindustrial technologies and pay rent or taxes. Three major varieties of peasants can be distinguished: feudal, agromanagerial, and capitalist. Their structured inferiority depends in the first case on the inability to acquire land; in the second, on the existence of a powerful managerial elite that sets production and labor quotas; and in the third, on the operation of a price market in land and labor controlled by big landlords, corporations, and banks.

Among peasant classes, an image of limited good is widespread. However, there are also contradictory values and attitudes that lead to innovations under appropriate structural and infrastructural conditions. In Tzintzuntzan, despite the image of limited good, men struggled for a chance to work as migrant laborers, and both men and women participated in a series of ill-fated development experiments in the hope of bettering their lives.

The counterpart of the image of limited good for urban subordinate classes is the culture of poverty. This concept focuses on the values and the traditions of the urban poor as an explanation for poverty. However, many of the values in the culture of poverty, such as distrust of authority, consumerism, and improvidence, are also found in more affluent classes. The irrelevance of the emphasis people place on the value of work for understanding the genesis of poverty classes can be seen in the case of Squid Cove. Newfoundlanders are known the world over for their work ethic, yet when mechanization and resource depletion left them without year-round jobs, they had no alternative but to accept welfare assistance. The broken fountain of Naples tells a similar story.

Racial and ethnic minorities and majorities are present in virtually all state societies. These groups differ from classes in having or in formerly having distinctive life-styles derived from another society, internal class differences, and a high degree of group consciousness. Minorities and majorities struggle for access to and control over the sources of wealth and power, aided or hindered by their adaptive strengths and weaknesses in relation to specific arenas of competition. Many minorities acquire the life-styles of the majority and marry exogamously without assimilating.

Neither assimilationist nor pluralist commitments may suffice to overcome the effects of segregation, discrimination, and exploitation. It can be argued that racial and ethnic chauvinism benefits the ruling class more than the ordinary members of either the minority or majority.

Social scientists usually identify a third type of stratified group known as castes. Castes are epitomized by the case of Hindu India. Traditional views of Indian castes have been dominated by top-down idealizations in which the lower castes are represented as voluntarily accepting their subordinate status. Bottom-up studies show that Indian castes struggle for upward mobility in a flexible and adaptive fashion, and that they closely resemble ethnic and racial minorities in other societies.

Chapter 20

Gender and Hierarchy

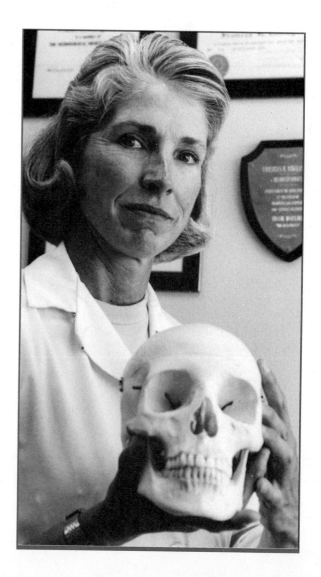

Male and female and other genders are culturally constructed categories that are subject to the same kinds of hierachical distinctions, advantages, and disabilities as classes, castes, and the other stratified groups discussed in the previous chapter. Here are some of the questions this chapter gets into: Do men and women interpret gender differences from the same perspective, or do they have different versions of who is up and who is down? Are males always dominant in public roles? Have male ethnographers underreported or ignored women's influence? Are matriarchies real or imagined? What is the effect of living in matrilineal societies on the position of women? Are men and women separate but equal in band-organized societies? Why are gender relations more equal in some agricultural societies than in others? Is there a relationship between warfare and male domination? Why is low female status so closely associated with the use of the plow? And finally, what kinds of changes in gender roles can we expect as the industrial nations continue to develop high-tech infrastructures and service and information economies?

SEX VERSUS GENDER

The etic sexual identity of human beings can be established by examining an individual's chromosomes, interior and exterior sex organs, and secondary sexual characteristics such as body build, size of breasts, and fat deposits. While all societies recognize a distinction between male and female based on some of these features, the emic definition of being male or female, or some other gender, varies considerably from one society to another. Anthropologists therefore prefer to use the term *gender* to denote the variable emic meanings associated with culturally defined sexual identities, and the phrase *gender roles* (instead of "sex roles") when referring to the expected patterns of thought and behavior that are associated with gender identities (Gilmore 1990; Jacobs and Roberts 1989; Ortner and Whitehead 1981).

Margaret Mead's (1950) study of three New Guinea tribes—the Arapesh, Mundugumor, and Tchambuli—is the classic anthropological work on the spectrum of gender roles. Mead discovered that among the Arapesh, both men and women are expected to behave in a mild, sympathetic, and cooperative manner, reminiscent of what Americans expect from an ideal mother. Among the Mundugumor, men and women are expected to be equally fierce and aggressive. Among the Tchambuli, the women shave their heads, are prone to hearty laughter, show comradely solidarity, and are aggressively efficient as food providers. Tchambuli men, on the other hand, are preoccupied with art, spend a great deal of time on their hairdos, and are always gossiping about the opposite sex. Although Mead's interpretations have been challenged as too subjective (Errington and Gewertz 1987), there is no doubt that marked contrasts in gender roles exist in different cultures.

GENDER IDEOLOGIES

In many cultures, males believe they are spiritually superior to females and that females are dangerous and polluting, weak and untrustworthy. For example, one of the most widespread of all gender ideologies has as its explicit aim the retention of a male monopoly on knowledge of the myths and rituals of human origins and of the nature of supernatural beings. This complex involves secret male initiation rites; male residence in a separate men's house (Fig. 20.1) from which women and children are excluded; masked male dancers who impersonate the gods and other spiritual beings; the bull roarer, which is said to be the voice of the gods and which is whirled about in the bush or under cover of darkness to frighten the women and uninitiated boys (see p. 393); storage of the masks, bull roarer, and other sacred paraphernalia in the men's house; threat of death or actual execution of any woman who admits to knowing the secrets of the cult; and threat of death or execution of any man who reveals the secrets to women or uninitiated boys (Gregor 1985:94ff; Hays 1988).

Ecclesiastical types of religions (see p. 397) are also characterized by a pervasive functional interconnection between male-dominated rituals and myths on the one hand and male political-religious

FIGURE *20.1*

INTERIOR OF MEN'S HOUSE, NEW GUINEA
The men use masks to terrify the women and children.

supremacy on the other. The established high priests of Rome, Greece, Mesopotamia, Egypt, ancient Israel, and the entire Muslim and Hindu world were or are men. High-ranking priestesses with autonomous control over their own temples, as in Minoan Crete, are the exception, even when the ecclesiastical cults include female deities. Males traditionally dominated the ecclesiastical organization of all the major world religions. All three chief religions of Western civilization—Christianity, Judaism, and Islam—stressed the priority of the male principle in the formation of the world. They identified the creator god as "He," and to the extent that they recognized female deities, as in Catholicism, traditionally assigned them a secondary role in myth and ritual. They all held that men were created first, and women second, out of a piece of a man (Fig. 20.2).

THE RELATIVITY OF GENDER IDEOLOGIES

How much of the male claim to spiritual superiority is believed by women? To begin with, as we have seen in Chapter 19, one must be skeptical that any subjugated group really accepts the reasons the subjugators give to justify their claims to superior status. In addition, much new evidence suggests that women have their own gender ideologies, which have not been properly recorded because earlier generations of ethnographers were primarily males and neglected or were unable to obtain the woman's point of view.

For example, the seclusion of menstruating women among the Yurok Indians of Northern Califor-

FIGURE *20.2*

RECREATED *CREATION*
(A) Michelangelo's *Creation*, from the Sistine Chapel. God, depicted as a male, creates Adam first. (B) Redrawing of the creation scene, with female God touching Eve.

BOX *20.1* ## A YUROK WOMAN'S VIEW ## OF MENSTRUAL SECLUSION A menstruating woman should isolate herself because this is the time when she is at the height of her powers. Thus, the time should not be wasted in mundane tasks and social distractions, nor should one's concentration be broken by concerns with the opposite sex. Rather, all of one's energies should be applied in concentrated meditation on the nature of one's life, "to find out the purpose of your life," and toward the "accumulation" of spiritual energy. The menstrual shelter, or room, is "like the men's sweathouse," a place where you "go into yourself and make yourself stronger." SOURCE: Buckley 1982:48–49.	**BOX *20.2*** ## A !KUNG WOMAN'S ## POINT OF VIEW Women are strong; women are important. Zhun/twa [!Kung San] men say that women are the chiefs, the rich ones, the wise ones. Because women possess something very important, something that enables men to live: their genitals. A woman can bring a man life even if he is almost dead. She can give him sex and make him alive again. If she were to refuse, he would die! If there were no women around, their semen would kill men. Did you know that? If there were only men, they would all die. Women make it possible for them to live. SOURCE: The words of Nisa, a !Kung San woman, as recorded by Marjorie Shostak (1981:288).

nia has consistently been interpreted by male ethnographers as a demonstration of the need to protect men from the pollution of menstrual blood. Only recently has it become clear that Yurok women had a completely different sense of what they were doing (Buckley 1982; Child and Child 1985). Rather than feeling that they were being confined for the benefit of Yurok men, they felt that they were enjoying a privileged opportunity to get away from the chores of everyday life, to meditate on their life goals, and to gather spiritual strength (Box 20.1). Similarly, while men may have one idea about which gender is more valuable, women may have quite a different idea.

Among the !Kung, who are generally regarded as having complementary and egalitarian gender roles, one woman at least felt that men were dependent on women far more than women were dependent on men. Men would die without women, she said (Box 20.2). As for the exclusion of women from male-centered rituals, women do not necessarily resent being excluded, because they do not attach much importance to what the men are doing with their bull roarers and masked dancing. Dorothy Counts tells how an old blind woman among the Kaliai of Papua New Guinea turned down the "honor" of being invited to remain in the village while the men performed their secret ceremonies. She left with the other women as she had always done, to feast and make lewd fun of the men's "secrets" (1985:61).

MALE BIAS: TROBRIAND REVISITED

There is much evidence, supplied principally by women ethnographers (Kaberry 1970; Mathews 1985; Sacks 1971; Sanday 1981), that the power of women has often been substantially underestimated or misconstrued by male anthropologists, who until recently were the main sources of cross-cultural data on gender roles. Even one of the greatest ethnographers, Bronislaw Malinowski, could fall short of providing a balanced view of gender roles in his classic study of the Trobriand Islanders. As discussed in Chapter 16, at harvest time in the Trobriands, brothers give their sisters' husbands gifts of yams. These yams provide much of the material basis for the political power of the Trobriand chiefs. Malinowski viewed the harvest gift as a kind of annual tribute from the wife's family to her husband, and therefore as a means of enhancing and consolidating male power. Annette Weiner has shown, however, that the harvest yams are given in the name of the wife and are actually as much a means of bolstering the value of being a woman as a means of conferring power on men. Malinowski did not record the fact that the gift of yams had to be reciprocated, and that the counter-gift had to go not to a man's wife's brother but to a man's wife. In return for the yams received in his wife's name, the Trobriand husband had to provide her with a distinct form of wealth consisting of women's skirts or bundles of pan-

FIGURE *20.3*

TROBRIAND ISLAND SAGALI
Women dominate the gift-giving display
that is part of mortuary rituals.

or eliminate their yam harvest gift if their sister cannot display and give away large quantities of bundles and skirts to relatives of the deceased. In Weiner's account, not only are men more dependent on women for their power than in Malinowski's account, but women also emerge as having far more influence in their own right. She concludes that all too often anthropologists "have allowed 'politics by men' to structure our thinking about other societies...leading us to believe erroneously that if women are not dominant in the political sphere of interaction, their power, at best, remains peripheral" (1976:228).

The distribution of power between the sexes is seldom simply a matter of women being completely at the mercy of men (or vice versa). As the Trobriand study shows, male anthropologists in the past may not have grasped the more subtle aspects of gender hierarchies. Yet, by emphasizing the ability of subordinates to manipulate the system in their favor, we must not fall into the trap of minimizing the real power differences embodied in many gender hierarchies. It is well known that slaves can sometimes outwit masters, that privates can frustrate generals, and that children can get parents to wait on them like servants. The ability to buffer the effects of institutionalized inequality is not the same as institutionalized equality.

danus and banana leaves, the materials used for making skirts. Much of a husband's economic activity is devoted to trading pigs and other valuables in order to supply his wife with large quantities of women's wealth. The skirts and bundles of leaves are publicly displayed and given away at huge funeral ceremonies known as *sagali* (which Malinowski knew about but did not describe in detail because he only paid limited attention to female culture). Weiner (1976:118) states that the sagali is one of the most important public events in Trobriand life (Fig. 20.3):

Nothing is so dramatic as women standing at a sagali surrounded by thousands of bundles. Nor can anything be more impressive than watching the deportment of women as they attend to the distribution. When women walk to the center [of the plaza] to throw down their wealth, they carry themselves with a pride as characteristic as that of any Melanesian bigman.

Failure of a husband to equip his wife with sufficient women's wealth to make a good showing at the sagali adversely affects his own prospects for becoming a big man. His brothers-in-law may reduce

GENDER HIERARCHY

Despite varying definitions of masculine and feminine, males tend in the majority of societies to be assigned more aggressive and violent roles than females (Schlegel 1972). From our previous discussions (Chs. 17 and 19) of the evolution of political organization, it is clear that males often preempt the major centers of public power and control. Headmen rather than headwomen dominate both egalitarian and stratified forms of trade and redistribution. The same male preeminence is evidenced by the Semai and Mehinacu headmen; the Solomon Island mumis and the New Guinea big men (but see Counts 1985); the Nuer leopard skin chief; the Kwakiutl, Trobriand, and Tikopian chiefs; the Bunyoro Mukama; the Inca, the pharaohs, and the emperors of China and Japan. If queens reigned, it was always as temporary holders of power that belonged to the males of the lineage. Nothing more dramatically exposes the political subordination of women than the fact that women comprise only 12.7 percent of the members of the world's legislative bodies. Fewer than 5 percent of heads of state are women (*The New York Times* 1989).

It was formerly believed that political control by women, or *matriarchy* (the opposite of *patriarchy*, or political control by men), occurred as a regular stage in the evolution of social organization. Today, virtually all anthropologists doubt the existence of matriarchies at any phase of cultural evolution (Rosaldo and Lamphere 1974:3). Claims for the existence of such societies often exaggerate the political significance of matrilineal descent and matrilocal residence. Ruby Rohrlich-Leavitt (1977:57), for example, argues that in Minoan Crete, "Women participated at least equally with men in political decision making, while in religion and social life they were supreme." This contention, however, is based on inferences from archaeological data that can be given contradictory interpretations (Ehrenberg 1989:109, 118). It seems likely that Minoan Crete was matrilineal and that women enjoyed a relatively high political status. However, the basis of Crete's economy was maritime trade and it was men, not women, who dominated this activity. Rohrlich-Leavitt contends that the Cretan matriarchy was made possible by the absence of both warfare and a male military complex. However, it seems likely that military activities were focused on naval encounters that have left little archaeologically retrievable evidence (Reed 1984).

The Iroquois of New York State are another society that has been offered as an example of a matriarchy. According to Daniel McCall (1980), women dominated both domestic and political affairs in this matrilineal, matrilocal society prior to the coming of the Europeans and the intensification of warfare (but see Albers 1989:140–142). However, McCall admits that after the arrival of the Europeans, male war chiefs dominated the tribal council. The question of Iroquois matriarchy, therefore, depends on their not being very warlike in former times. This seems doubtful because of the high correlation between matrilineal-matrilocal chiefdoms and intense external warfare (see p. 283). There is no doubt, however, that Iroquois women wielded a great deal of power in political as well as in domestic affairs (see p. 351).

The absence of matriarchies is an important fact about gender hierarchies, but its significance should not be exaggerated. It does not mean that males universally dominate females, for there are many societies in which gender roles do not involve marked inequalities.

GENDER AND EXPLOITATION

When males enjoy power advantages over females with respect to access to strategic resources (Josephides 1985), ideas about female pollution, whether shared by women or not, will in all likelihood be associated with significant deprivations and disadvantages (Goodale 1971). While the work of reinterpreting gender roles from a female point of view is pressed forward, one should not lose sight of the existence of real exploitation of women by men in both prestate and state societies.

The linking of negative stereotypes with various disadvantages has been stressed by Shirley Lindenbaum with respect to two strongly male-biased societies in which she has done fieldwork. In Bangladesh, Lindenbaum encountered an elaborate ideology of male supremacy expressed in symbols and rituals (see Box 20.3). She found similar beliefs and rituals among the Foré of highland New Guinea. In both instances, women were subject to important material deprivations. Among the Foré, pregnant women were secluded in special huts, not to celebrate and concentrate female powers but to limit them.

Her seclusion there is a sign of the half-wild condition brought on by the natural functions of her own body. Other women bring the food, for if she visited her gardens during this period of isolation she would blight all domesticated crops. Nor should she send food to her husband: ingesting food she had touched would make him feel weak, catch a cold, age prematurely. [Lindenbaum 1979:129]

If a Foré woman gives birth to a deformed or stillborn child, the woman is held solely responsible. Her husband and the men of the hamlet denounce her, accuse her of trying to obstruct male authority, and kill one of her pigs. Among the Foré as among many other New Guinea societies, men appropriate the best sources of meat for themselves. The men argue that women's animal foods—frogs, small game, and insects—would make men sick. These prejudices can have lethal effects. Throughout New Guinea, they are associated with much higher death rates for young girls than for young boys (Buchbinder 1977). The same lethal results are evident in Bangladesh:

The male child receives preferential nutrition. With his father he eats first, and if there is a choice, luxury foods or scarce foods are given to him rather than to his female siblings. The result is a Bengalese population with a preponderance of males, and a demographic picture in which the mortality rate for females under 5 years of age is in some years 50% higher than that for males. [Lindenbaum 1975:143]

SEXUAL SYMBOLISM IN BANGLADESH

BOX *20.3*

Men are associated with the right, preferred side of things, women with the left. Village practitioners state that a basic physiological difference between the sexes makes it necessary to register a man's pulse in his right wrist, a woman's in her left, and they invariably examine patients in this way. Most villagers wear amulets to avert illness caused by evil spirits; men tie the amulet to the right upper arm, women to the left. Similarly, palmists and spiritualists read the right hands of men and the left hands of women. In village dramas, where both male and female parts are played by male actors, the audience may identify men gesturing with the right arm, women with the left. During religious celebrations there are separate entrances at such public places as the tombs of Muslim saints or Hindu images, the right avenue being reserved for men and the left for women. In popular belief, girls are said to commence walking by placing the left foot forward first, men the right.

In some instances, this right-left association indicates more than the social recognition of physiological difference, carrying additional connotations of prestige, honour and authority. Women who wish to behave respectfully to their husbands say they should, ideally, remain to the left side while eating, sitting and lying in bed. The same mark of respect should be shown also to all social superiors: to the rich, and in present times to those who are well educated.

Thus, the right-left dichotomy denotes not only male-female but also authority-submission. It also has connotations of good-bad and purity-pollution. Muslims consider the right side to be the side of good augury, believing that angels dwell on the right shoulder to record good deeds in preparation for the Day of Judgment, while on the left side, devils record misdeeds. The left side is also associated with the concept of pollution. Islam decrees that the left hand be reserved for cleansing the anus after defecation. It must never, therefore, be used for conveying food to the mouth, or for rinsing the mouth with water before the proscribed daily prayers.

SOURCE: Lindenbaum 1977:142.

VARIATIONS IN GENDER HIERARCHIES: HUNTER-GATHERERS

In the words of Eleanor Leacock (1978:247), we cannot go from the proposition that "women are subordinate as regards political authority in most societies" to "women are subordinate in all respects in all societies." The very notions of "equality" and "inequality" may represent an ethnocentric misunderstanding of the kinds of gender roles that exist in many societies. Leacock (1978:225) does not dispute the fact that when "unequal control over resources and subjugation by class and by sex developed," it was women who in general became subjugated to men (recognizing, of course, that the degree of subjugation varied depending on local ecological, economic, and political conditions). In the absence of classes and the state, Leacock argues that gender roles were merely different, not unequal. There is certainly much evidence to indicate that power of any sort, whether of men over men or men over women, was trivial or nonexistent in many (but not all) band and village so-cieties, for reasons discussed in Chapter 17. Writing of her fieldwork among the Montagnais-Naskapi foragers of Labrador, Leacock (1983:116) notes, "They gave me insight into a level of respect and consideration for the individuality of others, regardless of sex, that I had never before experienced."

In his study of the forest-dwelling Mbuti of Zaire, Colin Turnbull (1982) also found a high level of cooperation and mutual understanding between the sexes, with considerable authority and power vested in women. Despite his skills with bow and arrow, the Mbuti male does not see himself as superior to his wife. He "sees himself as the hunter, but then he could not hunt without a wife, and although hunting is more exciting than being a beater or a gatherer, he knows that the bulk of his diet comes from the foods prepared by the women" (1982:153).

Marjorie Shostak's (1981) biography of Nisa shows the !Kung to be another foraging society in which nearly egalitarian relationships between the sexes prevail. Shostak states that the !Kung do not show any preference for male children over female children. In matters relating to child rearing, both parents guide their offspring, and a mother's word carries about the same weight as a father's. Mothers play a major role in deciding whom their children will marry, and after marriage, !Kung couples live near the wife's family as often as the husband's. Women dispose of whatever food they had and bring back to camp what they see fit.

All in all !Kung women have a striking degree of autonomy over their own and their children's lives. Brought up to respect their own importance in community life, !Kung women become multifaceted adults and are likely to be competent and assertive as well as nurturant and cooperative. [Shostak 1981:246]

However, one should not lose sight of the fact that many hunter-gatherers do not have equal gender roles. This seems to have been especially true of the Aborigines of Australia (Burbank 1989; Goodale 1971). In northern Queensland, for example, polygyny was common, some men acquiring as many as four wives. Men discriminated against women in the distribution of food. A man "often keeps the animal food for himself, while the woman has to depend principally on vegetables for herself and her child." The sexual double standard prevailed: Men beat or killed their wives for adultery, but wives did not have similar recourse. Furthermore, the division of labor between the sexes was anything but equal, with women doing most of the drudge work (D. Harris 1987).

GENDER HIERARCHIES IN MATRILINEAL SOCIETIES

While matrilineal, matrilocal societies should not be confused with matriarchies, women in matrilineal societies often dominated domestic life and exercised important prerogatives in political affairs. From their palisaded villages in upstate New York, the matrilocal and matrilineal Iroquois dispatched armies of up to 500 men to raid targets as far away as Quebec and Illinois. On returning to his native land, the Iroquois warrior joined his wife and children at their hearth in a village longhouse. The affairs of this communal dwelling were directed by a senior woman who was a close maternal relative of the man's wife. It was this matron who organized the work that the women of the longhouse performed at home and in the fields. She took charge of storing harvested crops and drawing on them as needed. When husbands were not off on some sort of expedition—absences of a year were common—they slept and ate in the female-headed longhouses but had virtually no control over how their wives lived and worked. If a hus-

band was bossy or uncooperative, the matron might at any time order him to pick up his blanket and get out, leaving his children behind to be taken care of by his wife and the other women of the longhouse.

Turning to public life, the formal apex of political power among the Iroquois was the Council of Elders, consisting of elected male chiefs from different villages. The longhouse matrons nominated the members of this council and could prevent the seating of the men they opposed. But they did not serve on the council itself. Instead, they influenced the council's decisions by exercising control over the domestic economy. If a proposed action was not to their liking, the longhouse matrons could withhold the stored foods, wampum belts, feather work, moccasins, skins, and furs under their control. Warriors could not embark on foreign adventures unless the women filled their bearskin pouches with the mixture of dried corn and honey men ate while on the trail. Religious festivals could not take place, either, unless the women agreed to release the necessary stores. Even the Council of Elders did not convene if the women decided to withhold food for the occasion (J. Brown 1975; Gramby 1977).

WOMEN IN WEST AFRICA

Favorable female gender relationships among chiefdoms and states occurred in the forested areas of West Africa. Among the Yoruba, Ibo, Igbo, and Dahomey, women had their own fields and grew their own crops. They dominated the local markets and could acquire considerable wealth from trade. To get married, West African men had to pay bride-price—iron hoes, goats, cloth, and, in more recent times, cash—a transaction which in itself indicated (p. 266) that the groom and his family and the bride and her family agreed that the bride was a very valuable person and that her parents and relatives would not "give her away" without being compensated for her economic and reproductive capabilities (Bossen 1988; Schlegel and Eloul 1988). West Africans believed that to have many daughters was to be rich.

Although men practiced polygyny, they could do so only if they consulted their senior wives and obtained their permission. Women, for their part, had considerable freedom of movement to travel to market towns, where they often had extramarital affairs. Furthermore, in many West African chiefdoms and states, women themselves could pay bride-price and "marry" other women. Among the Dahomey (see p. 264), a female husband built a house for her "wife" and arranged for a male consort to get her pregnant. By paying bride-price for several such "wives," an ambitious woman could establish control over a busy compound and become rich and powerful.

West African women also achieved high status outside the domestic sphere. They belonged to female clubs and secret societies, participated in village councils, and mobilized en masse to seek redress against mistreatment by men.

Among the Igbo of Nigeria, women met in council to discuss matters that affected their interests as traders, farmers, or wives. A man who violated the woman's market rules, let his goats eat a woman's crops, or persistently mistreated his wife ran the risk of mass retaliation. The miscreant would be awakened in the middle of the night by a crowd of women banging on his hut. They danced lewd dances, sang songs mocking his manhood, and used his backyard as a latrine until he promised to mend his ways. They called it "sitting-on-a-man" (Van Allen 1972).

The supreme rulers of these West African chiefdoms and states were almost always males. However, their mothers and sisters and other female relatives occupied offices that gave women considerable power over both men and women. In some Yoruba kingdoms, the king's female relatives directed the principal religious cults and managed the royal compounds. Anyone wanting to arrange rituals, hold festivals, or call up communal labor brigades had to deal with these powerful women first, before gaining access to the king. Among the Yoruba, women occupied an office known as "mother of all women," a kind of queen over females, who coordinated the voice of women in government, held court, settled quarrels, and decided what positions women should take on the opening and maintenance of markets, levying of taxes and tolls, declarations of war, and other important public issues. And in at least two Yoruba kingdoms, Ijesa and Ondo, the office of queen-over-women may have been as powerful as the office of king-over-men. Every grade of male chief under the king-over-men had a corresponding grade of female chief under the queen-over-women. The king-over-men and the queen-over-women met separately with their respective councils of chiefs to discuss matters of state. They then conferred with each other. No action was taken unless both councils were in agreement (Awé 1977; Hart 1985; Sudarkasa 1973).

WOMEN IN INDIA

In contrast to couples in West Africa, those in northern India express a strong preference for sons over daughters. As Barbara Miller (1981, 1987a, b) has shown, the women of India are an "endangered sex"

FIGURE *20.4*

INDIAN DOWRY
Indian groom displays the gifts from his bride's parents at their wedding.

as a result of the high rate of female infant and child death caused by parental neglect. A north Indian man who had many daughters regarded them as an economic calamity rather than an economic bonanza. Instead of receiving bride-price, the north Indian father paid each daughter's husband a dowry (see p. 267) consisting of jewelry, cloth, or cash (Fig. 20.4). In recent years, disgruntled or merely avaricious husbands have taken to demanding supplementary dowries. This has led to a spate of "bride-burnings" in which wives who fail to supply additional compensation are doused with kerosene and set on fire by husbands who pretend that the women killed themselves in cooking accidents (Crossette 1989; Sharma 1983).

North Indian culture has always been extremely unfriendly to widows. In the past, a widow was given the opportunity of joining her dead husband on his funeral pyre. Facing a life of seclusion with no hope of remarrying, subject to food taboos that brought them close to starvation, and urged on by the family priest and their husbands' relatives, many women chose fiery death rather than widowhood.

CAUSES OF VARIATION IN GENDER HIERARCHIES

Warfare is a major factor influencing the status of women in band and village societies. Since males in every human population on average have a physical advantage over females (Gray and Wolfe 1980:442; Percival and Quinkert 1987:136) with respect to the force they can exert with a club; the distance they can throw a spear, shoot an arrow, or hurl a stone; and the speed with which they can run short distances (see Table 20.1), males constitute the main fighting force in every known society (see Box 20.4 and Fig. 20.5). Males, therefore, are trained to be fierce and aggressive and to kill with a weapon far more often than women (Fig. 20.6). The training, combat experience, and the monopoly that men possess over the weapons of war empower them to dominate women. Thus the gender-equal !Kung and Mbuti seldom if ever engage in warfare, whereas the Australian Aborigines and other hunter-gatherers with marked gender hierarchies do engage in frequent warfare. Brian Hayden (Hayden et al. 1986) has tested the theory that wherever conditions favored the develop-

TABLE *20.1* WORLD RECORDS		
Event	Men (min:sec)	Women (min:sec)
100-meter dash	0:09.92	0:10.49
1 mile	3:46.32	4:15.71
400-meter hurdle	0:47.02	0:52.94[a]
	(ft) (in.)	(ft) (in.)
High jump	8 0	6 10

[a]Women's hurdles are set lower than men's.
SOURCE: *The World Almanac & Book of Facts 1990,b.*

ment of warfare among hunter-gatherers, the political and domestic subordination of women increased. Using a sample of 33 hunter-gatherer societies, he found that the correlation between low status for

BOX *20.4*

THE BODY AND CULTURE

Like everything else about human beings, the anatomical and physiological differences between men and women that are important for assigning combatant roles to males in preindustrial warfare are a product of the interaction of genetic and cultural influences. Feminist author Anne Oakley (1985:28) has shown that the shape and strength of the human body can be greatly altered by the type of work each sex performs and the quality and quantity of food they consume. In some societies such as Bali, where men and women perform similar kinds of work, they are even difficult to tell apart. Indeed, theoretically, the strength and swiftness differences between the sexes could not only be effaced but completely reversed by sufficiently favoring the physical training and diet of women and by drastically curtailing male activities and food consumption (see Fig. 20.5). However, the point being made here is that any band or village society that chose to make its women physically better suited for hand-to-hand combat than its men would not survive combat with groups that invested primarily in conditioning its males for combat; genetic differences still guarantee that a maximum of

investment in males will produce a brawnier and swifter combat team than a maximum investment in females.

FIGURE *20.5*
FEMALE BODYBUILDING CHAMPION
Gladys Portugese celebrates her victory at Madison Square Garden.

FIGURE *20.6*

AGGRESSIVE MALE GAMES

There is evidence of a close correlation between warfare and aggressive male sports.
(A) The sporting life in England—rugby; **(B)** the gentle art of football,
in the United States; **(C)** mock combat in Indonesia; **(D)** Afghan
game requires daring feats of horsemanship.

(A)

(C)

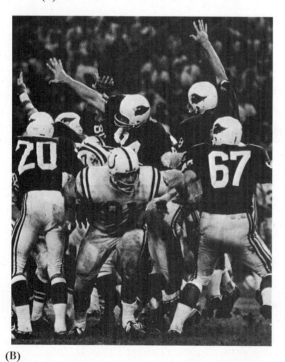

(B)

(D)

females and deaths due to armed combat was "unexpectedly high."

The reasons for overwhelming male dominance in societies where warfare is pronounced seem relatively straightforward. The lives of group members depend to a greater degree on males and male assessment of social and political conditions. Male tasks during times of warfare are simply more critical to the survival of everyone than is female work. Moreover, male aggressiveness and the use of force engendered by warfare and fighting renders female opposition to male decisions not only futile but dangerous. [Ibid.:458]

A similar relationship holds between the intensity of warfare and male dominance among village peoples and simple patrilineal chiefdoms. Thus the Yanomamö, with their high level of warfare, are well-known for strong male biases and their practice of female infanticide. Eastern highland New Guinea, noted for its male-centered communal cults and physical mistreatment of women, is also famous for its incessant warfare. As Daryl Feil (1987:69) puts it, war was "general, pervasive, and perpetual." The treatment of women by men was proportionately brutal:

Women were severely punished for adultery by having burning sticks thrust into their vaginas, or they were killed by their husbands; they were whipped with cane if they spoke out of turn or presumed to offer their opinions at public gatherings; and were physically abused in marital arguments. Men could never be seen to be weak or soft in dealings with women. Men do not require specific incidents or reasons to abuse or mistreat women; it is part of the normal course of events; indeed, in ritual and myth, it is portrayed as the essential order of things. [Ibid.:203]

Finally, as we have seen (p. 304), there is a strong correlation between unbalanced gender ratios and the practice of warfare (Divale and Harris 1976) among prestate societies in general. We must remember, however, that the correlation between intense warfare and female subordination does not hold in the case of matrilocal and matrilineal societies where warfare is practiced against distant foes, and forestalls rather than encourages male control over production and domestic life (see p. 283).

The correlation between frequency and intensity of warfare and male dominance also does not

hold for advanced chiefdoms and states. While stratified societies have bigger armies and wage war on a much grander scale than classless societies, the effect of warfare on women is less direct and generally less severe than in bands and villages (but not as favorable as in matrilineal societies). What makes the difference is that in state societies, soldiering is a specialty reserved for professionals. Most males no longer train from infancy to be killers of men, or even killers of animals (since there are few large animals left to hunt, except in royal preserves). Instead, they themselves became unarmed peasants and are no less terrified of professional warriors than their wives and children. Warfare does create a demand for suitably macho men to be trained as warriors, but in state societies, most women do not have to deal with husbands whose capacity for violence has been honed in battle. Nor does women's survival depend on training their sons to be cruel and aggressive. Female status in advanced chiefdoms and states therefore depends less on the intensity, frequency, and scale of warfare than on whether the anatomical differences between men and women endow males or females with a decisive advantage in carrying out some crucial phase of production.

HOES, PLOWS, AND GENDER HIERARCHIES

The contrasting gender hierarchies of West Africa and northern India are correlated with two very different forms of agriculture. In West Africa, the main agricultural implement was not an ox-drawn plow, as in the plains of northern India, but a short-handled hoe (Goody 1976). The West Africans did not use plows because in their humid, shady habitat, the tsetse fly made it difficult to rear plow animals. Besides, West African soils do not dry out and become hard-packed as in the arid plains of northern India, so that women using nothing but hoes were as capable as men of preparing fields and had no need for men to grow, harvest, or market their crops. In northern India, on the other hand, men maintained a monopoly over the use of ox-drawn plows. These implements were indispensable for breaking the long dry season's hard-packed soils. Men achieved this monopoly for essentially the same reasons that they achieved a monopoly over the weapons of hunting and warfare: Their greater bodily strength enabled them to be 15 to 20 percent more efficient than women. This advantage often means the difference between a family's survival and starvation, especially during prolonged dry spells when every fraction of an inch to which a plowshare penetrates beneath the surface and every minute less it takes a pair of oxen to complete a furrow are crucial for retaining moisture. As Morgan Maclachlan (1983) found in a study of the sexual division of labor in India, the question is not whether peasant women could be trained to manage a plow and a pair of oxen but whether in most families, training men to do it leads to larger and more secure harvests (Fig 20.7).

Further support for this theory can be found in the more female-favorable gender roles that characterize southern India and much of Southeast Asia and Indonesia (Peletz 1987). In these regions, noted for their strong matrifocal and complementary gender relationships, rice rather than wheat is the principal crop, and the principal function of traction animals in agriculture is puddling (softening and mixing the mud of rice paddies in preparation for planting) rather than plowing. This operation can be performed as efficiently by women and children as by men. Moreover, the operation of transplanting, which is as crucial as that of plowing or puddling, can also be carried out by women at least as efficiently as by men.

Is a factor as simple as male control over plowing sufficient to explain female infanticide, dowry, and widows throwing themselves onto their husbands' funeral pyres? Not if one thinks only of the direct effects of animal-drawn implements on agriculture itself. In evolutionary perspective, this male specialty was linked to a chain of additional specializations that cumulatively do point to a plausible explanation of many features of the depressed status of women in northern India as well as in other agrarian state societies with similar forms of agriculture in Europe, southwestern Asia, and northern China. Wherever men gained control over the plow, they became the master of large traction animals. Wherever they yoked these animals to the plow, they also yoked them to all sorts of carts and vehicles. Therefore, with the invention of the wheel and its diffusion across Eurasia, men yoked animals to the principal means of land transport. This gave them control over the transportation of crops to market, and from there it was a short step to dominating local and long-distance trade and commerce. With the invention of money, men became the first merchants. As trade and commerce increased in importance, records had to be kept, and it was to men active in trade and commerce that the task fell of keeping these records. Therefore, with the invention of writing and arithmetic, men came to the fore as the first scribes and accountants. By extension, men became the literate sex; they did reading, writing, and arithmetic. Therefore, men, not women, were the first historically known philosophers, theologians, and mathematicians in the early agrarian states of Europe, southwestern Asia, India, and China.

All of these indirect effects of male control over traction animals acted in concert with the continuing gender-role effects of warfare. By dominating the armed forces, men gained control over the highest administrative branches of government, including state religions. And the continuing need to recruit male warriors made the social construction of aggressive manhood a focus of national policy in every known state and empire. It is therefore no wonder that at the dawn of industrial times, men dominated politics, religion, art, science, law, industry, and commerce, as well as the armed forces, wherever animal-drawn plows had been the basic means of agricultural production.

GENDER AND INDUSTRIALISM

During the smokestack phase of industrialism, women had little opportunity to overthrow the heritage of the classic Eurasian gender hierarchy. After an initial period of intense exploitation in factory employment, married women were excluded from industrial work and were confined to domestic tasks in order to assure the reproduction of the working class. Factory-employed male breadwinners collaborated in this effort in order to preserve their privileges while fending off the threat that women posed to the male wage rate. A decisive break came after World War II with the shift in the mode of production

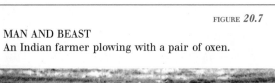

FIGURE *20.7*

MAN AND BEAST
An Indian farmer plowing with a pair of oxen.

FIGURE *20.8*

BREAKING THE GENDER BARRIER
(A) Neurosurgeon Frances Conley; (B) cowgirl; (C) construction engineer.

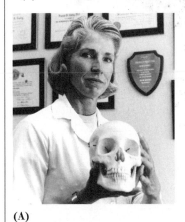

(A)   (B)   (C)

to information and service production. This led to a call-up of literate women into low-paid, nonunionized information and service jobs, the feminization of the labor force, a fall in fertility rates to historic lows, and the destruction of the male breadwinner family (Harris 1981).

Today's hyperindustrial mode of production is almost totally indifferent to the anatomical and physiological differences between men and women (except to the extent that women still may wish to have children). It is no accident that women's rights are rising as the strategic value of masculine brawn declines. Who needs extra muscle power when the decisive processes of production take place in automated factories or while people sit at desks in computerized offices? Men continue to fight for the retention of their old privileges, but they have been routed from one bastion after another as women fill the need for service and information workers by offering competent performance at lower wage rates than males. Even more than the market women of West Africa, women in today's advanced industrial societies have moved toward gender parity based on ability to earn a living without being dependent on husbands or other males (Fig. 20.8). We will return to the subject of modern-day gender roles in Chapter 26.

SUMMARY

Human sexual identity is mediated by culturally constructed gender roles. The gender roles of Western society in which men are "masculine" and women

are "feminine" are not representative of the variations that occur around the world.

In many cultures, males believe that they are spiritually superior to females and that women are a source of pollution. These beliefs are present in the male-centered religions of Western civilization, which hold that women were created out of a piece of man. Women often do not accept these male versions of gender roles, as illustrated by the examples of the Yurok and Kaliai. Moreover, as demonstrated in the restudy of the Trobriand Islanders, male ethnographers have often underestimated the etic power of women. Nonetheless, men have more frequently dominated women while the mirror image of patriarchy—matriarchy—is unknown. As illustrated by the consequences of gender roles in Bangladesh and the Foré, antifemale prejudices are often associated with high rates of illness and death among women.

Gender roles among hunter-gatherers are often egalitarian, as among the !Kung, Naskapi, and Mbuti, but in other hunter-gatherers—for example, the Queensland Aborigines—males are dominant. Female-favorable gender roles are also found in many matrilineal societies such as the Iroquois, but perhaps the most powerful women in preindustrial societies lived in West Africa among the Yoruba, Ibo, Igbo, and Dahomey. In contrast, the male-dominant gender roles of northern India, like those of Bangladesh, endanger the survival and well-being of females, especially when they are very young or very old.

Variations in gender hierarchies among hunter-gatherers and village societies are closely correlated with the frequency and intensity of warfare carried out against nearby groups. By contrast, long-distance warfare between village groups tends to promote matrilocality and a higher status for women. At the advanced chiefdom and state levels, only specialist warriors receive training for armed combat; consequently, variations in gender hierarchies depend less on the frequency and intensity of warfare than on the significance of the anatomical differences of men and women for carrying out certain crucial agricultural tasks. Underlying the contrast between West African gender relations and those of northern India are two different modes of agricultural production: hoe agriculture and plow agriculture, respectively. Women can use hoes as effectively as men, which leads to their controlling their own food supply, being involved in trade and markets, having an equal say in the management of household affairs, and wielding considerable political power. In northern India, men outperform women in the critical task of preparing hardpacked soils for planting by means of ox-drawn plows, leading to the preference for sons, female infanticide,

dowry, and the mistreatment of widows, in contrast to the preferences for daughters, bride-price, and the levirate in West Africa.

Further consequences of the Eurasian animal-drawn plow complex include male control over trade, accounting, mathematics, literacy, and church and state bureaucracies, as well as continued control over the army. Southern India, Southeast Asia, and Indonesia, with their contrastive use of animals for puddling rather than plowing rice paddies and their more female-favorable gender roles, lend additional support to this theory.

In the smokestack phase of the industrial revolution, married women were excluded from factory work and confined to the home as dependents in male breadwinner families. After World War II, male muscular aptitudes were no longer significant in the emerging information and service economy; women entered the labor force in unprecedented numbers, leading to increased independence from men and radical changes in gender roles, gender hierarchy, and family life.

Chapter 21

Sexuality

There is no single pattern of human sexuality. As in all other domains of human life, the definition of what is normal or natural sex varies drastically from one culture to another. Categories such as "gay" and "straight" as defined in Western cultures are not meaningful elsewhere. Homosexual behavior occurs to some extent in every society, but is as variegated as heterosexual behavior. This chapter is not intended either to change or to reinforce anyone's sexual preferences and practices. However, when we begin to see that our own preferences and activities seem strange to others, perhaps we will be more tolerant of those who seem strange to us.

HUMAN SEXUALITY

Because of the pervasive effects of culturally constructed gender roles, knowledge about human sexuality that is gained from the study of people living in one culture can never be taken as representative of human sexual behavior in general (Frayser 1985; Gregersen 1982). All aspects of sexual relationships, from infantile experiences through courtship and marriage, exhibit an immense amount of cultural variation (see Box 21.1). For example, consider the different modes of sexuality found among the Mangaians of Polynesia as compared with those of Hindu India.

SEX IN MANGAIA

According to Donald Marshall (1971), Mangaian boys and girls never hold hands in public nor do Mangaian husbands and wives embrace in public. Brothers and sisters must never be seen together. Mothers and daughters and fathers and sons do not discuss sexual matters with one another. And yet both sexes engage in intercourse well before puberty. After puberty, both sexes enjoy an intense premarital sex life. Girls receive varied nightly suitors in the parents' house, and boys compete with their rivals to see how many orgasms they can achieve. Mangaian girls are not interested in romantic protestations, extensive petting, or foreplay. Sex is not a reward for masculine affection; rather, affection is the reward for sexual fulfillment:

Sexual intimacy is not achieved by first demonstrating personal affection; the reverse is true. The Mangaian... girl takes an immediate demonstration of sexual virility and masculinity as the first test of her partner's desire for her and as the reflection of her own desirability.... Personal affection may or may not result from acts of sexual intimacy, but the latter are requisite to the former—exactly the reverse of the ideals of Western society. [Marshall 1971:181]

BOX *21.1*

A SEXY SPECIES

Humans are one of the sexiest species in the animal kingdom. The human penis is longer and thicker than that of any other primate, and the testes are heavier than in gorilla or orang. Our kind spends more time in precopulatory courtship, and copulatory sessions last longer than among other primates. The capacity for female orgasm, while not unique to humans as once thought, is highly developed. Copulatory frequency is not as high as among chimpanzees, but then again humans confront the greatest amount of socially imposed restrictions on sexuality. These restrictions lead to peculiarly human nocturnal emissions among males—wet dreams—and to rates of masturbation among both human males and females that are matched only in primates kept in zoos or laboratories. The human male's psychological preoccupation with sex has no parallel in other species. American adolescents aged twelve to nineteen report thinking about sex on average every five minutes during their waking hours, and even at age fifty, American males think about sex several times a day.

SOURCE: Harris 1989:180.

According to a consensus of Marshall's informants, males sought to reach orgasm at least once every night, and women expected each episode to last at least 15 minutes. They agreed on the data presented in Table 21.1 as indicative of typical male sexual activity.

| MANGAIAN MALE SEXUALITY | | | TABLE *21.1* |
Approximate age	Average number of orgasms per night	Average number of nights per week	
18	3	7	
28	2	5–6	
38	1	3–4	
48	1	2–3	

SOURCE: Marshall 1971:123.

FIGURE *21.1*

HINDU EROTIC ART
Erotic themes are common in the sacred art of India. Shown, Lord Shiva and Parvati.

SEX IN INDIA

A very different attitude toward sexual activity appears to be characteristic of Hindu India. There is a widespread belief among Hindu men (and shared by men in many other societies; see p. 363) that semen is a source of strength and that it should not be squandered.

Everyone knew that semen was not easily found; it takes forty days and forty drops of blood to make one drop of semen....Everyone was agreed...that the semen is ultimately stored in a reservoir in the head, whose capacity is twenty tolas (6.8 ounces).... Celibacy was the first requirement of true fitness, because every sexual orgasm meant the loss of a quantity of semen, laboriously formed. [Carstairs 1967; quoted in Nag 1972:235]

Contrary to popular stereotypes concerning Hindu eroticism (Fig. 21.1), there is evidence that coital frequency among Hindus is considerably less than among U.S. whites in comparable age groups. Moni Nag gives a summary (Table 21.2) of average weekly coital frequency for Hindu women and for white U.S. women. It is also clear, again contrary to popular impressions, that India's high level of fertility and population growth is not the result of sexual overindulgence caused by "not having anything else to do for entertainment at night."

MALE HOMOSEXUALITY

Attitudes toward homosexuality range from horror to chauvinistic enthusiasm (Box 21.2). Knowledge of male homosexuality is more extensive than knowledge of female homosexuality. Several cultures studied by anthropologists incorporate

| AMERICAN AND HINDU FEMALE COITAL FREQUENCY | | TABLE *21.2* |
Age group	White U.S. average weekly	Hindu average weekly
10–14	—	0.4
15–19	3.7	1.5
20–24	3.0	1.9
25–29	2.6	1.8
30–34	2.3	1.1
35–39	2.0	0.7
40–44	1.7	0.2
Over 44	1.3	0.3

SOURCE: Adapted from Nag 1972:235.

BOX *21.2*

SEXUAL PREFERENCES AND AVERSIONS

Given the many ways in which humans separate sexual pleasure from unwanted reproduction, the widespread occurrence of homosexual behavior should come as no surprise. More surprising are the many people who masturbate themselves or their partners, who take birth control pills, use condoms and spermicidal jellies, have abortions, and practice various gymnastic forms of noncoital heterosexuality, but who condemn and ridicule homosexual behavior on the grounds that is "unnatural." Nor does the linkage between homosexual behavior and AIDS render the fierce prejudices against those who find pleasure in homophile or lesbian relationships any less irrational. Were it not for medical advances, good clean "natural" heterosexual men and women would still be dying in vast numbers from syphilis.

To say that homosexuality is as natural as heterosexuality is not to say that the majority of men and women find same-sex individuals to be as arousing and erotically satisfying as members of the opposite sex. But there is no evidence that people endowed with opposite-sex preferences are also endowed with a predisposition to loathe and avoid same-sex relationships. And this holds the other way as well. That is, it is doubtful that the small numbers of humans who are predisposed to prefer same-sex relationships are born with phobic tendencies toward the opposite sex.

Humans have sex to spare. We are unfettered by breeding seasons or estrus cycles. Human males possess a penis that is the largest and testicles that are next to the largest among the primates. Human females possess a clitoris whose prominence surpasses all others except that of some chimpanzees. Our skins are uniquely glabrous and more erotically sensitive than that of any furry ape. If pygmy chimps engage in daily heterosexual encounters plus frequent bouts of genitogenital rubbing and homosexual pseudocopulatory thrusting, why should one expect *Homo sapiens,* the sexiest and most imaginative of the primates, to be any less versatile? In truth, it takes a great deal of training and conditioning, parental disapproval, social ridicule, threats of fiery hell, repressive legislation, and, now, the threat of AIDS to convert our kind's bountiful sexual endowment into an aversion against even the mere thought of homosexual congress. Most societies—about 64 percent, according to one survey—don't make the effort to create this aversion and either tolerate or actually encourage some degree of same-sex along with opposite-sex erotic behavior. If one includes clandestine and noninstitutionalized practices, then it is safe to say that homosexual behavior occurs to some extent in every human population. But, homosexual behavior in different cultural contexts is as variegated as heterosexual behavior. I think this astonishing variety testifies not only to the protean potential of human sexual needs and drives, but also to the even more protean ability of human cultures to sever the connection between sexual pleasure and reproduction.

SOURCE: Adapted from Harris 1989:236–237.

male homosexuality into their systems for developing masculine male personalities. For example, among native Americans of the Great Plains certain men donned female attire and dedicated themselves to providing sexual favors to great warriors. Known as *berdache,* these homosexuals were regarded as a separate gender and were honored in turn (Fig. 21.2). For a warrior to be served by a berdache was proof of manliness (Callender and Kochems 1983; Williams 1986).

Similarly, among the Azande of the Sudan, also renowned for their prowess in warfare, the un-married warrior-age grade, which lived apart from women for several years, had homosexual relations with the boys of the age grade of warrior apprentices (Fig. 21.3). After their experiences with "boy-wives," the warriors graduated to the next age status, got married, and had many children (Evans-Pritchard 1970).

Male homosexuality was highly ritualized in many New Guinea and Melanesian societies. It was ideologically justified in a manner that has no equivalent in Western notions of sexuality. It was not viewed as a matter of individual preference but as a social

FIGURE *21.2*

BERDACHE
Finds-Them-and-Kills-Them,
last of the Crow male homosexual
transvestites.

FIGURE *21.3*

AZANDE

obligation. Men were not classifiable as homosexual, heterosexual, or bisexual. All men were obliged to be bisexual as a matter of sacred duty and practical necessity. For example, among the Etoro, who live on the slopes of the central Papua New Guinea highlands, the emics of homosexuality revolve around the belief that semen is the source not only of babies but of manhood as well. Like the men of Hindu India, the Etoro believe that each man has only a limited supply of semen. When the supply is exhausted, a man dies. While coitus with their wives is necessary to prevent the population from becoming too small, husbands stay away from wives most of the time. Indeed, sex

is taboo between husband and wife for over 200 days of the year. The Etoro males regard wives who want to break this taboo as witches. To complicate matters, the supply of semen is not something that a man is born with. Semen can be acquired only from another male. Etoro boys get their supplies by having oral intercourse with older men. But it is forbidden for young boys to have intercourse with each other and, like the oversexed wife, the oversexed adolescent boy is regarded as a witch and condemned for robbing his age-mates of their semen supply. Such wayward youths can be identified by the fact that they grow faster than ordinary boys (Kelly 1976).

Among the Sambia of the southeastern highlands of New Guinea, boys are allowed to play with girls only until age 4 or 5. Subsequently, they are strictly regulated and all heterosexual play is forcefully punished. It is normal for young boys to hold hands with each other. But Sambia males and females never kiss, hold hands, or hug each other in public. Late in childhood, boys are initiated into the men's secret society and are taught how to act as warriors. Obedience to the male elders is rigidly enforced. Younger men, as among the Etoro, obtain the gift of semen from their seniors. Males must continue to avoid any heterosexual contact until they are married (Herdt 1987).

Homosexuality in New Guinea and Melanesia is closely associated with a heightened level of male-female sexual antagonism, fear of menstrual blood, and exclusive male rituals and dwellings. From an etic perspective, there seems to be a strong association between socially obligatory homosexuality and intense warfare. Warfare justified and rationalized an ethos of masculine prowess that placed men above women as desirable sexual partners. New Guinea societies that have ritualized male homosexuality to the greatest extent appear to be refugees from more densely populated regions (Herdt 1984a:169). As in other patrilocal warlike village societies (see p. 304), their juvenile sex ratios show a marked imbalance favoring males over females, attaining ratios as high as 140:100 (Herdt 1984b:57).

It is difficult to avoid the conclusion, therefore, that ritual homosexuality in New Guinea and Melanesia is part of a population-regulating negative feedback (see p. 313) system. As Dennis Werner (1979) has shown, societies that are strongly antinatalist (against having large numbers of children) tend to accept or encourage homosexual and other nonreproductive forms of sex. In addition, Melvin Ember (1982) has demonstrated that warfare in New Guinea is correlated with competition for scarce and/or depleted resources. However, much controversy surrounds these relationships.

Whatever the explanation for obligatory male homosexuality may be, its existence should serve as a warning against equating one's own culturally determined expressions of sexuality with human nature.

FEMALE HOMOSEXUALITY

Less is known about female homosexuality than about male homosexuality because of the predominance of male-biased ethnographies. Unlike males, females seldom seem to be subjected to initiation rituals that entail homosexual relationships. It is reported, however, that among the Dahomey, adolescent girls prepared for marriage by attending all-female initiation schools where they learned how to "thicken their genitalia" and engaged in sexual intercourse (Blackwood 1986).

Since women seldom bear the brunt of military combat, they have little opportunity to use same-sex erotic apprenticeships to form solidaristic teams of warriors. Similarly, enforced absence from the classical Greek academies precluded women's partici-

pation in homosexual philosophical apprenticeships, and since men regarded women as their sexual "objects," the incidence of overt lesbian behavior between women of rank and slave girls or other social inferiors could never be very high. More commonly, women do adopt socially sanctioned "not-man-not-woman" gender roles; dressing like men, performing manly duties such as hunting, trapping, and going to war, and using their in-between gender status to establish their credibility as shamans. Thirty-three American Indian societies are reported to have accepted gender transformations in women (Albers 1989:135). Among several western Native American tribes, female not-men-not-women entered into enduring lesbian relationships with women, whom they formally "married" (Blackwood 1984).

Several reported cases of institutionalized lesbianism are related to the migration of males in search of work. On the Caribbean island of Carriacou, where migrant husbands stay away from home for most of the year, older married women bring younger single women into their households and share the absent husband's remittances in exchange for sexual favors and emotional support. A similar pattern exists in South Africa, where it is known as the "mummy-baby game" (Gay 1986).

One of the most interesting forms of institutionalized lesbianism occurred in mid-nineteenth-century to early twentieth-century China in several of the silk-growing districts of the Pearl River Delta region in southern Kwangtung. Single women provided virtually all of the labor for the silkworm factories. Although poorly paid, they were better off than their prospective husbands. Rather than accept the subordinate status that marriage imposed on Chinese women, the silk workers formed antimarriage sisterhoods that provided economic and emotional support. While not all of the 100,000 sisters formed lesbian relationships, enduring lesbian marriages involving two and sometimes three women were common (Sankar 1986).

It seems clear that even when allowance is made for blind spots in the ethnographic reports of male observers, there are fewer forms of institutionalized female than of male homosexuality. Does this mean that females engage in homosexual behavior less often than males? Probably not. More likely, most female homosexuality has simply been driven underground or has been expressed in noninstitutionalized contexts that escape observation. Although seldom reported, adolescence is probably an occasion for a considerable amount of female homosexual experimentation the world over. Only recently, for example, has it come to light that among the Kalahari !Kung, young girls engage in sexual play with other girls before they do so with boys (Shostak 1981:114).

Polygynous marriage is another context in which lesbian relationships probably flourish. The practice seems to have been common in West Africa among the Nupé, Haussa, and Dahomey, and among the Azande and Nyakusa in East Africa. In Middle Eastern harems, where co-wives seldom saw their husbands, many women entered into lesbian relationships despite the dire punishment such male-defying behavior could bring (Blackwood 1986; Lockard 1986).

SUMMARY

Cross-cultural variations in gender roles prevent any single culture from serving as the model for what is natural in the realm of sex. Mangaian heterosexual standards contrast with those of Hindu India, which contrast with those of contemporary industrial societies. Homosexuality also defies neat stereotyping, as can be seen in the examples of the Crow and the Azande. Ritual male homosexuality, as among the Etoro, Sambia, and other New Guinea and Melanesian societies, is an elaborate, compulsory form of sexuality that has no equivalent in Western societies. It was probably selected for by the need to rear male warriors under conditions of environmental stress and competition.

Female homosexuality is less frequently reported, possibly as a result of male bias among ethnographers and the suppression of female liberties by dominant males.

PART VI

SUPERSTRUCTURE

Part VI shifts our focus from the organizations and groups that carry out the principal productive and reproductive functions of sociocultural systems to their mental, symbolic, and ideational aspects. Once again it should be pointed out that superstructure does not denote a superfluous, insignificant, or unimportant part of human social life. Moral values, religious beliefs, and aesthetic standards are the most distinctively human aspects of our species. Human sociocultural systems can no more exist without their symbolic and ideational superstructures than they can exist without structures or infrastructures. But a separate question remains: how shall we explain the differences and similarities in the values that people hold around the world? To what extent do our ideas and beliefs evolve under the constraints imposed by infrastructural conditions? Or is there another way to account for them?

Chapter 22

Personality and Culture

Personality is shaped not only by an individual's genes but also by one's culture. According to the followers of Sigmund Freud, however, there are some personality complexes that are found universally. We shall see if this is true. There is no doubt that culturally prescribed differences in childhood training greatly influence adult personality. But can it be said that all adults brought up in a particular culture have the same basic personality? Do the Japanese, for example, have a distinctive national character? And what of the relationship between culture and mental health? Are there certain forms of mental illness that occur in only one culture? And finally, when people have dreams and visions do they dream and hallucinate in culturally prescribed ways?

CULTURE AND PERSONALITY

Culture refers to the patterned ways in which the members of a population think, feel, and behave. *Personality* also refers to patterned ways of thinking, feeling, and behaving, but the focus is on the individual. Personality, as defined by Victor Barnouw (1985:8), "is a more or less enduring organization of forces within the individual associated with a complex of fairly consistent attitudes, values, and modes of perception which account, in part, for the individual's consistency of behavior." More simply, "personality is the tendency to behave in certain ways regardless of the specific setting" (Whiting and Whiting 1978:57).

The concepts employed in describing the thinking, feeling, and behavior of personality types are different from those employed in describing infrastructure, structure, and superstructure. In describing personalities, psychologists use concepts such as *aggressive, passive, anxious, obsessive, hysterical, manic, depressed, introverted, extroverted, paranoid, authoritarian, schizoid, masculine, feminine, infantile, repressed, dependent,* and so forth. Here is a part of a more extensive list of terms appropriate for the study of personality that appeared in a study of culture and personality in a Mexican village (Fromm and MacCoby 1970:79):

practical	anxious
economical	orderly
steadfast, tenacious	methodical
composed under stress	loyal
careful	unimaginative
reserved	stingy
patient	stubborn
cautious	indolent
imperturbable	inert
suspicious	pedantic
cold	obsessive
lethargic	possessive

If such concepts are employed to describe an entire population, the result will not add up to a description of modes of production and reproduction, domestic and political economy, systems of war and peace, or magico-religious rites and institutions. Rather, they will add up to a description of the kinds of personalities found in that population.

FREUD'S INFLUENCE

According to Sigmund Freud, the founder of psychoanalysis, adult personality is largely shaped by an individual's experiences in resolving certain recurrent conflicts during infancy and childhood. The most important conflict is known as the *Oedipus complex* (Oedipus, according to ancient Greek legend, killed his father and committed incest with his mother). The conflict is allegedly caused by biologically determined sexual strivings and jealousies within the nuclear family.

Freud held that a young boy's first sexual feelings are directed toward his mother. But the boy soon discovers that mother is the sexual object of his father and that he is in competition with his father for sexual "mastery" of the same woman. The father, while providing protection, also provides stern discipline (Fig. 22.1). He suppresses his son's attempt to express sexual love for mother. The son is frustrated and fantasizes that he is strong enough to kill his father. This arouses fear and guilt in the young boy: fear, because the father in fact or in the boy's fantasy, threatens to cut off the child's penis; and guilt, because the father is loved as well as feared. To resolve this conflict successfully, the young boy must learn to control his hostility and to redirect his sexuality toward females other than his mother.

For the young girl, Freud envisioned a parallel but fundamentally different trauma. A girl's sexuality is also initially directed toward her mother, but she

FIGURE *22.1*

FREUD'S MILIEU
A turn-of-the-century middle-class father with his two sons. He is stern but protective.

soon makes a fateful discovery: She lacks a penis. She blames her mother for this and redirects her sexual desires away from her mother and toward her father: "because he has the valued organ which she aspires to share with him" (Hall and Lindzey 1967).

However, her love for the father and for other men is mixed with a feeling of envy for they possess something she lacks. Penis envy is the female counterpart of castration anxiety in the boy. [Ibid:18]

Freud believed that women suffer from penis envy all their lives. In this fashion, Freud sought to ground the subordination of women to the unalterable facts of anatomy—hence the aphorism "anatomy is destiny." Thus, women were relegated to a passive and secondary role, the role of the "second sex." The best hope of overcoming her penis envy is for a woman to be passive and attractive, get married, and have babies:

Her happiness is great if later on this wish for a baby finds fulfillment in reality, and quite especially so if the baby is a little boy who brings the longed-for penis with him. [Freud, in Millett 1970:185]

For Freud, the most important part of a man's or woman's personality depends on the severity of each individual's Oedipal conflict and the degree to which it is resolved in growing up.

It is clear that Freud's notions about gender roles were projections of his own experiences as a male in highly male-centered late nineteenth-century Vienna where he lived and formulated his ideas. Sexual politics aimed at perpetuating the gender hierarchy, not science, provided the basis for his idea that women necessarily envied men and were destined always to be the "second sex."

IS THE OEDIPUS COMPLEX UNIVERSAL?

Starting with Bronislaw Malinowski's (1927) research on the avunculocal Trobriand family (see Chapter 18), anthropologists have criticized the Oedipus complex on the grounds that it imposes on the rest of the world a view of personality development appropriate to monogamous, patriarchical, nineteenth-century middle-class Vienna. Malinowski pointed out that Trobriand males couldn't develop the same kind of complex because it was their mother's brother and not their father who exercised authority over them. Thus, Trobriand males grew up without the hate-love feelings toward their father that Freud postulated as being universal.

Melford Spiro (1982) has attempted to rescue the Freudian position by separating the hate-love engendered by sexual jealousy from the hate-love engendered by authority. The Trobriand male lives with his father and mother until he is an adolescent. While his father is an easy-going and nonauthoritarian figure, there is still plenty of opportunity for father and son to develop feelings of sexual rivalry over the mother and wife. Spiro concludes, therefore, that Malinowski did not prove that the Trobrianders were without any basis for developing the Oedipus complex. It remains true, however, that the intensity and importance of the Oedipus complex must vary in relation to the amount and quality of the control that parents exercise over their children, and such control varies with the structure of the domestic group.

Most anthropologists interested in culture and personality studies today reject the idea that the Oedipus complex is universal (Parsons 1976). Freud's continuing influence, however, can be seen in the idea that personality is largely determined as a result of the individual's experiences during infancy and childhood. What anthropologists have added is the qualification that these experiences vary widely in conformity with the specific forms of family life and gender roles characteristic of particular sociocultural systems.

CHILDHOOD TRAINING AND PERSONALITY

Parents in a particular culture tend to follow similar childhood training practices involving the feeding, cleaning, and handling of infants and children. These childhood training practices vary widely from one society to another and are probably responsible for some cross-cultural differences in adult personalities (Box 22.1). In many cultures, for example, infants are constrained by swaddling bandages or cradle boards that immobilize their limbs. Elsewhere, freedom of movement is encouraged. Similarly, nursing may be either on demand at the first cry of hunger or at regular intervals at the convenience of the mother. Nursing at the mother's breast may last for a few months or several years, or may not take place at all. Supplementary foods may be taken in the first few weeks; they may be stuffed into the baby's mouth, prechewed by the mother, played with by the baby, or omitted entirely.

Weaning may take place abruptly, as when the mother's nipples are painted with bitter substances, and it may or may not be associated with the birth of another child. In some cultures infants are kept next to their mother's skin and carried wherever the mother goes (Fig. 22.2); elsewhere, they may be left behind with relatives or other caretakers. In some cultures infants are fondled, hugged, kissed, and fussed over by large groups of adoring children and adults; in others they are kept relatively isolated and touched infrequently.

Toilet training may begin as early as 6 weeks or as late as 24 months. The mode of training may involve many different techniques, some based on intense forms of punishment, shame, and ridicule, and others involving suggestion, emulation, and no punishment (Fig. 22.3).

Treatment of infant sexuality also varies widely. In many cultures mothers or fathers stroke their babies' genitals to soothe them and stop them from crying; elsewhere, even the baby is prevented from touching its own genitals, and masturbation is severely punished.

Another series of variables relevant to personality formation consists of later childhood and adolescent experiences: numbers of siblings, their relationships and mutual responsibilities (Fig. 22.4), patterns of play, opportunities to observe adult intercourse, opportunities to engage in homosexual or heterosexual experimentation, incest restrictions, and type of threat and punishment used against culturally prohibited sexual practices (Weisner and Gilmore 1977).

Figure 22.5 depicts one theory of how these childhood training practices may be related to per-

---

BOX *22.1*

TAKING CARE OF BABY AMONG HUNTER-GATHERERS

AMONG THE AGTA

"The infant is eagerly passed from person to person until all in attendance have had an opportunity to snuggle, nuzzle, sniff, and admire the newborn....A child's first experience, then, involves a community of relatives and friends. Thereafter, he enjoys constant cuddling, carrying, loving, sniffing, and affectionate genital stimulation" (Peterson 1978:16).

AMONG THE MBUTI

"The Mother emerges and presents the child to the camp...and she hands the boy to a few of her closest friends and family, not just for them to look at him but for them to hold him close to their bodies....In this way an initial model of predictability and security becomes multi-

plied, and so it is throughout the educational process: vital lessons, such as non-aggressivity, are learned through a plurality of models." (Turnbull 1978:172).

AMONG THE EFE PYGMY

"A recent study of Efe Pygmy infant caring practices (Tronick et al. 1987) found that the mother often was *not* the first one to nurse her infant and that other women frequently nursed the child during infancy. Four-month old infants spent only 40 percent of their time with their mother and were transferred among caretakers frequently—8.3 times per hour on average. Many individuals contributed to an infant's care: an average of 14.2 different people cared for an infant during eight hours of observation" (Hewlett 1991:15).

FIGURE *22.2*

CARE OF CHILDREN

Cultures vary greatly in the amount of body contact between mother and infant. **(A)** Swazi mother and child. **(B)** Arunta mother and child; mother has all-purpose carrying dish on her head and a digging stick in her hand.

(A)

(B)

FIGURE *22.3*

TOILET TRAINING, SOVIET STYLE

Soviet children were toilet trained in their nursery schools by their teachers. How might this have influenced their personalities in comparison with American children, who are toilet trained by their parents before they go to nursery school?

FIGURE *22.4*

JAVANESE GIRL AND BROTHER

One way to free mother for work in the fields is to turn over the care of infants to a 7-year-old sister.

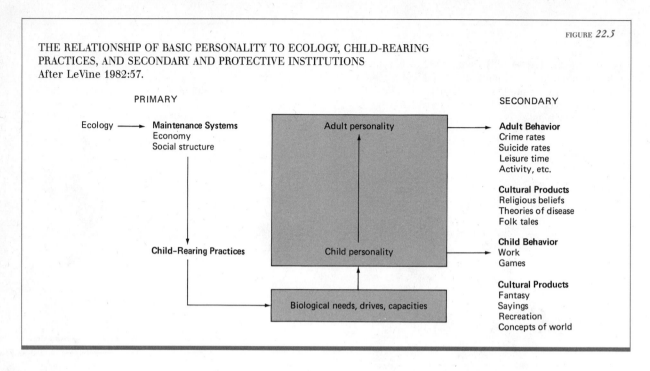

FIGURE *22.5*

THE RELATIONSHIP OF BASIC PERSONALITY TO ECOLOGY, CHILD-REARING PRACTICES, AND SECONDARY AND PROTECTIVE INSTITUTIONS
After LeVine 1982:57.

PRIMARY

Ecology → Maintenance Systems
Economy
Social structure

Child-Rearing Practices

Adult personality

Child personality

Biological needs, drives, capacities

SECONDARY

Adult Behavior
Crime rates
Suicide rates
Leisure time
Activity, etc.

Cultural Products
Religious beliefs
Theories of disease
Folk tales

Child Behavior
Work
Games

Cultural Products
Fantasy
Sayings
Recreation
Concepts of world

sonality and to other aspects of culture. The basic variables influencing child-rearing patterns are influenced by the nature of the culture's domestic, social, political, and economic institutions. These in turn are influenced by ecological factors. Child-rearing practices are also constrained by the necessity of satisfying certain biologically determined universal needs, drives, and capacities that all human infants share (e.g., oral, anal, and genital urges). The interaction between the child-rearing practices and these biological needs, drives, and capacities molds personality; personality, in turn, expresses itself in secondary institutions—that is, roughly what we have been calling "superstructure" in this text.

MALE INITIATION AND CHILDHOOD TRAINING

John Whiting (1969) and his associates have developed an interesting theory that relates childhood experiences to the formation of adult personality. Whiting has shown that statistical correlations exist among (1) protein scarcities, (2) nursing of children for 1 year or more, (3) prohibition of sexual relations between husband and wife for 1 year or more after the birth of their child, (4) polygyny, (5) domestic sleeping arrangements in which mother and child sleep together and father sleeps elsewhere, (6) child training by women, (7) patrilocality, and (8) severe male initiation rites.

Following our model, the following chain develops: Low protein availability and the risk of Kwashiorkor [a protein-deficiency disease] were correlated with an extended postpartum sex taboo to allow the mother time to nurse the infant through the critical stage before becoming pregnant again. The postpartum sex taboo was significantly correlated with the institution of polygyny, providing alternate sexual outlets for the male. Polygyny, in turn, is associated with mother-child households, child training by women, resultant cross-sex identity, and where patrilocality is also present, with initiation rites to resolve the conflict and properly inculcate male identity. [Harrington and Whiting 1972:491]

"Cross-sex identity" refers to the psychodynamic process by which boys who are reared exclusively by their mothers and older women identify themselves with their mothers and other women. Where patrilocality is present, reasons Whiting, functional consistency demands that adult males must make a strong identification with their fathers and other males. Hence, there is a conflict between what the male must do and think as an adult and what

FIGURE *22.6*

PSYCHODYNAMIC MODEL OF RELATIONSHIP BETWEEN LOW-PROTEIN
DIET AND SEVERE MALE INITIATION

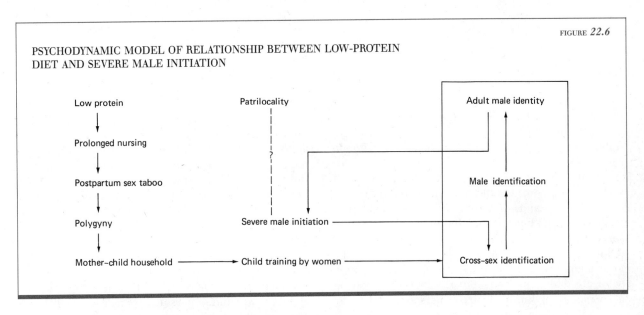

he is trained to do and think as an infant. Severe male initiation ceremonies involving circumcision or other forms of mutilation, prolonged seclusion, beatings, and trials of courage and stamina are thus required to resolve this conflict by breaking the prepubescent identity. The functional-causal links in Whiting's model are diagramed in Figure 22.6.

PATTERNS AND THEMES

Many other proposals have been made concerning how to treat the relationship between personality and culture. One popular option acknowledges that culture and personality represent two different ways of looking at the propensity to think, feel, and behave that are characteristic of a given population, and uses psychological terms to characterize both personality and the cultural system. For example, Ruth Benedict, in her famous book *Patterns of Culture* (1934), characterized the institution of the Kwakiutl potlatch (see p. 245) as a "megalomaniacal" performance-behavior dominated by fantasies of wealth and power. She saw potlatch as part of a "Dionysian" pattern that was characteristic of all the institutions of Kwakiutl culture. By *Dionysian* she meant the desire to achieve emotional excess, as in drunkenness or frenzy. Other cultures, such as that of the Pueblo Indians, she saw as Apollonian—given to moderation and the "middle of the road" in all things. Benedict's patterns were psychological elements reputedly found throughout a culture, "comparable to the chromosomes found in

most of the cells of a body" (Wallace 1970:149). Most anthropologists have rejected such attempts to use one or two psychological terms to describe whole cultures. Even the most simple hunter-gatherer cultures have too many different kinds of personalities to be summed up in such a manner.

Rather than attempt to sum up whole cultures under one or two psychological concepts, some anthropologists point to dominant themes or values that express the essential or main thought and feeling of a particular culture. The "image of limited good" is one such theme (see p. 330). Themes and values are readily translatable into personality traits.

For example, the image of limited good reputedly produces personalities that are jealous, suspicious, secretive, and fearful. The culture of poverty (see p. 334) also has its psychological components—improvidence, lack of future time orientation, and sexual promiscuity. An important theme in Hindu India is the "sacredness of life," and an important theme in the United States is "keeping up with the Joneses."

The problem with attempts to portray cultures in terms of a few dominant values and attitudes is that contradictory values and attitudes can usually be identified within the same cultures and even within the same individuals. Thus, although Hindu farmers believe in the sacredness of life (Opler 1968), they also believe in the necessity of having more bullocks than cows (see p. 408); and although many people in the United States believe in trying to keep up with the Joneses, there are others who believe that conspicuous consumption is foolish and wasteful.

BASIC PERSONALITY AND NATIONAL CHARACTER

A somewhat different approach to culture and personality postulates that every culture produces a basic or deep personality structure that can be found in virtually every individual member of the culture. When the populations involved are organized into a state, the basic personality is often called *national character*.

The notion of basic personality structure has always enjoyed considerable popularity among travelers to foreign lands as well as among scholars (Fig. 22.7). One often hears it said that the English are "reserved," the Brazilians "carefree," the French "sexy," the Italians "uninhibited," the Japanese "orderly," the Americans "outgoing," and so forth. Gerardus Mercator, the father of mapmaking, wrote the following descriptions of European basic personalities in the sixteenth century (see if you can guess Mercator's nationality):

Franks: Simple, blockish, furious.
Bavarians: Sumptuous, gluttons, brazenfaced.
Swedes: Light, babblers, boasters.
Saxons: Dissemblers, double-hearted, opinionative.
Spaniards: Disdainful, cautious, greedy.
Belgians: Good horsemen, tender, docile, delicate.

Modern scholarly versions of basic personality structure make use of more sophisticated psychological concepts.

The concept of basic personality type must not be permitted to obscure the fact that there is a great range of personalities in every society and that the more populous, complex, and stratified the society, the greater the variability. In every society many individuals have personalities that deviate widely from the statistical mode (most frequent type), and the range of individual personalities produces wide overlaps among different cultures. For example, it would certainly be correct to characterize the basic type of Plains native American male personality as an aggressive, independent, and fearless person. Yet, as we have seen (p. 362), there were always some young men who found themselves temperamentally unsuited to the male role. Very little is actually known about the amount of personality variance in different societies. It is certain, however, that complex state-level populations consisting of millions of people contain an enormous variety of personality types.

If one attempts to get away from one-word portrayals of a group's personality, another problem arises. The more criteria used to define the basic personality, the more likely that the modal type will only be found in relatively few individuals. Anthony Wallace (1952), for example, used 21 dimensions to de-

FIGURE *22.7*

NATIONAL CHARACTER
Allen Funt's popular TV show *Candid Camera* frequently explored national character differences by means of informal cross-cultural experiments. The three scenes represented here show the same young woman in three different countries, standing at a curb with a suitcase filled with 100 pounds of bricks. In each scene, she solicits a male passerby to help her get her suitcase across the street. In Country A, the man tugs and pulls at the suitcase with all his might, finally managing to get it across the street. In Country B, the man tries to move the suitcase, but when he finds it unexpectedly heavy, he gives up and goes on his way. In Country C, on finding the bag too heavy for one person to pick up, the man enlists the aid of another male passerby, and the two of them carry it across with no difficulty. Can you guess which country each scene depicts? In view of the recent changes in gender roles, what other scenarios might be likely to occur today?

Answers: (A) England; (B) France; (C) USA.

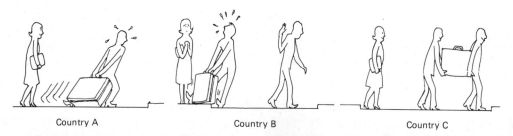

Country A   Country B   Country C

fine basic personality among the Iroquois. He found that the modal type was shared by only 37 percent of the total sample.

JAPANESE NATIONAL CHARACTER

Despite the varieties of personalities found in a given society, many psychological traits and their associated behaviors may be rare, "strange," or utterly alien to certain societies and not to others. This follows logically from the fact that a society's personality is culture described in psychological terms (see p. 370). Valid interpretations of personality configurations in alien cultures, however, require great familiarity with the language and deep immersion in the context of everyday life. The lived experience of being a member of another society often cannot be adequately represented by simple contrasts and conventional categories.

For example, the Japanese are stereotyped by Westerners as a people who are deferential, shy, self-effacing, conformist and dependent on group approval. "Few Japanese," writes one anthropologist, "achieve a sense of self that is independent of the attitude of others" (cited in Kumagai and Kumagai 1986:314, cf. Plath 1983). Examples of exaggerated deference are found in the frequent bowing and elaborate courtesy of Japanese business conferences, and the readiness with which Japanese identify themselves as a work team or a corporation rather than as individuals. Indeed, self-effacement has been linked by many observers to the secret of Japan's industrial success. Japanese management style plays down the difference between executives and workers. Everyone eats in the same company cafeteria and groups of workers regularly join with management to solve problems of mutual interest in a cooperative rather than adversarial manner.

However, there is another side of the Japanese personality that is reserved for private and intimate occasions. For anyone who is not a member of a Japanese family group and who does not interact with family members when there are no guests or outside observers present, it is difficult to witness the strength of individual ego-assertion that is also part of Japanese daily life (Box 22.2).

Most Japanese are brought up to be adept at changing back and forth between the private assertive self and the deferential public self. The significance of these different modes of presenting one's self has little if anything to do with the inner psychological strength of the Japanese ego. Since there is no real equivalent in the West to such a public-formal mode

---

BOX *22.2*

THE JAPANESE AT HOME

"People are relaxed and do not worry about formalities.... They can talk and joke about their innermost concerns.... Even the most formal of women may be informal with close friends.... They even tease each other about the formalities which they notice on other occasions.... With close friends, one can argue, criticize, and be stubborn without endangering the relationship. There is inevitably a great deal of laughter mixed with mutual support and respect.... It is partly the sharp contrast between seeing a close friend and a mere acquaintance that makes contacts with outsiders seem so stiff.... The visitor to Japan who does not appreciate the difference in behavior toward friends and acquaintances is likely to consider the Japanese as more formal than they actually are."

SOURCE: Quoted in Sugimoto and Mouer 1983.

---

of self-effacement, Japanese personality has often been incorrectly and unfavorably perceived by Westerners. Lacking a Western equivalent, Westerners interpret the posture of self-effacement as indicative of hypocrisy and deviousness. On the other side, the Japanese are equally befuddled by the failure of Westerners to make a distinction between expressions of one's ego in public-formal versus intimate-private situations. As recounted by a Japanese social scientist, being a dinner guest in an American home can be especially perplexing:

Another thing that made me nervous was the custom whereby an American host will ask a guest, before the meal, whether he would prefer a strong or a soft drink [and after dinner] whether [he takes] coffee or tea, and—in even greater detail—whether one wants it with sugar, and milk, and so on. [Kumagai 1986:12]

While the visitor soon realized that the hosts were trying to be polite, he felt extremely uncomfortable with having to say what he would like, since in the self-effacing and deferential posture appropriate to being a guest in a Japanese home, one avoids expressions of personal preference with respect to what is being served. Guests are dependent on hosts and surrender all vestiges of personal preference. The hosts in turn must avoid embarrassing their guests by asking them to choose their own food. Unlike Americans, Japanese hosts do not discuss how they prepared the main dish. They say, "This may not suit your taste, but it is the best we could do." The guests are not supposed to be interested in knowing any of the details of this effort.

COMPLIANT JAPANESE?

Japan's managerial and governing elites have long advocated and extolled the virtues of team spirit, loyalty to firm and state, and peaceful family-style acquiescence to authority. But it is often forgotten that social conflict is also part of Japan's traditions.

In 1897 Oka Minoru, later the chief architect of Japan's first factory law, predicted that Japanese labor relations would resemble the "beautiful customs" of "master and retainer" that had prevailed during feudalism. He envisioned the factory as "one big family" and predicted that "strikes will become unthinkable" (quoted in Garon 1987:30). But early in its career as an industrial nation, Japan was troubled by labor unrest. Although the right to strike was severely curtailed in 1900, there were bitter labor management confrontations in 1906, during and after World War I, and during the 1920s. Over one hundred thousand workers went out on strike in 1918 and 1919 (Garon 1987:40–41) in the aftermath of the great rice riots of 1918 (see below). Labor-management relations reached crisis proportions in the 1920s and again in the 1940s. During the American occupation, the Japanese were at first encouraged to develop national trade unions as a step toward democratization. "From an insignificant base of five thousand in October, 1945, union membership soared to nearly five million by December 1946" (Gordon 1987: 238). Strikes occurred at a rate that was similar to U.S. rates but with a far more radical and disharmonious objective: The unions planned a general strike for February 1, 1947. Frightened by the specter of a communist-inspired class war, the Americans stepped in and reversed course on unionization.

In addition to labor unrest and strikes, there is much additional evidence that Japan, like the rest of the industrial world, is not exclusively under the sway of harmony-promoting values. Peasant revolts were commonplace during the past century. For the decade 1868–1877, there are accounts of 499 peasant uprisings and 24 urban mass disturbances (Mouer and Sugimoto 1986:101). A sharp increase in the price of rice led to widespread rioting and looting in 1918

FIGURE *22.8*

JAPANESE RIOT
Police and demonstrators clash during a protest against expansion of Tokyo airport.

that lasted 53 days, spread to 42 prefectures, and required the attention of 92,000 troops before order was restored (ibid.; Garon 1987:40–41). Every major city was affected. The number of rioters who took to the streets was over 200,000 in Osaka; 130,000 in Nagoya; and 50,000 in Tokyo (Lewis 1990:97). Teachers engaged in massive boycotts and demonstrations against political censorship in the 1950s, complete with fistfights in the Japanese Diet between socialist and conservative members. In more recent times, dissent often accompanied by violence has been registered by various antipollution and environmental movements, the student movement, the consumer movement, the movement against nuclear weapons, the movement against noise pollution, and the decade-long farmers movement to prevent the expansion of Tokyo's Narita airport (Fig. 22.8).

Little credence should be given to the view that because these movements and demonstrations are themselves structured by groupist values, they therefore merely confirm the pervasiveness of such values and correspondingly fail to demonstrate the existence of alternative confrontational ideologies. There is nothing in the notion of protest that requires activists to act like a mob, especially in an age when performance for the media is the key to winning public support.

CULTURE AND MENTAL ILLNESS

Anthropologists do not agree on the role that cultural differences play in the incidence and nature of mental illness. Recent medical research has shown that there are probably important viral genetic and chemical-neurological bases for such classic mental disorders as schizophrenia and manic-depressive psychosis (Torrey 1980). This accords with the evidence that the rates of those diseases among groups as diverse as Swedes, Innuits, the Yoruba of West Africa, and modern Canadians do not show marked differences (Murphy 1976). However, there is no doubt that, while broad symptoms of the same mental diseases can be found cross-culturally, there is considerable variation in the specific symptoms found in different cultures. For example, a comparison of schizophrenic patients of Irish and Italian descent in a New York hospital revealed that substantially different sets of symptoms were associated with each group. The Irish patients tended to be obsessed with sexual guilt and to be much more withdrawn and quiet than the Italian patients, while the Italian patients were sexually aggressive and far more prone to violent fits and tantrums (Opler 1959). Just as Crow Indians have a particular visionary experience based on their cultural expectations (see p. 382), so too the specific content of psychotic hallucinations varies from culture to culture.

For example, American patients have delusions about putting Cadillac engines into people's heads or of talking with angels in spacesuits, themes that one does not expect to occur among people who do not own cars or watch rocket lift-offs. Westerners began to have delusions about being controlled by rays of electricity only around the beginning of the century. Similarly, a common delusion of modern schizophrenics is that they have become robots. This delusion did not exist before the word and concept of robot was introduced in 1921 in a play by Karel Capek (Barnouw 1985:361).

Moreover, as psychiatrist Richard Warner (1985) has shown, the severity of schizophrenia and the prospects of spontaneously recovering from it vary from culture to culture. In pre-industrial societies with extended families, small face-to-face communities, and religions that stress the existence of a multitude of ever-present spirit beings (see p. 390), the schizophrenic individual is not regarded as a shameful or threatening presence or even as a person who has gone crazy. Relatives continue to render emotional and physical support, while the community blames the schizophrenic's bizarre behavior on some pesky spirit. In contrast, schizophrenics in industrial societies are often expelled from both family and community, deprived of emotional and physical support, isolated, and made to feel worthless and guilty. These culturally constructed conditions make the prospect for recovery much poorer in industrial societies despite the availability of modern medical therapies.

CULTURE-SPECIFIC PSYCHOSES

Evidence for more powerful effects of culture on mental illness can be found in culture-specific psychoses—disorders that have a distinctive set of symptoms limited to only one or a few cultures.

One of the best known of these culture-specific psychoses occurs among the Innuits and is called Arctic hysteria, or *pibloktoq* (Fig. 22.9). Unlike classic psychoses, pibloktoq strikes suddenly. Its victims leap up, tear off their clothes, move their limbs convulsively, and roll about naked in the snow and

FIGURE *22.9*

ARCTIC HYSTERIA
The victim is an Innuit woman from Greenland.

ice. One explanation for this behavior likens it to a severe case of "cabin fever." Cooped up in their small,
crowded dwellings for long periods during which they
are unable to vent their feelings of hostility, pibloktoq
victims may become hysterical as a means of dealing
with their pent-up frustrations. It seems more likely,
however, that the underlying cause also lies in the
highly carnivorous diet of the Innuits. Lacking plant
foods and solar radiation, the Innuits are forced to rely
on the consumption of sea mammal and polar bear livers for their supply of vitamin A and vitamin D. Eating
too much of these livers produces a poisonous excess
of vitamin A, but eating too little can result in a deficit
of vitamin D, which in turn leads to a deficit of calcium
in the bloodstream (see p. 95). Both conditions—too
much vitamin A and too little calcium in the blood—
are known to be associated with convulsions and psychotic episodes (Landy 1985; Wallace 1972). Thus, pibloktoq is probably a consequence of the interaction
between culturally determined living conditions and
the chemistry of nutrition.

WINDIGO PSYCHOSIS?

Among the hunter-gatherer northern Ojibwa and
Cree of the Canadian subarctic forest, there is a
widespread belief that humans can become possessed by the spirit of Windigo, a cannibal monster
whose heart is made out of ice. This belief has given
rise to the hypothesis that the Cree and Ojibwa are
subject to a culture-specific malady called Windigo
psychosis. Those who are possessed by Windigo are
said to experience an overwhelming desire to kill
and eat their campmates. Living in a harsh environment, the Cree and Ojibwa often find themselves
snowbound and close to starvation in their isolated
winter camps. The likelihood of someone becoming a
Windigo is said to have been greatest under such conditions. Various reports verify the fact that famished
campmates did sometimes eat the bodies of their deceased companions in order to keep themselves alive.
(Similar accounts of "crisis cannibalism" have been
reported from many parts of the world, most recently
from a soccer team whose plane crashed in the Andes
Mountains.) Once having experienced human flesh,
human Windigos are said to crave more. They lose
their taste for ordinary food, their hearts feel like a
lump of ice, and the people around them no longer
look like people but like deer, moose, or other game
animals. Unless they are killed first, they will kill and
devour their companions.

As Louis Marano (1982) has shown, there are
many authenticated cases of the killing of people said

to be Windigos by their alarmed campmates. Recurrently, Windigo killers cite evidence that justifies their
homicides: The victims looked at them strangely,
tossed about and mumbled in their sleep, had saliva
dripping from their mouths, or tried to attack and
bite their companions. In one instance, the alleged
Windigo even seemed to hover off the ground and had
to be pulled down by his attackers. Recurrently, the
alleged Windigos themselves are said to have asked
that they be killed lest they eat their campmates one
by one. What is lacking in all of these accounts, however, is any hard data showing that the alleged Windigos thought and acted in the manner described by
their executioners. Without such data, the existence
of a genuine Windigo psychosis remains in doubt
and a much simpler explanation can be offered for
the belief in Windigo possession (Box 22.3). Under
conditions of extreme hunger and stress, the northern Ojibwa and Cree accused certain troublesome
campmates of being Windigos as a justification for
getting rid of them, thereby increasing the chances
of survival for the rest of the camp. Thus, the typical
executed Windigo was a sickly individual delirious
with a high fever, someone who was too ill to walk, a
senile old man or woman, or a stranger from another
ethnic group. In Marano's words, the Windigo beliefs
were not evidence of a psychosis but of a system of

BOX *22.3*

SCAPEGOATING THE WINDIGO

"Upon close scrutiny the Windigo psychosis
discloses itself not as a culturally isolated an-
thropophagic (i.e., cannibal) obsession, but instead as a rather predictable—though culturally conditioned—variant of triage homicide
and witch hunting typical of societies under
stress. In this process, as in all witch hunts,
the victims of the aggression are socially rede-
fined as the aggressors. Here the specific form
of the redefinition was determined by the constant threat of starvation, a situation in which
cannibalism has proved to be a tempting recourse for persons of all cultures throughout
history. By attributing society's most salient
fear to the scapegoat, the group was able to
project its modal anxiety onto the individual,
thus generating a rationale for homicide with
which everyone could identify."

SOURCE: Marano 1982:385.

"triage homicide" (i.e., letting some die in order that others might live) in which the fear of being eaten was used to overcome the fear of breaking the taboo on killing a campmate.

DREAMS AND HALLUCINATIONS

The cultural patterning of mental life affects the content of dreams, visions, and drug-induced hallucinations. For example, a form of individualistic religion (see p. 390) common in North and South America involves the acquisition of a personal guardian spirit or supernatural protector. Typically, this spirit protector is acquired by means of a visionary experience induced by fasting, self-inflicted torture, or hallucinogenic drugs (see p. 383). Although each vision is slightly different from the next, they all follow a similar culturally constructed pattern.

For many native North Americans an hallucinatory vision was the central experience of life (Fig. 22.10). Young men needed this hallucinatory experience to be successful in love, warfare, horse stealing, trading, and all other important endeavors. In keeping with their code of personal bravery and endurance, they sought these visions primarily through self-inflicted torture.

Among the Crow, for example, a youth who craved a visionary experience went alone into the mountains, stripped off his clothes, and abstained from food and drink. If this was not sufficient, he chopped off part of the fourth finger of his left hand.

Coached from childhood to expect that a vision would come, most of the Crow vision-seekers were successful. A buffalo, snake, chicken hawk, thunderbird, dwarf, or mysterious stranger would appear; miraculous events would unfold; and then these strange beings would "adopt" the vision-seeker and disappear. Scratches-face, who was one of Robert Lowie's informants, prayed to the morning star:

Old woman's grandson, I give you this [finger joint]. Give me something good in exchange...a good horse ...a good-natured woman...a tent of my own to live in. [Lowie 1948:6]

Lowie reports that after cutting off his finger, Scratches-face had a successful vision. "As a consequence of his blessing Scratches-face struck and

---

FIGURE *22.10*

SIOUX VISION
Section of pictographic biography done by Rain in the Face. **(A)** In a dream,
the lightning tells him that unless he gives a buffalo feast, the lightning will kill him.
He gives the feast, one part of which consists of filling a kettle with red-hot buffalo
tongues, of which he eats in order to save his life. **(B)** He dreams of buffalo again.
While dancing, he is shot by an arrow that enters the feathers. In removing it,
he soon vomits and, grabbing a handful of earth, rubs it into the wound, healing it rapidly.

(A)

(B)

killed an enemy without ever getting wounded. He also obtained horses and married a good-tempered and industrious woman."

Although each Crow's vision had some unique elements, they were usually similar in the following regards: (1) Some revelation of future success in warfare, horse raiding, or other acts of bravery was involved; (2) the visions usually occurred at the end of the fourth day—four being the sacred number of the native North Americans; (3) practically every vision was accompanied by the acquisition of a sacred song; (4) the friendly spirits in the vision adopted the youth; and (5) trees or rocks often turned into enemies who vainly shot at the invulnerable spirit being. Lowie concludes:

He sees and hears not merely what any faster, say in British Columbia or South Africa, would see and hear under like conditions of physiological exhaustion and under the urge of generally human desires, but what the social tradition of the Crow tribe imperatively suggests. [1948:14]

SUMMARY

Culture and personality are closely related concepts concerned with the patterning of thoughts, feelings, and behavior. Personality is primarily a characteristic of individuals; culture is primarily a characteristic of groups. Yet it is possible to speak of the personality of a group—of a basic, modal, or typical personality. The two approaches, however, use different technical vocabularies to describe the patterning of thought, feelings, and behavior.

Anthropologists who study personality generally accept the Freudian premise that personality is molded by childhood experiences. This has led to an interest in how adults interact with and relate to infants and young children, especially in such matters as toilet training, nursing, weaning, and sexual dis-

cipline. In some theories these experiences are seen as determining the nature of "secondary" institutions such as art and religion, or, as John Whiting has shown, the practice of severe male puberty rituals.

Other approaches to culture and personality attempt to characterize whole cultures in terms of central themes, patterns, basic personality, or national character. Care is necessary in order to avoid overgeneralizing the applicability of such concepts. A wide range of personality types is found in any large population.

This is not to deny that profound differences exist between personality patterns in different cultures. The Japanese, for example, have a distinctive disposition to separate ego-effacing from ego-asserting situations. This disposition, however, cannot be reduced to the stereotype that Japanese are hypocritical or devious. Similarly, the notion that the Japanese are compliant and respectful of authority fails to take into account a history of civil and industrial conflict.

The relationship between culture and mental disease remains problematical. Classic disorders such as schizophrenia and manic-depressive psychosis are somewhat modified by cultural influences, yet they occur in many different societies and probably are the result of interactions among cultural, biochemical, and genetic variables. Culture-specific psychoses such as pibloktoq indicate that cultural factors may powerfully influence the state of mental health, but, as the case of Windigo psychosis shows, caution is needed in evaluating allegations concerning the existence of such psychoses.

The pervasive effect of culture on mental life is further revealed by the patterning of dreams and hallucinations. As in the vision quests of native North and South Americans, the content of what is seen when under the influence of trance-inducing substances and procedures is specific to each culture's traditions.

Chapter 23

Religion

Now we are entering the inner sanctum of superstructure, the domain of religion, myth, magic, ritual and all the other aspects of cultures that are intended to mediate between ordinary beings and forces, on the one hand, and extraordinary beings and forces on the other. First some basic definitions will be needed. Then we shall try to classify the basic types of religious organizations and rituals. Finally, we shall range over the vast variety of religious behaviors, from puberty rites to messianic cults, from prayer to cannibal feasts, and from abominable pigs to sacred cows. Can aspects of religion be explained in terms of structure and infrastructure? To a considerable degree. Yet religion can frequently become a powerful force in its own right. Although infrastructural and structural conditions provide a means for understanding the origin of many specific beliefs and rituals, religion frequently plays a crucial role in strengthening the impulses leading toward major transformations in social life.

ANIMISM

What is religion? The earliest anthropological attempt to define religion was that of E. B. Tylor (1871). In his book *Primitive Culture,* he demonstrated that members of every society believe that inside the ordinary, visible, tangible body there is a normally invisible, normally intangible being: the soul. He gave the name *animism* to this belief. Throughout the world people believe that souls can be seen in dreams, trances, visions, shadows, and reflections, and that souls are implicated in fainting, loss of consciousness, and birth and death. Tylor reasoned that the basic idea of soul must have been invented in order to explain all these puzzling phenomena. The basic soul idea then led to belief in a variety of soul-like beings, including the souls of animals, plants, and material objects, as well as gods, demons, spirits, devils, ghosts, saints, fairies, gnomes, elves, angels, and so forth.

Tylor has been criticized by twentieth-century anthropologists for his suggestion that animism arose merely as a result of the attempt to understand puzzling human and natural phenomena. Today we know that religion is much more than an attempt to explain puzzling phenomena. Like other aspects of superstructure, religion serves a multitude of economic, political, and psychological functions.

Another important criticism of Tylor's stress on the puzzle-solving function of religion concerns the role of hallucinations in shaping religious beliefs. During drug-induced trances and other forms of hallucinatory experience, people "see" and "hear" extraordinary things that seem even more "real" than ordinary people and animals. One can argue, therefore, that animistic theories are not intellectual attempts to explain trances and dreams, but direct expressions of extraordinary psychological experiences. Nonetheless, it cannot be denied that religion and the doctrine of souls also serve the function of providing people with answers to fundamental questions about the meaning of life and death and the causes of events.

Although certain animistic beliefs are universal, each culture has its own distinctive animistic beings and its own specific elaboration of the soul concept. Some cultures insist that people have two or more souls; some cultures believe that certain individuals have more souls than others. Among the Jivaro of eastern Ecuador (Harner 1972), for example, three kinds of souls are recognized: an ordinary, or *true,* soul; an *arutam* soul; and a *musiak* soul (Box 23.1).

ANIMATISM AND MANA

As Robert Marett (1914) pointed out, Tylor's definition of religion as animism is too narrow. When people attribute lifelike properties to rocks, pots, storms, and volcanoes, they do not necessarily believe that souls are the cause of the lifelike behavior of these objects. Hence, there is a need to distinguish a concept of a supernatural force that does not derive its effect from souls. Marett therefore introduced the term *animatism* to designate the belief in such nonsoul forces. Possession of concentrated animatistic force can give certain objects, animals, and people extraordinary powers independent of power derived from souls and gods. To label this concentrated form of

BOX *23.1*

THREE SOULS OF THE JIVARO

The Jivaro believe that the true soul is present from birth inside every living Jivaro, male and female. Upon a person's death, this soul leaves the body and undergoes four additional changes. First it returns to its body's birthplace and relives its former life in an invisible form. Next it changes into a demon, and roams the forest, solitary, hungry, and lonely. The true soul then dies again and becomes a wampang, a species of giant moth that is occasionally seen flitting about. It too is perpetually hungry. In its fourth and final phase, the true soul turns to mist:

After a length of time about which the Jivaro are uncertain, the wampang finally has its wings damaged by raindrops as it flutters through a rainstorm, and falls to die on the ground. The true soul then changes into water vapor amidst the falling rain. All fogs and clouds are believed to be the last form taken by true souls. The true soul undergoes no more transformations and persists eternally in the form of mist. [Harner, 1972:151]

No one is born with the second Jivaro soul—the arutam. To obtain an arutam, one must fast, bathe in a sacred waterfall, and drink tobacco water or the juice of Datura, a plant that contains an hallucinogenic substance. The arutam comes out of the depths of the forest in the form of a pair of giant jaguars or a pair of huge snakes rolling over and over toward the soul seeker. When the apparition gets close, the seeker must run forward and touch it. The arutam will then enter the body at night.

People who possess an arutam soul speak and act with great confidence and feel an irresistible craving to kill their enemies. As long as they keep their arutam, they themselves are immortal. Unfortunately, arutam souls cannot be kept forever. They leave their temporary abode just before their possessor kills someone. Eventually, wandering in the forest, they will be recaptured by other soulseekers brave enough to touch them.

FIGURE *23.1*

JIVARO TROPHY HEAD

The third Jivaro soul is the musiak—the avenging soul. The musiak comes into existence when people who formerly possessed an arutam are killed by their enemies. The musiak develops inside the victim's head and tries to get out and attack the killer. To prevent this from happening, the best thing to do is to cut off the victim's head, "shrink" it, and bring it back home (Fig. 23.1). If it is handled properly in various rituals and dances, the musiak can make the killer strong and happy. After the musiak has been used to the killer's advantage, a ritual is performed to send it back to the village from which it came. To get it to go back, the women sing this song (Harner 1972:146):

Now, now, go back to your house where you lived. Your wife is there calling from your house. You have come here to make us happy. Finally we have finished. So return.

animatistic force, Marett used the Melanesian word *mana.* An adze that makes intricate carvings, a fishhook that catches large fish, a club that kills many enemies, or a horseshoe that brings "good luck" have large amounts of mana. People, too, may be spoken of as having more or less mana. A woodcarver whose work is especially intricate and beautiful possesses mana, whereas a warrior captured by the enemy has obviously lost his mana.

In its broadest range of meaning, mana simply indicates belief in a powerful force. Many vernacular relationships not normally recognized as religious beliefs in Western cultures can be regarded as mana. For example, vitamin pills are consumed by many millions of people in expectation that they will exert a powerful effect on health and well-being. Soaps and detergents are said to clean because of "cleaning power"; gasolines provide engines with "starting power" or "go-power"; salespeople are prized for their "selling power"; and politicians are said to have charisma or "vote-getting power." Many people fervently believe that they are "lucky" or "unlucky," which can be interpreted as a belief that they control varying quantities of mana.

NATURAL AND SUPERNATURAL

If belief in hidden forces constitutes religion, then what prevents us from regarding a belief in gravity or X-rays as religion? One way out of this dilemma is to associate religion with a realm of *supernatural* forces. This has its limitations also, because few preindustrial cultures make a neat distinction between natural and supernatural phenonena. In a culture where people believe ghosts are always present, it is not necessarily either natural or supernatural to provide dead ancestors with food and drink. The culture may simply lack emic categories for "natural" and "supernatural." Similarly, when a shaman blows smoke over a patient and triumphantly removes a sliver of bone allegedly inserted by the patient's enemy, the question of whether the performance is natural or supernatural may have no emic meaning.

Writing of the Gururumba (Fig. 23.2) of the highlands of western New Guinea, Philip Newman notes that they "have a series of beliefs postulating the existence of entities and forces we would call supernatural." Yet the contrast between natural and supernatural is not emically relevant to the Gururumba themselves:

It should be mentioned . . . that our use of the notion "supernatural" does not correspond to any Guru-

FIGURE *23.2*

GURURUMBA MEDICINE
This man is inducing vomiting by swallowing a 3-foot length of cane. After he has pushed it all the way into his stomach, he will work it up and down until he vomits. It is thought to be necessary to do this to rid the individual of contaminating influences gotten through contact with women.

rumba concept: they do not divide the world into natural and supernatural parts. Certain entities, forces, and processes must be controlled partially through lusu, *a term denoting rituals relating to growth, curing, or the stimulation of strength, while others need only rarely be controlled in this way.... However,* lusu *does not contrast with any term denoting a realm of control where the nature of controls differ from* lusu. *Consequently* lusu *is simply part of all control techniques and what it controls is simply part of all things requiring human control.* [Newman 1965:83]

SACRED AND PROFANE

Some anthropologists have suggested that beliefs or practices are religious when they produce a special emotional state or "religious experience." Robert Lowie (1948:339) characterized this experience as consisting of "amazement and awe," a feeling that one is in the presence of something extraordinary, weird, sacred, holy, divine. Lowie was even willing to rule that beliefs about gods and souls were not religious beliefs if the existence of these beings was taken for granted and if, in contemplating them, the individual did not experience awe or amazement.

The theoretician who made the greatest contribution to this way of looking at religion was Emile Durkheim. Like many others, Durkheim proposed that the essence of religious belief was that it evoked a mysterious feeling of communion with a sacred realm. Every society has its sacred beliefs, symbols, and rituals, which stand opposed to ordinary or profane events (Fig. 23.3). Durkheim's distinctive contribution was to relate the realm of the sacred to the control exercised by society and culture over each individual's consciousness. When people feel they are in communion with occult and mysterious forces and supernatural beings, what they are really experiencing is the force of social life. In our awe of the sacred, we express our dependence on society in symbolic form. Thus, according to Durkheim, the idea of "god" is but one form of the worship of society.

Every culture does make a distinction between sacred and profane realms, and there is probably some element of truth in Durkheim's idea that the sacred represents the worship of collective life. As we will see, the ability to appeal to the sacred character of certain beliefs and practices has great practical value in diminishing dissent, compelling conformity, and resolving ambiguities (see Rappaport 1971a and b).

FIGURE *23.3*

SACRED AND PROFANE
Shoes are left outside the mosque, symbolizing the transition from ordinary, mundane affairs to the realm of the holy and extraordinary.

MAGIC AND RELIGION

Sir James Frazer attempted to define religion in his famous book *The Golden Bough.* For Frazer, the question of whether a particular belief was religious or not centered on the extent to which the participants felt that they could make an entity or force do their bidding. If the attitude of the participants was one of uncertainty, if they felt humble and were inclined to supplicate and request favors and dispensations, their beliefs and actions were essentially religious. If they thought they were in control of the entities and forces governing events, felt no uncertainty about the outcome, and experienced no need for humble supplication, their beliefs and practices were examples of magic rather than of religion.

Frazer regarded prayer as the essence of religious ritual. But prayers are not always rendered in a mood of supplication. For example, prayers among the Navajo must be letter-perfect to be effective. Yet the Navajo do not expect that letter-perfect prayers will always get results. Thus, the line between prayers and "magical spells" is actually hard to draw. Supplication cannot be taken as characteristic of verbal communication between people and their gods. As Ruth Benedict (1938:640) pointed out, "cajolery and bribery and false pretense are common means of influencing the supernatural." Thus the Kai of New Guinea swindle their ancestral ghosts as they swindle each other. Other cultures try to outwit the spirits by lying to them. The Tsimshian of the Canadian Pacific Coast stamp their feet and shake their fists at the heavens and call their gods "slaves" as a term of reproach. The Manus of the Bismarck Archipelago keep the skulls of their ancestors in a corner of the house and try their best to please "Sir Ghost." However, if someone gets sick, the Manus may angrily threaten to throw Sir Ghost out of the house. This is what they tell Sir Ghost:

This man dies and you rest in no house. You will but wander about the edges of the island [used for excretory functions]. [Fortune 1965:216]

Thus, Frazer's definition of religion has not withstood the test of fieldwork. Religious thought and behavior is a complex mixture of awe and wonder, boredom and excitement, power and weakness.

THE ORGANIZATION OF RELIGIOUS BELIEFS AND PRACTICES

Anthony Wallace (1966) has distinguished four principal varieties of religious "cults"—that is, forms of organization of religious doctrines and activities—that have broad evolutionary implications. The four principal forms are (1) individualistic cults, (2) shamanistic cults, (3) communal cults, and (4) ecclesiastical cults, defined as follows:

1. Individualistic cults The most basic form of religious life involves individualistic (but culturally patterned) beliefs and rituals. Each person is a specialist; each one enters into a relationship with animistic and animatistic beings and forces as each personally experiences the need for control

FIGURE *23.4*

SAN CURING
Shaman in a trance.

and protection. One might call this "do-it-yourself" religion.

2. Shamanistic cults As Wallace points out, no culture known to anthropology has a religion that is completely individualistic, although the Innuit and other hunters and gatherers lean heavily in this direction. Every known society also exhibits at least the shamanistic level of religious specialization (Fig. 23.4). The term *shaman* derives from the word used by the Tungus-speaking peoples of Siberia to designate the part-time religious specialist consulted in times of stress and anxiety. In cross-cultural applications, however, *shaman* may refer to individuals who act as diviners, curers, spirit mediums, and magicians for other people in return for gifts, fees, prestige, and power.

3. Communal cults At a more complex level of political economy, communal forms of beliefs and practices become more elaborate. Groups of nonspecialists organized in terms of age grades, men's societies, clans, or lineages assume responsibility for regular or occasional performance of rituals deemed essential for their own welfare or for the survival of the society. While communal rituals may employ specialists such as shamans, orators, and highly skilled dancers and musicians, once the ritual performance is concluded, the participants revert to a common daily routine. There are no full-time religious specialists.

4. Ecclesiastical cults The ecclesiastical level of religious organization involves a full-time professional clergy or priesthood. These professionals form a bureaucracy that monopolizes the performance of certain rites on behalf of individuals, groups, and the whole society. Ecclesiastical bureaucracies are usually closely associated with state-level political systems. In many instances the leaders of the ecclesiastical hierarchy are members of the ruling class and, in some cases, a state's political and ecclesiastical hierarchies are indistinguishable.

Wallace notes that the individualistic, shamanistic, communal, and ecclesiastical form of beliefs and rituals constitute a scale. That is, each of the more complex levels contains the beliefs and practices of all the less complex levels. Consequently, among societies with ecclesiastical cults, there are also communal cults, shamanistic cults, and strictly individualistic beliefs and rituals (Fig 23.5). In the following sections, examples of each of these forms of religious organization will be given.

FIGURE *23.5*

LEVEL OF RELIGIOUS ORGANIZATION
(A) A Guatemalan shaman obtaining personal power at a shrine. **(B)** This does not prevent him from participating in the ecclesiastical cult of the Catholic church.

(A)

(B)

INDIVIDUALISTIC BELIEFS AND RITUALS: THE INNUIT

The individualism of much of Innuit belief and ritual parallels the individualism of the Innuit mode of production. Hunters alone or in small groups constantly match their wits against the cunning and strength of animal prey and confront the dangers of travel over the ice and the threats of storms and month-long nights. The Innuit hunter was equipped with an ingenious array of technological devices that made life possible in the Arctic, but the outcome of the daily struggle remained in doubt. From the Innuit's point of view, it was not enough to be well equipped with snow goggles, fur parkas, spring-bone traps, detachable barbed harpoon points, and powerful compound bows. One also had to be equipped to handle unseen spirits and forces that lurked in all parts of nature and that, if offended or not properly warded off, could reduce the greatest hunter to a starving wretch. Vigilant individual effort was needed to deal with wandering human and animal souls, place spirits, Sedna (the Keeper of the Sea Animals), the Sun, the Moon, and the Spirit of the Air (Wallace 1966:89). Part of each hunter's equipment was his hunting song, a combination of chant, prayer, and magic formula that he inherited from his father or father's brothers or purchased from some famous hunter or shaman. This he would sing under his breath as he prepared himself for the day's activities. Around his neck he wore a little bag filled with tiny animal carvings, bits of claws and fur, pebbles, insects, and other items, each corresponding to some Spirit Helper with whom he maintained a special relationship. In return for protection and hunting success given by his Spirit Helpers, the hunter had to observe certain taboos, refrain from hunting or eating certain species, or avoid trespassing in a particular locale. A hunter should never sleep out on the ice edge. Every evening he had to return to land or to the old firm ice that lies some distance back from the open sea, because the Sea Spirit does not like her creatures to smell human beings while they are not hunting (Rasmussen 1929:76). Care also must be taken not to cook land and sea mammals in the same pot; fresh water must be placed in the mouth of recently killed sea mammals, and fat must be placed in the mouth of slain land mammals (Wallace 1966:90). Note that some of these "superstitions" may have alleviated psychological stress or have had a practical value for hunting or some other aspect of Eskimo life. Not sleeping out on the ice, for example, is a safety precaution.

SHAMANISTIC CULTS

Shamans are those who are socially recognized as having special abilities for entering into contact with spirit beings and for controlling supernatural forces. The full shamanistic complex includes some form of trance experience during which the shaman's powers are increased. Possession, the invasion of the human body by a god or spirit, is the most common form of shamanistic trance. The shaman goes into a trance by smoking tobacco, taking drugs, beating on a drum, dancing monotonously, or simply by closing his or her eyes and concentrating. The trance begins with rigidity of the body, sweating, and heavy breathing. While in the trance the shaman may act as a medium, transmitting messages from the ancestors. With the help of friendly spirits, shamans predict future events, locate lost objects, identify the cause of illness, prescribe cures, and give advice on how clients can protect themselves against the evil intentions of enemies.

There is a close relationship between shamanistic cults and individualistic vision quests. Shamans are usually personalities who are psychologically predisposed toward hallucinatory experiences. In cultures that use hallucinogenic substances freely in order to penetrate the mysteries of the other world, many people may claim shamanistic status (Fig. 23.6). Among the Jivaro, one out of every four men is a shaman, since the use of hallucinogenic vines makes it possible for almost everyone to achieve the trance states essential for the practice of shamanism (Harner 1972:154). Elsewhere, becoming a shaman may be restricted to people who are prone to having auditory and visual hallucinations.

An important part of shamanistic performance in many parts of the world consists of simple tricks of ventriloquism, sleight of hand, and illusion. The Siberian shamans, for example, signaled the arrival of the possessing spirit by secretly shaking the walls of a darkened tent. Throughout South America the standard shamanistic curing ceremony involves the removal of slivers of bone, pebbles, bugs, and other foreign objects from the patient's body. The practice of these tricks should not be regarded as evidence that the shaman has a cynical or disbelieving attitude toward the rest of the performance. Michael Harner (1982), a modern proponent of shamanic rituals, insists there is nothing fraudulent about the sucking cure (see Box 23.2). It is not the object itself that is in the patient's body and causing the trouble; rather it is the object's spiritual counterpart. Shamans put the material object in their mouth during the sucking

FIGURE *23.6*

FEMALE SHAMAN
Piegan "medicine woman." Not all shamans are men.

cure because this helps withdraw its spiritual counterpart.

Although trance is part of the shamanistic repertory in hundreds of cultures, it is not universal. Many cultures have part-time specialists who do not make use of trance but who diagnose and cure disease, find lost objects, foretell the future, and confer immunity in war and success in love. Such persons may be referred to variously as magicians, seers, sorcerers, witch doctors, medicine men or medicine women, and curers. The full shamanistic complex embodies all these roles.

Among the Tapirapé, a village people of central Brazil (Wagley 1977), shamans (Fig. 23.7) derive their powers from dreams in which they encounter

BOX *23.2*

THE TAPIRAPÉ SUCKING CURE

Unless the illness is serious enough to warrant immediate treatment, shamans always cure in the late evening. A shaman comes to his patient, and squats near the patient's hammock; his first act is always to light his pipe. When the patient has a fever or has fallen unconscious from the sight of a ghost, the principal method of treatment is by massage. The shaman blows smoke over the entire body of the patient; then he blows smoke over his own hands, spits into them, and massages the patient slowly and firmly, always toward the extremities of the body. He shows that he is removing a foreign substance by quick movement of his hands as he reaches the end of an arm or leg.

The more frequent method of curing, however, is by the extraction of a malignant object by sucking. The shaman squats alongside the hammock of his patient and begins to "eat smoke"—swallow large gulps of tobacco smoke from his pipe. He forces the smoke with great intakes of breath deep down into his stomach; soon he becomes intoxicated and nauseated; he vomits violently and smoke spews from his stomach. He groans and clears his throat in the manner of a person gagging with nausea but unable to vomit. By sucking back what he vomits he accumulates saliva in his mouth.

In the midst of this process he stops several times to suck on the body of his patient and finally, with one awful heave, he spews all the accumulated material on the ground. He then searches in this mess for the intrusive object that has been causing the illness. Never once did I see a shaman show the intrusive object to observers. At one treatment a Tapirapé [shaman] usually repeats this process of "eating smoke," sucking, and vomiting several times. Sometimes, when a man of prestige is ill, two or even three shamans will cure side by side in this manner and the noise of violent vomiting resounds throughout the village.

SOURCE: Wagley 1943:73–74.

FIGURE *23.7*

TAPIRAPÉ SHAMAN
The shaman has fallen into a tobacco-induced trance and cannot walk unaided.

spirits who become the shaman's helpers. Dreams are caused by souls leaving the body and going on journeys. Frequent dreaming is a sign of shamanistic talent. Mature shamans, with the help of the spirit familiars, can turn into birds or launch themselves through the air in gourd "canoes," visit with ghosts and demons, or travel to distant villages forward and backward through time.

Tapirapé shamans are frequently called on to cure illness. This they do with sleight of hand and the help of their spirit familiars while in a semitrance condition induced by gulping huge quantities of tobacco, which makes them vomit (Box 23.2). It is interesting to note in conjunction with the widespread use of tobacco in native American rituals that tobacco contains hallucinogenic alkaloids and may have induced visions when consumed in large quantities.

COMMUNAL CULTS

No culture is completely without communally organized religious beliefs and practices. Even the Innuit have group rites. Frightened and sick Innuit individuals under the cross-examinations of shamans publicly confess violations of taboos that have made them ill and that have endangered the rest of the community.

Among native Americans of the Western Plains there were annual public rites of self-torture and vision quest known as the Sun Dance (Fig. 23.8). Under the direction of shaman leaders, the sun dancers tied themselves to a pole by means of a cord passed through a slit in their skin. Watched by the assembled group, they walked or danced around the pole and tugged at the cord until they fainted or the skin ripped apart. These public displays of endurance and bravery were part of the intense marauding and warfare complex that developed after the coming of the Europeans. Communal rites fall into two major categories: (1) rites of solidarity and (2) rites of passage. In the rites of solidarity, participation in dramatic public rituals enhances the sense of group identity, coordinates the actions of the individual members of the group, and prepares the group for immediate or future cooperative action. Rites of passage celebrate the social movement of individuals into and out of groups or into or out of statuses of critical importance to the individual and to the community. Reproduction, the achievement of manhood and womanhood, marriage, and death are the principal worldwide occasions for rites of passage.

Communal Rites of Solidarity: Totemism

Rites of solidarity are common among clans and other descent groups. Such groups usually have names and emblems that identify group members and set one group off from another. Animal names and emblems predominate, but insects, plants, and natural phenomena such as rain and clouds also occur. These group-identifying objects are known as *totems*. Many totems such as bear, breadfruit, or kangaroo are useful or edible species, and often there is a stipulated descent relationship between the members of the group and their totemic ancestor. Sometimes the members of the group must refrain from harming or eating their totem. There are many variations in the specific forms of totemic belief, however, and no single totemic complex can be said to exist.

The Arunta of Australia provide one of the classic cases of totemic ritual. Here an individual identifies with the totem of the sacred place near which one's mother passed shortly before becoming pregnant (see p. 276). These places contain the stone

FIGURE *23.8*

DAKOTA SUN DANCE
Painted by Short-Bull, chief of the Oglala Dakota (Sioux), this painting represents
the Sun Dance of more than 90 years ago. The circle in the center represents
a windbreak formed of fresh cottonwood boughs. In the center is the Sun Dance pole,
and hanging from it are the figures of a man and buffalo. Outside the Sun Dance
enclosure, devotees perform. One of them is dragging four buffalo skulls by cords
run through openings in the skin on his back. He will continue to drag these until
they tear loose.

FIGURE *23.9*

BULL ROARER *CHURINGA*
String is tied through hole and used to whirl the bull roarer
around one's head. This specimen is from Australia.
It is made out of stone and is known as a *churinga*. It represents a human spirit.

objects known as *churinga,* which are the visible
manifestations of each person's spirit (Fig. 23.9). The
churinga are believed to have been left behind by the
totemic ancestors as they traveled about the countryside at the beginning of the world. The ancestors
later turned into animals, objects, and other phenomena constituting the inventory of totems. The sacred
places of each totem are visited annually.

These rituals have many meanings and functions. The participants are earnestly concerned with
protecting their totems and ensuring their reproduction. But the exclusive membership of the ritual group
also indicates that they are acting out the mythologi-
cal dogma of their common ancestry. The totem ceremonies reaffirm and intensify the sense of common
identity of the members of a regional community.

The handling of the *churinga* confirms the fact that the totemic group has "stones" or, in a more familiar metaphor, "roots" in a particular land.

Communal Rituals: Rites of Passage

Because they involve a web of interrelated status changes for the entire community, birth, puberty, marriage, and death are the most common occasions for rites of passage (Fig. 23.10) The individual who is born, who reaches adulthood, who takes a spouse, or who dies is not the only one implicated in these events. Many other people must adjust to these momentous changes. Being born not only defines a new life but brings into existence or modifies the position of parent, grandparent, sibling, heir, agemate, and many other domestic and political relationships.

FIGURE *23.10*

RELIGION AND LIFE CRISES
(A) Dogon funeral dancers. The Crow scaffold burial **(B)** shows a common means of disposing of the dead in sparsely inhabited regions. **(C)** The Peruvian mummies show another method, which is common in arid climates.

(A)

(B)

(C)

The main function of rites of passage is to give communal recognition to the entire complex of new or altered relationships and not merely to the changes experienced by the individuals who get born, marry, or die.

Rites of passage conform to a remarkably similar pattern among widely dispersed cultures (Eliade 1958; Schlegel and Barry 1979). First, the principal performers are separated from the routines associated with their earlier life. Second, decisive physical and symbolic steps are taken to extinguish the old status. Often these steps include the notion of killing the old personality. To promote "death and transfiguration," old clothing and ornaments are exchanged for new, and the body is painted or mutilated. Finally, the participants are ceremoniously returned to normal life.

The pattern of rites of passage can be seen in the male initiation ceremonies of the Ndembu of northern Zambia (Fig. 23.11). Here, as among many African and Middle Eastern peoples, the transition from boyhood to manhood involves the rite of circumcision. Young boys are taken from their separate villages and placed in a special bush "school." They are circumcised by their own kinsmen or neighbors, and after their wounds heal, they are returned to normal life (see Box 23.3).

In many cultures girls are subject to similar rites of separation, seclusion, and return in relationship to their first menses and their eligibility for marriage. Genital mutilation is also common among girls, and there is a widely practiced operation known

FIGURE *23.11*

NDEMBU RITES
(A) Although the women are supposed to be terrified of the "monster," they are actually amused and skeptical. **(B)** The circumcision camp— the "place of dying."

(A)

(B)

BOX *23.3*

NO RITES HURT TOO

Westerners are likely to be shocked and dismayed by examples of painful puberty rituals. But the system that has been substituted for such rituals may not have any clear advantage as far as eliminating pain and suffering. The passage from child to adult in advanced industrial societies is not marked by any rituals at all. No one is quite sure of when adulthood begins. As a result, the young girl or boy must pass through a prolonged period of stress, known as adolescence, which is marked by high rates of accidents, suicides, and antisocial behavior. Which system is more cruel?

as clitoridectomy. In this operation, the external tip of the clitoris is cut off. Among many Australian groups, both circumcision and clitoridectomy were practiced. In addition, the Australians knocked out the pubescent child's front tooth. Males were subject to the further operation of subincision, in which the underside of the penis was slit open to the depth of the urethra. In several parts of Africa, clitoridectomy was followed by a procedure in which the two sides of the vulva are attached to each other by stitching with silk or catgut sutures or by thorns, thus preventing vaginal intercourse until their removal at the time of marriage (Dualeh 1982; Gruenbaum 1988; Lightfoot-Klein 1989).

ECCLESIASTICAL CULTS

As stated above, ecclesiastical cults have in common the existence of a professional clergy or priesthood organized into a bureaucracy. This bureaucracy is usually associated with and under the control of a central temple. At secondary or provincial temple centers, the clergy may exercise a considerable amount of independence. In general, the more highly centralized the political system, the more highly centralized the ecclesiastical bureaucracy.

The ecclesiastic specialists are different from both the Tapirapé shamans and the Ndembu circumcisers and guardians. They are formally designated persons who devote themselves to the rituals of their office (Fig. 23.12). These rituals usually include a wide variety of techniques for influencing and controlling animistic beings and animatistic forces. The material support for these full-time specialists is usually closely related to power and privileges of taxation. As among the Inca (p. 316), the state and the priesthood may divide up the rent and tribute exacted from the peasants. Under feudalism (see p. 315), the ecclesiastical hierarchy derives its earnings from its own estates and from the gifts of powerful princes and kings. High officials in feudal ecclesiastical hierarchies are almost always kin or appointees of members of the ruling class.

The presence of ecclesiastical organizations produces a profound split among those who participate in ritual performances. On the one hand, there is an active segment, the priesthood; on the other, the passive "congregation," who are virtual spectators. The members of the priesthood must acquire intricate ritual, historical, calendrical, and astronomical knowledge. Often they are scribes and learned persons. It must be stressed, however, that the "congregation" does not altogether abandon individualistic shamanistic and communal beliefs and rituals. These are all continued, sometimes secretly, in neighborhoods, villages, or households, side by side with the "higher" rituals, despite more or less energetic efforts on the part of the ecclesiastical hierarchy to stamp out what it often calls idolatrous, superstitious, pagan, heathen, or heretical beliefs and performances.

FIGURE *23.12*

ECCLESIASTICAL CULT
A Roman Catholic high mass is celebrated.

THE RELIGION OF THE AZTECS

Many of the principal characteristics of belief and ritual in stratified contexts can be seen in the ecclesiastical organization of the Aztecs of Mexico. The Aztecs held their priests responsible for the maintenance and renewal of the entire universe. By performing annual rituals, priests could obtain the blessing of the Aztec gods, ensure the well-being of the Aztec people, and guard the world against collapse into chaos and darkness. According to Aztec theology, the world had already passed through four ages, each of which ended in cataclysmic destruction. The first age ended when the reigning god transformed himself into the sun and all the people of the earth were devoured by jaguars. The second age, ruled over by the feathered serpent (Fig. 23.13), was destroyed by hurricanes that changed people into monkeys. The third age, ruled over by the god of rain, was brought to a close when the heavens rained fire. Then came the rule of the goddess of water, whose time ended with a universal flood, during which people turned into fish. The

FIGURE *23.13*

TEMPLE OF QUETZALCOATL
The plumed serpent, Mexico City (formerly Tenochtitlán).

fifth age is in progress, ruled over by the sun god and doomed to destruction sooner or later by earthquakes.

The principal function of the 5000 priests living in the Aztec capital was to make sure that the end of the world came later rather than sooner. This could be assured only by pleasing the legions of gods reputed to govern the world. The best way to please the gods was to give them gifts, the most precious being fresh human hearts. The hearts of war captives were the most esteemed gifts, since they were won only at great expense and risk.

Aztec ceremonial centers were dominated by large pyramidal platforms topped by temples (Fig. 23.14). These structures were vast stages on which the drama of human sacrifice was enacted at least once a day throughout the year. On especially critical days there were multiple sacrifices. The set pattern for these performances involved first the vic-

tim's ascent of the huge staircase to the top of the pyramid; then, at the summit, the victim was seized by four priests, one for each limb, and bent face up, spread-eagled over the sacrificial stone. A fifth priest cut the victim's chest open with an obsidian knife and wrenched out the beating heart. The heart was smeared over the statue of the god and later burned. Finally, the lifeless body was flung over the edge of the pyramid where it was rolled back down the steps. It is believed that during a four-day dedication ceremony of the main Aztec temple in Tenochtitlan, 20,000 prisoners of war were sacrificed in the manner described above. A yearly toll estimated to have been as high as 15,000 people was sent to death to placate the bloodthirsty gods. Most of these victims were prisoners of war, although local youths, maidens, and children were also sacrificed from time to time (Berdan 1982; Coe 1977; Soustelle 1970; Vaillant 1966). The bodies of most of those who

FIGURE *23.14*

TENOCHTITLÁN
A reconstructed view of the Aztec capital, with its numerous temple-topped pyramids.

were sacrificed were rolled down the pyramid steps, dismembered, and probably cooked and eaten (Harner 1977; see Box 23.4 for evidence of Aztec cannibalism).

AZTEC CANNIBALISM

Prior to the emergence of the state, many societies practiced human sacrifice and ritually consumed all or part of the bodies of prisoners of war (Harris 1985, 1989). Lacking the political means to tax and conscript large populations, chiefdoms had little interest in preserving the lives of their defeated enemies. With the advent of the state, however, these practices tended to disappear. As we have seen (p. 312), conquered territories were incorporated into the state and the labor power of defeated populations was tapped through taxation, conscription, and tribute. Thus, the preservation of the lives of defeated peoples became an essential part of the process of state expansion.

The Aztec, however, were an exception to this general trend. Instead of tabooing human sacrifice and cannibalism and encouraging charity and kindness toward defeated enemy peoples, the Aztec state made human sacrifice and cannibalism the main focus of ecclesiastical beliefs and rituals (Fig. 23.15). As the Aztec became more powerful, they sacrificed more and more prisoners of war and became more rather than less cannibalistic (Fig. 23.16).

Although it is considered controversial, Michael Harner's (1977) explanation of the Aztec state's unique cannibal religion remains the best theory available. Harner starts from the fact that as a result of millennia of intensification and population growth, the central Mexican highlands had lost their best domesticable animal species. Unlike the Inca, who obtained animal foods from llama, alpaca, and guinea pigs—or the Old World states that had sheep, goats, pigs, and cattle—the Aztec had only semidomesticated ducks and turkeys, and hairless dogs. Wild fauna, such as deer and migrating waterfowl, were not abundant enough to provide the Aztecs with more than 1 or 2 grams of animal protein per capita per day (compared with over 60 grams in the United States). The depleted condition of the natural fauna is shown by the prominence in the Aztec diet of bugs, worms,

BOX *23.4*

THE EVIDENCE FOR AZTEC CANNIBALISM

Bernadino de Sahagún, who started collecting data on the Aztecs in the 1540s, is generally considered to be the most honest and reliable historian and ethnograper of Aztec Culture. This is what he wrote in his *General History of the Things of New Spain:*

After having torn their hearts from them and poured the blood into a gourd vessel, which the master of the slain man himself received, they started the body rolling down the pyramid steps. It came to rest upon a small square below. There some old men, whom they called Quaquacuitlin, laid hold of it and carried it to their tribal temple, where they dismembered it and divided it up in order to eat it. [Sahagún 1951:3].

Again and again Sahagún asserts that the common fate of the victim's corpse was to be eaten:

After they had slain them and torn out their hearts, they took them away gently, rolling them down the steps. When they had reached the bot-tom, they cut off their heads and inserted a rod through them, and they carried the bodies to the houses which they called calpulli, *where they divided them up in order to eat them.* [Ibid.:24]

Diego Durán, another major chronicler, clarifies the nature of the occasion on which the "masters"—warriors who had captured the victims and marched them to Tenochtitlán—devoured the corpses.

Once the heart had been wrenched out it was offered to the sun and blood sprinkled toward the solar deity. Imitating the descent of the sun in the west the corpse was toppled down the steps of the pyramid. After the sacrifice the warriors celebrated a great feast with much dancing, ceremonial and cannibalism. [Durán 1964:121]

Can there be any doubt that Aztec human sacrifice was the precise counterpart of the redistributive feasting that so many other early ecclesiastical religions carried out with animal rather than human offerings?

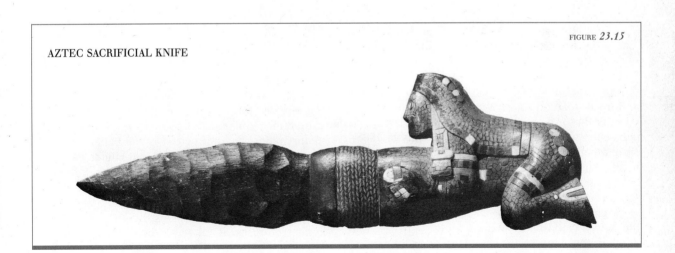

FIGURE *23.15*

AZTEC SACRIFICIAL KNIFE

and "scum cakes," which were made out of algae skimmed off the surface of Lake Texcoco (see Harris 1979b; Sahlins 1978).

Harner's theory is that the severe depletion of animal resources made it uniquely difficult for the Aztec state to prohibit the consumption of human flesh in order to facilitate its expansionist aims. Due to the severe depletion of animal resources, human flesh rather than animal flesh was redistributed as a means of rewarding loyalty to the throne and bravery in combat. Moreover, to have made serfs or slaves out of captives would only have worsened the animal food shortage. There was thus much to lose by prohibiting cannibalism and little to gain.

FIGURE *23.16*

SKULL RACK
One of the smaller racks in the Aztec capital.
The skulls in the photograph are sculpted in stone;
during Aztec times, real skulls were exhibited
on wooden structures raised on the sculpted base.
Part of the ongoing excavation in Mexico City.

BOX *23.5*

MEAT AND POLITICS IN THE SOVIET UNION

"If we could put 80 kilograms [176 pounds] of meat a year on the consumer's table, all other problems that we have would not be as acute as they are now. It is no exaggeration to say that the shortage of meat products is a problem that is worrying the whole nation."

SOURCE: Mikhail Gorbachev addressing the Soviet Central Committee. Quoted in Gumbel 1988.

It would have been far more puzzling if the Aztecs did not consume the flesh of their prisoners of war after expending so much effort in capturing and killing them. In etic perspective, it cannot be said that that the Aztecs went to war to obtain prisoners and meat. Like all states, the Aztec went to war for reasons that are associated with the inherently expansionist nature of the state (p. 312; Hassig 1988). From an emic perspective, as reported to the Spanish by the Aztecs, however, one could say that the desire to capture prisoners for sacrifice and consumption was an important objective of the participants.

This theory cannot be disproved by showing that the Aztecs could have obtained all of their essential nutrients from worms insects, algae, corn, beans, and other plant foods (Ortiz de Montellano 1978; 1983). Compared to meat, these are very inefficient packages of essential nutrients. Hence, the high value that the Aztecs placed on the consumption of human flesh was not a purely arbitrary consequence of their religious beliefs. Bear in mind that the perennial shortages of meat were an important source of discontent that contributed to the collapse of Soviet communism (Box 23.5). Rather, their religious beliefs (i.e.,

the cravings of their gods for human blood) reflected the importance of animal foods in relation to human dietary needs and the depleted supply of nonhuman animals in their habitat. (Note that most of the cultures of the world attach special value to the consumption of meat or other animal products rich in fat and protein. So-called "vegetarian cultures" are in reality lacto-vegetarians or ovo-vegetarians—that is, they spurn meat but eat dairy products and eggs.)

RELIGION AND POLITICAL ECONOMY: HIGH GODS

Full-time specialists, monumental temples, dramatic processions, and elaborate rites performed for spectator congregations are incompatible with the infrastructure and political economy of hunters and gatherers. Similarly, the complex astronomical and mathematical basis of ecclesiastical beliefs and rituals is never found among band and village peoples.

The level of political economy also influences the way in which gods are thought to relate to each other and to human beings. For example, the idea of a single high god who creates the universe is found among cultures at all levels of economic and political development. These high gods, however, play different kinds of roles in running the universe after they have brought it into existence. Among hunter-gatherers and other prestate peoples, the high gods tend to become inactive after their creation task is done (Sullivan 1987). It is to a host of lesser gods, demons, and ancestor souls that one must turn in order to obtain assistance (cf. Hayden 1987). On the other hand, in stratified societies the high god bosses the lesser gods and tends to be a more active figure to whom priests and commoners address their prayers (Swanson 1960), although the lesser gods may still be revered more actively by ordinary people.

A plausible explanation for this difference is that prestate cultures have no need for the idea of a central or supreme authority. Just as there is an absence of centralized control over people and strategic resources in life, so in religious belief, the inhabitants of the spirit would lack decisive control over each other. They form a more or less egalitarian group. On the other hand, the belief that superordination and subordination characterize relationships among the gods helps to obtain the cooperation of the commoner classes in stratified societies (Fig. 23.17; see p. 326).

One way to achieve conformity in stratified societies is to convince commoners that the gods demand obedience to the state. Disobedience and nonconformity result not only in retribution administered

	TABLE *23.1*
RELIGION, CLASS, AND MORALITY	

God interested in morality	Societies with social classes	Societies without social classes
Present	25	2
Absent	8	12

SOURCE: Adapted from Swanson 1960:166.

through the state's police-military apparatus but also in punishments in present or future life administered by the high gods themselves. In prestate societies, for reasons discussed in Chapter 17, law and order are rooted in common interest. Consequently, there is little need for high gods to administer punishments for those who have been "bad" and rewards for those who have been "good." But as Table 23.1 shows, where there are class differences, the gods are believed to take a lively interest in the degree to which each individual's thoughts and behavior are immoral or ethically subversive.

REVITALIZATION

The relationship of religion to structure and infrastructure can also be seen in the process known as *revitalization.* Under the severe stresses associated with colonial conquest and intense class or minority exploitation, religions tend to become movements concerned with achieving a drastic improvement in the immediate conditions of life and/or in the prospects for an afterlife. These movements are sometimes referred to as *nativistic, revivalistic, millenarian,* or *messianic.* The concept of revitalization is intended to embrace all the specific cognitive and ritual variants implied by these terms (see Wallace 1966).

Revitalization is a process of political and religious interaction between a depressed caste, class, minority, or other subordinate social group and a superordinate group. Some revitalization movements emphasize passive attitudes, the adoption of old rather than new cultural practices, or salvation through rewards after death; others advocate more or less open resistance or aggressive political or military action. These differences largely reflect the extent to which the subordinate groups are prepared to cope with the challenge to their power and authority. Revitalizations that take place under conditions of massive suffering and exploitation sooner or later

FIGURE *23.17*

RELIGION AND STRATIFICATION
Bishops and other high prelates of the Corpus Christi Cathedral in Cuzco, Peru, are an awe-inspiring sight to an Indian peasant.

result in political and even military probes or confrontations, even though both sides may overtly desire to avoid conflict (Worsley 1968). It should be kept in mind that Christianity and Islam began as revitalization movements. Protestantism and many of its subdivisions, such as the Amish, Hutterites, and Pentacostals, also resemble revitalization movements in several important respects, as do many of the current "electronic churches" (see p. 469).

NATIVE AMERICAN REVITALIZATIONS

Widespread revitalizations were provoked by the European invasion of the New World and the conquest and expulsion of the native American peoples and the destruction of their natural resources.

The most famous of the nineteenth-century revitalization movements was the Ghost Dance, also known (by whites) as the Messiah craze. This movement originated in 1870 near the California-Nevada border. A Paviotso prophet envisioned the return of the dead from the spirit world in a great train whose arrival would be signaled by a huge explosion. Simultaneously the whites would be swept from the land, but their buildings, machines, and other possessions would be left behind. (The resemblance to the neutron bomb is worth noting.) To hasten the arrival of the ancestors, there was to be ceremonial dancing accompanied by the songs revealed to the prophet during his visions.

A second version of the Ghost Dance was begun in 1889 under the inspiration of another Paviotso prophet, named Wovoka (Fig. 23.18). A vision in which all the dead had been brought back to life by the Ghost Dance was again reported. Ostensibly Wovoka's teachings lacked political content, and as the Ghost Dance spread eastward across the Rockies, its political implications remained ambiguous. Yet for the native Americans of the Plains, the return of the dead meant that they would outnumber the whites and hence be more powerful.

Among the Sioux, there was a version that included the return of all the bison and the extermination of the whites under a huge landslide. The Sioux warriors put on Ghost Dance shirts, which they believed would make them invulnerable to bullets. Clashes between the U.S. Army and the Sioux became more frequent, and the Sioux leader Sitting Bull was arrested and killed. The second Ghost Dance movement came to an end with the massacre of 200 Sioux at Wounded Knee, South Dakota (Fig. 23.19), on December 29, 1890 (Mooney 1965).

FIGURE *23.18*

WOVOKA
Leader of the Ghost Dance.

After all chance of military resistance was crushed, the native American revitalization movement became more introverted and passive. Visions in which all the whites were wiped out ceased to be experienced, confirming once again the responsiveness of religion to political reality. The development and spread of beliefs and rituals centering on peyote, mescal, and other hallucinogenic drugs are characteristic of many twentieth-century native American

FIGURE *23.19*

WOUNDED KNEE
(A) In the first battle, in 1890, 200 Sioux Indians were killed by the U.S. army.
(B) In the second battle, in 1973, militant Indians occupied the village of Wounded Knee, South Dakota, and exchanged gunfire with U.S. marshals.

(A)

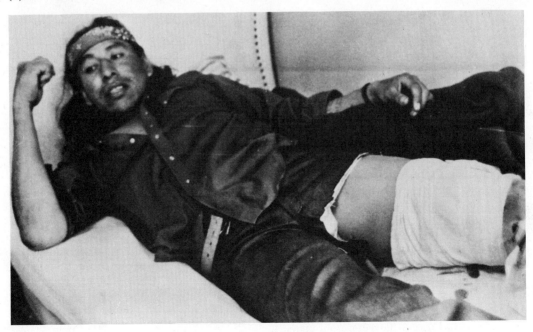

(B)

FIGURE *23.20*

PEYOTE CEREMONY
Delaware Indians of Oklahoma spend the night in prayer and meditation.
At right, they emerge to greet the dawn.

revitalizations. Peyote ritual, as practiced in the Native American Church, involves a night of praying, singing, peyote eating, and ecstatic contemplation followed by a communal breakfast (Fig 23.20). The peyote eaters are not interested in bringing back the buffalo or making themselves invulnerable to bullets; they seek self-knowledge, personal moral strength, and physical health (La Barre 1938; Stewart 1987; see Box 23.6).

Peyotism and allied cult movements do not, of course, signal the end of political action on the part of the native Americans. With the emergence of the "Red Power" movement, the native Americans' attempt to hold on to and regain their stolen lands is now being carried out through lawyers, politicians, novelists, Washington lobbyists, sit-ins, and land-ins (Fig. 23.21) (DeLoria 1969; Josephy 1982; Walker 1972).

BOX *23.6*

PEYOTE RELIGION

The peyote religion is a syncretistic cult, incorporating ancient Indian and modern Christian elements. The Christian theology of love, charity, and forgiveness has been added to the ancient Indian ritual and aboriginal desire to acquire personal power through individual visions. Peyotism has taught a program of accommodation for over 50 years and the peyote religion has succeeded in giving Indians pride in their native culture while adjusting to the dominant civilization of the whites.

SOURCE: Stewart 1968:108.

NATIVE AMERICAN MILITANTS
With Molotov cocktails and machine guns,
armed Mohawks near Montreal attempt
to prevent the takeover of their lands
for the building of a golf course.

CARGO CULTS

In New Guinea and Melanesia, revitalization is associated with the concept of *cargo*. The typical vision of the leaders of Melanesian revitalization movements is that of a ship bringing back the ancestors and a cargo of European goods. In recent times airplanes and spaceships have become the favorite means of delivering the cargo (see Worsley 1968).

As a result of the abundance of goods displayed by U.S. military forces during the Pacific island campaigns of World War II, some revitalizations stressed the return of the Americans. In Espiritu Santo in 1944, Tsek urged his people to destroy all trade goods and throw away their clothes in preparation for the return of the mysteriously departed Americans. Some of the American-oriented revitalizations have placed specific American soldiers in the role of cargo de-

liverers. On the island of Tana in the New Hebrides, the John Frumm cult cherishes an old GI jacket as the relic of one John Frumm, whose identity is not otherwise known (Fig. 23.22). The prophets of John Frumm build landing strips, bamboo control towers, and grass-thatched cargo sheds. In some cases beacons are kept ablaze at night and radio operators stand ready with tin-can microphones and earphones to guide the cargo planes to a safe landing.

An important theme is that the cargo planes and ships have been successfully loaded by the ancestors at U.S. ports and are on their way, but the local authorities have refused to permit the cargo to be landed. In other versions, the cargo planes are tricked into landing at the wrong airport. In a metaphorical sense these sentiments are applicable to the actual colonial contexts. The peoples of the South Seas have indeed often been tricked out of their lands and resources (Harris 1974).

In 1964 the island of New Hanover became the scene of the Lyndon Johnson cult. Under the leadership of the prophet Bos Malik, cult members demanded that they be permitted to vote for Johnson in the village elections scheduled for them by the Australian administration. Airplanes passing overhead at night were said to be President Johnson's planes searching for a place to land. Bos Malik advised that in order to get Johnson to be their president, they would have to "buy" him. This was to be done by

JOHN FRUMM
Members of this Tana, New Hebrides,
cargo cult.

paying the annual head tax to Malik instead of to the Australian tax collectors. When news reached New Hanover that an armed force had been dispatched to suppress the tax revolt, Malik prophesied that the liner Queen Mary would soon arrive bearing cargo and U.S. troops to liberate the islanders from the Australian oppressors. When the ship failed to materialize, Malik accused the Australian officials of stealing the cargo.

The confusion of the Melanesian revitalization prophets stems from lack of knowledge of the workings of cultural systems. They do not understand how modern industrial wage-labor societies are organized, nor comprehend how law and order are maintained among state-level peoples. To them, the material abundance of the industrial nations and the penury of others constitute an irrational flaw, a massive contradiction in the structure of the world. The belief system of the cargo cults vividly demonstrates why the assumption that all people distinguish between natural and supernatural categories is incorrect (see p. 386). Cargo leaders who have been taken to see modern Australian stores and factories in the hope that they would give up their beliefs return home more convinced than ever that they are following the best prescription for obtaining cargo. With their own eyes they have observed the fantastic abundance the authorities refuse to let them have (Lawrence 1964).

TABOO, RELIGION, AND ECOLOGY

As we have seen (p. 487), religion can be regarded as the concentration of the sense of the sacred. It follows that an appeal to the sacred nature of a rule governing interpersonal relations or of a rule governing the relationship between a population and its environment will be useful in resolving the uncertainties that people may sometimes experience concerning what they ought to do.

For example, the prohibition on incest within the nuclear family is widely seen as a sacred obligation. The violation of an incest taboo is looked on as a profane or antisacred act. One plausible explanation for these powerful sentiments is that people are strongly tempted to commit incest, but that the short-run satisfactions they might receive from such acts would have long-run negative consequences for them and for the continuity of social life because of the reduced ability of individuals and local groups to establish adaptive intergroup relationships (see p. 271). By surrounding incest prohibitions with the aura of

sacredness, the long-term individual and collective interests come to prevail, and the ambiguities and doubts individuals feel about renouncing the prohibited sexual relationships are resolved more decisively than would otherwise be possible. This does not mean that incest ceases to occur or that all psychological doubts are removed, but merely that such doubts are brought under more effective social control.

THE ABOMINABLE PIG

A similar tension between short-run and long-run costs and benefits may explain the origin of certain food taboos that are regarded as sacred obligations. For example, it seems likely that the ancient Israelite prohibition on the consumption of pork reflects the contradiction between the temptation to rear pigs and the negative consequences of raising animals that are useful only for meat. Pigs require shade and moisture to regulate their body temperature. With the progressive deforestation and desertification of the Middle East caused by the spread and intensification of agriculture and stock raising and by population growth, habitat zones suitable for pig rearing became scarce. Hence, an animal that was at one time reared and consumed as a relatively inexpensive source of fat and protein could no longer be reared and consumed by large numbers of people without reducing the efficiency of the main system of food production (Harris 1985). The temptation to continue the practice of pig raising persisted, however; hence the invocation of sacred commandments in the ancient Hebrew religion. Note that the explanation of the ancient origins of this taboo does not account for its perpetuation into the present. Once in existence, the taboo against pork (and other foods) acquired the function of demarcating or bounding Jewish ethnic minorities from other groups and of increasing their sense of identity and solidarity (see p. 337). Outside the Middle East the taboo no longer served an ecological function, but it continued to be useful on the level of structural relationships.

THE SACRED COW

The case of the sacred cow of India conforms to the general theory that the flesh of certain animals is made taboo when it becomes very expensive as a result of ecological changes. Like pigs in the Middle East, cattle were sacrificed and eaten quite freely in India during the Neolithic. With the rise of the state and of dense rural and urban populations, however, cattle could no longer be raised in sufficient numbers to be used both as a source of meat and as the principal source of traction power for pulling plows. But as the taboo on cattle use developed, it took a form quite different from the Israelite taboo on the pig. Whereas the pig was valued almost exclusively for its flesh, cattle were also valued for their milk and especially for their traction power. When pigs became too costly to be raised for meat, the whole animal became taboo and an abomination. But as cattle in India became too costly to be raised for meat, their value as a source of traction power increased (the land had to be plowed more intensively as population grew). Therefore, they had to be protected rather than abominated, and so the Hindu religion came to emphasize everyone's sacred duty to refrain from killing cattle or eating beef. Interestingly enough, the Brahmans, who at one time were the caste responsible for ritually slaughtering cattle, later became the caste most concerned with their protection and most opposed to the development of a beef slaughtering industry in India (Harris 1977, 1979a, 1985; cf. Simoons 1979).

What about the sacred cow today? Is the religious ban on the slaughter of cattle and the consumption of beef a functionally useful feature of modern Hinduism? Everyone agrees that the human population of India needs more calories and proteins, yet the Hindu religion bans the slaughter of cattle and taboos the eating of beef. These taboos are often held responsible for the creation of large numbers of aged, decrepit, barren, and useless cattle. Such animals are depicted as roaming aimlessly across the Indian countryside, clogging the roads, stopping the trains, stealing food from the marketplace, and blocking city streets (Fig. 23.23). A closer look at some of the details of the ecology and economy of the Indian subcontinent, however, suggests that the taboo in question does not decrease the capacity of the present Indian system of food production to support human life (see Box 23.7).

The basis of traditional Indian agriculture is the ox-drawn plow (see p. 356). Each peasant farmer needs at least two oxen to plow the fields at the proper time of the year. Despite the impression of surplus cattle, the central fact of Indian rural life is that there is a shortage of oxen, since one-third of the peasant households own less than the minimum pair. It is true that many cows are too old, decrepit, and sick to do a proper job of reproducing. At this point the ban on slaughter and beef consumption is thought to exert its harmful effect. For rather than kill dry, barren, and aged cows,

(A)

(B)

FIGURE *23.23*

SACRED COWS
(A) This resident of Calcutta is not wandering aimlessly; its owner knows where it is. **(B)** These cows are "parked," not blocking traffic. In India, cattle are ecologically more valuable than cars.

the Hindu farmer is depicted as ritually obsessed with preserving the life of each sacred beast, no matter how useless it may become. From the point of view of the poor farmer, however, these relatively undesirable creatures may be quite essential and useful. The farmer would prefer to have more vigorous cows, but

BOX *23.7*

OTHER FAVORABLE CONSEQUENCES OF THE TABOO ON THE CONSUMPTION OF BEEF

There are a number of additional reasons for concluding that the Hindu taboos against the slaughter of cattle and the consumption of beef have a positive rather than a negative effect on agricultural productivity in India. The ban on slaughter discourages the development of a meat-packing industry. Such an industry would be ecologically disastrous in a land as densely populated as India. In this connection it should be pointed out that the animal fat and protein output of the existing system is substantial. Although the Indian cows are very poor milkers by Western standards, they nonetheless contribute critical if small quantities of fat and protein to the diets of millions of people. Moreover, a considerable amount of beef does get eaten during the course of the year, since animals that die a natural death are consumed by carrion-eating outcastes. Finally, the critical function of the ban on slaughter during famines should be noted. When hunger stalks the Indian countryside, the slaughter taboo helps the peasants to resist the temptation to eat their cattle. If this temptation were to win out over religious scruples, it would be impossible for them to plant new crops when the rains began. Thus the intense resistance among Hindu saints to the slaughter and consumption of beef takes on a new meaning in the context of the Indian infrastructure. In the words of Mahatma Gandhi:

Why the cow was selected for apotheosis is obvious to me. The cow was in India the best companion. She was the giver of plenty. Not only did she give milk but she also made agriculture possible. [1954:3]

---

against slaughter but by the shortage of land and pasture.

Even barren cows, however, are by no means a total loss. Their dung makes an essential contribution to the energy system as fertilizer and as cooking fuel. Millions of tons of artificial fertilizer at prices beyond the reach of the small farmer would be required to make up for the loss of dung if substantial numbers of cattle were sent to slaughter. Since cattle dung is also a major source of cooking fuel, the slaughter of substantial numbers of animals would require the purchase of expensive dung substitutes, such as wood, coal, or kerosene. Cattle dung is relatively cheap because the cattle do not eat foods that can be eaten by people. Instead, they eat the stubble left in the fields and the marginal patches of grass on steep hillsides, roadside ditches, railroad embankments, and other nonarable lands. This constant scavenging gives the impression that cows are roaming around aimlessly, devouring everything in sight. But most cows have an owner, and in the cities, after poking about in the market refuse and nibbling on neighbors' lawns, each cow returns to its stall at the end of the day.

In a study of the bioenergetic balances involved in the cattle complex of villages in West Bengal, Stuart Odend'hal (1972) found that "basically, the cattle convert items of little direct human value into products of immediate human utility." Their gross energetic efficiency in supplying useful products was several times greater than that characteristic of agroindustrial beef production. He concludes that "judging the productive value of Indian cattle based on Western standards is inappropriate."

Although it might be possible to maintain or exceed the present level of production of oxen and dung with substantially fewer cows of larger and better breeds, the question arises as to how these cows would be distributed among the poor farmers. Are the farmers who have only one or two decrepit animals to be driven from the land?

Aside from the problem of whether present levels of population and productivity could be maintained with fewer cows, there is the theoretically more crucial question of whether it is the taboo on slaughter that accounts for the observed ratio of cattle to people. This seems highly unlikely. Despite the ban on slaughter, Hindu farmers cull their herds and adjust sex ratios to crops, weather, and regional conditions. The cattle are killed by various indirect means equivalent to the forms of neglect discussed in Chapter 13 with respect to human population controls. As a result of culling unwanted female calves, there are over 200 oxen for every 100 cows in the Gangetic plain, one of the most religiously orthodox regions of India (Vaidyanathan et al. 1982).

SUMMARY

Edward Tylor defined religion as animism or the doctrine of souls. According to Tylor, from the idea of the soul the idea of all godlike beings arose, while the idea of the soul itself arose as an attempt to explain phenomena such as trances, dreams, shadows, and reflections. Tylor's definition has been criticized for failing to consider the multifunctional nature of religion and for overlooking the compelling reality of direct hallucinatory contact with extraordinary beings.

As the Jivaro belief in three souls demonstrates, each culture uses the basic concepts of animism in its own distinctive fashion.

Tylor's definition of religion was supplemented by Marett's concepts of animatism and mana. Animatism refers to the belief in an impersonal life force in people, animals, and objects. The concentration of this force gives people, animals, and objects mana, or the capacity to be extraordinarily powerful and successful.

The Western distinction between natural and supernatural is of limited utility for defining religion. As the case of the Gururumba indicates, in many cultures there are no supernatural versus natural controls, only controls.

The distinction between sacred and profane realms of human experience may have greater universal validity than that between natural and supernatural. According to Durkheim, the feeling that something is sacred expresses the awe in which the hidden force of social consensus is held. Frazer tried to cope with the enormous variety of religious experience by separating religion from magic. Humility, supplication, and doubt characterize religion; routine cause and effect characterize magic. This distinction is difficult to maintain in view of the routine and coercive fashion in which animistic beings are often manipulated. There is no sharp difference between prayers and magic spells. Religion is a mix of awe and wonder, boredom and excitement, power and weakness.

The principal varieties of beliefs and rituals show broad correlations with levels of political economic organization. Four levels of religious organizations or cults can be distinguished: individualistic, shamanistic, communal, and ecclesiastical.

Innuit religion illustrates the individualistic or do-it-yourself level. Each individual carries out a series of rituals and observes a series of taboos that are deemed essential for survival and well-being, without the help of any part-time or full-time specialist. Do-it-yourself cults, however, are not to be confused with "anything goes." Vision quests, beliefs, and rituals always follow culturally determined patterns. Even dreams are culturally patterned.

No culture is devoid of shamanistic cults, defined by the presence of part-time magico-religious experts, or shamans, who have special talents and knowledge, usually involving sleight of hand, trances, and possession. As the case of Tapirapé shamanism indicates, shamans are frequently employed to cure sick people, as well as to identify and destroy evildoers. Many shamans think they can fly and move backward and forward through time.

Communal cults, involving public rituals deemed essential for the welfare or survival of the entire social group, also occur to some extent at all political-economic levels. Two principal types of communal ritual can be distinguished: rites of solidarity and rites of passage. As illustrated by the Arunta totemic rituals, rites of solidarity reaffirm and intensify a group's sense of common identity and express in symbolic form the group's claims to territory and resources.

As illustrated in the Ndembu circumcision rituals, rites of passage symbolically and publicly denote the extinction or "death" of an individual's or group's socially significant status and the acquisition or "birth" of a new socially significant status.

Finally, ecclesiastical cults are those that are dominated by a hierarchy of full-time specialists or "priests" whose knowledge and skills are usually commanded by a state-level ruling class. To preserve and enhance the well-being of the state and of the universe, historical, astronomical, and ritual information must be acquired by the ecclesiastical specialists. Ecclesiastical cults are also characterized by huge investments in buildings, monuments, and personnel and by a thoroughgoing split between the specialist performers of ritual and the great mass of more or less passive spectators who constitute the "congregation."

With the development of the state, the objective of warfare shifted from that of routing enemy populations to incorporating them within imperial systems. This brought an end to the practice of sacrificing and eating prisoners of war.

A theory that explains the unique features of Aztec religion is that the animal resources of central Mexico had been depleted. It was difficult for the Aztec state to refrain from rewarding its armies with the flesh of enemy soldiers in its effort to justify, expand, and consolidate ruling-class power. The depleted nature of Aztec animal resources is shown by the prominence of insects, worms, and algae in their diet. While balanced protein rations can be obtained from such foods as well as from corn and beans, the emphasis on obtaining and consuming vertebrate flesh and dairy products reflects a universal adaptive strategy for maximizing protein, fat, mineral, and vitamin consumption. The Aztecs' consumption of human flesh was an expression of this adaptive strategy; it could not be suppressed because of the depletion of alternative sources of animal foods.

Revitalization is another category of religious phenomena that cannot be understood apart from political-economic conditions. Under political-economic stress, subordinate castes, classes, minorities, and ethnic groups develop beliefs and rituals concerned with achieving a drastic improvement in their immediate well-being and/or their well-being in a life after death. These movements have the latent capacity to attack the dominant group directly or indirectly through political or military action; on the other hand, they may turn inward and accommodate by means of passive doctrines and rituals involving individual guilt, drugs, and contemplation.

Native American revitalizations were initially violent protests against genocide and ethnocide. The Sioux put on Ghost Dance shirts to protect themselves against bullets. After the suppression of the Ghost Dance movement, revitalization returned to contemplative renewal of native traditions, as in the peyote religion. More recently, the struggle of native Americans has become more secular and legalistic.

Melanesian and New Guinea cargo revitalizations foresaw the ancestors returning in ships laden with European trade goods. Later, airplanes and spaceships were substituted for sailing ships and steamboats. Cargo cults reflect a misunderstanding of industrial state systems by peoples who were living on the big-man village level of political evolution when they were brought into the wage-labor system.

Religious beliefs and rituals also exhibit adaptive relationships in the form of taboos. Taboos often take the form of sacred injunctions that resolve ambiguities and control the temptation to engage in behavior, such as incest, that has short-term benefits but that is socially disruptive in the long run. Many taboos on animals whose exploitation leads to ambiguous ecological and economic consequences can be seen in the same light. The ancient Israelite pig taboo, for example, can be understood as an adaptation to the changing costs and benefits of pig-rearing brought about by population increase, deforestation, and desertification.

A final example of the way in which taboos and whole religions adapt to changing political, economic, and ecological contexts is represented by the sacred cow of India.

Art

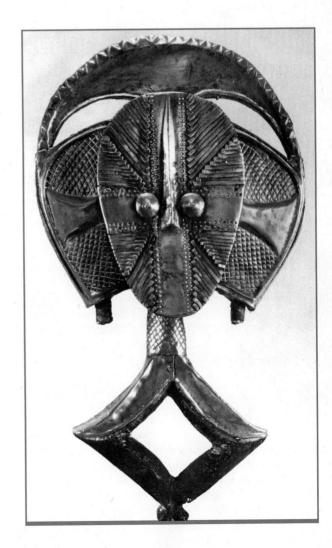

This chapter is concerned with additional aspects of superstructure—namely, the thought and behavior associated with painting, music, poetry, sculpture, dance, and other media of art. What is art? Is art as defined by Western art critics a valid definition of art in other cultures? How and why do the specific forms and styles of artistic expression vary from one culture to another? Is art ever only for art's sake? We shall see that art is not an isolated sector of human experience. It is intimately connected with and embedded in religion, politics, technology, and many other components of human social life.

WHAT IS ART?

Alexander Alland (1977:39) defines art as "play with form producing some aesthetically successful transformation-representation." The key ingredients in this definition are *play, form, aesthetic,* and *transformation.*

Play is an enjoyable, self-rewarding aspect of activity that cannot be accounted for simply by the utilitarian or survival functions of that activity.

Form designates a set of restrictions on how the art play is to be organized in time and space—the rules of the game of art.

Aesthetic designates the existence of a universal human capacity for an emotionally charged response of appreciation and pleasure when art is successful.

Transformation-representation refers to the communicative aspect of art. Art always represents something—communicates information—but this something is never represented in its literal shape, sound, color, movement, or feeling. To be art, as distinct from other forms of communication, the representation must be transformed into some metaphoric or symbolic statement, movement, image, or object that stands for whatever is being represented. A portrait, for example, no matter how "realistic," can only be a transformation-representation of the individual it depicts.

As Alland points out, play, adherence to form, and an aesthetic sense are found in many nonhuman animals. Chimpanzees, for example, like to play with paints (Fig. 24.1). Their adherence to form can be demonstrated by their placement of designs in the center of blank spaces or by their balancing of designs on different parts of a page. (They don't simply paint right off the page.) An aesthetic sense can be inferred by their repeated attempts to copy simple designs such as circles and triangles accurately. Moreover, as we have seen in Chapter 8, the capacity to use symbols and to learn rules of symbolic transfor-

mation is not entirely confined to human beings. The 3-year-old chimp Moja drew a bird and gave the sign for it. The trainer tried to make sure that it was a bird rather than a berry, so he asked her to draw a berry, which she promptly did (Hill 1978:98).

Nonetheless, just as grammatical language remains rudimentary among apes in nature, so too does their artistry. Although the rudiments of art can be found in our primate heritage, only *Homo sapiens* can justly be called the "artistic animal."

ART AS A CULTURAL CATEGORY

Although it is possible to identify art as an etic category of thought and behavior in all human cultures, an emic distinction between art and nonart is not universal (just as the distinction between natural and supernatural is not universal). What most Westerners mean by art is a particular emic category of modern Euramerican civilization. Euramerican schoolchildren are enculturated to the idea that art is a category of activities and products that stands opposed to the category of nonart. They learn to believe, in other words, that some paintings, carvings, songs, dances, and stories are not art. In Western civilization a particular performance is deemed artistic or not by a distinct group of authorities—an art establishment—who make or judge art and who control the museums, conservatories, critical journals, and other organizations and institutions devoted to art as a livelihood and style of life. Most cultures lack any semblance of an art establishment. This does not mean they lack art or artistic standards. A painted design on a pot or a rock, a carved mask or club, or a song or chant in a puberty ordeal is subject to critical evaluation by both performers and spectators. All cultures distinguish between less satisfactory and more satisfactory aesthetic experiences in decorative, pictorial, and expressive matters.

FIGURE *24.1*

CHIMPANZEE ARTISTS
(A), (B) A 2-year-old chimpanzee finger painting at the Baltimore Zoo. Note attempt to center painting. **(C)** A chimpanzee named Candy exhibits her artwork at the San Francisco Zoo.

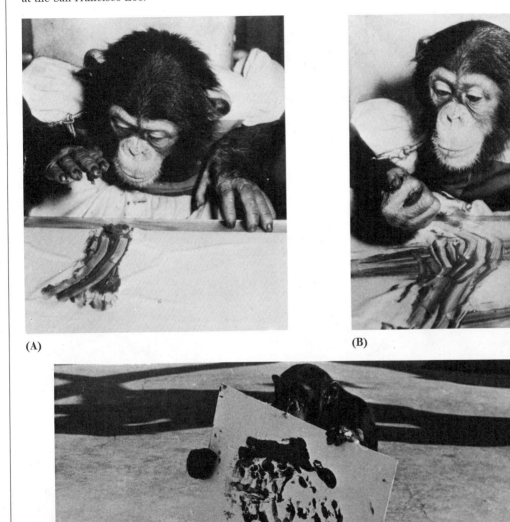

(A)

(B)

(C)

Basic to the modern Western idea of art and nonart is the exclusion of designs, stories, and artifacts that have a definite use in day-to-day subsistence activities and that are produced primarily for practical purposes or for commercial sale. Carpenters are distinguished from people who make wooden sculptures, bricklayers from architects, house painters from those who apply paint to canvas, and so forth. A similar opposition between art and practicality is seldom found in other cultures. Many works of art are produced and performed in complete harmony with utilitarian objectives. People everywhere, whether specialists or nonspecialists, derive pleasure from playfully embellishing and transforming the contours and surfaces of pots, fabrics, wood, and metal products (Fig. 24.2). All cultures, however, recognize that certain individuals are more skilled than others in making utilitarian objects and in embellishing them with pleasurable designs. Most anthropologists regard the skilled wood carver, basketmaker, potter, weaver, or sandalmaker as an artist.

ART AND INVENTION

As Alland (1977:24) suggests, play is a form of exploratory behavior that permits human beings to try out new and possibly useful responses in a controlled and protected context. The playful creative urge that lies behind art, therefore, is probably closely related to the creative urge that lies behind the development of science, technology, and new institutions. Art

FIGURE *24.2*

ART HAS MANY MEDIA
Native American cultures produced these objects. **(A)** Gold mummy mask with green stone eyes: Chumu, Peru. **(B)** Globular basket with coiled weave: Chumash, California. **(C)** Feathers of blue and yellow form the design of a Tapirapé mask: Brazil. **(D)** Painted wooden kero, or beaker, representing ocelot head: Inca, Peru. **(E)** Ceramic jar: Nazca, Peru. **(F)** Blanket, in blue, black, and white, with stripes and frets: Navajo.

FIGURE *24.3*

!KUNG SAN PLAYS THE BOW
Thumb plucks the string; mouth opens
and closes, moving along string
to control tone and resonance. Which
came first: bow for hunting, or bow
for making music?

and technology often interact and it is difficult to say where technology ends and art begins, or where art ends and technology begins. The beautiful symmetry of nets, baskets, and woven fabrics is essential for their proper functioning. Even in the development of media of musical expression there may be technological benefits. For example, there was probably some kind of feedback between the invention of the bow as a hunting weapon and the twanging of taut strings for musical effect (Fig. 24.3). No one can say which came first, but cultures with bows and arrows usually have musical strings. Wind instruments, blowguns, pistons, and bellows are all related. Similarly, metallurgy and chemistry relate to experimentation with the ornamental shape, texture, and color of ceramic and textile products. The first fired ceramics were figurines rather than utilitarian pots (Vandiver et al. 1989). Thus, it is practical to encourage craftworkers to experiment with new techniques and materials. Small wonder that many cultures regard technical virtuosity as mana (see p. 384). Others regard it as the gift of the gods, as in the classical Greek idea of the Muses—goddesses of oratory, dance, and music—whose assistance was needed if worthy artistic performances were to occur.

ART AND CULTURAL PATTERNING

Most artwork is deliberately fashioned in the image of preexisting forms. It is the task of the artist to replicate these forms by original combinations of culturally standardized elements—familiar and pleasing sounds, colors, lines, shapes, movements, and so on. Of course, there must always be some playful and creative ingredient, or it will not be art. On the other hand, if the transformation-representation is to communicate something—and it must communicate something if it is to be a successful work of art—the rules of the game cannot be the artist's own private invention. Complete originality, therefore, is not what most cultures strive after in their art.

It is the repetition of traditional and familiar elements that accounts for the major differences among the artistic products of different cultures. For example, Northwest Coast native American sculpture is well known for its consistent attention to animal and human motifs rendered in such a way as to indicate internal as well as external organs. These organs are symmetrically arranged within bounded geometrical forms (Fig. 24.4). Maori sculpture, on the other hand, requires that wooden surfaces be broken into bold but intricate filigrees and whorls (Fig. 24.5). Among the Mochica of ancient Peru, the sculptural medium was pottery, and Mochica pots are famous for their representational realism in portraiture and in depictions of domestic and sexual behavior (Fig. 24.6). Hundreds of other easily recognizable and distinctive art styles of different cultures can be identified. The continuity and integrity of these styles provide the basic context for a people's understanding and liking of art.

Establishment art in modern Western culture is unique in its emphasis on formal originality. It is taken as normal that art must be interpreted and explained by experts in order to be understood and appreciated. Since the end of the nineteenth century, the greatest artists of the Western art establishment are those who break with tradition, introduce new formal rules, and at least for a time render their work incomprehensible to a large number of people. Joined to this deemphasis of tradition is the peculiar and recent Western notion of artists as lonely people struggling in poverty against limitations set by the preexisting capability of their audience to appreciate and understand true genius.

Thus, the creative, playful, and transformational aspects of modern art have gotten the upper hand over the formal and representational aspects (Fig. 24.7). Contemporary Euramerican artists consciously strive to be the originators of entirely new formal rules. They compete to invent new transformations to replace the traditional ones. Modern aesthetic standards hold that originality is more important than intelligibility. Indeed, a work of art that is too easily understood may be condemned. Many art critics more or

(A)

FIGURE *24.4*

MASKS
(A) Mask within a mask within a mask. Whale conceals bird, which conceals human face, which conceals face of wearer; another Kwakiutl masterpiece. **(B)** Mask within a mask. Wearer of the Kwakiutl mask uses strings to pull eagle apart, revealing human face.

(B)

less consciously take it for granted that novelty must result in a certain amount of obscurity. What accounts for this obsession with being original?

One important influence is the reaction to mass production. Mass production leads to a downgrading of technical virtuosity. It also leads to a downgrading of all artwork that closely resembles the objects or performances others have produced. Another factor to be considered is the involvement of the modern artist in a commercial market in which supply peren-

nially exceeds demand. Part-time band- and village-level artists are not concerned with being original except to the extent that it enhances the aesthetic enjoyment of their work. Their livelihood does not depend on obtaining an artistic identity and a personal following.

Another factor to be considered is the high rate of cultural change in modern societies. To some extent, the emphasis on artistic originality merely reflects this rate of change.

FIGURE *24.5*

MAORI CANOE PROW
The Maori of New Zealand are among the world's greatest wood carvers.

FIGURE *24.6*

MOCHICA POT
A pre-Columbian portrait made
by the Mochica of northern Peru.

FIGURE *24.7*

WHAT DOES IT MEAN?
Fur-covered cup, saucer, and spoon
by Méret Oppenheim. (Cup, $4\frac{3}{8}''$ diameter;
saucer, $9\frac{3}{4}''$ diameter; spoon, 8'' long.)

Finally, the alienating and isolating tendencies of modern mass society may also play a role. Much modern art reflects the loneliness, puzzlement, and anxiety of the creative individual in a depersonalized and hostile urban, industrial milieu.

ART AND RELIGION

The history and ethnography of art are inseparable from the history and ethnography of religion. As we have seen (p. 141), art as an aspect of supernatural belief and ritual goes back at least 40,000 years.

Art is intimately associated with all four organizational levels of religion. For example, at the individualistic level, magical songs are often included among the revelations granted the vision seekers of the Great Plains. Even the preparation of trophy heads among the Jivaro must meet aesthetic standards, and singing and chanting are widely used during shamanistic performances. On the communal level, puberty rituals, as among the Ndembu (p. 395), provide occasions for dancing and myth and storytelling. Body painting is also widely practiced in communal ceremonies, as among the Arunta. Singing, dancing, and the wearing of masks are common at both puberty and funeral rituals. Much artistic effort is expended in the preparation of religiously significant funeral equipment such as coffins and graveposts (Figs. 24.8 and 24.9). Many cultures include among a deceased person's grave goods ceremonial artifacts such as pottery and clubs, points, and other weapons. Ancestors and gods are often depicted in statues and masks that are kept in men's houses or in shrines (Fig. 24.10). *Churingas* (p. 393), the Arunta's most sacred objects, are artfully incised with whorls and loops depicting the route followed by the ancestors during the dream time.

Finally, on the ecclesiastical level, art and religion are fused in pyramids, monumental avenues, stone statuary, monolithic calendar carvings, temples, altars, priestly garments, and a nearly infinite variety of ritual ornaments and sacred paraphernalia.

It is clear that art, religion, and magic satisfy many similar psychological needs in human beings. They are media for expressing sentiments and emotions not easily expressed in ordinary life. They impart a sense of mastery over or communion with unpredictable events and mysterious, unseen powers. They impose human meanings and values on an indifferent world—a world that has no humanly intelligible meanings and values of its own. They seek to

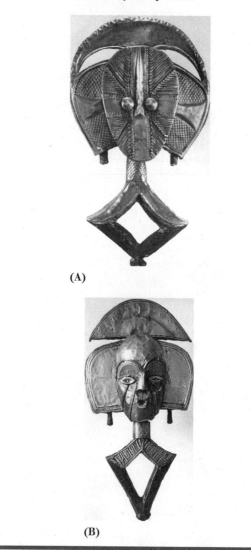

FIGURE *24.8*

BA KOTA FUNERARY FIGURES
The Ba Kota of the Gabon Republic place the skeletal remains of dead chiefs in bark boxes or baskets surmounted by Mbulu-ngulu guardian figures of wood, faced with brass or copper sheets or strips. Although the figures each express the creative individuality of the artist, they conform to the same stylistic pattern.

(A)

(B)

penetrate behind the facade of ordinary appearance into the true, cosmic significance of things. And they use illusions, dramatic tricks, and sleight of hand to get people to believe in them.

ASMAT GRAVEPOST
Around the world, much talent has been lavished on commemorating the dead, but styles and media vary enormously.

FIGURE *24.9*

ART AND ARCHITECTURE
Brightly painted faces on a men's house in Sepik River basin, New Guinea.

FIGURE *24.10*

ART AND POLITICS

Art is also intimately related to politics. This is especially clear in the context of state-sponsored art. As we have seen, in stratified societies, religion is a means of social control. The skills of the artist are harnessed by the ruling class to implant religious notions of obedience and to sanctify the sta-

tus quo (Fig. 24.11). Contrary to the popular modern image of the artist as a free spirit disdainful of authority, most state-level art is politically conservative (Paztory 1984:20). Ecclesiastical art generally interprets the world in conformity with prevailing myths and ideologies justifying inequities and exploitation. Art makes the gods visible as idols. Gazing on massive stone blocks carved as if by superhuman hands, commoners comprehend the necessity for subservience. They are awed by the immense size of pyramids and fascinated and befuddled by processions, prayers, pomp, and the sacrifices of priests

FIGURE *24.11*

GOLD DEATH MASK OF TUT
Another example of the interrelationship of art, religion, and politics.

FIGURE *24.12*

ART AND RELIGION
Notre Dame Cathedral, Paris. No one ever had to ask what it means, but how it was built remains a mystery.

in dramatic settings—golden altars, colonnaded temples, great vaulted roofs, huge ramps and stairways, windows through which only the light from heaven passes (Fig. 24.12).

The church and state have been the greatest patrons of the arts in all but the last few hundred years of history. With the rise of capitalism, ecclesiastical and civil institutions in the West became more decentralized, and wealthy individuals largely replaced church and state as patrons of the arts. Individualized sponsorship promoted greater flexibility and freedom of expression. Politically neutral, secular, and even revolutionary and sacrilegious themes became common. The arts became established as individualistic, secular forms of expression and entertainment. To protect and preserve its newfound autonomy, the art establishment adopted the doctrine of "art for art's sake." But once they were free to express themselves as they saw fit, artists were no longer sure what they wanted to express. They devoted themselves more and more to idiosyncratic and obscure symbols organized into novel and unintelligible patterns, as noted earlier in this chapter. And the patrons of art, concerned less and less with communication, increasingly looked toward the acquisition and sponsorship of art as a prestigious commercial venture that yielded substantial profits, tax deductions, and a hedge against inflation.

THE EVOLUTION OF MUSIC AND DANCE

Some anthropologists hold that the influence on art of structural and infrastructural components extends directly into the formal characteristics and aesthetic standards of different cultural styles. According to Allan Lomax and his associates (Lomax 1968; Lomax and Arensberg 1977), for example, certain broad characteristics of song, music, and dance are closely correlated with a culture's level of subsistence. Band and village peoples in general tend to have a different complex of music, song, and dance than do chiefdoms and states. Dividing cultures into those that are low and those that are high on the scale of subsistence technology leads to the following correlations:

Musical intervals The less advanced subsistence systems employ musical scales in which notes are widely separated—that is, have intervals of a third or more. Advanced subsistence systems employ scales that are marked by more and smaller intervals.

Repetition in song text The less advanced subsistence cultures employ more repetition in their lyrics—fewer words, over and over again.

Complexity and type of orchestra Advanced subsistence is correlated with musical performances involving more performers and a greater variety of instruments. Less advanced subsistence systems use only one or two kinds of instruments and small numbers of each.

Dance styles The advanced subsistence systems are correlated with dance styles in which many body parts—fingers, wrists, arms, torso, legs, feet, toes—have distinctive movements to make or "parts to play." Also, the more advanced the subsistence system, the more the dance style tends to emphasize complex curving motions, as opposed to simple up-and-down or side-to-side steps like hopping or shuffling.

Lomax sees these correlations between subsistence and art as resulting from direct and indirect influence of subsistence. Large, complex orchestration, for example, reflects the structural ability of a society to form large, coordinated groups. Dance styles, on the other hand, may simply express the characteristic movements employed in using such implements of production as digging sticks versus plows or complex machines. Some dances can be regarded as training for work, warfare, or self-defense. Obviously, there are many other functions of dance (Box 24.1).

Lomax's correlations have been criticized on technical grounds relating to sampling and coding procedures (see Kaeppler 1978). Nonetheless, Lomax's attempt to measure and compare music and dance styles, and to relate them to social structure and subsistence, constitutes an important avenue of approach.

THE COMPLEXITY OF PRIMITIVE ART: CAMPA RHETORIC

A common misconception about art among band and village societies is that it is necessarily more simple

---

> **BOX *24.1***
>
> ## SOME SOCIAL FUNCTIONS OF MUSIC, SONG, AND DANCE
>
> 1. Emotes: Lets people "blow off steam," makes them feel good.
> 2. Socializes: Teaches traditions.
> 3. Educates: Develops poise and confidence in performance.
> 4. Bonds: Creates a sense of togetherness among performers.
> 5. Rallies: Prepares for dangerous situations (e.g., warfare and journeys).
> 6. Aggresses: Lets people "show their stuff" harmlessly.
> 7. Worships: Brings people closer to the gods.
> 8. Seduces: Arouses sexual passions, displays charms.
> 9. Coordinates: Gets people to work or move together, as in sea chanties or military marches.
> 10. Entertains: Prevents boredom.

---

or naive than art in modern industrial societies (Titon et al. 1984). Although, as we have just seen, many stylistic aspects of art have undergone an evolution from simple to more complex forms, other aspects may have been as complex among Stone Age hunter-gatherers as they are today. The case of Campa rhetoric illustrates this point.

Rhetoric is the art of persuasive public discourse and is closely related to the theatrical arts. As Gerald Weiss (1977b) has discovered, the preliterate Campa, who live in eastern Peru near the headwaters of the Amazon River, use most of the important rhetorical devices cultivated by the great philosophers and orators of ancient Greece and Rome. Their object in public discourse is not merely to inform, but to persuade and convince. "Campa narration is 'a separate time,' where a spellbinding relationship between narrator and audience is developed, with powerful rhetorical devices employed to create and enhance the quality of that relationship" (1977b: 173).

Here are a few examples of these devices, as translated by Weiss from the Campa language, which belongs to the native American family of languages known as Arawak:

Rhetorical questions The speaker makes the point that the Campa are deficient in their worship of the sky god, the sun, by asking a question that he himself will then answer: "Do we supplicate him, he here, he who lives in the sky, the sun? We do not know how to supplicate him."

Iterations (effect by repetition) The speaker imparts an emphatic, graphic, cinematic quality to the point by repeating some key words: "The enemy comes out of the lake: And so they emerged in great numbers—he saw them emerge, emerge, emerge, emerge, emerge, emerge, emerge, emerge, emerge, all, all."

Imagery and metaphor Death is alluded to in the phrase "the earth will eat him." The body is described as "the clothing of the soul."

Appeal to evidence To prove that the oilbird was formerly human in shape: "Yes, he was formerly human—doesn't he have whiskers?"

Appeal to authority "They told me long ago, the elders, they who heard these words, long ago, so it was."

Antithesis (effect by contrast) A hummingbird is about to raise the sky rope, which the other larger creatures have failed to do: "They are all big whereas I am small and chubby."

In addition, the Campa orator uses a wide variety of gestures, exclamations, sudden calls for attention ("watch out, here it comes"); asides ("imagine it, then"; "careful that you don't believe, now"). Altogether, Weiss lists 19 formal rhetorical devices used by the Campa.

MYTH AND BINARY CONTRASTS

Anthropologists have found considerable evidence suggesting that certain kinds of formal structures recur in widely different traditions of oral and written literature, including myths and folktales. These structures are characterized by binary contrasts—that is, by two elements or themes that can be viewed as standing in diametric opposition to each other. Many examples of recurrent binary contrasts can be found in Western religion, literature, and mythology: good versus bad, up versus down, male versus female, cultural versus natural, young versus old, and so forth. According to the French anthropologist Lévi-Strauss, the founder of the research strategy known as structuralism (see Appendix), the reason these binary contrasts recur so often is that the human brain is "wired" in such a way as to make binary contrasts especially appealing, or "good to think." From the structuralist point of view, the main task of the anthropological study of literature, mythology, and folklore is to identify the common, unconscious binary contrasts that lie beneath the surface of human thought and

to show how these binary contrasts undergo unconscious transformation-representations.

Consider the familiar tale of Cinderella: A mother has two daughters and one stepdaughter. The two daughters are older, the stepdaughter is younger; the older ones are ugly and mean, while Cinderella is beautiful and kind. The older sisters are aggressive; Cinderella is passive. Through a kind fairy godmother, as opposed to her mean stepmother, Cinderella goes to the ball, dances with the prince, and loses her magical shoe. Her sisters have big feet, she has little feet. Cinderella wins the prince. The unconscious binary oppositions in the deep structure of this story might include:

passive	aggressive
younger	older
small	larger
good	evil
beautiful	ugly
culture	nature
(fairy godmother)	(stepmother)

Structuralists contend that the enjoyment people derive from such tales and their durability across space and time derive mainly from the unconscious oppositions and their familiar yet surprising representations.

Structuralist analyses can be extended from the realm of myth and ritual to the entire fabric of social life. According to David Hicks, who studied the Tetum of Timor in Indonesia, Tetum culture as a whole is structured by the following "binary matrix":

human beings	ghosts
secular	sacred
secular world	sacred world
above	below
men	women
right	left
superior	inferior
wife-givers	wife-takers
aristocrats	commoners
secular authority	sacred authority
elder brother	younger brother

Any single binary contrast can symbolize any other (Hicks 1976:107)—that is, in contrasting men with women, one could just as readily be contrasting elder brothers with younger brothers (among the Tetum, younger brothers must serve elder brothers just as women must serve men). The secular, above-ground, masculine world contrasts with the ghostly, sacred, below-ground, feminine world. Thus Tetum mythology recounts how the first human emerged from vagi-

FIGURE *24.13*

TETUM HOUSE
Women's entrance is around the back; men's entrance is through the front door.

nalike holes in the ground and how after leading a secular life on the surface of the earth, humans return to the sacred world below and to the ghostly ancestors. Tetum house architecture also participates in the same set of symbolic oppositions (Fig. 24.13). The house has two entrances; the back entrance for the women leads to the "womb" or women's part of the house, which contains the hearth and a sacred house post. The front entrance is for the men and leads to the male living quarters.

Structural analyses of literature, art, myths, rituals, and religion abound in anthropology. However, they are surrounded by considerable controversy, primarily because it is not clear whether the binary matrices discerned by the anthropologists really exist as unconscious realities in the minds of the people being studied. It is always possible to reduce complex and subtle symbols to less complex and gross symbols and then finally to emerge with such flat oppositions as culture versus nature or male versus female.

SUMMARY

Creative play, formal structure, aesthetic feelings, and symbolic transformations are the essential ingredients in art. Although the capacity for art is foreshadowed in the behavior of nonhuman primates, only humans are capable of art involving "transformation-representations." The distinctive human capacity for art is thus closely related to the distinctive human capacity for the symbolic transformations that underlie the semantic universality of human language.

Western emic definitions of art depend on the existence of art authorities and critics who place many examples of play, structured aesthetic, and symbolic transformation into the category of nonart. The distinction between crafts and art is part of this tradition. Anthropologists regard skilled craftspersons as artists.

Art has adaptive functions in relation to creative changes in the other sectors of social life. Art and technology influence each other, as in the case of instruments of music and the hunt, or in the search for new shapes, colors, textures, and materials in ceramics and textiles.

Despite the emphasis on creative innovation, most cultures have art traditions or styles that maintain formal continuity through time. This makes it possible to identify the styles of cultures such as the Northwest Coast, Maori, or Mochica. The continuity and integrity of such styles provide the basic context for a people's understanding of and liking for the artist's creative transformations. Establishment art in modern Western culture is unique in emphasizing structural or formal creativity as well as creative transformations. This results in the isolation of the artist. Lack of communication may be caused by factors such as the reaction to mass production, commercialization of art markets, a rapid rate of cultural change, and the depersonalized milieu of urban industrial life.

Art and religion are closely related. This can be seen in the Upper Paleolithic cave paintings, songs of the vision quest, preparation of shrunken heads, singing and chanting in shamanistic performances, Tapirapé shamanistic myths, Ndembu circumcision, storytelling, singing and dancing, Arunta *churingas*, and many other aspects of individual, shamanistic, communal, and ecclesiastical cults. Art and religion satisfy many similar psychological needs, and it is often difficult to tell them apart.

Art and politics are also closely related. This is clear in state-sponsored ecclesiastical art, much of which functions to keep people in awe of their rulers. It is only in recent times, with the rise of decentralized capitalist states, that art has enjoyed any significant degree of freedom from direct political control.

To the extent that bands, villages, chiefdoms, and states represent evolutionary levels, and to the extent that art is functionally related to technology, economy, politics, religion, and other aspects of the universal cultural pattern, it is clear that there has been an evolution of the content of art. A more controversial finding is that styles of song, music, and dance—including musical intervals, repetition in song texts, complexity and type of orchestra, body part involvement, and amount of curvilinear motion—have also undergone evolutionary changes. But as the example of Campa rhetoric shows, the art styles of band and village peoples can be highly sophisticated.

The structuralist approach to art attempts to interpret myths, rituals, and other expressive performances in terms of a series of unconscious universal binary oppositions. Common binary oppositions can be found in the Cinderella myth and in Tetum cosmology, ritual, and house architecture.

PART VII

ANTHROPOLOGY AND MODERN LIFE

*T**he findings of general anthropology are relevant to the understanding of social problems experienced in contemporary industrial as well as preindustrial societies. In Part VII we will examine a variety of situations in which anthropologists have attempted to use their knowledge to improve the well-being of disadvantaged social groups. Finally we shall attempt to show how the approach that has been presented in previous parts of this book can be applied to the study of advanced industrial societies such as the United States.*

Applied Anthropology

Up to now you have probably been thinking that some of this at least is pretty interesting stuff (I hope). But what good is it? Does it have any practical use? Well, it so happens that a lot of people (and not only anthropologists) think it does. Herein we explore some of the relationships between anthropological research and the attempt to achieve practical goals by organizations that sponsor or use such research. The sample of cases presented in this brief survey does not fairly represent the great variety of applied projects being carried out by anthropologists. This is a rapidly growing field that is hard to keep up with.

WHAT IS APPLIED ANTHROPOLOGY?

Since World War II, an increasing number of cultural anthropologists have become involved occasionally or regularly in research that has more or less immediate practical applications. They are known as practitioners of *applied anthropology.*

The core of applied anthropology consists of research commissioned by public or private organizations in the hope of achieving practical goals of interest to those organizations. Such organizations include federal, state, local, and international government bureaus and agencies, such as the U.S. Department of Agriculture, the Department of Defense, the National Park Service, the Agency for International Development, the Bureau of Indian Affairs, the World Bank, the World Health Organization, the Food and Agricultural Organization, various drug abuse agencies, education and urban planning departments of major cities, and municipal hospitals, to mention only a few. In addition, private organizations that have hired or contracted with anthropologists to carry out practical, goal-oriented research include major industrial corporations, research foundations such as Planned Parenthood and the Population Council, and various branches of the Rockefeller and Ford Foundations' International Crops Research Institutes (Chambers 1985; Willigen 1986).

It should be emphasized that cultural anthropologists do not have a monopoly on applied anthropology: Physical anthropology, archaeology, and linguistics also have their applied aspects. But here we shall deal mainly with the applied aspects of cultural anthropology.

RESEARCH, THEORY, AND ACTION

Although the hallmark of applied anthropology is involvement in research aimed at achieving a special practical result, the extent to which the applied anthropologist actually participates in bringing about the desired result varies from one assignment to another. At one extreme, the applied anthropologist may merely be charged with developing information the sponsoring organization needs in order to make decisions. In other instances, the applied anthropologist may be asked to evaluate the feasibility of a planned program or even to draw up a more or less detailed set of plans for achieving a desired goal (Husain 1976). More rarely, the anthropologist, alone or as a member of a team, may be responsible for planning, implementing, and evaluating a whole program from beginning to end. When anthropologists help to implement a program, they are spoken of as practicing *action anthropology.*

It is often difficult to draw a line between applied and nonapplied research. Abstract theorizing about the causes of sociocultural differences and similarities can itself be construed as applied anthropology if it provides a general set of principles to which any action program must conform if it is to achieve success. For example, general theories about the causes of peasant backwardness and of urban poverty (see pp. 331 and 334) can have considerable practical consequences even though the research behind these theories may not have been sponsored by organizations with the expressed goal of eliminating underdevelopment and urban poverty. Similarly, a better understanding of the processes that are responsible for the evolution of advanced industrial societies may be of immediate relevance to organizations that advise firms and governments on investment policies. Applied anthropology premised on blatantly incorrect theory is misapplied anthropology (Cohen 1984b).

WHAT DO APPLIED ANTHROPOLOGISTS HAVE TO OFFER?

The effectiveness of applied anthropology is enhanced by three distinctive attributes of general anthropology (see p. 4): (1) relative freedom from ethnocentrism and Western biases, (2) concern with holistic sociocultural systems, and (3) concern with ordinary etic behavioral events as well as with the emics of mental life.

Detecting and Controlling Ethnocentrism

The applied anthropologist can be of assistance to sponsoring organizations by exposing the ethnocentric, culture-bound assumptions that often characterize cross-cultural contacts and that prevent change-oriented programs from achieving their goals. For example, Western-trained agricultural scientists tend to dismiss peasant forms of agriculture as backward and inefficient, thereby overlooking the cumulative wisdom embodied in age-old practices handed down from generation to generation. The attitude of Western experts toward the use of cattle in India is a case in point (see p. 406). Anthropologists are more likely to reserve judgment about a traditional practice such as using cattle to plow fields, whereas a narrowly trained specialist might automatically wish to replace the animals with tractors. Again, applied anthropologists are likely to see that the attempt to model a health care delivery system after those with which Western-trained doctors are familiar may represent nothing more than an attempt to replace the culturally unfamiliar with the culturally familiar. Expensive staffs, costly hospitals, and the latest electronic gadgetry, for example, are not necessarily the way to improve the quality of health services (Cattle 1977:38). The American notion that milk is the "perfect food" has led to much grief and dismay throughout the world, since many populations in less developed countries to which tons of surplus milk in powdered form were sent as nutritional supplements lacked the enzyme needed to digest lactose, the predominant form of sugar in milk (Harris 1985). West-

ern notions of hygiene automatically suggest that mothers must be persuaded not to chew food and then put it in their babies' mouths. Yet it was found that in the case of the Pijoan Indians of the U.S. Southwest, premastication of infant foods was an effective way to combat the iron-deficiency anemia to which the infants who are fed exclusively on mother's milk are subject (Freedman 1977:8).

A Holistic View

As industrial society becomes increasingly specialized and technocratic (that is, dominated by narrowly trained experts who have mastered techniques and the use of machines others do not understand), the need for anthropology's holistic view of social life becomes more urgent. In diverse fields (e.g., education, health, economic development), there has been a convergence toward using narrow sets of easily quantified variables in order to verify objectively the accomplishment or lack of accomplishment of an organization's goals. All too often, however, the gain in verifiability is accomplished at the expense of a loss in "validity" (or "meaningfulness"). Easily quantified variables may represent only a small part of a much bigger system whose larger set of difficult-to-measure variables has the capacity to cancel out the observed effects of the small set of variables (Bernard 1981:5).

For example, after World War II the U.S. auto industry found it could earn more money by building heavier and more powerful cars without paying too much attention to the question of how long the cars would function without need of repairs. Other sets of variables—namely, the ecological consequences of auto emission pollution, the political and military conditions that made it possible for the United States to enjoy low oil prices, and the perception by foreign auto producers that there was a market for small, fuel-efficient, reliable, and long-lasting vehicles—were considered irrelevant to the task of maximizing the U.S. auto industry's profits. Hence, what appeared in a narrow context to be a highly objective measure of success (large profits and domination of the U.S. auto market) turned out in a longer time frame to be devoid of validity.

Thus, in commonsense language, anthropological holism boils down to being aware of the long term as well as the short term, the distant as well as the near, parts other than the one being studied, and the whole as well as the parts. Without these perspectives, even a seemingly straightforward and simple project can end up as a disaster (Box 25.1).

BOX *25.1*

WITHOUT HOLISM: AN ANDEAN FIASCO

Under the auspices of an international development program, experts from Australia tried to get the peasant Indians of Chimborazo Province in Ecuador to substitute high-yield Australian merino sheep for the traditional scrawny breeds the Indians owned. No one wanted the sheep, despite the offer to let the Indians have them free if used for breeding purposes. Finally, one "progressive" Indian accepted the offer and successfully raised a flock of cross-bred merinos that were far woolier and heavier than the traditional Indian flocks. Unfortunately, the Indians of Chimborazo live in a caste-structured society. Non-Indian farmers who live in the lower valleys resented the attention being paid to the Indians;

they began to fear that the Indians would be emboldened to press for additional economic and social gains, which would undermine their own positions. The merinos caught someone's attention, and the whole flock was herded into a truck and stolen. The rustlers were well protected by public opinion, which regarded the animals as "too good for the Indians anyway." The "progressive" innovator was left as the only one in the village without sheep. Variables such as ethnic and class antagonisms, opportunities for theft, and the political subservience of peasants are not part of the expertise of sheep breeders, but awareness of these factors nonetheless proved essential to the achievement of their goals.

Etic and Emic Views of Organizations

Technification and specialization are usually accompanied by the growth of bureaucracy. An essential component of bureaucracy is an emic plan by which the units within an organization are related to each other and according to which individuals are expected to perform their tasks. As in most sociocultural systems, there is considerable likelihood that the etic behavioral substance of organizations and situations differs from the mental emics of the bureaucratic plan. Anthropologists who are trained to approach social life from the ground up, and who are concerned with everyday events as they actually unfold, often can provide a view of organizations and situations that the bureaucracy lacks. Anthropologists have studied schools, factories, corporations, and hospitals in a manner that provides both emic and etic viewpoints.

AGRICULTURAL DEVELOPMENT

One of the most important subfields of applied anthropology focuses on the problem of agricultural development in peasant and small farmer communities. As mentioned previously (p. 328) anthropologists have studied peasants more often than they have studied other kinds of groups. Their knowledge of the conditions and aspirations of peasant life makes anthropologists useful as consultants to or members of interdisciplinary projects aimed at raising Third World standards of living (Barlett and Brown 1985). More rarely, anthropologists have themselves been appointed to direct, plan, implement, and evaluate development projects from beginning to end.

THE VICOS PROJECT

A classic example of an anthropological development effort took place in the 1950s under the auspices of the Cornell-Peru Vicos project. Vicos was a *hacienda* (a large farm on which a variety of crops is grown, worked by resident peasants) in the Peruvian highlands inhabited by 373 economically serflike, depressed, and exploited families of Indian peasants (Fig. 25.1). Cornell University leased the *hacienda* and turned it over to anthropologist Allen Holmberg with the objective of raising the Indians' standard of living and making them economically independent. At the time of intervention, the people of Vicos were unable to grow enough food to feed themselves, their farming lands were broken up into thousands of tiny scattered plots, their potato crop was subject to frequent failure, and they lacked motivation for producing a surplus, since they were constantly in debt or at the beck and call of the landlords.

Under the feudal rules of the *hacienda* system, the peasants were required to labor on the owner's fields for three days per week. Holmberg decided

FIGURE *25.1*

VICOS
A community work party begins its potato harvest.

to take advantage of this obligation by using it to familiarize the peasants with improved varieties of potatoes, fertilizers, fungicides, and insecticides. After seeing how successful the new seeds and methods were during their obligatory labor on the new boss's plot, the peasants were more willing to do the same on their own plots. This was facilitated by advancing the seeds and other materials on a sharecrop basis. Anthropologists and technicians carefully supervised the use of the new methods to ensure their success.

Meanwhile, other activities were underway: a full-scale educational program; a school hot-lunch program that introduced fruits and eggs, previously not part of the diet; a demonstration garden for growing leafy vegetables; and sewing machine lessons that enabled the women to make their own clothes. In addition, through frequent communal meetings and discussions, the peasants gradually came to place more trust in one another and to seek cooperative, communal solutions to their problems.

The culmination of all these changes was the purchase of the *hacienda* by the families living on it. Along with higher incomes, better health, and literacy, this event was considered dramatic evidence of the success of the project (Dobyns 1972:201). Most importantly, the people of Vicos continued to improve their standard of living long after all the applied an-

thropologists had left the community. Studies show that other communities in the same region have had much lower rates of improvement in per capita income, literacy, health conditions, and political representation (Doughty 1987:152). As a model for developing the entire peasant sector of the Peruvian Andes, however, the plan has attracted certain criticisms. The per capita cash outlays were quite modest in comparison with those of other international development efforts, yet there were hidden investment costs that are not likely to be duplicated on a scale large enough to affect a significant portion of the Peruvian peasantry. Vicos benefited from highly trained, honest, and relatively unselfish experts (including Holmberg) who worked diligently to improve the lot of the peasants. They were paid by universities and foundations, and many of them worked for next to nothing as graduate students hoping to be compensated by getting their Ph.D.s and making their careers in anthropology. Although extremely interesting as a demonstration of what can be done by action anthropologists who had considerable power to manage the people in their charge, the Vicos project fell short of providing a more general solution to the problem of underdevelopment in the Peruvian Andes. But such criticisms fail to take into account the limited goals of the project. The organizers wanted to demonstrate that it was possible for a low-budget, face-to-face collaborative effort by anthropologists, preexisting government agencies, and the people themselves to overcome centuries of poverty, isolation, ignorance, and prejudice. Judged on this limited basis, the project was a success.

THE HAITIAN AGROFORESTRY PROJECT

If agricultural development is to be meaningful, it cannot be confined to one or two peasant communities. It must use scientific knowledge to ensure that beneficial innovations will be spread rapidly throughout a region or a country by local participants rather than by foreign experts.

The Haitian Agroforestry Project shows more promise in this regard than the Vicos project. Planned and directed in its initial phase by anthropologist Gerald Murray, the Agroforestry Project has successfully induced Haitian peasants to plant millions of fast-growing trees in steep hillside farmlands threatened by erosion. Depletion of soil as a result of rapid runoff from treeless hillsides has long been recognized as one of Haiti's greatest problems. In addition, trees are needed as a source of charcoal—the principal cooking fuel in poor households—and as a source of building materials. There have been many other reforestation programs in Haiti, but they have met with little or no success either because the funds for planting were squandered or diverted by government bureaucrats or because peasants refused to cooperate and protect the seedlings from hungry goats.

The Haitian Agroforestry Project was designed to avoid both pitfalls. In accepting a $4 million grant from the United States Agency for International Development (USAID), Murray insisted on an unusual stipulation: No funds were to be transferred to the Haitian government or through the Haitian government. Instead, the funds were to be given to local community groups—private voluntary organizations—interested in peasant welfare. In practice, the majority of these groups were grass-roots religious associations formed by Catholic or Protestant priests, pastors, or missionaries. The project provided these groups with seedlings of fast-growing species matched to local ecological conditions and with expert advisors. The private voluntary organizations, in turn, undertook to assemble and instruct the local farmers and to distribute the seedlings to them free of charge, provided each farmer agreed to plant a minimum of 500 (G. Murray 1984).

It was clear that unless the peasants themselves were motivated to plant the seedlings and to protect them, the project could not succeed. Murray's analysis of why previous projects had been unable to obtain the peasants' cooperation was based on his firsthand knowledge of Haitian peasant life and on certain principles of anthropological theory (see below). Haitian peasants are market-oriented—they produce crops for cash sale. Yet previous attempts to get them to plant trees stipulated that trees should not be sold. Instead the peasants were told that they were an unmarketable national treasure. Thus, trees were presented as exactly the opposite of the cash crops that the peasants planted on their own behalf.

Putting himself in the peasants' shoes, Murray realized that previous reforestation projects had created an adverse balance of costs over benefits for the peasants. It was perfectly rational for the peasants to let their goats eat the seedlings instead of donating their labor and land to trees that they would be forbidden to harvest (or could only harvest 30 or 40 years in the future). Accordingly, Murray decided to distribute the trees as a cash crop over which the peasants would have complete control. The project merely informed the peasants how to plant the trees and take care of them. They were also shown how to set the seedlings in rows between which other crops could be planted until the trees matured. They were told, too, how fast the trees would grow and how much lumber or charcoal they could expect to get at various stages of growth. Then the peasants were left on their own to decide when it would be in their best interest to cut some or all of them.

The project's goal was to assist 5000 peasant families to plant 3 million trees in four years. After 4 years (1981–1985), it had in fact assisted 40,000 families to plant 20 million trees (Fig. 25.2). Considerable numbers of trees have already been used for charcoal and for building purposes. While it remains to be seen how much extra income will eventually be generated and how much erosion has been curtailed, Murray's basic analysis appears to have been correct.

THE THEORY BEHIND THE HAITIAN REFORESTATION PROJECT

Murray predicts that cash-oriented *agroforestry* (see Box 25.2) will become a major feature of peasant agriculture throughout the Third World. He interprets cash-oriented agroforestry as a response to a set of infrastructural conditions that are similar to the conditions associated with the rise of agricultural modes of production out of hunting and gathering: widespread depletion of a natural resource, and population pressure (see p. 161). Peasants, having depleted the trees

FIGURE *25.2*

HAITIAN AGROFORESTRY PROJECT
These trees are of the species
Leucaena leucophala and are about
two and one-half years old. Several other
species are also being planted.

BOX *25.2*

CO-OPTING THE "DEMON" BEHIND DEFORESTATION

I propose that we look carefully at the "demon" which is currently blamed for putting the final touches on the environment of Haiti—the market which currently exists for charcoal and construction materials. It is this market, many would argue, which sabotages forever any hopes of preserving the few remaining trees in Haiti.

I would like to argue that it is precisely this market which can restore tree growth to the hills of Haiti. The demon can be "baptized" and joined in wedlock to the ecological imperatives whose major adversary he has been up till now. With creative programming we can turn the tables on history and utilize the awe-inspiring cash-generating energy present throughout Haitian society in a manner which plants trees in the ground faster than they are being cut down. If this is to be done, it must be the peasant who does it. But he will not do it voluntarily or spontaneously unless tree planting contributes to the flow of desperately needed cash into his home. I propose that the mechanism for achieving this is the introduction of cash-oriented agroforestry.

SOURCE: G. Murray 1984:147.

on which they depend for soil regeneration, fuel, and building material, will now find it to their advantage to plant trees as one of their basic crops. In Murray's words (personal communication):

The anthropologically most important element of the model...is the diachronic (evolutionary) component in which I am positing a scarcity-and-stress-generated readiness for a repeat in the domain of fuel and wood of the transition from foraging to planting which began some 15 millennia ago in the domain of food.

THE NOT-SO-GREEN REVOLUTION

A more typical role for the applied anthropologist is that of critic-observer of the change process. An important example of this role can be found in the anthropological critique of the "Green Revolution." This critique again illustrates the importance of a holistic perspective for development projects.

The Green Revolution had its origin in the late 1950s in the dwarf varieties of "wonder wheat" developed by Nobel Prize winner and plant geneticist Norman Borlaug at the Rockefeller Foundation's research center in northwest Mexico. Designed to double and triple yields per acre, wonder wheat was soon followed by dwarf varieties of "miracle rice" engineered at a joint Rockefeller and Ford Foundation research center in the Philippines. (The significance of the dwarfed forms is that short, thick stems can bear heavy loads of ripe grain without bending over.) On the basis of initial successes in Mexico and the Philippines, the new seeds were hailed as the solution to the problem of feeding the expanding population of the underdeveloped world and were soon planted in vast areas of Pakistan, India, and Indonesia (Cloud 1973). The new seeds did

TABLE *25.1*

REGIONAL AND WORLD GRAIN PRODUCTION PER PERSON, PEAK YEAR AND 1990

Region	Peak production		1990 production	Change since peak year
	(year)	(kilograms)	(kilograms)	(percent)
Africa	1967	169	121	−28
E. Europe and Soviet Union	1978	826	763	− 8
Latin America	1981	250	210	−16
North America	1981	1,509	1,324	−12
Western Europe	1984	538	496	− 8
Asia	1984	227	217	− 4
World	1984	343	329	− 4

SOURCE: Brown et al. 1991:13.

result in a rapid increase of grain production per capita for a brief period. However, the pace of agricultural development has been adversely affected by a number of side effects associated with intensification: a growing scarcity of suitable land, lack of water for irrigation, and floods caused by deforestation. In addition, the point of diminishing returns for the application of chemical fertilizer to the new seeds has been reached. Thus between 1984 and 1990, growth in rice yields per acre virtually ceased. And the overall rate of increase in per capita production of all grains fell to 1 percent per year while at the same time, the rate of population growth remained at 2 percent. As a result, grain production per person is declining throughout much of the world, despite the green revolution (Brown et al. 1991: 12–13; see Table 25.1).

The main problem with the miracle seeds is that they were engineered to outperform native varieties of rice and wheat only if grown in fields heavily irrigated and treated with large inputs of chemical fertilizers, pesticides, insecticides, and fungicides. Without such inputs, the high-yield varieties perform little better than the native varieties, especially under adverse soil and weather conditions.

How these inputs are to be obtained and how and to whom they are to be distributed are difficult questions. Most peasants in the underdeveloped world not only lack access to irrigation water, but they are unable to pay for expensive chemical fertilizers and other chemical inputs. This means that unless extraordinary efforts are made by the governments of countries switching to miracle seeds, the chief beneficiaries of the Green Revolution are the wealthy farmers who already occupy the irrigated lands and who are best

able to pay for the chemical inputs (Cummings 1978; Glaeser 1987; Mencher 1974a, 1978; Oasa 1985:220; Walsh 1991).

THE GREEN REVOLUTION IN JAVA

Anthropologist Richard Franke (1974) studied the Green Revolution in central Java. Despite the fact that yield increases of up to 70 percent were being obtained, in the village studied by Franke only 20 percent of the farming households had joined the program. The chief beneficiaries were the farmers who were already better off than average, owned the most land, and had adequate supplies of water. The poorest families did not adopt the new seeds. They made ends meet by working part-time for well-to-do farmers who lent them money to buy food or who paid them in kind (Fig. 25.3). The richer farmers prevented their part-time workers from adopting the new seeds. The wealthier farmers feared they would lose their supply of cheap labor, and the poor farmers feared that if they cut themselves off from their patrons, they would have no one to turn to in case of sickness or drought. Franke concludes that the theories behind the Green Revolution are primarily rationalizations for ruling elites trying to find a way to achieve economic development without the social and political transformation their societies need.

The lesson of the Green Revolution is similar to that of the attempt to give merino sheep to the people of Chimborazo (Box 25.1). In both cases, purely technological solutions failed to achieve their intended purpose because of the failure to take into account other and equally important parts of sociocultural systems.

FIGURE *25.3*

RICE HARVEST, JAVA
Harvesting is done with a small hand knife, known as the *ani-ani*. Each stalk is individually cut,
but with the large supply of labor, a single morning is enough for all but the very largest plots to be harvested.
The paddy is bound in bundles and carried to the house of the owner, where a one-tenth portion is divided among
the harvesters; no other wage is paid.

MEXICO'S SECOND GREEN REVOLUTION

Mexico was one of the earliest centers for the development of high-yield varieties of Green Revolution wheat. If one totals up the production of maize, wheat, beans, and sorghum, it seems as if Mexico has solved its food production problems: Per capita grain production in 1980 was double the per capita grain production in 1945. Yet Mexico had to import over 7 million tons of grains in 1989 (World Bank 1991:211), more per capita than at the beginning of the Green Revolution. And it is not wheat or any of the traditional grains such as maize and beans, but sorghum (Fig. 25.4) that accounts for the bulk of the domestic grain supply. The reason for these paradoxical developments have been studied by anthropologist Billie DeWalt (1984:44). Prior to 1960, sorghum, which is widely grown in Africa and Asia for human food, was practically unknown in Mexico. In a mere 20 years,

sorghum production increased by 2772 percent. Today the amount of land devoted to sorghum production is twice as great as the amount of land devoted to wheat. The principal advantage of sorghum over wheat is that although it responds to irrigation, it can also prosper as a rain-fed crop and survive dry spells. DeWalt calls this Mexico's "second green revolution," a revolution that has taken place "without the benefit of a government-sponsored program to encourage production, without the sponsorship of any bilateral mutual aid agency, and without the teaching and technical assistance of any extension grants" (ibid.:40).

The reason for Mexico's need to import grains—unanticipated by the planners of the Green Revolution—is that 100 percent of the sorghum, 14 percent of the maize, and 10 percent of the wheat are being fed to animals and converted into pork, beef, and chickens. This results in a loss of about 4

SORGHUM IN MEXICO
Only animals will eat this crop when it is harvested.

FIGURE *25.4*

out of every 5 calories in the grains (see p. 215). While increased animal food consumption is desirable, the people most in need of additional calories and proteins cannot afford to eat significant quantities of such foods. About 30 million Mexicans are too poor ever to eat meat, and 20 million are even too poor to eat enough maize, wheat, and beans to satisfy minimum nutritional standards.

In DeWalt's view, the spectacular rise in the amount of land planted in sorghum has had an adverse effect on the welfare of Mexico's poorest classes (Boxes 25.3 and 25.4). Instead of being planted primarily as a rain-fed crop for direct human consumption, the grain is being grown for animal consumption on some of the country's best-irrigated lands. Therefore, not only is it an inefficient source of proteins and calories because it is converted into meat, but it has preempted lands for which the government had built irrigation works, roads, and other facilities in order to wipe out hunger and make Mexico self-sufficient in the production of staple grains (DeWalt 1984).

MEDICAL ANTHROPOLOGY

Another central focus of applied anthropology is the interaction among culture, disease, and health care

(Johnson and Sargent 1990). Anthropologists have, for example, studied the ethnography of everyday life in hospitals, organizations that are a rich source of jarring discrepancies between the emics of various staff specialists and the etics of patient care. From the perspective of the hospital bureaucracy, its various rules and regulations are designed to promote the health and well-being of patients. In fact, numerous studies have shown that the main effect of many rules and regulations is to shock and depersonalize the patients and to create in them a level of apprehension comparable to that which can be observed in an Ndembu boy awaiting the rite of circumcision in the "place of death" (see p. 395). On entering the hospital, patients are stripped of their clothing and their money. They become a case in a numbered room wearing a numbered bracelet for identification (the same way newborn babies are numbered). Groups of costumed personnel (some even wearing masks) speak to them in a strange new dialect: "Did you void this morning?" "When was your last B.M.?" (bowel movement). "You're going to have an EEG" (electroencephalogram). Patients are awakened, fed, and put to sleep according to a rigid schedule, and they are often kept uninformed about their condition and what is happening to them (Fig. 25.5). One might conclude that many hospital rules exist primarily for the convenience of the staff and have an adverse effect on the health

BOX *25.3*

DIETARY AFFLUENCE FOR SOME, SCARCITY FOR THE MASSES

Mexico has experienced two Green Revolutions in the past quarter century, yet finds that its agricultural situation is relatively and absolutely in a worse condition than before. In spite of excellent yields of wheat and sorghum, and somewhat better yields of maize and beans, the country is woefully short of meeting its basic grain needs. There are those who would lay the blame for this problem on the Mexican agricultural sector because it is backward and not productive enough. Others would suggest that population growth which is outstripping the productive capacity of the land is the problem. The evidence, however, indicates that Mexico's food problem is not a production problem but that it is simply another symptom of the country's unequal development.

It is unlikely that further technological advances by themselves will eliminate world hunger.... As we have seen, by any technical standards, the revolution in wheat and sorghum production would have to be judged as successes. Yet increased production has done little to make any real impact on the plight of the poor and the malnourished. Despite Mexico's heavy investment in building irrigation works, transportation facilities, storage structures, and other parts of the infrastructure; although the government has subsidized the purchase of agricultural machinery, fertilizers, and other inputs; and despite the application of green revolutionary technology, the country is no closer to solving the nutritional needs of a large part of its population than it was in 1940.

SOURCE: DeWalt 1985:44, 54.

BOX *25.4*

A CONTRARY POINT OF VIEW

Stagnation and a dampening of initiative do not serve the interests of the rural or urban poor. Few Third World countries can afford to bypass the opportunity to maximize production in their better lands.

Some critics contend that high-yielding varieties reduce labor demand because of mechanization. But none of the varieties requires machines to produce high yields. Where tractors, mechanical threshers, and harvesters are in use, labor demand usually increases. Animals rather than people are replaced, freeing land for the cultivation of crops for human consumption. By permitting more intensive cropping, machinery can increase the need for labor by 20 to 50 percent.

The increased food supplies generated by the spread of high-yielding varieties have created additional employment opportunities in such ser-

vice industries as the marketing of crop products and the manufacture, sale, and maintenance of vehicles, fertilizers, herbicides, and pesticides. Furthermore, food prices have been moderated by the increased volume of cereal production— a bonus for the rural and urban poor. (It is not unusual for low-income people to spend three-fourths of their income on food.) In Colombia, for example, the real price of rice dropped after the introduction of high-yielding varieties.

Excessive concern over the distribution of income in rural areas could lead to agricultural policies that extinguish initiative and impede food production. This would be to the detriment of poor people, especially those residing in towns and cities. In many developing countries close to half the population now lives in urban areas.

SOURCE: Plucknett and Smith 1982:218.

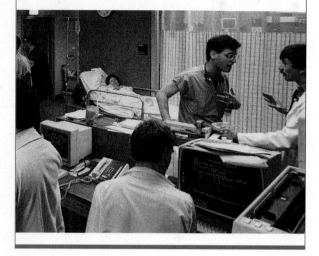

FIGURE *25.5*

EMERGENCY ROOM OF A METROPOLITAN HOSPITAL
Where are the patients?

and well-being of the patients (Foster and Anderson 1978:170–171).

Unfortunately, discovering what is wrong with hospitals and health care delivery is easier than discovering how to change them for the better. As Melvin Konner, who is an M.D. and an anthropologist, has pointed out, medical anthropologists may be lessening their effectiveness as agents of change by adopting an adversarial and negative tone. "Modern medicine," writes Konner (1991:81), is "not a conspiracy against humanitarianism, cost efficiency, comprehensible language, patient compliance, patient autonomy, cultural differences, folk beliefs about health, or any of the other nonmedical dimensions it handles less than perfectly." Konner does not deny that physicians tend to ignore cultural factors in disease, practice "defensive medicine" aimed more at protecting themselves against lawsuits than at curing their patients, and rely excessively on technology. But these defects arise from systemic forces rather than the venality of physicians as a group:

If third party payers [insurance companies] prefer to pay for expensive hospital care of the dying rather than dignified hospices or home care, that is not the fault of physicians. If society lacks compassion for the ill poor, making the doctor-patient encounter intolerably brief, stressful and inadequate for both, it is neither fair or analytically satisfying to blame the doctor or to rail against 'bourgeois' medicine. [Ibid.]

Marijuana

It has long been recognized that the mood, expectations, and personalities of drug users affect their reaction to psychoactive (mind-altering) drugs as much as the specific chemicals in the drugs themselves. Since culture denotes the total complex of behavioral and mental traditions surrounding individuals, one can expect that marked differences in reactions to psychoactive drugs will be found in different cultures. The study of the cultural component in drug-induced thoughts and behavior is therefore a source of essential information for anyone concerned with formulating or administering drug control policies.

Early in the 1970s a team of anthropologists and other behavioral and medical scientists led by Vera Rubin and Lambros Comitas (Rubin and Comitas 1975) undertook a cross-cultural study of marijuana use. Funds for the research were supplied by the National Institute of Mental Health's Center for Studies of Narcotic and Drug Abuse. Because they were interested in examining the long-term effects of marijuana on the health and well-being of chronic users, Rubin and Comitas selected the Caribbean island of Jamaica as the site for their study. Although marijuana is an illegal substance in Jamaica, Jamaicans are probably the most inveterate users of marijuana in the Western Hemisphere (Fig. 25.6). In the rural areas of the island, the researchers found that between 60 and 70 percent of working-class people use marijuana by smoking it, drinking it in tea, or eating it mixed with food. The most important difference between the marijuana complex in Jamaica and the marijuana complex in the United States is that working-class Jamaicans do not smoke marijuana to "turn on" or to achieve the hedonistic effects valued by middle-class American users. Rather, the Jamaicans are motivated to smoke marijuana because they believe it helps them work better and makes them healthier and stronger than nonusers. While weeding fields, for example, farmers said they were able to concentrate more on their tasks after smoking. Videotapes of farmers weeding with and without smoking suggested that their work was in fact more thorough and detailed after smoking. No evidence was found that those who smoked on the job worked less rapidly or less efficiently than those who did not. Rubin and Comitas conclude:

In all Jamaican settings observed, the workers [who smoke] are motivated to carry out difficult tasks with no decrease in heavy physical exertion, and their perception of increased output is a significant factor in bolstering their motivation to work. [1975:75]

FIGURE *25.6*

JAMAICAN RASTAFARIANS
These two men are members of a movement in which the smoking of marijuana is
viewed as a religious sacrament.

Many other aspects of the marijuana complex were studied. To assess the impact of chronic use on the health and personalities of users, a group of 30 smokers and a group of 30 nonsmokers with similar backgrounds and personal attributes were given a broad battery of clinical tests at the University Hospital in Jamaica. Aside from impairment of respiratory functions, which may be attributable to the fact that heavy marijuana smokers are also heavy tobacco smokers, the physical health of the Jamaican smokers was not significantly different from that of the nonsmokers. As for psychological states—intelligence, neurological fitness, sensory perception, memory, and attention—"There is no evidence that long-term use of cannabis [marijuana] is related to chronic impairment" (1975:119). It must be emphasized that this finding is not necessarily applicable to other cultures. It may very well be that in other cultural settings, such as the United States, the long-term use of marijuana does lead to impairment—the effects of cultural factors being no less real than those of physical or chemical factors.

A second intensive cross-cultural study of marijuana smoking has led to conclusions similar to those drawn by Rubin and Comitas. This study was carried out in the Central American country of Costa Rica by a multidisciplinary team whose leaders included anthropologists William Carter (1980) and Paul Doughty. It employed a research design based on "matched pairs"—each of 41 male users was carefully paired with a male nonuser for age, marital status, education, occupation, alcohol consumption, and tobacco consumption. As a result of this design, all the above factors could be ruled out as causes of any of the observed differences in the behavior and physical condition of the users and nonusers.

Initially, the Costa Rican study seemed to corroborate the widely held view that long-term marijuana use leads to lack of motivation for work and economic advancement. It was found that the users tended to have more part-time jobs, more unemployment, more job changes, and fewer material possessions than the nonusers. Yet there was an alternative explanation for these findings. It was possible that the users had become users because they were subject to greater economic and personal stress than the nonusers. If marijuana use caused economic failure and apathy, corroboration could be found by showing that economic failure and apathy increased in direct proportion to the quantity of marijuana used. When comparisons within the user group were made, the results did not support the hypothesis that higher dose levels were correlated with more marginal economic status. The reverse, in fact, was found to be the case. The more marijuana smoked, the more likely the user was to hold a steady, full-time job. Those who were working were smoking nearly twice as much marijuana per day as those who were unemployed. Those who had the shortest periods of unemployment were the heaviest users (Carter 1980:152ff).

Thus we can see that systematic cross-cultural comparisons are essential if we are to distinguish between the cultural and physical-chemical aspects of psychoactive substances.

Kuru

Medical anthropology has an important role to play in helping physical anthropologists and medical researchers understand the interaction between cultural and natural factors that cause people to become ill. The solution of the mystery of Kuru is a classic instance of how medical knowledge can be advanced by examining the interaction between cultural and natural causes of a deadly disease.

During the late 1950s, reports that a previously unknown disease was rampant among the Foré peoples of highland New Guinea made headlines around the world. Victims of the disease, called Kuru, were said to be laughing themselves to death. As reliable accounts began to replace rumor, Kuru turned out to be no laughing matter. Its victims progressively lost control over their central nervous systems, including the nerves controlling their facial muscles, so that their faces were often contorted by ghastly grimaces and smiles. The disease was always fatal within a year or two of its first symptoms (Fig. 25.7).

Researchers led by Carleton Gajdusek found a puzzling *epidemiological* pattern (i.e., distribution and incidence of the disease in the population). Most of the victims were women and girls. Although a few young men came down with it, adult men never did.

FIGURE *25.7*

YOUNG GIRL WITH ADVANCED KURU DISEASE

None of the neighboring tribespeople ever got Kuru, nor was it ever passed on to the Europeans who were in close contact with the Foré.

The first hypothesis was that the disease was genetic and was passed on in family lines from generation to generation. But genetics could not explain the preponderance of female victims plus the occasional young man. Rejecting the genetic explanation, Gajdusek, who was trained as a physical anthropologist and as a virologist (one who studies viruses), began to explore the possibility that Kuru was caused by a type of virus known as a slow virus, whose existence in human beings had never been demonstrated but had been long suspected. Beginning in 1963, Gajdusek inoculated chimpanzees with brain extracts of Kuru victims. After long incubation periods, the chimpanzees began to show the Kuru symptoms. The demonstration that humans could harbor slow viruses has important implications for the study of many puzzling diseases, such as multiple sclerosis, acquired immune deficiency syndrome (AIDS), and certain forms of cancer. For his work, Gajdusek received the Nobel Prize for medicine in 1976.

It was left to two cultural anthropologists, Robert Glasse and Shirley Lindenbaum, however, to complete the explanations for the puzzling epidemiological pattern. Glasse and Lindenbaum drew attention to the fact that in years prior to the outbreak of Kuru, the Foré had begun to practice a form of cannibalism as part of their funeral rituals. Female relatives of the deceased consumed the dead person's brain. Since it was women who were always charged with the task of disposing of the dead, and never men, the Kuru virus never infected adult males. But what about the young men who also occasionally got Kuru? As in many cultures, the Foré's distinction between male and female roles was held less rigidly before puberty than after. Occasionally, therefore, a boy would be permitted to partake of what otherwise was defined as strictly female food. And some years later, this occasional youth would succumb to Kuru along with the much greater number of girls and women (Lindenbaum 1979).

Since neither Gajdusek nor Lindenbaum actually witnessed the eating of human flesh by the Foré, the suggestion has been made that the virus was spread merely by contact with the corpse rather than by consumption of infected morsels. Yet Foré women themselves freely told several researchers that they had previously engaged in cannibalism as part of mortuary rituals (Gajdusek 1977; Harris 1985; Steadman and Merbs 1982). Today, since the Foré have given up their cannibalistic rites, Kuru has virtually ceased to exist among them.

The Case of the Unused Clinic

During the 1970s, a series of community health centers was established by the Department of Health and Hospitals of a large northeastern city. These centers were located in poor neighborhoods and designed to provide health care for the local people. All but one of the centers was used to capacity. Anthropologist Delmos Jones (1976) was charged with the task of discovering why this particular facility was underused.

Jones proceeded on the assumption that the main reasons for the underutilization of the health center would be found not in the characteristics of the population it was designed to serve, but in certain traits of the center itself. Initial investigation showed that many people in the neighborhood did not know about the center's existence. Unlike the other centers, this one was located inside a hospital and could not be seen from the street. Moreover, among those who had heard about the center, few were aware of where it was or what it did. In addition, many people had tried to use the center but had failed to do so. Probing further, Jones discovered that the neighborhood people had a negative image of the hospital in which

the clinic was located. It had the reputation of being very "fancy" and not for poor people. This led to disbelief that somewhere inside the hospital there was a free clinic. Rumor had it that poor people were even turned away from the hospital's emergency room.

People who had persisted in trying to use the clinic reported that they couldn't find it. When they got to the hospital they couldn't find any signs telling them where to go. Even some of the hospital's receptionists didn't know where it was, or refused to say. Jones suspected the latter was the case, because key members of the staff expressed displeasure at having a free clinic in their fancy hospital.

As at the other centers, this one had several neighborhood representatives. But these representatives had developed a defeatist attitude toward the client population and made little effort to contact people in the neighborhood. This apparently pleased the clinic's staff, who let it be known that they preferred to be under- rather than overworked.

Jones set about correcting the situation. First, signs were placed in obvious spots to direct patients to the clinic. Second, receptionists were told where the clinic was. Third, leaflets were printed up and distributed throughout the neighborhood. Finally, new neighborhood representatives were hired who had a more positive attitude toward the population and the clinic. Attendance rose, but the story does not have a happy ending.

Although the new neighborhood representatives were initially enthusiastic, they began to perceive that the hospital staff continued to frown on having the clinic in the hospital, and they became increasingly hesitant to recommend the clinic to the neighborhood people.

Despite the fact that the reasons for the clinic's underuse seemed rather obvious, the hospital's administration refused to accept Jones's explanation. They preferred to continue to think that the problem lay with the attitudes of the neighborhood people. "I, the researcher," reports Jones, "became an advocate for my own research findings...when policy makers don't listen, this could mean we are not telling them what they want to hear" (Jones 1976:227).

ADVOCACY ANTHROPOLOGY

The fact that the implementation phase of a project is often controlled by administrators or politicians who will not accept the anthropologist's analysis or suggestions has led a number of applied anthropologists like Delmos Jones to adopt the role of advocate. Advocacy anthropologists have fought to improve conditions in women's jails, lobbied in state legislatures for raising welfare allotments, submitted testimony before congressional committees in support of child health care programs, lobbied against the construction of dams and highways that would have an adverse effect on local communities, and engaged in many other consciousness-raising and political activities.

WITNESSING FOR THE HUNGRY AND HOMELESS

It is important to preserve the distinction between acting on behalf of a group's interests and serving as an expert witness concerning the violation of a group's rights. Anthropologist Anna Lou Dehavenon (1989–1990) has studied the causes of urban hunger and homelessness in New York City. She denies that she is an advocacy anthropologist. Her work has focused on two problems: the plight of individuals and families who need food and shelter on an emergency basis, and the plight of individuals and families whose welfare entitlements have lapsed as a result of bureaucratic apathy and ineptitude.

By doing fieldwork in the City's Emergency Assistance Units, Dehavenon was able to document the failure of these units to find temporary shelter for homeless families until the early hours of the morning. A lawsuit brought against the city used her data to compel the city's Human Resource Administration to find suitable shelter during regular working hours if possible but in no case later than midnight.

Dehavenon discovered that there was also a close connection between the appearance of families seeking emergency food help and the administrative phenomenon known as "churning." Churning results when people on welfare lose their entitlements as a result of a real or inaccurately recorded failure on their part to comply with bureaucratic requirements. The requirements most often at issue have to do with failure to keep appointments with a caseworker as indicated in a mailed notification, or failure to send a reply for a request for information, or to fill out a questionnaire. The most common reasons for not complying with these administrative rules stem from problems of communication. Mailboxes are frequently broken into; postmen give up trying to find the persons being contacted and write "whereabouts unknown." And, of course, a considerable amount of correspondence sent by people in compliance to welfare offices is not routed to the proper desk. Moreover, many welfare recipients are ill and cannot keep their appointments. Regardless of the reason, the welfare recipients lose their entitlement until the case

can be reopened pending completion of proper forms and other procedures that may take as long as two or three months. While this administrative churning is going on, an estimated 18,000 people a month who are legally entitled to assistance find themselves in a food emergency, which often means that an individual or family has been without solid food for two days or incurred considerable weight loss over the previous month. Others find themselves without money for rent—hence, the connection between churning and the people showing up at the Emergency Assistance Units (see Box 25.5).

By documenting and measuring these problems, by bringing them to the attention of high-ranking administrators in the city government, by proposing administrative reforms, and by releasing information to the news media, DeHavenon's research has helped to bring about a substantial reduction in the amount of churning. For example, welfare recipients are now alerted to look for mail setting up appointments. The Human Resources Administration has also made a start toward abandoning the policy of dropping people whose mail comes back "whereabouts unknown" or who fail to return questionnaires. But much remains to be done.

Some of DeHavenon's additional targets include these goals:

People who have medical problems or lack a fixed address should receive important notices by messenger.

BOX *25.5*

APATHY OR HOSTILITY?

A profound indifference to the plight of the poor may explain their ever-worsening condition of the past several years. Churning, however, is difficult to explain as a product of indifference alone. Rather, it is the direct and logical consequence of a government policy that places a high premium on preventing the erroneous issuance of benefits, but often seems to care much less if eligible recipients are denied the assistance they desperately need to survive. Unless our society is one consumed by hostility to the poor, it must put a stop to this perverse policy and secure for poor people the benefits to which they are entitled.

SOURCE: DeHavenon 1990:254.

All missed appointments should be automatically rescheduled once.

Recipients should have 60 days to comply with an administrative requirement. Their cases should not be closed but suspended so that as soon as they are in compliance, their payments can resume retroactively.

TO ADVOCATE OR NOT TO ADVOCATE: IS THAT THE QUESTION?

Some anthropologists hold the view that the only legitimate professional function of the applied anthropologist is to provide administrators, politicians, or lawyers with an objective analysis of a situation or organization, and that at most, action should be limited to suggesting but not implementing a plan. In this way it is hoped that anthropology will be able to preserve its scientific standing, since it is clear that an all-out attempt to achieve a practical goal frequently involves rhetorical skills and cajolery, and may increase the risk of biased presentations.

Against this view, advocacy anthropologists insist that the objectivity of anthropology and the other social sciences is illusory and that failure to push for the implementation of a goal represents a form of advocacy in itself. The objectivity is illusory, they argue, because political and personal biases control the commitment to study one situation rather than another (to study the poor rather than the wealthy, for example; see p. 452). And refraining from action is itself a form of action and therefore a form of advocacy, because one's inaction assures that someone else's actions will weigh more heavily in the final outcome. Anthropologists who do not actively use their skills and knowledge to bring about what they believe to be a solution simply make it easier for others with opposite beliefs to prevail. Such anthropologists are themselves part of the problem (Cohen 1984b).

No consensus exists among anthropologists about how to resolve these different views of the proper relationship between knowledge and the achievement of controversial practical goals. Perhaps the only resolution of this dilemma is the one that now exists: We must search our individual consciences and act accordingly.

In conclusion, it should be emphasized that we have looked at only a few of the many faces of applied anthropology. As Box 25.6 suggests, many other equally important and interesting cases could have been presented.

SUMMARY

Applied anthropology is concerned with research that has practical applications. Its core consists of re-

---

BOX *25.6*

PUTTING ANTHROPOLOGY TO PRACTICAL USE

TYPE OF ACTION	ANTHROPOLOGIST
Designed and spread inexpensive storage facilities for potatoes in highland Peru and the Philippines	Rhoades (1984); Werge (1979)
Prevented construction of dam that threatened a preexisting irrigation system in the Southwest	Jacobs (1978)
Evaluated community health projects in Tumaco, Colombia	Buzzard (1982)
Helped mothers to feed babies a life-saving remedy for dehydration resulting from diarrhea in Third World countries	Kendall (1984)
Helped to prepare litigation for a $47 million award to the Pembina Chippewa Indians for the loss of their tribal lands	Feraca (1984).
Helped to get fraud charges against Bannock-Shoshoni women dismissed, on grounds of cultural misunderstanding by English-speaking social workers	Joans (1984)
Developed quality-control procedures for the hotel industry	Glover et al. (1984)
Designed, implemented, and evaluated a community health program in Miami to take account of ethnically diverse medical needs	Weidman (1983)

search sponsored by public and private organizations with an interest in achieving practical goals. The role of the applied cultural anthropologist may consist merely in researching the possible means of attaining such goals; sometimes it includes drawing up plans and helping to implement them, as well as evaluating the results of implementation. Applied anthropologists involved in implementation are known as practitioners of action anthropology.

Beyond that core, other forms of research may also be considered part of applied anthropology. Abstract theorizing often has important practical implications, as in the case of alternative theories about the causes of underdevelopment or urban poverty. Much research that is not sponsored by a particular organization with a definite goal in view may nonetheless be aimed at achieving such a goal, such as the independence of a colony or the development of a newly independent state.

Applied anthropology has three major and distinctive contributions to make to the analysis and solution of urgent practical problems: (1) exposure of ethnocentric biases; (2) a holistic viewpoint stressing the long- as well as the short-term, the interconnectedness of the parts of a sociocultural system, and the whole of the system as well as its parts; and (3) a commitment to distinguishing etic behavioral events from emic plans and ideologies. All too often the intended effects of an organization's plans and policies differ sharply from their actual everyday etic consequences.

One important focus of applied anthropology is the problem of underdevelopment. Several examples follow.

The Cornell-Peru Vicos project illustrates applied anthropology functioning over the entire range of research, planning, implementation, and evaluation. This project substantially improved the standard of living of the serflike peasants who lived on the Vicos *hacienda*. An important ingredient in this success was the use of the authoritarian powers of the new manager to introduce new forms of agriculture and other innovations. While successful in its own sphere, it is doubtful if Vicos provides a model for the development of the Peruvian highlands, because of the hidden costs of the experts who guided the Vicosinos from day to day over a 10-year period.

The case of the Merino sheep in Ecuador is an example of what can happen in the absence of a holistic perspective.

The Haitian Agroforestry Project is another example of anthropological research, planning, implementation, and evaluation—in this case, applied to the goal of getting peasants to plant and protect trees. By appealing to the peasants' self-interest in using trees as a cash crop, this project shows signs of achieving a solution to one of Haiti's most serious problems.

The case of the Not-So-Green Revolution illustrates the importance both of a holistic perspective for development projects and of the role of the applied anthropologist as critic rather than change agent. Anthropologists have recurrently pointed out that high-yield miracle seeds benefit large landowners more than poor small farmers because the seeds require heavy inputs of water and expensive chemicals. The case of sorghum and wheat in Mexico point up the futility of seeking a purely technical solution to poverty and underdevelopment, since the effects on every technological innovation are modified by the total sociocultural context into which it is introduced.

Another focus of applied anthropology is medical anthropology. Studies of health care delivery systems and of everyday life in hospitals have attracted considerable interest among anthropologists. Other examples of applied medical anthropology follow.

The studies of marijuana use in Jamaica and Costa Rica illustrate the importance of controlling for ethnocentric biases in research related to problems of health and welfare. Just as technological innovations must be seen in a definite sociocultural context, so too must the use of psychoactive drugs. The Jamaican and Costa Rican studies show that marijuana cannot be seen as a purely chemical-physiological problem. Its effects are different in different cultures. By contrast to the United States, marijuana use in Jamaica and Costa Rica serves to relieve the burden of work rather than to provide relaxation after work.

The case of Kuru illustrates the importance of knowing the cultural context in which diseases occur. Understanding the role of cannibalism in funerary rituals and the development of distinct dietary patterns among men and women provided the key to solving the disease's mysterious epidemiology.

A final example of medical anthropology is the case of the underused urban clinic in the northeastern United States. The administrators in charge of the clinic program either do not recognize or will not admit the discrepancy between their stated plans and their own behavior. In such a situation, the administrators create the chief obstacle to implementation. This brings us to yet another dimension of applied anthropology. As brought out in the case of the "churning" of welfare recipients in a merciless bureaucratic machine, there is a legitimate role for anthropologists who hope to see their research used to help people who cannot help themselves.

Chapter 26

The Anthropology of a Hyperindustrial Society

Now the moment has arrived for us to apply what we have learned to the main social and cultural features of a modern industrial society. I have chosen the United States as an example. Naturally, it is impossible to cover all or even most of the features of so large and complex a society in a single chapter. Therefore, I have decided to concentrate on topics that relate to some of the acute social problems confronted by the people of the United States: boredom and alienation in the workplace; poverty; unemployment; the concentration of wealth; ethnic and race relations; crime; welfare; changing family structure and gender roles; and the challenge of new forms of religious expression. We shall see that these problems are related to the continuing evolution of the industrial mode of production, from smokestack manufacturing to the high tech production of services and information. Perhaps you will find the portrait painted here to be too negative and unflattering. But I would rather make you think than feel good.

MODE OF PRODUCTION

The mode of production in the United States is an advanced, increasingly high tech form of industrialism. *Industrialism* denotes the mass production of goods, services, and information by means of a highly detailed division of labor in which workers use electronic and other kinds of machines in routinized, repetitive ways. *Detailed division of labor* refers to the separation of production tasks into many tiny steps carried out by different workers.

The United States remains the top-ranking industrial manufacturing country in the world. Nonetheless, two-thirds of its work force is no longer engaged in manufacturing, and two-thirds of the gross domestic product consists of non-goods production (Fig. 26.1). Three-quarters of all employees produce information and services rather than tangible objects (Howe and Parks 1989:6). Most employed adult Americans work in offices, stores, restaurants, schools, clinics, and moving vehicles rather than on factory assembly lines. They wait on customers, repair broken machines, keep accounts, write letters, transfer funds, and provide grooming, schooling, training, information, counseling, and therapy to students, clients, customers, and patients.

Farming, which once accounted for the vast majority of American workers, now occupies only 3 percent of the work force. With the industrialization and automation of agriculture, large numbers of workers were displaced. Migration from farm to city provided much of the labor supply for the growth of the manufacturing sector of the economy. But the percentage of workers employed in manufacturing peaked in 1950, as more and more jobs were created in the service and information industries. Also, large numbers of service and information workers were recruited from the ranks of married housewives, with consequences to be discussed below.

The rise of the service and information sectors has led to the characterization of the United States as a "postindustrial society" (Bell 1973). It would seem more appropriate, however, to call the United States and other advanced industrial societies such as Germany and Japan, "hyperindustrial" (*hyper* means extra strong) rather than "postindustrial" since the shift to services and information processing has merely resulted in extending the detailed division of labor and the use of mass-production machines—office computers, word processors, duplicators, supermarket bar code scanners, electronic mail, automatic dialing machines—into additional kinds of production (Harris 1987; Sanderson 1988:451). Offices are factories whose product is information, blurring the distinction between blue-collar and white-collar workers (Fig. 26.2).

POLITICAL ECONOMY

Although Americans think of the United States as being a capitalist country, its political economy is actually best characterized as a mixture of capitalism and democratic state socialism—the same mixture that to varying degrees constitutes the political economies of Western Europe and Japan. Some 17 million people are directly employed by federal, state, and local governments. Another 36.7 million depend largely

FIGURE 26.1

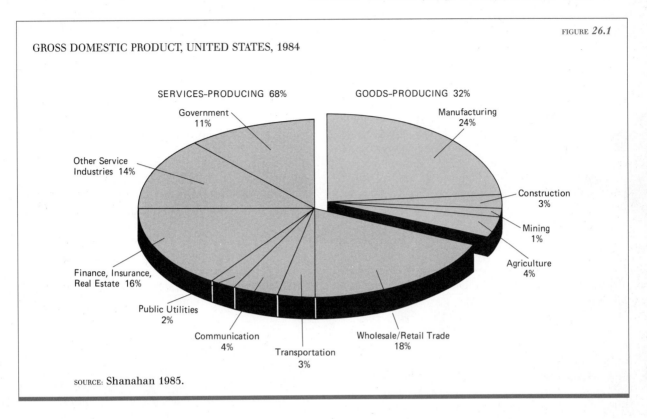

GROSS DOMESTIC PRODUCT, UNITED STATES, 1984

SERVICES-PRODUCING 68%

GOODS-PRODUCING 32%

Government 11%

Manufacturing 24%

Other Service Industries 14%

Construction 3%

Mining 1%

Agriculture 4%

Finance, Insurance, Real Estate 16%

Public Utilities 2%

Communication 4%

Transportation 3%

Wholesale/Retail Trade 18%

SOURCE: Shanahan 1985.

FIGURE 26.2

INFORMATION FACTORY
The accounting department of a large insurance company. Numbers and words instead of nuts and bolts are the basics of the work, but it's still an assembly line. Note the sex of the workers.

on government social security payments. Other forms of state, local, and federal pensions support an additional 5.2 million people. Welfare in the form of aid to dependent children, home relief, and aid to the hand-

icapped supports about 14 million people. There are 2 million people in the armed forces and 2.3 million receiving unemployment benefits. At least 1 million farm families depend on government subsidies. Then there are an estimated 6 million people whose jobs in private industry depend on government purchases of military equipment, construction contracts, government "bailout" loans to companies on the verge of bankruptcy, and assorted forms of government subsidies. Adding the dependents of these workers raises the total in this category to at least 10 million. By conservative estimate, therefore, over 80 million U.S. citizens depend on the redistribution of tax money rather than a share of profits made as a result of capitalist free enterprise.

OLIGOPOLY CAPITALISM

The essence of capitalist enterprise is the freedom to buy and sell in competitive price-making markets. Price-making markets exist where there are enough buyers and sellers to enable buyers to compete with buyers, buyers to compete with sellers, and sellers to compete with sellers for the prices that best suit their respective interests. It has long been recognized that in order to preserve the free enterprise system, limitations must be placed on the ability of small groups of powerful buyers or sellers to gain control over a market to the extent that the prices they offer effectively determine the price that must be paid by anyone who wants a particular product or service. Early in this century, the U.S. Congress passed laws against the formation of monopolies and actively pursued the breakup of companies that then dominated the railroad, meat-packing, and petroleum industries. The antimonopoly laws stopped short, however, of prohibiting the formation of semimonopolies or *oligopolies*—that is, companies that control not all, but a major share of the market for a particular product.

The trend toward oligopoly was already well advanced in the earlier part of this century. But after the end of World War II, the pace of acquisitions and expansions quickened. As a result, by 1980 the 50 largest U.S. manufacturing corporations owned 42 percent of all assets used in manufacturing, while the top 500 owned 72 percent of these assets (Silk 1985). In 1988, there were 3487 mergers worth $227 billion among corporations worth more than $1 million (U.S. Bureau of the Census 1990:534).

Despite the growth of oligopoly, there remain millions of small-scale owner-operated companies in the United States. Many of these, however, are franchise operations in service and retail trades and in the gasoline and fast-food industries. Their policies, prices, and products are controlled by giant parent companies.

INDUSTRIAL BUREAUCRACY AND ALIENATION

As a result of the growth of government and oligopolistic corporations and the spread of industrialism to information and service occupations, the majority of Americans work for organizations (including government workers) employing more than 100 people (ibid:528). These organizations do not reward individual initiative or free enterprise so much as the willingness of workers to perform standardized routine tasks. This has led to the appearance of what has been called "alienation": on factory assembly lines and in offices, stores, hospitals, and shops. Workers in large bureaucratized enterprises, government or private, tend to become bored with their tasks, hostile to management, indifferent to the quality of their product, and uninterested in the welfare of the ultimate consumers of the goods and the services they help to produce.

Some observers contend that automation is eliminating jobs that previously allowed for a considerable amount of style and self-expression. For example, as the fast-food chains take over the restaurant business, they do away with the need for qualified cooks and chefs, personalized menus, and knowledgeable waiters, waitresses, and stewards. They use "equipment and products designed to be operated (or sold) by minimally trained, unskilled persons, of whom high turnover rates are expected," whose jobs consist of sorting out boxed uniform portions of food prepared and frozen off-premises (Job 1980:41). There is considerable evidence that automation of the service and information sectors leads to an increase in the detailed division of labor, to the elimination of many interesting and versatile secretarial positions, and to a downgrading of skills and wages (Belsham 1988; Glenn and Feldberg 1977; Nelson 1986). Karen Nussbaum, of the National Association of Office Workers, writes:

Office automation as it is being introduced today requires that a great many people tediously enter the data, push the right buttons, fill out forms for the computer with perfect accuracy, and feed the forms to the computer. Each worker must discipline herself to the system imposed by the machine. Most often, clericals work with computer terminals which have been strictly programmed to perform only one task. (1980:3)

The new office machines themselves supervise and discipline their operators, virtually eliminating contact and conversation with other workers except those who perform similar functions nearby (Box 26.1).

For typists, telephone operators, cashiers, stock clerks, and mail sorters, automation means progressively less to know and less to think. By using optical scanning machines, file clerks can dispense with knowing the sequence of the alphabet. Supermarket cashiers no longer have to know how to add or subtract. Airline reservationists no longer need to know anything about timetables. Bank tellers, in Harry Braverman's words (1974:340), have become "mere check out clerks at a money supermarket."

On the other hand, some observers contend that as a result of automation, jobs are actually becoming more complex. In the textile industry, for example, those who operate and repair the new generation of automated looms must be able to read and interpret complex manuals. One study predicts that the percentage of jobs that require the highest skill levels will rise from 6 percent in 1984 to 13 percent in 2000 (Storper 1989:159–164; Swasy and Hymowitz 1990).

MODERN TIMES: WORKING FOR A LARGE OIL COMPANY AS A CUSTOMER SERVICE OPERATOR

The pace is strenuous (an average of 160 calls per day) and automatically set by the computer's automatic call distributor; tasks are repetitive, and workers are isolated in carrels on duty, while their movement is restricted by their headsets and the necessary concentration on the VDT [Video Display Terminal] screen. Machine-measured performance statistics are the basis for promotion: for each operator the computer measures the number of calls taken, the length of each call, the number of callers who "abandoned" before being answered, and the amount of time spent off the telephone or away from the work station. In order to monitor performance, supervisors listen in on 10% of each operator's daily call volume (approximately 16 calls) each month, using a telephone pickup that cannot be heard by the operator. More than three errors places the operator below the shop standard for "accuracy." One supervisor and former operator observed, "You can tell when they've been working the phones too long; their voices on the phone get louder and louder without their noticing it."

SOURCE: Nelson 1986:158.

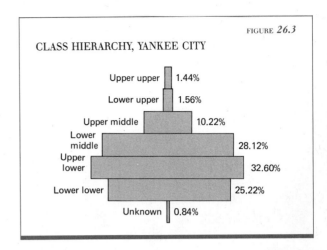

FIGURE *26.3*

CLASS HIERARCHY, YANKEE CITY

Upper upper 1.44%
Lower upper 1.56%
Upper middle 10.22%
Lower middle 28.12%
Upper lower 32.60%
Lower lower 25.22%
Unknown 0.84%

CLASS STRATIFICATION

Most Americans do not think of themselves as being members of a class, and class has always been downplayed as a factor in American History. Thus, according to George Bush, "class is for European democracies or something else—it isn't for the United States of America. We are not going to be divided by class" (quoted in DeMott 1990:11). But like all state-organized societies, the United States is a stratified society and has a complex system of classes, minorities, and other hierarchical groups.

Emic versions of U.S. stratification hierarchies differ from one class to another and bear little resemblance to etic accounts. James West (1945), who studied class relations in a small Midwestern community he called Plainville, concluded that there were different class hierarchies, depending on whether one

took the viewpoint of the "upper crust," "good religious people," "non-church people," "all us good honest working people," Methodists, Baptists, and so on. At the bottom of all these hierarchies there was a category called "people who live like animals."

Lloyd Warner (Warner et al. 1949) attempted to study the class structure of Yankee City (pseudonym for Newburyport, Massachusetts) by classifying people according to occupation, source of income, house type, and dwelling area. Warner's picture of Yankee City's classes (Fig. 26.3) represents a mixture of emic and etic criteria.

There is no doubt that the United States is a highly stratified society (Fig. 26.4). This can be seen from the data on the distribution of wealth among U.S. families. According to a Federal Reserve research survey, the richest 1 percent of U.S. families in 1989 owned 37 percent of the total net wealth; the next 9 percent owned 31 percent; and the remaining 90 percent owned 33 percent. That is, the top 10 percent owned more than twice the total of what the bottom 90 percent owned (Kinnickell and Woodburn 1992).

IS THERE A RULING CLASS IN THE UNITED STATES?

The most important question that can be asked about class in the United States is whether there is a ruling class. Paradoxically, this is a subject about which relatively little is known.

The existence of a ruling class in the United States seems to be negated by the ability of the people as a whole to vote political officeholders in or out of office by secret ballot. Yet the fact that less than half of the voting-age population votes in presidential elections (Fig. 26.5 and Table 26.1) suggests

FIGURE *26.4*

HOMELESS
This tragic figure haunts the streets of Washington, D.C., the capital of the richest country in the world.

that the majority of citizens distrust the candidates' promises or doubt that one candidate can do anything more than any other to make life significantly better (Hadley 1978; Ladd 1978). The actual selection of political candidates and the financing and conduct of election campaigns are controlled through special interest groups and political action committees. Small coalitions of powerful individuals working through lobbyists, law firms, legislatures, the courts, executive and administrative agencies, and the mass media can decisively influence the course of elections and of national affairs. The great bulk of the decision-making process consists of responses to pressures exerted by special interest groups (Drew 1983; Sabato 1989; Thomas 1986). In the campaigns for Congress the candidate who spends the most money usually wins.

Those who claim that there is no ruling class in the United States argue that power is dispersed among many different contending blocs, lobbies, associations, clubs, industries, regions, income groups, ethnic groups, states, cities, age groups, legislatures, courts, and unions, and that no coalition powerful enough to dominate all the others can form (Dahl 1981). In the terminology of the economist John Kenneth Galbraith (1958, 1967), there is no ruling class; there is only "countervailing" power (Roach et al. 1969).

But the crucial question is this: Is there a category of people who share a set of underlying interests in the perpetuation of the status quo and who by virtue of their extreme wealth are able to set limits to the kinds of laws and executive policies that are enacted and followed out? The evidence for the existence of such a category of people consists largely of studies of the extent of interlocking memberships on corporate boards of directors and the concentration of ownership and wealth in giant corporations and well-to-do families. This kind of data alone cannot prove the existence of a ruling class, since there remains

Candidates	Percent of eligible voters who voted	Number of votes cast
1960 Kennedy—Nixon	63.1%	68,838,000
1964 Johnson—Goldwater	61.8%	70,645,000
1968 Humphrey—Nixon	60.7%	73,212,000
1972 McGovern—Nixon	55.1%	77,625,000
1976 Carter—Ford	53.6%	81,603,000
1980 Carter—Reagan	52.6%	86,497,000
1984 Mondale—Reagan	53.1%	92,631,000
1988 Bush—Dukakis	50.1%	91,584,820

FIGURE *26.5*

APATHY
Percentage of eligible voters who vote for president is declining.

SOURCE: U.S. Bureau of the Census, *Congressional Quarterly,* Jan. 21, 1989.

TABLE 26.1

PRESIDENTIAL MANDATES?

Year	Winner (Party)	Percentage of total popular vote	Percentage of voting-age population
1932	Roosevelt (D)	57.4	30.1
1936	Roosevelt (D)	60.8	34.6
1940	Roosevelt (D)	54.7	32.2
1944	Roosevelt (D)	53.4	29.9
1948	Truman (D)	49.6	25.3
1952	Eisenhower (R)	55.1	34.0
1956	Eisenhower (R)	57.4	34.1
1960	Kennedy (D)	49.7	31.2
1964	Johnson (D)	61.1	37.8
1968	Nixon (R)	43.4	26.4
1972	Nixon (R)	60.7	33.5
1976	Carter (D)	50.1	26.8
1980	Reagan (R)	50.7	26.7
1984	Reagan (R)	58.8	31.2
1988	Bush (R)	53.4	26.8

Even the most "popular" presidents have been elected by only about one-third of the voting-age population.
SOURCE: Cook, 1989:137.

the problem of how boards of directors and wealthy families actually influence decisions on crucial matters such as the rate of inflation, unemployment, national health service, energy policy, tax structure, resource depletion, pollution, military spending, urban blight, and so forth. As we will see in the next section, the concentration of wealth and economic power in the United States shows at least that there is a real potential for such influence to be exerted (Roberts and Brintnall 1982:259).

THE CONCENTRATION OF WEALTH

According to the Federal Reserve Board (Kennickell and Woodburn 1992) 1 percent of U.S. families owned:

45 percent of all nonresidential real estate
49 percent of all publicly held stock
78 percent of all trusts
62 percent of all business assets

The concentration of economic power is far greater than even these statistics suggest. The reason is that for most of the population, the main form of wealth consists of residences and automobiles. These forms of wealth are not capital. They cannot be used to create more capital nor can they be used to control economic decisions. On the other hand, people who own large amounts of business assets—stocks, bonds, and commercial real estate—own capital and can exert control over those who do not. Moreover, the fact that 1 percent of the population owns one half of the corporate stock does not tell us how much capital is actually controlled by these individuals. To control a large corporation, one does not need to own 51 percent of the stock. Since most private investors hold only small quantities of stock, investors who own as little as 15 percent of the stock control corporate policy.

About half of stocks and bonds are owned by institutional investors, who administer pension funds, trust funds, and insurance companies. It is the corporations, families, and people who control these institutional investors that have the greatest economic power.

As a result of the wave of buyouts and mergers that took place in the United States during the 1980s, the concentration of economic power has continued to increase. A rough idea of the trend toward greater concentration of economic power can be derived from changes in family income. Between 1977 and 1989 the average pretax incomes of the top 1 percent of American families rose 77 percent while the pretax incomes of the bottom 40 percent of families fell by between 1 percent and 9 percent. The top 1 percent of families earned an average of $560,000 each in 1989 and their combined earnings were half a trillion dollars,

FIGURE *26.6*

MEMBERS OF THE RULING CLASS?
(A) H. Ross Perot; **(B)** Donald Trump; **(C)** David Rockefeller.

(A)   (B)   (C)

an amount almost equivalent to the sum of all federal tax revenues. Another revealing statistic is the change in the disparity between the incomes of employees and employers. In the 1970s employers made 35 times what employees made; in 1990 they were making 120 times more (Noah 1992).

It is entirely possible, therefore, that a small group of individuals and families exerts a decisive influence over the policies of a small but immensely powerful group of corporations. Some of the individuals and families involved are well known. Besides the Mellons, they include Rockefellers, Du Ponts, Fords, Hunts, Pews, and Gettys (Fig. 26.6). But it is a testament to the ability of the super-rich to live in a world apart that the names of many other powerful families are unknown to the general public. Anthropologists have been remiss in not studying the patterns of thoughts and actions of the super-rich (Nader 1972).

POVERTY AND UPWARD MOBILITY IN THE UNITED STATES

Modern industrial democracies attribute great importance to the achievement of mobility from the subordinate to the superordinate classes. In the United States, it was traditionally held that by diligent effort poor people could work their way up from poverty to riches within a lifetime. It is clear, however, that only a tiny fraction of the population can hope to move into the ruling class.

At the lower levels, the U.S. stratification system is fairly open—but not as open as was traditionally believed. The main factor that determines a person's

chances of upward mobility is the level at which one starts: "There is much upward mobility in the United States, but most of it involves very short social distances" (Blau and Duncan 1967:420). A child whose father was in the bottom 5 percent income group has a 1 percent chance of entering the top 10 percent income group. A child whose father was in the top 5 percent has a 1 percent chance of falling to the bottom 10 percent (Solon 1992).

According to official government standards, 13.5 percent of the individuals in the United States were living in poverty in 1990 (Noah 1991). This burden falls disproportionately on America's children, who make up the bulk of the poverty class. Close to 25 percent of Americans age 6 and under must contend with this burden. The adequacy of the government's definition of poverty remains in doubt, however. At least one-third of a low-income family's budget must be spent on food in order to maintain minimum nutritional standards. Families with incomes twice as high as the poverty cutoff ($13,359 for a family of four) do not necessarily enjoy a comfortable standard of living. The costs of housing, education, transportation, and medical attention have risen more rapidly than income, and such families have had to contend with the declining quality of goods, services, utilities, roads, streets, public buildings, parks, and public transportation (Harrington 1980).

What is the reason for the persistence of a large poverty class in the United States? The perennial favorite explanation is that the poor are victims of their own mental, behavioral, and cultural shortcomings. But as we have seen (p. 334), values said to be distinctive of the culture of poverty are actually shared by the middle-class. Many middle-class Americans seem to believe that the poorer you are, the more you should save, and the harder you should work: "The first principle is that in order to move up, the poor must not only work, they must work harder than the classes above them" (Gilder 1981:256). But isn't this a case of expecting more from those who have least? According to anthropologist Anthony Leeds, the poor in the United States are not victims of their own values; rather they are the victims

of certain kinds of labor markets which are structured by the condition of national technology, available capital resources, enterprise location, training institutions, relations to foreign and internal markets, balance-of-trade relations, and the nature of the profit system of capitalist societies.... These are not independent [characteristics] of some suppressed culture [of poverty] but characteristics or indices of certain kinds of total economic systems. [Leeds 1970:246]

What this boils down to is that due to factors beyond their control, most of the poor are doomed to remain poor, even when they try harder than the people above them (Thurow 1987).

STREETCORNER MEN

The view that America's poor refuse to work hard and to save because of a culture of poverty fails to take into account the types of work and opportunities that are open to them. In his book *Tally's Corner* (1967), Elliot Liebow, an ethnographer who has studied the black streetcorner men of Washington, D.C., describes the conditions shaping the work patterns of the unskilled black male. The streetcorner men are full of contempt for the menial work they must perform, but this is not a result of any special tradition they acquire from the culture of poverty. Historically, the dregs of the job market in the United States have been left for blacks and other minorities—jobs whose conditions and prospects are the mark of failure, that are demeaned and ridiculed by the rest of the labor force, and that pay only the minimum wage or less; jobs that are dull, as in dishwashing or floor polishing; dirty, as in garbage collecting and washroom attending; or backbreaking, as in truck loading or furniture moving (Fig. 26.7).

The duller, dirtier, and more exhausting the work, the less likely that extra diligence and effort will be rewarded by anything but more of the same. There is no "track" leading from the night maid who

FIGURE *26.7*

DEAD-END JOB
Nonunion employment at a construction site in Washington, D.C.

cleans the executive's office to the firm's vice-president; from the dishwasher to the restaurant owner; from the unskilled, unapprenticed construction worker to journeyman electrician or bricklayer. These jobs are dead ends from the beginning. As Liebow points out, no one is more explicit in expressing the worthlessness of the job than the boss who pays so little for it. The rest of society, contradicting its professed values concerning the dignity of labor, also holds the job of dishwasher or janitor in low esteem. "So does the streetcorner man. He cannot do otherwise. He cannot draw from a job those social values which other people do not put into it" (Liebow 1967:59).

According to Liebow, an additional mark of the degradation is that wages for menial work in hotels, restaurants, hospitals, and office and apartment buildings take into account the likelihood that the workers will steal food, clothing, or other items in order to bring their take-home pay above subsistence. The employer then sets the wages so low that stealing must take place. Although implicitly acknowledging the need for theft, the employer nonetheless tries to prevent it and will call the police if someone is caught stealing.

Liebow tells the story of Richard, a black man in his twenties who had tried to support his family with extra jobs ranging from shoveling snow to picking peas and who had won the reputation of being one of the hardest-working men on the street. "I figure you got to get out there and try. You got to try before you can get anything," said Richard. But after five years of trying, Richard pointed to a shabby bed, a sofa, a couple of chairs, and a television set, and gave up:

"I've been scuffling for five years from morning till night. And my children still don't have anything, my wife don't have anything, and I don't have anything." [Ibid.:67]

RACIAL, ETHNIC, AND CLASS CONFLICT

The intensity and clarity of racial and ethnic conflict in the United States presents a counterpoint to the generally unconscious and confused nature of class relations. Rather than classes, racial and ethnic minorities and majorities are the stratified groups that manifest a sense of their own identity, consciousness of a common destiny, and collective purpose. Why has this been the case? The persecution, segregation, and exploitation of minority enclaves by racial and ethnic majorities, and the activism of minorities on their own behalf, can be viewed as forms of political and economic struggle that preserve the overall pattern of class stratification. Instead of uniting to improve schools, neighborhoods, jobs, and health services, ethnic and racial groups seek to achieve their own advancement at one another's expense (Fig. 26.8). Ethnic chauvinism thus pits "have-nots" against "have-littles," and thereby allows the "haves" to maintain their wealth and power (see Bottomore 1966; Perlo 1976; Sowell 1983).

Once again the emic-etic distinction is vital to the comprehension of this situation. Ethnic pluralism in the United States has not arisen as the result of conscious, conspiratorial effort. The formation of ethnic and racial consciousness took precedence over the formation of class consciousness because of the relatively high rate of upward mobility enjoyed by white immigrants. Class consciousness did not develop because in the short run it was disadvantageous for the white working class, with its relatively high mobility, to make an alliance with the black working

FIGURE *26.8*

WHEN RACIAL AND ETHNIC TENSIONS EXPLODE **(A)** Members of the large gang known as the Crips played an important role in the Los Angeles riots of 1992. **(B)** The morning after the looting and burning in Los Angeles.

(A)

(B)

class. Blacks were abandoned and actively persecuted by working-class whites and left behind to suffer the worst effects of low wages, unemployment, and exploitation because large numbers of whites, by abandoning blacks, increased or (thought they increased) their own chances of rising to middle-class status. However, it can be argued that working-class whites have had to pay an enormous penalty for failing to unite with black poverty and working-classes. For example, in her study of the working-class neighborhood of Greenpoint-Williamsburg in Brooklyn, New York, Ida Susser (1982:208) found that racial divisions debilitated collective action and allowed elected officials and commercial developers a free hand that benefited middle and upper-class whites: "So long as racial issues kept white voters loyal, elected officials could ignore the needs of a poor white working-class constituency."

THE NEW RACISM

One of the reasons for the limited success of the black power movement in the United States is that it provoked a reactive increase in the solidarity sentiments and activities of the white ethnic groups. In response to real or imagined threats to their schools, neighborhoods, and jobs, "white ethnics"—people of Italian, Polish, Irish, and Jewish descent—fought back against black power. They mounted antibusing campaigns and created new private and public school systems based on segregated suburban residence patterns (Glasser 1989; Katz and Taylor 1988; Stein and Hill 1977).

During the 1980s and 1990s, tensions between whites and blacks and other minorities increased in different regions and cities all across the United States. A wave of racially motivated verbal and physical abuse affected not only urban neighborhoods (such as New York's Howard Beach, Crown Heights, and Bensonhurst) but college campuses as well. This resurgence of overt racism results in part from the fact that successive conservative governments have devalued civil rights, encouraged resentment against affirmative action, and fostered racial polarization by cutting back on critical social programs (Glasser 1989; C. Murray 1984). But there is a deeper level of sociocultural causation that needs to be explored. One must ask why such a political program became attractive during the 1980s.

It seems likely that the electoral success of political leaders who were indifferent or even vindictive about the plight of the country's minorities was related to the marked deterioration in the economic prospects of the white majority. Polls reveal that many working- and middle-class whites have grown apprehensive about being able to improve or even maintain their level of socio-economic well-being. For the first time in U.S. history, many young people are convinced that they will not be able to live as comfortably as their parents. These are not groundless fears. The wave of racial and ethnic unrest coincides with

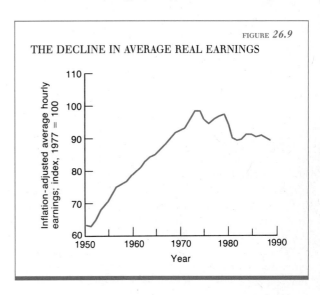

FIGURE *26.9*

THE DECLINE IN AVERAGE REAL EARNINGS

a period during which the average real weekly earnings of production and nonsupervisory employees declined by 18 percent (Mishel and Frankel 1990; Morehouse and Dembo 1988:7; see Fig. 26.9). During the same period U.S. hourly take-home wages for the first time slipped below those of the other major industrial powers (see Table 26.2) It is understandable, therefore, why whites should increasingly regard any form of affirmative action as "reverse discrimination," and have lost interest in extending a helping hand to the poor, especially to poor blacks and Hispanics. Coming from segregated neighborhoods and segregated schools, blacks and whites seldom form friendships in their youth. They grow up as if they came from entirely different societies. It is no wonder, then, that when blacks are thrown together in predominantly white high schools and colleges, they feel insecure and huddle together for protection against insensitive or openly hateful treatment (Fleming 1984; Hacker 1989, 1992).

TABLE *26.2*

HOURLY PAY LEVELS (FOR PRODUCTION WORKERS, IN U.S. DOLLARS)

	1985	1986	1987	1988
United States	$12.95	$13.19	$13.44	$13.62
Japan	6.47	9.47	11.14	13.80
West Germany	9.56	13.35	16.87	20.19
Italy	7.40	10.01	12.33	14.77
France	7.52	10.27	12.42	14.03
Britain	6.19	7.50	8.96	11.06

SOURCE: Malabre 1989.

VALUES AND THE MATRIFOCAL FAMILY

One of the explanations for poverty in the urban ghettos focuses attention on the problem of so-called fatherless, or matrifocal, families (see p. 264). (The most common explanation for black poverty continues to be based on notions of racial inferiority. See p. 95 for a discussion of this explanation.)

The main structural features of matrifocality are as follows: The domestic unit consists of a mother and her children by several different men. Some of the woman's coresident adult daughters may also have children. The fathers provide only temporary and partial support. Men who move in and out of the domestic unit are etically "married" to mothers—they act out all the typical husband-father roles. Yet emically, the relationship is distinguished from "true marriage," and the children are legally regarded as "illegitimate" (Gonzalez 1970).

In 1965, with the release of a report by Daniel P. Moynihan, then U.S. Assistant Secretary of Labor, matrifocality received official recognition as the prime cause of the perpetuation of poverty among blacks in the United States. According to Moynihan, black youths are not properly motivated to take jobs that are actually available because of the absence of a male father figure in their family. They are reared in households where only the women are regularly employed. Adult males drift in and out of these households, and thus black youths grow up without the aid and inspiration of a stable male figure holding a steady job and providing comfort and security for wife and children. Moynihan proposed that matrifocality was a cause not only of poverty but of crime and drug addiction as well.

Explanations of poverty that appeal to enculturation experience within matrifocal households don't explain very much because the phenomenon of matrifocality is itself a response to poverty.

Like all domestic arrangements, the matrifocal family in the United States represents an adjustment to certain conditions that are beyond the control of its members. The conditions in question are these: (1) Both men and women lack access to strategic resources—that is, they own no significant property; (2) wage labor is available to both men and women; (3) women earn as much as or more than men; and (4) a man's wages are insufficient to provide subsistence for a dependent wife and children, or the combined incomes of husband and wife are insufficient to pay for day care.

The official welfare policies of the U.S. government greatly strengthen the tendency to form matrifocal families. Households that seek welfare support usually cannot contain able-bodied "fathers." Mothers whose husbands or children's fathers do not earn enough money to support the household can claim Aid to Families with Dependent Children (AFDC) welfare allotments, provided that able-bodied fathers are not coresident with their children. Since poor fathers cannot stay home with their children and claim AFDC allotments, the law confers upon poor women an extra economic value that makes it inevitable that they will become the center of domestic life as long as the men cannot earn enough to make the AFDC allotments unnecessary. Since it is the woman who is favored for AFDC payments, it is she who gets the lease in public housing projects and who controls (but does not own) the family's dwelling space. Of course, there are other, more general reasons for matrifocality. These have been discussed on page 264.

THE FLATS

In her study of the Flats, a black ghetto in a midwestern city (Fig. 26.10), anthropologist Carol Stack (1974) provides an account of the strategies that poverty-level families follow in attempting to maximize their security and well-being in the face of the AFDC laws and the inadequate wages of the unskilled male. Nuclear families do not exist in the Flats because the material conditions necessary for such families do not exist. Instead, the people of the Flats are organized into large female-centered networks of kinfolk

FIGURE *26.10*

CHILDREN OF THE FLATS
Area of Carl Stack's study.

and neighbors. The members of these networks engage in reciprocal economic exchanges, take care of one another's children, provide emergency shelter, and help one another in many ways not characteristic of middle-class domestic groups.

In the Flats the most important single factor that affects interpersonal relationships between men and women is unemployment and the difficulty that men have in finding secure jobs:

Losing a job, or being unemployed month after month, debilitates one's self-importance and independence, and for men, necessitates that they sacrifice their role in the economic support of their families. Then they become unable to assume the masculine role as defined by American society. [Stack 1974:112]

Ironically, as Stack points out:

Attempts by those on welfare to formulate nuclear families are efficiently discouraged by welfare policy. In fact, welfare policy encourages the maintenance of non-coresidential cooperative domestic networks. [Ibid.:127]

A woman can be cut off from welfare as soon as her husband gets out of the army or comes home from prison, or if she is single and gets married. Thus, "Women come to realize that welfare benefits and ties with kin networks provide greater security for them and their children" (ibid.:113).

CRIME

The United States has one of the highest rates of violent crime found among industrial nations. More than one-fifth of the inhabitants of America's largest cities feel "very unsafe" when they have to go out at night in their own neighborhoods. Women and old people have the greatest fear. Over half of all U.S. women say that they are afraid to go out alone after dark. Senior citizens are afraid to leave their apartments during the day. People also feel insecure indoors: One-third of all U.S. households contain firearms purchased for protection against intruders (U.S. National Criminal Justice Information and Statistics Service 1978). Crime victimization surveys indicate that in 1987 there were 4.5 million victims of assaults, 1 million victims of personal robberies, 141,000 victims of rapes or attempted rape, and 21,000 victims of homicides. One and a half million people had their car stolen. Altogether, 22 million households were touched by crime (U.S. Bureau of the Census 1990:173, 174, 176).

There are 5 times more homicides, 10 times more rapes, and 17 times more robberies in the United States than in Japan; and there are 7 times more homicides, 12 times more rapes, and 8 times more robberies in the United States than in Great Britain (Ross and Benson 1979).

One reason for the higher rate of violent crime in the United States is that U.S. citizens own far more pistols and rifles per capita than the Japanese or British. The right to "bear arms" is guaranteed by the U.S. Constitution. But the failure to pass stricter gun control laws itself reflects, in part at least, the pervasive, realistic fear of being robbed or attacked and the consequent desire to defend person and property. Hence, the cause of the high incidence of violent crimes must be sought at deeper levels of U.S. culture.

THE CRIME AND POVERTY CONNECTION

Much evidence links the unusually high rate of crime in the United States to the long-term, grinding poverty and economic hopelessness of America's inner-city minorities, especially of blacks and Hispanics. Although suburban crime is also on the rise, the principal locus of violent crime remains the inner cities. Blacks, who constitute 12 percent of the population, account for 61 percent of arrests for robbery and 55 percent of arrests for murder and manslaughter (Hacker 1992:181).

One should note, however, that proportionately, blacks themselves suffer more from violent crimes than do whites. A poor black is 25 times more likely than a wealthy white to be a victim of a robbery resulting in injury, and eight times more likely to be a homicide victim. In fact, homicide is the ranking killer of black males between 15 and 24 years of age. More black males die from homicide than from motor vehicle accidents, diabetes, emphysema, or pneumonia. (Two out of five black male children born in an American city in 1980 will not reach age 25.)

The basic reason for all this crime is long-term chronic unemployment and poverty. During and after World War II, U.S. blacks migrated in unprecedented numbers from farms to cities in search of factory jobs just when the economy was beginning to change from goods production to service and information production. Today their poverty rate is about three times greater than that of whites, and their unemployment rate has been twice as high as whites' for decades (Hacker 1992:102). In 1988, 44 percent of all black children (and 38 percent of Hispanic children) were living in poverty (Mishel and Frankel 1990).

Most of these children will not be able to compete successfully for jobs that pay higher than the minimum wage. Without special assistance and affirmative action, there is little hope that these children will be able to work their way out of poverty.

Over half of all black teenagers are unemployed; and in ghettos like Harlem in New York City, the unemployment rate among young black youth may be as high as 86 percent (Brown 1978; National Urban League 1990; see Fig. 26.11).

There is a body of scholarly opinion claiming that poverty in general has little to do with the high rate of criminal violence in the United States and therefore that black unemployment and poverty are not sufficient in themselves to account for the high rates of U.S. crime. It is true that if one simply compares crime rates by state or city, those with low per capita incomes do not necessarily have high rates of criminal violence. But the poverty of the black ghetto is different from the poverty of rural whites or of an earlier generation of urban ethnics. Unlike the rural poor, inner-city blacks have the opportunity as well as the motive to commit violent crimes. The city is an ideal setting for finding and surprising victims and successfully eluding the police. Most important, unlike the European immigrants of previous generations, blacks have with the passage of time become more and not less concentrated inside their ghettos (Fig. 26.12). Under these conditions, the benefits of criminal behavior may seem to outweigh the risks of getting caught and being sent to jail. John Conyers, a member of the black congressional caucus, writes:

When survival is at stake, it should not be surprising that criminal activity begins to resemble an opportunity rather than a cost, work rather than deviance, and a possibly profitable undertaking that is superior to a coerced existence directed by welfare bureaucrats. [1978:678]

THE DRUG CONNECTION

The high odds against attaining economic success by going to school and acquiring the skills necessary to compete with whites for the better jobs lies behind the decision of many black, Hispanic, and other minority youth to traffic in illicit drugs. A week spent selling crack can bring more wealth than a year of working as a dishwasher or a fast-food server. Ironically, the most successful drug businesses are run by young men who refrain from taking drugs themselves and who display many of the characteristics associated with entrepreneurship in legitimate businesses. They break into the trade with a small investment, hire employees, keep careful accounts, strive to establish good relationships with their regular customers, encourage the consumption of their product, adjust prices to market conditions, and keep careful tabs on what their competitors are doing. Of course, the use of crack and other addictive substances has a devastating effect on the consumers who use drugs to escape from a squalid reality. The people of the United States pay an enormous price for the drug trade in the form of increased crime rates, overburdened courts and jails, and drug-related health problems such as AIDS (Massing 1989; T. Williams 1989).

THE WELFARE CONNECTION

A disproportionate share of violent urban crime in the United States is committed by black and Hispanic ju-

FIGURE *26.11*

YOUTH ON A STOOP
The alternatives are dishwashing, floor polishing, and truck loading.

FIGURE *26.12*

LOW-COST HOUSING
(A) Pruitt-Igoe-public housing complex in St. Louis;
(B) Scudder Homes housing project in Newark; **(C)** a building in New York City's South Bronx—cheerful decals cover the empty windows.

(A)

(B)

(C)

veniles brought up in matrifocal families that receive AFDC allotments. This connection between juvenile delinquency and matrifocality reflects the fact that AFDC benefits are set below poverty-level incomes. Almost all inner-city AFDC women, therefore, count on supplementary incomes from husbands-in-hiding, coresident male consorts, or former consort fathers of their children.

Anthropologist Jagna Sharff (1981) found that all the mothers in a group of 24 Hispanic AFDC families living in New York City's Lower East Side had some kind of male consort (Fig. 26.13). While few of the men in the house held regular full-time jobs, even those who were unemployed chipped in something toward food and rent from selling stolen goods, dealing

in marijuana or cocaine, and an occasional burglary or mugging. Some women had more than one consort, while others picked up money and gifts through more casual relationships.

In their early teens, young inner-city boys make substantial contributions to their household's economic balance through their involvement in street crime and dope peddling. In addition, they confer an important benefit on their mothers in the form of protection against the risk of rape, mugging, and various kinds of ripoffs to which the ghetto families are perpetually exposed.

Sharff found that AFDC mothers value sons for streetwise "macho" qualities, especially their ability to use knives or guns, which are needed to protect the

FIGURE *26.13*

LOWER EAST SIDE
The vicinity of Jagna Sharff's study.

family against unruly or predatory neighbors. While the AFDC mothers did not actively encourage their sons to enter the drug trade, everyone recognized that a successful drug dealer could become a very rich man. To get ahead in the drug business, one needs the same "macho" qualities that are useful in defending one's family. When a young man brings home his first drug profits, mothers have mixed feelings of pride and apprehension. In her sample of AFDC families, Sharff compiled a record of 10 male homicides in three years (see Table 26.3). Since young ghetto males have a 40 percent chance of dying by age 25, a

TABLE *26.3*

MALE HOMICIDES IN 24 AFDC FAMILIES, 1976–1979

Victim's age	Immediate cause of death
25	Shot in drug-related incident
19	Shot in dispute in grocery store
21	Shot in drug-related incident
28	Stabbed in drug-related incident
32	"Suicide" in a police precinct house
30	Stabbed in drug-related incident
28	Poisoned by adulterated heroin
30	Arson victim
24	Shot in drug-related incident
19	Tortured and stabbed in drug-related incident

SOURCE: Sharff 1980.

ghetto mother has to have more than one son if she hopes to enjoy the protection of a streetwise male.

One must be careful not to conclude that every family on AFDC conforms to this pattern. For some mothers, AFDC represents a one-time emergency source of funds used in the aftermath of divorce or separation until they can find a job and arrange for child care. But several million inner-city women, mostly black and Hispanic, use AFDC not as a temporary crutch but as a regular or recurrent source of subsistence. It has been found that long-term welfare dependency is especially characteristic of unwed mothers who begin to receive AFDC when they have a first child. Almost 40 percent of these women will stay on welfare for 10 or more years (Besharov 1989:151).

HYPERINDUSTRIAL FAMILY AND GENDER ROLES

The rise of the information and service economy was dependent on and has contributed to a dramatic shift in the sexual composition of the U.S. labor force and to a rise in the cost of rearing children (see p. 226); these changes in turn are responsible for other notable shifts at the structural and ideological levels of U.S. social life.

Since World War II, two out of three new jobs have been taken by calling up a "reserve army" of married women. Concurrently, partially as a result of the premium placed on education for upward mobility in a service and information economy, and partially as a result of the call-up of married women, middle-income families with only one wage earner have difficulty in raising even one or two children who will maintain middle-class standards of consumption. These infrastructural changes account for other changes on the structural and superstructural levels, affecting marriage patterns, family organization, and behavioral and ideological aspects of gender roles and sexuality, such as the post–World War II rise of feminist doctrines and the politics of female liberation (Margolis 1984).

Four major categories of effects can be traced to the shifting sexual composition of the work force and the increased cost of rearing children: (1) declining rates of fertility, (2) falling marriage and rising divorce rates, (3) new forms of family structures, and (4) new gender roles and new forms of sexuality.

Fertility

After World War II, U.S. fertility rates rose rapidly, producing the phenomenon of the "baby boom" that reached its peak in 1957. Subsequently, the completed fertility rate fell to levels that are still at a historic low, a full 50 percent from the peak of the baby boom— from 3.69 to 1.81. While it is true that the crude birthrate per 1000 women has risen slightly since 1975, the all-important completed fertility rate has remained unchanged at its historic low. The reason the crude birthrate per 1000 women has risen slightly is due entirely to the fact that the age cohort of baby boom children has been in its prime reproductive years. There is no indication, however, that the completed fertility rate is about to rise (Newitt 1985; Westoff 1986).

There are many ideological expressions of the trend toward smaller numbers of children per woman. For example, surveys show that the number of women between age 18 and 34 who say that they do not expect to have children has quintupled since 1967 to 11 percent. Among those who want children, the number of offspring desired dropped from four to two during the decade 1970–1980. In 1970, 53 percent of women cited motherhood as "one of the best parts of being a woman"; in 1983, only 26 percent did (Dowd 1983).

Marriage and Divorce Rates

One out of three U.S. marriages now ends in divorce, a threefold increase since 1960. Among couples under 30 years old, the rate of divorce is rapidly approaching one out of two marriages, four times higher than it was in 1960. (These figures represent the number of current marriages divided by the number of current divorces. They do not reflect the total number of past marriages and past divorces.)

This has been accompanied by a great deal of remarriage. Over one-fifth of all marriages are remarriages involving at least one previously divorced partner. Fifty percent of divorced women remarry within 2 years (Sachs 1985:761). But among single women aged 15–44, marriage rates per 1000 have fallen by 36 percent since 1960 (U.S. Bureau of the Census Statistical Abstract 1990:87). And Americans are waiting longer to get married. In 1990 only 39 percent of women ages 20 to 24 were or had been married, down from 63 percent in 1975. For women ages 25 to 29 the percentage fell from 87 percent to 69 percent (Otten 1991). Moreover, the probability of divorce increases with remarriage: 33 percent overall for the first time, 50 percent for the second (Sachs 1985:761). So marriage itself as an institution is not in decline. What is in decline is monogamous marriages that last until one of the partners dies.

Family Structure

At the beginning of the century, most marriages were entered into for life, and families were headed by male breadwinners. Each married pair had on the average three or more children, and the children were brought up by their natural parents unless the marriage was terminated through death.

Today, matrifocal domestic groups are the fastest-growing form of family, up by 80 percent since 1960. Currently 22 percent of all children under age 18 live in mother-present, father-absent households. As we have seen (p. 456), matrifocality is especially common among blacks: 55 percent of all black children under 18 are living in mother-present, father-absent households (U.S. Bureau of the Census 1990:52). But this kind of family is growing even faster among whites and now constitutes 16 percent of all white households with children present (ibid.). Largely as a result of divorce, separation, and growth of female-headed families, 45 percent of all children born today in the United States can expect to live with only one parent for some period before they reach the age of 18. To look at it slightly differently, 33 percent of all children are already living either with only one natural parent or with one natural parent and a stepparent. Very little is known as yet about how parents, stepparents, stepsiblings, children, and stepchildren are dealing with each other—what kinds of bonds they form, what kinds of responsibilities they accept, and what kinds of conflicts they experience (Stacey 1990; Weitzman 1985; see Box 26.2). It seems likely, however, that higher divorce rates for second and third marriages are linked to the strains of coping with the nation's 6.5 million stepchildren under age 18 (Collins 1985:15).

New Gender Roles and Forms of Sexuality

Surveys show that a profound change has taken place in the United States with respect to attitudes toward premarital and extramarital intercourse. The number of adults who in response to questionnaire surveys say that they sanction or accept premarital and extramarital intercourse rose from 20 percent of adults to over 50 percent in the period from 1960 to 1980. During the same period, the number of unmarried couples who say they are living together increased almost as fast as the number of female-headed families (Herbers 1985).

Considerable evidence points to an increase in premarital sexual activity among unwed juveniles and young adults. Planned Parenthood studies show that one-half of the teenagers graduating from high

BOX *26.2*

FUTURE FAMILY?

On a spring afternoon half a century from today, the Joneses are gathering to sing "Happy Birthday" to Junior.

There's Dad and his third wife, Mom and her second husband, Junior's two half brothers from his father's first marriage, his six stepsisters from his mother's spouse's previous unions, 100-year-old Great-Grandpa, all eight of Junior's current "grand-parents," assorted aunts, uncles-in-law and stepcousins.

While one robot scoops up the gift wrappings and another blows out the candles, Junior makes a wish—that he didn't have so many relatives.

The family tree by the year 2003 will be rooted as deeply as ever in America's social landscape, but it will be sprouting some odd branches (U.S. News & World Report, quoted in Stacey 1990:3).

Do you agree with this projection? What alternative forms of birthday parties and family reunions are more likely to take place in the next century?

aspects of sexual relations. One derivative of this trend is the increased production and consumption of pornographic materials, including "adult" books and *Playboy, Hustler,* and *Penthouse*-type magazines (Fig. 26.14). Pornographic video cassettes make up a substantial percent of the rental volume of stores that rent cassettes to home users. "What would have been off-limits even in a red-light district a few years ago is now available for people to see in their living rooms" (Lindsey 1985:9).

The relaxation of U.S. laws against homosexuality can also be viewed as an expression of the same trend. As we have seen (p. 364), societies that interdict homosexuality are strongly pronatalist and tend to condemn all forms of sex that do not lead to childbirth and parenting. Heterosexual couples committed to the separation of sex from reproduction do not differ from homosexual couples in this regard. The in-

FIGURE *26.14*

PORN
Making money out of sex is a big industry in the United STates.

school have an active sex life. Given the wide resistance to intensive, publicly supported contraceptive programs for teenagers (New York City is an exception), it is not surprising that the rate of teenage pregnancies has doubled since 1965 and that the United States now finds itself with the highest rate in the industrial world. This distinction is partially attributable to the very high rate of pregnancies among U.S. black teenagers, but the rate for white teenagers (93 per 1000) is double that of England and quadruple that of the Netherlands (Brozan 1985, Hacker 1992:77). Four out of ten American women will have become pregnant by the time they reach 20 years. With the spread of AIDS, condoms have become the first line of defense against teenage pregnancies ending with the birth of AIDS-infected infants.

The basic shift in U.S. attitudes toward sexuality can be described in terms of an ever-widening separation of the hedonistic from the reproductive

FIGURE *26.15*

OUT OF THE CLOSET
A gay rights march in New York City.

crease in the numbers of self-identified homosexuals
testifies to the general liberalization of sexual rules of
conduct since World War II (Fig. 26.15). It remains to
be seen, however, how far the fear of AIDS will force
homosexuals "back into the closet" (Fig. 26.16). Since
heterosexuals can contract AIDS from heterosexual
as well as bisexual partners, sexual promiscuity is in
decline throughout the population. If no vaccine or
cure for AIDS is found, marriage rates or long-term,
living-together arrangements may increase substantially. Fertility rates, however, will probably remain
unaffected.

A THEORY OF CULTURE CHANGE
IN THE UNITED STATES

All of the changes we have described can be related
to the hyperindustrial mode of production. The trend
away from factory employment required and facilitated the call-up of female labor previously locked up
in child care; concurrently the premium placed on
education for employment in nonmanufacturing jobs,
together with the increase in the "opportunity costs"
of pregnancy and parenting (that is, the amount of income forgone when women stop working to bear and

FIGURE *26.16*

AIDS MARCH
There are indications that the AIDS epidemic is
reducing sexual promiscuity among homosexuals
and heterosexuals.

raise children), inflated the costs of rearing children, weakened the marriage bond, depressed the fertility rate, and furthered the separation of the reproductive from the hedonistic components of sexuality.

The principal change that has occurred in the labor force is not merely an increase in the proportion of women who are employed (Table 26.4) but a growth in the proportion of employed women who are married and have children. Prior to World War II, only 15 percent of women living with husbands worked outside the home. In 1988 this proportion had risen to 56.5 percent. In 1988, 57 percent of married women with children 6 years and under and 72.5 percent of all women with children aged 6 to 17 were in the labor force (Hayghe 1985:31). What do these women do? Over 83 percent of them hold nonmanufacturing, service- and information-producing jobs—mostly low-level jobs that pay on the average only 70 percent of the wages earned by males (Serrin 1984:1, U.S. Bureau of the Census Statistical Abstract 1990:409).

The link between feminization and the information and service economy is reciprocal: Women, especially married women, had formerly been barred from unionized, male-dominated manufacturing jobs in which they were seen by husbands and unions as a threat to the wage scale. In the nonunionized and traditionally feminine information and service occupations—secretaries, schoolteachers, health workers, saleswomen, and so on—there was less resistance. Seen from the perspective of capital investment, the reserve army of housewives constituted a source of cheap, docile labor that made the processing of information and people a profitable alternative to investment in factories devoted to goods production (Fig. 26.17). In fact, U.S. firms were able to find an equivalent class of cheap labor for manufacturing enterprises only by transferring a considerable share of their goods production facilities to less developed countries, especially to Asia and Latin America. Thus the feminization of the labor force and the decline of goods manufacturing are closely related phenomena, although, as we have seen (p. 356), this relationship has nothing to do with the inherent capacities of the sexes for physical labor and factory work.

Why did U.S. women respond in such large numbers to the service and information call-up? Ironically, their primary motivation was to strengthen the traditional multichild, male breadwinner family in the face of rising costs of food, housing, and education. The real costs of these goods and services have risen faster than has the average male breadwinner's take-home pay. After 1965, family income in the United States was able to keep up with inflation only because of the contribution from working wives (Zoanna 1984). The incomes of families in the age group 25 to 34 has dropped steadily since 1965 when compared with all family households, despite the prevalence of two-earner households (Mariano:1984). Despite their lower rate of remuneration, married women's wages became critical for maintaining or achieving middle-class status, especially, as shown by Valery Oppenheimer in her book *Work and the Family* (1982), during "life-cycle squeezes" when young couples are just starting out and when older couples have to face the costs of sending children to college. The U.S. Department of Agriculture's Family Economics Research Group projects that the cumulative cost of raising a child who will be 17 years old in 2007 will be $151,170 for low-income families; $210,070 for middle-income families; and $293,400 for high-income families (Exter 1991). Add between $50,000 and $100,000 for four years of college, and the cost of raising an upper-middle-class child to adulthood will easily reach half a million dollars. The more the economy shifts toward services, information, and high tech jobs, the greater the amount of schooling needed to achieve or maintain middle-class status. In other words, "higher-quality" children cost more. In this respect the current costs of rearing children represent the climax of the long-term shift from agricultural to industrial modes of production and from rural to urban ways of life associated with the demographic transition (see p. 232). It is this substitution of quality for quantity that underlies the decade-by-decade drop in U.S. fertility prior to the baby boom, and the historic low fertility rate achieved after 1970. These lower fertility rates also reflect a decline in the counterflow of economic benefits from children to parents as children work apart from parents, establish sep-

TABLE *26.4*

LABOR FORCE PARTICIPATION RATES OF WOMEN BY AGE, SELECTED YEARS, 1948–1987

Age	Participation rate (%) in			
	1948	1967	1977	1987
Total, 16 years and over	32.7	41.1	48.4	56.0
16 to 19 years	42.0	41.9	51.2	53.3
20 to 24 years	45.3	53.3	66.5	73.0
25 to 34 years	33.2	41.9	59.7	72.4
35 to 44 years	36.9	48.1	55.8	74.5
45 to 54 years	35.0	51.8	55.8	67.1

SOURCE: Jacobs et al. 1989:16.

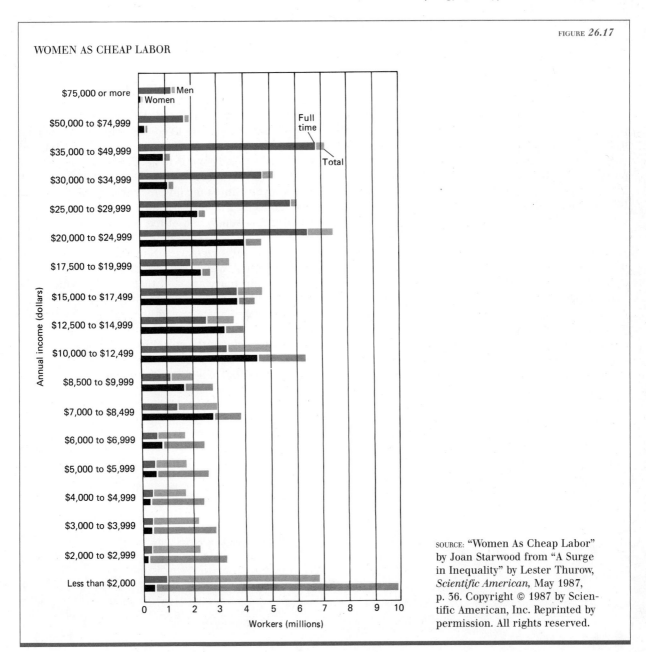

WOMEN AS CHEAP LABOR

FIGURE *26.17*

SOURCE: "Women As Cheap Labor" by Joan Starwood from "A Surge in Inequality" by Lester Thurow, *Scientific American*, May 1987, p. 36. Copyright © 1987 by Scientific American, Inc. Reprinted by permission. All rights reserved.

arate households, and are no longer capable of paying the medical and housing costs of their aged fathers and mothers.

While the average U.S. family cannot rear more than one or two "high-quality" children without a second income, wives are generally incapable of providing that second income if they have to raise more than one or two children (given the absence of adequate subsidized day-care facilities in the nation).

It is this contradiction that explains why married women accept low-paying and dead-end jobs. But this situation is changing. There is a positive feedback effect (p. 313) between working in the labor force, staying in it, and paying the cost of rearing children. The more a woman puts into a job, the more she earns and the more it costs her in the form of "forgone income" to give it up. As forgone income increases, so does the cost of staying home to rear children—and the likelihood that fewer children will be born.

Attitudes about motherhood have changed accordingly. In 1970, when women were asked to name the most enjoyable things in life, 53 percent mentioned being a mother and raising a family, while only 9 percent mentioned career, jobs, or pay. In 1983, 26 percent mentioned being a mother and raising a family, 26 percent mentioned career, jobs, and pay, but only 6 percent mentioned being a wife, down from 22 percent in 1970 (Fig. 26.18).

A common misunderstanding of the declining U.S. fertility rate is that it was caused by the introduction of birth control pills. This is incorrect, since the decline began in 1957 and it was not until 1963–1964 that the pill was widely adopted. Beyond that, many contraceptive devices and practices were available in the 1930s, as demonstrated by the fact that the current fertility rate was much lower than it became immediately after World War II. Moreover, as we have seen (Ch. 13), even preindustrial populations have effective means of limiting family size in relation to the costs and benefits of rearing children.

Divorce rates obviously reflect the falling fertility rate as well as married women's participation in the work force. Not having children tends to facilitate divorce; conversely, having large numbers of children makes divorce extremely difficult. And the more a married woman becomes involved in the labor force, the more independent she becomes of the male income, the more likely she is to accept the idea that she can get along without having a husband, and so the more likely she is to get divorced.

Finally, the feminization of the work force, mediated by declining fertility, higher divorce rates, and the demise of the male breadwinner family, is implicated in the separation of the reproductive from the hedonistic aspects of sexuality. The marital and procreative imperative of Victorian and early twentieth-century times, which stated that all sex was to take place within marriage and that all sex within marriage was to lead to reproduction, cannot appeal to men and women who are either not married or who, if married, are not having children. This, as already pointed out, places the structure of the households of many middle-class heterosexual couples on the continuum with that of homosexual couples, while simul-

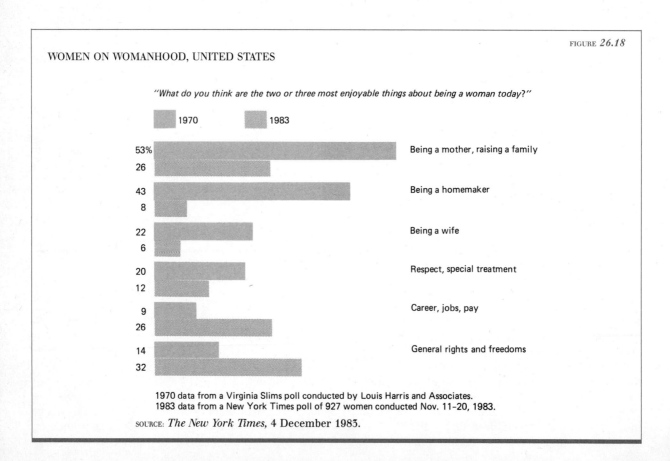

FIGURE *26.18*

WOMEN ON WOMANHOOD, UNITED STATES

"What do you think are the two or three most enjoyable things about being a woman today?"

1970   1983

53% / 26	Being a mother, raising a family
43 / 8	Being a homemaker
22 / 6	Being a wife
20 / 12	Respect, special treatment
9 / 26	Career, jobs, pay
14 / 32	General rights and freedoms

1970 data from a Virginia Slims poll conducted by Louis Harris and Associates.
1983 data from a New York Times poll of 927 women conducted Nov. 11-20, 1983.

SOURCE: *The New York Times*, 4 December 1983.

taneously explaining the overt acceptance of casual sexual encounters (prior to the AIDS epidemic) and the rapid expansion of commerce in pornography.

As we have seen (Chapters 14 and 15), family structure is closely correlated with demographic, technological, economic, and environmental variables. It is impossible in the present case to mistake the direction of causality. While multiple and complex feedbacks have operated at all stages of the process, the main thrust emanated from changes occurring at the infrastructural level—the shift from goods production to service and information production. Alterations at the structural level—marriage and the organization of the family—did not show up until a substantial commitment to the new mode of production had taken place. For example, the number of women who had husbands present and who were participating in the work force had already risen from 15 percent to 30 percent by 1958. Yet it was not until 1970 that the feminist movement attained a level of national consciousness, when women shed their bras, held crockery-smashing parties, and marched down New York's Fifth Avenue shouting slogans like "Starve a rat tonight; don't feed your husband." These antics expressed the pent-up frustration of wives who were already in the labor force and experiencing the contradictions of the old and new gender roles. As noted by Maxine Margolis in her book *Mothers and Such:* "While the media devoted much space to 'bra-burning' and other supposed atrocities of the women's movement, little attention was paid to the reality of women's work which had set the stage for the revival of feminism" (1984:231). Writing from an economist's perspective, Valery Oppenheimer, in her book *Work and the Family,* makes the same point:

There is no evidence that these substantial shifts in women's labor force participation were precipitated by prior changes in sex-role attitudes. On the contrary, they [changes in sex role attitudes] lagged behind behavioral changes, indicating that changes in behavior have gradually brought about changes in sex role norms rather than the reverse. Moreover, the evidence clearly indicates that the start of the rapid changes in women's labor force behavior greatly preceded the rebirth of the feminist movement. [1982:30]

As Oppenheimer explains further, this is not to say that "more equalitarian sex-role attitudes and a feminist ideological perspective are not major motivating forces," but "that these attitudes reinforce or provide an ideological rationale (or normative justification)" (ibid.).

To identify the infrastructural conditions of a social movement and to assign them a causal priority

over values and ideas is not to diminish the role of values and ideas or of volition in the dynamism of history. We have seen (p. 401) that the extent to which action is mobilized under ideological and sentimental auspices alters the odds favoring the fulfillment of a particular infrastructural potential. Nonetheless, it is essential in this case, as well as in other controversial social movements, that both those who favor and those who oppose a particular change comprehend that some outcomes are more probable than others. In the present instance, for example, it seems highly improbable that women in the United States can be restored to their former situation as housewives. In order to resurrect the male breadwinner family and put women back behind the sink, the nation would have to revert to a more primitive phase of capitalism and industrialization, a course that even the most conservative antifeminists do not propose to take.

RELIGION

It might be supposed that as one of the world's technologically most advanced industrial societies, the United States would also be one of the societies in which the majority of citizens reject traditional forms of animism and animatism (see Chapter 23). Science is the principal source of modern technology, which in turn underlies the industrial mass production and consumption of goods, services, and information. While science is not necessarily opposed to a belief in souls, gods, or luck, scientific principles of knowledge do require that propositions based on faith, tradition, hunches, or visions be subjected to systematic logical and empirical tests. One might expect, therefore, that in a society in which science and scientific technology play a prominent role, most people would be agnostics, neither believing nor disbelieving in animism or animatism, if not outright atheists.

Yet a mere 4 percent of Americans tell pollsters that they do not believe in God; 94 percent of U.S. citizens profess a belief in a god or a universal spirit; only 13 percent say that religion is not important in their lives; and barely 9 percent believe that God played no role in the creation or evolution of the human species (Gilbert 1988). While there are signs that the established U.S. churches are having difficulty holding their own (or are slowly losing influence), many novel forms of religious belief and practice seem to be taking their place.

Some observers detect signs of a large-scale religious "awakening." This awakening involves more than a reaffirmed belief in an active, personal deity. The forms of awakening range from weekend encounter groups to messianic prophets. As seen by sociologist Robert Bellah (1976), the most representative aspect of this awakening is the acceptance of "Asian spirituality" as an antidote for Western "utilitarian individualism." According to Bellah, aspects of Zen, Taoism, Buddhism, Hinduism, Sufism, and other Asian religions first began to strike a responsive chord in the counterculture of the late 1960s, as many Americans began to feel that the struggle to achieve material gains by and for individuals was hollow and meaningless. Helped along by drugs and meditation, the counterculture generation realized the "illusoriness of worldly striving." "Careerism and status-seeking, the sacrifice of present fulfillment for some ever-receding future goal, no longer seemed worthwhile" (Bellah 1976:341).

Recognizing that the United States had many unsolved material problems such as racism and poverty, Bellah nonetheless insists that the religious awakening was brought on as much by "the success of the society" and by the "realization that education and affluence did not bring happiness or fulfillment" as by its failures. Following this line of reasoning to its logical outcome, we are led to conclude that the basic cause of the religious awakening in the United States is a crisis of spirit and meaning rather than a crisis of practical material needs. Writes Bellah: "The deepest cause, no matter what particular factors contributed to the actual timing, was, in my opinion, the inability of utilitarian individualism to provide a meaningful pattern of personal and social existence" (ibid.:39).

It can be argued against this view, however, that the deepest and most characteristic impulse of America's religious awakening is not the search for ultimate meaning but the search for solutions to America's unsolved economic and social problems. The role of "Asian" spirituality in the formation and propagation of new religious groups and rituals in the United States is easily exaggerated. The number of people involved in new individualistic, shamanistic, communal, and ecclesiastical cults and revitalization movements that have as their principal concern contemplation, withdrawal from worldly affairs, and other supposedly "Asian" motifs is actually quite small. Much more prominent are cults and movements that have a definite "Western" program for mastering worldly problems and enhancing individual material welfare (Fig. 26.19).

The point seems self-evident for those Americans who want to predict the future from horoscopes (like Nancy Reagan), cure illness through shamanistic trances, or disable their boss or teacher by sticking pins in dolls. These are all techniques for mastering the world rather than retreating from it.

FIGURE *26.19*

REVEREND ROBERT SCHULER IN HIS CRYSTAL CATHEDRAL
Ten thousand one-way mirrors set in filigreed steel, Orange, California.

Utilitarian motives are also self-evident in the seemingly endless varieties of weekend encounter groups and mind-body therapies that are part of the "human-potential movement." Executives prescribe encounter groups and sensitivity training courses to improve relationships among employees and to step up sales.

In the more etherealized and spiritualized "trainings," the predominant, recurring theme is that of mind over matter. Not only do participants expect to control others by improving their control over themselves, but they expect to control physical happenings by the imposition of their thoughts on matter. Erhard Seminars Training (est), for example, claims that "nobody has to die unless he chooses to; all deaths are suicides, and there are no accidents. And you can fly if you allow yourself to know how" (Conway and Siegelman 1978:169). Similar extreme forms of mentalism—belief in the omnipotence of thought—characterize the principles and goals of the more "meditative" human potential disciplines. Scientology, for example, holds forth the promise of "not worrying and bogging myself down with a burden of problems," "freedom from my compulsions," "no longer feel[ing] afraid of anything," "ability to change body size," "ability to see through walls,"

FIGURE 26.20

HARE KRISHNA
One of the Asian-derived cults that offer a life-style opposed to mainstream
U.S. culture.

and "ability to hear other people's thoughts" (Wallis 1977:121). Even cults such as the "Moonies" (the Unification Church), the Hare Krishnas (Fig. 26.20), and the Divine Light Mission have a definite worldly commitment—a yearning for control—contradicting the notion that the current religious awakening in the United States is best understood as an Asian-inspired "critique of the expansion of wealth and power." Former "Moonie" Barbara Underwood, for example, confessed that she wanted to make "millions of dollars" to purchase and maintain hotels, resorts, palatial residences from Chicago to New Orleans, training and living centers, college campuses, yachts, and even the Empire State and Pan Am buildings. "Instilled in us was the firm belief that Moon must reclaim all ownership of money and land from Satan's stockpile."

"Christians think that the Messiah must be poor and miserable," says a Unification Church training manual. "He did not come for this. Messiah must be the richest. Only He is qualified to have dominion over things. Otherwise, neither God nor Messiah can be happy" (Underwood and Underwood 1979:76; Welles 1978:255).

THE ELECTRONIC CHURCH

Whatever the balance may be between worldly and otherworldly themes in the cults that have adopted aspects of Asian religions, such cults are not representative of the main thrust of religious change in the United States today. Far more powerful are Protestant fundamentalism and the various born-again Christian revitalization movements that have been able to use television to expand membership and raise funds. These so-called electronic churches, or TV cults, to a large extent recruit their membership through a personal "gospel of wealth"—they promise material success and physical well-being to the true believer. Their message appeals especially to people who are sick, old, or isolated, impoverished by inflation, bewildered by the changes in sex mores and the family, and frightened by crime in the streets. According to TV preacher Jim Bakker: "The scripture says, 'Delight yourself in the Lord and he'll give you the desire of your heart.'...Give and it shall be given unto you." Bakker tells how one man prayed for a Winnebago mobile home, color brown, and got just that. Says

Bakker: "Diamonds and gold aren't just for Satan—they're for Christians, too" (Bakker 1976). (Unfortunately, Bakker's appetite for diamonds and gold led him to sell lifetime vacations in nonexistent condos and he was sentenced to jail for fraud and embezzlement.)

On his "Old Time Gospel Hour," Moral Majority leader Jerry Falwell (Fig. 26.21) asks the faithful to turn over one-tenth of their income: "Christ has not captured a man's heart until He has your pocketbook." Two million potential contributors whose names and addresses are kept in a computer data bank receive frequent requests for money, one of which reads: "Maybe your financial situation seems impossible. Put Jesus first in your stewardship and allow him to bless you financially" (*Time*, 1 October 1979:68).

Finding himself $50 million short of the funds needed to complete his City of Faith hospital complex near Tulsa, Oklahoma, video evangelist Oral Roberts raised money with the aid of swatches from a "miracle cloth." "My hands feel as if there is a super-natural heat in them," he declared. "My right hand is especially hot right now." Following God's instructions, Roberts began to turn out millions of swatches imprinted with his right hand. In return, those who acquire the cloth are promised "special miracles" (*Newsweek*, 10 September 1979).

Another TV evangelist, Pat Robertson, recruits followers and raises funds through what he calls the Kingdom Principles: The Bible says the more you give to Jesus the more you will get back in return. And the harder it is to give, the greater will be the increase. Thus, as described in Rifkind and Howard (1979:108), a woman in California who was on a limited income and in poor health

decided to trust God and to step out in faith on the Kingdom Principles. She was already giving half her disability money to the 700 Club to spread the gospel of Jesus Christ. But just last week, she decided to go all the way, and give God the money she spends for cancer medicine—$120 a month. And three days

FIGURE *26.21*

THE ELECTRONIC CHURCH
Jerry Falwell's "Old Time Gospel Hour" being televised live from Lynchburg, Virginia, to a network of 391 television stations. Cameras can be seen on the balcony and in the center of the audience.

later—get this!—from an entirely unexpected source, she got a check for three thousand dollars!

Since all the other aspects of U.S. culture are in flux, it is not surprising that religious beliefs and practices are going through a period of change and ferment. The experience of other cultures and historical epochs demonstrates that stresses brought on by rapid cultural change usually find expression in spiritual yearning, questing, and experimenting that lead to an expansion and intensification of religious activity, broadly defined.

All the major world religions were born during times of rapid cultural transformations. Buddhism and Hinduism arose in the Ganges Valley of northern India during an epoch of deforestation, population increase, and state formation. Judaism arose during the prolonged migrations of the ancient Israelites. Christianity arose in conjunction with attempts to break the yoke of Roman imperialism. Islam arose during the transition from a life of pastoral nomadism to that of trade and empires in Arabia and North Africa. Protestants split from Catholicism as feudalism gave way to capitalism. As we have seen (p. 402), messianic and millenarian cults swept across the Great Plains as the American Indians lost their lands and hunting grounds, while in the wake of the European colonization of New Guinea and Melanesia, hundreds of cargo cults, devoted to acquiring worldly wealth with the assistance of ancestors returned from the dead, spread from island to island.

There is reason to believe, therefore, that the rising intensity of religious activity in the United States constitutes an attempt to solve or to escape from the problems of malfunctioning consumerism, unemployment, the upending of sex roles, the breakup of the breadwinner family, alienation from work, oppressive government and corporate bureaucracies, feelings of isolation and loneliness, fear of crime, and bewilderment about the root cause of why so many changes are happening at once.

SUMMARY

As a result of the recent expansion of the service and information sectors, the United States is best described as a hyperindustrial society, since virtually all forms of economic activity now involve mass production, the detailed division of labor, and mechanical or electronic machinery.

Although from an emic perspective the political economy of the United States is said to be capitalism, from an etic perspective it is a mixture of socialism and capitalism. Again, from an emic perspective, the capitalist sector of the economy is viewed as being based on free enterprise price competition; etically, however, the degree of concentration of economic resources in the largest conglomerate corporations creates a situation of oligopoly that does not set prices through competitive market supply and demand.

The majority of Americans work for bureaucratized organizations that do not reward individual initiative so much as they reward the willingness of people to carry out routine, standardized tasks. As a consequence, there is widespread alienation not only on the assembly line but in information and service jobs as well. While some observers look to the automation of information and services as a means of overcoming the problem, there is evidence that the electronic office of the future will further routinize and de-skill the labor force.

The emics and etics of the system of social stratification in the United States offer sharply contrasting views. Emic versions downgrade the degree of separation between the classes and deny the existence of a ruling class. From an etic perspective, however, there is considerable evidence that, despite countervailing sources of political influence, a ruling elite exists that decisively influences the overall shape of U.S. social, economic, and military policies. This evidence consists of the concentration of wealth in super-rich families and in the interlocking stock-voting powers of a handful of top institutional investors. In contrast to the many studies of the poor, however, very little is known about the super-rich; anthropologists have been remiss in not studying "up" as well as "down."

The persistence of a large poverty class again points to a serious split between emic and etic versions of U.S. life. Upward mobility is not as rapid or extensive as most Americans believe. There is a tendency to blame the perpetuation of the poverty class on the victims of poverty, as seen in the notion of a "culture of poverty" and in the demand that the poor must work harder than the affluent. The poor, however, share most values with the middle class, and there is little evidence that by trying harder they can overcome the structural conditions that lead to unemployment and underemployment. Evidence to the contrary can be seen in Elliot Liebow's account of Washington's streetcorner men.

In contrast to the emic blurring of class lines in the United States, racial and ethnic minorities and majorities consciously conceive of themselves as sharply defined and competitive groups. Ethnic and social chauvinism pits black "have-nots" against white "have-littles" and thereby helps the "have-lots" maintain wealth and power. The black power movement has aided many privileged blacks, but it has further entrapped the majority of blacks in the nation's urban ghettos. The worsening plight of America's black underclass is often attributed to the allegedly pathological nature of the black matrifocal family. But matrifocality among the poor is produced by poverty, unemployment, and the rules of the AFDC welfare program, as shown in Carol Stack's study of the Flats.

The United States pays a huge hidden cost for its failure to ameliorate the situation in which the black underclass finds itself. The long-term high unemployment of blacks and Hispanic ghetto males has created a situation of hopelessness and envy that has led a disproportionate percentage of blacks and Hispanics to make crime their career. America's racial and ethnic dilemma accounts to a large extent for the marked difference between rates of violent crime in the United States and in the Western industrial nations and Japan. AFDC is also implicated in the high rates of violent crime in America's inner cities. As Jagna Sharff's study of Hispanic women on AFDC in New York shows, the AFDC stipends are set too low for families to live on, thereby encouraging young men to resort to criminal behavior to fill the gap in family budgets.

The development of the United States's hyperindustrial service and information economy has had a powerful effect on middle-class family life. After World War II, married women entered the labor force in unprecedented numbers, taking the rapidly expanding lower-paying service and information jobs.

As inflation wiped out the possibility of achieving or maintaining middle-class status on their husbands' incomes, married women became locked into the labor force. Their role as wage earners conflicted with their role as mothers, subverted the traditional marital and procreative imperative, and undermined the male breadwinner family. It has also led to the separation of sex from reproduction, the spread of single-parent families, consensual trial unions, declining first-time marriage rates, and historically low fertility rates. The separation of sex from reproduction in turn has encouraged the expression of once-prohibited forms of sexuality, including homosexuality and pornographic movies, books, and videotapes.

The rapid pace of change and the problems induced by inflation; the bureaucratization, oligopolization, alienation, and feminization of the economy and the labor force; the challenge to the marital and procreative imperative; the prevalence of crime; and the persistence of poverty and sharp inequalities in wealth and power may supply the basic reasons for America's current religious awakening. The history of other cultures demonstrates that stresses brought on by rapid cultural change and social unrest usually find expression in spiritual yearning, questing, and experimenting that lead to an expansion and intensification of religious activity. Although some aspects of America's religious awakening can be attributed to an attempt to reject the material world, the center of religious ferment as seen in the video cults and human potential movement consists of attempts to overcome practical and mundane problems.

A History of Theories of Culture

This appendix serves as a brief outline of the history of the development of anthropological theories. It also presents the main research strategies employed by contemporary anthropologists.

The impulse lying behind the development of cultural anthropology is probably as old as our species. Members of different human groups have always been curious about the customs and traditions of strangers. The fact that people who live in different societies build different kinds of shelters, wear different kinds of clothing, practice different kinds of marriages, worship different spirits and gods, and speak different languages has always been a source of puzzlement. The most ancient and still most common approach to these differences is to assume that one's own beliefs and practices are normal expressions of the true or right way of life, as justified by the teachings of one's ancestors and the commandments or instructions of supernatural beings. Most cultures have origin myths that set forth the sequence of events leading to the beginning of the world and of humanity, and to the adoption of the group's way of life. The failure of other groups to share the same way of life can then be attributed to their failure to be true, real, or normal human beings.

THE ENLIGHTENMENT

As Europe entered the age of exploration and mercantile expansion, interest in describing and explaining cultural diversity increased. The discovery and exploration of a whole "New World"—the Americas—opened the eyes of philosophers, political leaders, theologians, and scientists to astonishing contrasts in the human condition.

Toward the middle of the eighteenth century, during the period known as the *Enlightenment,* the first systematic attempts to offer scientific theories of cultural differences began to emerge. The common theme of these theories was the idea of progress. It was held by scholars such as Adam Smith, Adam Ferguson, Jean Turgot, and Denis Diderot that cultures were different not because they expressed innate differences in human capacities or preferences, but because they manifested different levels of rational knowledge and achievement. It was believed that humankind, including Europe's ancestors, had at one time lived in an "uncivilized" condition, lacking a knowledge of farming and animal husbandry, laws,

and governments. Gradually, however, guided by the ever-expanding role of reason in human affairs, humankind progressed from a "state of nature" to a state of enlightened civilization. Cultural differences were thus largely a result of the different degrees of intellectual and moral progress achieved by different peoples.

NINETEENTH-CENTURY EVOLUTIONISM

The idea of cultural progress was the forerunner of the concept of cultural evolution that dominated theories of culture during the nineteenth century. Cultures were usually seen as moving through various stages of development, ending up with something resembling Euramerican life-styles. Auguste Comte postulated a progression from theological to metaphysical to positivistic (scientific) modes of thought. Georg Wilhelm Friedrich Hegel saw a movement from a time when only one man was free (the Asiatic tyrant) to a time when some were free (Greek city-states) to a time when all would be free (European constitutional monarchies). Others wrote of an evolution from status (such as slave, noble, or commoner) to contract (employee and employer, buyer and seller); from small communities of people who knew each other's faces to large, impersonal societies; from slave to military to industrial societies; from animism to polytheism to monotheism; from magic to science; from female-dominated horticultural societies to male-dominated agricultural societies; and from many other hypothetical earlier and simpler stages to later and more complex ones.

One of the most influential schemes was that proposed by the American anthropologist Lewis Henry Morgan in his book Ancient Society. Morgan divided the evolution of culture into three main stages: savagery, barbarism, and civilization. These stages had figured in evolutionary schemes as early as the sixteenth century, but Morgan subdivided them and filled them out in greater detail and with greater reference to ethnographic evidence than had anyone else. (Morgan himself carried out a lifelong study of the Iroquois, who lived near his hometown of Rochester, New York.) Morgan held that "lower savagery" subsistence had been gained exclusively by gathering wild foods, that people mated promiscuously, and that the basic unit of society was the small nomadic "horde" that owned its resources communally. By the period of "upper savagery," the bow and arrow had been invented, brother-sister marriage was prohibited, and descent was reckoned primarily through women. With the invention of pottery and the beginning of farming came the transition to barbarism. Incest prohibitions were extended to include all descendants in the female line, and clan and village became the basic structural units.

The development of metallurgy marked the upper phase of barbarism; descent shifted from the female to the male line, men married several women at one time (polygyny), and private property appeared. Finally, the invention of writing, the development of civil government, and the emergence of the monogamous family marked the beginning of "civilization."

SOCIAL DARWINISM

In addition to the greater complexity and detail of the nineteenth-century evolutionary schemes, there was one fundamental difference between them and the eighteenth-century notions of universal progress. Almost all the nineteenth-century schemes (with the conspicuous exception of Marxism) postulated that cultures evolved in conjunction with the evolution of human biological types and races. Not only were the cultures of modern-day Europe and America seen as the pinnacle of cultural progress, but the white race (especially its male half) was seen as the epitome of biological progress.

This fusion of biological evolutionism with cultural evolutionism is often but incorrectly attributed to the influence of Charles Darwin. In fact, the development of biological interpretations of cultural evolution preceded the appearance of Darwin's *Origin of Species,* and Darwin was himself greatly influenced by social philosophers such as Thomas Malthus and Herbert Spencer. Malthus's notion that population growth led to an inevitable "struggle for existence" had been elaborated by Spencer into the idea of the "survival of the fittest" in social life before Darwin published his theories of biological evolution.

The success of Darwin's biological theory of the survival of the fittest (he called it "natural selection") greatly enhanced the popularity of the view that social and cultural evolution also depended on biological evolution. After the publication of Darwin's *Origin of Species,* there appeared a movement known as *Social Darwinism,* based on the belief that cultural and biological progress depended on the free play of competitive forces in the struggle of individual against individual, nation against nation, and race against race. The most influential Social Darwinist was Herbert Spencer, who went so far as to advocate the end of all attempts to provide charity and relief for the unemployed and impoverished classes and the so-called backward races on the grounds that such assistance interfered with the operation of the "law of the survival of the fittest" and merely prolonged the agony and deepened the misery of those who were "unfit." Spencer used Social Darwinism to justify the capitalist free enterprise system, and his influence continues to be felt among advocates of unrestrained capitalism as well as among advocates of white supremacy.

MARXIST EVOLUTIONISM

It is important to realize that while the writings and thoughts of Karl Marx were diametrically opposed to Social Darwinism, *Marxism* was also heavily influenced by the prevailing nineteenth-century notions of cultural evolution and progress. Marx saw cultures passing through the stages of primitive communism, slave society, feudalism, capitalism, and communism. Also, like many of his contemporaries, Marx stressed the importance of the role of struggle in achieving cultural evolution and progress. All history, according to Marx, was the outcome of the struggle between social classes for control over the means of production. The proletarian class, brought into existence by capitalism, was destined to abolish private property and bring about the final stage of history: communism. Upon reading Morgan's *Ancient Society,* Marx and his associate Friedrich Engels thought they had found a confirmation of their idea that during the first stage of cultural evolution there was no private property and that the successive stages of cultural progress had been brought about by changes in the "mode of production"—as, for example, in the co-occurrence of the development of agriculture and the transition between savagery and barbarism in Morgan's scheme. Morgan's *Ancient Society* provided the basis for Engels's *The Origin of the Family, Private Property and the State,* which, until the middle of the twentieth century, served as a cornerstone of Marxist anthropology.

THE REACTION TO NINETEENTH-CENTURY EVOLUTIONISM

Early in the twentieth century, anthropologists took the lead in challenging the evolutionary schemes and doctrines of both the Social Darwinists and the Marxist Communists. In the United States, the dominant theoretical position was developed by Franz Boas and his students, and is known as *historical particularism.* According to Boas, nineteenth-century attempts to discover the laws of cultural evolution and to schematize the stages of cultural progress were founded on insufficient empirical evidence. Boas argued that each culture has its own long and unique history. To understand or explain a particular culture, the best one can do is to reconstruct the unique path it had followed. The emphasis on the uniqueness of each culture amounted to a denial of the prospects for a generalizing science of culture. Another important feature of historical particularism is the notion of cultural relativism, which holds that there are no higher or lower forms of culture. Such terms as *savagery, barbarism,* and *civilization* merely express the ethnocentrism of people who think that their way of life is more normal than those of other peoples.

To counter the speculative "armchair" theories and ethnocentrism of the evolutionists, Boas and his students also stressed the importance of carrying out ethnographic fieldwork among non-Western peoples. As the ethnographic reports and monographs produced by the historical particularists multiplied, it became clear that the evolutionists had indeed misrepresented or overlooked the complexities of so-called primitive cultures and that they had grossly underestimated the intelligence and ingenuity of the non-Caucasoid, non-European peoples of the world.

Boas's most important achievement was his demonstration that race, language, and culture were independent aspects of the human condition. Since both similar and dissimilar cultures and languages are found among people of the same race, there was no basis for the Social Darwinist notion that biological and cultural evolution were part of a single process.

DIFFUSIONISM

Another early twentieth-century reaction to nineteenth-century evolutionism is known as *diffusionism.* According to its advocates, the principal source of cultural differences and similarities is not the inventiveness of the human mind, but the tendency of humans to imitate one another. Diffusionists see cultures as a patchwork of elements derived from a haphazard series of borrowings from near and distant peoples. In the critical case of the origin of native American civilizations, for example, diffusionists argued that the technology and architecture of

the Inca of Peru and the Aztecs of Mexico were diffused from Egypt or from Southeast Asia, rather than invented independently (see p. 108 for a critique of diffusionism).

BRITISH FUNCTIONALISM AND STRUCTURAL-FUNCTIONALISM

In Great Britain, the dominant early-twentieth-century research strategies are known as *functionalism* and *structural-functionalism.* According to the functionalists, the main task of cultural anthropology is to describe the recurrent functions of customs and institutions, rather than to explain the origins of cultural differences and similarities. According to one of the leading functionalists, Bronislaw Malinowski, the attempt to discover the origins of cultural elements was doomed to be speculative and unscientific because of the absence of written records. Once we have understood the function of an institution, argued Malinowski, then we have understood all we will ever understand about its origins.

A. R. Radcliffe-Brown was the principal advocate of structural-functionalism. According to Radcliffe-Brown, the main task of cultural anthropology was even narrower than that proposed by Malinowski. Whereas Malinowski emphasized the contribution of cultural elements to the biological and psychological welfare of individuals, Radcliffe-Brown and the structural-functionalists stressed the contribution of the biological and psychological welfare of individuals to the maintenance of the social system. For the structural-functionalists, the function of maintaining the system took precedence over all others. But like Malinowski, the structural-functionalists labeled all attempts to find origins as speculative history.

Thus, the functionalists and structural-functionalists evaded the question of the general, recurrent causes of cultural differences, while emphasizing the general, recurrent functional reasons for similarities. This set the functionalists and structural-functionalists apart from the diffusionists as much as from the nineteenth-century evolutionists. Nor were the functionalists and structural-functionalists sympathetic to Boas's historical particularism. But like Boas and his students, the British functionalists and structural-functionalists stressed the importance of carrying out fieldwork, insisting that only after two or more years of immersion in the language, thoughts, and events of another culture could anthropologists provide valid and reliable ethnographic descriptions.

CULTURE AND PERSONALITY

In turning away from the nineteenth-century notions of causality and evolution, many anthropologists, influenced by the writings of Sigmund Freud, attempted to interpret cultures in psychological terms. The writings of Freud and the anti-evolutionism of Boas set the stage for the development of the approach known as *culture and personality*. Two of Boas's most famous students, Ruth Benedict and Margaret Mead, pioneered in the development of culture and personality theories. Such theories in general may be described as psychological forms of functionalism that relate cultural beliefs and practices to individual personality, and individual personality to cultural beliefs and practices. As we saw in Chapter 22, many advocates of the culture and personality approach stress the importance of early childhood experiences such as toilet training, breast feeding, and sex training in the formation of a basic or modal type of adult personality or national character. Some culture and personality theories attempt to explain cultural differences and similarities as a consequence of basic or modal personality. In general, however, culture and personality advocates do not deal with the problem of why the beliefs and practices that mold particular personality types or national characters occur in some cultures but not in others.

THE NEW EVOLUTIONISM

After World War II, increasing numbers of anthropologists became dissatisfied with the anti-evolutionism and lack of broad generalizations and causal explanations characteristic of the first half of the century. Under the influence of Leslie White, an effort was launched to reexamine the works of the nineteenth-century evolutionists such as Lewis Henry Morgan, to correct their ethnographic errors, and to identify their positive contribution to the development of a science of culture. White pioneered in postulating that the overall direction of cultural evolution was largely determined by the quantities of energy that could be captured and put to work per capita per year (see p. 216).

At the same time (about 1940 to 1950), Julian Steward laid the basis for the development of the approach known as *cultural ecology*, which stressed the role of the interaction of natural conditions such as soils, rainfall, and temperature with cultural factors such as technology and economy as the cause of both cultural differences and similarities.

The return to broad evolutionary points of view in the second half of the twentieth century among American cultural anthropologists was stimulated by archaeological evidence that diffusion could not account for the remarkable similarities between the development of states and empires in the New and Old Worlds (see p. 196). The step-by-step process by which native American peoples in the Andean and Mesoamerican regions independently developed their own elaborate civilizations is now fairly well known, thanks to modern archaeological research.

Julian Steward was especially impressed with the parallels in the evolution of the ancient civilizations of Peru, Mexico, Egypt, Mesopotamia, and China, and called for a renewed effort on the part of anthropologists to examine and explain these remarkable uniformities. Yet Steward was careful to distinguish his scheme of cultural evolution from the more extreme versions of nineteenth-century evolutionism. According to Steward, the problem with these earlier evolutionists was that they postulated a single or *unilinear* set of stages for all cultures, whereas there are actually many, or *multilinear*, paths of development depending on initial environmental, technological, and other conditions.

DIALECTICAL MATERIALISM

Both White and Steward were influenced by Marx and Engels's emphasis on changes in the material aspects of modes of reproduction as the mainspring of cultural evolution. However, neither accepted the full set of Marxist propositions embodied in the point of view known as *dialectical materialism*, which gained considerable popularity among Western anthropologists for the first time in the 1960s and 1970s. Dialectical materialists hold that history has a determined direction—namely, that of the emergence of communism and of classless society. The sources of this movement are the internal contradictions of sociocultural systems. To understand the causes of sociocultural differences and similarities, social scientists must not only study these contradictions but must take part in the "dialectical" resolutions that lead to progress toward communism. The most important contradiction in all societies is that between the means of production (roughly, the technology) and the relations of production (who owns the means of production). In the words of Karl Marx: "The mode of production in material life determines the general character of the social, political, and spiritual process of life. It is not the consciousness of men that determines their existence, but on the contrary, their social existence determines their consciousness" (1970 [1859]:21).

CULTURAL MATERIALISM

Further elaboration of the theoretical perspectives of Marx, White, and Steward has led to the appearance of the point of view known as *cultural materialism.* This research strategy holds that the primary task of anthropology is to give causal explanations for the differences and similarities in thought and behavior found among human groups. Like dialectical materialists, cultural materialists hold that this task can best be carried out by studying the material constraints to which human existence is subjected. These constraints arise from the need to produce food, shelter, tools, and machines, and to reproduce human populations within limits set by biology and the environment. These are called material constraints or conditions in order to distinguish them from constraints or conditions imposed by ideas and other mental or spiritual aspects of human life such as values, religion, and art. For cultural materialists, the most likely causes of variation in the mental or spiritual aspects of human life are the differences in the material costs and benefits of satisfying basic needs in a particular habitat.

Cultural materialists differ from dialectical materialists mainly in rejecting the notion that anthropology must become part of a political movement aimed at destroying capitalism and at furthering the interests of the proletariat. Cultural materialists allow for a diversity of political motivation among anthropologists united by a common commitment to the development of a science of culture. In addition, cultural materialists reject the notion that all important cultural changes result from the playing out of dialectical contradictions, holding that much of cultural evolution has resulted from the gradual accumulation of useful traits through a process of trial and error.

SOCIOBIOLOGY

Sociobiology is a research strategy that attempts to explain some sociocultural differences and similarities in terms of natural selection. It is based on a refinement of natural selection known as the *principle of inclusive fitness.* This principle states that natural selection favors traits that spread an individual's genes by increasing not only the number of an individual's offspring, but the number of offspring of close relatives, such as brothers and sisters, who carry many

of the same genes. What controls biological evolution, therefore, is whether a trait increases the inclusive total of an individual's genes in succeeding generations and not merely the number of one's own progeny.

Applied to cultural evolution, human sociobiology states that cultural traits are selected if they maximize an individual's reproductive success reckoned in terms of inclusive fitness. Selection does not necessarily bring about a one-to-one correlation between genes and behavior, but between genes and tendencies to behave in certain ways rather than others. For example, sociobiologists hold that the tendency for humans to forage in a manner that optimizes energy produced per unit of time is selected because it maximizes reproductive success (Wilson 1975, 1978; Lewontin et al. 1984).

From a cultural materialist perspective it is not necessary to posit that useful traits are always selected because they maximize reproductive success. In the case of optimal foraging theory, for example (see p. 211), the favorable balance of energetic benefits over costs in satisfying an individual's nutritional needs is sufficient to understand why certain animals are captured and others are not, without reference to its effects on reproductive success. Moreover, it is clear, contrary to sociobiological principle, that humans do not always seek to maximize reproductive success. The most glaring discrepancy is the low rate of reproductive success characteristic of the affluent classes in industrial society. The behavior of one-child American families scarcely seems to be dominated by the urge to have as many children as possible.

STRUCTURALISM

Not all post–World War II approaches to cultural theory are aimed at explaining the origin of cultural differences and similarities.

In France, under the leadership of Claude Lévi-Strauss, the point of view known as structuralism has been widely accepted. Structuralism is concerned only with the psychological uniformities that underlie apparent differences in thought and behavior. According to Lévi-Strauss, these uniformities arise from the structure of the human brain and of unconscious thought processes. The most important structural feature of the human mind is the tendency to dichotomize, or to think in terms of binary oppositions, and then, to attempt to mediate this opposition by a third concept, which may serve as the basis for yet another opposition. A recurrent opposition present in many myths, for example, is culture versus nature.

From the structuralist point of view, the more cultures change, the more they remain the same, since they are all merely variations on the theme of recurrent oppositions and their resolutions. Structuralism, therefore, is concerned with explaining the similarities among cultures, but not with explaining the differences. See the section "Myth and Binary Contrasts" in Chapter 24 for an example of a structuralist analysis.

PARTICULARIZING APPROACHES

Mention must also be made of the fact that many anthropologists continue to reject all general causal viewpoints, holding that the chief aim of ethnography ought to be the study and interpretation of the emics of different cultures—their world views, symbols, values, religions, philosophies, and systems of meanings. During the 1980s, these approaches grew in popularity and were characterized by rejection of the distinction between observer and observed, etics and emics, and science and nonscience. Extreme relativism (see page 105) and anti-evolutionism reminiscent of Franz Boas's historical particularism also characterize recent approaches. For many contemporary cultural anthropologists the main task of ethnography is to become familiar with a culture in the way one becomes familiar with a book or a poem, and then to "read" or interpret it as if one were a literary critic. The goal of these anthropologists is not to discover the scientific truth about a culture but to compose interpretations about the "other"—the other culture—that are elegant and convincing.

One recent manifestation of this line of development is called *deconstructionism*. It focuses on the hidden intentions and unexpressed biases of the author of an ethnography rather than on the question of what the culture being described is really like.

Although deconstructionists make valid points about the need to expose biases and prejudices in scientific descriptions (remember Malinoswski), their flat rejection of scientific truth as a goal of ethnography results in fragmented, contradictory, and essentially nihilistic notions about the human condition.

GLOSSARY

ADAPTATION The process by which organisms, or cultural elements, undergo change in form or function in response to threats to their existence and replication.

ADAPTIVE CAPACITY Previously established ability of a minority to compete for upward mobility in a given sociocultural context.

AFFINAL A relationship based on marriage.

AFFIXES Bound MORPHEMES that occur at the initial position in a word.

AGE GRADES In some societies, formally institutionalized segmentation of the population, by sex and chronological age, with RITES OF PASSAGE announcing the transition from one status to the next.

AGRICULTURE The cultivation of domesticated crops.

ALLELES Variants of GENES that occupy the same location on corresponding CHROMOSOMES.

ALLOPHONE A variant of a PHONEME; all the contrastive sounds with the class of sounds designated by a particular phoneme.

AMBILINEAL DESCENT The reckoning of descent through a combination of male and female ancestors establishing a descent relationship with a particular ancestor; resembles BILATERAL DESCENT but maintains a narrow rather than a broadening span of kin on each ascending generation.

AMBILOCALITY Residence of a couple after marriage alternatively with either the husband's or wife's kin.

ANIMATISM The attribution of humanlike consciousness and powers to inanimate objects, natural phenomena, plants, and animals.

ANIMISM Belief in personalized yet disembodied beings such as souls, ghosts, spirits, and gods. Compare ANIMATISM.

ANTHROPOLOGICAL LINGUISTICS The study of the great variety of languages spoken by human beings.

ARCHAEOLOGY The scientific study of the remains of cultures of past ages.

ARTIFACTS Material objects made by human hands, and having specifiable uses and functions.

ASCRIBED STATUS The attributes of an individual's position in SOCIETY that are involuntary and often inevitable, based on sex or descent.

ASCRIPTION See ASCRIBED STATUS.

ASSEMBLAGE In the archaeological sense, a patterned set of artifacts used by an occupational group that represents the sum of its social activities.

ASSIMILATION Disappearance of a group—usually a MINORITY—through the loss of biological and/or cultural distinctiveness.

AVUNCULOCALITY Residence of a couple after marriage with or near the groom's mother's brother.

BAND, LOCAL A small, loosely organized group of hunter-gatherer families, occupying a specifiable territory and tending toward self-sufficiency.

BASIC PERSONALITY Certain culturally defined traits expected to characterize generally members of a societal group.

BERDACHE A male transvestite who assumes a sanctioned female role among the native American peoples of the Great Plains.

BERGMANN'S RULE Warm-blooded species tend to develop larger, heavier bodies in the colder limits of their range.

BIFACE TOOLS Modules worked by percussion on both surfaces to yield well-formed cutting and scraping edges.

BILATERAL DESCENT Rule by which ego traces descent equally through both parents and through both sexes in all ascending and descending generations and collateral lines.

BIOGRAM The basic genetically determined propensities for behavior characteristics of a species.

BIPEDALISM Two-leggedness.

BLADE TOOLS Long, thin flakes with relatively parallel edges, struck from a core.

BLOOD FEUD Vengeful confrontation between opposing groups of kin, set off by real or alleged homicide or other crimes, and involving continuing alternative retaliation in kind.

BLOOD GROUPS The several types of blood cells classified according to their ability to provoke an immunological reaction when combined with one another.

BRACHIATION Locomotion, usually through trees, by swinging by the forelimbs held overhead. Gibbons are especially noted for this.

BREEDING POPULATION A segment of a population, usually delimited on geographical or cultural lines, characterized by a high level of interbreeding in which one or more distinctive genes occur with particular frequency. See also GENE POOL.

BRIDE-PRICE Goods or valuables transferred by the groom's kin to recompense the bride's relatives for her absence.

CARGO CULT A REVITALIZATION MOVEMENT native to Melanesia based on the expectation of the imminent return of ancestors in ships, planes, and trains bringing treasures of European-manufactured goods.

CARRYING CAPACITY The population of a species that a particular area or ECOSYSTEM can support without suffering irreversible deterioration.

CASTE Widely applied as a term to a self-enclosed CLASS or MINORITY; a stratified, endogamous descent group.

CHARISMA The personal magnetism of extraordinary individuals.

CHOPPERS Stone core BIFACE implements with broad, crude cutting edges at one end.

CHROMOSOMES Threadlike structures within the cell nucleus, containing DNA, that transmit information that determines heredity.

CIRCULATING CONNUBIA A system of marriages in which several groups exchange spouses in one direction in a circle or in directions that alternate in each generation.

CIRCUMCISION The ritual removal of the foreskin of a male's penis.

CLANS Kin groups whose members assume—but need not demonstrate—descent from a common ancestor.

CLASS, SOCIAL One of the stratified groupings within a society, characterized by specific attitudes and behavior and by differential access to power and to basic resources. Less endogamous and more open than CASTES or MINORITIES.

CLINES The gradual changes in traits and gene frequencies displayed by the populations of a species as the distance between them increases.

CLITORIDECTOMY The ritual removal of a portion of a female's clitoris.

COGNATIC LINEAGE A group whose members trace their descent genealogically from a common ancestor through the application of ambilineal descent.

COLLATERALS Persons who are CONSANGUINEAL kin, possessing a common ancestor, but in different lines of descent, such as cousins.

COMMUNAL RITES Ceremonies, largely religious, carried out by the social group—usually by nonprofessional specialists and celebrants.

COMPLEMENTARY OPPOSITION The process by which groups unite into more and more inclusive units as they are confronted with more and more inclusive coalitions of antagonistic groups.

CONSANGUINEAL A relationship between persons based on descent, in contrast to the AFFINAL relationship of marriage.

CORE TOOLS Stone implements made by shaping a large lump or core, such as the hand ax; the tool consists of the core rather than of the pieces detached from it, as in the case of flake tools.

CORVÉE A forced labor draft imposed by a government for public road and building construction, often in lieu of taxes.

COUVADE Customary restrictions on the activities of a man often associated with his wife's lying-in and birth of their child.

CRANIUM The part of the skull that encloses the brain.

CROSS COUSINS Persons of either sex whose parents are siblings of the opposite sex; offspring of a father's sister and mother's brother. Compare PARALLEL COUSINS.

CULTURAL ANTHROPOLOGY The analysis and description of cultures of past and present ages.

CULTURAL MATERIALISM The research strategy that attempts to explain the differences and similarities in thought and behavior found among human groups by studying the material constraints to which humans are subjected. These material constraints include the need to produce food, shelter, tools, and machines, and to reproduce human populations within limits set by biology and the environment.

CULTURAL RELATIVISM The principle that all cultural systems are inherently equal in value and that the traits characteristic of each need to be assessed and explained within the context of the system in which they occur.

CULTURE The learned patterns of behavior and thought characteristic of a societal group.

CULTURE AREA A geographical region characterized by a certain complex of trait elements, occurring as shared by several cultural groups, because of common ecological adaptation and or history.

DEEP STRUCTURE The form of an utterance that is not directly observable but that accounts for the intelligibility of its SURFACE STRUCTURE.

DENTAL FORMULA A coding of the numbers of incisor, canine, premolar, and molar teeth, in sequence, in one quadrant of the lower and upper jaws. Used as a trait in anthropoid classification.

DESCENT RECKONING The rule for ascertaining an individual's kinship affiliation from among the range of actual or presumed connections provided by birth to a particular culturally defined father and/or mother.

DETERMINISM The assumption that in cultural phenomena, as in physiochemical and biological spheres, similar causes under similar conditions give rise to similar effects.

DIFFUSION The process by which cultural traits, ways, complexes, and institutions are transferred from one cultural group to another.

DIMORPHISM, SEXUAL The occurrence of differentiation as in color, structure, size, and other traits between male and female members of the same species.

DISPLACEMENT The ability to communicate about items or events with which the communicators are not in direct contact.

DIVINATION Arrival at an expectation or judgment of future events through the interpretation of omens construed as evidence.

DNA (DEOXYRIBONUCLEIC ACID) The long-stranded molecules that are the principal component of CHROMOSOMES. Varied arrangements of DNA determine the GENETIC CODE and the GENOTYPE.

DOMESTICATE A domesticated plant or animal.

DOUBLE DESCENT Customary reckoning of affiliation of an individual in unilineal KIN GROUPS of both parents.

DOWRY Compensation given at marriage to a husband or his group by his wife's group; in some instances, it is the wife who controls the compensation, in which case the transfer of wealth resembles a predeath form of inheritance for the bride.

DUALITY OF PATTERNING The use of a limited set of code units in different combinations and sequences to generate different messages.

ECOLOGY The study of the total system of relationships among all the organisms and environmental conditions characteristic of a given area or region.

ECONOMY The management of the production, distribution, and consumption of the natural resources, labor, and other forms of wealth available to a cultural system.

ECOSYSTEM The community of plants and animals—including humans—within a habitat, and their relations to one another.

EGALITARIAN A type of societal group at the cultural level lacking formalized differentiation in access to, and power over, basic resources among its members.

EGO The person of reference at the center of kin terminological systems.

EMICS Descriptions or judgments concerning behavior, customs, beliefs, values, and so on, held by members of a societal group as culturally appropriate and valid. See also ETICS.

ENCULTURATION The process by which individuals—usually as children—acquire behavioral patterns and other aspects of their culture from others, through observation, instruction, and reinforcement.

ENDOGAMY The principle that requires ego to take a spouse from a group or status of which ego is a member.

EPICANTHIC FOLDS Flaps over the eyes, giving them a slanted look.

ETHNOCENTRISM The tendency to view the traits, ways, ideas, and values observed in other cultural groups as invariably inferior and less natural or logical than those of one's own group.

ETHNOCIDE The deliberate extinction of one culture by another.

ETHNOGRAPHY The systematic description of contemporary cultures.

ETICS The techniques and results of making generalizations about cultural events, behavior patterns, artifacts, thought, and ideology that aim to be verifiable objectively and valid cross-culturally. See also EMICS.

EVOLUTION, GENERAL The observation that in cultural systems as well as in living organisms there has been a directional emergence of progressively more complex levels of organization, integration, adaptation, and efficiency.

EXOGAMY The rule that forbids an individual from taking a spouse from within a prescribed local, kin, status, or other group with which they are both affiliated.

EXTENDED FAMILY A domiciliary aggregate of the members of two or more NUCLEAR FAMILIES, comprising siblings and their spouses and children, and often including their parents and married children.

FAMILY, LINGUISTIC A group of related languages historically derived from a common antecedent language.

FAMILY, SOCIETAL A domiciliary and or kin grouping, variously constituted of married and related persons and their offspring, residing together for economic and reproductive purposes. See also NUCLEAR FAMILY; EXTENDED FAMILY.

FAMILY, TAXONOMIC A category employed in the phylogenetic classification of plants and animals, just above the level of genus.

FEUDAL SYSTEM A type of historical socioeconomic organization involving a network of obligations, in which the PEASANTS are structured inferiors to their lord and are bound to provide certain payments and services in exchange for apparent privileges.

FOSSILS Remains or traces of plants or animals preserved—usually by mineralization—from the geological past.

FUNCTIONS The systemic needs served by artifacts, patterns of behavior, and ideas; the ways in which cultural traits contribute toward maintenance, efficiency, and adaptation of the cultural system.

GENE FLOW The movement of genetic material from one GENE POOL to another as a consequence of interbreeding.

GENE POOL The sum and range of variety of genes present within a given BREEDING POPULATION.

GENES The basic chemical units of heredity, found at particular loci on the CHROMOSOMES.

GENETIC CODE The arrangement of chemical components in the DNA molecules and on CHROMOSOMES, carrying information concerning the inheritance of traits.

GENITOR The etic male source of the sperm responsible for the birth of a particular child.

GENOCIDE The deliberate extinction of one population by another.

GENOTYPE The total gene complement received by an individual organism from its parents; as distinguished from the external appearance manifest in the PHENOTYPE.

GEOGRAPHIC RACE A BREEDING POPULATION, usually of considerable spatial extent, that can be expressed in terms of the frequencies of specifiable, characterizing genetic traits.

GHOST DANCE A REVITALIZATION MOVEMENT that appeared on the North American Plains during the nineteenth century, awaiting the departure of the whites and the restoration of Indian traditional ways.

GLOTTOCHRONOLOGY The reckoning of the time at which two languages diverged, from an examination of the extent to which their basic vocabularies are the same.

GROOM PRICE Compensation given to a man's MATRILINEAL GROUP when he resides with his wife's matrilineal group. Very rare.

HEADMAN In an EGALITARIAN group, the titular head who may lead those who will follow, but is usually unable to impose sanctions to enforce his decisions or requests, or deprive others of equal access to basic resources.

HERITABILITY In biology, the extent to which the manifestation of a particular trait can be attributed to transmission by genetic inheritance under a specific set of environmental conditions.

HOMINIDS (HOMINIDAE) The taxonomic family, including all living and extinct types and races of humans and protohumans. See also HOMINOIDS.

HOMINOIDS (HOMINOIDEA) The taxonomic superfamily of the anthropoids, including all extinct and contemporary varieties of apes and humans, and excluding the monkeys and prosimians. See also HOMINIDS.

ICONOGRAPHIC SYMBOLS Symbols that bear a direct resemblance to the items they symbolize.

IDEOLOGY Cognitive and emotional aspects of the emic superstructure.

INCEST Socially prohibited mating and or marriage, as within certain specified limits of real or putative KINSHIP.

INDEPENDENT ASSORTMENT The process by which hereditary information on one chromosome is passed on independently of the information on all other CHROMOSOMES.

INDUSTRIALIZATION An advanced stage of techno-economic development observed particularly in modern states and colonizing powers, characterized by centralized controls of tools, labor input, the techniques and organization of production, the marketing of goods, and cash wages.

IRRIGATION CIVILIZATION An advanced type of preindustrial society associated with the control of extensive man-made facilities for crop irrigation and land drainage. Usually characterized by highly centralized political institutions.

KINDRED A BILATERAL KIN GROUP in which ego traces relationships in ever-widening collateral and lineal descent and ascent through both ego's maternal and paternal kin and ego's sons and daughters.

KIN GROUP A social aggregate of individuals related by either CONSANGUINEAL ties of descent or AFFINAL ties of marriage.

KIN SELECTION An exclusion of the principle of NATURAL SELECTION that takes into consideration the reproductive success not only of individuals but of their close biological kin in explaining the frequency of GENES and ALLELES.

KINSHIP The network of culturally recognized interpersonal relations through which individuals are related to one another by ties of descent or marriage.

KINSHIP TERMINOLOGY The system of terms by which members of a KIN GROUP customarily address or refer to one another, denoting their relationship.

KITCHEN MIDDENS Seacoast mounds formed by the debris of centuries of Mesolithic shellfish eating.

LEVIRATE Custom favoring the remarriage of a widow to her deceased husband's brother.

LIEBIG'S LAW Points out that in biological evolution the processes of adaptation and selection respond to the given minimal potentialities of the environment.

LINEAGE A KIN GROUP whose members can actually trace their relationship through specific, known genealogical links along the recognized line of descent, as either MATRILINEAL or PATRILINEAL.

MAGIC The practice of certain rituals that are presumed to coerce desired practical effects in the material world, or in persons.

MAJORITY The superordinate group in a hierarchy of racial, cultural, or religious minorities. The majority is usually, but not necessarily, not only politically and economically dominant but more numerous as well.

MANA A term for the impersonal pervasive power expected in certain objects and roles. See also ANIMATISM.

MARRIAGE A socially sanctioned form of heterosexual mating and coresidence establishing duties and obligations with respect to sex and reproduction; variant forms are homosexual matings and childless marriages.

MATRIARCHY The political and economic dominance of men by women; no cases have been confirmed.

MATRIFOCAL FAMILY A domiciliary group comprising one or more adult women, and their offspring, within which husbands-fathers are not permanent residents.

MATRILINEAL GROUPS Persons whose descent reckoning is through females exclusively.

MATRILOCALITY Residence of a couple after marriage in or near the wife's mother's domicile.

MESSIANIC MOVEMENT A movement offering REVITALIZATION or salvation through following the spiritual or activist leadership of a prophetic individual or messiah; often against vested authority.

MICROLITHS Small, trapezoidal-shaped flakes of flinty stone; usually set in rows in wooden or bone hafts.

MIDDEN See KITCHEN MIDDENS.

MINORITY Subordinate endogamous descent groups based on racial, cultural, or religious criteria found in all state societies.

MODAL PERSONALITY The type of basic PERSONALITY perceived to be characteristic of a cultural system, or of one of its strata or subgroups.

MONOGAMY Marriage between one man and one woman at a time.

MORPHEME The smallest sequence of sounds to which a definite meaning is attached.

MUTATION Innovative change in hereditary material, transmitted to the offspring.

NATURAL SELECTION The process by which differential reproductive success changes the frequency of genes in populations. One of the major forces of EVOLUTION.

NEOLOCALITY Residence of a couple after marriage apart from the parental domicile of either spouse.

NUCLEAR FAMILY The basic social grouping comprising married male and female parents and their offspring.

OEDIPUS CONFLICT Sexually charged hostility, usually repressed, between parents and children of the same sex.

PARALLEL COUSINS Persons whose parents are siblings of the same sex; the sons and daughters of two sisters or of two brothers.

PARALLEL CULTURAL EVOLUTION Represented by instances in which significant aspects, patternings, or institutions in two or more cultural systems undergo similar adaptations and transformations; presumably in response to the operations of similar causal and dynamic factors.

PASTORAL NOMADS Peoples who raise domesticated animals and do not depend on hunting, gathering, or the planting of their own crops for a significant portion of their diets.

PATRILINEAL GROUPS Persons whose descent reckoning is through males exclusively.

PATRILOCALITY Residence of a couple after marriage in or near the husband's father's domicile.

PEASANTS Food-producing farm workers who form the lower economic stratum in preindustrial and underdeveloped societies, subject to exploitative obligations in the form of rent, taxes, tribute, forced labor service (CORVÉE), and the like.

PERSONALITY The structuring of the inherent constitutional, emotional, and intellectual factors that determine how a person feels, thinks, and behaves in relation to the patterning of a particular cultural context.

PHENOTYPE The characteristics of an individual organism that are the external, apparent manifestations of its hereditary genetic composition, resulting from the interaction of its genotype with its environment. See also GENOTYPE.

PHONEME A single vocal sound (PHONE), or the several variants of such a sound (ALLOPHONES), which a listener recognizes as having a certain linguistic function.

PHONES The emic units of sound that contrast with one another and that are the building blocks of PHONEMES.

PHONETIC LAWS Statements about the shifts in the sound values of certain vowel and consonant PHONEMES that have occurred regularly in time within languages and reveal past historic relations between languages.

PHYLETIC GRADUALISM The theory of speciation (held by Darwin) that populations evolve gradually, by the slow accumulation of adaptive changes, so that eventually they become unable to interbreed with other populations. Compare PUNCTUATED EQUILIBRIUM.

PHYSICAL ANTHROPOLOGY The study of the animal origins and biologically determined nature of humankind and of physical variations among human populations.

PLACENTA Nutrient-and-waste-exchanging structure that enhances fetal development within the mother's body.

PLURALISM Where a national or regional population is composed of several social, cultural, or religious minorities concerned with maintaining their separate identities.

POLITICAL ECONOMY Treating the role of political authority and power in production, distribution, and consumption of goods and services.

POLYANDRY Marriage of one woman with two or more males simultaneously.

POLYGAMY Marriage involving more than one spouse of either sex.

POLYGYNY Marriage of one male with two or more women simultaneously.

POLYMORPHISM Genetic traits for which there are two or more ALLELES at the same chromosome locus.

PUNCTUATED EQUILIBRIUM A theory of speciation holding that evolutionary changes are triggered by species-forming "events" representing disturbances in the equilibrium between a population and its environment, and that such changes may occur within a relatively short span of time—for example, several centuries. Compare PHYLETIC GRADUALISM.

RACE Large populations characterized by a bundle of distinctive gene frequencies and associated with continents or extensive regions.

RACIOLOGY The scientific study of the relationship between race and culture.

RACISM The attitude that the genetic composition of various RACES determines the principal cultural differences manifested by different groups of people.

RECIPROCITY The principle of exchanging goods and/or valuables without overt reckoning of economic worth or overt reckoning that a balance need be reached, to establish or reinforce ties between persons.

REDISTRIBUTION A system of exchange in which the labor products of several different individuals are brought to a central place, sorted by type, counted, and then given away to producers and nonproducers alike.

RENT A payment in kind or in money for the opportunity to live or work on the owner's land.

REPRODUCTION The process by which an organism makes a copy of itself and of its plans or heredity instructions.

REVITALIZATION MOVEMENT Reaction by a minority group to coercion and disruption, often under MESSIANIC leadership, aiming to reclaim lost status, identity, and well-being.

RITES OF PASSAGE Communally celebrated rituals that mark the transition of an individual from one institutionalized STATUS to another.

RITES OF SOLIDARITY Rites that confirm the unity of a group.

ROLES Patterns of behavior associated with specific statuses.

SEMANTIC UNIVERSALITY Potential of all human languages for generating utterances capable of conveying information relevant to all aspects of experience and thought, without limits as to time or place.

SHAMAN A part-time practitioner of magico-religious rites of DIVINATION and curing, skilled in sleight of hand and the techniques of trance and possession.

SISTER EXCHANGE A form of marriage in which two males marry each other's sister (or sisters).

SOCIETY A group within which all aspects of the UNIVERSAL PATTERN occur with a high density of interaction among its members and having a geographical locus.

SODALITY A group based on nonkinship principles such as a club or a professional association.

SORORATE Custom by which a deceased wife is replaced by a sister.

STATUS Position or standing, socially recognized, ascribed to be achieved by an individual or group. Compare ROLE.

SUBCULTURE A culture associated with a MINORITY, MAJORITY, CLASS, CASTE, or other group within a larger sociocultural system.

SUITOR SERVICE BRIDE-PRICE rendered in the form of labor.

SURFACE STRUCTURE The directly observed form of an utterance.

TABOO A culturally determined prohibition on an activity, plant, animal, person, or place.

TAXONS The groups of organisms designated by the taxonomic labels of biology.

TOOL An object, not part of the user's body, that the user holds or carries during or just prior to use and that is used to alter the form or location of a second object with which it was previously unconnected.

TOTEMS Plants, animals, phenomena, or objects symbolically associated with particular descent groups as identifying insignia.

UNILINEAL DESCENT The reckoning of descent either exclusively through males or exclusively through females.

UNIVERSAL PATTERN A set of categories comprehensive enough to afford logical and classificatory organization for the range of artifacts, traits, ways, and institutions to be observed in any or all cultural systems.

UXORILOCAL RESIDENCE When the husband lives in the wife's home.

VIRILOCAL RESIDENCE When the wife lives in the husband's home.

WARFARE Formalized armed combat by teams of people who represent rival territories or political communities.

ZYGOTE A fertilized egg; the first cells of a new individual.

ABRUZZI, WILLIAM. **1982** "Ecological Theory and Ethic Differentiation Among Human Populations." *Current Anthropology* 23:13–35.

ACHESON, JAMES M. **1972** "Limited Good or Limited Goods: Response to Economic Opportunity in a Tarascan Pueblo." *American Anthropologist* 74:1152–1169.

———. **1974** "Reply to George Foster." *American Anthropologist* 76:57–62.

ACKERMAN, SANDRA. **1989** "European Prehistory Gets Even Older." *Science* 246:28–30.

ADAMS, KENNETH. **1992** "Dowry As a Compensatory Marriage Payment." Unpublished paper.

ADAMS, M., AND J. V. NEIL. **1967** "The Children of Incest." *Pediatrics* 40:55–62.

ADAMS, RICHARD N. **1968** "An Inquiry into the Nature of the Family." In *Selected Studies in Marriage and the Family,* R. F. Winch and L. W. Goodman, eds., pp. 45–57. New York: Holt, Rinehart and Winston.

ADAMS, RICHARD, W. BROWN, AND T. P. CULBERT. **1981** "Radar Mapping, Archaeology and Ancient Maya Land Use." *Science* 213:1457–1463.

ADAMS, ROBERT McC. **1966** *The Evolution of Urban Society: Early Mesopotamia and Mexico.* Chicago: Aldine.

———. **1972** "Patterns of Urbanization in Early Southern Mesopotamia." In *Man, Settlement, and Urbanism,* P. J. Ucko et al., eds., pp. 735–749. Cambridge, Mass.: Schenkman.

———. **1983** "Natural and Social Science Paradigms in Near Eastern Prehistory." In *The Hilly Flanks and Beyond,* T. Young et al., eds., pp. 369–374. Studies in Ancient Oriental Civilization Publication No. 36. Chicago: Oriental Institute.

ADOVASIO, J. M., J. DONAHUE, AND R. STUCKENRATH. **1990** "The Meadowcraft Rockshelter Radiocarbon Chronology 1975–1990." *American Antiquity* 55(2):348–354.

———. **1992** "Never Say Never Again: Some Thoughts on Could Haves and Might Have Beens." *American Antiquity* 57:327–331.

ALBA, RICHARD. **1990** *Ethnic Identity: The Transformation of White America.* New Haven: Yale University Press.

ALBERS, PATRICIA. **1989** "From Illusion to Illumination: Anthropological Studies of American Indian Women." In *Gender and Anthropology,* Sandra Morgan, ed., pp. 132–170. Washington D.C.: American Anthropological Association.

ALEXANDER, RICHARD. **1977** "Natural Selection and the Analysis of Human Sociology." In *The Changing Scenes in the Natural Sciences, 1776–1976,* C. E. Goulden, ed., pp. 283–337. Philadelphia: Academy of Natural Science, Special Publication 12.

ALLAND, ALEXANDER, JR. **1977** *The Artistic Animal: An Inquiry into the Biological Roots of Art.* Garden City, N.Y.: Doubleday/Anchor Books.

ALTUNA, JESUS. **1983** "On the Relationship Between Archaeofaunal and Parietal Art in the Cantabrian Region." In *Animals and Archaeology: Hunters and Their Prey,* J. Clutton-Brock and C. Grigson, eds., pp. 227–238. Oxford: BAR International Series 163.

AMERICAN ANTHROPOLOGICAL ASSOCIATION. **1990–1991** *AAA Guide.* Washington, D.C.

ANDREWS, E. WYLLYS V, AND NORMAN HAMMOND. **1990** "Redefinition of the Swasey Phase at Cuello Belize." *American Antiquity* 55(3):570–584.

ANNATI, EMMANUEL. **1986** "Comments on W. Davis's 'The Origins of Image Making.' " *Current Anthropology* 27:202.

ARDREY, ROBERT. **1961** *African Genesis: A Personal Investigation into the Animal Origins and Nature of Man.* New York: Atheneum.

ARENSBURG, B., L. A. SCHEPARTZ, A. M. TILLIER, B. VANDERMEERSCH, AND Y. RAK. **1990** "A Reappraisal of the Anatomical Basis for Speech in Middle Paleolithic Hominoids." *American Journal of Physical Anthropology* 83:137–146.

ARESHIAN, GREGORY. **1990** "Further Thoughts on the Uruk Expansion." *Current Anthropology* 31: 396–399.

ARIEL, IRVING (ED.). **1981** *Malignant Melanoma.* New York: Appleton-Century Crofts.

ARMELAGOS, GEORGE, AND A. MCARDLE. **1975** "Population, Disease, and Evolution." *American Antiquity* 40:1–10.

AWÉ, BOLANLIE. **1977** "The Iyalod in Traditional Yoruba Political Systems." In *Sexual Stratification: A Cross Cultural View,* Alice Schlegel, ed., pp. 270–291. New York: Columbia University Press.

BADA, JEFFREY. **1985** "Aspartic Acid Racemization Ages of California Paleoindian Skeletons." *American Antiquity* 50:645–647.

BADRIAN A., AND N. BADRIAN. **1984** "Social Organization of *Pan Paniscus* in the Lomako Forest, Zaire." In *The Pygmy Chimpanzee,* R. Susman, ed., pp. 325–346. New York: Plenum Press.

BAKKER, JIM. **1976** *Move That Mountain.* Plainfield, N.J.: Logos International.

BAKSH, MICHAEL. **1985** "Faunal Food as a 'Limiting Factor' on Amazonian Cultural Behavior: A Machiguenga Example." *Research in Economic Anthropology* 7:145–175.

BALEE, WILLIAM. **1984** "The Ecology of Ancient Tupi Warfare." In *Warfare, Culture and Environment,* Brian Ferguson, ed., pp. 241–265. Orlando, Fla.: Academic Press.

BARASH, DAVID P. **1977** *Sociology and Behavior.* New York: Elsevier.

BARBER, BERNARD. **1968** "Social Mobility in Hindu India." In *Social Mobility in the Caste System,* J. Silverberg, ed., pp. 18–35. The Hague: Mouton.

BARINAGA, MARCIA. **1992** "'African Eve' Backers Beat a Retreat." *Science* 255:686–687.

BARLETT, PEGGY, AND PETER BROWN. **1985** "Agricultural Development and the Quality of Life: An Anthropological View." *Agriculture and Human Values* 2:28–35.

BARNES, J. A. **1960** "Marriage and Residential Continuity." *American Anthropologist* 62:850–866.

BARNOUW, VICTOR. **1985** *Culture and Personality* (4th ed.). Homewood, Ill.: Dorsey Press.

BARRAU, JACQUES. **1967** "De l'homme cueilleur à l'homme cultivateur: L'exemple océanien." *Cahiers d'Histoire Mondiale* 10:275–292.

BARTH, FREDERICK. **1974** "Ecological Relationships of Ethnic Groups in Swat, North Pakistan." In *Man in Adaptation,* Yehudi Cohen, ed., pp. 378–385. Chicago: Aldine.

BARTRAM, WILLIAM. **1958** *The Travels of William Bartram;* Francis Harper, ed. New Haven, Conn.: Yale University Press.

BAR-YOSEF, O. **1986** "The Walls of Jericho: An Alternative Interpretation." *Current Anthropology* 27:157–162.

———. **1992** "The Role of Western Asia in Modern Human Origins." Unpublished paper.

BAR-YOSEF, O., AND A. BELFER-COHEN. **1991** "From Sedentary Hunter-Gatherers to Territorial Farmers in the Levant." In *Between Bands and States,* Susan Gregg, ed., pp. 181–202. Center for Archaeological Investigations, Occasional Paper 9. Carbondale, Ill.: Southern Illinois University Press.

BAR-YOSEF, O., AND F. VALLA. **1990** "The Natufian Culture and the Origin of the Neolithic in the Levant." *Current Anthropology* 31:433–436.

BATRA, RAVI. **1987** "Are the Rich Getting Richer?" *The New York Times,* May 3, Sec. 3, p. 2.

BAYLISS-SMITH, TIMOTHY. **1977** "Human Ecology and Island Populations: The Problems of Change." In *Subsistence and Survival: Rural Ecology in the Pacific,* T. Bayliss-Smith and R. Feachem, eds., pp. 11–20. New York: Academic Press.

BEADLE, GEORGE. **1981** "The Ancestor of Corn." *Scientific American* 242(1):96–103.

BEALS, K., C. SMITH, AND S. DODD. **1984** "Brain Size: Cranial Morphology, Climate and Time Machines." *Current Anthropology* 25(3):301–330.

BEATTIE, JOHN. **1960** *Bunyoro: An African Kingdom.* New York: Holt, Rinehart and Winston.

BEAUMONT, PETER, AND J. C. VOGEL. **1972** "On a New Radiocarbon Chronology for Africa South of the Equator." *African Studies* 31:155–182.

BECK, BENJAMIN. **1975** "Primate Tool Behavior." In *Socioecology and Psychology of Primates,* R. H. Tuttle, ed., pp. 413–447. The Hague: Mouton.

BELKIN, LISA. **1985** "Parents Weigh Costs of Children." *The New York Times,* May 23, pp. 19, 21.

BELL, DANIEL. **1973** *The Coming of Post-Industrial Society: A Venture in Social Forecasting.* New York: Basic Books.

BELLAH, ROBERT. **1976** "New Religious Consciousness and the Crisis in Modernity." In *The New Religious Consciousness,* Robert Bellah and Charles Clock, eds., pp. 297–330. Berkeley: University of California Press.

BELMONTE, THOMAS. **1979** *The Broken Fountain.* New York: Columbia University Press.

BENDER, DONALD. **1967** "A Refinement of the Concept of Household: Families, Co-Residence, Domestic Functions." *American Anthropologist* 69:493–503.

BELSHAM, MARTHA. **1988** "The Clerical Worker's Boss: An Agent of Job Stress." *Human Organization* 47:361–367.

BENDIX, REINHARD, AND S. M. LIPSET (EDS.). **1966** *Class, Status, and Power: Social Stratification in Comparative Perspective.* New York: Free Press.

BENEDICT, RUTH. **1934** *Patterns of Culture.* Boston: Houghton Mifflin.

———. **1938** "Religion." In *General Anthropology,* F. Boas, ed., pp. 627–665. New York: Columbia University Press.

BENTHAM, JEREMY. **1978** "Offenses Against One's Self: Pederasty." *Journal of Homosexuality* 3:389–405.

BENZ, BRUCE F., AND HUGH H. ILTIS. **1990** "Studies in Archaeological Maize: The 'Wild' Maize from San

Marcos Cave Reexamined." *American Antiquity* 55(3):500–511.

BERDAN, FRANCES. **1982** *Aztecs of Central Mexico.* New York: Holt, Rinehart and Winston.

BEREITER, CARL, AND S. ENGLEMANN. **1966** *Teaching Disadvantaged Children in Preschool.* Englewood Cliffs, N.J.: Prentice-Hall.

BERMEJO, M., G. ILLERA, AND J. SABATER-PI. **1989** "New Observations on the Tool-behavior of Chimpanzees from Mt. Assirik (Senegal, West Africa)." *Primates* 30(1):65–73.

BERNARD, H. RUSSELL. **1981** "Issues in Training in Applied Anthropology." *Practicing Anthropology* 3:(Winter).

BERNARDI, BERNADO. **1985** *Age Class Systems: Social Institutions and Politics Based on Age.* New York: Cambridge University Press.

BERRA, TIM M. **1990** *Evolutionism and the Myth of Creationism: A Basic Guide to the Facts in the Evolution Debate.* Stanford Calif.: Stanford University Press.

BERREMAN, GERALD. **1966** "Caste in Cross-cultural Perspective." In *Japan's Invisible Race: Caste in Culture and Personality,* G. de Vos and H. Wagatsuma, eds., pp. 275–324. Berkeley: University of California Press.

———. **1975** "Bazar Behavior: Social Identity and Social Interaction in Urban India." In *Ethnic Identity: Cultural Continuity and Change,* L. Romanucci-Ross and G. de Vos, eds., pp. 71–105. Palo Alto, Calif.: Mayfield.

———. **1981** *Social Inequality.* New York: Academic Press.

BERRY, MICHAEL S. **1985** "The Age of Maize in the Greater Southwest: A Critical Review." In *Prehistoric Food Production in North America,* Richard I. Ford, ed., pp. 279–308. Ann Arbor: University of Michigan Museum of Anthropology.

BESHAROV, DOUGLAS J. **1989** "Targeting Long-Term Welfare Recipients." In *Welfare Policy for the 1990's,* Phoebe H. Cottingham and David T. Ellwood, eds., pp. 146–164. Cambridge, Mass.: Harvard University Press.

BICKERTON, DEREK. **1990** *Language and Species.* Chicago: University of Chicago Press.

BINFORD, LEWIS. **1983** *In Pursuit of the Past.* New York: Thames and Hudson.

———. **1986** *An Archaeological Perspective.* New York: Seminar Press.

BINFORD, LEWIS R., AND NANCY STONE. **1986** "Zhoukoudian: A Closer Look." *Current Anthropology* 27:453–475.

BIOLSI, THOMAS. **1984** "Ecological and Cultural Factors in Plains Indians Warfare." In *Warfare, Culture and Environment,* Brian Ferguson, ed., pp. 141–168. Orlando, Fla.: Academic Press.

BIRD, ROBERT MCKELVY. **1990** "What Are the Chances of Finding Maize in Peru Dating Before 1000 B.C.?

Reply to Banavia and Grobman." *American Antiquity* 55(4):828–840.

BIRDSELL, JOSEPH B. **1981** *Human Evolution: An Introduction to the New Physical Anthropology.* Boston: Houghton Mifflin.

BITTLES, ALAN, ET AL. **1991** "Reproductive Behavior and Health in Consanguineous Marriages." *Science* 2(52):789–794.

BIXLER, RAY. **1982** "Comment on the Incidence and Purpose of Royal Sibling Incest." *American Ethnologist* 9:580–582.

BLACK, FRANCIS. **1975** "Infectious Disease in Primitive Societies." *Science* 187:515–518.

BLACKWOOD, EVELYN. **1984** "Sexuality and Gender in Certain North American Indian Tribes: The Case of Cross-Gender Females." *Signs* 10:27–42.

———. **1986** "Breaking the Mirror: The Construction of Lesbianism and the Anthropological Discourse on Homosexuality." In *Anthropology and Homosexual Behavior,* Evelyn Blackwood, ed., pp. 1–18. New York: Haworth Press.

BLAKE, JUDITH. **1961** *Family Structure in Jamaica: The Social Context of Reproduction.* New York: Free Press.

BLAU, PETER, AND O. D. DUNCAN. **1967** *The American Occupational Structure.* New York: Wiley.

BLOCH, MARC. **1964** "Feudalism as a Type of Society." In *Sociology and History: Theory and Research,* W. J. Cahnman and A. Boskoff, eds., pp. 163–170. New York: Free Press.

BLUMLER, MARK A., AND ROGER BYRNE. **1991** "The Ecological Genetics of Domestication and the Origins of Agriculture." *Current Anthropology* 32:23–54.

BODLEY, JOHN H. **1975** *Victims of Progress.* Menlo Park, Calif.: Cummings.

BODMER, WALTER FRED, AND L. L. CAVALLI-SFORZA. **1976** *Genetics, Evolution, and Man.* San Francisco: Freeman.

BOESCH, CHRISTOPE, AND HEDWIGE BOESCH. **1984** "Mental Map in Wild Chimpanzees: An Analysis of Hammer Transports for Nut Cracking." *Primates* 25(2): 169–170.

———. **1991** "Dim Forest, Bright Chimps." *Natural History* (September):50–56.

BOHANNAN, PAUL. **1973** "Rethinking Culture: A Project for Current Anthropologists." *Current Anthropology* 14:357–372.

BÖKÖNYI, SANDOR, R. J. BRAIDWOOD, AND C. A. REED. **1973** "Earliest Animal Domestication Dated?" *Science* 182:1161.

BONAVIA, DUCCIO, AND ALEXANDER GROBMAN. **1989** "Preceramic Maize in the Central Andes: A Necessary Clarification." *American Antiquity* 54(4):836–840.

BONGAARTS, JOHN. **1980** "Does Malnutrition Affect Fertility? A Summary of the Evidence." *Science* 208:564–569.

BONGAARTS, JOHN, AND F. ODILE. **1984** "The Proximate Determinants of Fertility in Sub-Saharan

Africa." *Population and Development Review* 10:511–537.

BOSERUP, ESTER. **1965** *The Condition of Agricultural Growth: The Economics of Agrarian Change Under Population Pressure.* Chicago: Aldine.

BOSSEN, LAUREL. **1988** "Toward a Theory of Marriage: The Economic Anthropology of Marriage Transactions." *Ethnology* 27:127–144.

BOTTOMORE, T. B. **1966** *Classes in Modern Society.* New York: Random House/Vintage Books.

BOUCHARD, THOMAS, ET AL. **1991** "Letters." *Science* 252:191–192.

BOURGUIGNON, ERIKA. **1980** "Comparisons and Implications: What Have We Learned?" In *A World of Women: Anthropological Studies of Women in the Societies of the World*, Erika Bourguignon et al., eds., pp. 321–342. South Hadley, Mass.: Praeger Scientific a J. F. Bergin Publisher Book.

BOWLES, S., AND H. GINTIS. **1976** *Schooling in Capitalist America.* New York: Basic Books.

BRAIDWOOD, LINDA, AND R. BRAIDWOOD. **1986** "Prelude to the Appearance of Village-Farming Communities in Southwestern Asia." In *Ancient Anatolia: Aspects of Change and Cultural Development*, J. V. Canby et al., eds., pp. 3–11. Madison: University of Wisconsin Press.

BRAIDWOOD, ROBERT J., AND L. S. BRAIDWOOD ET AL. (EDS.). **1983** *Prehistoric Archaeology Along the Zagros Flanks.* Chicago: Oriental Institution Publications No. 105.

BRAIDWOOD, ROBERT J., AND G. R. WILLEY (EDS.). **1962** *Courses Toward Urban Life: Archaeological Considerations of Some Cultural Alternates.* Chicago: Aldine.

BRAIN, CHARLES K. **1988** "New Information from the Swartkrans Cave of Relevance to 'Robust' Australopithecines." In *Evolutionary History of the 'Robust' Australopithecines*, Frederick E. Grine, ed., pp. 311–316. New York: A. de Gruyter.

BRAUER, GUNTER. **1984** "A Craniological Approach to the Origin of Anatomically Modern *Homo sapiens* in Africa and Implications for the Appearance of Modern Europeans." In *The Origins of Modern Humans: A World Survey of the Fossil Evidence*, Fred Smith and Frank Spencer, eds., pp. 327–410. New York: Alan R. Liss.

BRAVERMAN, HARRY. **1974** *Labor and Monopoly Capital: The Degradation of Work in the Twentieth Century.* New York: Monthly Review Press.

BRICKER, HARVEY. **1976** "Upper Paleolithic Archeology." *Annual Review of Anthropology* 5:133–148.

BROWMAN, DAVID. **1976** "Demographic Correlations of the Wari Conquest of Junin." *American Antiquity* 41:465–477.

BROWN, JUDITH K. **1975** "Iroquois Women: An Ethnohistoric Note." In *Toward an Anthropology of Women*,

Rayna Reiter, ed., pp. 235–251. New York: Monthly Review Press.

——— **1985** *In Her Prime: A New View of Middle-Aged Women.* South Hadley, Mass.: Bergin and Garvey.

BROWN, LESTER. **1978** *The Global Economic Prospect: New Sources of Economic Stress.* Washington, D.C.: World Watch Institute.

BROWN, LESTER, ET AL. **1991** *State of the World 1991: A Worldwatch Institute Report on Progress Toward a Sustainable Society.* New York/London: Norton.

BROWN, PETER. **1985** "Microparsites and Macroparasites." Paper read at the 1985 annual meeting of the American Anthropological Association, Washington, D.C.

BROWN, RONALD. **1978** Testimony: Hearings Before the Subcommittee on Crime, House of Representatives. Ninety-fifth Congress, Serial No. 47. Washington, D.C.: U.S. Government Printing Office.

BROZAN, NADINE. **1985** "U.S. Leads Industrialized Nations in Teen Age Births and Abortions." *The New York Times*, March 13, pp. 1, 22.

BRUNTON, RON. **1975** "Why Do the Trobriands Have Chiefs?" *Man* 10(4):545–550.

BRYAN, ALAN (ED.). **1987** "Points of Order." *Natural History* 6:6–11.

BRYAN, ALAN, ET AL. **1978** "An El Jobo Mastodon Kill at Taima-Taima, Venezuela." *Science* 200:1275–1277.

BUCHBINDER, GEOGEDA. **1977** "Nutritional Stress and Population Decline Among the Maring of New Guinea." In *Malnutrition, Behavior and Social Organization*, Lawrence S. Greene, ed., pp. 109–142. New York: Academic Press.

BUCKLEY, THOMAS. **1982** "Menstruation and the Power of Yurok Women." *American Ethnologist* 9:47–90.

BULLOUGH, VERNE, AND BONNIE BULLOUGH. **1978** *Prostitution: An Illustrated and Social History.* New York: Crown.

BUNN, HENRY, AND ELLEN KROLL. **1986** "Systematic Butchery by Plio/Pleistocene Hominids at Olduvai Gorge, Tanzania." *Current Anthropology* 27:431–452.

BURBANK, VICTORIA. **1989** "Gender and the Anthropology Curriculum: Aboriginal Australia." In *Gender and Anthropology*, Sandra Morgan, ed., pp. 116–131. Washington, D.C.: American Anthropological Association.

BURTON, MICHAEL, LILYAN BRUDNER, AND DOUGLAS WHITE. **1977** "A Model of the Sexual Division of Labor." *American Ethnologist* 4(2):227–251.

BURTON, MICHAEL, AND D. WHITE. **1987** "Sexual Division of Labor in Agriculture." In *Household Economies*, M. Maclachlan, ed. Lanham, Md.: University Press of America.

BUZZARD, SHIRLEY. **1982** *The PLAN Primary Health Care Project, Tumaco, Colombia: A Case Study.* Warwick, R.I.: Foster Parents Plan International.

CACCONE, A., AND J. POWELL. **1989** "DNA Divergence among Hominoids." *Evolution* 43:925–942.

CAIN, MEADE. **1977** "The Economic Activities of Children in a Village in Bangladesh." *Population and Development Review* 3:201–227.

CALDWELL, JOHN. **1982** *Theory of Fertility Decline.* New York: Academic Press.

CALDWELL, J., ET AL. **1983** "The Causes of Demographic Change in Rural South India: A Micro Approach." *Population and Demographic Review* 8:689-727.

CALLENDER, CHARLES, AND LEE KOCHEMS. **1983** "The North American Berdache." *Current Anthropology* 24: 443–470.

CANN, R., ET AL. **1987** "Mitochondrial DNA and Human Evolution." *Nature* 352:31–36.

CARASCO, PEDRO. **1978** "Le economía del México prehispánico." In *Economía política e ideologia en el México prehispánico*, Pedro Carasco and Johanna Broda, eds., pp. 15–76. Mexico City: Editorial Nueva Imagen.

CARLSTEIN, TONY. **1983** *Time Resources: Society and Ecology.* London: George Allen & Unwin.

CARNEIRO, ROBERT. **1970** "A Theory of the Origin of the State." *Science* 169:733–738.

———. **1981** "Chiefdom: Precursor of the State." In *The Transition to Statehood in the New World*, Grant Jones and Robert Kautz, eds., pp. 37–75. New York: Cambridge University Press.

CARNEIRO, ROBERT, AND DAISY F. HILSE. **1966** "On Determining the Probable Rate of Population Growth During the Neolithic." *American Anthropologist* 68: 177–181.

CARPENTER, CLARENCE. **1940** "A Field Study in Siam of the Behavior and Social Relations of the Gibbons, Hylobateslar." *Comparative Psychological Monographs* 16:1–212.

CARRIER, DAVID. **1984** "The Energetic Paradox of Human Running and Hominid Evolution." *Current Anthropology* 25:483–495.

CARROLL, LUCY. **1977** "'Sanskritization,' 'Westernization,' and 'Social Mobility': A Reappraisal of the Relevance of Anthropological Concepts to the Social Historian of Modern India." *Journal of Anthropological Research* 33(4):355–371.

CARSTAIRS, G. M. **1967** *The Twice Born.* Bloomington: Indiana University Press.

CARTER, WILLIAM, ED. **1980** *Cannabis in Costa Rica: A Study of Chronic Marihuana Use.* Philadelphia: ISHI.

CARTMILL, MATT. **1974** "Rethinking Primate Origins." *Science* 184(4135): 436–443.

CATTELL, R. B. **1940** "A Culture-free Intelligence Test." *Journal of Educational Psychology* 31:161–179.

CATTLE, DOROTHY. **1977** "An Alternative to Nutritional Particularism." In *Nutrition and Anthropology in Action*, Thomas Fitzgerald, ed., pp. 35–45. Amsterdam: Van Gorcum.

CAVALLI-SFORZA, L. L. **1972** "Origins and Differentiation of Human Races." Proceedings of the Royal Anthropological Institute for 1972, London, pp. 15–26.

CAVALLI-SFORZA, L. L., AND W. F. BODMER. **1965** *The Genetics of Human Populations.* San Francisco: Freeman.

CHAGNON, NAPOLEON. **1974** *Studying the Yanomamö.* New York: Holt, Rinehart and Winston.

CHAGNON, NAPOLEON, AND RAYMOND HAMES. **1979** "Protein Deficiency and Tribal Warfare in Amazonia: New Data." *Science* 203:910–913.

CHAMBERS, ERVE. **1985** *Applied Anthropology: A Professional Guide.* Englewood Cliffs, N.J.: Prentice-Hall.

CHAMPION, TIMOTHY, ET AL. (EDS.). **1984** *Prehistoric Europe.* New York: Academic Press.

CHANG, K. C. **1973** "Radiocarbon Dates from China: Some Initial Interpretations." *Current Anthropology* 14:525–528.

———. **1980** *Shang Civilization.* New Haven, Conn.: Yale University Press.

———. **1983** *Art, Myth, and Ritual: The Path to Political Authority in Ancient China.* Cambridge, Mass.: Harvard University Press.

———. **1984a** "China." *American Antiquity* 49(4): 754–756.

———. **1984b** "Concluding Remarks." In *The Origins of Chinese Civilization*, David Keightley, ed., pp. 565–581. Berkeley: University of California Press.

———. **1986** *The Archaeology of Ancient China* (4th ed.). New Haven, Conn.: Yale University Press.

CHARLTON, THOMAS. **1978** "Teotihuacán, Tepeapulco, and Obsidian Exploitation." *Science* 200:1227–1236.

CHARNOV, ERIC. **1976** "Optimal Foraging: The Marginal Value Theorem." *Theoretical Population Biology* 9:129–136.

CHARTERIS, J., J. C. WALL, AND J. NOTTRODT. **1982** "Pliocene Hominid Gait: New Interpretations Based on the Available Footprint Data from Laetoli." *American Journal of Physical Anthropology* 58:133–144.

CHASE, P., AND H. DIBBLE. **1987** "Middle Paleolithic Symbolism: A Review of Current Evidence and Interpretations." *Journal of Anthropological Archaeology* 6:263–296.

CHILD, ALICE, AND J. CHILD. **1985** "Biology, Ethnocentrism, and Sex Differences." *American Anthropologist* 87:125–128.

CHILDE, V. GORDON. **1952** *New Light on the Most Ancient East.* London: Kegan Paul.

CHOMSKY, NOAM. **1973** "The General Properties of Language." In *Explorations in Anthropology: Readings in Culture, Man, and Nature*, Morton Fried, ed., pp. 115–123. New York: Crowell.

———. **1989** *Necessary Illusions; Thought Control in Democratic Societies.* Boston: South End Press.

CICCHETTI, DANTE, AND VICKI CARLSON (EDS.). **1989** *Child Maltreatment: Theory and Research on the Causes and Consequences of Child Abuse and Neglect.* New York: Cambridge University Press.

CIOCHON, RUSSEL. **1985** "Hominoid Cladistics and the Ancestry of Modern Apes and Humans." In *Primitive Evolution and Human Origins*, R. L. Ciochon and

J. G. Fleagle, eds., pp. 345–362. Menlo Park, Calif.: Benjamin/Cummings.

CLARK, G. A., AND J. M. LINDLEY. **1989** "Modern Human Origins in the Levant and Western Asia: The Fossil and Archaeological Evidence." *American Anthropologist* 91:962–985.

CLARK, GUY. **1981** "On Preagricultural Adaptations." *Current Anthropology* 22:444–445.

CLARK, J. D. **1983** "The Significance of Culture Change in the Early Later Pleistocene in Northern and Southern Africa." In *The Mousterian Legacy: Human Biocultural Change in the Upper Pleistocene,* Eric Trinkhaus, ed., pp. 1–9. Oxford: BAR International Series, No. 164.

CLARK, WILLIAM. **1976** "Maintenance of Agriculture and Human Habitats Within the Tropical Forest Ecosystem." *Human Ecology* 4(3):247–259.

CLOUD, WALLACE. **1973** "After the Green Revolution." *The Sciences* 13(8):6–12.

COCKBURN, T. A. **1971** "Infectious Diseases in Ancient Populations." *Current Anthropology* 12:45–62.

COE, MICHAEL. **1968** *America's First Civilization: Discovering the Olmec.* New York: American Heritage.

———. **1977** *Mexico* (2nd ed.). New York: Praeger.

COHEN, MARK N. **1977** *The Food Crisis in Prehistory.* New Haven, Conn.: Yale University Press.

———. **1987** "The Significance of Long-Term Changes in Human Diet and Food Economy." In *Food and Evolution: Toward a Theory of Human Food Habits,* M. Harris and E. Ross, eds., pp. 261–283. Philadelphia: Temple University Press.

COHEN, MARK, AND G. ARMELAGOS (EDS.). **1984** *Paleopathology and the Origin of Agriculture.* New York: Academic Press.

COHEN, MYRON. **1976** *House United, House Divided.* New York: Columbia University Press.

COHEN, RONALD. **1978** "Ethnicity." *Annual Review of Anthropology,* 7:379–403.

COHEN, RONALD, AND ELMAN SERVICE (EDS.). **1978** *Origins of the State: The Anthropology of Political Evolution.* Philadelphia: Institute for the Study of Human Issues.

———. **1984a** "Warfare and State Foundation: Wars Make States and States Make Wars." In *Warfare, Culture and Environment,* Brian Ferguson, ed., pp. 329–355. Orlando, Fla.: Academic Press.

———. **1984b** "Approaches to Applied Anthropology." *Communication and Cognition* 17:135–162.

COHEN, YEHUDI. **1978** "The Disappearance of the Incest Taboo." *Human Nature* 1(7):72–78.

COHN, BERNARD. **1955** "Changing Status of a Depressed Caste." In *Village India: Studies in the Little Community,* M. Mariott, ed. *American Anthropological Memoirs* 83:55–77.

COHN, NORMAN. **1962** *The Pursuit of the Millennium.* New York: Harper & Row/Torchbooks.

COLE, DOUGLAS. **1991** "Underground Potlatch." *Natural History* (October):50–53.

COLE, JOHN, AND L. GODFREY. **1985** "The Paluxy River Footprint Mystery Solved." *Creation/Evolution* 15:5(1). Special Issue.

COLLIER, GEORGE, RENATO ROSALDO, AND JOHN WORTH (EDS.). **1982** *The Inca and Aztec States, 1400–1800: Anthropology and History.* New York: Academic Press.

COLLINS, GLENN. **1985** "Remarriage: Bigger Ready-Made Families." *The New York Times,* May 13, p. 15.

CONDOMINAS, GEORGE. **1977** *We Have Eaten the Forest.* New York: Hill and Wang.

CONRAD, NICHOLAS J. **1990** "Laminar Lithic Assemblages from the Last Interglacial Complex in Northwestern Europe." *Journal of Anthropological Research* 46:243–262.

CONWAY, FLO, AND JIM SIEGELMAN. **1978** *Snapping: America's Epidemic of Sudden Personality Change.* Philadelphia: Lippincott.

CONYERS, JOHN. **1978** "Unemployment Is Cruel and Unusual Punishment." Hearings before the House Subcommittee on Crime, House of Representatives. Ninety-fifth Congress, Serial No. 47, pp. 647–679. Washington, D.C.: U.S. Government Printing Office.

COOK, R. **1989** "Turnout Hits 64-Year Low in Presidential Race." *Congressional Quarterly Weekly Report* 47(January 21): 135–138.

COOK, S. F. **1972** *Prehistoric Demography.* Reading, Mass.: Addison-Wesley.

COON, CARLETON. **1965** *The Living Races of Man.* New York: Knopf.

CORDELL, LINDA. **1984** *Prehistory of the Southwest.* Orlando, Fla.: Academic Press.

COUNTS, DOROTHY. **1985** "Tamparonga: The Big Women of Kaliai (Papua New Guinea)." In *In Her Prime: A New View of Middle-Aged Women,* J. Brown and V. Kerns, eds., pp. 49–64. South Hadley, Mass.: Bergin and Garvey.

COWGILL, G. L. **1964** "The End of Classic Maya Culture." *Southwestern Journal of Anthropology* 20: 145–159.

CRAIG, DANIEL. **1979** "Immortality Through Kinship: The Vertical Transmission of Substance and Symbolic Estate." *American Anthropologist* 81:94–96.

CROSBY, ALFRED. **1986** *Ecological Imperialism: The Biological Expansion of Europe 900–1900.* New York: Cambridge University Press.

CROSSETTE, BARBARA. **1989** "India Studying the 'Accidental' Deaths of Hindu Wives." *The New York Times,* January 15, p. 4.

CULBERT, T. P. **1988** "The Collapse of Classic Maya Civilization." In *The Collapse of Ancient States and Civilizations,* Norman Yoffee and George Cowgill, eds., pp. 69–101. Tucson: University of Arizona Press.

CUMMINGS, R. C. **1978** "Agriculture Change in Vietnam's Floating Rice Region." *Human Organization* 37:235–245.

CURVIN, ROBERT, AND BRUCE PORTER. **1978** "The Myth of Blackout Looters." *The New York Times,* July 13, p. 21.

DAHL, ROBERT. **1981** *Democracy in the United States* (4th ed.). Boston: Houghton Mifflin.

DALTON, GEORGE. **1969** "Theoretical Issues in Economic Anthropology." *Current Anthropology* 10: 63–102.

———. **1972** "Peasantries in Anthropology and History." *Current Anthropology* 13:385–416.

———. **1974** "How Exactly Are Peasants Exploited?" *American Anthropology* 76:553–561.

D'ALTROY, TERRENCE. **1988** *Political and Domestic Economy in the Inca Empire.* New York: Columbia University Institute of Latin American and Iberian Studies.

D'ALTROY, T., AND T. K. EARLE. **1985** "Staple Finance, Wealth Finance, and Storage in the Inca Political Economy." *Current Anthropology* 26:187–206.

DANIEL, GLYNN. **1980** "Megalithic Monuments." *Scientific American* 243:78–91.

DAS GUPTA, MONICA. **1978** "Production Relations and Population: Rampur." *Journal of Development Studies* 14(4):177–185.

DAVIS, SHELTON. **1977** *Victims of the Miracle: Development and the Indians of Brazil.* New York: Cambridge University Press.

DEHAVENON, ANNA LOU. **1989–1990** "Charles Dickens Meets Franz Kafka: The Maladministration of New York City's Public Assistance Programs." *New York University Review of Law and Social Change* 17:231–254.

DE LAGUNA, FREDERICA. **1968** "Presidential Address: 1967." *American Anthropologist* 70:469–476.

DELORIA, VINE. **1969** *Custer Died for Your Sins.* London: Collier-Macmillan.

DELSON, ERIC. **1986** "Human Phylogeny Revised Again." *Nature* 322:496–497.

DE MOTT, BENJAMIN. **1980** "The Pro-Incest Lobby." *Psychology Today* (March):11–16.

———. **1990** *The Imperial Middle: Why Americans Can't Think Straight About Class.* New York: Morrow.

DENNELL, ROBIN. **1983** *European Economic Prehistory: A New Approach.* New York: Academic Press.

DENTAN, ROBERT. **1968** *The Semai: A Non-Violent People of Malaya.* New York: Holt, Rinehart and Winston.

D'ERRICO, FRANCESCO. **1989** "Paleolithic Lunar Calendars: A Case of Wishful Thinking?" *Current Anthropology* 30:117–118.

DESPRES, LEO. **1975** "Ethnicity and Resource Competition in Guyanese Society." In *Ethnicity and Resource Competition in Plural Societies,* L. Despres, ed., pp. 87–117. The Hague: Mouton.

DEVEREAUX, GEORGE. **1967** "A Typological Study of Abortion in 350 Primitive, Ancient, and Pre-Industrial Societies." In *Abortion in America,* H. Rosen, ed., pp. 95–152. Boston: Beacon Press.

DEVINE, JOHN. **1985** "The Versatility of Human Locomotion." *American Anthropologist* 87:550–570.

DE WAAL, F. **1983** *Chimpanzee Politics.* New York: Harper & Row.

DeWALT, BILLIE. **1984** "Mexico's Second Green Revolution: Food for Feed." *Mexican Studies/Estudios Mexicanos* 1:29–60.

———. **1985** "El Sorgo y la Crisis Alimentaria Mexicana." In *El Sorgo En Sistemas de Produccion En America Latina,* Paul Compton and Billie DeWalt, eds., pp. 153–166. Mexico City: Intsormil/ICRISAT/ILIMMYT.

DIAMOND, JARED. **1989** "Blood, Genes, and Malaria." *Natural History* (February):8–18.

DICKSON, D. BRUCE. **1981** "Further Simulations of Ancient Agriculture at Tikal, Guatemala." *American Antiquity* 46:922–928.

———. **1987** "Circumscription by an Anthropogenic Environmental Destruction: An Expansion of Carneiro's (1970) Theory of the Origin of the State." *American Antiquity* 52(4):709–716.

DILLEHAY, T. D. **1984** "A Late Ice Age Settlement in Southern Chile." *Scientific American* 25(4):547–550.

DILLEHAY, T. D., AND M. B. COLLINS. **1988** "Early Cultural Evidence from Monte Verde in Chile." *Nature* 332:150–152.

DILLINGHAM, BETH, AND B. ISAAC. **1975** "Defining Marriage Cross-culturally." In *Being Female: Reproduction, Power and Change,* D. Raphael, ed., pp. 55–63. The Hague: Mouton.

DINCAUZE, DENA. **1984** "An Archaeo-Logical Evaluation of the Case for Pre-Clovis Occupations." *Advances in World Archaeological Theory* 3:275–323.

DIVALE, WILLIAM. **1972** "Systematic Population Control in the Middle and Upper Paleolithic: Inferences Based on Contemporary Hunters and Gatherers." *World Archaeology* 4:221–243.

———. **1974** "Migration, External Warfare, and Matrilocal Residence." *Behavior Science Research* 9:75–133.

DIVALE, WILLIAM, AND MARVIN HARRIS. **1976** "Population, Warfare and the Male Supremacist Complex." *American Anthropologist* 78:521–538.

DIVALE, WILLIAM, M. HARRIS, AND D. WILLIAMS. **1978** "On the Misuse of Statistics: A Reply to Hirschfeld et al." *American Anthropologist* 80:379–386.

DJERASSI, CARL. **1990** "Fertility Awareness: Jet-Age Rhythm Method?" *Science* 248:1061–1062.

DJILAS, MILOVAN. **1957** *The New Class: An Analysis of the Communist System.* New York: Praeger.

DOBYNS, HENRY. **1972** "The Cornell-Peru Project: Experimental Intervention in Vicos." In *Contemporary Societies and Cultures of Latin America,* Dwight Heath, ed., pp. 201–210. New York: Random House.

———. **1983** *Their Numbers Became Thinned: Native American Population Dynamics in Eastern North America.* Knoxville: University of Tennessee Press.

DOLE, GERTRUDE. **1966** "Anarchy Without Chaos: Alternatives to Political Authority Among the Kui-Kuru." In *Political Authority,* M. J. Swartz, V. W. Turner, and A. Tuden, eds., pp. 73–88. Chicago: Aldine.

DOUGHTY, PAUL. **1987** "Against the Odds: Collaboration and Development at Vicos." In *Collaborative Research and Social Change: Applied Anthropology in Action,* Donald Stull and J. Schensul, eds., pp. 129–157. Boulder, Colo.: Westview Press.

DOWD, MAUREEN. **1983** "Many Women in Poll Equate Value of Job and Family Life." *The New York Times,* December 4, I-3.

DREW, ELIZABETH. **1983** *Politics and Money: The New Road to Corruption.* New York: Macmillan.

DUALEH, RAQIYA. **1982** *Sisters in Affliction: Circumcision and Infibulation of Women in Africa.* London: Zed Press.

DUMOND, DON. **1975** "The Limitation of Human Population: A Natural History." *Science* 1987:713–721.

DUMONT, LOUIS. **1970** *Homo Hierarchicus: The Caste System and Its Implications,* Mark Sainsbury, trans. Chicago: University of Chicago Press.

DURAN, DIEGO. **1964** *The Aztecs: The History of the Indies of New Spain.* New York: Orion Press.

EARLE, TIMOTHY. **1989** "The Evolution of Chiefdoms." *Current Anthropology* 30:84–88.

ECKHARDT, R. B. **1987** "On Hominid Brain Expansion." *Current Anthropology* 28(2):206–207.

EHRENBERG, MARGARET. **1989** *Women in Prehistory.* Norman: University of Oklahoma Press.

ELDREDGE, NILES, AND S. GOULD. **1972** "Punctuated Equilibria: An Alternative to Phyletic Gradualism." In *Models in Paleobiology,* J. M. Schopf, ed., pp. 82–115. San Francisco: Freeman, Cooper.

ELDREDGE, NILES, AND IAN TATTERSALL. **1982** *The Myths of Human Evolution.* New York: Columbia University Press.

ELIADE, M. **1958** *Birth and Rebirth: The Religious Meaning of Initiation in Human Culture.* New York: Harper & Row.

EMBER, CAROL, MELVIN EMBER, AND B. PASTERNACK. **1974** "On the Development of Unilineal Descent." *Journal of Anthropological Research* 30:69–94.

EMBER, MELVIN. **1982** "Statistical Evidence for an Ecological Explanation of Warfare." *American Anthropologist* 84:645–649.

EMBER, MELVIN, AND CAROL EMBER. **1971** "The Conditions Favoring Matrifocal Versus Patrifocal Residence." *American Anthropologist* 73:571–594.

———. **1988** "Fear of Disasters as an Engine of History: Resource Crisis, Warfare and Interpersonal Aggression." Paper read at the multidisciplinary conference on "What Is the Engine of History?" at Texas A&M University, October 27–29.

EMERSON, T. E., AND R. B. LEWIS, (EDS.). **1986** *Cahokia and Its Neighbors: Mississippian Cultural Variation in the American Midwest.* Urbana: University of Illinois Press.

EPSTEIN, T. SCARLETT. **1968** *Capitalism, Primitive and Modern: Some Aspects of Tolai Economic Growth.* East Lansing: Michigan State University Press.

ERRINGTON, FREDRICK, AND DEBORAH GEWERTZ. **1987** *Cultural Alternatives and a Feminist Anthropology: An Analysis of Culturally Constructed Gender Interest in Papua, New Guinea.* New York: Cambridge University Press.

ESPENSHADE, THOMAS. **1984** *Investing in Children: New Estimates of Parental Expenditures.* Washington, D.C.: Thomas J. Espenshade.

EVANS-PRITCHARD, E. E. **1940** *The Nuer, A Description of the Modes of Livelihood and Political Institutions of a Nilotic People.* Oxford: Clarendon Press.

———. **1970** "Sexual Inversion Among the Azande." *American Anthropologist* 72:1428–1433.

EXTER, THOMAS. **1991** "The Cost of Growing Up." *American Demographics* 13(8):59ff.

EYSENCK, H. J. **1973** *The Inequality of Man.* London: Temple Smith.

FAGAN, BRIAN M. **1984** *The Aztecs.* New York: Freeman.

———. **1989** *People of the Earth.* Glenview, Ill.: Scott, Foresman.

FALLERS, L. **1977** "Equality and Inequality in Human Societies." In *Horizons of Anthropology* (2nd ed.), S. Tax and L. Freeman, eds., pp. 257–268. Chicago: Aldine.

FARNSWORTH, PAUL, ET AL. **1985** "A Re-Evaluation of the Isotopic and Archaeological Reconstructions of Diet in the Tehuacan Valley." *American Antiquity* 50: 102–116.

FEI, HSIAO-T'UNG, AND CHANG CHIH-I. **1947** *Earthbound China: A Study of Rural Economy in Yunnan.* Chicago: University of Chicago Press.

FEIBEL, CRAIG S., FRANCIS H. BROWN, AND IAN McDOUGAL. **1989** "Stratigraphic Context of Fossil Hominids from the Omo Group Deposits: Northern Turkana Basin, Kenya and Ethiopia." *American Journal of Physical Anthropology* 78:595–622.

FEIL, DARYL. **1987** *The Evolution of Highland Papua New Guinea Societies.* New York: Cambridge University Press.

FEINMAN, G., AND J. NEITZEL. **1984** "Too Many Types: An Overview of Sedentary Prestate Societies in the Americas." In *Advances in Archaeological Method and Theory,* M. B. Schiffer, ed., pp. 39–102. New York: Academic Press.

FERACA, STEPHEN. **1984** Personal Communication. (See Pl. 97-403, 97th Congress, Second Session, 1982.)

FERGUSON, BRIAN R. **1979** "War and Redistribution on the Northwest Coast." Paper read at the meetings of the American Ethnological Association, Vancouver, B.C.

————. **1984** "Introduction: Studying War." In *Warfare, Culture and Environment,* Brian Ferguson, ed., pp. 1–61. Orlando, Fla.: Academic Press.

————. **1989a** "Game Wars? Ecology and Conflict in Amazonia." *Journal of Anthropological Research* 45:179–206.

————. **1989b** "Ecological Consequences of Amazonian Warfare." *Ethnology* 27:249–264.

FIALKOWSKI, KONRAD R. **1986** "A Mechanism for the Origin of the Human Brain: A Hypothesis." *Current Anthropology* 27:288–290.

————. **1990** "On the Origins of the Brain and Heat Stress: New Facts." *Current Anthropology* 31: 187–188.

FIRTH, RAYMOND. **1957** *We, the Tikopia: A Sociological Study of Kinship in Primitive Polynesia.* Boston: Beacon Press.

FITTKAU, E. J., AND H. KLINGE. **1973** "On Biomass and Trophic Structure of the Central Amazon Rain Forest Ecosystem." *Biotropica* 5:1–14.

FLADMARK, KNUT. **1986** "Getting One's Berings." *Natural History,* November, pp. 8ff.

FLANNERY, KENT. **1972** "The Origin of the Village as a Settlement Type in Mesoamerica and the Near East: A Comparative Study." In *Man, Settlement, and Urbanism,* P. J. Ucko, R. Tringham, and G. W. Dimbleby, eds., pp. 23–53. Cambridge, Mass.: Schenkman.

————. **1973** "The Origins of Agriculture." *Annual Review of Anthropology* 2:270–310.

————. **1982** *Maya Subsistence: Studies in Memory of Dennis E. Puleston.* New York: Academic Press.

FLEAGLE, JOHN G. **1988** *Primate Adaptation and Evolution.* New York: Academic Press.

FLEAGLE, J., ET AL. **1987** "Age of the Earliest African Anthropoids." *Science* 234:1247–1249.

FLEMING, STUART. **1977** *Dating in Archaeology: A Guide to Scientific Techniques.* New York: St. Martin's Press.

FOLBRE, NANCY. **1991** "Women on Their Own: Global Patterns of Female Headship." Washington, D.C.: International Center for Research on Women.

FORTES, MEYER. **1969** *Kinship and the Social Order: The Legacy of Lewis Henry Morgan.* Chicago: Aldine.

FORTUNE, REO. **1965** *Manus Religion.* Lincoln: University of Nebraska Press.

FOSTER, GEORGE M. **1967** *Tzintzuntzan: Mexican Peasants in a Changing World.* Boston: Little, Brown.

————. **1974** "Limited Good or Limited Goods: Observations on Acheson." *American Anthropologist* 76: 53–57.

FOSTER, GEORGE, AND BARBARA ANDERSON. **1978** *Medical Anthropology.* New York: Wiley.

FOUTS, ROGER S., AND DEBORAH H. FOUTS. **1985** "Signs of Conversation in Chimpanzees." Paper given at meeting of AAAS, Los Angeles, May 28–31.

————. **1989** "Loulis in Conversation with the Cross-Fostered Chimpanzees." In *Teaching Sign Language to Chimpanzees,* R. Allen Gardner, Beatrix T. Gardner, and Thomas E. Van Cantfort, eds., 293–307. Albany: State University of New York Press.

FOWLER, WILLIAM R., JR. **1984** "Late Preclassic Mortuary Patterns and Evidence for Human Sarifice at Chalchuapa, El Salvador." *American Antiquity* 49(3):603–618.

FRANKE, RICHARD W. **1973** *The Green Revolution in a a Javanese Village.* Ph.D. dissertation, Harvard University.

————. **1974** "Miracle Seeds and Shattered Dreams." *Natural History* 83(1):10ff.

FRAYSER, SUZANNE. **1985** *Varieties of Sexual Experience: An Anthropological Perspective on Human Sexuality.* New Haven, Conn.: HRAF.

FRAZER, JAMES. **1911–1915** *The Golden Bough* (3rd ed.). London: Macmillan.

FREDRICK, J., AND P. ADELSTEIN. **1973** "Influence of Pregnancy Spacing on Outcome of Pregnancy." *British Medical Journal* 4:753–756.

FREEDMAN, ROBERT. **1977** "Nutritional Anthropology: An Overview." In *Nutrition and Anthropology in Action,* Thomas Fitzgerald, ed., pp. 1–23. Amsterdam: Van Gorcum.

FRIED, MORTON, H. **1967** *The Evolution of Political Society: An Essay in Political Anthropology.* New York: Random House.

————. **1968** "The Need to End the Pseudoscientific Investigation of Race." In *Science and the Concept of Race,* M. Mead et al., eds., pp. 122-131. New York: Columbia University Press.

————. **1972** *The Study of Anthropology.* New York: Crowell.

————. **1975** *The Notion of Tribe.* Menlo Park, Calif.: Cummings.

————. **1978** "The State, the Chicken, and the Egg; or What Came First?" In *Origins of the State,* Ronald Cohen and Elman Service, eds., pp. 35–47. Philadelphia: Institute for the Study of Human Issues.

FRIEDEL, D. **1986** "On the Mayan Collapse." In *Peer Polity Interaction and Socio-Political Change,* C. Renfrew and J. Cherry, eds. New York: Cambridge University Press.

FRISANCHO, A. R., J. MATOS, AND P. FLEGEL. **1983** "Maternal Nutritional Status and Adolescent Pregnancy Outcome." *American Journal of Clinical Nutrition* 38:739–746.

FRISCH, R. **1984** "Body Fat, Puberty and Fertility." *Science* 199:22–30.

FRISON, GEORGE C. **1989** "Experimental Use of Clovis Weaponry and Tools on African Elephants." *American Antiquity* 54(4):766–784.

FROMM, ERICH, AND M. MACCOBY. **1970** *A Mexican Village: A Sociopsychoanalytic Study.* Englewood Cliffs, N.J.: Prentice-Hall.

FURSTENBERG, FRANK, THEODORE HERSHBERG, AND JOHN MEDELL. **1975** "The Origin of the Female-Headed Black Family: The Impact of the Urban Experience." *Journal of Interdisciplinary History* 6(2): 211–233.

GAJDUSEK, D. C. **1977** "Unconventional Viruses and the Origin and Disappearance of Kuru." *Science* 197:943–960.

GALATY, JOHN G., AND DOUGLAS L. JOHNSON. **1990** *The World of Pastoralism: Herding Systems in Comparative Perspective.* London: Belhaven Press.

GALBRAITH, JOHN K. **1958** *The Affluent Society.* New York: Houghton Mifflin.

———. **1967** *The New Industrial State.* Boston: Houghton Mifflin.

GALDIKAS-BRINDAMOUR, B. **1975** "Orangutans, Indonesia's 'People of the Forest.'" *National Geographic* 184:444–473.

GAMBLE, CLIVE. **1986** *The Paleolithic Settlement of Europe.* New York: Cambridge University Press.

GANDHI, MOHANDAS K. **1954** *How to Serve the Cow.* Ahmedabad: Navajivan Publishing House.

GARDNER, B. T., AND R. A. GARDNER. **1971** "Two-Way Communication with a Chimpanzee." In *Behavior of Non-Human Primates,* A. Schrier and F. Stollnitz, eds., vol. 4, pp. 117–184. New York: Academic Press.

———. **1975** "Early Signs of Language in Child and Chimpanzee." *Science* 187:752–753.

GARGETT, R. **1989a** "Grave Shortcomings: The Evidence for Neandertal Burial." *Current Anthropology* 30:326–330.

———. **1989b** "On Neanderthal Burials: Reply." *Current Anthropology* 30:326–330.

GARON, SHELDON M. **1987** *The State and Labor in Modern Japan.* Berkeley: University of California Press.

GAULIN, STEPHEN, AND JAMES S. BOSTER. **1990** "Dowery as Female Competition." *American Anthropologist* 92:994–1005.

GAY, JUDITH. **1986** "'Mummies and Babies' and Friends and Lovers in Lesotho." In *Anthropology and Homosexual Behavior,* Evelyn Blackwood, ed., pp. 97–116. New York: Haworth Press.

GIBBONS, ANN. **1991** "Déjà Vu All Over Again: Chimp Language Wars." *Science* 251:1561–1562.

———. **1992** "Neandertal Language Debate." *Science* 256:33–34.

GILBERT, DENNIS A. **1988** *Compendium of American Public Opinion.* New York: Facts on File Publications.

GILDER, GEORGE. **1981** *Wealth and Poverty.* New York: Basic Books.

GILMORE, DAVID. **1990** *Manhood in the Making: Cultural Concepts of Masculinity.* New Haven, Conn.: Yale University Press.

GLAESER, BERNARD (ED.). **1987** *The Green Revolution Revisited.* London: Allen and Unwin.

GLASER, DANYA, AND S. FROSH. **1988** *Child and Sexual Abuse.* Chicago: Dorsey Press.

GLASSER, IRA. **1989** "How Long America?" *Civil Liberties,* Summer, pp. 12ff.

GLASSOW, MICHAEL. **1978** "The Concept of Carrying Capacity in the Study of Social Process." In *Advances in Archaeological Theory and Method,* Michael Schiffler, ed., pp. 31–48. New York: Academic Press.

GLENN, EVELYN, AND ROSALYN FELDBURG. **1977** "Degraded and Deskilled: The Proletarianization of Clerical Work." *Social Problems* 25:52–64.

GLOVER, G., ET AL. **1984** "Making Quality Count: Boca Raton's Approach to Quality Assurance." *The Cornell Hotel and Restaurant Administration Quarterly,* November, pp. 39–45.

GLUCKMAN, MAX. **1955** *Custom and Conflict in Africa.* Oxford: Blackwell.

GODFREY, LAURIE. **1981** "The Flood of Anti-evolutionism." *Natural History,* June, pp. 4–10.

GODFREY, L., AND J. COLE. **1979** "Biological Analogy, Diffusionism, and Archaeology." *American Anthropologist* 81:37–45.

GONZALEZ, NANCY L. **1970** "Towards a Definition of Matrilocality." In *Afro-American Anthropology: Contemporary Perspectives,* N. E. Whitten and J. F. Szwed, eds., pp. 231–243. New York: Free Press.

GOOD, KENNETH. **1987** "Limiting Factors in Amazonian Ecology." In *Food and Evolution: Toward a Theory of Human Food Habits,* M. Harris and E. Ross, eds., pp. 407–426. Philadelphia: Temple University Press.

———. **1989** *Yanomami Hunting Patterns: Trekking and Garden Relocation as an Adaptation to Game Availability in Amazonia, Venuzuela.* Ph.D. dissertation, the University of Florida.

GOODALE, JANE. **1971** *Tiwi Wives.* Seattle: University of Washington Press.

GOODALL, JANE. See VAN LAWICK-GOODALL, JANE.

GOODMAN, M., ET AL. **1990** "Primate Evolution at the DNA Level and a Classification of Hominoids." *Journal of Molecular Evolution* 30:260–266.

GOODY, JACK. **1976** *Production and Reproduction.* New York: Cambridge University Press.

GORDON, ANDREW. **1987** "The Right to Work in Japan: Labor and State in the Depression." *Social Research* 54(2):247–272.

GORMAN, CHESTER F. **1969** "Hoabinhian: A Pebble Tool Complex With Early Plant Associations in Southeast Asia." *Science* 163:671–673.

———. **1978** "A Priori Models and Thai History: A Reconsideration of the Beginnings of Agriculture in Southeastern Asia." In *Origins of Agriculture,* C. Reed, ed., pp. 321–355. The Hague: Mouton.

GOUGH, E. KATHLEEN. **1959** "Criterion of Caste Ranking in South India." *Man in India* 39:115–126.

———. **1968** "The Nayars and the Definition of Marriage." In *Marriage Family and Residence,* Paul Bohannon and J. Middleton, eds., pp. 49–71. Garden City, N.Y.: Natural History Press.

GOULD, RICHARD. **1982** "To Have and Not to Have: The Ecology of Sharing Among Hunter-Gatherers." In *Resource Managers: North American and Australian Hunter-Gatherers,* Nancy Williams and Eugene Hunn, eds., pp. 69–91. Boulder, Colo.: Westview Press.

GOULD, R., D. KOSTER, AND A. SONTZ. **1971** "The Lithic Assemblages of the Western Desert of Aborigines of Australia." *American Antiquity* 36:149–169.

GRAMBY, RICHARD. **1977** "Deerskins and Hunting Territories: Competition for a Scarce Resource of the Northeastern Woodlands." *American Antiquity* 42:601–605.

GRAY, PATRICK, AND LINA WOLFE. **1980** "Height and Sexual Dimorphism and Stature Among Human Societies." *American Journal of Physical Anthropology* 53: 441–456.

GREENBERG, JOSEPH. **1968** *Anthropological Linguistics: An Introduction.* New York: Random House.

GREENBERG, JOSEPH C., CHRISTY TURNER, AND S. ZEGURA. **1986** "The Settlement of the Americas: A Comparison of the Linguistic, Dental and Genetic Evidence." *Current Anthropology* 27:477–497.

GREGERSON, EDGAR. **1982** *Sexual Practices: The Story of Human Sexuality.* London: Mitchell Beazley.

GREGOR, THOMAS. **1969** *Social Relations in a Small Society: A Study of the Mehinacu Indians of Central Brazil.* Ph.D. dissertation, Columbia University.

———. **1985** *Anxious Pleasure: The Sexual Lives of an Amazonian Peoples.* Chicago: University of Chicago Press.

GRINE, FREDERICK E. **1988** *Evolutionary History of the "Robust" Australopithecines.* New York: Aldine de Gruyter.

GROSS, DANIEL R. **1975** "Protein Capture and Cultural Development in the Amazon Basin." *American Anthropologist* 77:526–549.

———. **1981** "Reply to Beckerman" mss.

———. **1984** "Time Allocation: A Tool for the Study of Cultural Behavior." *Annual Review of Anthropology* 13:519–558.

GRUENBAUM, ELLEN. **1988** "Reproductive Ritual and Social Reproduction: Female Circumcision and the Subordination of Women in the Sudan." In *Economy and Class in Sudan*, Norman O'Neil and Jay O'Brien, eds., pp. 308–322. Brookfield, Vt.: Gower.

GUIDON, NIEDE, AND G. DELIBRIAS. **1986** "Carbon 14 Dates Point to Man in the Americas 32,000 Years Ago." *Nature* 321:769–771.

GUMBEL, PETER. **1988** "Down on the Farm: Soviets Try Once More to Straighten Out Old Agricultural Mess." *The Wall Street Journal,* December 2. Orlando, Fla.: Dow Jones & Company.

GUTHRIE, R. D. **1983** "Osseus Projectile Points: Biological Consideration Affecting Raw Materials Selection and Design Among Paleolithic and Paleoindian Peoples." In *Animals and Archaeology: Hunters and Their Prey,* J. Clutton-Brock and C. Grigson, eds., pp. 273–194. Oxford: BAR International Series, No. 163.

HAAS, JONATHAN. **1982** *The Evolution of the Prehistoric State.* New York: Columbia University Press.

HACKER, ANDREW. **1989** "Affirmative Action: The New Look." *The New York Review of Books,* October 12, pp. 63–68.

———. **1992** *Two Nations: Black and White, Separate, Hostile, Unequal.* New York: Scribner's.

HADLEY, ARTHUR. **1978** *The Empty Polling Booth.* Englewood Cliffs, N.J.: Prentice-Hall.

HAHN, J. **1972** "Aurignacian Signs, Pendants, and Art Objects in Central and Eastern Europe." *World Archaeology* 3:252–266.

HALL, CALVIN, AND G. LINDZEY. **1967** "Freud's Psychoanalytic Theory of Personality." In *Personalities and Cultures: Readings in Psychological Anthropology*, Robert Hunt, ed., pp. 3–29. Garden City, N.Y.: Natural History Press.

HAMBLIN, DORA JANE. **1973** *The First Cities.* New York: Time Life.

HAMLIN, R. L., AND B. L. PITCHER. **1980** "The Classic Maya Collapse: Testing the Class-Conflict Model." *American Antiquity* 45:246–247.

HAMILTON, SAHNI, B. POPKIN, AND D. SPICE. **1984** *Women and Nutrition in Third World Countries.* South Hadley, Mass.: Bergin Garvey.

HAMILTON, WILLIAM. **1987** "Omnivorous Primate Diets and Human Over-Consumption of Meat." In *Food and Evolution: Toward a Theory of Human Food Habits,* M. Harris and E. Ross, eds., pp. 117-132. Philadelphia: Temple University Press.

HAMMOND, NORMAN (ED.). **1978** *Social Processes in Maya Prehistory.* New York: Academic Press.

HAMMOND, NORMAN, AND CHARLES MIKSICEK. **1981** "Ecology and Economy of a Formative Maya Site at Cuello, Belize." *Journal of Field Archaeology* 8:259–269.

HANDWERKER, W. P. **1983** "The First Demographic Transition: An Analysis of Subsistence Choices and Reproductive Consequences." *American Anthropologist* 85:5–27.

HANSEN, RICHARD. **1991** "The Road to Nakbe." *Natural History* 5:8–13.

HARDING, ROBERT. **1975** "Meat Eating and Hunting in Baboons." In *Socioecology and Psychology of Primates,* R. H. Tuttle, ed., pp. 245–257. The Hague: Mouton.

HARLAN, JACK. **1978** "Origins of Cereal Argiculture in the Old World." In *Origins of Agriculture,* C. Reed, ed., pp. 357–383. The Hague: Mouton.

HARLOW, HARRY, M. DODSWORTH, AND A. ARLING. **1966** "Maternal Behavior of Rhesus Monkeys Deprived of Mothering and Peer Association in Infancy." *Proceedings of the American Philosophical Society* 110:58–66.

HARNER, MICHAEL J. **1970** "Population Pressure and the Social Evolution of Agriculturalists." *Southwestern Journal of Anthropology* 26:67–86.

————. **1972** *The Jívaro: People of the Sacred Waterfalls.* Garden City, N.Y.: Natural History Press.

————. **1977** "The Ecological Basis for Aztec Sacrifice." *American Ethnologist* 4:117–135.

————. **1982** *The Way of the Shaman: A Guide to Power and Healing.* New York: Bantam.

HARRINGTON, CHARLES, AND J. WHITING. **1972** "Socialization Process and Personality." In *Psychological Anthropology,* Francis Hsu, ed., pp. 469–507. Cambridge, Mass.: Schenkman.

HARRINGTON, MICHAEL. **1980** *Decade of Decision.* New York: Simon & Schuster.

HARRIS, DAVID. **1976** "Traditional System of Plant Food Production and the Organization of Agriculture in West Africa." In *Origins of African Plant Domestication,* J. Harlan, J. de Wet, and A. Stemler, eds., pp. 311–356. The Hague: Mouton.

————. **1987** "Aboriginal Subsistence in a Tropical Rain Forest Environment: Food Procurement, Cannibalism and Population Regulation in Northeastern Australia." In *Food and Evolution: Toward a Theory of Human Food Habits,* Marvin Harris and Eric Ross, eds., pp. 357–385. Philadelphia: Temple University Press.

HARRIS, DAVID AND G. HILLMAN (EDS.). **1989** *Foraging and Farming: Evolution of Plant Domestication.* London: Unwin and Hyman.

HARRIS, J. W. K. **1983** "Cultural Beginnings: Plio-Pleistocene Archaeological Occurrences from the Afar, Ethiopia." In *African Archaeological Review,* N. David, ed., pp. 3–31. Cambridge: Cambridge University Press.

HARRIS, MARVIN. **1970** "Referential Ambiguity in the Calculus of Brazilian Racial Identity." *Southwestern Journal of Anthropology.* 26:1–14.

————. **1971** *Culture, Man, and Nature* (1st ed.). New York: Crowell.

————. **1974** *Cows, Wars, Pigs, and Witches: The Riddles of Culture.* New York: Random House.

————. **1977** *Cannibals and Kings: The Origins of Cultures.* New York: Random House.

————. **1979a** "Comments on Simoons' Questions in the Sacred Cow Controversy." *Current Anthropology* 20:479–482.

————. **1979b** "Reply to Sahlins." *The New York Review of Books,* June 28, pp. 52–53.

————. **1981** *America Now: The Anthropology of a Changing Culture.* New York: Simon & Schuster.

————. **1984** "Animal Capture and Yanomamö Warfare: Retrospective and New Evidence." *Journal of Anthropological Research* 40:183–201.

————. **1985** *Good to Eat: Riddles of Food and Culture.* New York: Simon & Schuster.

————. **1989** *Our Kind: Who We Are, Where We Came From, Where We Are Going.* New York: Harper & Row.

HARRIS, MARVIN, AND ERIC ROSS (EDS.). **1987a** *Food and Evolution: Toward a Theory of Human Food Habits.* Philadelphia: Temple University Press.

————. **1987b** *Death, Sex, and Fertility.* New York: Columbia University Press.

HARRISON, GAIL. **1975** "Primary Adult Lactase Deficiency: A Problem in Anthropological Genetics." *American Anthropologist* 77:812–835.

HARRISON, PETER. **1982** "Subsistence and Society in Eastern Yucatán." In *Maya Subsistence: Studies in Memory of Dennis E. Puleston,* Kent Flannery, ed., pp. 119–128. New York: Academic Press.

HARRISON, PETER, AND B. L. TURNER (EDS.). **1978** *Prehispanic Maya Agriculture.* Albuquerque: University of New Mexico Press.

HARRISON, R. J., AND W. MONTAGNA. **1969** *Man.* Englewood Cliffs, N.J.: Prentice-Hall.

HART, C. W. M., AND A. R. PILLING. **1960** *The Tiwi of North Australia.* New York: Holt, Rhinehart and Winston.

HART, KEITH. **1985** "The Social Anthropology of West Africa." *Annual Review of Anthropology* 14:243–272.

HARTUNG, JOHN. **1985** Review of *Incest: A Biosocial View,* by J. Shepher. *American Journal of Physical Anthropology* 67:169–171.

HASEGAWA, TOSHIKAZU, ET AL. **1983** "New Evidence of Scavenging Behavior in Wild Chimpanzees." *Current Anthropology* 24:231–232.

HASSAN, FEKRI. **1978** "Demographic Archaeology." In *Advances in Archaeological Method and Theory,* Michael Schiffer, ed., pp. 49–103. New York: Academic Press.

————. **1981** *Demographic Archaeology.* New York: Academic Press.

HAUGEN, EINAR. **1977** "Linguistic Relativity: Myths and Methods." In *Language and Thought: Anthropological Issues,* W. C. McCormack and S. A. Worms, eds., pp. 11–28. The Hague: Mouton.

HAVILAND, WILLIAM. **1970** "Tikal, Guatemala and Mesoamerican Urbanism." *World Archaeology* 2:186–198.

HAWKES, KRISTEN, KIM HILL, AND J. O'CONNELL. **1982** "Why Hunters Gather: Optimal Foraging and the Aché of Eastern Paraguay." *American Ethnologist* 9:379–398.

HAYDEN, BRIAN. **1987** "Alliances and Ritual Ecstasy: Human Responses to Resource Stress." *Journal for the Scientific Study of Religion* 26:81–91.

HAYDEN, BRIAN, M. DEAL, A. CANNON, AND J. CASEY. **1986** "Ecological Determinants of Women's Status Among Hunter/Gatherers." *Human Evolution* 1(5):449–474.

HAYGHE, L. **1984** "Working Mothers Reach Record Numbers in 1984." Bureau of Labor Statistics, *Monthly Labor Review,* December, p. 31.

HAYS, TERENCE E. **1988** " 'Myths of Matriarchy' and the Sacred Flute Complex of the Papua New Guinea Highlands." In *Myths of Matriarchy Reconsidered,* Deborah Gewertz, ed., pp. 98–120. Sydney, Australia: University of Sydney.

HEADLAND, THOMAS N., KENNETH L. PIKE, AND MARVIN HARRIS. **1990** *Emics and Etics: The Insider/Outsider Debate.* Newbury Park, Calif.: Sage.

HEDGES, S. B., ET AL. **1991** "Technical Comment: Human Origins and Analysis of Mitochondrial DNA Sequences." *Science* 255:737–739.

HEIDER, KARL G. **1969** "Visiting Trading Institutions." *American Anthropologist* 71:462–471.

———. **1972** *The Dani of West Irian.* Reading, Mass.: Addison-Wesley.

HENDERSON, JOHN. **1981** *The World of the Ancient Maya.* Ithaca, N.Y.: Cornell University Press.

HENRY, DONALD. **1985** "Preagricultural Sedentism: The Natufian Example." In *Prehistoric Hunter-Gatherers: The Emergence of Cultural Complexity,* D. Price and J. Brown, eds., pp. 365–381. New York: Academic Press.

HERBERS, J. **1985** "Non-Relatives and Solitary People Make Up Half of New Households." *The New York Times,* November 20, p. 1.

HERDT, GILBERT. **1984a** "Semen Transactions in Sambia Cultures." In *Ritualized Homosexuality in Melanesia,* Gilbert Herdt, ed., pp. 167–210. Berkeley: University of California Press.

———. **1984b** "Ritualized Homosexuality Behavior in the Male Cults of Melanesia 1862–1983: An Introduction." In *Ritualized Homosexuality in Melanesia,* Gilbert Herdt, ed., pp. 1–81. Berkeley: University of California Press.

———. **1987** *The Sambia: Ritual and Custom in New Guinea.* New York: Holt, Rinehart and Winston.

HERMAN, EDWARD S., AND NOAM CHOMSKY. **1988** *Manufacturing Consent: The Political Economy of the Mass Media.* New York: Pantheon Books.

HERRE, WOLF, AND M. ROHRS. **1978** "Zoological Considerations in the Origins of Farming and Domestication." In *Origins of Agriculture,* C. Reed, ed., pp. 245–279. The Hague: Mouton.

HERRNSTEIN, R. J. **1973** *I.Q. in the Meritocracy.* Boston: Little, Brown.

HERSKOVITZ, M. **1938** *The Dahomey.* New York: J. J. Augustin.

HERTZLER, JOYCE O. **1965** *A Sociology of Language.* New York: Random House.

HEWLETT, BARRY S. **1991** "Demography and Childcare in Preindustrial Societies." *Journal of Anthropological Research* 47(1):1–37.

HICKS, DAVID. **1976** *Tetum Ghosts and Kin.* Palo Alto, Calif.: Mayfield.

HIERNAUX, JEAN. **1969** *Egalité ou Inegalité des Races?* Paris: Hachette.

HIGHAM, CHARLES. **1988** *The Archaeology of Mainland Southeast Asia.* Cambridge: Cambridge University Press.

HILL, JANE. **1978** "Apes and Language." *Annual Review of Anthropology* 7:89–112.

HIRSCH, JERRY. **1981** "To Unfrock the Charlatans." *Sage Race Relations Abstracts* 6:1–67.

HIRSCHFELD, LAWRENCE, J. HOWE, AND B. LEVIN. **1978** "Warfare, Infanticide and Statistical Inference: A Comment on Divale and Harris." *American Anthropologist* 80:110–115.

HO, PING. **1975** *The Cradle of the East: An Inquiry into the Indigenous Origins of Techniques and Ideas of Neolithic and Early Historic China, 5000–1000 B.C.* Chicago: University of Chicago Press.

HOCKETT, CHARLES, AND R. ASCHER. **1964** "The Human Revolution." *Current Anthropology* 5:135–147.

HOGBIN, H. IAN. **1964** *Guadacanal Society: The Koaka Speakers.* New York: Holt, Rinehart and Winston.

HOLE, FRANK. **1984** "A Reassessment of the Neolithic Revolution." *Paleorient* 10:49–60.

———. **1987** "Chronologies in the Iranian Neolithic." In *Chronologies du Proche Orient,* Olivier Aurenche, et al., eds., pp. 353–379. B.A.R. International Series, No. 379. Oxford: British Archaeological Reports.

HOMMON, ROBERT. **1986** "Social Evolution in Ancient Hawai'i." In *Island Societies: Archaeological Approaches to Evolution and Transformation,* Patrick Kirch, ed., pp. 55–69. New York: Cambridge University Press.

HOPKINS, KEITH. **1980** "Brother–Sister Marriage in Ancient Egypt." *Comparative Studies in Society and History* 22:303–354.

HOWE, W., AND WILLIAM PARKS. **1989** "Labor Market Completes Sixth Year of Expansion in 1988." *Monthly Labor Review* 112:3–12.

HUBLIN, J. J. **1985** "Human Fossils from the North African Middle Pleistocene and the Origin of *Homo sapiens.*" In *Ancestors: The Hard Evidence,* Eric Delson, ed., pp. 283–288. New York: Alan R. Liss.

HULSE, FREDERICK. **1973** *Human Species: An Introduction to Physical Anthropology* (2nd ed.). New York: Random House.

HUNN, EUGENE. **1982** "Did the Aztec Lack Potential Animal Domesticates?" *American Ethnologist* 9: 578–579.

HUNT, ROBERT. **1988** "Size and Structure of Authority in Canal Irrigation Systems." *Journal of Anthropological Research* 44:335–355.

HUSAIN, TARIQ. **1976** "The Use of Anthropologists in Project Appraisal by the World Bank." In *Development from Below: Anthropologists and Development Situations,* David Pitt, ed., pp. 71–81. The Hague: Mouton.

HUTTERER, KARL. **1976** "An Evolutionary Approach to the Southeast Asian Cultural Sequence." *Current Anthropology* 17:221–242.

HYMES, DELL. **1971** "Introduction." In *The Origin and Diversification of Language,* M. Swadesh and J. F. Sherzer, eds. Chicago: Aldine.

HYSLOP, JOHN. **1984** *The Inka Road System.* Orlando, Fla.: Academic Press.

IRVING, WILLIAM. **1985** "Contact and Chronology of Early Man in the Americas." *Annual Review of Anthropology* 14:529–555.

IRWIN, GEOFFREY. **1983** "Chieftanship, Kula and Trade in Massim Prehistory." In *The Kula: New Perspectives on Massim Exchange*, J. Leach and E. Leach, eds., pp. 29–72. Cambridge: Cambridge University Press.

ISAAC, BARRY. **1988** "Introduction." In *Prehistoric Economies of the Pacific Northwest Coast*, Barry Isaac, ed., pp. 1–16. Greenwich, Conn.: JAI Press.

ISAAC, G., AND D. CRADER. **1981** "To What Extent Were Early Hominids Carnivorous? An Archaeological Perspective." In *Omnivorous Primates: Gathering and Hunting in Human Evolution*, R. Harding and G. Teleki, eds., pp. 37–103. New York: Columbia University Press.

ISBELL, W., AND K. SCHREIBER. **1978** "Was Huari a State?" *American Antiquity* 43:372–389.

ITANI, JUN'ICHIRO. **1961** "The Society of Japanese Monkeys." *Japan Quarterly* 8:421–430.

ITANI JUN'ICHIRO, AND A. NISHIMURA. **1973** "The Study of Infra-Human Culture in Japan." In *Precultural Primate Behavior*, E. W. Menzell, ed., pp. 26–50. Basel: S. Karjer.

JACOBS, EVA, S. SHIPP, AND G. BROWN. **1989** "Families of Working Wives Spending More on Services and Nondurables." *Monthly Labor Review* 117(February):15–23.

JACOBS, KENNETH. **1985** "Climate and the Hominid Post-Cranial Skeleton in Wurm and Early Holocene Europe." *Current Anthropology* 26:512–514.

JACOBS, SUE. **1978** "Top-down Planning: Analysis of Obstacles to Community Development in an Economically Poor Region of the Southwestern United States." *Human Organization* 37(3):246–256.

JACOBS, SUE, AND C. ROBERTS. **1989** "Sex, Sexuality, Gender, and Gender Variance." In *Gender and Anthropology*, Sandra Morgan, ed., pp. 438–462. Washington, D.C.: American Anthropological Association.

JACOBSON, JEROME. **1979** "Recent Developments in South Asian Prehistory and Protohistory." *Annual Review of Anthropology* 8:467–502.

JAMES, STEVEN R. **1989** "Hominid Use of Fire in the Lower and Middle Pleistocene: A Review of the Evidence." *Current Anthropology* 31:1–26.

JANZEN, DANIEL. **1973** "Tropical Agroecosystems." *Science* 182:1212–1219.

JELLIFFE, D. B., AND E. F. JELLIFFE. **1978** "The Volume and Composition of Human Milk in Poorly Nourished Communities: A Review." *American Journal of Clinical Nutrition* 31:492–515.

JENNINGS, JESSE. **1974** *Prehistory of North America* (2nd ed.). New York: McGraw-Hill.

———. **1983** *Ancient South America*. San Francisco: Freeman.

JENSEN, ARTHUR. **1969** "How Much Can We Boost I.Q. and Scholastic Achievement?" *Harvard Educational Review* 29:1–123.

JENSEN, NEAL. **1978** "Limits to Growth in World Food Production." *Science* 201:317–320.

JERISON, H. J. **1973** *Evolution of the Brain and Intelligence*. New York: Academic Press.

JIOBU, ROBERT. **1988** *Ethnicity and Assimilation*. Albany: State University of New York Press.

JOANS, BARBARA. **1984** "Problems in Pocatello in Linguistic Misunderstanding." *Practicing Anthropology* 6(3,4):6ff.

JOB, BARBARA COTTMAN. **1980** "Employment and Pay Trends in the Retail Trade Industry." *Monthly Labor Review*, March, pp. 40–43.

JOCHIM, MICHAEL. **1983** "Paleolithic Cave Art in Ecological Perspective." In *Hunter-Gatherers' Economy in Prehistory: A European Perspective*, G. Bailey, ed., pp. 212–219. New York: Cambridge University Press.

JOHANSON, DONALD, AND MAITLAND EDEY. **1981** *Lucy: The Beginnings of Humankind*. New York: Warner.

JOHANSON, DONALD, AND JAMES SHREEVE. **1989** *Lucy's Child: The Discovery of a Human Ancestor*. New York: Morrow.

JOHANSON, DONALD, ET AL. **1987** "New Partial Skeleton of *Homo habilis* from Olduvai Gorge, Tanzania." *Nature* 327:205–209.

JOHNSON, ALLEN W. **1975** "Time Allocation in a Machiguenga Community." *Ethnology* 14:301–310.

JOHNSON, ALLEN, AND TIMOTHY EARLE. **1987** *The Evolution of Human Societies from Foraging Groups to Agrarian States*. Stanford, Calif.: Stanford University Press.

JONAITIS, ALDONA. **1991** *Chiefly Feasts: The Enduring Kwakiutl Potlatch*. Seattle: University of Washington Press.

JONES, DELMOS. **1976** "Applied Anthropology and the Application of Anthropological Knowledge." *Human Organization* 35:221-229.

JONES, RHYS. **1989** "East of Wallace's Line: Issues and Problems in the Colonization of the Australian Continent." In *The Human Revolution*, Paul Mellars and Chris Stringer, eds., pp. 743–782. Rutgers, N.J.: Princeton University Press.

JORGENSEN, JOSEPH. **1971** "On Ethics and Anthropology." *Current Anthropology* 12(3):321–334.

JOSEPH, SUAD. **1978** "Muslim-Christian Conflicts in Lebanon: A Perspective on the Evolution of Sectarianism." In *Muslim-Christian Conflicts: Economic, Political and Social Origins*, S. Joseph and B. Pillsbury, eds., pp. 63–98. Boulder, Colo.: Westview Press.

JOSEPHIDES, LISETTE. **1985** *The Production of Inequality: Gender and Exchange Among the Kewa*. New York: Tavistock.

JOSEPHY, ALVIN. **1982** *Now That the Buffalo's Gone: A Study of Today's American Indians*. New York: Knopf.

JUNOD, HENRI. **1912** *Life of a South African Tribe*. Neuchatel, Switz.: Imprimerie Attinger Frères.

KABERRY, PHYLLIS, **1970(1939)** *Aboriginal Woman, Sacred and Profane.* London: Routledge.

KAEPPLER, ADRIENNE. **1978** "Dance in Anthropological Perspective." *Annual Review of Anthropology* 7:31–49.

KAMIN, L. J. **1974** *The Science and Politics of I.Q.* New York: Halstead Press.

KANG, ELIZABETH. **1979** "Exogamy and Peace Relations of Social Units: A Cross-Cultural Test." *Ethnology* 18:85–99.

KANO, TAKAYOSHI. **1990** "The Bonobos' Peaceable Kingdom." *Natural History* 11:62–71.

KAPLAN, L., T. LYNCH, AND C. SMITH. **1973** "Early Cultivated Beans *(Phaseolus vulgaris)* from an Intermontane Peruvian Valley." *Science* 179:76–77.

KARODA, S. **1984** "Interaction Over Food Among Pygmy Chimpanzees." In *The Pygmy Chimpanzee,* R. L. Susman, ed., pp. 301–324. New York: Plenum.

KATZ, PHYLLIS, AND S. A. TAYLOR. **1988** *Eliminating Racism: Profiles in a Controversy.* New York: Plenum.

KATZ, SOLOMON, AND MARY VOIGT. **1986** "Bread and Beer: The Early Use of Cereals in the Human Diet." *Expedition* 28:23–34.

KAY, PAUL, AND W. KEMPTON. **1984** "What Is the Sapir–Whorf Hypothesis?" *American Anthropologist* 86:65–79.

KEEGAN, WILLIAM F., AND MORGAN D. MACLACHLAN. **1989** "The Evolution of Avunculocal Chiefdoms: A Reconstruction of Taino Kinship and Politics." *American Anthropologist* 91:613–630.

KEELEY, LAWRENCE. **1988** "Hunter-Gatherer Economic Complexity and 'Population Pressure': A Cross-Cultural Analysis." *Journal of Anthropological Archaeology* 7:373–411.

KEELEY, LAWRENCE H., DANIEL CAHEN. **1989** "Early Neolithic Forts and Villages in NE Belgium: A Preliminary Report." *Journal of Field Archaeology* 16:157–177.

KEIGHTLEY, DAVID N. **1978** "The Religious Commitment: Shang Theology and the Genesis of Chinese Political Culture." *History of Religions* 17:211-225.

KEIGHTLEY, DAVID (ED.). **1983** *The Origins of Chinese Civilization: Studies in China.* Berkeley: University of California Press.

KELLY, RAYMOND. **1976** "Witchcraft and Sexual Relations." In *Man and Woman in the New Guinea Highlands,* P. Brown and G. Buchbinder, eds., pp. 36–53. Washington, D.C.: Special Publication No. 8, American Anthropological Association.

KELSO, A. J. **1974** *Physical Anthropology* (2nd ed.). Philadelphia: Lippincott.

KENDALL, CARL. **1984** "Ethnomedicine and Oral Rehydration Therapy: A Case Study of Ethnomedical Investigation and Program Planning." *Social Science and Medicine* 19(3):253–260.

KENYON, KATHLEEN. **1981** *Excavations at Jericho,* Vol. III. London: British School of Archaeology in Jerusalem.

KERTZER, DAVID. **1978** "Theoretical Developments in the Study of Age Group Systems." *American Ethnologist* 5(2):368–374.

KHARE, RAVINDRA. **1984** *The Untouchable as Himself: Identity and Pragmatism Among the Lucknow Charmer.* New York: Cambridge University Press.

KHAZANOV, K. M. **1984** *Nomads and the Outside World.* Cambridge: Cambridge University Press.

KINNECKELL, ARTHUR, AND R. L. WOODBURN. **1992** "Technical Working Paper." Washington, D.C.: Federal Reserve.

KIRCH, PATRICK. **1984** *The Evolution of Polynesian Chiefdoms.* New York: Cambridge University Press.

KITAHARA-FRISCH, J. **1980** "Apes and the Making of Stone Tools." *Current Anthropology* 21:359.

KLASS, MORTON. **1979** *Caste: The Emergence of the South Asian Social System.* Philadelphia: ISHI.

KLEIN, RICHARD. G. **1989** *The Human Career: Human Biolological Origins.* Chicago: University of Chicago Press.

KLEUGEL, JAMES, AND E. R. SMITH. **1981** "Beliefs About Stratification." *Annual Review of Sociology* 7:29–56.

KNIGHT, ROLF. **1974** "Grey Owl's Return: Cultural Ecology and Canadian Indigenous Peoples." *Reviews in Anthropology* 1:349–359.

KOLATA, ALAN. **1986** "The Agricultural Foundations of the Tiwanaku State: A View from the Heartland." *American Antiquity* 51:748–762.

KONNER, MELVIN. **1991** "The Promise of Medical Anthropology: An Invited Commentary." *Medical Anthropology Quarterly* 5:78–82.

KORTLANDT, A. **1967** "Experimentation with Chimpanzees in the Wild." In *Progress in Primatology,* D. Starck, R. Schnieder, and H. Kuhn, eds., pp. 185–194. Stuttgart: Gustav Fischer.

———. **1984** "Habitat Richness, Foraging Range, and Diet in Chimpanzees and Some Other Primates." In *Food Acquisition and Processing in Primates,* D. Chivers, A. Wood, and A. Bilsborough, eds., pp. 119–159. New York: Plenum.

KOSKOFF, DAVID. **1978** *The Mellons: The Chronicle of America's Richest Family.* New York: Crowell.

KOTTAK, CONRAD. **1990** *Prime-time Society: An Anthropological Analysis of Television and Culture.* Ann Arbor: University of Michigan Press.

KRAMER, ANDREW. **1991** "Modern Human Origins in Australasia: Replacement or Evolution?" *American Journal of Physical Anthropology* 86:455–473.

KROEBER, ALFRED L. **1948** *Anthropology.* New York: Harcourt Brace.

KRZYZANIAK, LECH. **1981** "Origin and Early Development of Food-producing Cultures in Northeastern Africa." *Current Anthropology* 22:693–694.

KUMAGAI, HISA, AND ARNO KUMAGAI. **1986** "The Hidden 'I' in Amae: Passive Love and Japanese Social Perception." *Ethos* 14:305–320.

KURTZ, DONALD. **1987** "The Economics of Urbanization and State Formation at Teotihuacán." *Current Anthropology* 28:329–353.

LA BARRE, WESTON. **1938** *The Peyote Cult.* Yale University Publications in Anthropology, No. 19. New Haven, Conn.: Yale University Press.

LABOV, WILLIAM. **1972** *Language in the Inner City.* Philadelphia: University of Pennsylvania Press.

LADD, EVERETT, JR., **1978** *Where Have All the Voters Gone?* New York: Norton.

LAITMAN, JEFFREY. **1985a** "Evolution of the Hominid Upper Respiratory Tract: The Fossil Evidence." In *Hominid Evolution: Past, Present and Future,* P. Tabias, ed., pp. 281–286. New York: Alan R. Liss.

———. **1985b** "Later Middle Pleistocene Hominids." In *Ancestors: The Hard Evidence,* Eric Delson, ed., pp. 265–267. New York: Alan R. Liss.

LAKOFF, ROBIN. **1973** "Language and Woman's Place." *Language in Society* 2:45–79.

LANDY, DAVID. **1985** "Pibloktok and Inùit Nutrition: Possible Implications of Hypervitaminosis A." *Social Science and Medicine* 21:173–185.

LANG, H., AND R. GÖHLEN. **1985** "Completed Fertility of the Hutterites: A Revision." *Current Anthropology* 26(3):395.

LANGDON, STEVE. **1979** "Comparative Tlingit and Haida Adaptation to the West Coast of the Prince of Wales Archipelago." *Ethnology* 18:101–119.

LANNING, EDWARD P. **1974** "Western South America." In *Prehispanic America,* S. Gorenstein, ed., pp. 65–86. New York: St. Martin's Press.

LANPO, JIA. **1989** "On Problems of the Beijing-Man Site: A Critique of New Implications." *Current Anthropology* 30:200–204.

LATIMER, BRUCE, AND C. OWEN LOVEJOY. **1990** "Metatarsophalangeal Joints of *Australopithecus afarensis.*" *American Journal of Physical Anthropology* 83:13–23.

LATTIMORE, OWEN. **1962** *Inner Asian Frontiers of China.* Boston: Beacon Press.

LAWRENCE, PETER. **1964** *Road Belong Cargo: A Study of the Cargo Movement in the Southern Madang District, New Guinea.* Manchester, England: University of Manchester Press.

LEACH, EDMUND R. **1968** "Polyandry, Inheritance, and the Definition of Marriage, with Particular Reference to Sinhalese Customary Law." In *Marriage, Family, and Residence,* P. Bohannan and J. Middleton, eds., pp. 73–83. Garden City, N.Y.: Natural History Press.

LEACOCK, ELEANOR BURKE. **1973** "The Montagnais-Naskapi Band." In *Cultural Ecology: Readings on the Canadian Indians and Eskimos,* B. Cox, ed., pp. 81–100. Toronto: McClellan and Stewart.

———. **1978** "Women's Status in Egalitarian Society: Implication for Social Evolution." *Current Anthropology* 19:247–275.

———. **1983** "Ideologies of Male Dominance as Divide and Rule Politics: An Anthropologist's View." In *Women's Nature,* Marian Lowe and Ruth Hubbard, eds., pp. 111–121. New York: Pergamon Press.

LEAKEY, MARY. **1979** "Footprints Frozen in Time." *National Geographic* 155:446–457.

LEAVITT, GREGORY. **1989** "Disappearance of the Incest Taboo." *American Anthropologist* 91:116–131.

———. **1990** "Sociobiological Explanations of Incest Avoidance: A Critical Review of Evidential Claims." *American Anthropologist* 91:971–993.

LEE, RICHARD. **1968** "What Do Hunters Do for a Living, or How to Make Out on Scarce Resources." *Man the Hunter,* R. B. Lee and I. DeVore, eds., pp. 30–43. Chicago: Aldine.

———. **1969** "!Kung Bushman Subsistence: An Input-Output Analysis." In *Environment and Cultural Behavior: Ecological Studies in Cultural Anthropology,* A. P. Vayda, ed., pp. 47–79. Garden City, N.Y.: Natural History Press.

———. **1979** *The !Kung San: Men and Women in a Foraging Society.* Cambridge: Cambridge University Press.

———. **1990** "Primitive Communism and the Origin of Social Inequality." In *The Evolution of Political Systems: Sociopolitics of Small-Scale Sedentary Societies,* Steadman Upham, ed., pp. 225–246. New York: Cambridge University Press.

LEE, R., AND M. HURLICH. **1982** "From Forager to Fighters: South Africa's Militarization of the Namibian San." In *Politics and History in Band Society,* Eleanor Leacock and Richard Lee, eds., pp. 327–345. Cambridge: Cambridge University Press.

LEEDS, ANTHONY. **1970** "The Concept of the Culture of Poverty: Conceptual, Logical, and Empirical Problems, with Perspectives from Brazil and Peru." In *The Culture of Poverty: A Critique,* E. Leacock, ed., pp. 226–284. New York: Simon & Schuster.

LEES, SUSAN, AND D. BATES. **1974** "The Origins of Specialized Nomadic Pastoralism: A Systemic Model." *American Antiquity* 39:187–193.

LEIGH, STEVEN R. **1992** "Cranial Capacity Evolution in *Homo erectus* and Early *Homo sapiens.*" *American Journal of Physical Anthropology* 87:1–13.

LENTZ, DAVID. **1991** "Maya Diets of the Rich and Poor." *Latin American Antiquity* 2:269–287.

LEONARD, KAREN I. **1978** *Social History of an Indian Caste.* Berkeley: University of California Press.

LESSER, ALEXANDER. **1968** "War and the State." In *War: The Anthropology of Armed Conflict and Aggression,* M. Fried, M. Harris, and R. Murphy, eds., pp. 92–96. Garden City, N.Y.: Natural History Press.

LE VINE, ROBERT. **1982** *Culture, Behavior, and Personality* (2nd ed.). New York: Aldine.

LEWIN, ROGER. **1984** "Man the Scavenger." *Science* 224:861–862.

———. **1987** "Four Legs Bad: Two Legs Good." *Science* 235:969–972.

LEWIS, MICHAEL. **1990** *Rioters and Citizens: Mass Protest in Imperial Japan.* Berkeley: University of California Press.

LEWIS, OSCAR. **1961** *The Children of Sanchez: Autobiography of a Mexican Family.* New York: Random House.

———. **1964** *Pedro Martinez: A Mexican Peasant and His Family.* New York: Random House.

———. **1966** *La Vida: A Puerto Rican Family in the Culture of Poverty—San Juan and New York.* New York: Random House.

LEWONTIN, R. **1972** "The Appearance of Human Diversity." In *Evolutionary Biology,* Vol. 6, Th. Dobzhansky et al., eds., pp. 381–398. New York: Plenum.

LEWONTIN, R., S. ROSE, AND L. KAMIN. **1984** *Not in Our Genes: Biology, Ideology, and Human Nature.* New York: Pantheon.

LIEBERMAN, PHILIP. **1984** *The Biology and Evolution of Language.* Cambridge, Mass.: Harvard University Press.

———. **1985** "On the Evolution of Human Syntactic Ability: Its Pre-adaptive Bases—Motor Control and Speech." *Journal of Human Evolution* 14:657–668.

———. **1991** *The Evolution of Speech, Thought, and Selfless Behavior.* Cambridge Mass.: Harvard University Press.

LICK, JOHN. **1983** "Ranked Exchange in Yela (Rossel Island)." In *The Kula: New Perspectives on Massim Exchange,* J. Leach and E. Leach, eds., pp. 503–528. Cambridge: Cambridge University Press.

LIEBOW, ELLIOT. **1967** *Tally's Corner: A Study of Negro Street Corner Men.* Boston: Little, Brown.

LIGHTFOOT-KLEIN, HANNY. **1989** *Prisoners of Ritual: An Odyssey into Female Genital Circumcision in Africa.* New York: Harrington Park Press.

LINDEBAUM, SHIRLEY. **1975** "The Last Course: Nutrition and Anthropology in Asia." In *Nutrition and Anthropology in Action,* Thomas Fitzgerald, ed., pp. 141–155. Atlantic Highlands, N.J.: Humanities Press.

———. **1979** *Kuru Society.* Palo Alto, Calif.: Mayfield.

LINDLEY, J. M., AND G. A. CLARK. **1990** "Symbolism and Modern Human Origins." *Current Anthropology* 31(3):233–261.

LINDSEY, ROBERT. **1985** "Official Challenge Outlets That Offer Explicit Videotapes." *The New York Times,* June 3, pp. 1, 9.

LINTON, RALPH. **1959** "The Natural History of the Family." In *The Family: Its Function and Destiny,* R. Anshen, ed., pp. 30–52. New York: Harper & Row.

LITTLEFIELD, ALICE, L. LIEBERMAN, AND L. REYNOLDS. **1982** "Redefining Race: The Potential Demise of a Concept in Physical Anthropology." *Current Anthropology* 23:641–655.

LIVINGSTONE, FRANK B. **1969** "Genetics, Ecology, and the Origins of Incest and Exogamy." *Current Anthropology* 10:45–62.

———. **1982** "Comment on Littlefield, Lieberman, and Reynolds." *Current Anthropology* 23:651.

LIZOT, JACQUES. **1977** "Population, Resources and Warfare Among the Yanomamö." *Man* 12:497–517.

———. **1979** "On Food Taboos and Amazon Cultural Ecology." *Current Anthropology* 20:150–151.

LLOYD, SETON. **1978** *The Archaeology of Mesopotamia: From the Old Stone Age to the Persian Conquest.* London: Thames and Hudson.

LOCHLIN, J. C., AND R. C. NICHOLS. **1976** *Heredity, Environment and Personality.* Austin: University of Texas Press.

LOCKARD, DENYSE. **1986** "The Lesbian Community: An Anthropological Approach." In *Anthropology and Homosexual Behavior*, Evelyn Blackwood, ed., pp. 83–96. New York: Haworth Press.

LOMAX, ALAN (ED.). **1968** *Folksong Style and Culture.* Washington, D.C.: American Association for the Advancement of Science, Publication No. 88.

LOMAX, ALAN, AND CONRAD ARENSBERG. **1977** "A Worldwide Evolutionary Classification of Cultures by Subsistence Systems." *Current Anthropology* 18:659–708.

LONG, BRUCE. **1987** "Reincarnation." In *Encyclopedia of Religion,* Vol. 12, pp. 265–269. New York: Macmillan.

LOWIE, ROBERT. **1948(1924)** *Primitive Religion.* New York: Liveright.

LYNCH, THOMAS F. **1983** "The Paleo-Indians." In *Ancient South Americans,* Jessie Jennings, ed., pp. 87–137. San Francisco: Freeman.

———. **1990** "Glacial-Age Man in South America? A Critical Review." *American Antiquity* 55(1):12–36.

LYNN, RICHARD. **1978** "Ethnic and Racial Differences in Intelligence: International Comparison." In *Human Variation: The Biopsychology of Age, Race, and Sex,* R. T. Osborne, C. Noble, and N. Weyl, eds., pp. 261–286. New York: Academic Press.

MCCALL, DANIEL. **1980** "The Dominant Dyad: Mother-Right and the Iroquois Case." In *Theory and Practice,* Stanley Diamond, ed., pp. 221–261. The Hague: Mouton.

MACCORMACK, CAROL P. **1982** "Adaptation in Human Fertility and Birth." *Ethnography of Fertility and Birth,* Carol P. MacCormack, ed., pp. 1–23. New York: Academic Press.

MCCORRISTON, JOY, AND FRANK HOLE. **1991** "The Ecology of Seasonal Stress and the Origins of Agriculture in the Near East." *American Anthropologist* 93:46–69.

MACDOUGAL, A. **1984** "Gap Between Rich, Poor Is Widening." *Los Angeles Times,* October 21.

MACDOUGALL, J. D. **1976** "Fission-Track Dating." *Scientific American* 235(6):114–122.

MCGREW, W. C. **1977** "Socialization and Object Manipulation of Wild Chimpanzees." In *Primate Bio-Social Development,* Susan Chevalier-Skolinkoff and Frank Poirier, eds., pp. 261–288. New York: Garland.

McGREW, W. C., AND C. E. G. TUTIN. **1973** "Chimpanzee Tool Use in Dental Grooming." *Nature* 241:477–478.

McGREW, W. C., C. TUTIN, AND P. BALDWIN. **1979** "New Data on Meat Eating by Wild Chimpanzees." *Current Anthropology* 20:238–239.

McGURK, F. C. J. **1975** "Race Differences Twenty Years Later." *Homo* 26:219–239.

McHENRY, HENRY M. **1991a** "Femoral Lengths and Stature in the Plio-Pleistocene Hominids." *American Journal of Physical Anthropology* 85:149–158.

———. **1991b** "Petite Bodies of the 'Robust' Australopithecines." *American Journal of Physical Anthropology* 86:445–454.

———. **1992** 'How Big Were Early Hominids?" *Evolutionary Anthropology* 1:15–20.

McINTOSH, SUSAN, AND RODERICK McINTOSH. **1983** "Current Directions in West African Prehistory." *Annual Review of Anthropology* 12:215–258.

MACLACHLAN, MORGAN. **1983** *Why They Did Not Starve: Biocultural Adaptation in a South Indian Village.* Philadelphia: Institute for the Study of Human Issues.

MacLEISH, KENNETH. **1972** "The Tasadays: The Stone Age Cavemen of Mindanao." *National Geographic* 142:219–248.

MACNEISH, RICHARD. **1978** *The Science of Archaeology?* Belmont, Calif.: Duxbury Press.

———. **1981** "The Transition to Statehood as Seen from the Mouth of a Cave." In *The Transition to Statehood in the New World,* Grant Jones and Paul Kautz, eds., pp. 123–154. New York: Cambridge University Press.

MAIR, LUCY. **1969** *Witchcraft.* New York: McGraw-Hill.

MALABRE, ALFRED. **1989** "Is the Bill Arriving for the Free Lunch?" *The Wall Street Journal,* January 9, pp. A1ff.

MALINOWSKI, BRONISLAW. **1920** "War and Weapons Among the Natives of the Trobriand Islands." *Man* 20:10–12.

———. **1927** *Sex and Repression in Savage Society.* London: Routledge & Kegan Paul.

———. **1935** *Coral Gardens and Their Magic* (2 vols.). London: Allen and Unwin.

MALKENSON, FREDERICH, AND J. KEANE. **1983** "Radiobiology of the Skin." In *Biochemistry and Physiology of the Skin,* Lowell Goldsmith, ed., pp. 769–814. New York: Oxford University Press.

MALONEY, WILLIAM. **1987a** "Dharma." *Encyclopedia of Religion,* Vol. 4, pp. 239–332. New York: Macmillan.

———. **1987b** "Karman." *Encyclopedia of Religion,* Vol. 8, pp. 261–266. New York: Macmillan.

MAMDANI, MAHMOOD. **1973** *The Myth of Population Control: Family, Caste, and Class in an Indian Village.* New York: Monthly Review Press.

MARANO, LOU. **1982** "Windigo Psychosis: The Anatomy of an Emic-Etic Confusion." *Current Anthropology* 23:385–412.

MARCUS, JOYCE. **1983** "Lowland Maya Archaeology at the Crossroads." *American Antiquity* 48:454–488.

MARETT, ROBERT. **1914** *The Threshold of Religion.* London: Methuen.

MARGOLIS, MAXINE. **1984** *Mothers and Such.* Berkeley: University of California Press.

MARIANO, ANN. **1984** "Baby Boomers Face Housing and Job Market Bummers." *Salt Lake Tribune,* September 23, p. F7. (Orig. *Washington Post.*)

MARKS, JOHN. **1991** "What's Old and New in Molecular Phylogenetics." *American Journal of Physical Anthropology* 85:207–219.

MARSHACK, ALEXANDER. **1985** *Hierarchical Evolution of the Human Capacity: The Paleolithic Evidence.* New York: American Museum of Natural History.

———. **1989** "Evolution of the Human Capacity: The Symbolic Evidence." *Yearbook of Physical Anthropology* 32: 1–34.

MARSHALL, DONALD. **1971** "Sexual Behavior on Mangaia." In *Human Sexual Behavior,* D. Marshall and R. Suggs, eds., pp. 103–162. Englewood Cliffs, N.J.: Prentice-Hall.

MARTIN, PAUL. **1984** "Prehistoric Overkill: The Global Model." In *Quaternary Extinctions: A Prehistoric Revolution,* Paul S. Martin and R. Klein, eds., pp. 354–403. Tucson: University of Arizona Press.

MARX, KARL. **1970(1859)** *A Contribution to the Critique of Political Economy.* New York: International Publishers.

MASON, J. ALDEN. **1957** *The Ancient Civilizations of Peru.* Harmondsworth, Eng.: Penguin.

MASSING, MICHAEL. **1989** "Crack's Destructive Sprint Across America." *The New York Times Magazine,* October 1, pp. 38ff.

MATHENY, RAY. **1976** "Maya Lowland Hydraulic Systems." *Science* 193:639–646.

———. **1982** "Ancient Lowland and Highland Maya Water and Soil Conservation Strategies." In *Maya Subsistence: Essays in Memory of Dennis E. Puleston,* K. Flannery, ed., pp. 157–178. New York: Academic Press.

MATHENY, RAY, AND D. GURR. **1983** "Variations in Prehistoric Agricultural Systems of the New World." *Annual Review of Anthropology* 12:79–103.

MATHEWS, HOLLY. **1985** "We Are Mayordomo: A Reinterpretation of Women's Roles in the Mexican Cargo System." *American Ethnologist* 12:285–301.

MAYR, ERNST. **1982** *The Growth of Biological Thought: Diversity, Evolution, and Inheritance.* Cambridge, Mass.: Harvard University Press.

MEACHAM, WILLIAM. **1977** "Continuity and Local Evolution in the Neolithic of South China." *Current Anthropology* 18:419–440.

MEAD, MARGARET. **1950** *Sex and Temperament in Three Primitive Societies.* New York: Mentor.

———. **1970** *Culture and Commitment.* Garden City, N.Y.: Natural History Press.

MEGGITT, MERVYN. **1964** "Male–Female Relationships in the Highlands of Australian New Guinea." *American Anthropologist* 66:204–224.

MEINTEL, DEIRDRE. **1978** *Cape Verde Americans: Their Cultural and Historical Background.* Unpublished Ph.D. dissertation, Brown University.

MELLAART, JAMES. **1975** *The Earliest Civilizations in the Near East.* London: Thames and Hudson.

MELLARS, PAUL. **1985** "The Ecological Basis of Social Complexity in the Upper Paleolithic of Southwestern France." In *Prehistoric Hunter-Gatherers: The Emergence of Cultural Complexity,* D. Price and J. Brown, eds., pp. 271–297. New York: Academic Press.

———. **1989** "Technological Changes Across the Middle-Upper Paleolithic Transition: Economic, Social, and Cognitive Perspectives." In *The Human Revolution,* Paul Mellars and Chris Stringer, eds., pp. 338–365. Rutgers, N.J.: Princeton University Press.

MENCHER, JOAN. **1974a** "Conflicts and Contradictions in the Green Revolution: The Case of Tamil Nadu." *Economic and Political Weekly* 9:309–323.

———. **1974b** "The Caste System Upside Down: Or, the Not So Mysterious East." *Current Anthropology* 15:469–478.

———. **1978** *Agriculture and Social Structure in Tamil Nadu.* New Delhi: Allied Publishers.

MENZEL, E. W., JR., ET AL. **1985** "Chimpanzee *(Pan troglodytes)* Spatial Problem Solving with the Use of Mirrors and Televised Equivalents of Mirrors." *Journal of Comparative Psychology* 99:211–217.

MILLER, BARBARA. **1981** *The Endangered Sex: Neglect of Female Children in Rural North India.* Ithaca, N.Y.: Cornell University Press.

———. **1987a** "Wife-beating in India: Variations on a Theme." Paper read at the annual meetings of the American Anthropological Association, November.

———. **1987b** "Female Infanticide and Child Neglect in Rural North India." In *Child Survival,* Nancy Scheper-Hughes, ed., pp. 95–112. Boston: D. Redidel.

MILLETT, KATE. **1970** *Sexual Politics.* Garden City, N.Y.: Doubleday.

MILLON, RENÉ. **1970** "Teotihuacán: Completion of the Map of the Giant Ancient City in the Valley of Mexico." *Science* 170:1077–1082.

———. **1973** *The Teotihuacán Man.* Austin: University of Texas Press.

MINTURN, LEIGH, AND JOHN T. HITCHCOCK. **1963** "The Rajputs of Khalapur, India." In *Six Cultures, Studies of Child Rearing.* B. B. Whiting, ed., pp. 203–361. New York: Wiley.

MINTURN, L., AND J. STASHAK. **1982** "Infanticide as a Terminal Abortion Procedure." *Behavior Science Research* 17:70–90.

MINTZ, SYDNEY. **1985** *Sweetness and Power.* New York: Viking Penguin.

MISHEL, LAWRENCE, AND DAVID FRANKEL. **1990** "The State of Working America." A report released by the Economic Policy Institute, Washington, D.C.

MITCHELL, D., AND L. DONALD. **1988** "Archaeology and the Study of Northwest Coast Economies." In *Prehistoric Economies of the Pacific Northwest Coast,* Barry Isaac, ed., pp. 293–351. Greenwich, Conn.: JAI Press.

MITCHELL, WILLIAM. **1973** "The Hydraulic Hypothesis: A Reappraisal." *Current Anthropology* 14:532–535.

MIYADI, D. **1967** "Differences in Social Behavior Among Japanese Macaque Troops." In *Progress in Primatology,* D. Starck, R. Schneider, and H. Kuhn, eds., pp. 228–231. Stuttgart: Gustav Fischer.

MOLNAR, STEPHEN. **1983** *Human Variation: Races, Types, and Ethnic Groups* (2nd ed.). Englewood Cliffs, N.J.: Prentice-Hall.

MONTAGU, ASHLEY. **1972** *Statement on Race* (3rd ed.). New York: Oxford University Press.

———. **1974** *Man's Most Dangerous Myth: The Fallacy of Race.* New York: Oxford University Press.

MOONEY, JAMES. **1965(1896)** *The Ghost Dance Religion.* Chicago: University of Chicago Press.

MOORE, ANDREW. **1985** "The Development of Neolithic Societies in the Near East." *Advances in World Archaeology* 4:1–69.

MORAN, EMILIO. **1982** *Human Adaptability: An Introduction to Ecological Anthropology.* Boulder, Colo.: Westview Press.

MOREHOUSE, WARD, AND DAVID DEMBO. **1985a** *The Underbelly of the U.S. Economy: Joblessness and Pauperization of Work in America.* Special Report No. 2 (February). New York: Council on International Public Affairs.

———. **1985b** *The Underbelly of the U.S. Economy: Joblessness and Pauperization of Work in America.* Special Report No. 4 (August). New York: Council on International Affairs.

———. **1988** Background Paper. *Joblessness and the Pauperization of Work in America.* New York: Council on International and Public Affairs.

MORLAN, RICHARD. **1978** "Early Man in North Yukon Territory: Perspectives as of 1977." In *Early Man in America from a Circum-Pacific Perspective,* Alan Bryan, ed., pp. 78–95. Edmonton: University of Alberta.

MORREN, GEORGE. **1984** "Warfare in the Highland Fringe of New Guinea: The Case of the Mountain Ok." In *Warfare, Culture and Environment,* Brian Ferguson, ed., pp. 169–208. Orlando, Fla.: Academic Press.

MORRIS, C. **1976** "The Master Design of the Inca." *Natural History* 85(10):58–87.

MORRIS, JOHN. **1974a** *Scientific Creationism for Public Schools.* San Diego, Calif.: Institute for Creation Research.

————. **1974b** *The Troubled Waters of Evolution.* San Diego, Calif.: Creation Life.

————. **1986** "The Paluxy River Mystery." *Impact* 151:i–iv. El Cajon, Calif.: Institute for Creation Research.

MOSELEY, MICHAEL E. **1983** "Central Andean Civilization." In *Ancient South America,* Jessie Jennings, ed., pp. 179–239. San Francisco: Freeman.

————. **1992** *The Inca and Their Ancestors.* London: Thames and Hudson.

MOUER, ROSS E., AND YOSHIO SUGIMOTO. **1986** *Images of Japanese Society: A Study in the Structure of Social Reality.* London: Kegan Paul.

MOYNIHAN, DANIEL P. **1965** *The Negro Family, the Case for National Action.* Washington, D.C.: U.S. Department of Labor.

MUNZEL, MARK. **1973** *The Aché Indians: Genocide in Paraguay.* International Work Group for Indigenous Affairs (IWGIA), 11.

MURDOCK, GEORGE P. **1949** *Social Structure.* New York: Macmillan.

————. **1967** *Ethnographic Atlas.* Pittsburgh: University of Pittsburgh Press.

MURDOCK, GEORGE AND C. PROVOST. **1973** "Factors in the Division of Labor by Sex." *Ethnology* 12:203–225.

MURPHY, ROBERT. **1956** "Matrilocality and Patrilineality in Mundurucu Society." *American Anthropologist* 58:414–434.

————. **1976** "Man's Culture and Women's Nature." *Annals of the New York Academy of Sciences* 293: 15–24.

MURRAY, CHARLES. **1984** *Losing Ground: American Social Policy 1950–1980.* New York: Basic Books.

MURRAY, GERALD. **1984** "The Wood Tree as a Peasant Cash Crop: An Anthropological Strategy for the Domestication of Energy." In *Haiti—Today and Tomorrow: An Interdisciplinary Study,* Charles Fost and A. Valdman, eds., pp. 141–160. Lanham, Md.: University Press of America.

NADEL, S. F. **1952** "Witchcraft in Four African Societies." *American Anthropologist* 54(1): 18–29.

NADER, LAURA. **1972** "Up the Anthropologist—Perspectives Gained from Studying Up." In *Reinventing Anthropology,* Dell Hymes, ed., pp. 284–311. New York: Random House.

————. **1980** *No Access to Law.* New York: Academic Press.

NAG, MONI. **1972** "Sex, Culture, and Human Fertility: India and the United States." *Current Anthropology* 13:231–238.

————. **1983** "The Impact of Sociocultural Factors on Breastfeeding and Social Behavior." In *Determinants of Fertility in Developing Countries,* Rodolfo A. Bulatao, Ronald D. Lee, with Paula E. Hollerbach and John Bongaarts, eds., pp. 163–198. New York: Academic Press.

NAG, MONI, AND N. KAK. **1984** "Demographic Transition in the Punjab Village." *Population and Development Review* 10:661–678.

NAG, MONI, BENJAMIN WHITE, AND ROBERT PEET. **1978** "An Anthropological Approach to the Study of the Economic Value of Children in Java and Nepal." *Current Anthropology,* pp. 239–306.

NAPIER, JOHN. **1970** *The Roots of Mankind.* Washington, D.C.: Smithsonian Institution.

NARDI, BONNIE. **1983** "Reply to Harbison's Comments on Nardi's Modes of Explanation in Anthropological Population Theory." *American Anthropologist* 85:662–664.

NAROLL, RAUL. **1973** "Introduction." In *Main Currents in Anthropology,* R. Naroll and F. Naroll, eds., pp. 1–23. Englewood Cliffs, N.J.: Prentice-Hall.

NASAR, SYLVIA. **1992** "The 1980's: A Very Good Time for the Very Rich." *The New York Times,* March 5, p. A1.

NASH, JILL. **1974** "Matriliny and Modernization: The Nagovisi of South Bougainville." *New Guinea Research Bulletin,* No. 55. Canberra, Australia.

NATIONAL RESEARCH COUNCIL. **1974** *Agricultural Production Efficiency.* Washington, D.C.: National Academy of Sciences.

NEEDHAM, JOSEPH. **1970** *Clerks and Craftsmen in China and the West.* Cambridge: Cambridge University Press.

NELSON, HARRY, AND ROBERT JURMAIN. **1988** *Introduction to Physical Anthropology.* St. Paul, Minn.: West.

NELSON, KRISTEN. **1986** "Labor Demand, Labor Supply, and the Suburbanization of Low-Wage Office Work." In *Production, Work, Territory: The Geographical Anatomy of Industrial Capitalism,* A. Scott and M. Storper, eds., pp. 149–171. Boston: Allen and Unwin.

NELSON, SARAH M. **1990** "Diversity of the Upper Paleolithic 'Venus' Figurines and Archeological Mythology." In *Powers of Observation: Alternative Views in Archaeology,* Sarah M. Nelson and Alice B. Kehoe, eds. Archaeological Papers of the American Anthropological Association, No. 2.

NETTING, ROBERT McC., RICHARD R. WILK, AND ERIC J. ARNOULD. **1984** *Households: Comparative and Historical Studies of the Domestic Group.* Berkeley: University of California Press.

NEVILLE, GWEN. **1979** "Community Form and Ceremonial Life in Three Regions of Scotland." *American Ethnologist* 6:93–109.

NEWCOMER, PETER. **1977** "Toward a Scientific Treatment of Exploitation: A Critique of Dalton." *American Anthropologist* 79:115–119.

NEWITT, JANE. **1985** "How to Forecast Births." *American Demographics,* January, pp. 30–33, 51.

NEWMAN, PHILIP L. **1965** *Knowing the Gururumba.* New York: Holt, Rinehart and Winston.

NEWMEYER, FREDERICK. **1978** "Prescriptive Grammar: A Reappraisal." In *Approaches to Language: Anthro-*

pological Issues, W. C. McCormack and S. A. Wurm, eds., pp. 581–593. The Hague: Mouton.

NEW YORK TIMES, THE. **1989** "Women in Parliaments," August 25, p. A7.

NICHOLS, DEBORAH. **1982** "A Middle Formative Irrigation System Near Santa Clara Coatitlán in the Basin of Mexico." *American Antiquity* 47:133–144.

NISHIDA, TOSHISADA. **1973** "The Ant-Gathering Behavior by the Use of Tools Among Wild Chimpanzees of the Mahali Mountains." *Journal of Human Evolution* 2:357–370.

NOAH, TIMOTHY. **1991** "Number of Poor Americans Is Up." *The Wall Street Journal,* September 27, p. A2.

NUSSBAUM, KAREN. **1980** *Race Against Time.* Cleveland: National Association of Office Workers.

OAKLEY, A. **1985** *Sex, Gender, and Society.* London: Gower/Maurice Temple Smith.

OASA, EDMUND. **1985** "Farming Systems Research: A Change in Form But Not in Content." *Human Organization* 44:219–227.

ODEND'HAL, STUART. **1972** "Energetics of Indian Cattle in Their Environment." *Journal of Human Ecology* 1:3–22.

ODUM, HOWARD. **1970** *Environment, Power, and Society.* New York: Wiley.

OLIVER, DOUGLAS. **1955** *A Solomon Island Society: Kinship and Leadership Among the Sivai of Bougainville.* Cambridge, Mass.: Harvard University Press.

OLSON, GERALD. **1978** "Effects of Activities of the Ancient Maya Upon Some of the Soils in Central America." Paper read at the meetings of the Society for American Archaeology, Tucson, Arizona.

OLZAK, S., AND J. NAGEL. **1986** *Competitive Ethnic Relations.* Orlando, Fla.: Academic Press.

OPLER, MORRIS. **1959** "Cultural Differences in Mental Disorders: An Italian and Irish Contrast in Schizophrenias—U.S.A." In *Culture and Mental Health,* Morris Opler, ed., pp. 425–442. New York: Atherton.

———. **1968** "The Themal Approach in Cultural Anthropology and Its Application to North Indian Data." *Southwestern Journal of Anthropology* 24:215–227.

OPPENHEIMER, VALLERY. **1982** *Work and the Family: A Study in Social Demography.* New York: Academic Press.

ORANS, MARTIN. **1968** "Maximizing in Jajmaniland: A Model of Caste Relations." *American Anthropologist* 70:875–897.

ORTIZ DE MONTELLANO, B. R. **1978** "Aztec Cannibalism: An Economic Necessity?" *Science* 200:611–617.

———. **1983** "Counting Skulls: Comments on the Aztec Cannibalism Theory of Harner-Harris." *American Anthropologist* 85:403–406.

ORTNER, SHERRY, AND H. WHITEHEADS (EDS.). **1981** *The Cultural Construction of Gender and Sexuality.* Cambridge: Cambridge University Press.

OSBERG, LARS. **1984** *Economic Inequality in the United States.* New York: M. E. Sharpe.

OSBORNE, R. T. **1978** "Race and Sex Differences in Heritability of Mental Test Performance: A Study of Negroid and Caucasoid Twins." In *Human Variation: The Biopsychology of Age, Race, and Sex,* R. T. Osborne, C. Noble, and N. Weyl, eds., pp. 137–169. New York: Academic Press.

OTTEN, ALAN. **1991** "Drop in Early Marriages May Have Lasting Impact." *The Wall Street Journal,* November 26, p. B1.

OTTENHEIMER, MARTIN. **1984** "Some Problems and Prospects in Residence and Marriage." *American Anthropologist* 86:351–358.

OTTERBEIN, KEITH. **1973** "The Anthropology of War." In *The Handbook of Social and Cultural Anthropology,* J. Honigman, ed., pp. 923–958. Chicago: Rand McNally.

PAIGE, DAVID, AND THEODORE BAYLESS (EDS.). **1978** *Lactose Digestion: Clinical and Nutritional Implications.* Baltimore: Johns Hopkins University Press.

PARENTI, MICHAEL. **1986** *Inventing Reality: The Politics of Mass Media.* New York: St. Martin's Press.

PARKER, SEYMOUR, AND R. KLEINER. **1970** "The Culture of Poverty: An Adjusted Dimension." *American Anthropologist* 75:516–527.

PARKER, SUE. **1985** "A Social-Technological Model for the Evolution of Languages." *Current Anthropology* 26:617–639.

PARSONS, JEFFREY. **1976** "The Role of Chinampa Agriculture in the Food Supply of Aztec Tenochtitlán." In *Culture Change and Continuity: Essays in Honor of James Bennett Griffin,* C. Cleland, ed., pp. 233–257. New York: Academic Press.

PARSONS, TALCOTT. **1970** "Equality and Inequality in Modern Society, or Social Stratification Revisited." In *Social Stratification: Research and Theory for the 1970's,* Edward Laumann, ed., pp. 13–72. New York: Bobbs-Merrill.

PASTERNAK, BURTON, CAROL EMBER, AND MELVIN EMBER. **1976** "On The Conditions Favoring Extended Family Households." *Journal of Anthropological Research* 32(2):109–123.

PAZTORY, ESTHER. **1984** "The Function of Art in Mesoamerica." *Archeology,* January–February, pp. 18–25.

PELETZ, MICHAEL G. **1987** "Female Heirship and the Autonomy of Women in Negeri Sembilan, West Malaysia." In *Research in Economic Anthropology: A Research Annual,* Vol. 8, Barry L. Isaac, ed., pp. 61–101. Greenwich, Conn.: JAI Press.

PELTO, PERTTI, AND GRETEL PELTO. **1973** "Ethnography: The Fieldwork Enterprise." In *Handbook of Social* *and Cultural Anthropology,* J. Honigman, ed., pp. 241–248. Chicago: Rand McNally.

———. **1976** *The Human Adventure: An Introduction to Anthropology.* New York: Macmillan.

PERCIVAL, L., AND K. QUINKERT. **1987** "Anthropometric Factors." In *Sex Differences in Human Performance,* Mary Baker, ed., pp. 121–139. New York: Wiley.

PERLO, VICTOR. **1976** *Economics of Racism U.S.A.: Roots of Black Inequality.* New York: International Press.

PETERSON, J. T. **1978** *The Ecology of Social Boundaries: Agta Foragers of the Philippines.* Urbana: University of Illinois Press.

PFEIFFER, JOHN E. **1982** *The Creative Explosion: An Enquiry into the Origins of Art and Religion.* New York: Harper & Row.

PHILIPS, SUSAN. **1980** "Sex Differences and Language." *Annual Review of Anthropology* 9:523–544.

PHILLIPSON, DAVID. **1985** *African Archaeology.* New York: Cambridge University Press.

PICKERSGILL, B., AND C. B. HEISER. **1975** "Origins and Distributions of Plants in the New World Tropics." In *The Origins of Agriculture,* C. A. Reed, ed., pp. 803–835. The Hague: Mouton.

PIDDOCKE, STUART. **1965** "The Potlatch System of the Southern Kwakiutl: A New Perspective." *Southwestern Journal of Anthropology* 21:244–264.

PIGGOTT, STUART. **1965** *Ancient Europe.* Chicago: Aldine.

PILBEAM, DAVID. **1985** "Patterns of Hominoid Evolution." In *Ancestors: The Hard Evidence,* Eric Delson, ed., pp. 51–59. New York: Alan R. Liss.

PIMENTEL, DAVID, L. E. HURD, A. C. BELLOTTI, ET AL. **1973** "Food Production and Energy Crisis." *Science* 182:443–449.

PIMENTEL, D., AND M. PIMENTEL. **1985** "Energy Use for Food Processing for Nutrition and Development." *Food and Nutrition Bulletin* 7(2):36–45.

PIMENTEL, DAVID, ET AL. **1975** "Energy and Land Constraints in Food Protein Production." *Science* 190:754–761.

PIVEN, FRANCES, AND R. CLOWARD. **1971** *Regulating the Poor: The Functions of Public Welfare.* New York: Random House/Vintage Books.

PLATH, DAVID, ED. **1983** *Work and Life Course in Japan.* Albany: State University of New York Press.

PLUCKNETT, D., AND N. SMITH. **1982** "Agricultural Research and Third World Food Production." *Science* 217:215–219.

PODOLEFSKY, AARON. **1984** "Contemporary Warfare in the New Guinea Highlands." *Ethnology* 23:73–87.

POPE, GEOFFREY G. **1988** "Recent Advances in Far Eastern Paleoanthropology." *Annual Review of Anthropology* 17:43–77.

POSPISIL, LEOPOLD, **1963** *The Kapauku Papuans of West New Guinea.* New York: Holt, Rinehart and Winston.

———. **1968** "Law and Order." In *Introduction to Cultural Anthropology,* J. Clifton, ed., pp. 200–224. Boston: Houghton Mifflin.

POST, JOHN. **1985** *Food Shortage, Climatic Variability, and Epidemic Disease in Pre-Industrial Europe.* Ithaca, N.Y.: Cornell University Press.

POTTS, RICHARD. **1984** "Hominid Hunters?" In *Hominid Evolution and Community Ecology,* Robert Foley, ed., pp. 129–166. Orlando, Fla.: Academic Press.

PREMACK, DAVID. **1971** "On the Assessment of Language Competence in the Chimpanzee." In *The Behavior of Nonhuman Primates,* Vol. 4, A. M. Schrier and F. Stollnitz, eds., pp. 185–228. New York: Academic Press.

———. **1976** *Intelligence in Ape and Man.* Hillsdale, N.J.: Erlbaum.

PRICE, DAVID. **1992** *Irrigation in Egypt.* Ph.D. dissertation, University of Florida.

PRICE, DOUGLAS. **1983** "The European Mesolithic." *American Antiquity* 48:761–778.

———. **1991** "The Mesolithic of Northern Europe." *Annual Review of Anthropology* 20:211–233.

PROTSCH, REINER, AND RAINER BERGER. **1973** "Earliest Radiocarbon Dates for Domesticated Animals." *Science* 179:235–239.

RAMIREZ, F., AND J. MEYER. **1980** "Comparative Education: The Social Construction of the Modern World System." *Annual Review of Sociology* 6:369–399.

RAPPAPORT, ROY. **1968** *Pigs for the Ancestors: Ritual in the Ecology of a New Guinea People.* New Haven, Conn.: Yale University Press.

———. **1971a** "Ritual, Sanctity, and Cybernetics." *American Anthropologist* 73:59–76.

———. **1971b** "The Sacred in Human Evolution." In *Explorations in Anthropology,* Morton Fried, ed., pp. 403–420. New York: Crowell.

———. **1984** *Pigs for the Ancestors: Ritual in the Ecology of a Papuan New Guinea People* (2nd ed.). New Haven, Conn.: Yale University Press.

REDFORD, KENT, AND JOSE DOREA. **1984** "The Nutritional Value of Invertebrates with Emphasis on Ants and Termites as Food for Mammals." *Journal of the Zoological Society of London* 203: 385–395.

REITE, MARTIN, AND NANCY CAINE (EDS.). **1983** *Child Abuse: The Nonhuman Primate Data.* New York: Alan R. Liss.

RENFREW, COLIN. **1973** *Before Civilization: The Radiocarbon Revolution and Prehistoric Europe.* New York: Knopf.

REYNA, S. P. **1989** "Grudge Matching and War: Considerations of the Nature and Universality of War." Paper presented at the American Anthropological Association annual meeting, Washington, D.C., November 15.

RHOADES, ROBERT. **1984** *Breaking New Ground: Agricultural Anthropology.* Lima, Peru: International Potato Center.

RIBEIRO, DARCY. **1971** *The Americas and Civilization.* New York: Dutton.

RICE, PATRICIA, AND A. PATTERSON. **1986** "Validating the Cave Art—Archaeofaunal Relationship in Cantabrian Spain." *American Anthropologist* 88:658–667.

RICHARDS, PAUL. **1973** "The Tropical Rain Forest." *Scientific American* 229:58–68.

RIFKIND, JEREMY, AND TED HOWARD. **1979** *The Emerging Order: God in the Age of Scarcity.* New York: Putnam.

RIGHTMIRE, G. P. **1984** "*Homo sapiens* in Sub-Saharan Africa." In *The Origin of Modern Humans: A World Survey of the Fossil Evidence,* Fred Smith and Frank Spencer, eds., pp. 295–325. New York: Alan R. Liss.

———. **1991** *The Evolution of* Homo erectus: *Comparative Anatomical Studies of an Extinct Human Species.* Cambridge: Cambridge University Press.

RILEY, CARROLL L., J. CHARLES KELLEY, CAMBELL W. PENNINGTON, AND ROBERT L. RANDS. **1971** *Man Across the Sea.* Austin: University of Texas Press.

ROACH, JACK L., L. GROSS, AND O. R. GURSSLIN (EDS.). **1969** *Social Stratification in the United States.* Englewood Cliffs, N.J.: Prentice-Hall.

ROBERTS, PAUL. **1964** *English Syntax.* New York: Harcourt Brace Jovanovich.

ROBERTS, RON, AND D. BRINTNALL. **1982** *Reinventing Inequality.* Boston: Schenkman.

ROHNER, RONALD. **1969** *The Ethnography of Franz Boas.* Chicago: University of Chicago Press.

ROHRLICH-LEAVITT, RUBY. **1977** "Women in Transition: Crete and Sumer." In *Becoming Visible: Women in European History,* Renate Bridenthal and C. Koonz, eds., pp. 38–59. Boston: Houghton Mifflin.

ROSALDO, MICHELLE, AND LOUISE LAMPHERE (EDS.). **1974** *Women, Culture, and Society.* Stanford, Calif.: Stanford University Press.

ROSS, ERIC. **1979** "Reply to Lizot." *Current Anthropology* 20:151–155.

ROSS, PHILLIP. **1991** "Hard Words." *Scientific American,* April, pp. 137–147.

ROSS, RUTH, AND G. BENSON. **1979** "Criminal Justice from East to West." *Crime and Delinquency* 25:76–86.

RUBIN, VERA, AND LAMBROS COMITAS. **1975** *Ganja in Jamaica: A Medical Anthropology Study of Chronic Marijuana Use.* The Hague: Mouton.

RUMBAUGH, D. M. **1977** *Language Learning by a Chimpanzee: The Lana Project.* New York: Academic Press.

RUSSELL, KENNETH. **1988** *The Behavioral Ecology of Early Food Production in the Near East and North Africa.* London: B.A.R. Series 391.

RUYLE, EUGENE E. **1973** "Slavery, Surplus, and Stratification on the Northwest Coast: The Ethnoenergetics of an Incipient Stratification System." *Current Anthropology* 14:603–631.

———. **1975** "Mode of Production and Mode of Exploitation: The Mechanical and the Dialectical." *Dialectical Anthropology* 1:7–23.

SABATO, LARRY. **1989** *Paying for Elections: The Campaign Finance Thicket.* New York: Priority Press.

SACHS, BERNICE. **1985** *Vital Speeches of the Day* 50(4):757–762.

SACKS, KAREN B. **1971** *Economic Bases of Sexual Equality: A Comparative Study of Four African Societies.* Ph.D. dissertation, University of Michigan.

SAFA, HELEN I. **1967** *An Analysis of Upward Mobility in Lower Income Families: A Comparison of Family and Community Life Among American Negro and Puerto Rican Poor.* Syracuse, N.Y.: Youth Development Center.

———. **1986** "Economic Autonomy and Sexual Equality in Caribbean Society." *Social and Economic Studies* 35(3):1–20.

SAHAGUN, BERNARDINO DE. **1951** "Book 2—The Ceremonies." In *General History of the Things of New Spain: Florentine Codex,* A. J. O. Anderson and C. E. Dibble, trans. (from Aztec). In *Thirteen Parts,* Part III. Santa Fe, N.M.: School of American Research, and Salt Lake City: University of Utah.

SAHLINS, MARSHALL. **1972** *Stone Age Economics.* Chicago: Aldine.

———. **1978** "Culture as Protein and Profit." *The New York Review of Books,* November 23, pp. 45–53.

SALZMAN, PHILIP. **1971** "Comparative Studies of Nomadism and Pastoralism." *Anthropological Quarterly* 44(3):104–210.

SANDAY, PEGGY. **1981** *Female Power and Male Dominance: On the Origins of Sexual Inequality.* New York: Cambridge University Press.

SANDERS, WILLIAM T. **1972** "Population, Agricultural History, and Societal Evolution in Mesoamerica." In *Population Growth: Anthropological Implications,* B. Spooner, ed., pp. 101–153. Cambridge, Mass.: M.I.T. Press.

SANDERS, WILLIAM T., AND B. PRICE. **1968** *Mesoamerica: The Evolution of a Civilization.* New York: Random House.

SANDERS, WILLIAM T., R. SANTLEY, AND J. PARSONS. **1979** *The Basin of Mexico: Ecological Processes in the Evolution of a Civilization.* New York: Academic Press.

SANDERS, WILLIAM, AND DAVID WEBSTER. **1978** "The Mesoamerican Urban Tradition." *American Anthropologist* 90:521–546.

SANDERSON, STEPHEN. **1988** *Macrosociology: An Introduction to Human Societies.* New York: Harper & Row.

SANJEK, ROGER. **1972** *Ghanian Networks: An Analysis of Interethnic Relations in Urban Situations.* Ph.D. dissertation, Columbia University.

———. **1977** "Cognitive Maps of the Ethnic Domain in Urban Ghana: Reflections on Variability and Change." *American Ethnologist* 4:603–622.

SANKAR, ANDREA. **1986** "Sisters and Brothers, Lovers and Enemies: Marriage Resistance in Southern

Kuangtung." In *Anthropology and Homosexual Behavior*, Evelyn Blackwood, ed., pp. 69–81. New York: Haworth Press.

SANTLEY, ROBERT 1987 "Comment on Kurtz." *Current Anthropology* 28:344–345.

SAPIR, EDWARD. 1921 *Language: An Introduction to the Study of Speech.* New York: Harcourt, Brace.

SARICH, VINCENT. 1974 "Just How Old Is the Hominid Line?" *Yearbook of Physical Anthropology* 17:98–112.

SAVAGE-RUMBAUGH, SUE. 1987 "Communication, Symbolic Communication, and Language: Reply to Seidenberg and Petitto." *Journal of Experimental Psychology: General* 116:288–292.

SAVAGE-RUMGAUGH, SUE, ET AL. 1990 "Symbols: Their Communicative Use, Comprehension, and Combination by Bonobos *(Pan paniscus)*." In *Advances in Infancy Research,* Vol. 6, Carolyn Rovee-Collier and Lewis P. Lipsitt, eds., pp. 222–254. Norwood, N.J.: ABLEX.

SCARBOROUGH, VERNON L. 1983 "A Preclassic Maya Water System." *American Antiquity* 48:720–744.

SCARBOROUGH, VERNON L., AND GARY G. GALLOPIN. 1991 "A Water Storage Adaptation in the Maya Lowlands." *Science* 251:658–662.

SCARR, SANDRA, ANDREW J. PAKSTIS, SOLOMON H. KATZ, AND WILLIAM B. BARKER. 1977 "Absence of a Relationship Between Degree of White Ancestry and Intellectual Skills Within a Black Population." *Human Genetics* 39:69–86.

SCARR, S., AND R. A. WEINBERG. 1976 "I.Q. Test Performance of Black Children Adopted by White Families." *American Psychologist* 31:726–739.

SCHEFFLER, HAROLD. 1973 "Kinship, Descent, and Alliance." In *Handbook of Social and Cultural Anthropology,* J. Honigman, ed., pp. 747–793. Chicago: Rand McNally.

SCHEPER-HUGHES, NANCY. 1984 "Infant Mortality and Infant Care: Cultural and Economic Constraints on Nuturing in Northeast Brazil." *Social Science and Medicine* 19(5):535–546.

SCHERMERHORN, R. A. 1970 *Comparative Ethnic Relations.* New York: Random House.

SCHLEGEL, ALICE (ED.). 1972 *Male Dominance and Female Autonomy.* New Haven, Conn.: Human Relations Area Files.

SCHLEGEL, ALICE, AND H. BARRY. 1979 "Adolescent Initiation Ceremonies: A Cross-Cultural Code." *Ethnology* 18:199–210.

——. 1986 "The Cultural Consequences of Female Contributions to Subsistence." *American Anthropologist* 88:142–150.

SCHLEGEL, ALICE, AND R. ELOUL. 1988 "Marriage Transactions: Labor, Property and Status." *American Anthropologist* 90:291–309.

SCHNEIDER, HAROLD. 1977 "Prehistoric Transpacific Contact and the Theory of Culture Change." *American Anthropologist* 79:9–25.

SCHWARTZ, JEFFREY, I. TATTERSAL, AND N. ELDREDGE. 1978 "Phylogeny and Classification of the Primates Revisited." *Yearbook of Physical Anthropology* 21:95–133.

SCODITTI, G. 1983 "Kula on Kitava." In *The Kula: New Perspectives in Massim Exchange,* J. Leach and E. Leach, eds., pp. 249–273. New York: Cambridge University Press.

SCRIMSHAW, NEVIN. 1977 "Through a Glass Darkly: Discerning the Practical Implications of Human Dietary Protein-Energy Interrelationships." *Nutrition Reviews* 35:321–337.

SCRIMSHAW, SUSAN. 1983 "Infanticide as Deliberate Fertility Regulation." In *Determinants of Fertility in Developing Nations: Supply and Demand for Children,* R. Bulatao and R. Lee, eds. New York: Academic Press.

SEEMAN, MARK F. 1988 "Ohio Hopewell Trophy-Skull Artifacts as Evidence for Competition for Middle Woodland Society Circa 50 B.C.–A.D. 350." *American Antiquity* 53(3):565–577.

SENGAL, RANDAL. 1973 "On Mechanism of Population Growth During the Neolithic." *Current Anthropology* 14:540–542.

SERRIN, WILLIAM. 1984 "Experts Say Job Bias Against Women Persists." *The New York Times,* November 25, pp. 1, 18.

SERVICE, ELMAN R. 1975 *Origins of the State and Civilization: The Processes of Cultural Evolution.* New York: Norton.

SHANAHAN, EILEEN. 1985 "Measuring the Service Economy." *The New York Times,* October 21, p. 4.

SHANKMAN, PAUL. 1991 "Culture Contact, Cultural Ecology, and Dani Warfare." *Man* 26:299–321.

SHARER, ROBERT J., AND DAVID C. GROVE. 1989 *Regional Perspectives on the Olmec.* New York: Cambridge University Press.

SHARFF, JAGNA. 1980 "Life on Dolittle Street: How Poor People Purchase Immortality." Final report, Hispanic Study Project No. 9. Department of Anthropology, Columbia University, New York.

——— 1981 "Free Enterprise and the Ghetto Family." *Psychology Today,* March.

SHARMA, URSULA. 1983 "Dowry in North India: Its Consequences for Women." In *Women and Property,* Renee Hirschon, ed., pp. 62–74. London: Croom Helm.

SHEETS, JOHN, AND JAMES A. GAVAN. 1977 "Dental Reduction from *Homo erectus* to Neanderthal." *Current Anthropology* 18:587–589.

SHEPHER, JOSEPH. 1983 *Incest: A Biosocial Point of View.* New York: Academic Press.

SHERRATT, ANDREW. 1982 "Mobile Resources: Settlement and Exchange in Early Agricultural Europe." In *Ranking Resource, and Exchange: Aspects of the Archaeology of Early European Society,* C. Renfrew and S. Shennan, eds., pp. 13–26. Cambridge: University of Cambridge Press.

SHIPMAN, PAT. **1986** "Scavenging or Hunting in Early Hominids: Theoretical Framework and Tests." *American Anthropologist* 88:27–43.

SHORT, RICHARD. **1984** "On Placing the Child Before Marriage, Reply to Birdsell." *Population and Development Review* 9:124–135.

SHOSTAK, MARJORIE. **1981** *Nisa, The Life and Words of a !Kung Woman.* Cambridge, Mass.: Harvard University Press.

SHUEY, AUDREY M. **1966** *The Testing of Negro Intelligence.* New York: Social Science Press.

SIBLEY, CHARLES, AND JON ALQUIST. **1987** "DNA Hybridization Evidence of Hominoid Phylogeny: Results from an Expanded Data Set." *Journal of Molecular Evolution* 26:99–121.

SIBLEY, CHARLES G., JOHN A. COMSTOCK, AND JON E. ALQUIST. **1990** "DNA Hybridization Evidence of Homonoid Phylogeny: A Reanalysis of the Data." *Journal of Molecular Evolution* 30: 202–236

SILK, JOAN, AND RICHARD BOYD. **1989** "Anthropology: Human Evolution." U.C.L.A. Lecture Notes.

SILK, LEONARD. **1985** "The Peril Behind the Takeover Boom." *The New York Times,* December 29, Sec. 3, p. 1.

SIMMONS, ALAN. **1986** "New Evidence for the Early Use of Cultigens in the American Southwest." *American Antiquity* 51:73–89.

SIMONS, ELWYN L. **1968** "A Source for Dental Comparison of *Ramapithecus* and *Australopithecus* and *Homo.*" *South African Journal of Science* 64:92–112.

———. **1985** "Origins and Characteristics of the First Hominids." In *Ancestors: The Hard Evidence,* Eric Delson, ed., pp. 37–41. New York: Alan R. Liss.

SIMONS, ELWYN L., AND P. ETTEL. **1970** "Gigantopithecus." *Scientific American* 222(1):77–85.

SIMOONS, FREDERICK. **1979** "Questions in the Sacred Cow Controversy." *Current Anthropology* 20:467–493.

———. **1982** "Geography and Genetics as Factors in the Psychobiology of Human Food Selection." In *Psychobiology of Human Food Selection,* L. M. Barker, ed., pp. 205–224. Westport, Conn.: AVI.

SIMPSON, GEORGE, AND J. M. SINGER. **1972** *Racial and Cultural Minorities* (2nd ed.). New York: Harper & Row.

SINGER, R., AND J. WYMER. **1982** *The Middle Stone Age at the Klasies River Mouth in South Africa.* Chicago: University of Chicago Press.

SKINNER, WILLIAM. **1987** "Gender and Power in Japanese Families: Consequences for Reproductive Behavior and Longevity." Paper prepared for Symposium No. 103, Wenner-Gren Foundation for Anthropological Research: An International Symposium. "Gender Hierarchies," January 10–18.

SMITH, C. T. **1970** "Depopulation of the Central Andes in the 16th Century." *Current Anthropology* 11:453–460.

SMITH, CURTIS. **1985** *Ancestral Voices: Language and the Evolution of Consciousness.* Englewood Cliffs, N.J.: Prentice-Hall.

SMITH, E. A. **1983** "Anthropological Applications of Optimal Foraging Theory: A Critical Review." *Current Anthropology* 24:625–651.

SMITH, F. H. **1983** "Behavioral Interpretations of Changes in Craniofacial Morphology Across the Achaic/Modern *Homo sapiens* Transition." In *The Mousterian Legacy: Human Biocultural Change in the Upper Pleistocene,* E. Trinkhaus, ed., pp. 141–163. Oxford: BAR Reports S164.

SMITH, M. G. **1968** "Secondary Marriage Among Kadera and Kagoro." In *Marriage, Family, and Residence,* P. Bohannan and J. Middleton, eds., pp. 109–130. Garden City, N.Y.: Natural History Press.

SMITH, RAYMOND T. **1988** *Kinship and Class in the West Indies: Genealogical Study of Jamaica and Guyana.* Cambridge Studies in Social and Cultural Anthropology 65. New York: Cambridge University Press.

SNOWDON, CHARLES T. **1990** "Language Capacities of Nonhuman Animals." *Yearbook of Physical Anthropology* 33:215–243.

SOFFER, OLGA. **1985** *Upper Paleolithic of the Central Russian Plain.* Orlando, Fla.: Academic Press.

———. **1987** "Upper Paleolithic Connubia, Refugia, and the Archaeological Record from Eastern Europe." In *The Pleistocene Old World: Regional Perspectives,* Olga Soffer, ed., pp. 333–348. New York: Plenum.

SOLECKI, RALPH. **1980** "An Early Village Site at Azwi Chemi Shanidar." *Bib Mes* 13.

SOLHEIM, WILLIAM. **1970** "Relics from Two Diggings Indicate the Thais Were the First Agrarians." *The New York Times,* January 12.

SOLON, GARY. **1992** *The American Economic Review.* In Press.

SOLOWAY, JAQUELINE S., AND RICHARD B. LEE. **1990** "Foragers, Genuine or Spurious?" *Current Anthropology* 31(2):109–146.

SORENSON, RICHARD. **1972** "Socio-Ecological Change Among the Foré of New Guinea." *Current Anthropology* 13:349–383.

SORENSON, RICHARD, AND P. E. KENMORE. **1974** "Proto-Agricultural Movement in the Eastern Highlands of New Guinea." *Current Anthropology* 15:67–72.

SOUSTELLE, JACQUES. **1970** *Daily Life of the Aztecs.* Stanford, Calif.: Stanford University Press.

SOUTHWORTH, FRANKLIN. **1969** " 'Standard' Language and Social Structure." Paper read at the annual meeting of the American Anthropological Association, New Orleans.

SOWELL, THOMAS. **1983**. *The Economics and Politics of Race.* New York: Morrow.

SOWUNMI, M. **1985** "The Beginnings of Agriculture in West Africa: Botanical Evidence." *Current Anthropology* 26:127–129.

SPENCER, P. **1965** *The Samburu: A Study of Gerontocracy in a Nomadic Tribe.* Berkeley: University of California Press.

SPIRO, MELFORD. **1954** "Is the Family Universal?" *American Anthropologist* 56:839–846.

———. **1982** *Oedipus in the Trobriands.* Chicago: University of Chicago Press.

SPUHLER, JAMES. **1985** "Anthropology, Evolution, and Scientific Creationism." *Annual Review of Anthropology* 14:103–133.

SRINIVAS, M. N. **1955** "The Social System of a Mysore Village." In *Village India: Studies in the Little Community,* M. Marriot, ed., pp. 1–35. Memoir 83. Washington, D.C.: American Anthropological Association.

STACEY, JUDITH. **1990** *Brave New Families: Stories of Domestic Upheaval in Late Twentieth Century America.* New York: Basic Books.

STACK, CAROL. **1974** *All Our Kin: Strategies for Survival in a Black Community.* New York: Harper & Row.

STAHL, ANN. **1984** "Hominid Dietary Selection Before Fire." *Current Anthropology* 25:151–168.

STEADMAN, LYLE, AND C. MERBS. **1982** "Kuru: Early Letters and Field-Notes from the Collection of D. Carleton Gajdusek." *American Anthropologist* 84:611–627.

STEIN, HOWARD, AND R. F. HILL. **1977** *The Ethnic Imperative: Examining the New White Ethnic Movement.* University Park: Pennsylvania State University Press.

STEINHART, JOHN, AND CAROL STEINHART. **1974** "Energy Use in the U.S. Food System." *Science* 184:307–317.

STEPHENS, THOMAS. **1989** *Dictionary of Latin American Racial and Ethnic Terminology.* Gainesville: University of Florida Press.

STERN, CURT. **1973** *Principles of Human Genetics* (3rd ed.). San Francisco: Freeman.

STERN, JACK, AND RANDALL SUSMAN. **1983** "The Locomotor Anatomy of *Australopithecus afarensis.*" *American Journal of Physical Anthropology* 60:279–318.

STERN, STEVE J. **1988** "Feudalism, Capitalism, and the World System in the Perspective of Latin America and the Carribean." *American Historical Review* 93:829–897.

STEWART, OMER. **1968** "Lorenz Margolin on the Ute." In *Man and Aggression,* M. F. Ashley Montagu, ed., pp. 103–110. New York: Oxford University Press.

———. **1987** *Peyote Religion: A History.* Norman: University of Oklahoma Press.

STOLTMAN, JAMES. **1978** "Temporal Models in Prehistory: An Example from Eastern North America." *Current Anthropology* 19:703–746.

STONEKING, MARK, AND REBECCA L. CANN. **1989** "African Origin of Human Mitochondrial DNA." In *The Human Revolution,* Paul Mellars and Chris Stringer, eds., pp. 17–30. Rutgers, N.J.: Princeton University Press.

STORPER, MICHAEL. **1989** *The Capitalist Imperative: Territory, Technology, and Industrial Growth.* New York: Basil Blackwell.

STRAUS, LAWRENCE. **1982** "Comments on White's Middle/Upper Paleolithic Transition." *Current Anthropology* 23:185–186.

STRAUSS, GUY. **1989** "On Early Hominid Use of Fire." *Current Anthropology* 30:488–491.

STREET, JOHN. **1969** "An Evaluation of the Concept of Carrying Capacity." *Professional Geographer* 21(2):104–107.

STRINGER, CHRIS B. **1985** "Middle Pleistocene Hominid Variability and the Origins of Late Pleistocene Humans." In *Ancestors: The Hard Evidence,* Eric Delson, ed., pp. 289–295. New York: Alan R. Liss.

STURTEVANT, EDGAR H. **1964** *An Introduction to Linguistic Science.* New Haven, Conn.: Yale University Press.

SUDARKASA, N. **1973** *Where Women Work: : A Study of Yoruba Women in the Marketplace and in the Home.* Ann Arbor: University of Michigan Museum.

SUGIMOTO, Y., AND R. MOUER. **1983** *Japanese Society: A Study in Social Reconstruction.* London: Kegan Paul.

SULLIVAN, LAWRENCE. **1987** "Supreme Beings." In *The Encyclopedia of Religion,* M. Eliade ed. New York: Macmillan and Free Press.

SUSMAN, RANDAL L. **1989** "New Hominid Fossils from the Swartkrans Formation (1979–1986 Excavations): Postcranial Specimens." *American Journal of Physical Anthropology* 79:451–474.

SUSSER, IDA. **1982** *Norman Street.* New York: Oxford University Press.

SUSSMAN, ROBERT. **1972** "Child Transport, Family Size, and Increase in Population During the Neolithic." *Current Anthropology* 13:258–259.

SUTTLES, WAYNE. **1960** "Affinal Ties, Subsistence, and Prestige Among the Coast Salish." *American Anthropologist* 62:269–305.

SUZUKI, AKIRA. **1975** "The Origins of Hominid Hunting: A Primatological Perspective." *Socioecology and Psychology of Primates,* R. H. Tuttle, ed., pp. 259–278. The Hague: Mouton.

SWANSON, GUY E. **1960** *The Birth of the Gods: The Origin of Primitive Beliefs.* Ann Arbor: University of Michigan Press.

SWASY, ALECIA, AND C. HYMOWITZ. **1990** "The Workplace Revolution." *The Wall Street Journal Reports,* February 9, pp. R6–R8.

TANNER, NANCY. **1974** "Matrifocality in Indonesia and Africa and Among Black Americans." In *Woman, Culture and Society,* M. Rosaldo and L. Lamphere, eds., pp. 129–156. Stanford, Calif.: Stanford University Press.

———. **1983** "Hunters, Gatherers, and Sex Roles in Space and Time." *American Anthropologist* 85:335–341.

TAYLOR, PAUL. **1985** "Notice Regarding the Motion Picture, 'Footprints in Stone.' " Mesa, Ariz.: Films for Christ Association.

TAYLOR, R. E., ET AL. **1985** "Major Revisions in the Pleistocene Age Assignment for North American Human Skeletons by C-14 Accelerator Mass Spectometry, None Older than 11,000 C-14 Years B.P." *American Antiquity* 50:136–140.

TEFFT, STANTON. **1975** "Warfare Regulation: A Cross-Cultural Test of Hypotheses." In *War: Its Causes and Correlates,* Martin Nettleship et al., eds., pp. 693–712. Chicago: Aldine.

TELEKI, GEZA. **1973** "The Omnivorous Chimpanzee." *Scientific American* 288(1):32–42.

———. **1981** "The Omnivorous Diet and Eclectic Feeding Habits of Chimpanzees in Gombe National Park, Tanzania." In *Omnivorous Primates: Gathering and Hunting in Human Evolution,* G. Teleki and S. O. Harding, eds., pp. 303–343. New York: Columbia University Press.

TEMPLETON, ALAN. **1991** "Technical Comment: Human Origins and Analysis of Mitochondrial DNA Sequences." *Science* 255:737.

TERRACE, HERBERT. **1979** "Is Problem Solving Language?" *Journal of the Experimental Analysis of Behavior* 31:161–175.

TESTART, ALAIN. **1982** "The Significance of Food-Storage Among Hunter-Gatherers: Residence Patterns, Population Densities and Social Inequalities." *Current Anthropology* 23(3):523–537.

THOMAS, DAVID HURST, ED., **1989** *Columbian Consequences: Archaeological and Historical Perspectives on the Spanish Borderlands West,* Vol. 1. Washington D.C.: Smithsonian Institution Press.

———. **1991** "Columbian Consequences, the Spanish Borderlands in Cubist Perspective." In *Columbian Consequences: Archaeological and Historical Perspectives on the Borderlands East,* Vol. 3. Washington D.C.: Smithsonian Institution Press.

THOMAS, LEWIS. **1986** "Peddling Influence." *Time,* March 3, pp. 26–36.

THOMPSON-HANDLER, NANCY, RICHARD K. MALENKY, AND N. BADRIAN. **1984** "Sexual Behavior of *Pan paniscus* under Natural Conditions in the Lomako Forest." In *The Pygmy Chimpanzee,* R. Susman, ed., pp. 347–368. New York: Plenum.

THORNER, ALAN, AND M. WOLPOFF. **1992** "The Multiregional Evolution of Humans." *Scientific American* (April):76–83.

THUROW, LESTER. **1987** "A Surge in Inequality." *Scientific American* 256(5):30–35.

TILAKARATNE, M. W. **1978** "Economic Change, Social Differentiation, and Fertility: Aluthgana." In *Population and Development: High and Low Fertility in Poorer Countries,* G. Hawthorn, ed., pp. 186–197. London: Frank Cass.

TITON, J. T., ET AL. **1984** *Worlds of Music: An Introduction to the Musics of the World's Peoples.* New York: Schirmer Books.

TODD, I. A. **1978** *Catal Hüyük in Perspective.* Menlo Park, Calif.: Cummings.

TORREY, E. F. **1980** *Schizophrenia and Civilization.* New York: Jason Aronson.

TOTH, NICHOLAS, AND K. SCHICK. **1986** "The First Million Years: The Archaeology of Protohuman Culture." *Archaeology Method and Theory* 9:1-96.

TREVATHAN, WENDA. **1982** "Comment on Littlefield, Lieberman, and Reynolds 1982." *Current Anthropology* 23:657–662.

TRIGGER, BRUCE. **1978** "Iroquois Matriliny." *Pennsylvania Archaeologist* 48:55–65.

TRINKHAUS, ERIC. **1983** "Neanderthal Postcrania and the Adaptive Shift to Modern Humans." In *The Mousterian Legacy: Human Biocultural Change in the Upper Pleistocene,* E. Trinkhaus, ed., pp. 165–200. Oxford: BAR Reports S164.

———. **1986** "The Neanderthals and Modern Human Origins." *Annual Review of Anthropology* 15:193–218.

TRONICK, E. Z., G. A. MORELLI, AND S. WINN. **1987** "Multiple Caretaking of Efe (Pygmy) Infants" *American Anthropologist* 89:96–106.

TRUSSELL, JAMES, AND ANNE PEBLY. **1984** "The Potential Impact of Changes in Fertility on Infant, Child, Maternal Mortality." *Studies in Family Planning* 15:267–280.

TURNBULL, COLIN M. **1978** "The Politics of Non-Aggression." In *Learning Non-Aggression,* Ashley Montagu, ed. Oxford: Oxford University Press.

———. **1982** "The Ritualization of Potential Conflict Between the Sexes Among the Mbuti." In *Politics and History in Band Societies,* Eleanor Leacock and Richard Lee, eds., pp. 133–155. Cambridge: Cambridge University Press.

TURNER, B. L. **1974** "Prehistoric Intensive Agriculture in the Mayan Lowlands." *Science* 185:118–124.

TURNER, B. L., II. **1990** "The Rise and Fall of Population and Agriculture in the Central Maya Lowlands: 300 BC to Present." In *Hunger and History: Food Shortage, Poverty, and Deprivation,* Lucille F. Newman, and William Crossgrove et al., eds., pp. 178–211. New York: Blackwell.

TURNER, B. L., AND PETER HARRISON. **1981** "Prehistoric Raised Field Agriculture in the Mayan Lowlands." *Science* 213:399–405.

TURNER, TERRENCE. **1991** "Report of the Special Commission to Investigate the Situation of the Brazilian Yanomami." Washington, D.C.: American Anthropological Association.

TUTTLE, RUSSEL H. **1969** "Knuckle-Walking and the Problem of Human Origins." *Science* 166:953–961.

TYLOR, EDWARD B. **1871** *Primitive Culture.* London: J. Murray.

UNDERWOOD, BARBARA, AND BETTY UNDERWOOD. **1979** *Hostage to Heaven.* New York: Clarkson W. Potter.

UNGER-HAMILTON, ROMANA. **1989** "The Epi-Paleolithic Southern Levant and the Origins of Cultivation." *Current Anthropology* 30:89–103.

U.S. BUREAU OF THE CENSUS. **1985** *Statistical Abstract of the United States.* Washington, D.C.: U.S. Bureau of the Census.

———. **1989** *Statistical Abstract of the United States.* Washington, D.C.: U.S. Bureau of the Census.

———. **1990** *Statistical Abstract of the United States.* Washington, D.C.: U.S. Bureau of the Census.

U.S. NATIONAL CRIMINAL JUSTICE INFORMATION AND STATISTICS SERVICE. **1978** *Myths and Realities About Crime.* Washington, D.C.: U.S. Government Printing Office.

U.S. SENATE COMMITTEE ON GOVERNMENTAL AFFAIRS. **1978** *Voting Rights in Major Corporations.* Ninety-fifth Congress, 1st session. Washington, D.C.: U.S. Government Printing Office.

UPHAM, STEADMAN. **1990** *The Evolution of Political Systems: Sociopolitics in Small-Scale Sedentary Societies.* New York: Cambridge University Press.

VAIDYANATHAN, A., N. NAIR, AND M. HARRIS. **1982** "Bovine Sex and Age Ratios in India." *Current Anthropology* 23:365–383.

VAILLANT, GEORGE C. **1966(1941)** *The Aztecs of Mexico.* Baltimore: Penguin.

VALENTINE, CHARLES. **1970** *Culture and Poverty: Critique and Counterproposals.* Chicago: University of Chicago Press.

VAN ALLEN, J. **1972** "Sitting on a Man: Colonialism and the Lost Political Institutions of Igbo Women." *Canadian Journal of African Studies* 6(2):165–182.

VANDIVER, PAMELA B., ET AL. **1989** "The Origins of Ceramic Technology at Dolni Vestonice, Czechoslovakia." *Science* 246:1002–1008.

VAN LAWICK-GOODALL, JANE. **1965** "Chimpanzees on the Gombe Stream Reserve." In *Primate Behavior,* I. Devore, ed., pp. 425–473. New York: Holt, Rinehart and Winston.

———. **1986** *The Chimpanzees of Gombe.* Cambridge, Mass.: Harvard University Press.

VIGILANT, LINDA, ET AL. **1991** "African Populations and the Evolution of Human Mitochondrial DNA." *Science* 253:1503–1507.

VILLA, PAOLA, ET AL. **1986** "Cannibalism in the Neolithic." *Science* 233:431–437.

VISHNU-MITTRE. **1975** "The Archaeobotanical and Palynological Evidence for the Early Origin of Agriculture in South and Southeast Asia." In *Gastronomy, the Anthropology of Food and Food Habits,* M. Arnott, ed., pp. 13–21. The Hague: Mouton.

VOGT, EVON Z. **1969** *Zinacantan.* Cambridge, Mass.: Harvard University Press.

VOIGT, MARY. **1986** "Review of T. Young, P. Smith, and I. Mortensen, eds., *The Hilly Flanks and Beyond.*" *Paleorient* 12(1):52–53.

———. **1990** "Reconstructing Neolithic Societies and Economies in the Middle East." *Archeomaterials* 4:1–14.

WADEL, CATO. **1973** *Now, Whose Fault Is That? The Struggle for Self-Esteem in the Face of Chronic Unemployment.* Institute of Social and Economic Research, Memorial University of Newfoundland.

WAGLEY, CHARLES. **1943** "Tapirapé Shamanism." *Boletim Do Museu Nacional (Rio de Janeiro) Anthropologia* 3:1–94.

———. **1977** *Welcome of Tears.* New York: Oxford University Press.

WAGLEY, CHARLES, AND M. HARRIS. **1958** *Minorities in the New World.* New York: Columbia University Press.

WALKER, ALAN, ET AL. **1986** "2.5 Myr *Australopithecus boisei* from West of Lake Turkana, Kenya." *Nature* 322:517–522.

WALKER, DEWARD. **1972** *The Emergent Native Americans.* Boston: Little, Brown.

WALKER, PHILLIP L. **1988** "Cranial Injuries as Evidence of Violence in Prehistoric California." *American Journal of Physical Anthropology* 80:313–323.

WALLACE, ANTHONY F. C. **1966** *Religion: An Anthropological View.* New York: Random House.

———. **1970** *Culture and Personality* (2nd ed.). New York: Random House.

———. **1972** "Mental Illness, Biology and Culture." In *Psychological Anthropology,* Francis Hsu, ed., pp. 363–402. Cambridge, Mass.: Schenkman.

WALLACE, WILSON. **1952** "The Modal Personality Structure of the Tuscarora Indians, as Revealed by the Rorschach Test." Bulletin 150, Bureau of American Ethnology. Washington, D.C.: U.S. Government Printing Office.

WALLIS, ROY. **1977** *The Road to Total Freedom: A Sociological Analysis of Scientology.* New York: Columbia University Press.

WALSH, JOHN. **1991** "The Greening of the Green Revolution." *Science* 252:26.

WARD, STEVEN, AND ANDREW HILL. **1987** "Pliocene Hominid Partial Mandible from Tabarin, Baringo, Kenya." *American Journal of Physical Anthropology* 72:21–37.

WARNER, RICHARD. **1985** *Recovery from Schizophrenia: Psychiatry and Political Economy.* London: Routledge and Kegan Paul.

WARNER, W. LLOYD. **1958** *A Black Civilization.* New York: Harper & Row.

WARNER W. LLOYD, M. MEEKER, AND K. EELLS. **1949** *Social Class in America: A Manual for the Social Status.* Chicago: Chicago Research Association.

WATSON, JAMES. **1977** "Pigs, Fodder, and the Jones Effect in Postipomean New Guinea." *Ethnology* 16:57–70.

WEATHERFORD, JACK. **1988** *Indian Givers: How the Indians of the Americas Transformed the World.* New York: Crown.

WEBSTER, DAVID. **1985** "Surplus, Labor, and Stress in Late Classic Maya Society." *Journal of Anthropological Research* 41:375–399.

WEBSTER, GARY S. **1990** "Labor Control and Emergent Stratification in Prehistoric Europe." *Current Anthropology* 31:337–366.

WEIDMAN, HELEN. **1983** "Research, Service, and Training Aspects of Clinical Anthropology." In *Clinical Anthropology,* D. Shimkin and P. Golde, eds., pp. 119–153. Washington, D.C.: University Press of America.

WEIL, PETER. **1986** "Agricultural Intensification and Fertility in the Gambia (West Africa)." In *Culture and Reproduction: An Anthropological Critique of Demographic Transition Theory,* W. P. Handwerker, ed., pp. 294–320. Boulder, Colo.: Westview Press.

WEINER, ANNETTE. **1976** *Women of Value, Men of Renown.* Austin: University of Texas Press.

WEISMAN, STEVEN. **1978** "City Constructs Statistical Profile in Looting Cases." *The New York Times,* August 14, p. 1.

WEISNER, THOMAS, AND RONALD GILMORE. **1977** "My Brother's Keeper: Child and Sibling Caretaking." *Current Anthropology* 18:169–190.

WEISS, GERALD. **1977a** "The Problem of Development in the Non-Western World." *American Anthropologist* 79:887–893.

———. **1977b** "Rhetoric in Campa Narrative." *Journal of Latin American Lore* 3:169–182.

WEITZMAN, LENORE. **1985** *The Divorce Revolution: Consequences for Women and Children in America.* New York: Free Press.

WELLES, CHRIS. **1978** "The Eclipse of Sun Myung Moon." In *Science, Sin and Scholarship,* Irving Horowitz, ed., pp. 243–258. Cambridge, Mass.: MIT Press.

WENDORF, F., AND R. SCHILD. **1981** "The Earliest Food Procedures." *Archaeology* 34:30–36.

WENKE, ROBERT. **1990** *Patterns in Prehistory* (3rd ed.). New York: Oxford University Press.

WERGE, R. **1979** "Potato Processing in the Central Highlands of Peru." *Ecology of Food and Nutrition* 7:229–234.

WERNER, DENNIS. **1979** "A Cross-Cultural Perspective on Theory and Research on Male Homosexuality." *Journal of Homosexuality* 4:345–362.

WEST, JAMES. **1945** *Plainville, U.S.A.* New York: Columbia University Press.

WESTERMARK, E. **1894** *The History of Human Marriage.* New York: Macmillan.

WESTOFF, CHARLES. **1986** "Fertility in the United States." *Science* 234:544–559.

WEYER, E. **1932** *The Eskimos.* New Haven, Conn.: Yale University Press.

WHITE, BENJAMIN. **1982** "Child Labour and Population Growth in Rural Asia." *Development and Change* 13:587–610.

———. **1983** *"Agricultural Involution" and Its Critics: Twenty Years After Clifford Geertz.* The Hague: Institute of Social Studies.

WHITE, LESLIE. **1949** *The Science of Culture.* New York: Grove Press.

WHITE, RANDALL. **1989** "Production Complexity and Standardization in Early Aurignacion Bead and Pendant Manufacture: Evolutionary Implications." In *The Human Revolution,* Paul Mellars and Chris Stringer, eds., pp. 366–390. Rutgers, N.J.: Princeton University Press.

———. **1990** "Comment on Lindly and Clark." *Current Anthropology* 31:250–251.

WHITE, TIM, AND GEN SUWA. **1987** "Hominid Footprints at Laetoli: Facts and Interpretations." *American Journal of Physical Anthropology* 72(4):485–514.

WHITESIDES, GEORGE. **1985** "Nut Cracking by Wild Chimpanzees in Sierra Leone, West Africa." *Primates* 26:91–94.

WHITING, JOHN (ED.). **1969** "Effects of Climate on Certain Cultural Practices." In *Environmental and Cultural Behavior: Ecological Studies in Cultural Anthropology,* A. P. Vayda, ed., pp. 416–455. Garden City, N.Y.: Natural History Press.

WHITING, JOHN, AND BEATRICE WHITING. **1978** "A Strategy for Psychocultural Research." In *The Making of Psychological Anthropology,* George Spindler, ed., pp. 41–61. Berkeley: University of California Press.

WHITTLE, A. W. R. **1985** *Neolithic Europe: A Survey.* New York: Cambridge University Press.

———. **1988** *Problems in Neolithic Archaeology.* New York: Cambridge University Press.

WHORF, BENJAMIN. **1956** *Language, Thought, and Reality.* New York: Wiley.

WILLEY, GORDON. **1977** "The Rise of the Maya Civilization: A Summary View." In *The Origins of Maya Civilization,* Richard E. Adams, ed., pp. 383–423. Albuquerque: University of New Mexico Press.

WILLEY, G. R., AND D. B. SHIMKIN. **1971** "Why Did the Pre-Columbian Maya Civilization Collapse?" *Science* 173:656–658.

WILLIAMS, BARBARA J. **1989** "Contact Period Rural Overpopulation in the Basin of Mexico: Carrying Capacity Models Tested with Documentary Data." *American Antiquity* 54(4):715–732.

WILLIAMS, TERRY. **1989** *The Cocaine Kids: The Inside Story of a Teenage Drug Ring.* Reading Mass.: Addison-Wesley.

WILLIAMS, WALTER. **1986** *The Spirit and the Flesh: Sexual Diversity in American Indian Culture.* Boston: Beacon Press.

WILLIGEN, JOHN VAN. **1986** *Applied Anthropology: An Introduction.* South Hadley, Mass.: Bergin and Garvey.

WILMSEN, EDWIN N. **1982** "Biological Variables in Forager Fertility Performance: A Critique of Bongaart's Model." Working Paper No. 60, African Studies Center. Boston University.

WILMSEN, EDWIN N., AND JAMES R. DENBOW. **1990** "Paradigmatic History of San-speaking Peoples and Current Attempts at Revision." *Current Anthropology* 31:489–524.

WILSON, E. O. **1975** *Sociobiology: The New Synthesis.* Cambridge, Mass.: Harvard University Press.

———. **1978** *Human Nature.* Cambridge, Mass.: Harvard University Press.

WILSON, MONICA. **1963** *Good Company: A Study of Nyakyusa Age-Villages.* Boston: Little, Brown.

WIRSING, ROLF. **1985** "The Health of Traditional Societies and the Effects of Acculturation." *Current Anthropology* 26:303–322.

WITOWSKI, STANLEY, AND CECIL A. BROWN. **1978** "Lexical Universals." *Annual Review of Anthropology* 7:427–451.

———. **1985** "Climate, Clothing, and Body-Part Nomenclature." *Ethnology* 24:197–214.

WITTFOGEL, KARL A. **1957** *Oriental Despotism: A Comparative Study of Total Power.* New Haven, Conn.: Yale University Press.

WOLF, ARTHUR P. **1968** "Adopt a Daughter-in-Law, Marry a Sister: A Chinese Solution to the Problem of the Incest Taboo." *American Anthropologist* 70:864–874.

WOLF, A. P., AND C. S. HUANG. **1980** *Marriage and Adoption in China, 1845–1945.* Stanford, Calif.: Stanford University Press.

WOLF, ERIC R. **1959** *Sons of the Shaking Earth.* Chicago: University of Chicago Press.

———. **1969** *Peasants' Wars of the Twentieth Century.* New York: Harper & Row.

———. **1982** *Europe and the People Without History.* Berkeley: University of California Press.

WOLPOFF, MILFORD H. **1980** *Paleoanthropology.* New York: Knopf.

———. **1989** "Multiregional Evolution: The Fossil Alternative to Eden." In *The Human Revolution: Behavioural and Biological Perspectives on the Origins of Modern Humans,* Vol. 1, P. Mellars and C. Stringer, eds., pp. 62–108. Edinburgh: Edinburgh University Press.

WOOD, CORINNE. **1975** "New Evidence for the Late Introduction of Malaria into the New World." *Current Anthropology* 16:93–104.

WOODBURN, JAMES. **1982a** "Egalitarian Societies." *Man* 17:431–451.

———. **1982b** "Social Dimension of Death in Four African Hunting and Gathering Societies." In *Death and the Regeneration of Life,* Maurice Block and Jonathan Parry, eds., pp. 187–210. New York: Cambridge University Press.

WORLD BANK. **1991** *World Development Report 1991: The Challenge of Development.* Oxford: Oxford University Press.

WORSLEY, PETER. **1968** *The Trumpet Shall Sound: A Study of "Cargo" Cults in Melanesia.* New York: Schocken.

WRANGHAM, R. W., AND E. V. Z. B. RISS. **1990** "Rates of Predation on Mammals by Gombe Chimpanzees, 1972–1975." *Primates* 31:157–170.

WU, R., AND S. LIN. **1985** "Chinese Paleoanthropology: Retrospect and Prospect." In *Paleoanthropology and Paleolithic Archaeology in the People's Republic of China,* R. Wu and J. W. Olsen, eds., pp. 1–27. Orlando, Fla.: Academic Press.

YATES, ROBIN D. S. **1990** "War, Food Shortages, and Relief Measures in Early China." In *Hunger in History: Food Shortage, Poverty, and Deprivation,* Lucile F. Newman et al., eds., pp. 147–176. Cambridge, Mass.: Basil Blackwell.

YEN, DOUGLAS. **1977** "Hoabhinian Horticulture: The Evidence and Questions From Northern Thailand." In *From Sunda to Sahel,* J. Allen, J. Golson, and Rhys Jones, eds., pp. 567–600. New York: Academic Press.

YESSNER, DAVID. **1987** "Life in the Garden of Eden: Causes and Consequences of the Adoption of Marine Diets by Human Societies." In *Food and Evolution: Toward a Theory of Human Food Habits,* M. Harris and E. Ross, eds., pp. 285–310. Philadelphia: Temple University Press.

YI, SEONBOK, AND G. A. CLARK. **1983** "Observations on the Lower Paleolithic of Northeast Asia." *Current Anthropology* 24:181–202.

———. **1985** "The Dyuktai Culture and New World Origins." *Current Anthropology* 26:1–20.

YOUNG, T. CUYLER, P. E. L. SMITH, AND P. MORTENSEN (EDS.). **1983** *The Hilly Flanks and Beyond: Essays on the Prehistory of Southwestern Asia.* Studies in Ancient Oriental Civilization No. 36. Chicago: The Oriental Institute.

YOUNG, L. M. **1982** "The Shang of Ancient China." *Current Anthropology* 23:311–314.

ZIHLMAN, ADRIENNE, AND J. LOWENSTEIN. **1985** *"Australopithecus afarensis:* Two Sepes or Two Species? In *Hominid Evolution: Past, Present and Future,* Philip Tobias, ed., pp. 213–220. New York: Alan R. Liss.

ZOANNA, J. **1984** "Is the U.S. Middle Class Shrinking Alarmingly? Economists Are Split." *The Wall Street Journal,* June 20, pp. 1, 26.

ZOHARY, DANIEL, AND M. HOPF. **1988** *Domestication of Plants in the Old World.* New York: Oxford University Press.

CREDITS

8.5 (A) Michael Grecco, Stock, Boston; (B) Patrick Ward, Stock, Boston.

8.6 John Running, Stock, Boston.

8.8 The Bettmann Archive.

9.3 (A) After H. Martin; (B) Alexander Marshack.

9.6 Lee Boltin.

9.9 Mazonwicz, Gallery of Prehistoric Art.

9.10 Musée de l'Homme, courtesy of Alexander Marshack.

9.11 From "Upper Paleolithic of the Can Connubia, Refugia, and the Archaeological Record from Eastern Europe," in Olga Soffer, ed., *The Pleistocene Old World: Regional Perspectives* (New York: Plenum Publishing). Copyright © 1987 by Plenum Publishing Corporation. Reprinted by permission of the publisher and Olga Soffer.

9.12 Tass, Sovfoto.

9.13 From Timothy Champion et al., *Prehistoric Europe* (New York: Academic Press, 1984). Copyright © 1984 by Academic Press, Inc. Reprinted by permission of Academic Press and Timothy Champion.

10.2 Ralph S. Solecki.

10.3 From Romana Unger-Hamilton, "The Epi-Paleolithic Southern Levant and the Origins of Cultivation." *Current Anthropology* 30:90. Copyright © 1989 The University of Chicago Press. Reprinted by permission.

10.4 Ralph S. Solecki.

10.5 Ralph S. Solecki.

10.7 Robert Braidwood and Oriental Institute, University of Chicago.

10.8 Sheridan, Ancient Art and Architecture Collection, Click/Chicago.

10.9 (A) Ralph S. Solecki; (B) AP/Wide World; (C) Guler, Magnum.

10.10 Sheridan, Ancient Art and Architecture Collection, Click/Chicago.

10.11 Robert Harding Picture Library.

10.12 Rogers, Monkmeyer.

10.13 Menzel, Stock, Boston.

10.14 AP/Wide World Photos.

10.15 (A) Historical Museum, Beijing; (B) Institute of Archaeology, Beijing.

10.16 Mazonowicz, Gallery of Prehistoric Art.

11.4 George Frison.

11.6 Dr. J. M. Adovasio, Dept. of Anthropology, University of Pittsburgh.

B11.1 "View One" from Dena F. Dincauze, "An Archaeo-Logical Evaluation of the Case for Pre-Clovis Occupations." *Advances in World Archaeology* 3:275–323. Copyright © 1984 by Academic Press, Inc. Reprinted by permission of Academic Press and the author. "View Two" from William Irving, "Contact and Chronology of Early Man in the Americas." *Annual Review of Anthropology* 14:529–555. Copyright © 1985 by Annual Reviews Inc. Reprinted by permission.

11.7 The American Museum of Natural History.

11.10 Gordon Ekholm and The American Museum of Natural History.

11.11 Norman Hammond.

11.12 Copyright © President & Fellows of Harvard College 1992. All rights reserved. Peabody Museum, Harvard University.

11.13 The American Museum of Natural History.

11.14 Menzel, Stock, Boston.

11.15 (A) Reed, Anthro-Photo; (B) AP/Wide World Photos.

11.17 © George W. Gardner.

11.18 Greene, Frederic Lewis.

11.19 Chaco Culture National Historic Park, NPS.

11.20 From Jesse Jennings, *Prehistory of North America*, second edition (New York: McGraw-Hill, 1974). Copyright © 1974 by Jesse Jennings. Reprinted by permission of the author.

11.21 Adapted from *Prehistory of North America*, second edition, by Jesse Jennings. Copyright © 1974 by McGraw-Hill.

11.22 The American Museum of Natural History.

11.23 UPI/Bettmann Archive.

11.24 The American Museum of Natural History.

B11.4 Adapted from Carroll L. Riley et al., eds., *Man Across the Sea* (Austin: University of Texas Press, 1971). Copyright © 1971 University of Texas Press. Reprinted by permission of the author and the University of Texas Press.

12.1 AP/Wide World.

12.2 Robert Carneiro and The American Museum of Natural History.

19.10 Richard Farley, Topham, The Image Works.

B19.3 From Thomas Belmonte, *The Broken Fountain* (New York: Columbia University Press, 1979). Copyright © 1979 Columbia University Press, New York. Reprinted with the permission of the publisher.

19.11 (A), (B), (C), and (D) Israeli Information Service.

19.12 P. Durand, Sygma.

19.13 UPI.

20.1 The American Museum of Natural History.

20.2 (A) The Granger Collection, New York.

B20.2 From Marjorie Shostak, *Nisa: The Life and Words of a !Kung Woman* (Cambridge, Mass: Harvard University Press, 1981). Copyright © 1981 by Marjorie Shostak. Reprinted by permission of the publishers.

20.3 Courtesy, Annette B. Weiner.

20.4 Bettmann.

20.5 Christopher Morrow, Black Star.

20.6 (A) and (D) Eugene Gordon; (B) George Gardner; (C) UPI; (E) UPI.

20.7 McLaren, Photo Researchers.

20.8 (A) AP/Wide World; (B) Beryl Goldberg; (C) Bruce Roberts, Photo Researchers.

21.1 Sharma, DPI.

21.2 Museum of the American Indian, Heye Foundation, New York.

21.3 Bloss, Anthro-Photo.

22.1 The Bettmann Archive.

22.2 (A) and (B) The American Museum of Natural History.

22.3 Neil Goldstein, Stock, Boston.

22.4 United Nations.

22.8 Reuters, Bettmann.

22.9 The American Museum of Natural History.

22.10 (A) and (B) Museum of the American Indian, Heye Foundation, New York.

23.1 Hector Aceves, Photo Researchers.

23.2 The American Museum of Natural History.

23.3 UPI/Bettmann Archive.

23.4 DeVore, Anthro-Photo.

23.5 (A) Eugene Gordon; (B) United Nations.

23.6 Museum of the American Indian, Heye Foundation, New York.

23.7 Charles Wagley.

23.8 The American Museum of Natural History.

23.9 Neg. no. 324767, The American Museum of Natural History.

23.10 (A) © 1989 Eugene Gordon; (B) Museum of the American Indian, Heye Foundation, New York; (C) Neg. no. 31592. Photo by J. Otis Wheelock. Courtesy Department Library Services, The American Museum of Natural History.

23.11 (A) and (B) Victor Turner, *The Forest of Symbols*, Cornell University Press.

23.12 Laimute Druskis, Photo Researchers.

23.13 Mexican National Tourist Council.

23.14 Photograph by Egyptian Expedition, The Metropolitan Museum of Art.

23.15 The American Museum of Natural History.

23.16 © Peter Menzel.

23.17 Segio Larrain, Magnum.

23.18 Nevada Historical Society.

23.19 (A) Museum of the American Indian, Heye Foundation, New York; (B) AP/Wide World Photos.

23.20 Painting by Ernest Spybuck, Museum of the American Indian, Heye Foundation, New York.

23.21 Reuters/Bettmann.

23.22 © Muller, 1982, Woodfin Camp.

23.23 (A) Moni Nag; (B) UPI.

24.1 (A), (B), and (C) Wide World.

24.2 (A), (B), (C), (D), (E), and (F) Museum of the American Indian, Heye Foundation, New York.

24.3 Lee, Anthro-Photo.

24.4 (A) and (B) The American Museum of Natural History.

24.5 The American Museum of Natural History.

24.6 The American Museum of Natural History.

24.7 Oppenheim, Meret, *Object* (1936). Fur-covered cup, saucer, and spoon; cup, $4\frac{3}{8}''$ diameter; saucer, $9\frac{3}{8}''$ diameter; spoon, $8''$ long; overall height $2\frac{7}{8}''$. Collection, The Museum of Modern Art, New York. Purchase.

24.8 (A) and (B) de Havenon Collection.

24.9 Eugene Gordon.

24.10 UPI.

24.11 Photograph by Egyptian Expedition, The Metropolitan Museum of Art.

24.12 French Government Tourist Office.

24.13 Maxine Hicks.

NAME INDEX